Political Power: *A Reader in Theory and Research*

POLITICAL POWER

A Reader in Theory and Research

Roderick Bell

David V. Edwards

R. Harrison Wagner

The Free Press, New York

Collier-Macmillan Limited, London

To the discipline and profession
which make this book
possible and necessary,
and to The Rule of Anticipated Reactions.

Preface

THIS collection of articles originated in a seminar on political power which the three of us taught together during the spring of 1968. We all shared an interest in the problems of theory and methodology in political science, and the literature on power seemed to provide a good opportunity to confront these problems in a concrete way. It seemed likely to us that this literature exemplified three of the central problems of scientific method in political science—concept formation, theory construction, and measurement—in a way which emphasized both the distinctive concerns of the discipline and its underlying unity. These expectations were fulfilled, and they provide the main justification for this volume. But they were fulfilled in an unexpected way, which accounts for the particular form this volume has taken.

To state the matter briefly, we concluded that much of the literature on political power suffered from an overemphasis on the definition of concepts and measurement techniques, and an underemphasis of theory. Yet it seems to us that these three tasks must be pursued simultaneously if any of them are to serve any useful scientific purpose. If a collection of readings can have any unifying theme, that is the central theme of this book. The essays by Wagner and Bell argue for this point directly, the first in the course of an examination of the concept, and the second in the course of a discussion of the relationship between theory and measurement. And the readings are organized in such a way as to emphasize these problems.

The articles collected in Section II seem to us to exemplify the concerns of students of politics which lead one to think seriously about the concept of power in the first place. The presumption that the distribution of power is the key to many other properties of political systems is shared by students of all forms of politics from the local to the international level. But it is notoriously difficult to answer the questions posed by this presumption in a noncontroversial way.

One type of effort to reduce the scope of the resulting controversies is represented by the articles in Section III, all of which attempt to state the meaning of the concept more precisely than ordinary usage. Another type of attack on the problem is represented by many of the articles in Section IV, which seek to elaborate ways by which power can be measured noncontroversially. Bell argues in his essay in Section I that measurement can be accomplished only in the context of a theory. The articles in Section IV exemplify a wide range of types of theory, implicitly or explicitly, which help to make the measurement devices they suggest meaningful. They are all theories of interpersonal influence of one form or another.

It is a long way from interpersonal influence to the sorts of properties of political systems to which the writings of Section II were addressed. Accordingly, Section V contains a series of articles which are explicitly devoted to theories of political systems organized around some version of the concept of power. The reader may judge for himself how much of an advance these articles represent over the more traditional efforts to characterize political systems with the concept of power. We believe that any further advancement must come through greater development of the diverse sorts of empirical theories which have been implied by much of the literature on political power.

The construction of such theories can attract the efforts even of social scientists who do not believe a concentration on power is a useful approach. It is in that sense that we believe the essays collected in this volume represent a contribution to the unity of the discipline.

Our efforts in teaching the seminar and collecting and preparing these materials benefitted from clerical assistance from Peter E. van Leuven and Janet L. Allaway, and from clerical support from the University of Texas.

R.B.
D.V.E.
R.H.W.

Contents

Political Power: *A Reader in Theory and Research*

The Study of Political Power:

An Introduction to the Problems

of Theory and Measurement

The Concept of Power and the Study of Politics

R. Harrison Wagner

THERE ARE three main problems which lead one to think carefully about the ordinary meaning of the word "power" as it is used in descriptions of politics. The first is posed by the fact that it is extraordinarily difficult to reach agreement about the answer to the questions "Who has power?" and "How much power does he (or they) have?" when asked of any political system. The second is that it is similarly difficult to define the word in a way everyone will accept. The third is that the relationship between the meanings of "power" and "politics" seems puzzling. To some people, the study of political power seems synonymous with the study of politics. On the other hand, "power politics" does not seem to be a redundant expression.

If "politics" could be defined by "power," then political science could be given clear boundaries (assuming one can define "power"), and a theory of power might then be a general theory of politics. If it cannot, then the relevance of the attribution and measurement of power to the development of a cumulative science of politics is not so obvious. Other so-called "approaches" might be more important, for example, "decision-making," or "systems theory."

Efforts to define the word have given rise to subsidiary puzzles. Is power an attribute of someone, or a certain kind of relationship between people? Does it imply coercion, and if so, what does "coercion" mean? What is the relationship between the meaning of "power" and the meanings of other words, for example, "influence," "authority," "force," or "to govern?"

I will try to show that some of these problems are false, in the sense that they are puzzles based on a misunderstanding of the way the word "power" is normally used. Others are the result of genuine problems of observation and explanation similar to many others in the social sciences. It is important to eliminate the former in order that attention can be concentrated on the latter.

Problems of the former kind are simply the result of the fact that we can do things without being able to explain how we do them, for example, tie our shoes. The same is true of the use of words. It is possible to know how to use a word without being able to describe how it is used (and hence to report accurately what it means). Words can be defined in any way we like, of course, but one cannot both define a word in any way one likes and clarify its ordinary meaning. One could define "power" as "the degree of blackness of one's skin," but that would not help political science or Negro militants very much.

It is helpful in examining ordinary usage to think of as many examples as one can. Power is ascribed to many different things on many different grounds. We speak of horsepower, and the power of ideas; of economic power, social power, and political power; of healing power and brain power; of purchasing power and military power; and of the executive, legislative, and judicial powers of the American government. In all these instances the word "power" behaves in much the same way as the word "ability." In fact, the English word "power" derives from the Latin and French words which mean "to be able," and the German word "*Macht*" derives from "*mögen*," which has that as one of its meanings.

The origins of words are not always helpful. "Strength," for example, seems to derive from a Latin word meaning "to tighten or strain." But in this case I maintain that origins are helpful—that to say that X has the power to do something is to say that X *is able* to do something, that X *can* do something. The power of a truck is not something akin to its gasoline; it is simply its *ability* to move a specified weight a specified distance in a specified period of time. The power of a lens is its ability to magnify an image a certain amount. The mental power of a man is his ability to do certain things with his mind. The purchasing power of a dollar is described when one states how much it can buy. It thus appears that one social scientist was being rather arbitrary when he maintained that "when we speak ... of the power of an idea ... we are using figurative language, speaking truly, as it were, but metaphorically ...."[1] The power of an idea is what an idea can do.

Another social scientist has complained that "unfortunately in the English language 'power' is an awkward word, for unlike 'influence' and 'control' it has no convenient verb form, nor can the subject and object of the relation be supplied noun forms without resort to barbaric neologisms."[2] It should be noticed that, while there is no such verb form in English, there is one in French, "*Il peut.*" It is the beginning of wisdom to see that that verb has no object whatever. "Power" does not mean a relationship.

The notion that "power" must stand for a relationship between people has two origins. One is that politics is a collective phenomenon; political power must therefore entail some human relationships. This is true. But to say that "political power" *implies* such relationships is not the same as saying that it stands for them. I will return to this point.

The other source of this mistake is the fact that "Sam has power" is an incomplete sentence. Just as the statement "Sam can" ought to evoke the reply, "Sam can do what?"; so the statement "Sam has power" ought to be followed by the query, "the power to do what?" When the context is known, of course, this is not necessarily true, just as, when one knows the context, the statement "Sam has a lot of ability" can make sense. But if one does not know whether Sam is a student applying for a

scholarship or a professional football player, the sentence is incomplete. Similarly, if one doesn't know whether Sam is Secretary of Defense or Mayor of Peking, the statement that he has a lot of power is incomplete, even if one knows it is political power and not brain power that Sam has.

The fact that the statement "Sam has a lot of power" is incomplete probably lies behind the complaints of some people that power is spoken of as though it could be smelled and touched, or stored in a keg. It is a short step from this complaint to the assertion that power is not something which can be possessed, but a relationship. And it is a short step from this assertion to the belief that "power" must refer to a specific kind of relationship, a "power relationship." To say this is to be misled by the English language. "Sam has a lot of power" is obscure, not because "power" is there the object of the verb "to have," but because it is incomplete. We must know *what* Sam has the power to do. To assume that "power" stands for a relationship is to assume that "Sam has a lot of power" must mean "Sam has a lot of power over Joe." But suppose the sentence is completed by saying "Sam has the power to declare war." Sam cannot declare war, of course, unless he has the requisite relationships with other people. But what other people? And what sorts of relationships? The sentence implies these relationships, but it does not refer to them, and one can believe the statement without knowing what they are.

So far I have talked about the meaning of "power." What of "political power?" It should be obvious that "power" as I have discussed it cannot be used to define "politics." It is reasonable to assume, then, that "politics" must be used to define "political power." To say that someone has the power to do something would mean that he was able to do it, and consequently that under certain specified conditions he might do it. Clearly, then, if we understand what it means to say that Sam *did* a political thing, or performed a political deed, we will know what political power is; for if Sam did it, he manifestly had the power to do it. Thus it is only necessary to know what a political act is, and to know how to ascribe responsibility for a political act to an individual, in order to know what political power means.

What, then, is a political act? Examples of political acts would include declaring war, raising taxes, appointing public officials, making a budget, etc. What do all such acts have in common? One thing they certainly have in common is that they are collective acts—they are acts which require the cooperation of more than one person. This common attribute may not be enough to define politics unambiguously, but it is enough to get the process of analysis started. The question now becomes: What does it mean to ascribe responsibility for a collective act to only a portion of the people who had to cooperate to perform it? Lyndon Johnson decided to bomb North Vietnam, but to my knowledge he has never personally bombed anyone. Why do we say that he did it, instead of saying that he and the pilots and everyone else involved did it?

Before I answer that question, I should point out that there is a distinction between a collective decision and a collective act. A decision might be made in which more than one person participated, but the decision resulted in an individual's action, *e.g.*, a professor and a student might jointly decide what books the student will read. A collective act, however, is one which requires the cooperation of more than one person to perform it, *e.g.*, the bombing of North Vietnam. In each of these two cases, it is possible that the participants will either agree or disagree in their evaluation of the consequences of the act. These distinctions can be presented in the following table:

I propose to concentrate for the moment on individual acts which are decided upon by more than one person. The first question

I will ask is: What does it mean to say that one person or the other made the decision? If one cannot understand this question when asked of acts performed by individuals it will be impossible to understand it when asked of collectivities. I will return to this table later, when it will be necessary to define "politics" more carefully.

The class of instances I have chosen to begin with is, of course, that class referred to by those who define "power" as "A's ability to get B to do something he would not otherwise have done." Why, then, refer to it in such a peculiar way, that is, as decisions made by more than one individual, with the responsibility unequally distributed between them? The reason is that this way of speaking, I believe, raises important questions which are obscured by the other way of speaking. It emphasizes that *both* are involved in making the decision, and raises explicitly the question of why responsibility for the act is focused on the person attempting to participate in the decision rather than on the person performing the act.

For it is clear that A's intervention is not a sufficient condition for B's decision. B had to decide to act in the direction desired by A. This is true even in the famous case where A says to B "your money or your life." B *could* say "fire away." At most, then, A's intervention is a *necessary* condition for B's action, and is therefore an incomplete explanation of it.

Why, then, concentrate so much attention on it? For the same reason that we say that my turning on a switch explains why the light went on—for purely practical

	Collective Acts		Individual Acts	
	Agree	*Disagree*	*Agree*	*Disagree*
Collective Decisions				
Individual Decisions				

reasons. We desire to concentrate on the point at which intervention by someone will change things. We assume other necessary conditions will be constant, but that this one might vary. But this is a chancy assumption. One might encounter a burned-out fuse, or an uncooperative victim.

If we wish to answer practical questions, like how to get the lights on or how to get a bill passed, we will be content with singling out certain necessary conditions as those most likely to vary significantly for our purposes. If, on the other hand, we are interested in complete explanations we will be interested in all those necessary conditions which are, together, sufficient for the occurrence of B's action, or the light's going on. For the latter, one would have to investigate B's desires as well as A's intervention.[3]

How, then, does A's intervention, together with some attributes of B, alter B's decision? I can only think of two main ways. Either A merely informs B that the consequences of acting differently from A's suggestion would be contrary to B's own desires (as when he tells B he is about to be struck down by a falling brick unless he moves), or he alters the expected consequences of B's intended action, so that B now prefers something else (as when he threatens to hit B with a brick unless he moves). Either case may warrant the attribution of power to A. It is the latter case which I would like to analyze further.[4]

Speaking less anecdotally, suppose B prefers x to y, while A prefers that B do y rather than x. What can A do which will have the effect of B's doing y rather than x, which he prefers? A must simply find a q which B prefers to some r, and which he also prefers to x. He must then act so that B must choose, not between x and y, but between $x + r$ and $y + q$. If B prefers q to x and x to y and y to r ($q > x > y > r$) he will prefer $y + q$ to $x + r$ ($y + q > x + r$). B will therefore do y rather than x, which he otherwise would have preferred to do.

Another asset of this phraseology should

now be apparent. By speaking of the exercise of influence as interdependent decisions, it becomes possible to employ two different theoretical languages in describing them, and to use the theorems which already exist in those languages to explain the decisions. These languages are those of utilities and the theory of games on the one hand, and preference, indifference, exchange, and economic theory on the other hand.[5]

I propose to use the latter for a while to make a few analytical points. I want to examine first the relevance of two distinctions: the distinction between inducements and sanctions on the one hand; and the distinction between coercion and persuasion on the other hand. First I must emphasize that they are different distinctions. The former distinguishes between offering a man something, and denying it to him. The second is more obscure, but it seems to have something to do with the extent to which B might feel constrained by A's intervention. It is not clear what that means, but it rests on the difference between being threatened with a horsewhipping and being threatened with expressions of disapproval. It may be empirically true, of course, that all inducements are merely persuasive, while all sanctions are coercive. But what of masochists? And is the offer of a meal to a starving man in exchange for a confession less coercive than the denial of approval to one's child for failing to wipe his shoes before entering the house?

The analysis given above of A's influence on B ignores both these distinctions. Let x, for example, be keeping a horse and y losing a horse to B. Let q be gaining a pig and r be not gaining a pig. If B prefers pigs to horses, he can be offered $y + q$ by A, and he will choose that over $x + r$. He will swap his horse for B's pig.

On the other hand, let x be keeping one's wife, and y be giving one's wife to A. Let q be earning a living wage, and r be starving to death. If B prefers living to keeping his wife, then A can offer him $y + q$, and he will prefer it to $x + r$. He will swap A his wife for a living wage. But he will report that he has been coerced into giving up his wife. In this example, q is an inducement; but q could as easily have been an offer not to shoot, and r the prospect of being murdered. Once again, then, the distinction between inducement and sanction does not seem to coincide with the distinction between persuasion and coercion.

What aspects of the primitive situation which I have described would seem to be relevant to these distinctions? Obviously, one is the intensity of B's preference for x over y. Intensity of preference is a difficult notion to define precisely, but perhaps one could think of it as the distance between x and y on B's entire schedule of preferences, or the quantity of some standard good, such as money, which B would be prepared to give up in order to be allowed to have x rather than y. This helps distinguish B's horse from his wife, for example.

It may usually be true, as I have said, that gaining inducements lies lower on everyone's schedule of preferences than avoiding sanctions. But this clearly depends on the good. Food, clothing, and shelter will be preferred intensely to their opposites whether one already has them or not. For many other goods, however, it is undoubtedly true that keeping what one has is preferred to gaining what one does not have. A utilitarian argument against the redistribution of incomes rests on this distinction.

But the distinction between inducements and sanctions may refer to another aspect of this primitive situation. The relation between A and B is one of exchange. Given the choices available, both benefit by the exchange. But B would benefit much more by having different choices available. This is true of all exchange relationships. If I trade money for beer, both the liquor dealer and I gain, even though I lose money and he loses beer. But I would gain much more if I had my money plus his beer, and he would gain more by the reverse. Why, then, would B accept the terms offered by A?

There would seem to be only two broad kinds of reason. He might have no alternative, or he might regard the terms of exchange as legitimate for some reason. Whether B had any alternative would

depend on what choices he could present A with, and A's schedule of preferences. Whether B regarded the terms of exchange as legitimate would depend on many factors less easily established, but one of them might be whether A was offering B something which A had, or was denying B something which B had or had reason to expect.

These two sets of attributes (intensities of preference and attitudes toward the terms of exchange) also affect B's description of this relationship. For the same relationship can be described as the exercise of power by A, as exchange between A and B, and as a conflict between A and B. I do not regard liquor dealers as having a great deal of power. But if I needed liquor much more than I do, and if the rate of exchange of money for liquor were much less favorable to me, then I might. Or I might retaliate against them, thereby initiating a conflict, which could also be described as the reciprocal exercise of power.

I conclude from this that the notion of "power," when used to describe such situations, is ambiguous. It singles out one party to a joint decision, and it does so for reasons which are left unclear. It is therefore preferable for purposes of analysis to avoid the word, and speak rather of interdependent decisions, specifying the sort of interdependence which is involved.

It is now necessary to examine the notion of collective *acts*. There will be some people who wish to deny, of course, that such things exist, for they seem to imply the personification of collectivities. But our language is full of such acts, and I think it would be extremely difficult to eliminate them from it. I have already mentioned several of them, for example, the bombing of North Vietnam. The appointment of a Cabinet officer is another. If a very large number of people do not cooperate by behaving as though Robert McNamara is Secretary of Defense, he cannot be Secretary of Defense.

There are two separate characteristics of

such ways of speaking relevant here. The first is that, although collective acts require the cooperation of many people, the people and the nature of their cooperation are often left undefined. Consider the appointment of a Secretary of Defense. One knows that many people must cooperate, but which people, and how? This leads to confusion only because of the second attribute of such ways of speaking: the fact that we often assign responsibility for such collective acts to one person, or a few people. It is this, as I argued earlier, which makes it possible to say that these people have power: they have the power to do whatever we say they did.

I suggest that such ascriptions of power are even more ambiguous than those involving merely decisions for acts performed by individuals. For they fail to specify who is involved, or what sort of cooperative actions the people involved perform. Consider the President's decision to appoint Clark Clifford Secretary of Defense. The President made the appointment, and therefore he had the power to do it. But how did he do it, and what constitutes a complete explanation of Clark Clifford's successful emergence as Secretary of Defense subsequent to the President's decision? That is left unclear. Furthermore, when the answer is known, it might be somewhat different from the answer to the question of what explains the earlier appearance of Charles Wilson as Secretary of Defense. Yet it is both convenient and meaningful to say that one of the elements of the President's power is his power to appoint the Secretary of Defense.

Furthermore, it should be clear that such collective acts cannot be explained by a whole series of dyadic relations such as the one I examined earlier. For the President has no direct dealings with many of the people whose cooperation is necessary to make Clark Clifford Secretary of Defense. One cannot say that the President's power to appoint Secretaries of Defense *is* his ability to get some B to do something he

would not otherwise do. Let us assume, for example, that I do not know that the Secretary of Defense is appointed by the President, and yet I know that Clark Clifford is Secretary of Defense. I will treat him as such (and thereby contribute to his being such) nonetheless. But it would be hard to say that the President *got* me to treat him as such.

This suggests that such ascriptions of power are very convenient ways of speaking, but are useless for most analytical purposes. To explain the appearance of Clark Clifford as Secretary of Defense by the President's ability to get someone else (*e.g.*, a Congressional committee chairman) to do something he would not otherwise do would be doubly incomplete: it would omit reference to the preference schedules of the committee chairman and the bargaining relationship between him and the President, and it would omit reference to all the other people whose cooperation is required, but who were not directly affected by any action of the President.

Once again, then, the word "power" diverts our attention from the interesting problems. In this instance the interesting problems concern the explanation for the cooperation of all those involved in the performance of the collective act. The word "power" merely involves the ascription of responsibility for such acts, something which is useful for only practical purposes.

I conclude, then, that "political power" is not a relationship, but that it assumes relationships without specifying what they are. Use of the term therefore assumes the answers to the interesting questions, rather than providing an answer. As the central focus for political science it is therefore sterile. At the same time, it is a mistake to believe that a concentration on political power could be a very different approach from any other. It is sterile not because it is different from others and useless, but because it is merely a misleading way of stating other so-called "approaches." It assumes, for example, a theory of interdependent decisions. Thus it is a little part of decision-making theories, rather than something different from them.

I argued earlier that "politics" as well as "power" was necessary to define "political power." Thus far I have been talking merely about interdependent decisions and collective acts. This does not seem to be enough to define "politics" unambiguously. There are two ways of defining the word. One is by reference to institutions which are ordinarily thought of as political, for example, governments. The other is by reference to interpersonal relations which are also thought to be political, for example, office politics. Either would conform to some ordinary usage. The question is: Which is more theoretically productive?

It begins to appear that the latter is. The task, therefore, is to specify such interpersonal relations unambiguously, and in such a way that both ordinary language and the demands of theory can be satisfied. I suggest as such a definition the following: politics consists of those human relationships in which two or more people are affected by the consequences of a decision, they both (or all) find it more advantageous (or find it necessary) to submit to the consequences of the decision rather than avoid them, they disagree about their evaluation of the consequences, and they all try to influence the decision. I suggest that this definition conforms to most ordinary usage, but at the same time lends itself to both game theory and economic theory. Such a definition implies that politics is very widespread. But it is distinguishable from other social relationships. If a boy asks a girl for a date, for example, that is not politics (although it is an attempt to influence her). If he marries her, however, a dispute about where they are to live would be a political dispute.

Utilizing the definition of politics offered above, it is possible to interpret the table presented on page 5.

Individual decisions about collective acts can only be interpreted as occasions in which an individual physically transports another individual (or several individuals), for only then can they be said to play no role in the decision at all. Such an instance which would involve agreement about the evaluation of consequences might be a husband's carrying his wife across the threshold of their new home. Disagreement about the consequences would characterize a policeman's transporting his prisoner to jail. It is not clear that these present any interesting analytical problems. Individual decisions about individual acts whose consequences do not adversely affect anyone else, and which no one else attempts to influence, are similarly uninteresting to students of politics.

But individual decisions about individual acts, whose consequences affect other individuals with different evaluations of the consequences, represent the raw materials of politics. When the latter individuals attempt to alter the decision, a simple or primitive political system has been created. Two sorts of transformation in such primitive relationships can occur. One is the transformation of conflict into agreement. The other is the development of the capacity to perform collective acts among such individuals.

There are three prevalent non-institutional definitions of politics: politics is the

	Collective Acts		Individual Acts	
	Agree	*Disagree*	*Agree*	*Disagree*
Collective Decisions	Religious movements	Complex politics	Advice ——— Exchange	Simple politics
Individual Decisions				The raw materials of politics

exercise of influence (or, more ambiguously, power); politics is the resolution of conflict (including conflict over the allocation of scarce goods); and politics is the pursuit of collective goals. It is easy to see that these definitions, far from being mutually exclusive, merely single out aspects of more complex relationships. Politics involves all these things. One of the more important tasks of political analysis must be the investigation of the relations among them.

What role should the concept of political power play in that analysis? Much of the literature in political science devoted to the study of political power (of which the community power literature is the most prominent part) concentrates on the task of attributing power to individuals or groups, or, in other words, finding out how power is distributed. Much less effort has been devoted to developing theories which explain the outcomes of interdependent decisions which such attributions of power merely point to, or to developing theories which would tell one the significance of the distribution of power for the working of the broader political system. It is commonly assumed that if one knows who has power, one will know why, and one will also have the explanation for much else that happens in the political system. Yet these assumptions are far from being obviously true.

Indeed, it is impossible even to attribute power to individuals or groups non-controversially without a theory which explains the causal relationships which such attributions assume. Perhaps a partly fictitious example will make this point clearer. I once attended a faculty meeting at which an issue of interest to me was to be resolved. Before the meeting, it appeared that the outcome was almost certainly to be the one which I preferred. In the course of the meeting, however, a colleague who opposed the measure raised some objections which no one else had thought of, and after some discussion the outcome I desired (and had expected) failed. After the meeting, another colleague who had shared my desires and expectations remarked that we had just witnessed another instance of the remarkable power of colleague X to get his way in spite of opposition to his views. This interpretation surprised me, for I had thought that this had merely been one more instance of a committee being able to think of more objections to a proposal than individuals can. We had a rather unproductive argument about this.

What lay behind this argument? It seems clear to me in retrospect that one major source of our disagreement was a difference in our practical orientations toward the issue. My colleague had been actively involved in the effort to affect the outcome in the way I desired. I, however, had merely agreed with this view without doing much to get it adopted. To my more active colleague, X was the difference between success and failure—*if* X had not spoken, the outcome would probably have been different. To me, on the other hand, X's thoughts might have occurred to anyone; and they could not have affected the outcome if many people had not agreed with them. To my colleague, X was a sufficient condition for the failure of the proposal. To me, X was certainly not a necessary condition for its failure, nor, if one looked closely enough, a sufficient condition either.

It seems clear to me that only a theory which explained the outcome could resolve the differences in the viewpoints of my colleague and myself which arose out of different practical concerns. I suspect that much of the literature on political power suffers from the same defects as this little discussion. To some observers, the power elite are the people who must be influenced or removed to accomplish some desired goal. To more passive observers, the role of the elite seems much more complex. I doubt that these differences can be eliminated. But it seems more likely to me that there can be agreement on the theory which explains the outcome than that there can be agreement on who is responsible for it.

There have been two common efforts to cope with this problem. One has been the attempt to define "power" more precisely. The other has been the attempt to measure it. I have tried to show in this essay that a precise definition of "power" is not much help. Roderick Bell argues in the following essay that measurement does not help much either. We both believe that the definition of concepts and measurement must occur simultaneously with the effort to construct theory.

One implication of what I have said thus far is that the concept of power, while indispensable as an abbreviation of complex phenomena, does not unambiguously refer to anything, and therefore is not likely to play a major part in any useful theory. On the other hand, genuine nonsense is very rare, in spite of what the logical positivists believed. People who have concentrated on power have usually meant something, however obscurely. A more relevant question, therefore, is this: What sorts of theories need to be developed around the concerns which have preoccupied the people who have focused on the study of power?

The most obvious of these seems to me to be a theory of interdependent decisions in conflict situations. It is wrong, of course, to think that "power" must refer to such situations. Many different kinds of inter-action may be used to justify the attribution of power. Moreover, the criteria which are employed in attributing power even in conflict situations are ambiguous, as I argued earlier. But it is such situations to which many statements about the "exercise of power" refer. And it is because of that fact that the theory of games seems much more relevant to such problems than, say, a theory of opinion change, although power may properly be attributed on the basis of A's having changed B's opinions as well.

A part of such a theory would be an attempt to state the relationship between what are commonly called "political re-sources," and the outcome of such collective decisions. A political resource is simply a way in which A can alter the consequences of B's actions. But what counts as a political resource, and what effect it has on the outcome, cannot be known in the absence of a theory which explains and predicts the outcome. In some instances, a frown is an important resource, a resource which is obviously widely distributed. In other instances, the possession of complicated

weapons of great destructive force is not an important resource. There is a great deal of debate among students of both inter-national and domestic politics about the significance of such resources which could be made more productive by greater con-centration on the theory of interdependent decision which would be required to settle the matter.

It is only in the context of such a theory that the concept of power can acquire explanatory significance. It might then have two main kinds of significance. First, it can be a dispositional term similar to "brittle-ness," as applied to glass.[6] That is, it can refer to a tendency of some object to behave in a certain way in certain circumstances, which may be said to constitute part of a very low-level explanation of its behavior in a particular circumstance. One can, of course, attribute brittleness to glass without necessarily having a theory which explains its brittleness. But I have been contending that one cannot unambiguously use "power" even as a dispositional term without a theory which justifies its use. The reason for this is that in the case of power it is harder to get agreement about what one is observing. The practical orientations of observers differ significantly, and the non-experimental nature of most observations of social relationships allows great latitude in the sorts of dispositions which can be attributed to individuals without directly contradicting the evidence. Furthermore, the word "power," as ordinarily used, does not refer unambiguously to any particular disposition.

Second, "power" may refer to a resource, the significance of which is deducible from the theory. As such, it may refer either to a physical ability of some sort (*e.g.*, fire-power); or it may refer to an individual's tendency (or ability) to produce certain outcomes in certain kinds of interdependent choice situations. In the latter instance, "power" would not refer to a tendency which was in itself sufficient to cover the individual case (*e.g.*, A's power to declare war explains this particular declaration of war), but to a tendency which requires other generalizations as well to explain the outcome (*e.g.*, A's power to declare war on B coupled with B's desire to avoid war explains B's decision to submit to A's demands when threatened with the prospect of war).

The second type of relevant theory would be a theory of collective decisions, in the sense of that term which I used earlier. That is, it would be a theory which explained how many individual decisions become pyramided in the complex ways which make ordinary references to collective decisions (the declaration of war, the nomination of a presidential candidate) possible, but which such references do not, in themselves, refer to unambiguously. It is not immediately obvious what the relationship might be between this second type of theory and the first. But "power theories" of politics suggest, implicitly or explicitly, that political systems (or entities which make such political decisions as I have just referred to) are somehow built on or derived from inter-personal relationships of conflict. How such relationships might form the basis of complex social entities is a question which has recently been explored in abstract terms by Kenneth Boulding, Talcott Parsons, and Peter Blau.[7]

Finally, there is the problem of the relationship between the distribution of power and the outcomes produced by complex political systems. This is undoubtedly the central question raised by efforts to characterize political systems as elitist or pluralist. But I hope I have made clear by now that, when put in such general terms, it is not even clear what the question means. Of course, if one believed that some single person or group could be unambigu-ously said to be responsible for a decision or set of decisions, then to point to them would be an explanation of the decisions. But that is surely not often true, even in the case of totalitarian dictatorships. Yet if one does not believe that, what does the question refer to, and what is its explanatory significance?

First one must recognize that the question does not unambiguously refer to anything. But the unnamed things to which it might refer can be divided into two broad classes. The "power" which is distributed might be resources, in the sense in which that term was defined above, or it might be the capacity to perform a political act. In the latter case, one might be interested in such capacities either as dispositional explanations for particular performances of those acts, or as resources which form part of the explanation of other acts.

It follows that if one is interested in explaining more than the acts immediately covered by this dispositional term, one must be referring to the distribution of resources of one form or another. Such resources may be either physical assets such as weapons, or capacities dependent on social relationships (which include money and complex weapons systems, as well as administrative authority). It is not at all obvious that the decentralization of one sort of resource (*e.g.*, administrative authority) has similar effects to the decentralization of others (*e.g.*, six-shooters, or nuclear weapons). Such a question cannot be answered until a theory of interdependent decisions is specified to cover the case in question, and probably a theory of political systems as well.

These, then, seem to me to be the genuine problems raised for political science by the concept of political power. They are difficult problems. It would be unfortunate if one were distracted from them by the puzzles which have been produced by the mysterious word "power."

IN SEVERAL recent essays on power (or influence) attempts have been made to offer usable measures for the concept. On its face, this is an important task; not until we can really measure power can we test propositions about it which assert quantity relationships. Here we consider some representative attempts to measure power, and the difficulties attending such endeavors. Harrison Wagner argued above that ambiguities associated with uses of the word "power" in ordinary discourse have diverted our attention from more tractable, productive orientations. Since it can be shown that measurement itself depends upon observations which are impossible in the absence of such orientations, those same ambiguities return to plague us again.

A lucid discussion of the measurement of power will require at the very least that we be specific within the limits of ordinary language about what it is we are attempting to measure. Moreover, we shall certainly need to be able to be explicit about those actual observations which are required in the measurement process. But the question whether an observation constitutes measurement cannot be answered save by appeal to theory; very loosely speaking, we can never know that we have correctly assigned numbers to empirical phenomena until the results are useful to explain things. We can begin with a discussion of general concepts of measurement, returning then to the concept of power and some attempts to measure it.

I

The Nature of Measurement[1]

We may, with Stevens, say that "measurement [consists of] the assignment of numerals to objects or events according to rule—any rule."[2] Clearly it will be necessary to say something about those rules, as well as the objects or events. Turning our attention to the latter for the moment, we can avoid some confusion by considering the usual criteria for the construction of

2

Political Power: The Problem of Measurement

Roderick Bell

scientific concepts. The language of science consists wholly of declarative sentences, and those sentences contain but two kinds of words: logical words and factual words.[3] The non-logical words must conform to certain criteria, most especially Hempel's two principles of scientific concept formation—*i.e.*, a scientific concept must possess both theoretical and empirical import. A word has empirical import if it refers, directly or indirectly, to the world of sense experience (thus it is connected to our "experiential vocabulary"). It has theoretical import if it can be used in sentences (more formally, "well-formed formulations") which connect the concept to others in the theory.[4]

Ordinarily, the meanings of most of the factual words of a scientific theory are given by definition. But if each and every word in a theory were defined in terms of one or more other words in the theory, mere circularity would obtain. At least one of the factual words must be "primitive," in the sense that it is undefined within the theory. Its meaning must be given ostensively; it must be part of our experiential vocabulary (if the theory in question is to have anything to do with the world of our experience).[5] Now, philosophers of science have given less attention than one might expect to the problem of primitive terms. It should be clear that if the primitive terms of a theory lack unequivocal meaning, then the intersubjectivity of the theory is threatened. In part, it is the function of measurement to establish rules by which observable data are linked unequivocally to theoretical constructs.[6] If we can measure something, we can assign numerals to it according to a rule. The actual operations by which we accomplish this often constitute the all-important link between defined terms in a theory and the world of experience. In other words, measurement is one important way—though not the only way—to give empirical import to the non-logical terms of scientific theory. I shall elaborate upon this point presently as I say more about how we measure something; first I want to point up the relevance of measurement to that other principle of concept formation, theoretical import.

If theories consist of two kinds of words, what of the logical terms? Purely formal (logical) systems vary infinitely, from simple syllogisms whose validity can be ascertained by inspection to formidable axiomatic systems whose entailments are even still not worked out by logicians and mathematicians. With only a few notable exceptions, political scientists have not troubled laymen with any very sophisticated deductions. It is interesting to speculate why. May Brodbeck points out that "arithmetic is a subtle and strong logic permitting deductions which, without it, might be quite impossible."[7] Why, then, do political scientists so often neglect it in the formulation of theories?[8] Part of the answer is, I suppose, that to employ it would be like using an elephant gun to hunt rabbits, *i.e.*, such theories as we have mustered have few nonobvious entailments. But at least part of the answer must be that many of our key concepts are not, at present, amenable to mathematical treatment. Laws and theorems cannot be stated in terms of mathematical relationships unless numbers of appropriate sorts can be assigned to the concepts involved. (To take a rather famous example, we could not insert any old concepts into the formula $E = mc^2$ and expect the resulting empirical statement to be true. Moreover, the statement would not even *mean* anything—true or not—unless the inserted concepts had

certain number characteristics; if c were "charisma," I for one could not make sense of "charisma squared.") Thus Ellis' remark, "measurement is the link between mathematics and science."[9] "Theoretical import" refers to whether a concept fits into useful law-like statements; only measured concepts will fit into law-like statements of arithmetical form.

What we usually mean by measurement is accomplished by applying arithmetic to something observable. Now it is important to realize that in observation we already classify as we predicate this of that.[10] Torgerson argues that "measurement pertains to properties of objects, and not to the objects themselves,"[11] but it is not possible to name an object ("this is a stick") without introducing a classificatory concept. How would I know a stick from a nonstick? Presumably because items in the class of sticks have some properties which differentiate them from things not in that class. Thus if we can observe anything at all, we can measure in some fundamental sense: "it does not seem possible to imagine a world in which the conditions for *enumeration* are not satisfied, but in which the formal system [for enumeration] is yet constructable."[12] Enumeration depends upon identification and re-identification; the construction of a formal system likewise depends upon this condition. Of course we have not done anything very spectacular if all we can do is assign a numeral to a class of objects, but no more. We will have established what Stevens calls a *nominal* scale (assigning numbers to football players is an example of the application of such a scale); Torgerson, for one, does not consider such a scale true measurement since, as he uses the term, measurement "refers to the relative amount or degree of a property ...."[13] To talk about relative amounts is to talk about the concept of a quantity, which in turn leads us to a consideration of scales.

I said above that to observe something is to classify it, in the sense that we must be able to distinguish the "something" from all other objects. Our classification is thus rudimentarily comparative. Now suppose that we were to distinguish "sweet" things from "nonsweet" things (our domain of discourse would presumably be all edible things). The same facility—being able to taste—will allow us to further subclassify the class of sweet things. Three elements (x, y and z), say, all belong in the set of sweet things. But y and z may be put into a subset of sweetness which we are able to discern (y and z taste sweeter than x); finally, z alone among the three elements might be put into a subset of that second set (y, z), such that z tastes sweeter than y. Now, we can do that simply because we can taste degrees of sweetness. Our ability thus to order the elements is no more nor less mysterious than our ability to differentiate sweet from nonsweet. And if we were to construct our sets and subsets in elementary set-theoretic terms, it would turn out that the formal characteristics of the relationships between the sets are isomorphic with other notations, including that of the set of ordinal numbers (or, the relation among degrees of sweetness is asymmetrical, transitive and connected).[14]

Some will object that my account so far has begged some important questions. For instance, is it not the case that John and Mary may disagree about how to order things in terms of sweetness? And would it not help them if they had something by which to *measure* sweetness?

That "something" would be a scale of measurement: I will come to that presently. Here it should be noticed that *if* John and Mary had a "sweet-tester" (a black box to them) which indicated sweetness on a finely calibrated scale, they well might disagree upon the location of the needle. (Is it *precisely* on, say, 3.1128? Or is it closer to 3.1129?) If anyone, on the other hand, believes that it makes no sense to differentiate between degrees of sweetness at all, then restaurant owners, small children and artificial sweetener manufacturers will disagree with him. Indeed, faced with this evidence and more, he might decide to see a doctor to remedy an apparent deficiency of his senses. The problem of accuracy of observation ("observation" refers euphemistically to the five senses) is always with us; what kind of

observations are sufficient depends upon our purposes.

If I told you that I have three piles of pipe in my yard, and that the pipes in pile a are shorter than the pipes in pile b which are in turn shorter than the pipes in c, you would not know which pile to take if I offered one. The "middle pile" (b) might contain pipes about six inches long or 100 feet long. There is no question of precision here, for I have carefully checked to see that no pipe in pile b is shorter than any pipe in pile a. You require more information than is conveyed by *nominal* or *ordinal* measurement. For I have already provided an *ordinal scale* when I assigned numerals (1, 2 and 3) to the pipes.

Clearly we are not yet in any position to say that pipes in pile b are twice as long as pipes in a, or, in general, to say anything about "how much of" the property (length) these pipes have. Yet it is instructive to note that we can, by direct observation, ascertain that one is longer than another. In the same way we can observe that one pipe is the same length as another and we may, if we like, adopt a piece of pipe as a *standard* against which to compare others. Then I can pass along additional information to you about the pile of pipes: they are all less than or equal to the standard pipe. (Of course, this is one of the functions served by keeping standard meter bars, etc., in official places.) But it would certainly be useful to go further, so that we could say that pipe x is twice as long as y, for instance. Certainly we can (and commonly do) say of a series of numbers that they are (a) ordered, and that (b) the differences between the numbers are ordered. We have seen that just in our ability to observe degrees of a property, we can often assign numbers with characteristic (a) to that property. Apparently we must specify further operations in order to achieve characteristic (b), the *interval scale*. Such a scale would allow us to pass along the additional information just mentioned.

We add numbers together, so that $1 + 1 = 2$; why not define additive measurement as the *operation* of adding magnitudes together (as, laying two equal lengths of pipe together)? Indeed, this is often suggested, but it is plainly not enough.[16] First, it is difficult to know what one would mean by adding, say, sweetness together. Second, how would one know that two lengths of pipe put together are twice as long as one? As Wartofsky points out, "checking" against a double length is circular, "because we are only performing the same operation twice, once in establishing the 'double length,' then again, in 'checking' it."[17] We can only get part way out of the difficulty. A cardinal set of numbers is a collection of units which are invariant in magnitude and which may be numbered by counting.[18] Likewise a standard unit of length is taken to be invariant in magnitude (standards are kept in special conditions for this reason) and may be counted. If we "define *quantity* as that which is measurable in terms of this countability of invariant units and of their correspondence with other sets of such units, then this magnitude . . . *is* number." But " . . . the discovery that this relationship is true of some magnitudes and not of others is an empirical discovery."[19] In other words, to measure something additively, we must discover laws which assert a relationship between the units of magnitude isomorphic with the relationship between cardinal numbers. And no empirical law can be established unequivocally. Our best assurance that it is true lies in the law's interconnectedness with other laws. To establish that weight is an additive magnitude requires the acceptance of knowledge about magnitudes and quantities other than weight. To measure at the interval level it is necessary to discover additive relations among degrees of some magnitude. Only then can cardinal numbers be assigned to degrees of magnitude.

I believe that it is worth emphasizing that we have indeed *discovered* that length is an additive relationship. We have considerable confidence in this assertion because Euclid-ean geometry, interpreted as an empirical theory about properties of rigid bodies in space, seems to work in all sorts of applications.[20] If length were *not* an additive property, then predictions from Euclid's theory would not hold.

By now it should be clear that in order to pass along information about how *much* of a quantity some object has, it is necessary to adopt a *scale* of measurement. In fact, we must indicate that changes in degree of some magnitude are correlated to changes in degree of some other, which is taken as a scale.[21] In additive measurement (the interval scale), the important characteristics of such a scale are (a) standard empirical units which (b) display in actual observation the relationships of arithmetical additivity. Both characteristics seem to imply direct observation which, notoriously enough, is not easy to do if one is talking about power. I can think of two replies to such an objection, and they must be made separately.

First, standard works on measurement distinguish between kinds of measurement, and the distinction will probably be relevant to any attempt to measure power. It appears that, with some scales, one is able to compare the ratio between scale units and the quantity *directly*. When I measure length, I compare my standard foot-rule directly to the object which I am measuring. But I cannot directly compare hotnesses, for "the measurement of a quantity or degree of hotness depends on its definition in terms of volumes, lengths, and so on."[22] I can only directly observe hotness in a crude, rank-order way (I can feel it, and I can see water turning to steam, etc.); the construction of a thermometric scale depends upon extensive scientific knowledge about temperature relationships and volume. Campbell called the first kind of measurement *fundamental*, and Torgerson accepts the distinction between that and derived, or *associative* measurement, of which a thermometer is an example.[23] So if someone objects that we cannot think of observable units of "power," our first response is that we may not need to. We cannot think of observable units of hotness, yet it has been possible to construct additive scales for it given experimentation with volumes and temperature laws.[24]

My second reply is more complicated—or more subtle, at any rate. Some students of measurement accept Campbell's distinction, but others do not. For, as I indicated earlier on, it is not easy to think of a quantity which is, on the face of it, additive. Length and time are often regarded as fundamental quantities (in terms of which others are derived). But it turns out that neither can be established as an additive quantity without reference to something else as a standard.[25] Measurement (and observation itself) depends at every turn upon one's theory or, more broadly, orienting device. Now I am not claiming that there is nothing "really" in the world. But I am saying that how we view the world depends upon how we are oriented to view it, and that in turn surely depends upon a complex of historical accidents, environmental demands, etc. If we cannot think of units of power, or of other quantities which would allow us to derive units of power, then it *may* reflect not upon the "way the world is," but upon the way we are *viewing* the world.

There is a great deal more to be said about measurement in general, but that would take us far afield. Here I have tried to suggest the important features of three levels of measurement—nominal, ordinal and interval—and the interconnectedness of observation, measurement and theory. I will now turn to a consideration of "power" as viewed from some representative perspectives. I think it is clear by now why we should pay special attention to the question, What can we actually *observe* when we think of political things in the ways suggested? Once such matters are clarified, we can turn to the problem of scale construction.

II

Theoretical Perspectives and the Observation of Power

We shall attempt now to discern the theoretical orientations in several approaches to the measurement of power. It

seems to me that some are unduly pessimistic about the possibility of asserting coherent, rigorous theories about politics, and this for a paradoxical reason. Many of us in the discipline have been downright pugnacious in our insistence that it is, indeed, possible to construct empirical theories which could explain political phenomena. As we talked about that, and made our arguments, we have often appealed to the physical sciences as a model. Physics has been a favorite discipline in this respect, and I think rightly so. Apparently, however, these arguments have given the erroneous impression—to some behavioralists not less than the "traditionalists"—that if we had a correct theory of politics we would be able to explain and predict virtually any very interesting political phenomenon. If that is the state of affairs to which we aspire, it is small wonder that we are chary of coming right out with an attempt at theory. All attempts seem meager, even ludicrous, when set against that mighty and glorious standard. Traditionalists scoff, and behavioralists ponder and hanker after the elusive insight which will make all of the seemingly disparate pieces fit together.

I would suppose that politics, like another ancient concern of man, the weather, will remain intractable for some time to come. Meteorologists know a very great deal about the weather and what causes it. If it rains, they can explain why it rained. If it does not rain, they can explain that as well. Nevertheless, most of us have at one time or another been made to reflect, blackly, upon the inability of weathermen to tell us just when, how much, and precisely where it is going to rain. To some, that just goes to show. (It "shows," I suppose, that to have relevant scientific information is not necessarily to know everything you might, in every circumstance, like to know.) Others, reflecting upon the analogy, may reach my own conclusion, namely, that an explanation of most political phenomena will require appeal to more than one theory. To use the weather analogy once again, it happens that rainfall is sometimes affected by air pollution from industrial cities. A full explanation of such rainfall would require not only physical and chemical theories, but reference to the sources of the pollution as well. Depending upon how far back we wanted to push the explanatory process, we might find ourselves appealing to economic theory in order to explain rainfall! Even then, of course, we would have explanation but not necessarily prediction. While scientific explanation and prediction are ordinarily regarded as logically identical processes (the difference being that in predicting the event to be explained has not yet occurred), the practical difficulties of prediction can be enormous. It is easy to explain why a building burned down after the evidence is in; however, fire chiefs know—with mixed feelings, I suppose—that it is nearly impossible to predict that a building will in fact burn down. In any case, the central point here is that a relevant theory for the observation and measurement of power will in all likelihood be one which does not nearly entail all interesting political phenomena.

As Wagner points out, many scholars persist in talking about "power" or "influence" when, upon inspection, it turns out that they are interested in phenomena which require no such concept for their explanation. Indeed, when we try to discern different approaches to the measurement of influence, it begins to appear that those approaches are about different things altogether. I propose to examine three of these approaches in the hope that by revealing their logical underpinnings we can see more clearly how the process of measurement is informed by them.

Many authors, when they write about power, seem to be interested in the degree of centralization evinced by the political system in question. Exactly what it is that the system is centralized (or not) with respect to is sometimes not altogether clear, as I shall show. But I want to emphasize here that it is this system characteristic

which interests many political scientists. Other political scientists, it seems to me, have taken the position that we must proceed to sort out the nature of relationships between individuals, and impacts of various sorts upon individuals. The approach is thus psychological, or social-psychological and I will, after Lane, characterize it as S-O-R (stimulus-organism-response).[26] As a rudimentary classification scheme, it allows us to sort out important variables; clearly, it is a framework for causal analysis, and much of the literature on power and influence depends upon implicit or explicit causal analysis. When the "cause" (stimulus) of certain behaviors (response) is someone's conscious intent, then we can name the process a power relationship or some such. A third logical framework is game-theoretical. Game theory has several putative applications, one being a theory of rational decision-making. From such a perspective, it is plausible to name certain strategic advantages which accrue to a player (due to his defined resources or player-position in the game) by the term, "power."

It will come as no revelation to students of political science when I say that much of the so-called "community power" literature has been concerned with the *density*, so to speak, of power in the community. That, is who has the power? Is it spread around, or is it concentrated in the hands of a few? Indeed, so much attention has been directed to this sort of question that students of community power are routinely classified as "elitist," "neo-elitist" or "pluralist," depending upon their views about power concentration. I shall not attempt to trace out the surprising proliferation of issues which has arisen out of early arguments about the concentration of power in communities. (Polsby summarizes many of the issues succinctly enough; Dahl reviews some of the issues as well.) Here I want to discuss some problems inherent in attempts to characterize collectivities (groups, systems, etc.) in empirical terms.

As Wagner points out, it is not surprising that we find ourselves attributing acts to individuals (Napoleon, say) when in fact many people participated. Alternatively, we often refer to complex arrays of individuals and activities as individualized things (*e.g.*, the United States). Ordinarily these are shorthand terms, and they do no harm, but sometimes such uses actually confuse us, deceiving us to believe that a nonsense statement makes sense after all. Philosophers of science have given considerable attention to what they call the "fallacy of methodological holism," or, less formidably, "emergentism."[27] Briefly, the argument against the claim that properties inhere in groups or collectivities which cannot be defined in individual terms rests upon the first principle of scientific concept formation, empirical import. Any term not definable in terms of our experiential vocabulary only destroys the scientific validity of the theory (or statement) in which it is used. I think it is fair to say that the community power studies have suffered from a failure to clarify the connection between their statements about the collectivity and the vocabulary of direct experience. In what sense is it possible (meaningful) to make statements about, say, the concentration of power in a collectivity? I can think of two notions of "concentrated" in this context (although I am not claiming that no others could be thought of). First, we could be speaking of discrete entities, so that they can be observed to occur in variable proximity to one another. If I were speaking of marbles in a circle, I could notice whether they were equally spaced or unevenly distributed. A measure of concentration would no doubt be some appropriate averaging statistic where distance was the relevant quantity. But the ordinary concept of distance does not appear to be very important in social contexts anymore (if it ever was); neither is it easy to think of discrete entities of power.

Economists can speak of the concentration of wealth because money can be conceptualized in the appropriate way. It is evenly or unevenly distributed not in some area, but among a certain population. (If one wishes to call that "power," he may, but it is certainly confusing.) Political scientists have tried to treat "decisions" or, less often, "interactions," as observable,

discrete events. After the fashion of the sociogram, we might record the number and patterns of interactions and/or decisions in a community. Out of the laboratory this is difficult if not impossible to do, however. In a laboratory it is possible to specify behaviors which count as interactions of a certain kind; in the natural environment cabdrivers and policemen and wives and lovers tend to augment the scope of interactions beyond the range of any theory I know of.

I would not say that it is impossible to record interactions or relationship patterns in a natural setting, for sociologists do it all of the time, and some students of community power, employing the "reputational approach," record the number of individuals who attribute influence to others, etc. But none of these attempts satisfactorily deals with the problem of unequivocal empirical import. They may be useful as low-level description, or as exploratory analysis; they do not differentiate very rigorously between relevant and irrelevant interactions, or between informed and careless attributions of power (or, indeed, between one meaning of "power" and another). Treating decisions as discrete entities meets with similar difficulties. Which decisions are relevant to one's theory? What actually counts as a decision?

I think that most political scientists would object to my even talking about concentration in terms of observable patterns of discrete entities, for they do not seem to be thinking in that way. I do it in order to make perfectly clear what sort of assumptions might be required in order to attribute, say, power concentration to a community.

Another way of speaking about concentration in a system would be to examine the patterns of presumed connections between events or objects. If we can posit relationships between events or objects, then we may be able to say something interesting about the patterns of relationships, in addition to the relationships themselves. But we should remain cautious about such a tactic. Assertions are empirical if they can be disconfirmed; surely it will not be sufficient to the ends of scientific theory if we try to make empirical assertions about patterns of relationships if the relationships themselves are not amenable to empirical test. I will return to this point when we consider Brams' article.

What I have called S-O-R approaches to the study of political behavior warrant attention in this essay since, as Riker points out, ambiguities traceable to ideas of "cause" often crop up in attempts to measure power or influence. For example, Wagner argues that if "we are interested in complete explanations we will be interested in all those necessary conditions which are, together, sufficient for the occurrence of B's action . . . ."[28] To speak of necessary and sufficient conditions is one way (indeed, usually the preferred way) of speaking about causal relations. Riker is matter-of-fact about it, and Simon is witty about it, but both point out that social scientists, at least, do not like the term, "cause," in their vocabulary. But speaking of stimuli and responses cannot be very different from speaking of causes and effects, though it may be useful thus to disavow any claims to metaphysical knowledge about "real" connections. Nevertheless, we may miss some important and troublesome issues if we too assiduously avoid the word.

Specifically, if we think in terms of necessary and sufficient conditions, then how do we know when we know "everything?" It is all well and good to say that we are interested in all those necessary conditions which are sufficient to some response, but does that mean that we want to include, as necessary conditions, that B hears what A says? If that is "understood," then do we understand as well how modulations in the air are transformed through the ear into some sort of nervous reaction? Do we, in short, have to—or even want to—include every "condition" between stimulus and response? And if we do not, upon what

basis do we exclude variables? That question, out of theoretical context, is unanswerable. Once again, if we insist upon trying to explain the totality of politics (or those contexts in which "power" has intuitive appeal), we shall founder upon what I expect will turn out to be the limited scope of any given theory. But if we do formulate limited theories, then the queston of what conditions may be excluded is answered by referring to the *completeness* of the theory. Newtonian mechanics is a complete theory in the sense that one can compute the values for any variable in the theory solely on the basis of the values of the other variables in the theory. Every relevant variable is named in the theory, which is *not* to say that any concrete phenomenon can be explained solely in terms of the theory. A complete theory of, say, opinion change will admit a limited number of empirical terms, and only these will be relevant to a statement of necessary and sufficient conditions. It is my guess that we will be unable to establish a complete theory of opinion change without recourse to laboratory experimentation. In any case, general S-O-R-treatments of political behavior surely are subject to the pitfalls of causal analysis. Causal analysis, in turn, only makes sense in the context of a theory that admits but a limited number of empirical terms to its vocabulary. Interesting treatments of influence seem to try to include far too much, as I shall argue.

A third logical background to influence analysis is game-theoretic in nature. Game theory can be baffling, and this for several reasons. Of course it may be complex mathematically, a feature not calculated to endear it to most political scientists. Beyond that, it is not very clear whether the formal theory of games could be an empirical theory about human behavior in certain situations. In game theory it is easy to give empirical content to the player terms—these are simply designated individuals. It is not always easy to give empirical interpretation to the concept of utilities, however. We may, if we choose, give an interpretation of player utilities in terms of physical units, *e.g.*, dollars. But then game theory does not yield encouragingly accurate predictions of actual behavior.[29] However, if we persist in referring to utilities as theoretical, unoperationalized terms, then we can always *assume* that player A was rational (regardless of the outcome), he just has unusual values and hence unordinary utilities. It will be seen that the measurement of utilities is a problem quite circumscribed by the formal properties of game theory. We turn our attention now to some attempts to measure power or influence.

III

The Measurement of Power

There is always something dangerous in pretending to have selected "representative" works from a school or approach within a subject area. Quite a few different attempts to measure influence are included in this book; I propose to examine briefly Brams' "Measuring the Concentration of Power in Political Systems," since it is a recent addition to that first approach I mentioned above (degree of centralization in a system). Two somewhat older articles by Simon remain, in my judgement, excellent examples of the problems and issues raised by the second approach (S-O-R), while Shapley and Shubik provide a standard game-theoretic measure. I have selected these essays for specific treatment not necessarily because I regard them as the best of their kind, but because they are less mixed than other measurement attempts in this book.

MEASURING DEGREE OF CENTRALIZATION
Steven Brams defines his index of power concentration as follows:

$$PC = 1 - \frac{N_{mc}}{N_t}$$

where N_{mc} = the number of decision-makers in all minority control sets, and N_t = the total number of decision-makers in the political system. Brams refines the index in order to take account of hierarchical levels of influence (the index yields paradoxical results without such refine-

ment), but that need not concern us for the moment. In what sense does this index measure power concentration in political systems? Basically, it is merely the ratio of rulers to ruled; its interesting feature is that the index focuses attention upon sets of individuals rather than the individuals themselves. It is rather like trying to figure out a log jam. Ten logs might be leaning together in such a way that to dislodge one would release the rest. But whether that would break a jam of, shall we say, 10,000 logs would depend upon how other subsystems of logs were dependent—if at all—upon any of those ten logs. Lumberjacks yearn to find the "key log"; political scientists relentlessly track the "real" powerholders. Brams' index, by expressing a ratio of rulers to ruled (about which more, later), tells us whether the system is like a log jam with a few key logs, or whether it is more like a stack of wood with each log more or less holding its own. Now, Brams devotes quite a lot of space to the proposition that such an index is useful in that it directs our attention to *system* properties and the possibilities of comparative laws. I agree with Brams in some degree. It seems to me that buildings would never be so strong if architects did not know something about the comparative strengths and weaknesses of divers geometric distributions of beams, as well as the strength of the beams themselves. And—again, analogously—that is the sort of thing in which Brams is interested: What can we say about power-concentrated systems as opposed to non-concentrated systems?

Where I must demur is with the implicit claim that this article is toward a theory of power in political systems. It *may* be toward a theory of organization, but not power. For Brams consistently avoids or glosses over the question, What observations are required in order to effect the suggested measurement of power concentration? The answer to this question reveals that, in its present form, the index is not of "power" concentration at all—unless one is addicted to a peculiar usage of the term.

In order to use Brams' power concentration index, one would first have to identify and count all of the decision-makers in the political system. Now, by itself this is an observation not readily made, for one would have to decide whom to include and exclude from the system. And finding out just who the decision-makers are in a community was the task which Hunter, and others, set out to accomplish. They, at any rate, did not think the answer obvious. Neither do I. This is one reason why I think Brams' index more appropriate for formal organizations rather than political systems generally: identifying the boundaries of the system, and the elements for inclusion, remains a formidable problem quite unsolved by Brams.

But suppose that we *can* solve that problem, if only by fiat. That is, suppose we are willing to restrict our attention to formal decision-making posts in an organization or government (then we are beginning a theory of formal organizations, of course). If we can identify the members of the set, we can count them; I think this is not a particularly mysterious part of the index. It remains then for us to identify the elements in all "minority control sets," count them, and perform the elementary operations indicated in the formula. A minority control set is a mutual influence set which "directly influences one or more other mutual influence sets containing a total of more constituent decision-makers."[30] Mutual influence sets are subsets in which the decision-makers "can influence (directly or indirectly), and be influenced . . . only by every other decision-maker in their sets."[31] Manifestly, there is no way to observe members of such sets without being able to observe influence. That, of course, is a trick most of us have not learned; let us see how Brams handles the problem.

As a very rudimentary approach to this problem, we shall consider two actors to be in a power relationship when they appear to be responsive to each other's behavior. When one actor responds more frequently than the other, we shall assume that the actor responding less frequently exercises asymmetrical influence . . .; when the actors respond . . . with equal frequency, we shall assume that they are involved in a symmetrical influence relationship.[32]

What stands out here is that there is nothing in Brams' approach to guide us in interpreting the term, "respond." Do facial expressions count? Must the responder do what the initiator asks? Many of the essays included in this book address themselves—not notably successfully—to just such problems. I think Brams' approach might prove valuable within a clearer substantive framework; he erroneously assumes what this collection of essays disproves: that all of that literature about "power" signifies such a framework. I think that we will lose much of the power of Brams' approach if we are not careful about what terms we introduce into the logical framework. The following approaches concern themselves more directly with the problem which is, in Brams' larger framework, a secondary one.

MEASURING CAUSED CHANGES

The eclectic Herbert Simon turned his attention, a few years ago, to the general problem of sorting out causes from effects in social contexts. I think that his efforts remain timely, though heirs to his ideas have refined some of his techniques considerably.[33] As Simon points out in "Notes . . . ," there are implications in viewing a social structure as a network of asymmetrical relationships. I think the most important one is that to view the world in this way makes the definition of power or influence a matter of determining causal relationships: "A has power over B" becomes an if-then statement in which A's behavior is asymmetrically related to B's response. The units of observation that Simon talks about in this article are ones which make sense in an asymmetrical causal framework. It argues, for example, that "a measurement of authority will be a measurement of at least one form of influence."[34] A's authority over B is measured by observing the relative size of the set of behaviors that B will perform at A's command; as the size of the set increases and decreases, so do we observe that A's authority increases and decreases. Now, two related considerations are relevant here.

Earlier on, I said that to observe something is to classify it, for we must distinguish the thing in question from all other things. Thus, if we can observe what actions B will perform at A's command, we can define a set. I said as well, above, that we can sometimes discern subsets within a set (as sweeter things in a set of sweet things); the formal characteristics of the relationships between the sets will be isomorphic with other notations, thus determining the level of measurement. Simon thinks that authority can be measured at a weak ordinal scale level (a "partial ordering," since the subsets within the set of B's responses may overlap occasionally). The first consideration is that there is no sense in talking about sets, subsets and the relationships between them unless it is possible to specify exactly what properties of objects or events define those sets (*e.g.*, red things, sweet foods, strong men, etc.). But the related consideration here is that in order to observe the set of behaviors B will perform at A's command, we must somehow be able to observe an asymmetrical relationship. Much of Simon's article is devoted to clarifying the difficulties which beset us when we try to sort out the directions of relationships between individuals (the "rule of anticipated reactions," etc.). But nothing of what Simon talks about really answers the fundamental objections to causal analysis raised long ago by David Hume. How can we know whether a set of behaviors is in response to A's command? Who can observe "cause?"

The second Simon article I want to talk about ("Spurious . . .") deals with the problems of distinguishing spurious correlation from "true" correlation. No purpose is served, presumably, by merely repeating what Simon says, so I shall leave it to the reader to wade through this and related works.[35] Here I only want to emphasize that it is by no means impossible

to test for causal connections, provided one is willing to make certain limiting assumptions. The main point to be grasped is that "cause," in this sense, refers to the *form* of the theory (or partial theory) which describes empirical reality. In the simple three-variable cause which Simon illustrates,

$$x + a_{12}y + a_{13}z = u_1,$$
$$y + a_{23}z = u_2,$$
$$z = u_3,$$

where u = "error terms."[36] In these equations, a change in u_3 changes z, hence y and x; a change in u_2 changes y and hence x, but not z. Now what Simon is attempting to show is that, with limiting assumptions, it is possible to reject the entire "model" by showing that certain entailments (specifically, that particular coefficients will equal zero) do not obtain. It is by this same logic that we formulate null hypotheses in order to reject them rather than trying to verify them. Similarly we test hypotheses which are entailed by theories in order to reject those theories. Even so, we can formulate causal models with a limited number of non-testable entailments; if one of the testable entailments can be falsified, the model is rejected.

It would be misleading if I did not point out that the formulation of multi-variable models for testing is exceedingly difficult. The number of possible models for a given number of variables quickly becomes astronomical, and it is not usually easy to rule out large numbers of combinations prior to testing. This is a problem of scientific discovery and does not, by itself, militate against the logic of causal model testing. Some social scientists have tried to devise defensible inductive procedures which are related to Simon's approach; others—and I lean to this view—have gravitated to small-group laboratory experimental work in order to effect the manipulation of presumed causal factors.

It would appear that we are now somewhat closer to being able to measure power, although formidable difficulties remain. Simon's work suggests that we should try to identify sets of behaviors such that specific subsets of all possible behaviors are in response to commands from certain individuals. To do this, I would argue, we must be prepared to make appropriate assumptions which allow causal analysis; then the size of the above-mentioned subsets indicates (at, Simon suspects, a partially-ordered level of measurement) degree of authority. What is lacking now is any theoretical framework to guide us in the selection of relevant behaviors. Would the same theory explain why B responds obediently to A when A (1) tells B to shoot on sight and when A (2) tells B to undress? With little more than intuitive notions as to what induces people to comply with orders of various sorts, we become aware of the problems confronting anyone who would measure power in the absence of adequate theory. However, when rigorous theory is supplied, the range of topics originally considered under the rubric of power is drastically reduced.

DECISION-MAKING AND THE MEASUREMENT
OF UTILITIES

A third approach to the measurement of power is to adopt a theory which predicts decision-making strategies under certain conditions. The mathematical theory of games—by itself a nonempirical, formal axiomatic system—has intrigued social scientists with its apparent applicability to real-life situations. Appropriate axioms of the theory of games are given empirical content by transforming them into postulates of "rationality" on the part of game-players (i.e., decision-makers in situations formally analogous to some game). Thus it may be postulated that in a two-person, zero-sum game, both players will always minimize their maximum possible losses. In many kinds of games (and they may be two- or n-person, constant- or variable-sum, etc.), it is possible, though not usually simple, to show that there is a best winning

strategy for each player. (This is not to say that any player can "win," of course.) The "power" of a player thus becomes a function of his position in the game, or—since we are postulating rational players—his relative ability to win.

Game theory abstracts certain presumed characteristics of decision-making in conflict situations and, as Anatol Rapoport points out, whether the essential aspects have indeed been abstracted from real-life situations is a moot question.[37] Not only may we doubt whether "rational" players actually do try to maximize the pay-offs to themselves while guarding against loss; it could be that pay-offs are not in fact the important, dominant feature of real-life conflict situations. Perhaps these are only elaborate rationalizations to mask a lust for conflict—mere aggressiveness—which actually motivates us to combat others. Before we consider such questions (for these are questions about the descriptive accuracy of the theory, not the logic of it), I want to indicate how the formal properties of mathematical game theory affect the measurement of utilities.

In the first part of this essay, I talked about three levels of measurement, nominal, ordinal and interval. These are classifications of scales, of course, and one can grasp intuitively the differences between the three types. The original classifications were, however, based upon criteria of more intersubjective import than intuitive grasp. Coombs based his classification upon the kinds of applications of arithmetic represented by the different scales. Thus, the nominal scale is "any scale on which only arithmetical formulae of the form $a \gneqq b$ have any analytic application."[38] An ordinal scale applies formulae of the form $a \gneqq b$, and so forth. An alternative means of classification which seems to accomplish similar types is that of Stevens, who bases his upon the kinds of transformations which will yield a new scale that serves all of the purposes of the original one. For example, with a nominal scale we simply assign numbers to objects (football players) in order to differentiate them. It follows that any system of numbering would do, provided no object ends up with the same number as another. We may permute these numbers in any way we please, and the resulting new scale would serve the same purpose as the original; for Stevens, a nominal scale is one which retains its usefulness under any permutation transformation.

Since ordinal scales indicate transitive order, then they may be subjected to any order-preserving transformation. Interval scales may be subject to any order-preserving and interval-preserving preserving transformation; there is only one, $y = mx + c$, where $m > 0$.[39] In other words, if a scale of measurement can be transformed according to the above formula, and if it retains all of its original uses upon transformation, then it is an interval scale.

Now consider the problem of the measurement of "payoffs" in game theory. In many games, as I said above, it is possible to find the "best" way to play the game, in the sense that rational players would always choose the same strategies. But it is easy to imagine a rational player playing the game differently for different stakes; indeed, "serious" poker players will seldom participate in a very low-stakes poker game not, apparently, because they are all rich but because they have found players to be wildly incautious when the money stakes are trivial. Contract bridge players, on the other hand, often play quite carefully where there is no money at all at stake. This merely illustrates that the risks and payoffs associated with various strategies in a game vary according to the situation and the nature of the stakes involved.

Game theory assumes rational players, and this means "to get as much as possible in terms of utilities [the "psychological" or subjective worth of outcomes]."[40] In other words, it should make no difference that utilities may be measured in different units under different circumstances. Thus we should be able to transform utilities measured on a scale Y into units of X according to the formula, $y = mx$ ($m > 0$), and the payoff scale should remain invariant.[41] Now suppose that a constant sum is added to all of the possible payoffs to a player in a certain game (such as a fixed

bonus being attached to all of the payoffs). Logically, the player should not alter his strategy, since the constant will not affect the relative attractiveness of any of the payoffs; the payoff scale should remain invariant with respect to the transformation $y = x + c$ (c constant).[42] Combining these transformations, we have $y = mx + c$ ($m > 0$), which is the transformation formula characterizing Stevens' interval scale.

It is particularly important to note that the logic of most game-theoretic analysis is based upon the idea that utilities can be specified in the manner suggested above, *i.e.*, that payoffs can be specified on an interval scale. The whole structure of game theory depends upon such a premise; in turn, measurement of utilities is informed by the theory. But since people seem incapable of consistent replies to questions like "How many times greater is your preference for Congress over the Presidency than your preference of the Presidency over the Supreme Court?" we must seek alternative means of measurement.

Surely it would take us quite far afield to attempt to recapitulate the literature on psychophysics and psychometrics here. Suffice it to say that much has been—and is being—written about techniques for measuring subjective responses to events and objects.[43] The important criterion for game theory is whether the numbers obtained would retain their validity after linear transformation.

Shapley and Shubik ("A Method . . . ") calculate the distribution of power in a committee system on the basis of the chance a member has of being critical to the success of a winning coalition. It is easy to see, however, that the authors' index nowise measures "power" in a descriptive sense. For example, we can imagine a congressman who assiduously avoids being on the winning side of certain issues (perhaps civil rights bills) in order to remain in the favor of his constituency. Of course such an individual would turn out to be relatively powerless by the Shapley–Shubik index, even though such tactics might assure continued re-election. Eventually this same congressman would assume high office within the committee system of Congress (assuming that current seniority norms continue to prevail), giving him great manipulative capacities vis-à-vis certain kinds of legislation—perhaps civil rights legislation. This and untold further examples convince me that even an accurately descriptive game theory would not tell us nearly everything we would want to know about the distribution of influence in Congress. Of course, scientific theories rarely *do* tell one everything he might want to know about a concrete phenomenon.

One reason, then, why Riker's test of the adequacy of the power index yielded ambiguous results is probably that a theory of rational decision-making in conflict situations simply is inadequate to account for anything like the full range of motives for voting in committees. And there remains the other question, whether humans ever do actually order their preferences in such a way that interval-level measurement is realistic. If they do not, most game theory is irrelevant to a descriptive theory of decision-making.

Solutions to myriads of games are being sought, and new game situations are being devised. Concurrently, social scientists are testing to see whether certain solved games do provide models for descriptive theories of decision-making. There is little reason to be overly sanguine about the prospects for the development of an empirical theory of decision-making in conflict situations from mathematical game theory nor, in Rapaport's view, can we expect game theory to serve as a useful prescriptive theory.[44] Truly it is dangerous to prejudge such questions in any case. My only point here is that game theory as a descriptive theory would surely lack the broad scope which characterizes less rigorous discussions of influence and power.

Conclusion

Measurement is not a process which takes place independently of theory. In the first part of this essay I tried to indicate some general features of measurement which require the acceptance of a theoretical framework; it may be helpful to recapitulate parts of my argument here.

If we construe measurement rather narrowly, then we have in mind the application of arithmetic to our field of inquiry. Arithmetic helps us to accomplish complicated deductions; measurement links concepts to arithmetic. But as Simon points out, it will do us no good to insist that concepts have properties similar to cardinal numbers if, in fact, those properties do not obtain.[45] We discussed the logic by which numbers are assigned to objects or events, concluding that in order to assign cardinal numbers to objects (which is, roughly, to measure at the interval level) one must already have a theory which implies that the observed units have the same properties as cardinal numbers. In other words, one must establish isomorphism between certain axioms of a theory of numbers and an empirical theory about the concepts in question.

If we construe measurement more broadly (the assignment of numbers to objects or events according to any rule), then the very processes of observation and classification constitute measurement at some (perhaps very low) level of measurement. We are inclined therefore to look to the theoretical orientation which informs one's view of power; if we can explicate the theory, then the level of measurement is indicated.

The three approaches I have talked about are not, I should say, each about "power." One approach is concerned to explain system concentration and diffusion; a system may be concentrated in terms of *resources* (which can be observed, counted, etc.) and/or in terms of linkages. Brams attempts to classify systems according to the degree to which influence is concentrated or dispersed; he attaches numbers (at a partially-ordered level) to different classifications of *patterns* of influence. Brams is working on a theory about system properties.

Simon appears to be concerned to explain interactions between persons. His approach is explicitly causal but, in the essays we examined, he does not go very far toward identifying exactly which concepts should be included (and therefore what should be excluded) in the theory. Lacking clear guidelines, causal analysis cannot be carried to its conclusion. Of course Simon recognizes the difficulty, and suggests that game theory might be an appropriate theoretical framework.

Whether game theory is "appropriate" in the sense of being descriptively accurate remains an open question. Clearly, its potential descriptive application is not nearly so broad as the apparent scope of many of the essays on power in this book. But it is interesting to see how the logic of

game theory determines the level of measurement of payoffs; here is a theory which asserts that preferences in certain situations are ordered by the same properties as cardinal numbers.

If our achievements in the field of power measurement are meager and disappointing, we should not blame our measurement techniques. It should be clear that our theories are to blame. But it is certainly not at all clear that a theory of power, as such, is somewhere in the offing. If we eventually develop several theories (like game theory) which, together, subsume much of the amorphous phenomenon we call "power," then we will no doubt be faced with several different measures, none of which is a measure of power.

Political Power and Political Science

ALTHOUGH today social scientists still sometimes settle for "pure" description in their work, they generally agree that they must eventually go beyond description to explanation and perhaps eventually to prediction. Thus it is as an explanatory device that the notion of power must prove itself if it is to be useful to us as students of society and politics. Although some scholars originally sought simply to determine just where "power" lay or resided in a political unit or relationship, most of this early work was founded on the belief that such knowledge would prove to be explanatory—that knowing what was termed "the distribution of power" would enable one to understand political actions and outcomes.

Thus there is a large and extensive body of literature in political science and sociology which concerns itself with who has power in a given political unit—whether it be a committee or the international system. Further work by students of politics and society—as will be clear in subsequent sections of this book—significantly altered the terms in which political analysis was undertaken. But even in the earlier work which concentrated on the distribution of power there were disputes about approaches and emphases. These controversies varied with the level of politics under analysis.

At the local level, debate has been over whether there is a small group of men who rule—men whose role in community government is consistently larger than that of the rest of the populace. This focus upon individuals and a small group results largely from the widespread presumption that any society or population will have an elite plus the fact that the study of an elite is most possible at the level of a small populace. But if everyone grants that it is possible to discover which residents matter, there remains considerable debate over whether there is one group which dominates all decisions—the "elitist" or "community power structure" school—or whether the dominant group changes as the issues change—the "pluralist" school. The "pluralist" tends to view political decisions as resulting from the skillful employment of "power resources" (such as patronage, popularity, voting credit, etc.) by various small special interest groups with incompletely overlapping memberships and resources.

The debate between the elitists and the pluralists can be extended, on a grander scale, to the study of American national politics. The argument here is over whether or not a discrete group or special interest—such as the very wealthy or the military-industrial complex—manages to control political outcomes. In other words, at the state and national level, the debate has been over whether policy decisions are determined primarily by the operation of the electoral political process or by the influence-peddling of lobbies and private interests.

At the international level, the prime question has not been who rules or why he decides as he does, but rather whether states conduct themselves primarily as seekers after power over each other and whether some distributions of power among states are more stable than others, as is argued in "balance of power" theory.

At each of these levels, the early quarrels arose from differing interests and presuppositions and were compounded because for a time many people thought they were answering similar questions when they were not. The selections in this section are works which reveal the disputes and which also helped significantly to straighten out the debates. They were milestones along the path toward the advancement of the explanatory study of power in politics, and they remain insightful analyses of key issues in the debates that raged in study of the local, national, and international levels of politics.

POLITICAL SCIENTISTS are beginning to view certain major contributions to the study of community politics less favorably than one would have expected after hearing the fanfare surrounding the original acceptance of these works.[1] Often billed as studies of "community power structure," these works have been produced mostly by sociologists, whose orientation has been to study the politics of American communities as a subsidiary aspect of social structure.[2] "The political organization of Jonesville," writes one such scholar, "fits the rest of the social structure . . . curving or bulging with the class outlines of the body politic."[3]

The faults which critics have found with studies following this general conception of politics as an epiphenomenon of social stratification are many, varied and serious. They include the charges that this conception encourages research designs which generate self-fulfilling prophecies,[4] and that it leads to the systematic misreporting of facts[5] and to the formulation of ambiguous and unprovable assertions about community power.[6] It would be gratuituous for me to re-explore these criticisms here. It would be more profitable, instead, to describe some of the ways in which students have evaded—apparently with success—the various disabilities of the stratification approach to the study of community power. With judicious unoriginality, I shall call the alternative research strategy to be outlined here the "pluralist" approach. Old, familiar pluralistic presumptions[7] about the nature of American politics seem to have given researchers strategies for the study of community power which are both feasible to execute and comparatively faithful to conditions in the real world.[8] What follows is an attempt to explain why this seems to be the case for pluralist studies, but not for stratification studies.

The first, and perhaps most basic presupposition of the pluralist approach, is that nothing categorical can be assumed about power in any community. It rejects the stratification thesis that *some* group necessarily dominates a community.[9] If anything, there seems to be an unspoken notion among pluralist researchers that at bottom *nobody* dominates in a town, so that their

3

How to Study Community Power: The Pluralist Alternative*

Nelson W. Polsby

Nelson W. Polsby, Associate Professor of Political Science at the University of California, Berkeley, wrote this article as part of a longer study, eventually published as Political Theory and Community Power. This work was a part of the study of community power in New Haven, Connecticut, directed by Robert Dahl. The article criticizes the stratification or elitist approach and argues for the pluralist position. It is reprinted from 22 Journal of Politics (1960), 474-84, with the permission of the author and the publisher.

first question to a local informant is not likely to be, "Who runs this community?," but rather, "Does anyone at all run this community?" It is instructive to examine the range of possible answers to each of these questions. The first query is somewhat like, "Have you stopped beating your wife?," in that virtually any response short of total unwillingness to answer will supply the researchers with a "power élite" along the lines presupposed by the stratification theory.[10] On the other hand, the second question is capable of eliciting a response which *could* lead to the discovery of a power élite (*i.e.*, "Yes"), or any of an infinite number of stable, but non-élitist patterns of decision-making (*i.e.*, "No but . . ."; "Yes, but . . ."), or total fragmentation, or disorganization (*i.e.*, "No").

* This article is a paper of the New Haven Community Leadership Study, and owes a great deal to Robert A. Dahl and Raymond E. Wolfinger. I am also grateful to George M. Belknap, Norton E. Long and Robert O. Schulze, but none of these gentlemen should be held responsible for the notions presented here.

31

What sort of question is likely to follow
"Who runs the community?" in a question-
naire? Obviously, something like "*How* do
the people named in the above response run
the community?" This entirely probable
pattern of investigation begs the question of
whether or not those said to rule actually do
rule. In the pluralist approach, on the other
hand, an attempt is made to study specific
outcomes, in order to determine who actually prevails in community decision-making.
Consonant with the desire to study actual
outcomes, which requires arduous and
expensive field work, outcomes in a few
(but, for reasons of expense, usually only a
few) issue-areas are studied closely. More
than a single issue-area is always chosen,
however, because of the presumption among
pluralist researchers that the same pattern
of decision-making is highly unlikely to
reproduce itself in more than one issue-
area. In this expectation, pluralist researchers
have seldom been disappointed.[11] They
recognize, however, the possibility that the
same pattern *could* reproduce itself in more
than one issue-area. Since actual behavior
is observed, or reconstructed from documents, witnesses, and so on, it is possible to
determine empirically whether or not the
same group rules two or more issue-areas.
The presumption that the existence of a
power élite is unlikely does not, in other
words, prevent the finding of such an élite
if the data so indicate.

A superficially persuasive objection to
this approach might be phrased as follows:
"Suppose research in a community discloses different patterns of decision-making
in each of three issue-areas. This does not
rule out the possibility that all other issue-
areas in the community are dominated by a
single power élite." How can pluralists
meet this objection? First, it is necessary to
acknowledge the *possibility* that this is the
case. However, pluralists can (and do)
protect themselves in part by studying
significant issues. In the New Haven study,
for example, of which this paper is an outgrowth, we studied (1) nominations by the
two political parties, which determine which
persons hold public offices; (2) the New
Haven Redevelopment program, which is
the largest in the country (measured by past
and present outlay per capita); (3) public
education, which is the most costly item in
the city's budget; and (4) a campaign to
revise the city charter.[12] In Bennington,
Scoble studied political nominations and
elections, the issue of consolidation of
various municipal governments, the formation of a union high-school district, and the
construction of a new high-school building.[13] A pilot study, by Long and Belknap,
of a large eastern city embraced the problems of transportation, race relations,
traffic, urban redevelopment and recrea-
tion,[14] while, in the San Francisco Bay area,
Belknap studied the issues of urban redevelopment, transportation and race relations.[15] None of these issues was trivial;
they probably were, in fact, the most
important issues before these communities
during the time these studies were being
carried out. What sort of a power élite is it
—it may appropriately be asked—which
asserts itself in relatively trivial matters, but
is inactive or ineffective in the most significant areas of community policy-making?

Stratification theory holds that power
élites fail to prevail only on trivial issues.[16]
By pre-selecting as issues for study those
which are generally agreed to be significant,
pluralist researchers can test stratification
theory without searching endlessly in one
issue-area after another, in order to
discover some semblance of a power élite.
After all, it cannot be reasonably required of
researchers that they validate someone
else's preconceived notions of community
power distributions. If the researchers'
design is such that any power distribution
has an equal chance of appearing in his
result, his result may not properly be criticized on the grounds that it did not conform
to expectations. The burden of proof is
clearly on the challenger in such a case to
make good his assertion that power is
actually distributed otherwise.[17]

Another presumption of the pluralist
approach runs directly counter to stratification theory's presumption that power
distributions are a more or less permanent
aspect of social structure. Pluralists hold

that power may be tied to issues, and issues can be fleeting or persistent, provoking coalitions among interested groups and citizens ranging in their duration from momentary to semi-permanent. There is a clear gain in descriptive accuracy involved in formulating power distributions so as to take account of the dimension of time, as pluralists do,[18] since it is easily demonstrated that coalitions *do* vary in their permanency. To presume that the set of coalitions which exists in the community at any given time is a timelessly stable aspect of social structure is to introduce systematic inaccuracies into one's description of social reality.

Why do pluralists reject the idea that *some* group necessarily dominates every community? The presumption that communities are likely to be less rather than more permanent in their patterns of decision-making is no doubt part of the answer, but another part is an even more fundamental conception of human behavior as governed in large part by inertia. This view leads pluralists to put a high value on overt activity as indicative of involvement in issues and to look upon the collection of "reputations" for leadership as a much less desirable research procedure.[19]

Pluralists consider as arbitrary the inclusion of certain groups as being "implicated" in decisions when these groups themselves reject such involvement.[20] For pluralists, "false class consciousness" does not exist, because it implies that the values of analysts are imposed on groups in the community. They reject the idea that there is any particular issue or any particular point in the determination of an issue where a group must assert itself in order to follow its expressed values. Rather, the pluralist assumes that there are many issues and many points at which group values can be realized. Further, pluralists presume that there are certain costs in taking any action at all. This refers not simply to the possibility of losing, of making political enemies, and so on, but also to the costs in personal time and effort involved in political mobilization, in becoming informed, in lobbying or campaigning and in taking the trouble to vote.[21]

It is a demonstrated fact that public

activity of all sorts is a habit more characteristic of the middle and upper classes than of the lower classes.[22] Vidich and Bensman, for the first time in a community study, depicted the life of the lowest-class groups in the community sufficiently well so that the personally functional aspects of withdrawal from the community were revealed.[23] The presumption of inertia permits the researcher to regard the public sector of activity as but one facet of behavior capable of giving people satisfaction, and discourages the inappropriate and arbitrary assignment of upper and middle-class values to all actors in the community.

The presumption of inertia also helps put economic and social notables into perspective. If a man's major life work is banking, the pluralist presumes he will spend his time at the bank, and not in manipulating community decisions. This presumption holds until the banker's activities and participations indicate otherwise. Once again, it is very important to make the point that this assumption is not scientifically equivalent to its opposite. If we presume that the banker is "really" engaged in running the community, there is practically no way of disconfirming this notion, even if it is totally erroneous. On the other hand, it is easy to spot the banker who really *does* run community affairs when we presume he does not, because his activities will make this fact apparent. In the absence of the requisite activities, we have no grounds for asserting that the banker, in fact, does run the community.[24]

The pluralist emphasis on the time-bounded nature of coalitions and on the voluntary aspect of political participation leads to a further contrast with stratification theory, since pluralists hold that the "interest group" and the "public" are the social collectives most relevant to the analysis of political processes. In the sociologist's patois, politically important groups would be called phenomena of "collective behavior" rather than of "social struc-

ture."[25] Social classes in stratification
theory are populations differentially ranked
according to economic or status criteria,
which embrace the entire community.
Everyone in a community is a member of at
least one but no more than one class at any
given moment, and no one in the community falls outside the system. This is a legitimate heuristic construction; however, it is a
mistake to impute to the apparently
inescapable fact of class membership any
sort of class consciousness. This sociologists
have long recognized.[26] But they seem less
willing to grant that it is equally incorrect to
presume that those sharing similar market
or status positions are also equidistant to all
the bases of political power, or in fact share
class interests. American society has never
been noted for its inter-class warfare, a fact
often reported with a great show of surprise
in stratification studies of American communities.[27]

Pluralists, who see American society as
fractured into a congeries of hundreds of
small "special interest" groups, with incompletely overlapping memberships, widely differing power bases, and a multitude of techniques for exercising influence
on decisions salient to them,[28] are not
surprised at the low priority which Americans give to their class membership as bases
of social action. In the decision-making of
fragmented government—and American
national, state and local governments are
nothing if not fragmented—the claims of
small, intense minorities are usually attended to.[29] Hence it is not only inefficient but
usually unnecessary for entire classes to
mobilize when the preferences of class-
members are pressed and often satisfied in a
piecemeal fashion. The empirical evidence
supporting this pluralist doctrine is overwhelming,[30] however much stratification
theorists may have missed its significance for
them, namely, that the fragmentation of
American governmental decision-making
and of American society makes class
consciousness inefficient, and, in most cases,
makes the political interests of members of
the same class different.

Pluralist research is not interested in
ascertaining an actor's ranking in a system
presumed to operate hierarchically. Rather,
pluralists want to find out about leadership
roles, which are presumed to be diverse and
fluid, both within a single issue-area over
time, and as between issue-areas. Long and
Belknap, for example, identify the following leadership roles in community decision-
making: Initiation, Staffing and Planning,
Communication and Publicity, Intra-élite
Organizing, Financing and Public Sanctioning.[31]

By describing and specifying leadership
roles in concrete situations, pluralists are in
a position to determine the extent to which
power structure exists. If there exist high
degrees of overlap among issue-areas in
decision-making personnel, or of institutionalization in the bases of power in
specified issue-areas, or of regularity in the
procedures of decision-making, then the
empirical conclusion is justified that some
sort of "power structure" exists. By specifying leadership roles and activities, the
pluralist research strategy makes it possible
for an empirical determination of the
bounds and durability of a community
"power structure"—if one exists—to be
described, and the stratification theory
presumption that community power is
necessarily general and relatively immutable
can be discarded as arbitrary.

The final contrast I want to make between
the pluralist and stratification methods has
to do with their differing conceptions of
what is meant by "power." I have already
noted that stratification theorists emphasize
the cataloguing of power bases, meaning
the resources available to actors for the
exercise of power.[32] Pluralists, on the other
hand, concentrate on power exercise itself.
This leads to two subsidiary discoveries.
First, there are a great many different kinds
of resources which can be turned to use in
the process of community decision-making
—many more resources, in fact, than stratification theorists customarily take account
of. One list, for example, includes: money
and credit; control over jobs; control over
the information of others; social standing;
knowledge and expertness; popularity,
esteem and charisma; legality, constitution-

ality and officiality; ethnic solidarity; and the right to vote.[33]

The second product of the pluralist emphasis on power exercise is the discovery that resources are employed only with variations in degree of skill. The elaboration of the ways in which resources are employed enables the pluralist researcher to pay attention to what practical politicians customarily see as the heart of their own craft: the processes of bargaining, negotiation, salesmanship and brokerage, and of leadership in mobilizing resources of all kinds. This approach also makes possible a more realistic evaluation of the actual disposable resources of actors. A corporation may be worth millions of dollars, but its policies and liquidity position may be such that it cannot possibly bring those monetary resources into play in order to influence the outcome of a community decision—even one in which the corporation is vitally interested. And interest itself, as noted above, is differentially distributed in a pattern which pluralists assume is rational for most actors, most of the time. For example, Long and Belknap observe:

> Just as business organizations may be disinterested in community affairs because of the national scope of its (sic) operations, individual businessmen who move or are shifted from city to city may have little opportunity or incentive to participate in community affairs. Some businesses have strong pressures on them to give attention to community and metropolitan problems. Large department stores are particularly tied up with the destiny of the city and must decide whether to keep to the central city or decentralize in suburban shopping centers. Businessmen with a "metropolitan view" would thus be expected to be found here rather than in the branch office of a national corporation.[34]

What practical recommendations emerge from this comparison of stratification and pluralist approaches to the study of com-

munity power?[35] First, the researcher should pick issue-areas as the focus of his study of community power. Second, he should be able to defend these issue-areas as being important in the life of the community. Third, he should study actual behavior, either at first hand, or by reconstructing behavior from documents, informants, newspapers and other appropriate sources. There is no harm in starting with a list of people whose behavior the researcher wishes to study *vis-à-vis* any issue-area. The harm comes, rather, in attributing some mystical significance to such a list, so that the examination of activity and of actual participation in decision-making becomes superfluous. This recommendation is not meant to discourage the researcher from collecting information about the reputation of actors, or their intentions with respect to community issue, or their evaluations about the "meanings" of community incidents. All of these kinds of data are of immeasurable value in tracing patterns of decision-making. However, these cultural data must be accompanied by information about behavior so that the researcher has some way of distinguishing between myths and facts.

The final recommendation is of the same order: researchers should study the outcomes of actual decisions within the community. It is important, but insufficient, to know what leaders want to do, what they intend to do, and what they think they can do. The researcher still has to decide on the basis of his own examination of the facts what actually emerges from these various intentions, and not conclude prematurely that the combination of intentions and resources inflexibly predetermines outcomes.

4

A Critique of the Ruling Elite Model

Robert A. Dahl

Robert A. Dahl, Sterling Professor of Political Science
at Yale University, is the most prominent of the
pluralist analysts of community power. He directed
the famed New Haven study and presented its results
in his classic book, Who Governs? This article,
an early criticism of elitist analysis, is reprinted from
52 American Political Science Review (1958) 463–69,
with the permission of the author and publisher.

A GREAT MANY people seem to believe that "they" run things: the old families, the bankers, the City Hall machine, or the party boss behind the scene. This kind of view evidently has a powerful and many-sided appeal. It is simple, compelling, dramatic, "realistic." It gives one standing as an inside-dopester. For individuals with a strong strain of frustrated idealism, it has just the right touch of hard-boiled cynicism. Finally, the hypothesis has one very great advantage over many alternative explanations: It can be cast in a form that makes it virtually impossible to disprove.

Consider the last point for a moment. There is a type of quasi-metaphysical theory made up of what might be called an infinite regress of explanations. The ruling elite model *can* be interpreted in this way. If the overt leaders of a community do not appear to constitute a ruling elite, then the theory can be saved by arguing that behind the overt leaders there is a set of covert leaders who do. If subsequent evidence shows that this covert group does not make a ruling elite, then the theory can be saved by arguing that behind the first covert group there is another, and so on.

Now whatever else it may be, a theory that cannot even in principle be controverted by empirical evidence is not a scientific theory. The least that we can demand of any ruling elite theory that purports to be

more than a metaphysical or polemical doctrine is, first, that the burden of proof be on the proponents of the theory and not on its critics; and, second, that there be clear criteria according to which the theory could be disproved.

With these points in mind, I shall proceed in two stages. First, I shall try to clarify the meaning of the concept "ruling elite" by describing a very simple form of what I conceive to be a ruling elite system. Second, I shall indicate what would be required in principle as a simple but satisfactory test of any hypothesis asserting that a particular political system is, in fact, a ruling elite system. Finally, I shall deal with some objections.

I

A Simple Ruling Elite System

If a ruling elite hypothesis says anything, surely it asserts that within some specific political system there exists a group of people who to some degree exercise power or influence over other actors in the system. I shall make the following assumptions about power:[1]

1) In order to compare the relative influence of two actors (these may be individuals, groups, classes, parties, or what not), it is necessary to state the scope of the responses upon which the actors have an effect. The statement, "A has more power than B," is so ambiguous as to verge on the meaningless, since it does not specify the scope.

2) One cannot compare the relative influence of two actors who always perform identical actions with respect to the group influenced. What this means as a practical matter is that ordinarily one can test for differences in influence only where there are cases of differences in initial preferences. At one extreme, the difference may mean that one group prefers alternative A and another group prefers B, A and B being mutually exclusive. At the other extreme, it may mean that one group prefers alternative A to other alternatives, and another

Notes to chapter 4 are found on page 366.

group is indifferent. If a political system displayed complete consensus at all times, we should find it impossible to construct a satisfactory direct test of the hypothesis that it was a ruling elite system, although indirect and rather unsatisfactory tests might be devised.

Consequently, to know whether or not we have a ruling elite, we must have a political system in which there is a difference in preferences, from time to time, among the individual human beings in the system. Suppose, now, that among these individuals there is a set whose preferences regularly prevail in all cases of disagreement, or at least in all cases of disagreement over key political issues (a term I propose to leave undefined here). Let me call such a set of individuals a "controlling group." In a fully-fledged democracy operating strictly according to majority rule, the majority would constitute a controlling group, even though the individual members of the majority might change from one issue to the next. But since our model is to represent a ruling elite system, we require that the set be *less than a majority in size*.

However, in any representative system with single member voting districts where more than two candidates receive votes, a candidate *could* win with less than a majority of votes; and it is possible therefore, to imagine a truly sovereign legislature elected under the strictest "democratic" rules that was nonetheless governed by a legislative majority representing the first preferences of a minority of voters. Yet I do not think we would want to call such a political system a ruling elite system. Because of this kind of difficulty, I propose that we exclude from our definition of a ruling elite any controlling group that is a product of rules that are actually followed (that is "real" rules) under which a majority of individuals could dominate if they took certain actions permissible under the "real" rules. In short, to constitute a ruling elite a controlling group must not be *a pure artifact of democratic rules*.

A ruling elite, then is a controlling group less than a majority in size that is not a pure artifact of democratic rules. It is a minority of individuals whose preferences regularly

prevail in cases of differences in preference on key political issues. If we are to avoid an infinite regress of explanations, the composition of the ruling elite must be more or less definitely specified.

II

Some Bad Tests

The hypothesis we are dealing with would run along these lines: "Such and such a political system (the U.S., the U.S.S.R., New Haven, or the like) is a ruling elite system in which the ruling elite has the following membership." Membership would then be specified by name, position, socio-economic class, socio-economic roles, or what not.

Let me now turn to the problem of testing a hypothesis of this sort, and begin by indicating a few tests that are sometimes mistakenly taken as adequate.

The first improper test confuses a ruling elite with a group that has a high *potential for control*. Let me explain. Suppose a set of individuals in a political system has the following property: there is a very high probability that if they agree on a key political alternative, and if they all act in some specified way, then that alternative will be chosen. We may say of such a group that it has a *high potential for control*. In a large and complex society like ours, there may be many such groups. For example, the bureaucratic triumvirate of Professor Mills would appear to have a high potential for control.[2] In the City of New Haven, with which I have some acquaintance, I do not doubt that the leading business figures together with the leaders of both political parties have a high potential for control. But a potential for control is not, except in a peculiarly Hobbesian world, equivalent to actual control. If the military leaders of this country and their subordinates agreed that it was desirable, they could most assuredly establish a military dictatorship of the most overt sort; nor would they need the aid of leaders of business corporations or the executive branch of our government. But they have not set up such a dictatorship. For what is lacking are the premises I mentioned earlier, namely agreement on a key political alternative and some set of specific implementing actions. That is to say, a group may have a high potential for control and a *low potential for unity*. The actual *political effectiveness* of a group is a function of its potential for control *and* its potential for unity. Thus a group with a relatively low potential for control but a high potential for unity may be more politically effective than a group with a high potential for control but a low potential for unity.

The second improper test confuses a ruling elite with a group of individuals who have more influence than any others in the system. I take it for granted that in every human organization some individuals have more influence over key decisions than do others. Political equality may well be among the most Utopian of all human goals. But it is fallacious to assume that the absence of political equality proves the existence of a ruling elite.

The third improper test, which is closely related to the preceding one, is to generalize from a single scope of influence. Neither logically nor empirically does it follow that a group with a high degree of influence over one scope will necessarily have a high degree of influence over another scope within the same system. This is a matter to be determined empirically. Any investigation that does not take into account the possibility that different elite groups have different scopes is suspect. By means of sloppy questions one could easily seem to discover that there exists a unified ruling elite in New Haven; for there is no doubt that small groups of people make many key decisions. It appears to be the case, however, that the small group that runs urban redevelopment is not the same as the small group that runs public education, and

neither is quite the same as the two small groups that run the two parties. Moreover the small group that runs urban redevelopment with a high degree of unity would almost certainly disintegrate if its activities were extended to either education or the two political parties.

III

A Proposed Test

If tests like these are not valid, what can we properly require?

Let us take the simplest possible situation. Assume that there have been some number —I will not say how many—of cases where there has been disagreement within the political system on key political choices. Assume further that the hypothetical ruling elite prefers one alternative and other actors in the system prefer other alternatives. Then unless it is true that in all or very nearly all of these cases the alternative preferred by the ruling elite is actually adopted, the hypothesis (that the system is dominated by the specified ruling elite) is clearly false.

I do not want to pretend either that the research necessary to such a test is at all easy to carry out or that community life lends itself conveniently to strict interpretation according to the requirements of the test. *But I do not see how anyone can suppose that he has established the dominance of a specific group in a community or a nation without basing his analysis on the careful examination of a series of concrete decisions.* And these decisions must either constitute the universe or a fair sample from the universe of key political decisions taken in the political system.

Now it is a remarkable and indeed astounding fact that neither Professor Mills nor Professor Hunter has seriously attempted to examine an array of specific cases to test his major hypothesis.[3] Yet I suppose these two works more than any others in the social sciences of the last few years have sought to interpret complex political systems essentially as instances of a ruling elite.

To sum up: The hypothesis of the existence of a ruling elite can be strictly tested only if:

1) The hypothetical ruling elite is a well-defined group.

2) There is a fair sample of cases involving key political decisions in which the preferences of the hypothetical ruling elite run counter to those of any other likely group that might be suggested.

3) In such cases, the preferences of the elite regularly prevail.

IV

Difficulties and Objections

Several objections might be raised against the test I propose.

First, one might argue that the test is *too weak*. The argument would run as follows: If a ruling elite *doesn't* exist in a community, then the test is satisfactory; that is, if every hypothetical ruling elite is compared with alternative control groups, and in fact no ruling elite exists, then the test will indeed show that there is no minority whose preferences regularly prevail on key political alternatives. But—it might be said—suppose a ruling elite *does* exist. The test will not *necessarily* demonstrate its existence, since we may not have selected the right group as our hypothetical ruling elite. Now this objection is valid; but it suggests the point I made at the outset about the possibility of an infinite regress of explanations. Unless we use the test on every possible combination of individuals in the community, we cannot be certain that there is not some combination that constitutes a ruling elite. But since there is no more *a priori* reason to assume that a ruling elite does exist than to assume that one does not exist, the burden of proof does not rest upon the critic of the hypothesis, but upon its proponent. And a proponent must specify what group he has in mind as his ruling elite. Once the group is specified, then the test I have suggested is, at least in principle, valid.

Second, one could object that the test is *too strong*, For suppose that the members of the "ruled" group are indifferent as to

the outcome of various political alternatives. Surely (one could argue) if there is another group that regularly gets its way in the face of this indifference, it is in fact the ruling group in the society. Now my reasons for wishing to discriminate this case from the other involve more than a mere question of the propriety of using the term "ruling elite," which is only a term of convenience. There is, I think, a difference of some theoretical significance between a system in which a small group dominates over another that is opposed to it, and one in which a group dominates over an indifferent mass. In the second case, the alternatives at stake can hardly be regarded as "key political issues" if we assume the point of view of the indifferent mass; whereas in the first case it is reasonable to say that the alternatives involve a key political issue from the standpoint of both groups. Earlier I refrained from defining the concept "key political issues." If we were to do so at this point, it would seem reasonable to require as a necessary although possibly not a sufficient condition that the issue should involve actual disagreement in preferences among two or more groups. In short, the case of "indifference vs. preference" would be ruled out.

However, I do not mean to dispose of the problem simply by definition. The point is to make sure that the two systems are distinguished. The test for the second, weaker system of elite rule would then be merely a modification of the test proposed for the first and more stringent case. It would again require an examination of a series of cases showing uniformly that when "the word" was authoritatively passed down from the designated elite, the hitherto indifferent majority fell into ready compliance with an alternative that had nothing to recommend it intrinsically.

Third, one might argue that the test will not discriminate between a true ruling elite and a ruling elite together with its satellites. This objection is in one sense true and in one sense false. It is true that on a series of key political questions, an apparently unified group might prevail who would, according to our test, thereby constitute a ruling elite. Yet an inner core might actually make the decisions for the whole group.

However, one of two possibilities must be true. Either the inner core and the front men always agree at all times in the decision process, or they do not. But if they always agree, then it follows from one of our two assumptions about influence that the distinction between an "inner core" and "front men" has no operational meaning; that is, there is no conceivable way to distinguish between them. And if they do not always agree, then the test simply requires a comparison at those points in time when they disagree. Here again, the advantages of concrete cases are palpable, for these enable one to discover who initiates or vetoes and who merely complies.

Fourth, it might be said that the test is either too demanding or else it is too arbitrary. If it requires that the hypothetical elite prevails in *every single case*, then it demands too much. But if it does not require this much, then at what point can a ruling elite be said to exist? When it prevails in 7 cases out of 10? 8 out of 10? 9 out of 10? Or what? There are two answers to this objection. On the one hand, it would be quite reasonable to argue, I think, that since we are considering only key political choices and not trivial decisions, if the elite does not prevail in *every* case in which it disagrees with a contrary group, it cannot properly be called a ruling elite. But since I have not supplied an independent definition of the term "key political choices," I must admit that this answer is not wholly satisfactory. On the other hand, I would be inclined to suggest that in this instance as in many others we ought not to assume that political reality will be as discrete and discontinuous as the concepts we find convenient to employ. We can say that a system approximates a true ruling elite system, to a greater or lesser degree, without insisting that it exemplify the extreme and limiting case.

Fifth, it might be objected that the test I have proposed would not work in the most obvious of all cases of ruling elites, namely in the totalitarian dictatorships. For the control of the elite over the expression of opinion is so great that overtly there is no disagreement; hence no cases on which to base a judgment arise. This objection is a fair one. But we are not concerned here with totalitarian systems. We are concerned with the application of the techniques of modern investigation to American communities, where, except in very rare cases, terror is not so pervasive that the investigator is barred from discovering the preferences of citizens. Even in Little Rock, for example, newspaper men seemed to have had little difficulty in finding diverse opinions; and a northern political scientist of my acquaintance has managed to complete a large number of productive interviews with White and Negro Southerners on the touchy subject of integration.

Finally, one could argue that even in a society like ours a ruling elite might be so influential over ideas, attitudes, and opinions that a kind of false consensus will exist—not the phony consensus of a terroristic totalitarian dictatorship but the manipulated and superficially self-imposed adherence to the norms and goals of the elite by broad sections of a community. A good deal of Professor Mills' argument can be interpreted in this way, although it is not clear to me whether this is what he means to rest his case on.

Even more than the others this objection points to the need to be circumspect in interpreting the evidence. Yet here, too, it seems to me that the hypothesis cannot be satisfactorily confirmed without something equivalent to the test I have proposed. For once again either the consensus is perpetual and unbreakable, in which case there is no conceivable way of determining who is ruler and who is ruled. Or it is not. But if it is not, then there is some point in the process of forming opinions at which the one group will be seen to initiate and veto, while the rest merely respond. And we can only discover these points *by an examination of a series of concrete cases where key decisions are made:* decisions on taxation and expenditures, subsidies, welfare programs, military policy, and so on.

It would be interesting to know, for example, whether the initiation and veto of alternatives having to do with our missile program would confirm Professor Mills' hypothesis, or indeed any reasonable hypothesis about the existence of a ruling elite. To the superficial observer it would scarcely appear that the military itself is a homogeneous group, to say nothing of their supposed coalition with corporate and political executives. If the military alone or the coalition together is a ruling elite, it is either incredibly incompetent in administering its own fundamental affairs or else it is unconcerned with the success of its policies to a degree that I find astounding.

Robert A. Dahl

However, I do not mean to examine the evidence here. For the whole point of this paper is that the evidence for a ruling elite, either in the United States or in any specific community, has not yet been properly examined so far as I know. And the evidence has not been properly examined, I have tried to argue, because the examination has not employed satisfactory criteria to determine what constitutes a fair test of the basic hypothesis.

"Power Elite" or "Veto Groups"?

William Kornhauser

William Kornhauser, Professor of Sociology at the
University of California, Berkeley, and author of
The Politics of Mass Society (New York, Free Press,
1959), here compares the work of a prominent
elitist, C. Wright Mills, with that of a prominent
pluralist, David Riesman. The essay, which appeared
as a chapter in a collection of essays in honor of
Riesman edited by S. M. Lipset and Leo Lowenthal,
Culture and Social Character (New York, Free Press,
1961), is reprinted with the permission of the author
and the publisher.

IN THE fifties two books appeared purporting to describe the structure of power in present-day America. They reached opposite conclusions: where C. Wright Mills found a "power elite," David Riesman found "veto groups." Both books have enjoyed a wide response, which has tended to divide along ideological lines. It would appear that *The Power Elite* has been most favorably received by radical intellectuals, and *The Lonely Crowd* has found its main response among liberals. Mills and Riesman have not been oblivious to their differences. Mills is quite explicit on the matter: Riesman is a "romantic pluralist" who refuses to see the forest of American power inequalities for the trees of short-run and discrete balances of power among diverse groups (244).[1] Riesman has been less explicitly polemical, but he might have had Mills in mind when he spoke of those intellectuals "who feel themselves very much out of power and who are frightened of those who they think have the power," and who "prefer to be scared by the power structures they conjure up than to face the possibility that the power structure they believe exists has largely evaporated" (257–258).[2]

I wish to intervene in this controversy just long enough to do two things: (1) locate as precisely as possible the items upon which Riesman and Mills disagree; and (2) formulate certain underlying issues in the analysis of power that have to be met before such specific disagreements as those between Riesman and Mills can profitably be resolved.

We may compare Mills and Riesman on power in America along five dimensions:

1) Structure of power: how power is distributed among the major segments of present-day American society.

2) Changes in the structure of power: how the distribution of power has changed in the course of American history.

3) Operation of the structure of power: the means whereby power is exercised in American society.

4) Bases of the structure of power: how social and psychological factors shape and sustain the existing distribution of power.

5) Consequences of the structure of power: how the existing distribution of power affects American society.

1

Structure of Power

It is symptomatic of their underlying differences that Mills entitles his major consideration of power simply "the power elite," whereas Riesman has entitled one of his discussions "who has the power?" Mills is quite certain about the location of power, and so indicates by the assertive form of his title. Riesman perceives a much more amorphous and indeterminate power situation, and conveys this view in the interrogative form of his title. These contrasting images of American power may be diagrammed as two different pyramids of power. Mills' pyramid of power contains three levels:

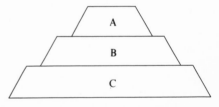

Notes to chapter 5 are found on page 366.

The apex of the pyramid (A) is the "power elite": a unified power group composed of the top government executives, military officials, and corporation directors. The second level (B) comprises the "middle levels of power": a diversified and balanced plurality of interest groups, perhaps most visibly at work in the halls of Congress. The third level (C) is the "mass society": the powerless maze of unorganized and atomized people who are controlled from above.

Riesman's pyramid of power contains only two major levels:

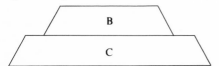

The two levels roughly correspond to Mills' second and third levels, and have been labeled accordingly. The obvious difference between the two pyramids is the presence of a peak in the one case and its absence in the other. Riesman sees no "power elite," in the sense of a single unified power group at the top of the structure, and this in the simplest terms contrasts his image of power in America with that of Mills. The upper level of Riesman's pyramid (B) consists of "veto groups": a diversified and balanced plurality of interest groups, each of which is primarily concerned with protecting its jurisdiction by blocking efforts of other groups that seem to threaten that jurisdiction. There is no decisive ruling group here, but rather an amorphous structure of power centering on the interplay among these interest groups. The lower level of the pyramid (C) comprises the more or less unorganized public, which is sought as an ally (rather than dominated) by the interest groups in their maneuvers against actual or threatened encroachments on the jurisdiction each claims for itself.

2

Changes in the Structure of Power

Riesman and Mills agree that the American power structure has gone through

four major epochs. They disagree on the present and prospective future in the following historical terms: Mills judges the present to represent a fifth epoch, whereas Riesman judges it to be a continuation of the fourth.

The first period, according to Mills and Riesman, extended roughly from the founding of the republic to the Jacksonian era. During this period, Riesman believes America possessed a clearly demarcated ruling group, composed of a "landed-gentry and mercantilist-money leadership" (239). According to Mills, "the important fact about these early days is that social life, economic institutions, military establishment, and political order coincided, and men who were high politicians also played key roles in the economy and, with their families, were among those of the reputable who made up local society" (270).

The second period extended roughly from the decline of Federalist leadership to the Civil War. During this period power became more widely dispersed, and it was no longer possible to identify a sharply defined ruling group. "In this society," Mills writes, "the 'elite' became a plurality of top groups, each in turn quite loosely made up" (270). Riesman notes that farmer and artisan groups became influential, and "occasionally, as with Jackson, moved into a more positive command" (240).

The third period began after the Civil War and extended through McKinley's administration in Riesman's view (240) and until the New Deal according to Mills (271). They agree that the era of McKinley marked the high point of the unilateral supremacy of corporate economic power. During this period, power once more became concentrated, but unlike the Federalist period and also unlike subsequent periods, the higher circles of economic institutions were dominant.

The fourth period took definite shape in the 1930's. In Riesman's view this period marked the ascendancy of the "veto groups," and rule by coalitions rather than by a unified power group. Mills judges it to

have been so only in the early and middle
Roosevelt administrations: "In these years,
the New Deal as a system of power was
essentially a balance of pressure groups
and interest blocs" (273).

Up to World War II, then, Mills and
Riesman view the historical development of
power relations in America along strikingly
similar lines. Their sharply contrasting
portrayal of present-day American power
relations begins with their diverging assessments of the period beginning about 1940.
Mills envisions World War II and its after-
math as marking a new era in American
power relations. With war as the major
problem, there arises a new power group
composed of corporate, governmental, and
military directors.

> The formation of the power elite, as we may
> now know it, occurred during World War II
> and its aftermath. In the course of the organi-
> zation of the nation for that war, and the
> consequent stabilization of the war-like
> posture, certain types of man have been
> selected and formed, and in the course of
> these institutional and psychological devel-
> opments, new opportunities and intentions
> have arisen among them.[3]

Where Mills sees the ascendancy of a
power elite, Riesman sees the opposite
tendency toward the dispersal of power
among a plurality of organized interests:

> There has been in the last fifty years a change
> in the configuration of power in America, in
> which a single hierarchy with a ruling class at
> its head has been replaced by a number of
> "veto groups" among which power is dis-
> persed (239).
> The shifting nature of the lobby provides us
> with an important clue as to the difference
> between the present American political scene
> and that of the age of McKinley. The ruling
> class of businessmen could relatively easily
> (though perhaps mistakenly) decide where
> their interests lay and what editors, lawyers,
> and legislators might be paid to advance
> them. The lobby ministered to the clear
> leadership, privilege, and imperative of the
> business ruling class. Today we have sub-
> stituted for that leadership a series of groups,
> each of which has struggled for and finally
> attained a power to stop things conceivably

inimical to its interests and, within far
narrower limits, to start things (246–247).

In short, both Mills and Riesman view
the current scene from an historical perspective; but where one finds a hitherto
unknown *concentration* of power, the other
finds an emerging *indeterminacy* of power.

3

Operation of the Structure of Power

Mills believes the power elite sets all
important public policies, especially foreign
policy. Riesman, on the other hand, does
not believe that the same group or coalition
of groups sets all major policies, but rather
that the question of who exercises power
varies with the issue at stake: most groups
are inoperative on most issues, and all
groups are operative primarily on those
issues that vitally impinge on their central
interests. That is to say that there are as
many power structures as there are distinctive spheres of policy (256).

As to the modes of operation, both
Mills and Riesman point to increasing
manipulation, rather than command or
persuasion, as the favored form of power
play. Mills emphasizes the secrecy behind
which important policy-determination occurs. Riesman stresses not so much manipulation under the guise of secrecy as manipulation under the guise of mutual tolerance
for one another's interests and beliefs.
Manipulation occurs, according to Riesman, because each group is trying to hide
its concern with power in order not to
antagonize other groups. Power relations
tend to take the form of "monopolistic
competition": "rules of fairness and fellow-
ship [rather than the impersonal forces of
competition] dictate how far one can go"
(247). Thus both believe the play of power
takes place to a considerable extent back-
stage; but Mills judges this power play to
be under the direction of one group, while
Riesman sees it as controlled by a mood and
structure of accommodation among many
groups.

Mills maintains that the mass media of communication are important instruments of manipulation: the media lull people to sleep, so to speak, by suppressing political topics and by emphasizing "entertainment." Riesman alleges that the mass media give more attention to politics and problems of public policy than their audiences actually want, and thereby convey the false impression that there is more interest in public affairs than really exists in America at the present time. Where Mills judges the mass media of communication to be powerful political instruments in American society (315–316), Riesman argues that they have relatively little significance in this respect (228–231).

4

Bases of the Structure of Power

Power tends to be patterned according to the structure of interests in a society. Power is shared among those whose interests coincide, and divides along lines where interests diverge. To Mills, the power elite is a reflection and solidification of a *coincidence of interests* among the ascendant institutional orders. The power elite rests on the "many interconnections and points of coinciding interests" of the corporations, political institutions, and military services (19). For Riesman, on the other hand, there is an amorphous power structure, which reflects a *diversity of interests* among the major organized groups. The power structure of veto groups rests on the divergent interests of political parties, business groups, labor organizations, farm blocs, and a myriad of other organized groups (247).

But power is not a simple reflex of interests alone. It also rests on the capabilities and opportunities for cooperation among those who have similar interests, and for confrontation among those with opposing interests. Mills argues in some detail that the power elite rests not merely on the coincidence of interests among major institutions but also on the "psychological

similarity and social intermingling" of their higher circles (19). By virtue of similar social origins (old family, upperclass background), religious affiliations (Episcopalian and Presbyterian), education (Ivy League college or military academy), and the like, those who head up the major institutions share codes and values as well as material interests. This makes for easy communication, especially when many of these people already know one another, or at least know many people in common. They share a common way of life, and therefore possess both the will and the opportunity to integrate their lines of action as representatives of key institutions. At times this integration involves "explicit co-ordination," as during war (19–20). So much for the bases of power at the apex of the structure.

At the middle and lower levels of power, Mills emphasizes the lack of independence and concerted purpose among those who occupy similar social positions. In his book on the middle classes,[4] Mills purports to show the weakness of white-collar people that results from their lack of economic independence and political direction. The white-collar worker simply follows the more powerful group of the moment. In his book on labor leaders,[5] Mills located the alleged political impotence of organized labor in its dependence on government. Finally, the public is conceived as composed of atomized and submissive individuals who are incapable of engaging in effective communication and political action (302 ff.).

Riesman believes that power "is founded, in large measure, on interpersonal expectations and attitudes" (253). He asserts that in addition to the diversity of interest underlying the pattern of power in America there is the psycho-cultural fact of widespread feelings of weakness and dependence at the top as well as at the bottom of the power structure: "If businessmen feel weak and dependent they do in actuality become weaker and more dependent, no matter what material resources may be ascribed to them" (235). In other words, the amorphousness of power in America rests in part

on widespread feelings of weakness and
dependence. These feelings are found
among those whose position in the social
structure provides resources that they could
exploit, as well as among those whose
position provides less access to the means
of power. In fact, Riesman is concerned to
show that people at all levels of the social
structure tend to feel weaker than their objective position warrants.

The theory of types of conformity that
provides the foundation of so much of
Riesman's writings enters into his analysis
of power at this point. The "other-
directed" orientation in culture and character helps to sustain the amorphousness of
power. The other-directed person in politics
is the "inside-dopester," the person who
possesses political competence but avoids
political commitment. This is the dominant
type in the veto groups, since other-direction
is prevalent in the strata from which their
leaders are drawn. "Both within the [veto]
groups and in the situation created by their
presence, the political mood tends to become one of other-directed tolerance" (248).
However, Riesman does not make the basis
of power solely psychological:

> This does not mean, however, that the veto
> groups are formed along the lines of charac-
> ter structure. As in a business corporation
> there is room for extreme inner-directed
> and other-directed types, and all mixtures
> between, so in a veto group there can exist
> complex "symbiotic" relationships among
> people of different political styles. . . . Des-
> pite these complications I think it fair to say
> that the veto groups, even when they are set
> up to protect a clearcut moralizing interest,
> are generally forced to adopt the political
> manners of the other-directed (249).

Riesman and Mills agree that there is
widespread apathy in American society,
but they disagree on the social distribution
of political apathy. Mills locates the
apathetic primarily among the lower social
strata, whereas Riesman finds extensive
apathy in higher as well as lower strata.
Part of the difference may rest on what
criteria of apathy are used. Mills conceives of

apathy as the lack of political meaning in
one's life, the failure to think of personal
interests in political terms, so that what
happens in politics does not appear to be
related to personal troubles.[6] Riesman extends the notion of apathy to include the
politically uninformed as well as the politically uncommitted.[7] Thus political indigna-
tion undisciplined by political understanding is not a genuine political orientation.
Riesman judges political apathy to be an
important *basis* for amorphous power
relations. Mills, on the other hand, treats
political apathy primarily as a *result* of the
concentration of power.

5

Consequences of the Structure of Power

Four parallel sets of consequences of
the structure of power for American society
may be inferred from the writings of Mills
and Riesman. The first concerns the impact
of the power structure on the interests of
certain groups or classes in American
society. Mills asserts that the existing power
arrangements enhance the interests of the
major institutions whose directors constitute
the power elite (276 ff.). Riesman asserts
the contrary: no one group or class is
decisively favored over others by the cul-
minated decisions on public issues (257).

The second set of consequences concerns
the impact of the structure of power on the
quality of politics in American society. Here
Mills and Riesman are in closer agreement.
Mills maintains that the concentration of
power in a small circle, and the use of manipulation as the favored manner of exercising
power, lead to the decline of politics as
public debate. People are decreasingly
capable of grasping political issues, and of
relating them to personal interests.[8] Riesman
also believes that politics has declined in
meaning for large numbers of people. This
is not due simply to the ascendancy of "veto
groups," although they do foster "the
tolerant mood of other-direction and hasten

the retreat of the inner-directed indignants" (251). More important, the increasing complexity and remoteness of politics make political self-interest obscure and aggravate feelings of impotence even when self-interest is clear.[9]

The third set of consequences of the American power structure concerns its impact on the quality of power relations themselves. Mills contends that the concentration of power has taken place without a corresponding shift in the bases of legitimacy of power: power is still supposed to reside in the public and its elected representatives, whereas in reality it resides in the hands of those who direct the key bureaucracies. As a consequence, men of power are neither responsible nor accountable for their power (316–317). Riesman also implies that there is a growing discrepancy between the facts of power and the images of power, but for the opposite reason from Mills: power is more widely dispersed than is generally believed (257–258).

Finally, a fourth set of consequences concerns the impact of the power structure on democratic leadership. If power tends to be lodged in a small group that is not accountable for its power, and if politics no longer involves genuine public debate, then there will be a *severe weakening of democratic institutions*, if not of leadership (the power elite exercises leadership in one sense of the term, in that it makes decisions on basic policy for the nation). Mills claims that power in America has become so concentrated that it increasingly resembles the Soviet system of power:

Official commentators like to contrast the ascendancy in totalitarian countries of a tightly organized clique with the American system of power. Such comments, however, are easier to sustain if one compares mid-twentieth-century Russia with mid-nineteenth-century America, which is what is often done by Tocqueville-quoting Americans making the contrast. But that was an America of a century ago, and in the century that has passed, the American elite have not remained as patrioteer essayists have described them to us. The "loose cliques" now head institutions of a scale and power not then existing and, especially since World War I, the loose cliques have tightened up (271).

If, on the other hand, power tends to be dispersed among groups that are primarily concerned to protect and defend their interests rather than to advance general policies and their own leadership, and if at the same time politics has declined as a sphere of duty and self-interest, then there will be a *severe weakening of leadership*. Thus Riesman believes that "power in America seems to [be] situational and mercurial; it resists attempts to locate it" (257). This "indeterminacy and amorphousness" of power inhibits the development of leadership: "Where the issue involves the country as a whole, no individual or group leadership is likely to be very effective, because the entrenched veto groups cannot be budged" (257). "Veto groups exist as defense groups, not as leadership groups" (248). Yet Riesman does not claim that the decline of leadership directly threatens American democracy, at least in the short run: the dispersion of power among a diversity of balancing "veto groups" operates to support democratic institutions even as it inhibits effective leadership. The long-run prospects of a leaderless democracy are of course less promising.

II

In the second part of this paper, I wish to raise certain critical questions about Riesman's and Mills' images of power.

One set of questions seeks to probe more deeply the basic area of disagreement in their views. A second set of questions concerns their major areas of disagreement.

Power usually is analyzed according to its distribution among the several units of a system. Most power analysts construe the structure of power as a *hierarchy*—a rank-order of units according to their amount of power. The assumption often is made that there is only one such structure, and that all units may be ranked vis-à-vis one another. Units higher in the hierarchy have power over units lower in the structure, so there is a one-way flow of power. Mills tends to adopt this image of the structure of power.

Riesman rejects this conception of the power structure as mere hierarchy:

> The determination of who [has more power] has to be made all over again for our time: we cannot be satisfied with the answers given by Marx, Mosca, Michels, Pareto, Weber, Veblen, or Burnham (255).
> The image of power in contemporary America presented [in *The Lonely Crowd*] departs from current discussions of power which are usually based on a search for a ruling class (260).

Riesman is not just denying the existence of a power elite in contemporary American society; he is also affirming the need to consider other aspects of power than only its unequal distribution. He is especially concerned to analyze common responses to power:

> If the leaders have lost the power, why have the led not gained it? What is there about the other-directed man and his life situation which prevents the transfer? In terms of situation, it seems that the pattern of monopolistic competition of the veto groups resists individual attempts at power aggrandizement. In terms of character, the other-directed man simply does not seek power; perhaps, rather, he avoids and evades it (275).

Whereas Mills emphasizes the *differences* between units according to their power, Riesman emphasizes their *similarities* in this respect. In the first view, some units are

Two Portraits of the American Power Structure

	Mills	Riesman
Levels	a. Unified power elite b. Diversified and balanced plurality of interest groups c. Mass of unorganized people who have practically no power over elite	a. No dominant power elite b. Diversified and balanced plurality of interest groups c. Mass of unorganized people who have some power over interest groups
Changes	a. Increasing concentration of power	a. Increasing dispersion of power
Operation	a. One group determines all major policies b. Manipulation of people at the bottom by group at the top	a. Who determines policy shifts with the issue b. Monopolistic competition among organized groups
Bases	a. Coincidence of interests among major institutions (economic, military, governmental)	a. Diversity of interests among major organized groups b. Sense of weakness and dependence among those in higher as well as lower status
Consequences	a. Enhancement of interests of corporations, armed forces, and executive branch of government b. Decline of politics as public debate c. Decline of responsible and accountable power—loss of democracy	a. No one group or class is favored significantly over others b. Decline of politics as duty and self-interest c. Decline of capacity for effective leadership

seen as dominated by other units, while in the second view, all units are seen as subject to constraints that shape and limit their use of power *in similar directions.*

The problem of power is not simply the differential capacity to make decisions, so that those who have power bind those who do not. Constraints also operate on those who are in decision-making positions, for if these are the places where acts of great consequence occur, so are they the targets for social pressures. These pressures become translated into restrictions on the alternatives among which decision-makers can choose. Power may be meaningfully measured by ascertaining the range of alternatives that decision-makers can realistically consider. To identify those who make decisions is not to say how many lines of action are open to them, or how much freedom of choice they enjoy.

A major advance in the study of power is made by going beyond a formal conception of power, in which those who have the authority to make decisions are assumed to possess the effective means of power and the will to use it. Nor can it be assumed that those not in authority lack the power to determine public policy. The identification of effective sources of power requires analysis of how *decision-makers are themselves subject to various kinds of constraint.* Major sources of constraint include (1) opposing elites and active publics; and (2) cultural values and associated psychological receptivities and resistances to power. A comparison of Mills and Riesman with respect to these categories of constraint reveals the major area of disagreement between them.

Mills implies that both sources of constraint are by and large inoperative on the highest levels of power. (1) There is little opposition among the top power-holders. Since they are not in opposition to one another, they do not constrain one another. Instead, they are unified and mutually supportive. Furthermore, there are few publics to constrain the elite. Groups capable of effective participation in broad policy determination have been replaced by atomized masses that are powerless to affect policy, since they lack the social bases for association and communication. Instead, people in large numbers are manipulated through organizations and media controlled by the elite. (2) Older values and codes no longer grip elites, nor have they been replaced by new values and codes that could regulate the exercise of power. Top men of power are not constrained either by an inner moral sense or by feelings of dependence on others. The widespread permissiveness toward the use of expedient means to achieve success produces "the higher immorality," that is to say, elites that are irresponsible in the use of power.

In sharp contrast to Mills, Riesman attaches great importance to both kinds of constraints on decision-makers. (1) There is a plethora of organized groups, "each of which has struggled for and finally attained a power to stop things conceivably inimical to its interests" (247). Furthermore, there is extensive opportunity for large numbers of people to influence decision-makers, because the latter are constrained by their competitive relations with one another to bid for support in the electoral arena and more diffusely in the realm of public relations. (2) The cultural emphasis on "mutual tolerance" and social conformity places a premium on "getting along" with others at the expense of taking strong stands. People are psychologically disposed to avoid long-term commitments as a result of their strong feelings of dependence on their immediate peers. "Other-directed" persons seek approval rather than power.

In general, the decisive consideration in respect to the restraint of power is the presence of multiple centers of power. Where there are many power groups, not only are they mutually constrained; they also are dependent on popular support, and therefore responsive to public demands. Now, there are many readily observable cases of institutionalized opposition among power groups in American society. In the economic sphere, collective bargaining between management and labor is conflict of this kind; and to the extent that "countervailing power" among a few large firms has been replacing competition among many small firms in the market place, there is a *de facto* situation of opposition among economic elites. In the political sphere, there is a strong two-party system and more or less stable factionalism within both parties, opposition among interest blocs in state and national legislatures, rivalry among executive agencies of government and the military services, and so forth.

Mills relegates these conflicting groups to the middle levels of power. Political parties and interest groups, both inside and outside of government, are not important units in the structure of power, according to Mills. It would seem that he takes this position primarily with an eye to the sphere of foreign policy, where only a few people finally make the big decisions. But he fails to put his argument to a decisive or meaningful test: he does not examine the pattern of decisions to show that foreign policy not only is made *by* a few people (this, after all, is a constitutional fact), but that it is made *for their particular interests*. Mills' major premise seems to be that all decisions are taken by and for special interests; there is no action oriented toward the general interests of the whole community. Furthermore, Mills seems to argue that because only a very few people occupy key decision-making *positions*, they are free to decide on whatever best suits their particular interests. But the degree of *autonomy* of decision-makers cannot be inferred from the *number* of decision-makers, nor from the *scope* of their decisions. It is determined by the character of decision-making, especially the dependence of decision-makers on certain kinds of *procedure* and *support*.

Just as Mills is presenting a distorted image of power in America when he fails to consider the pressures on those in high positions, so Riesman presents a biased picture by not giving sufficient attention to *power differentials* among the various groups in society. When Riesman implies that if power is dispersed, then it must be relatively equal among groups and interests, with no points of concentration, he is mak-

ing an unwarranted inference. The following statement conjures up an image of power in America that is as misleading on its side as anything Mills has written in defense of his idea of a power elite.

> One might ask whether one would not find, over a long period of time, that decisions in America favored one group or class . . . over others. Does not wealth exert its pull in the long run? In the past this has been so; for the future I doubt it. The future seems to be in the hands of the small business and professional men who control Congress, such as realtors, lawyers, car salesmen, undertakers, and so on; of the military men who control defense and, in part, foreign policy; of the big business managers and their lawyers, finance-committee men, and other counselors who decide on plant investment and influence the rate of technological change; of the labor leaders who control worker productivity and worker votes; of the black belt whites who have the greatest stake in southern politics; of the Poles, Italians, Jews, and Irishmen who have stakes in foreign policy, city jobs, and ethnic, religious and cultural organizations; of the editorializers and storytellers who help socialize the young, tease and train the adult, and amuse and annoy the aged; of the farmers—themselves a warring congeries of cattlemen, corn men, dairymen, cotton men, and so on—who control key departments and committees and who, as the living representatives of our inner-directed past, control many of our memories; of the Russians and, to a lesser degree, other foreign powers who control much of our agenda of attention; and so on (257).

It appears that Riesman is asking us to believe that power differentials do not exist, but only differences in the spheres within which groups exercise control.

If Riesman greatly exaggerates the extent to which organized interests possess equal power, nevertheless he poses an important problem that Mills brushes aside. For Riesman goes beyond merely noting the existence of opposition among "veto groups" to suggest that they operate to smother one another's initiative and leadership. It is one thing for interest groups to constrain one another; it is something else again when they produce stalemate. Riesman has pointed to a critical problem for a pluralist society: the danger that power may become fragmented among so many competing groups that effective general leadership cannot emerge.

On Mills' side, it is indisputable that American political institutions have undergone extensive centralization and bureaucratization. This is above all an *institutional* change wrought by the greatly expanded scale of events and decisions in the contemporary world. But centralization cannot be equated with a power elite. There can be highly centralized institutions and at the same time a fragmentation of power among a multiplicity of relatively independent public and private agencies. Thus Riesman would appear to be correct that the substance of power lies in the hands of many large organizations, and these organizations are not unified or coordinated in any firm fashion. If they were, surely Mills would have been able to identify the major mechanisms that could produce this result. That he has failed to do so is the most convincing evidence for their nonexistence.

To complete this analysis, we need only remind ourselves of the fundamental area of agreement between our two critics of American power relations. Both stress the *absence of effective* political action at all levels of the political order, in particular among the citizenry. For all of their differences, Mills and Riesman agree that there has been a decline in effective political participation, or at least a failure of political participation to measure up to the requirements of contemporary events and decisions. This failure has not been compensated by an increase in effective political action at the center: certainly Riesman's "veto groups" are not capable of defining and realizing the community's general aspirations; nor is Mills' "power elite" such a political agency. Both are asserting the inadequacy of political associations, including public opinion, party leadership, Congress, and the Presidency, even as they see the slippage of power in different directions. In consequence, neither is sanguine about the capacity of the American political system to provide responsible leadership, especially in international affairs.

If there is truth in this indictment, it also may have its sources in the very images of power that pervade Mills' and Riesman's thought. They are both inclined toward a negative response to power; and neither

shows a willingness to confront the idea of a political system and the ends of power in it. Riesman reflects the liberal suspicion of power, as when he writes "we have come to realize that men who compete primarily for wealth are relatively harmless as compared with men who compete primarily for power." That such assertions as this may very well be true is beside the point. For certainly negative consequences of power can subsist alongside of positive ones. At times Riesman seems to recognize the need for people to seek and use power if they as individuals and the society as a whole are to develop to the fullest of their capacities. But his dominant orientation toward power remains highly individualistic and negative.

Mills is more extreme than Riesman on this matter, since he never asks what is socially required in the way of resources of power and uses of power, but instead is preoccupied with the magnitude of those resources and the (allegedly) destructive expropriation of them by and for the higher circles of major institutions. It is a very limited notion of power that construes it only in terms of coercion and conflict among particular interests. Societies require arrangements whereby resources of power can be effectively used and supplemented for public goals. This is a requirement for government, but the use of this term should not obscure that fact that government either commands power or lacks effectiveness. Mills does not concern himself with the *ends* of power, nor with the conditions for their attainment. He has no conception of the bases of political order, and no theory of the functions of government and politics. He suggests nothing that could prevent his "power elite" from developing into a fullblown totalitarianism. The logic of Mills' position finally reduces to a contest between anarchy and tyranny.

The problem of power seems to bring out the clinician in each of us. We quickly fasten on the pathology of power, whether we label the symptoms as "inside-dopesterism" (Riesman) or as "the higher immorality" (Mills). As a result, we often lose sight

of the ends of power in the political system
under review. It is important to understand
that pivotal decisions increasingly are made
at the national level, and that this poses
genuine difficulties for the maintenance of
democratic control. It is also important to
understand that a multiplicity of public and
private agencies increasingly pressure decision-makers, and that this poses genuine
difficulties for the maintenance of effective
political leadership. But the fact remains
that there have been periods of centralized
decision-making *and* democratic control,
multiple constraints on power *and* effective
leadership. There is no simple relationship
between the extent to which power is
equally distributed and the stability of
democratic order. For a democratic order
requires strong government as well as
public consent by an informed citizenry.
Unless current tendencies are measured
against both sets of needs, there will be
little progress in understanding how either
one is frustrated or fulfilled. Finally, in the
absence of more disciplined historical and
comparative analysis, we shall continue to
lack a firm basis for evaluating such widely
divergent diagnoses of political malaise as
those given us by Mills and Riesman.

"THE SOVIET UNION is now engaged in an audacious attempt to upset the established balance of power prevailing in Europe." This statement was used by C. L. Sulzberger, writing in the *New York Times* for March 23, 1952, to open a discussion of the Soviet offer to establish a unified and neutral Germany. It symbolizes the startling renaissance of the balance of power concept in recent years not only in the pages of learned journals, but in the daily press and in radio as well. This rebirth is probably attributable to the effort to reconsider the notions concerning international relations generally held during the League of Nations period, notions which emphasized open diplomacy, collective security, and the use of arbitration instead of unilateral force. The apparent futility of these methods seemed to call for the reintroduction of more meaningful concepts into the analysis of international affairs, and the balance of power thus reappeared as part of the general trend to re-establish the primacy of power as the key to the understanding of interstate relations.

There would be no difficulty in this development if the term "balance of power" were free from philological, semantic, and theoretical confusion. Unfortunately, it is not. The term is defined differently by different writers; it is used in varying senses, even if not defined exactly at all; and, finally, it is the focal concept in several quite distinct theories of international relations. The purpose of this article is the clarification, not only of the *verbal* differences in meaning, but also of the *applied meanings* of the "balance of power" phrase as they vary in accordance with the intentions of the users. The necessity for such an attempt may be demonstrated by an introductory discussion of the variety of thought on this topic, in terms of substantive meanings no less than in terms of systems of classification.

Thus Leopold Ranke and Bishop Stubbs regarded the balance of power as the principle in modern history which weaves otherwise unintelligibly divergent strands into an

The Balance of Power: Prescription, Concept, or Propaganda

Ernst B. Haas

Ernst B. Haas, Professor of Political Science at the University of California, Berkeley, and author of several major books on international integration, in this classic article examines many of the varying uses of the term "balance of power" in writings on international relations and reveals contradictory uses which help to account for some of the long-lasting disputes over the nature of power in international politics. The article, which appeared in 5 World Politics (1953), 442–77, is here reprinted with the permission of the author and publisher.

understandable whole. The balance "is the principle which gives unity to the political plot of European history," said Stubbs.[1] Richard Cobden, by contrast, was constrained to propound that

> The balance of power—which has, for a hundred years, been the burden of kings' speeches, the theme of statesmen, the ground of solemn treaties, and the cause of wars—which has served down to the very year in which we write [1836], and which will, no doubt, continue to serve, for years to come, as a pretence for maintaining enormous standing armaments . . . the balance of power is a chimera: It is not a fallacy, a mistake, an imposture—it is an undescribed, indescribable, incomprehensible nothing; mere words, conveying to the mind not ideas, but sounds, like those equally barren syllables which our ancestors put together for the purpose of puzzling themselves about words . . . .[2]

One writer is certain the concept holds the key to understanding modern history; the other is equally convinced that it never had any actual historical existence at all. Other analysts—for instance, Gulick—are willing to concede that

> Balance of power policies today have a continuous history dating back to the time of

53

the Italian Renaissance. . . . The origin of the modern development of the Balance of Power coincided with the growth of the present state system. . . . It [the doctrine] spread rapidly to the rest of Europe in the wake of the development of the nation-states, and soon became one of the cardinal tenets of diplomacy throughout the West.

On the other hand, the same writers hasten to demonstrate that the theory of the balance of power—theories, would be more accurate—is not only illogical, but fallacious because it cannot efficiently realize policy aims, and harmful because it runs counter to moral law.[3] And, finally, while Gulick considers the theory as having a definite historical reality but as being fallacious, a very large number of writers since the Renaissance have not only insisted on the fact that the theory has been the mainspring of actual diplomatic decisions, but have concerned themselves with perfecting over-all theories of international relations on the basis of the balance of power. That the use of both the term and the theory is not free from semantic difficulties has not escaped the attention of Alfred Stern, for one. Stern noted that the term, in one breath, is used to describe an objective state of affairs, while in the next it implies a guide to the making of foreign policy. In one instance it means an equality of power, in the next a slight superiority, in the words of the same speaker or writer. "Usually the tendency is to use it in the former sense in peace time and in the latter during a time of diplomatic crisis or warfare," concludes Stern.[4] Clearly, the meaning of the term is obscured by the varying intentions of writers employing it. Apologists for a given policy are likely to resort to one meaning, while advocates of a radically new policy tend to emphasize others. The very vagueness of the term commends its application in the rough-and-tumble of policy-making in a democracy.

These multifarious usages have given rise to several attempts to classify both the meanings of the term and the theories associated with them. Thus Bucher, investigating only its philological meanings,

reached the conclusion that the term has three connotations: "balance" meaning an exact equality of political forces, in a two-state system; "balance" meaning the existence, in a three-state system, of two approximately equal forces, with a third one "holding the balance," i.e., enabling whichever side it decides to join to win the conflict; and "balance" meaning the same thing as hegemony, contradictory though this may sound.[5] Kaeber analyzed the content of numerous formulations of the theory and thought that this general classification is adequate: theories stating the term to mean the exact equality of two contending states, or state systems; theories implying such a distribution of power, in a multi-state system, that no single state would be able, with impunity, to overawe the other states; and "balance" meaning the existence of two contending state systems, with a third state again "holding the balance."[6]

Professor Hans Morgenthau, himself a well-known exponent of the balance of power theory, states that the term may carry these meanings in technical discussion: (1) a policy aimed at bringing about a certain power distribution; (2) a description of any actual state of affairs in international politics; (3) an approximately equal distribution of power internationally; and (4) a term describing any distribution of political power in international relations. When he states his own formulation of the theory and its meaning, it acquires the significance of a universal law of history.[7] Professor Quincy Wright, on the other hand, distinguishes between a "static balance of power" and a "dynamic" one. A static balance is "the condition which accounts for the continued coexistence of independent governments in contact with one another," whereas a dynamic balance "characterizes the policies adopted by governments to maintain that condition." This formulation is based on the assumption that states will inevitably struggle among themselves for predominance and aggrandizement, the index of power being the military potential. The static balance exists automatically—in close analogy to the equilibrium in mechanics—among all states seeking self-preservation and aggrandizement, without planning or analysis. The dynamic policy can be adopted only after conscious thought, implying that the statesmen so acting have some regard for the welfare of the community of states rather than for their self-preservation alone, and here the analogy to physics ends. It is the static sense of the definition, claims Professor Wright, which has enjoyed a large measure of actual historical application, while he is ready to admit that under contemporary conditions the entire theory has ceased to be wholly applicable.[8] It is apparent not only that the precise meaning of the term is in dispute, but that there is no agreement on the classification of the various meanings and their theoretical implications.

Classification of Verbal Meanings

The problem of classifying and analyzing the significance of these varying usages of the term "balance of power" is twofold. On the primary level, it is necessary to differentiate as precisely as possible between the various shades of verbal meaning given to the term by statesmen and commentators. Following this process, it will then be possible to classify and analyze these meanings in terms of the purposes—theoretical and practical—which the users of the phrase may have had in mind. Significance can thus be given to the revived balance of power concept in terms of the motivations impelling its proponents.

Among the various meanings of the term "balance of power," one of the more common is a mere factual description of the distribution of political power in the international scene at any one time. But, in another sense, the term is used to mean a theoretical principle acting as a guide to foreign policy-making in any and all international situations, so that the preponderance of any one state may be avoided. Expanding this notion and assuming that almost all states guide their policies by this principle, a general system of the balance of power is thought to come about, a system in which each participating state has a certain role. Such a system may take the form of two or more power blocs in mutual opposition to

each other and it may exist with or without the benefit of a balancer, i.e., a state willing and able to throw its weight on either scale of the balance, to speak in terms of the classical metaphor, and thus presumably bring about the diplomatic or military victory of the bloc so supported, or possibly prevent any change in existing conditions. In addition to these various shades of theoretical meaning implying some sort of system, the term "balance of power" has frequently been used to describe the existence of a political equilibrium, i.e., such a distribution of power that each state (or each major state) is the approximate equal of every other. On the other hand, the term is commonly employed to connote the exact opposite of the equilibrium notion; it then comes to be identical with a notion of hegemony. Still other commentators insist on the presence of general historical laws of the balance of power, a notion to which the term "natural law" has been given by some. By this they mean that the search for hegemony by one state will inevitably be met by a coalition of all other states, thus forming a "counterweight" against political preponderance and tending to re-establish the *status quo ante*. And, finally, balance of power very frequently means power politics generally and the establishment of certain military and strategic conditions specifically. Some writers equate the term with peace, others with war. This general differentiation now remains to be supported with apposite illustrative citations.[9]

1) Balance meaning "Distribution of Power." The simplest and most commonly found use of the term "balance of power" occurs in plain descriptive statements. Thus when Bolingbroke wrote that "Our Charles the First was no great politician, and yet he seemed to discern that the balance of power was turning in favor of France, some years before the treaty of Westphalia . . . ,"[10] he was merely saying that the Stuart ruler was noticing that the power of France was increasing as compared to that of Britain. Or, again, Henry Wallace once remarked that Japan's joining the Axis meant

> . . . that the old balance of power upon which the U.S. relied for safety is now gone. Only if we are speedy and efficient in our defense can we keep aggressor nations, or any combination of them, from coming to this country. . . . The old balance of power under which the Monroe Doctrine was easily defended is gone. We must look to our own defenses, relying on ourselves to repel any aggression.[11]

Balance of power, in usages such as these, means no more than distribution of power. It does not connote any "balancing" of weights at all. When a statesman says that the "balance of power has shifted," he wants to say that his opponent has grown more powerful than was the case previously.

2) Balance meaning "Equilibrium." An imposing array of politicians and political scientists has urged that the term "balance of power" means what it seems to imply to the uninitiated layman: an exact equilibrium of power between two or more contending parties. Wrote Réal de Curban, for instance:

> Speaking generally, the rulers regard Europe as a balance in which the heaviest side subdues the other side and believe that in order to retain Europe in a solid and peaceful condition it is necessary to maintain between the principal parties this point of equilibrium, which, preventing either side of the balance from sinking, proves that they are on an exactly equal level. . . . The House of France and the House of Austria have been regarded as the scales of the balance of Europe. One or the other of these scales have received their support from England and Holland, which acted as the balancers.[12]

His distinguished compatriots, Duplessis-Mornay and Rohan, agreed with this postulation in important seventeenth-century pamphlets on the nature of the balance of power, recommending, by the way, that the Bourbons subdue the Habsburgs in order to achieve this much-vaunted equilibrium.[13] In Germany

Konstantin Frantz, in 1859, urged the same definition and denounced the Vienna settlement for not having permitted Prussia and Austria to gain equality of power with the other three major states.[14] This juxtaposition of arguments gives considerable support to Professor Pollard's conclusion that the meaning of equilibrium should be taken with a great deal of reserve:

> One has a shrewd suspicion that those who believe in a balance of power, do so because they think it is like a balance at the bank, something better than mere equality, an advantage which they possess. Unconsciously they have both meanings in their minds when they use the phrase. The equality-meaning commends it as propaganda; the advantage is a mental reservation for private use. Statesmen and publicists have sometimes betrayed an uneasy consciousness of the ambiguity and incautiously talked about a just, good, or proper balance of power, admitting thereby that a mere balance was not good enough; and an eighteenth century biographer of Cardinal Wolsey lets the cat out of the bag when he refers to "that grand rule, whereby the counsels of England should always be guided, of preserving the balance of power *in her hands.*"[15]

These formulations of the balance of power as a purely external and international equilibrium between contending states or blocs of states take no account of the possible existence of a similar relationship between contending groups within the state. Such an addition to the theory, however, was furnished by Harold Lasswell.[16] Lasswell speaks of a balancing of power rather than a "balance," since the attempt toward equilibrium can never be a wholly successful one, owing to various non-objective factors which interfere with scientific balancing. Lasswell rounds out the conventional presentation of the search for equilibrium by pointing to the domestic political process as offering a parallel spectacle. Furthermore, he establishes a relationship between the domestic and international balancing processes by describing liaison and support between various societal groups in one state, working with or against certain other groups in the opposing state or in the "balancer" state.

3) *Balance meaning "Hegemony."* This analysis leads easily to the meaning of balance of power equivalent to hegemony. Examples from the literature are numerous and only two will be given: one from the eighteenth century and one modern. Thus, the Count of Hauterive, a pamphleteer for Napoleon I, argued that the balance of power demanded Napoleon's breaking the Treaty of Campo Formio, to enable France to bring about a confederation of the continent against England and in this way reduce the hegemonial superiority of Britain on the seas and, incidentally, establish the hegemony of France.[17] And Napoleon himself, in December of 1813, expressed his desire for a peace "based on the balance of rights and interests."[18]

Nicholas Spykman also understood the balance of power as implying a search for hegemony. His thesis—that all states seek a hegemonial position and therefore are in more or less continual conflict with each other—has for its natural corollary that this conflict, if it stops short of total war, has to result in some sort of equilibrium. This, however, can never be stable, because statesmen do not seek "balance" but hegemony:

> The truth of the matter is that states are interested only in a balance which is in their favor. Not an equilibrium, but a generous margin is their objective. There is no real security in being just as strong as a potential enemy; there is security only in being a little stronger. There is no possibility of action if one's strength is fully checked; there is a chance for a positive foreign policy only if there is a margin of force which can be freely used. Whatever the theory and the rationalization, the practical objective is the constant improvement of the state's own relative power position. The balance desired is the one which neutralizes other states, leaving the home state free to be the deciding force and the deciding voice.[19]

Should equilibrium be attained at one point, it would immediately be wiped out by the search for slight superiority.

4) *Balance meaning "Stability" and "Peace."* A number of analysts have persisted in identifying what they have called the "balance of power" with the kind of idyllic world they desire to establish. They do not mean that the balance of power is a method for realizing peace and stability, but that peace and stability are identical with a balance of power. Typical of this approach is Francis Gould Leckie.[20] Leckie's tome is free from the usual recommendations of balancing the power of state A against state B, with states C and D holding the balance between them. He confines himself to recommending that feudal succession law be abolished and Europe go in for large-scale colonization in Africa and America, thus creating a "stable balance of power." At other times he does, however, lapse into more conventional meanings of the balance —an inconsistency unfortunately found all too frequently in these writings. Similarly, Olof Höijer tends to use the term in this sense, arguing that whenever the powers decided peace was desirable and should be maintained on a given issue—e.g., the London Conference of 1830–1839—a true balance of power existed, though to some analysts it might appear as if here the term "concert" might be more appropriate.[21]

5) *Balance meaning "Instability" and "War."* Occasionally, by contrast, we find writers using the term "balance of power" as being synonymous with the very kind of world conditions they abhor: war, intervention, competition, and instability. Thus the Abbé de Pradt argued that the balance of power means war, while peace is identical with the settling of all issues on their moral, economic, and ethnographic merits.[22] This approach is also typical of that extraordinary eighteenth-century writer, Johann Gottlob Justi, of Cobden and Bright, of the elder Mirabeau, and of Kant, who called the balance of power a *Hirngespinst*.[23] It is true of de Pradt, however, that he tends to identify "balance of power" with power politics generally, a very common identification indeed.

6) *Balance meaning "Power Politics" generally.* Edmund Waller once exclaimed:

> Heav'n that has plac'd this island to give law,
> To balance Europe and her states to awe.

"Balance" in this jingle comes to mean the exertion of power pure and simple. And as the anonymous author of *The Present State of Europe* (ed. of 1757) stated, "The struggle for the balance of power, in effect, is the struggle for power."[24] Power, politics of pure power, *Realpolitik*, and the balance of power are here merged into one concept, the concept that state survival in a competitive international world demands the use of power uninhibited by moral considerations. Lord Bolingbroke, in his fascinating *Letters on the Study and Use of History*, expressed similar ideas. He argued, in effect, that the concept of the balance of power was simply an eminently practical contrivance by which the states of Europe could determine when to combine in defensive alliances against whichever state seemed to be working for hegemony, to "endanger their liberties," i.e., to absorb them. Since this desire was thought to be inherent in either France or Austria at all times, the balance of power comes to mean any power combination to stop "aggression."[25]

This formulation of the term is commonly expanded to include all the factors making for state power, and especially military installations, military potentials, and strategic positions. State A's position in the balance of power is "good" after the construction of a given line of fortresses, or "bad" if that line is obliterated by boundary changes. The point need not be labored. Use of the term "balance of power" in this very commonly employed meaning signifies the over-all power position of states in an international scene dominated by power politics. States are pictured as fighting for power, and only for power—for whatever reasons—and the struggle in or for a balance of power is equivalent to the power political process as a whole. Balance of power here is not to be understood as a refinement of the general process of power politics, but as being identical with it.

7) *Balance as implying a "Universal Law of History."* John Bassett Moore once wrote that

What is called the balance of power is merely a manifestation of the primitive instinct of "self-defense," which tends to produce combinations in all human affairs, national as well as international, and which so often manifests itself in aggression. Not only was the Civil War in the United States the result of a contest over the balance of power but the fact is notorious that certain sections of the country have, during past generations, constantly found themselves in general relations of mutual support because of a continuing common interest in a single question.[26]

The point of departure of these usages is again the assumed inevitable and natural struggle among states for preponderance, and the equally natural resistance to such attempts. Given these two considerations, it follows that as long as they continue in force, there is bound to be a "balance" of states seeking aggrandizement and states opposing that search. In Frederick L. Schuman's version of the balance, there is a tendency for all revisionist states to line up against the ones anxious to conserve given treaties, and in Professor Morgenthau's analysis the "imperialistic" states tend to line up against those defending the status quo, producing a balance in the process.[27] It is often inherent in this formulation to consider Europe as a great "confederation" unified by homogeneous morals and religion and tied together by international law. The balance of power struggle, equally, is part of that system and tends toward its preservation by avoiding the hegemony of a single member. And, of course, it is in this formulation that the analogy to the mechanical balance is most frequently found. As Rousseau put it:

The nations of Europe form among themselves a tacit nation.... The actual system of Europe has precisely the degree of solidity which maintains it in a constant state of motion without upsetting it. The balance existing between the power of these diverse members of the European society is more the work of nature than of art. It maintains itself without effort, in such a manner that if it sinks on one side, it reestablishes itself very soon on the other. ... This system of Europe is maintained by the constant vigilance which observes each disturbance of the balance of power.[28]

Ratzel gave this outlook a geographical orientation by arguing that during the "youth period" of states, a continuous process of expansion and contraction in a given *Raum* takes place, ending in a natural balance between the youthful contenders.[29] Whether in this version or without the benefit of geopolitical notions, the theory is a widely held one, corresponding roughly to what Professor Wright calls the "static balance of power." It was stated in detail by Donnadieu, who claimed that

> "Destiny takes along him who consents and draws along him who refuses!" said Rabelais. The balance of power is one of these necessary forces; in other words, it is the expression of a law in the life of nations.[30]

In the hands of Albert Sorel the universal law version of the balance of power underwent further sophistication. In the first place, Sorel made no claim for the "universality" of the principle, but confined its application to the Europe of the *ancien régime*, during which time politics among sovereign rulers was held to be entirely free from ideological determinants. Furthermore, while he treated balance of power policies as "natural" and largely instinctive, he admitted nevertheless that the practice of balancing was the result of reasoned decisions based on the principle of *raison d'état*. Political action is the result of the desire for "power after power," greed and covetousness. Aggrandizement is the policy motive which holds the key to the understanding of international relations. And *raison d'état*

> rules in all situations in which one feels oneself strong enough to follow with impunity the policies suggested by it. It inspires the same thoughts in Vienna and in Berlin. Young rulers and future ministers are taught about it. I read in the *Institutions politiques* of Bielfeld: "In whatever situation a state may find itself, the fundamental principle of *raison d'état* remains unchanged. This principle, accepted by all ancient and modern nations, is that the welfare of the people should always be the supreme law." "The great powers," wrote an Austrian diplomat in 1791, "must only conduct themselves in accordance with *raison d'état.... Interest* must win all varieties of resentment, however just they may be."

Something that can be taught to young rulers clearly is not instinctive. Yet Sorel holds that the very excesses of unrestrained and aggressive *raison d'état* doctrines result in their antithesis: moderation, willingness to forego expansion when the prize is small, and a willingness to abide by treaties if no undue sacrifice seems implied. Sorel sums up these restraints in the term "understood interest" (*intérêt bien entendu*), and maintains that if practiced they result in a balance of power:

> The converging of ambitions is the limit to aggrandizement. Since there are no more unclaimed territories in Europe, one state can only enrich itself at the expense of its neighbors. But all the powers agreed in not permitting a single one among them to rise above the others. He who pretends to the role of the lion must see his rivals ally themselves against him. Thus there arises among the great states a sort of society, through common concern; they want to preserve what they possess, gain in proportion to their commitment and forbid each of the associated states to lay down the law to the others.[31]

Balance of power thus comes to mean the instinctive antithesis to the reasoned thesis of *raison d'état*. Unconscious moderation, temporarily, restrains deliberate greed. A general dialectic of power relationships is thus created in which balances of power play a definite part. However, no balance is permanent and is subject to change at a moment's notice. It guarantees neither peace nor law; in fact, it implies war and its own destruction whenever a former counterweight state acquires sufficient power to challenge the very balance which it was called upon to maintain.

8) Balance as a "System" and "Guide" to policy-making. In the formulation of the balance of power as a universal law of history there was an element of instinctive, unconscious, and unplanned behavior which would defy any analysis in terms of conscious human motivations. Statesmen were represented as acting in accordance with the prescriptions of the balance of power as if they were the unconscious pawns of some invisible hand, to borrow a phrase from Adam Smith. In the formulation of the balance of power as a system of political organization and guide to policy-making, emphasis is firmly thrown on conscious and deliberate behavior and decision-making.

What is the balance of power as a system and guide? A few short definitions might suggest tentative answers. Thus, Professor Fay says: "It means such a 'just equilibrium' in power among the members of the family of nations as will prevent any of them from becoming sufficiently strong to enforce its will upon the others."[32] Or, again, in the words of Professor Gooch, the balance of power is

> the determination, partly conscious and partly instinctive, to resist by diplomacy or arms the growth of any European state at once so formidable and so actually or so potentially hostile as to threaten our liberties, the security of our shores, the safety of our commerce, or the integrity of our foreign possessions.[33]

Needless to add, this is a particularly British understanding of the balance of power, underlining once more the difficulty —if not the impossibility—of stating the theory in such terms that all governments could subscribe to it at any one time. Both definitions, however, are in very close agreement with some of the classical statements of the nature of the balance of power, understood as a guide to statesmen on how to prevent any other state from acquiring enough power to threaten their state in any way. Thus Fénelon, a moralist with considerable experience in policy-making, said:

> To hinder one's neighbor from becoming too strong is not to do harm; it is to guarantee one's self and one's neighbor from subjection; in a word it is to work for liberty, tranquility, and public safety. Because the aggrandizement of one nation beyond a certain limit changes the general system of

all nations connected with it . . . the excessive aggrandizement of one may mean the ruin and subjection of all the other neighbors. . . . This attention to the maintenance of a kind of equality and equilibrium between neighboring states is what assures peace for all.[34]

Leagues to preserve the balance of power are then advocated by the learned bishop, but he is careful to specify that they may not be used for offensive purposes. Moreover, the balancing process was to assure that no state was eliminated from the map of Europe, no matter how much it might have to be "limited" to assure the security of its neighbors. No less a thinker than David Hume also understood the balance in this sense. He postulated, first, the existence of a multi-state system, dominated by competition and hostility among the members. Statesmen ever since Thucydides, said Hume, have made good policy when they checked in due time, through alliances and coalition wars, the growth of a state potentially able to absorb them all, and made bad policy when they ignore this guiding principle.[35] It is interesting to note in passing that Hume approved of the balance of power as a guide to "good" policy-making while opposing the mercantilist balance of trade theory, whereas most of the other opponents of mercantilism in his age—e.g., the elder Mirabeau—attacked the balance of power as well.[36] This, in essence, is the formulation given by the majority of publicists to the theory of the balance of power, considered only as a conscious guide to policy-making. It is stated succinctly and incisively by Dupuis:

> The simple instinct of prudence would suffice to suggest the idea of the balance of power; the meditations of statesmen and the lessons of experience have transformed the instinct into a rule of conduct and raised the idea to the dignity of a principle. And in the role of political principle, the balance of power does not only have the advantage of reminding councils of the prudence confirmed by the teachings of the past; it has the merit of opening, during periods of crisis, a field for negotiation and if it cannot dictate the solutions of the conflict, it can prepare the setting for an alliance.[37]

The guide, therefore, merely tells statesmen to prevent the growth of any state which, merely because of its power, is potentially able to absorb or limit their own states . . . .

So much for the guide. How does the balance of power then become a system? It stands to reason that if all the states of Europe (or the world) were to base their policies on the prescription of the balance of power, a "system" would come about in the sense that the least movement toward hegemony by one would immediately result in the coalition of the other states into an opposing alliance. The ever-present readiness to do just that and the constant vigilance declared necessary to prevent any one state's hegemony would in themselves produce this system of the balance of power. It is at this point that the theory grows more fanciful. The earlier doctrines, based on the guide-and-system idea, contented themselves with the so-called simple balance. The analogy is that of a pair of scales, and the supposition was that there would be only two major states, with their satellites, in the "system." The idea of a strict physical equilibrium—or slight hegemony—would then apply. Later doctrines, however, introduced the notion of the complex balance, on the analogy of the chandelier. More than two states, plus satellites, were postulated, and the necessity for preserving the freedom of all from the lust for dominance by any one was thought to involve the setting into motion of various weights and counterweights on all sides of the chandelier. It is this system which is closely related to the idea of the "balancer," introduced into the theory by British writers during the seventeenth century and a commonplace in the eighteenth. It implied, of course, the existence of powers sufficiently unconcerned by the merits of whatever the issue of the crisis was to be willing to "add their weight" to whichever side was the weaker, and thus prevent the possible victory—and implied hegemony—of the stronger. The balance of power considered as a guide was the reasoning process at the base of the system.[38]

Meanings and the Intentions of Users

The foregoing analysis of verbal applications of the term "balance of power" has

resulted in the demonstration of eight more or less distinct meanings and connotations which the term may carry. Of more significance to the application of balance of power terminology in the discussion of international affairs, however, is the use to which these meanings may be put. For just as the emphasis on collective security and Wilsonian liberalism in international relations tends to exclude discussion of the balance of power—either as irrelevant or else as undesirable—for essentially ideological reasons, so can the application of the term by its proponents vary with their ideological, theoretical, and practical preoccupations. An attempt will therefore be made to correlate the application of various usages of the term with the intentions of its users, at least insofar as these intentions may be ascertained from the context of the writings and statements examined. Four areas of intention can thus be distinguished: a purely descriptive intent; a conscious or unconscious propagandistic intent; an intention of using the term as an analytical concept in the development of a theory of international relations; and an intention of using the term as a guide to foreign policy-making.

BALANCE OF POWER AS DESCRIPTION

Forswearing any theoretical or analytical purpose, writers commonly have recourse to the term "balance of power" in discussing international affairs. Current references to the balance of power by journalists and radio commentators most frequently fall into this category. And in most instances the meaning to be conveyed to the audience merely implies "distribution" of power, rather than "balance" in anything like the literal sense. The citations from Bolingbroke, the reference by C. L. Sulzberger, and the statement of Henry Wallace quoted above all meet these criteria. By using the term "balance of power" these writers were merely describing a particular distribution of power. Their intentions then did not carry them into any more ambitious realm . . . .

BALANCE OF POWER AS PROPAGANDA AND "IDEOLOGY"

A precise understanding of the verbal meaning of the term "balance of power" becomes especially important when it is used as a propagandistic slogan or as an ideological phrase, in the Mannheimian sense. The meanings of "balance" as being identical with either "peace" or "war" fall into this category. Obviously, while it might be correct to speak of a state of balance or imbalance *implying* or *engendering* either war or peace, the balance as such cannot logically be equated with conditions which might arise as a consequence of the balance, i.e., war or peace. In the cases in which the authors employed it to mean "peace" or "war," "balance of power" then became no more than a convenient catchword to focus individual aspirations into a generally acceptable mold; and there can be no doubt that at certain times the concept of balance was an extremely popular one, whether it was used for policy-making or not. If used in a patently forced manner, the term becomes indistinguishable from plain propaganda. . . .

BALANCE OF POWER AS ANALYTICAL CONCEPT

At the opposite pole of the propaganda-oriented application of the term "balance of power" lies the user's intention to employ the term as a tool of analysis. It is in this area of intentions that the term rose to the status of a theory of international relations during the eighteenth and nineteenth centuries, no less than it has in our own era. It is also true, however, that in this area as well as in the other fields of intentions analyzed so far not one but several of the verbal meanings of the term find application. Even as a tool of scholarly analysis the term has been used to mean "power politics," "equilibrium," "hegemony" and, finally, a "universal law" of state conduct.

"The basic principle of the balance of power," wrote Réal de Curban, "is incontestable: the power of one ruler, in the last analysis, is nothing but the ruin and diminution of that of his neighbors, and his power is nothing but the weakness of the others."[39] And in a Hobbesian state of nature which was presupposed to exist among sovereign states no other conclusion seemed possible. This reasoning has led numerous writers to equate the balance of power with power politics or *Realpolitik* generally. The struggle for self-preservation in the state of nature implies the formation of alliances and mutually antagonistic blocs which in turn make negotiations in "good faith" a contradiction in terms. Power politics are the only discernible pattern in which balancing is an inherent process. As such, it is not separate from but identical with competitive power struggles. Consequently, in dispassionate analyses of international affairs the "balance" of power carries no significance other than that usually associated with "power politics," unrefined by any conception of equilibrium or deliberate balancing measures.[40]

Furthermore, the concept of evenly balanced power, or "equilibrium," finds frequent application as a tool of analysis. In the preceding discussion the equilibrium concept found application merely as a descriptive phrase implying no generalized behavior pattern in international relations. In the present context the reverse is true. Lasswell, in speaking of the "balancing process," for instance, assumes that under conditions of expected future violence—domestic as well as international—any increase in the coercion potential of one power unit will lead to a compensatory increase in the competing unit or units. Further increases on the part of one side will always bring corresponding increases on the part of its competitors, so that in effect a rough equality of power potential will always prevail, a factor which may make for either open conflict or induce fear of refraining from hostilities, depending on circumstances, the nature of the elites in question, and the accuracy of intelligence reports concerning the degree of "balancing." The analytical application of the equilibrium-meaning of the balance of power, in short, generalizes the basic assumption of the absence of international consensus and the consequent inherent presence of conflict into a pattern of balancing.

Carrying the equilibrium-meaning one step further results in the application of the balance of power concept as implying the search for hegemony. This application again finds its counterpart in the intentions of detached analysts striving for a generalized understanding of phenomena rather than for description. Spykman, as demonstrated above, clearly sets forth the assumptions of this approach. His argument is that the search for power by sovereign states is an end in itself, since conflict—actual or potential—is the only consistent pattern in relations between state units. While the search for power originally implied the desire for self-preservation, a generalized desire for power-seeking over a long period of time converts this process into an end in itself. On this level, the discussion of the balance of power is identical with power politics generally. As in the case of Lasswell's balancing process, however, the generalized process of competitive power-seeking must result in equilibrium if war is avoided—temporarily. But statesmen, as indicated above, seek a margin of safety in superiority of power and not in equality of power. Hence the search for equilibrium in effect is the search for hegemony, and the balance of power as an analytical concept becomes another term for the simultaneous search for preponderance of power by all the sovereign participants. No wonder Spykman exclaims that

> He who plays the balance of power can have no permanent friends. His devotion can be to no specific state but only to balanced power. The ally of today is the enemy of tomorrow. One of the charms of power politics is that it offers no opportunity to grow weary of one's friends. England's reputation as *perfide Albion* is the inevitable result of her preoccupation with the balance of power.[41]

In this refined analysis, the balance of power comes to be considered as a special case—either in its equilibrium or its hegemony connotation—in the general pattern

of power politics, though Spykman in the passage just cited again tends to use the two terms interchangeably.

The supreme attempt to use the balance of power as an analytical concept arises in the case of those writers who make the balance the essence of a theory of international relations. It is here that the balance attains the quality of a "law of history," as indeed Rousseau and Donnadieu implied by their very choice of words, and many contemporary writers by their emphasis on the "naturalness" of state behavior in accordance with the dictates of balanced power. The universal law connotation of the balance of power presupposes state conduct in no way different from the assumptions of Spykman and Lasswell. But Professors Morgenthau and Schuman for instance, in giving the balance of power this extended meaning, go beyond the characterization of equilibrium and hegemony. They develop the thesis that it is inherent in the nature of a multi-state system based on sovereignty to engage in mutually hostile policies, for whatever motives. In this process the search for balanced power, the need to form blocs and counterblocs to prevent the feared attainment of hegemony by one or the other of the participants in the conflict is a natural, if not instinctive, choice of policy. A group of revisionist states always lines up against a group of states devoted to the maintenance of the status quo in such a way that approximate balance results. So general is this pattern that it attains the quality of a historical law. And the characteristic feature of this law is that it does not necessarily assume a conscious intention on the part of statesmen to "balance power with power" in a sense which would imply the official acceptance of a balance of power theory by governments. Statesmen, to be sure, may be consciously motivated by balancing notions. But, if they are not, the policies which they would most logically adopt would be those consistent with the balance of power. As Professor Morgenthau indicates, if they fail to do so, they do not make "logical" policy and thereby violate historically proven and generalized modes of conduct. The distinctive feature about the balance of power applied as a tool of analysis, then, is its possible separation from the motivations of governments.

BALANCE OF POWER AS PRESCRIPTION

While the analytical application of the term does not imply conscious acceptance of balancing rules by governments, there is a large body of thought—historical and contemporary—which does insist that the balance of power is—or should be—a guiding principle for decision-making on the part of governments. It is this application of the term which makes use of the meaning defined above as "guide-and-system." Once more international relations are pictured, in one version, as being in the Hobbesian state of nature, so that survival dictates the formation of alliances among those states committed to "preserving the balance" against the onslaught of the state(s) allegedly seeking world or regional domination or, as the eighteenth-century writers put it, "universal monarchy." In this sense, the balance is a conscious guide dictating the rules of survival. In another sense, however, the world (or Europe, in the earlier writing) is represented as a "system" of states tied together by mutual interdependence, common institutions, and a common system of law (the law of nations), and the search for hegemony of a single member of this "system" was then represented as an attack upon the whole organic unit.[42] The system was based on the continued independence of all members and their common will to resist the search for hegemony by any one of their number. The balance of power was inherent in the very system itself and also acted as a body of rules dictating the proper policies for preventing the attainment of hegemony, i.e., it acted as a "guide." . . .

Intentions and Their Significance to a Theory of International Relations

The breakdown of the "balance of power" phrase into a series of eight distinct verbal meanings has now been categorized into four possible applications which these meanings have found in political literature, and perhaps in diplomacy as well. It is not to be inferred that in these classifications there is one which alone is of general value and applicability to the analysis of international relations. This problem is inherent in the inevitably somewhat arbitrary basis of distinction adopted in the foregoing analysis. It is not claimed, of course, that the term "balance of power," in any of its eight possible connotations, is used as propaganda or description in the intentions of any one writer to the exclusion of other possible intended applications. The four categories here established, in short, cannot be regarded as mutually exclusive even in the intentions of the same writer, analyst, commentator, or statesman.[43] A basic barrier in communication is created by this apparently facile interchangeability of meanings and intentions. A theoretical analysis, therefore, cannot proceed on the basis of identifying one writer with one meaning or one category of intentions. Each meaning and intention must be considered separately in terms of the immediate context, even though meanings and intentions may change as the context changes, either in compliance with the user's overall scheme or in defiance of his thought. Nevertheless, it is clear that not all of these categories are of equal relevance to the effort to construct a theory of international relations. The effort to separate the theoretically meaningful categories from those which, while important in the total context of international relations, are based on inadequate logical or conceptual assumptions is one on which a few general observations must be made.

Thus, the theoretical significance of the descriptive intention may be open to several alternative interpretations. It may well be argued that as long as the distribution of power, in general terms, in terms of equilibrium or lack of equilibrium, i.e., the implied hegemony of one camp, is merely discussed with the intention of *describing* an objective state of affairs, there can be no question of theoretical implications. A reference to a "balance" of power in such a context would carry no more general meaning than the application of such terminology to a summary of the number of convention delegates pledged to a given presidential aspirant. And, in fact, it is precisely in such situations that the term is finding a new lease on life.

It can be argued, however, that even the meaning of "distribution" and "equilibrium" in an ordinary descriptive sense may carry with it theoretical implications. If it is desired to establish the general historical conditions to which the rise of certain institutions can be attributed, for instance, this meaning of "balance" may acquire a theoretical significance beyond the scope indicated above. Thus, it may be suggested that modern international law owes its growth to a "balance" of power—in the sense of "distribution" avoiding "hegemony"—during its crucial decades and that without such a "balance" it could not have developed at all, since the strongest state(s) would have had no interest in its growth.[44] It is in situations such as these that the user's context acquires tremendous significance, since it may well be that in applying the term in this sense what was intended was not description, but analysis or a correlation between the balance as prescription and its historical consequences.

Applications of balance of power terminology for propagandistic or self-deceptive purposes similarly may be interpreted in several ways. *A priori*, such application could not carry with it a significance to a general theory of international relations, since it is used for intellectually dishonest purposes. It is intended for dissimulation, not clarification, and certainly not as a consistent guide to action. Furthermore, the meanings of "balance" subsumed in this category are in themselves open to considerable logical and conceptual doubts. The usage of the term as connoting peace and stability or war and instability, again, is largely descriptive, or else a pure value

judgment of no theoretical significance whatever. The fact that some writers have indulged in this loose terminology merely indicates that the term "balance of power" had tended to become a catch-all to accommodate whatever policies writers wanted to recommend. The frankly propagandistic use of the term is thus merely an extreme species of the same genus.

To a general theory of politics based on Mannheimian concepts of ideology, however, even this category might prove to be of relevance. Should the theory be oriented toward the study of value systems—avowed and tacit—and toward the factors of manipulation of external and internal forces, this area of intentions might acquire some importance. What appears to the student of motivations as dishonesty and self-deception might assume far greater causative significance to a student of psychopathology in international relations.

In the area of concept, of course, the balance of power acquires immediate theoretical significance, deservedly or otherwise. It is deliberately chosen as the major support of a widely accepted method of analyzing intergroup relations. But even here some caution with respect to meanings is necessary. Thus, the usage which speaks of the balance of power in terms indistinguishable from power politics generally should not be given separate consideration, since the application of the phrase here is really misplaced in terms of logical consistency as well as of historical tradition. It would be absolutely correct to consider the balance of power as a refinement of a general system of power politics, should one be postulated, as indeed writers such as Dupuis, Donnadieu, Gentz, and Brougham did consider it. But the essential distinction between policies of power for the sake of power—unrefined by any thought of balancing some state's power with some other state's—and the balance of power as defined by Fay, Gooch, and Fénelon should still be maintained. History is full of examples of plain power policies, unqualified by balance notions.

It appears, however, that a theory of international relations which does not insist on the necessity of demonstrating general laws of conduct in terms of actual motivations leaves itself open to attack on grounds of lack of comprehensiveness. And it is this factor which has been responsible for a great deal of the skepticism with which the universal law version of the balance of power as an analytical concept has been treated ever since Justi. The treatment of the balance of power as prescription, in the sense of the guide-and-system connotation, therefore, acquires its theoretical significance in this context. The balancing of power is considered as the primary motivation of governments in this approach and, as Brougham clearly showed, the realization of this motivation assumes the subordination of all other possible policy motivations in international politics, at least insofar as they are inconsistent with the demands of balanced power. To a theory of international relations which relies on demonstrable motivations among policy-makers, therefore, the balance of power as prescription must be a fundamental point of departure.

The Concept of Power

THE ARTICLES in this section include the most important attempts to explicate the concept of power in such a way as to facilitate its observation and measurement. Herbert Simon and Robert Dahl agree in defining "power" as the ability of one person to alter the behavior of another. Peter Bachrach and Morton Baratz, in two important articles, criticize this definition for its failure to include some determinants of political outcomes, and incidentally argue that "power" should be restricted to certain types of interdependent choice situations. Finally, William Riker discusses these and other analyses of the concept, and concludes that they differ in their definitions of causality.

Riker's article is important for calling our attention to the need to construct theories which state the necessary and sufficient conditions for the political outcomes which interest us, rather than dispute about the attribution of power. It is an important bridge between writings on political power and other efforts to construct a cumulative science of political behavior. For an important effort to explicate the concept of power which is more directly tied to a specific theory of political behavior, see the articles by John Harsanyi reproduced in the following section.

7

IF POLITICAL power is taken as one of the central phenomena to be explained by political science, then the propositions of political science will necessarily contain sentences and phrases like "the power of A is greater than the power of B," "an increase (or decrease) in the power of A," "the distribution of political power," and the like. And if the empirical truth or falsity of such propositions is to be tested, there must be agreement as to the operational definition of the term "power" and the operational means that are to be used to determine the degree of its presence or absence in any situation.

All of this is elementary enough—but how far has the task been carried out; to what extent have the operational tools of observation and measurement been provided us? That a great deal remains to be done can be made clear, I think, by an outrageous example. Suppose that, in the presence of a boorishly critical skeptic, we were to assert: "Peron holds a monopoly of power in Argentina." Suppose that our skeptic were to reply: "Prove it." We could of course, adopt the tactics of Dr. Johnson who, when asked to prove the existence of the table at which he was sitting, suggested that his disputant kick it. While this reply has never been adjudged entirely adequate by metaphysicians, kicking a table would certainly settle the question of its existence to the satisfaction of most empirical scientists. But how, precisely, does one "kick" a dictatorship to find out if it exists? If I kicked Peron, I would go to jail; but I would also if I kicked the King of England, who is not usually regarded as a dictator.

Now I do not doubt that Peron is dictator of Argentina; nor (a slightly more difficult point to establish) that the King is not dictator of England; nor (an even more subtle point) that Stalin was dictator of Russia at a time when he held no official governmental position whatsoever. Nor will I ask the reader to doubt these propositions. I will ask the reader, however, to join me in an inquiry into the meanings of propositions like those just stated, and into the means for establishing the truth of such propositions—which truth, in spite of the

Notes on the Observation and Measurement of Power*

Herbert A. Simon

This article by Herbert Simon was one of the first efforts to give an operational definition of the concept of power. It remains one of the best. The article also contains some sensible remarks about the measurement of power. Originally published in 15 Journal of Politics (1953) 500–16, and reprinted in Herbert Simon, Models of Man (New York: John Wiley, 1957), it is reproduced here with the permission of the Journal of Politics and the author.

appearance of self-evidence, can certainly be confirmed only by empirical data. In general, our inquiry may be regarded as a series of footnotes on the analysis of influence and power by Lasswell and Kaplan in *Power and Society*, which we will take as the starting point.

SKETCH OF A DEFINITION OF THE TERM "POWER"

Like Humpty Dumpty, we will insist that a word means what we want it to mean. But if our aim is to construct a body of science, and if we already have in view the general range of phenomena to be explained, our definitions may be willful, but they must not be arbitrary.[1] If we were to say that we would measure a man's power by his height, this would be an internally consistent definition, but one hardly useful in exploring the phenomena referred to in common speech as the phenomena of power. If we were to say that we would measure a man's power by his wealth *or* his ability to influence the behavior of

* I should like to acknowledge my debt to the two men who introduced me to politics as power—Harold D. Lasswell and the late Charles E. Merriam.

69

Notes to chapter 7 are found on page 368.

others, the definition would not even be internally consistent, for these two criteria might in fact be only imperfectly correlated.[2]

Power and Value Position. I think that definitions which equate influence or power[3] with the values an individual possesses are unsuitable for political science. The difficulty is revealed when we try to state what we mean by a "value." If we list specific values—wealth, wisdom, or what not—then the statement that "A possesses certain of these values" is not what we *mean* when we say "A has power." For if these two statements are regarded as identical by definition, then a proposition like "the wealthy are the powerful"—dear to Marxists and anti-Marxists alike—ceases to be an empirical proposition in political science, and becomes true simply by definition.

A second defect of such definitions is that they confront us with the necessity of inventing new values to account for persons whom we wish to regard as powerful, but whose values lie outside the usual lists—Gandhi is a good example.

The situation becomes even worse if we admit power into the list of social values that define power. That power is a value, i.e., something desired and valued, is generally admitted; but if so, to define power as value position renders meaningless propositions like: "We can measure a person's power by his ability to acquire power."[4]

To summarize, I propose to define power and influence in such a way as to distinguish these concepts from value position. In doing so, I believe I am conforming to common usage, because (a) propositions, intended to be empirical, are often asserted with respect to the relation between power and value position, and (b) power is often asserted to be a value (but not the only value) that is desired.

If, having made a distinction between power and value position, we are able to establish an empirical relationship between the two, we can then use value position as an *index* of power—which is something quite different from using it as the defining

operation. I think that we can conjecture what the relationship is likely to be. When a society is in a state of stable equilibrium, there is likely to be a close correspondence between the distribution of power and the distribution of value. If this is so, then, *in equilibrium situations*, we can use the value distribution as an index of the power distribution when the latter is difficult to ascertain directly.

Power and Value Potential. Objections similar to those just mentioned can be raised against defining power or influence as synonymous with value potential. Value potential (see Lasswell and Kaplan, p. 58) is simply value position referred to some future date. As before, such a definition would transform from empirical propositions to definitional identities such statements as: "Those who have power will employ it to improve their value position" —which is roughly equivalent to: "Those who have power have high value potential."

In fact, the two definitional proposals examined thus far—relating power to value position and value potential, respectively— reveal that even at the empirical level we are not certain as to the relationship between the possession of values and of power. Does possession of power imply high value position or high potentiality of improving value position? In the previous section I suggested that, in equilibrium situations, we assume an empirical relationship to exist between value *position* and power in order to predict the latter from the former. In non-equilibrium situations, we often employ an assumed relationship between power and value *potential* to predict the latter from the former. These empirical dynamic relations may be represented diagrammatically thus:

Value Position— > Power— > Value Potential (Future Value Position).

An Alternative Definition. As an alternative to the definitions just discarded, we propose the definition of "influence process" employed by Lasswell and Kaplan: "The *exercise of influence* (influence process) consists in affecting policies of others than the self."[5]

This definition involves an asymmetrical relation between influencer and influencee. Now we are wary, in the social sciences, of asymmetrical relations. They remind us of pre-Humeian and pre-Newtonian notions of causality. By whip and sword we have been converted to the doctrine that there is no causation, only functional interrelation, and that functional relations are perfectly symmetrical. We may even have taken over, as a very persuasive analogy, the proposition that "for every action, there is an equal and opposite reaction." If, in spite of this, we persist in thinking that there is something asymmetrical about the influence (or power) relation, it may be reassuring that quite similar relations can be introduced into the most respectable of physical systems.[6]

It should be noticed also that the Lasswell-Kaplan definition refers to processes of change rather than to a state of equilibrium. Presumably, we observe the influence of A over B by noting the differences between the way B actually behaves and the way he *would* behave if A were not present (or if A's desires changed). Influence belongs to the theory of dynamics, or of comparative statics, rather than to the theory of equilibrium.

ASYMMETRY OF THE POWER RELATION

The notion that the power or influence relation of A to B is asymmetrical carries with it some implication as to how the phenomenon of power can be observed and measured. Let us first consider the case where the asymmetry is supposed to be complete; i.e., A influences B, but B does not influence A at all. Then, if we are dealing with a determinate system, the behavior of A can be predicted without any reference to his relation to B, while the behavior of B follows once we know the behavior of A. Stated otherwise, the social system as a whole must contain a subsystem, that determines the behavior of A, but in which B does not appear (or at least B's reactions to A's behavior do not appear).

Now to determine the influence of A upon B, we simply observe a number of situations in which the behavior of A varies, and note what is the concomitant variation in B's behavior. As a concrete example, let us suppose that a dictator is "unilaterally coupled" to his subjects—his decisions determine their behavior, but there is no "feedback" from their behavior to his. Then, if by manipulating the variables that determine his own expectations or desires we can change his decisions, we can also observe what changes this brings about in the behavior of the subjects.

Power in the Presence of Feedback. It will immediately be objected that we are never faced with a situation involving unilateral coupling in this extreme sense—that there is always some feedback from the influencee to the influencer. This difficulty can be handled in either of two ways: (1) we can give up the idea that the relation is asymmetrical; or (2) we can add an asymmetrical relation operating in the opposite direction from the first. *If the processes of influence take time,* and particularly if the time lags associated with the two asymmetrical relations are different, there is at least the possibility that we can make separate empirical observations of the two relations.[7]

If, in our previous example, our dictator makes a decision, and if he is sensitive to public approval and disapproval, then we will observe in sequence: (1) the decision, (2) subsequent changes in behavior of the subjects, (3) expressions of approval or disapproval by the subjects, and (4) modifications in the decision if it proves to be unpopular. In favorable cases, the feedback may involve large time lags. If, instead of a dictator, we have an elected president, the feedback might take the form of a change in the holder of the office at the next election.

Now, if there is any feedback at all, measurement of influence requires the observation of disequilibrium as well as equilibrium. In a state of equilibrium in the case of the elected president, the last previous election would have already put in office a president whose decisions would be acceptable to the citizens—it would be impossible to determine whether the chicken was mother or daughter of the egg.

The Rule of Anticipated Reactions. But an even graver difficulty must be admitted. Because of the phenomenon that Friedrich[8] has christened "the rule of anticipated reactions" and that the servomechanism engineer calls "anticipatory control," the time lags upon which we depend for measurement may be destroyed. If the President is elected, his decisions may be affected not only by what the citizens did in the last election, but also by his expectations of what they will do in the next.

I think it can be seen that the possibility of measuring the separate links in the chain of influence depend, in this instance, on the presence of some ignorance in the system. So long as the President is able to form exact expectations of the citizens' reactions, and they of what a candidate will do if elected, his influence on them cannot be distinguished from their influence on him, but let his or their forecasts be in error and the possibilities of disentangling the relations are re-established.

Fortunately for political scientists—who would otherwise be largely debarred from observation of the central phenomenon of their science—the members of the body politic are often far from accurate in their predictions. If President Roosevelt had foreseen the outcome of the 1938 "purges" he might not have undertaken them, and we should have been deprived of valuable information about influences on voting behavior. If the assassination of Lincoln had been anticipated, we would have lost instructive insights into the relative powers of President and Congress provided by the administration of Andrew Johnson. The unpredicted and the unexpected provide a break from the usual chain of intended connections and, serving as something of a substitute for controlled experimentation, permit us to observe the construction of the separate links.

Implications of the Definition. Apart from the question of measurement, the habit of viewing a social structure as a network of (generally) asymmetrical relationships can help to clarify some of the ambiguities that are commonly found in statements of power relationships. This formulation teaches us that, when we wish to speak of the influence of a particular element in a social system upon that system, we must specify whether we mean the influence of the element considered as independent, with all the reverse feedback relations ignored, or whether we mean the net influence of the element, taking into account all the reciprocal influences of other elements upon it. Concretely, how powerful we consider the President to be depends on whether we ignore, or take into consideration, the fact that he is an elected official, and the fact that he is advised by a corps of permanent civil servants.

If we regard the President as an "independent variable," then we arrive at one assessment of his influence. If we add to our system the environmental influences created by the administrative bureaucracy, which greatly restrict the variability that differences in personal qualities and beliefs would otherwise produce in the behavior of different presidents, we arrive at a smaller estimate of the influence of those personal qualities and beliefs.

As an exercise for developing his skill in handling both this distinction and the rule of anticipated reactions, the reader may like to test his wits on the proposition: "The power of the President can be measured by the number of bills he vetoes where the veto is not overridden."

The interpretation of influence as unilateral coupling corresponds reasonably well with our everyday intuitive notions. We would ordinarily argue that it makes a greater difference to events in the United States if a Justice of the Supreme Court or a United States Senator is replaced than if John Jones, an Idaho potato farmer, retires and turns over his farm to his son. What we are saying here is that the personal characteristics of the individual occupying a particular position (a judgeship or a senatorial seat) constitutes a variable upon which other variables in the system depend. The influence of any position, according to this notion, is proportional to the amount of change induced throughout the system by a change in the characteristics of the individual occupying the position in question.

THE EXERCISE OF INFLUENCE AND THE
INFLUENCE BASE

Direct measurements of influence are obtained when we can observe the ratio of change in behavior of influencee to change in behavior of influencer. If, starting with such measurements, we are able to determine empirically the conditions that make for influence—the characteristics of individuals and situations that permit us to predict that the influence of a particular individual will be large—then we can derive from these empirical relationships additional indirect measurements of influence. In particular, if we can measure the magnitude of the influence *base*,[9] we can infer from this the magnitude of the influence. (E.g., if wealth is the principal influence base in a particular situation—the principal means for exercising influence—then in that situation we may measure influence indirectly by wealth.)

Dynamic Relationships. Now there are generally intricate relationships among the bases of influence and the values that are sought. In the first place, influence is the means, in rational social behavior, of securing the values that are desired. Hence, influence itself, and consequently the bases of influence also become something valued as means to other values. Moreover, many of the bases of influence may be valued *both* as means for the exercise of influence and for other reasons as well.

Wealth will serve as an example. Wealth, in most societies, is a base of influence, hence, a means for securing values. But wealth is also valued for the consumption it permits and the deference it commands. Now consider the extreme case of a society in which wealth is the only influence base, and where consumption and deference are the only values. In such a society, *investment* is the use of influence to augment the influence base, *consumption* is the use of influence to augment other values without increase in the influence base.

Similar dynamic relationships apply to influence bases other than wealth. Political power, too, can be "invested"—control of a legislature may be employed to gerrymander legislative districts in order to ensure continued control. It can also be consumed, to obtain desired legislation, sometimes at the expense of future power.

I have spelled out these dynamic relationships to emphasize the point made earlier that it is essential to distinguish between the operations that measure influence directly, and the indirect estimates of influence that can be inferred from measurements of the influence base. It is often true that influence is used to obtain value. (This accounts for the relationship between influence and value potential.) It is often true that value position provides the influence base. (This accounts for the relationship between influence and value position.) It is often true that influence is employed to augment future influence. In the scheme proposed here, these are all empirical relationships that should not be confused with definitional identities.

Comments on the Nature of the Influence Base. The term "influence base" has been used here to refer to the conditions for the exercise of influence. The influence base is by no means synonymous with the value position, although there are two significant connections between them. First, when values are exchangeable, they can be given to others in return for desired behavior. It is in this sense that values provide a base for influence. Second, any condition that gives its possessor influence is likely to become a desideratum—a value. It is not because being a Supreme Court Justice is valued that such a Justice has influence; but, conversely, it is because he has influence that the position is valued.[10]

Because the connection between influence base and value is not always the same, a classification of influence bases in terms of the values related to them is rather superficial. A more fundamental basis for classification is with respect to the motivation of the influencee that leads him to accept influence. On this basis, Lasswell and Kaplan define three successively narrower terms: (a) influence (encompassing all motivations for acceptance); (b) power (acceptance motivated by sanctions); and (c) authority (acceptance motivated by attitudes toward legitimacy).[11]

There has been some tendency in the literature of political science to regard ordinary sanctions, like money and physical force, as the bases of "effective" power; and legitimacy as the base of "formal" power. The implication of this kind of language is that "effective" power is what determines actual behavior, while "formal" power is some kind of epiphenomenal rationalization of the power structure—window-dressing, so to speak.[12] Some political scientists, however, Charles Merriam being a notable example, insist on legitimacy as an important independent motivation for the acceptance of power.

Which of these viewpoints is correct—and to what extent—is an empirical question. The definitions we have thus far constructed indicate, at least schematically, what kinds of data would be needed to answer the question. What is required is a situation in which we can observe: (a) the distribution of power as indicated by behavior changes of influencees as a function of behavior changes of influencers; (b) the distribution of monetary, physical, and similar sanctions among the influencers; and (c) the attitudes of influencees toward legitimacy, and their beliefs as to where legitimate power lies. Situations where there is the greatest possible discrepancy between the possession of sanctions and the possession of legimacy would be the most rewarding. Many clearcut examples of the discrepancy between power bases can be found, of course, in revolutions. An example of a more subtle situation that could profitably be examined from this viewpoint is the behavior of the United States Senate in the 1937 fight over the Supreme Court bill. I will not try to prejudge the evidence except to state my personal conviction that legitimacy will turn out to

be a far from epiphenomenal aspect of the power structure.

Expectations and the Power Base. An empirical study of this problem will not proceed very far without disclosing another crucial behavioral variable: the *expectation* of each of the participants about the behavior of the others. I refer not merely to the obscuring effects of the rule of anticipated reactions, discussed earlier, but to the fact that the consequences an individual thinks will follow on his actions depend on what action he thinks other individuals will take.

A political régime prescribes appropriate behavior rôles to its participants; these rôles include appropriate actions to constrain any particular participant (or small group of participants) who departs from his rôle. But the constraints will be applied only if the remaining participants (or most of them) continue to play their rôles. Hence, most of the sanctions a political régime has at its disposal—whether they consist of money, force, attitudes toward legitimacy, or what not—disappear at once when a large number of the participants act in concert to depart from their rôles.

To each individual in a political régime, consequently, the régime looks exceedingly stable so long as he expects the other individuals to support it; it looks exceedingly unstable when he pictures himself as acting in concert with a large number of others to overthrow it. Hence, estimates of the stability of a political structure depends not only on observation of the distribution of actual power, or of the distribution of the power base; but equally upon estimates of the capacity of subgroups for co-ordinated action.

It follows from this that power and influence, measured in terms of the definitions we have proposed, are not additive quantities. Every observation of a power relationship makes an assumption, whether explicit or implicit, as to the pattern of expectation and of group co-ordination. Such an observation will have predictive value, in general, only so long as this assumption holds.

To take a specific example, if we were to make some observations as to the power of a political party to discipline an individual member, we would probably reach conclusions that would be completely inapplicable to the question of the party's power to discipline an organized dissenting clique.

Expectations as a Means of Measuring Power. At this point we might revert to a point raised at the beginning of this paper: how do we know that Peron is dictator of Argentina? If we accept the proposition we have just been urging, that expectations of consequences are a major determinant of behavior, then we can use such expectations, so long as the situation remains stable, to estimate where power lies.

We are faced here with an example of a self-confirming prophecy. Suppose we are able to ascertain that the people of Argentina really believe that Peron is dictator. It follows that they will expect sanctions to be applied to themselves if they do not accept the decisions of the Peron régime. Hence, so long as these expectations remain, they will behave as if Peron *were* dictator, and indeed, he will be.

It seems to me that this is the valid core of the naive method we commonly employ as political scientists when, seeking to determine the power structure in a particular situation, we ask the participants what the power structure is. This procedure is valid to the extent that the expectations of the participants constitute the power base. It gives us, in fact, an indirect measure of influence in the same way that data on wealth, or on attitudes of legitimacy, give us indirect measures of influence.

Now if this technique of observation is to be used sophisticatedly, certain cautions must be observed. First, such observations fail to reveal wheels within wheels in the power mechanism. Peron decides for Argentina, but who decides for Peron? Second, when expectations diverge from the other elements in the power base, they may conceal the fragility of the power structure. We have seen that revolution involves, above all, a change in the expectations, and

this will be revealed only at the moment of revolution.

Both of these points can be illuminated by looking at the phenomenon of the "figurehead." The holder of power begins to move toward the status of figurehead when his behavior is no longer an "independent variable" but is itself determined by his submission to power. This can take place in at least two ways. First, he may be aware of sanctions to which he is subject that are not apparent to others (if he makes the wrong decision, the secret police will assassinate him, or his mistress will refuse to sleep with him). In this case, he becomes a figurehead when the existence of these sanctions becomes known, for this knowledge will alter the expectations to conform to the "real" power structure. (Of course, other power bases enter to modify the course of events—he may continue to wield power because feelings of legitimacy attach to him.)

Second, the power holder may sense that the system of expectations is fragile—that revolution is imminent unless he anticipates the reactions to his exercise of power and restrains it within limits. Again, when awareness develops of his self-restraint, expectations will begin to change and he will begin to lose his power. It can hardly be doubted that this was a central process in the movement of England from a monarchical to a democratic government.

With this we may close our comments on the influence base—the conditions for the exercise of influence. We have seen that influence and the bases of influence are distinct and separately observable concepts; and that independent observation of them is required to assess the relative effectiveness of various influence bases in the influence process. Finally, we have seen that observations of the exercise of influence must, to be meaningful, be accompanied by observations of the expectations and capacities for co-operative action of the various subgroups acting in the power arena.

THE UNITS OF OBSERVATION

Our definition of influence leaves quite ambiguous the kinds of units in which degrees of influence might be expressed. The quantities with which we are most familiar are those measured in *cardinal numbers:* A weighs 200 pounds; he weighs twice as much as B. Sometimes we deal with a "weaker" kind of number, the *ordinal number*, which permits us to say that: "A is cleverer than B," but not: "A is twice as clever as B." We may also be aware of quantities that are not single numbers but pairs, triples, or n-tuples of numbers (usually called *vectors*). If A has five oranges and three apples, we may denote his possessions by the vector (5,3). We can say that A has more than B, who has (4,2); but we cannot compare A with C, who has (4,5). We cannot say that D has twice as many as A unless he has exactly twice as many apples *and* twice as many oranges.

All of these kinds of quantities, and others as well, occur in the physical sciences. Mass is a cardinal number, hardness an ordinal number, and force a vector. We should expect to find at least as rich a variety of quantities in the social sciences. Hence, we must ask ourselves what "kind" of a quantity best represents influence and power.[13]

I do not propose to tackle the problem in all its generality, but will, instead, examine one broad class of situations that I think is of significance. The particular class of power relations with which I shall be concerned is usually denoted by the term "authority," and I shall retain that term although it is used in a very different sense by Lasswell and Kaplan.[14]

We will say that an individual accepts *authority* when his choice among alternative behaviors is determined by the communicated decision of another. The acceptance of authority may stem from any combination whatsoever of the bases of power—monetary inducements, force, legitimacy, or any others. Authority is never unlimited—the range of alternative behaviors from which the superior may select the particular choice he desires of the subordinate is a finite range. The limits within which authority will be accepted we will call the *zone of acceptance*.

It is clear from the definition that authority is a form of influence: when A exercises authority over B, he exercises influence over B. Hence, a measurement of authority will be a measurement of at least one form of influence.

Let us regard each possible behavior that B can perform as an element in a set, and let us designate the set of all such possible behaviors by V. The set of behaviors that B will perform at A's command (the subset of V corresponding to B's zone of acceptance) we will designate by S. Then we can use the size of the set S as a measure of A's authority over B.

But what kind of a quantity is the size of S? Suppose that at one time B will accept any order in the set S, but at some later time he will only accept orders in S', which is a part of S. Then we are surely justified in saying that A's authority has decreased. Under such circumstances, comparisons of "greater" and "less" are possible. But it may happen that the zone of acceptance changes from S' to S'' where these are intersecting (overlapping) sets neither of which entirely includes the other. In this case we cannot say that A's authority has increased or that it has decreased—our sets are not completely ordered. The kind of quantity that appears most suitable for measuring the degree of authority of A over B is what the mathematician would call a "partial ordering."

Now this may seem a disappointing result—we started off with brave talk about "measuring" and have ended with some statements about more or less inclusive sets. The point is that whatever quantities we construct must reflect the characteristics of the phenomena we propose to measure with them. Ordinary cardinal (or even ordinal) numbers possess the property that they are completely ordered. If power relations are only partially ordered, then we shall certainly end up by talking nonsense about them if we insist that they should be represented by cardinal numbers, or that we should always be able to predicate "greater" or "less" of them. If we feel disappointment, it should be directed at the phenomena with which we are confronted rather than at the kind of quantity that appears to represent them.

I must hasten to point out that the above discussion does not in any sense prove that it is impossible to associate cardinal numbers with authority relations. It often happens that, starting with sets of elements, we can associate a cardinal number with each set in such a way that the resulting complete ordering is consistent with the partial ordering defined by the sets themselves. (The cardinal number associated with each set measures, in some sense, its "size.") This is precisely what the tax assessor does when he associates with Jones' set of tangible possessions a number that represents the (presumed) amount of money for which these possessions could be exchanged in the market.

Putting aside the question of using cardinal numbers to measure the "sizes" of different zones of acceptance, we may ask how the sets themselves may be observed and measured. The procedure is relatively straightforward; we observe what kinds of decisions are accepted and what kinds are not. If His Majesty's first minister decides that several hundred additional lords shall be created to establish the supremacy of the House of Commons, will His Majesty accede to the request? The observation falls within our general definition of influence: how does the behavior of the influencee vary with the behavior (in this case the decision) of the influencer?

The difficulties that are generally involved in the observation of influence are present here also. Because of the rule of anticipated reactions, the influencee may behave in accordance with the anticipated decision, never expressed, of the influencer; and the influencer will seldom issue commands that he knows in advance lie outside the zone of acceptance of the influencee— the limits will seldom be observed except when predictions are faulty. Because of the effect of expectations, the zone of acceptance may be suddenly narrowed when the influencee judges that he will be joined in resistance to authority by others.

To pursue these matters further would carry us rapidly into some rather difficult

mathematical questions. If we attempted to construct mathematical models for formulating and analyzing authority relations we would be led, I think, to models resembling very closely those employed by von Neumann and Morgenstern in their *Theory of Games and Economic Behavior*. I will not undertake such an analysis here, but will simply refer to some essays in this direction that have been published elsewhere.[15]

CONCLUSION

Let us now draw together the threads of our discussion. The problem posed at the outset was how we can make observations and measurements of the distribution of influence and power. The definition of the key terms—"influence" and "power"—is the first step toward an answer. The position taken here is that the phenomenon we wish to measure is an asymmetrical relation between the behavior of two persons. We wish to observe how a change in the behavior of one (the influencer) alters the behavior of the other (the influencee).

We have seen that in most situations, all sorts of reciprocal power relations are present, and that their observation is complicated by the anticipation of reactions. The more accurate the predictions of participants in the system of the reactions of others, the more difficult it becomes to observe influence. Our main hope must be that human beings will remain fallible in their predictions.

To the extent that we can establish empirically the conditions for the exercise of power, these conditions, or influence bases, provide an indirect means of measurement. Observations of the distribution of values and of attitudes regarding legitimacy constitute two significant kinds of indirect evidence about the distribution of power. A third, of critical significance, are the expectations of the participants in the power situation.

In a final section we examined the types of units in terms of which measurement might be expressed. Our principal conclusion here is that we must be prepared to admit into our measurement schemes many other kinds of units besides cardinal numbers. In particular, certain notions from set theory, such as the concept of partial ordering among sets, may be suggestive of fruitful schemes of measurement.

THAT SOME people have more power than others is one of the most palpable facts of human existence. Because of this, the concept of power is as ancient and ubiquitous as any that social theory can boast. If these assertions needed any documentation, one could set up an endless parade of great names from Plato and Aristotle through Machiavelli and Hobbes to Pareto and Weber to demonstrate that a large number of seminal social theorists have devoted a good deal of attention to power and the phenomena associated with it. Doubtless it would be easy to show, too, how the word and its synonyms are everywhere embedded in the language of civilized peoples, often in subtly different ways: power, influence, control, pouvoir, puissance, Macht, Herrschaft, Gewalt, imperium, potestas, auctoritas, potentia, etc.

I shall spare the reader the fruits and myself the labor of such a demonstration. Reflecting on the appeal to authority that might be made does, however, arouse two suspicions: First (following the axiom that where there is smoke there is fire), if so many people at so many different times have felt the need to attach the label power, or something like it, to some Thing they believe they have observed, one is tempted to suppose that the Thing must exist; and not only exist, but exist in a form capable of being studied more or less systematically. The second and more cynical suspicion is that a Thing to which people attach many labels with subtly or grossly different meanings in many different cultures and times is probably not a Thing at all but many Things; there are students of the subject, although I do not recall any who have had the temerity to say so in print, who think that because of this the whole study of "power" is a bottomless swamp.

Paradoxical as it may sound, it is probably too early to know whether these critics are right. For, curiously enough, the systematic study of power is very recent, precisely because it is only lately that serious attempts have been made to formulate the concept rigorously enough for systematic study.[1] If we take as our criterion for the efficiency of a scientific concept its usability in a theoretical system that possesses a high

8

The Concept of Power

Robert A. Dahl

Dahl's article, "A Critique of the Ruling Elite Model," appears in Section II above. This article contains some of Dahl's earliest reflections on the subject. Originally published in 2 Behavioral Science (1957) 201–215, it is reprinted here with permission of that journal and the author.

degree of systematic and empirical import, then we simply cannot say whether rigorous definitions of the concept of power are likely to be useful in theoretical systems with a relatively large pay-off in the hard coin of scientific understanding. The evidence is not yet in.

I think it can be shown, however, that to define the concept "power" in a way that seems to catch the central intuitively understood meaning of the word must inevitably result in a formal definition that is not easy to apply in concrete research problems; and therefore, operational equivalents of the formal definition, designed to meet the needs of a particular research problem, are likely to diverge from one another in important ways. Thus we are not likely to produce—certainly not for some considerable time to come—anything like a single, consistent, coherent "Theory of Power." We are much more likely to produce a variety of theories of limited scope, each of which employs some definition of power that is useful in the context of the particular piece of research or theory but different in important respects from the definitions of other studies. Thus we may never get through the swamp. But it looks as if we might someday get around it.

With this in mind, I propose first to essay a formal definition of power that will, I hope, catch something of one's intuitive notions as to what the Thing is. By "formal" I mean that the definition will presuppose the existence of observations of a kind that may not always or even frequently be possible. Second, I should like to indicate how operational definitions have been or might be modelled on the formal one for some specific purposes, and the actual or possible results of these operational definitions.

I should like to be permitted one liberty. There is a long and honorable history attached to such words as power, influence, control, and authority. For a great many purposes, it is highly important that a distinction should be made among them; thus to Max Weber, "*Herrschaft ist. . . ein Sonderfall von Macht*," Authority is a special case of the first, and Legitimate Authority a subtype of cardinal significance (11). In this essay I am seeking to explicate the primitive notion that seems to lie behind *all* of these concepts. Some of my readers would doubtless prefer the term "influence," while others may insist that I am talking about control. I should like to be permitted to use these terms interchangeably when it is convenient to do so, without denying or seeming to deny that for many other purposes distinctions are necessary and useful. Unfortunately, in the English language power is an awkward word, for unlike "influence" and "control" it has no convenient verb form, nor can the subject and object of the relation be supplied with noun forms without resort to barbaric neologisms.

POWER AS A RELATION AMONG PEOPLE

What is the intuitive idea we are trying to capture? Suppose I stand on a street corner and say to myself, "I command all automobile drivers on this street to drive on the right side of the road"; suppose further that all the drivers actually do as I "command" them to do; still, most people will regard me as mentally ill if I insist that I have enough power over automobile drivers to compel them to use the right side of the road. On the other hand, suppose a

policeman is standing in the middle of an intersection at which most traffic ordinarily moves ahead; he orders all traffic to turn right or left; the traffic moves as he orders it to do. Then it accords with what I conceive to be the bedrock idea of power to say that the policeman acting in this particular role evidently has the power to make automobile drivers turn right or left rather than go ahead. My intuitive idea of power, then, is something like this: *A* has power over *B* to the extent that he can get *B* to do something that *B* would not otherwise do.

If Hume and his intellectual successors had never existed, the distinction between the two events above might be firmer than it is. But anyone who sees in the two cases the need to distinguish mere "association" from "cause" will realize that the attempt to define power could push us into some messy epistemological problems that do not seem to have any generally accepted solutions at the moment. I shall therefore quite deliberately steer clear of the possible identity of "power" with "cause," and the host of problems this identity might give rise to.

Let us proceed in a different way. First, let us agree that power is a relation, and that it is a relation among people. Although in common speech the term encompasses relations among people and other animate or inanimate objects, we shall have our hands full if we confine the relationship to human beings. All of the social theory I mentioned earlier is interesting only when it deals with this limited kind of relationship. Let us call the objects in the relationship of power, actors. Actors may be individuals, groups, roles, offices, governments, nation-states, or other human aggregates.

To specify the actors in a power relation —*A* has power over *B*—is not very interesting, informative, or even accurate. Although the statement that the President has (some) power over Congress is not empty, neither is it very useful. A much more complete statement would include references to (*a*) the source, domain, or *base* of the President's power over Congress; (*b*) the *means* or instruments used by the President to exert power over Congress; (*c*) the *amount* or extent of his power over Congress; and (*d*) the range or *scope* of his power over Congress. The base of an actor's power consists of all the resources—opportunities, acts, objects, etc.—that he can exploit in order to effect the behavior of another. Much of the best writing on power—Bertrand Russell is a good example—consists of an examination of the possible bases of power. A study of the war potential of nations is also a study of the bases of power. Some of the possible bases of a President's power over a Senator are his patronage, his constitutional veto, the possibility of calling White House conferences, his influence with the national electorate, his charisma, his charm, and the like.

In a sense, the base is inert, passive. It must be exploited in some fashion if the behavior of others is to be altered. The *means* or instruments of such exploitation are numerous; often they involve threats or promises to employ the base in some way and they may involve actual use of the base. In the case of the President, the means would include the *promise* of patronage, the *threat* of veto, the *holding* of a conference, the *threat* of appeal to the electorate, the *exercise* of charm and charisma, etc.

Thus the means is a mediating activity by *A* between *A*'s base and *B*'s response. The *scope* consists of *B*'s responses. The scope of the President's power might therefore include such Congressional actions as passing or killing a bill, failing to override a veto, holding hearings, etc.

The *amount* of an actor's power can be represented by a probability statement: e.g., "the chances are 9 out of 10 that if the President promises a judgeship to five key Senators, the Senate will not override his veto," etc. Clearly the amount can only be specified in conjunction with the means and scope.

Suppose now we should wish to make a relatively complete and concise statement about the power of individual *A* over individual *a* (whom I shall call the respondent) with respect to some given scope of responses. In order to introduce the basic ideas involved, let us restrict ourselves to the 2 by 2 case, where the actor *A* does or

does not perform some act and the respondent *a* does or does not "respond." Let us employ the following symbols:

$(A, w) = A$ does w. For example, the President makes a nationwide television appeal for tax increases.

$(A, \bar{w}) = A$ does not do w.

$(a, x) = a$, the respondent, does x. For example, the Senate votes to increase taxes.

$(a, \bar{x}) = a$ does not do x.

$P(u|v) =$ Probability that u happens when v happens.

Then a relatively complete and concise statement would be symbolized:

$$P(a, x|A, w) = p_1$$
$$P(a, x|A, \bar{w}) = p_2$$

Suppose now, that $p_1 = 0.4$ and $p_2 = 0.1$. Then one interpretation might be: "The probability that the Senate will vote to increase taxes if the President makes a nationwide television appeal for a tax increase is 0.4. The probability that the Senate will vote to increase taxes if the President does not make such an appeal is 0.1."

PROPERTIES OF THE POWER RELATION

Now let us specify some properties of the power relation.

1) A necessary condition for the power relation is that there exists a time lag, however small, from the actions of the actor who is said to exert power to the responses of the respondent. This requirement merely accords with one's intuitive belief that *A* can hardly be said to have power over *a* unless *A*'s power attempts precede *a*'s responses. The condition, obvious as it is, is critically important in the actual study of power relations. Who runs the XYZ Corporation? Whenever the president announces a new policy, he immediately secures the compliance of the top officials. But upon investigation it turns out that every new policy he announces has first been put to him by the head of the sales department. Or again, suppose we had a full record of the times at which each one of the top Soviet leaders revealed his positions on various issues; we could then deduce a great deal about who is running the show and who is not. A good bit of the mystery surrounding the role of White House figures like Sherman Adams and Harry Hopkins would also be clarified by a record of this kind.

2) A second necessary condition is, like the first, obvious and nonetheless important in research: there is no "action at a distance." Unless there is some "connection" between *A* and *a*, then no power relation can be said to exist. I shall leave the concept of "connection" undefined, for I wish only to call attention to the practical significance of this second condition. In looking for a flow of influence, control, or power from *A* to *a*, one must always find out whether there is a connection, or an opportunity for a connection, and if there is not, then one need proceed no further. The condition, obvious as it is, thus has considerable practical importance for it enables one to screen out many possible relations quite early in an inquiry.

3) In examining the intuitive view of the power relation, I suggested that it seemed to involve a successful attempt by *A* to get *a* to do something he would not otherwise do. This hints at a way of stating a third necessary condition for the power relation. Suppose the chances are about one out of a hundred that one of my students, Jones, will read *The Great Transformation* during the holidays even if I do not mention the book to him. Suppose that if I mention the book to him and ask him to read it, the chances that he will do so are still only one out of a hundred. Then it accords with my intuitive notions of power to say that evidently I have no power over Jones with respect to his reading *The Great Transformation* during the holidays—at least not if I restrict the basis of my action to mentioning the book and asking him (politely) to read it. Guessing this to be the case, I tell Jones that if he does not read the book over the holidays I shall fail him in

my course. Suppose now that the chances he will read the book are about 99 out of 100. Assume further that nothing else in Jones's environment has changed, at least nothing relevant to his reading or not reading the book. Then it fully accords with my intuitive notions of power to say that I have some power over Jones's holiday reading habits. The basis of my power is the right to fail him in his course with me, and the means I employ is to invoke this threat.

Let me now set down symbolically what I have just said. Let

(D, w) = my threat to fail Jones if he does not read *The Great Transformation* during the holidays.

$(D, \bar{w})$ = no action on my part.

(J, x) = Jones reads *The Great Transformation* during the holidays.

Further, let

$p_1 = P(J, x | D, w)$ the probability that Jones will read *The Great Transformation* if I threaten to fail him.

$p_2 = P(J, x | D, w)$ the probability that Jones will read the book if I do not threaten to fail him.

Now let us define the *amount of power*. To avoid the confusion that might arise from the letter *p*, let us use the symbol *M* (from *Macht*) to designate the amount of power. Then in accordance with the ideas set out in the illustration above, we define *A*'s power over *a*, with respect to the response *x*, by means of *w*, as *M*, or, more fully:

$$M\left(\frac{A}{a} : w, x\right) = P(a, x | A, w)$$
$$- P(a, x | A, \bar{w}) = p_1 - p_2$$

Thus in the case of myself and Jones, *M*, my power over Jones, with respect to reading a book during the holidays, is 0.98.

We can now specify some additional properties of the power relation in terms of M:

a. If $p_1 = p_2$, then $M = 0$ and no power relation exists. The absence of power is thus equivalent to statistical independence.

b. M is at a maximum when $p_1 = 1$ and $p_2 = 0$. This is roughly equivalent to saying that A unfailingly gets B to do something B would never do otherwise.

c. M is at a minimum when $p_1 = 0$ and $p_2 = 1$. If negative values of M are to be included in the power relation at all—and some readers might object to the idea—then we shall have a concept of "negative power." This is not as foolish as it may seem, although one must admit that negative control of this kind is not ordinarily conceived of as power. If, whenever I ask my son to stay home on Saturday morning to mow the lawn, my request has the inevitable effect of inducing him to go swimming, when he would otherwise have stayed home, I do have a curious kind of negative power over him. The Legion of Decency sometimes seems to have this kind of power over moviegoers. Stalin was often said to wield negative power over the actions on appropriations for foreign aid by the American Congress. A study of the Senate that will be discussed later suggested that at least one Senator had this kind of effect on the Senate on some kinds of issues.

Note that the concept of negative power, and M as a measure, are both independent of the *intent* of A. The measure does, to be sure, require one to assign a positive and negative *direction* to the responses of the respondent; what one chooses as a criterion of direction will depend upon his research purposes and doubtless these will often include some idea as to the intent of the actors in a power relation. To take a specific case, p_1 *could* mean "the probability that Congress will defeat a bill if it is contained in the President's legislative program," and p_2 could mean "the probability that Congress will defeat such a bill if it is not contained in the President's legislative program." By assigning direction in this way, positive values of M would be associated with what ordinarily would be interpreted as meaning a "negative" influence of the President over

Congress. The point of the example is to show that while the measure does require that direction be specified, the intent of A is not the only criterion for assigning direction.

POWER COMPARABILITY

The main problem, however, is not to determine the existence of power but to make comparisons. Doubtless we are all agreed that Stalin was more powerful than Roosevelt in a great many ways, that McCarthy was less powerful after his censure by the Senate than before, etc. But what, precisely, do we mean? Evidently we need to define the concepts "more power than," "less power than," and "equal power."

Suppose we wish to compare the power of two different individuals. We have at least five factors that might be included in a comparison: (1) differences in the basis of their power, (2) differences in means of employing the basis, (3) differences in the scope of their power, i.e., in type of response evoked, (4) differences in the number of comparable respondents, and (5) differences in the change in probabilities, or M.

The first two of these may be conveniently thought of as differences in properties of the actors exercising power, and the last three may be thought of as differences in the responses of the respondents. Now it is clear that the pay-off lies in the last three—the responses. When we examine the first two in order to compare the power of individuals, rulers, or states, we do so on the supposition that differences in bases and means of actors are very likely to produce differences in the responses of those they seek to control.

As I have already indicated, much of the most important and useful research and analysis on the subject of power concerns the first two items, the properties of the actors exercising power, and there is good reason to suppose that studies of this kind will be as indispensable in the future as they have been in the past. But since we are concerned at the moment with a formal explication of the concept of power, and not with an investigation of research problems, (some of these will be taken up later on) it is important to make clear that analysis of the first two items does not, strictly speaking, provide us with a comparison of the power of two or more actors, except insofar as it permits us to make inferences about the last three items. If we could make these inferences more directly, we should not be particularly interested in the first two items—at least not for purposes of making comparisons of power. On the other hand, given information about the responses, we may be interested in comparing the efficiency of different bases or means; in this case, evidently, we can make a comparison only by holding one or both of the first two factors constant, so to speak. In general, the properties of the power wielder that we bring into the problem are determined by the goals of one's specific research. For example, one might be interested in the relative power of different state governors to secure favorable legislative action on their proposals by means of patronage; or alternatively, one might be interested in the relative effectiveness of the threat of veto employed by different governors.

In whatever fashion one chooses to define the relevant properties of the actors whose power he wishes to compare, strictly speaking one must compare them with respect to the responses they are capable of evoking. Ideally, it would be desirable to have a single measure combining differences in scope, number of comparable respondents controlled, and change in probabilities. But there seems to exist no intuitively satisfying method for doing so. With an average probability approaching one, I can induce each of 10 students to come to class for an examination on a Friday afternoon when they would otherwise prefer to make off for New York or Northampton. With its existing resources and techniques, the New Haven Police Department can prevent about half the students who park along the streets near my office from staying

beyond the legal time limit. Which of us has the more power? The question is, I believe, incapable of being answered unless we are ready to treat my relationships with my students as in some sense comparable with the relations of the Police Department to another group of students. Otherwise any answer would be arbitrary, because there is no valid way of combining the three variables—scope, number of respondents, and change in probabilities—into a single scale.

Let us suppose, for a moment, that with respect to two of the three variables the responses associated with the actions of two (or more) actors we wish to compare are identical. Then it is reasonable to define the power of A as greater than the power of B if, with respect to the remaining variable, the responses associated with A's acts are greater than the responses associated with B's acts. It will be readily seen, however, that we may have jumped from the frying pan into the fire, for the term "greater than" is still to be defined. Let us take up our variables one by one.

To begin with, we may suppose that the probability of evoking the response being the same for two actors and the numbers of comparable persons in whom they can evoke the response also being the same, then if the scope of responses evoked by A is greater than that evoked by B, A's power is greater than B's. But how can we decide whether one scope is larger than another? Suppose that I could induce my son to bathe every evening and to brush his teeth before going to bed and that my neighbor could induce his son to serve him breakfast in bed every morning. Are the two responses I can control to be counted as greater than the one response my neighbor can control? Evidently what we are willing to regard as a "greater" or "lesser" scope of responses will be dictated by the particular piece of research at hand; it seems fruitless to attempt to devise any single scale. At one extreme we may wish to say that A's scope is greater than B's only if A's scope contains in it every response in B's and at least one more; this would appear to be the narrowest definition. At the other extreme, we may be prepared to treat a broad category of responses as comparable, and A's scope is then said to be greater than *B*'s if the number of comparable responses in his scope is larger than the number in *B*'s. There are other possible definitions. The important point is that the particular definition one chooses will evidently have to merge from considerations of the substance and objectives of a specific piece of research, and not from general theoretical considerations.

Much the same argument applies to the second variable. It is clear, I think, that we cannot compare *A*'s power with respect to the respondents $a_1, a_2 \ldots a_n$ and *B*'s power with respect to the respondents $b_1, b_2 \ldots b_n$ unless we are prepared to regard the two sets of individuals as comparable. This is a disagreeable requirement, but obviously a sensible one. If I can induce 49 undergraduates to support or oppose federal aid to education, you will scarcely regard this as equivalent to the power I would have if I could induce 49 Senators to support or oppose federal aid. Again, whether or not we wish to treat Senators as comparable to students, rich men as comparable to poor men, soldiers as comparable to civilians, enlisted men as comparable to officers, military officers as comparable to civil servants, etc., is a matter that can be determined only in view of the nature and aims of the research at hand.

The third variable is the only one of the three without this inherent limitation. If scope and numbers are identical, then there can be no doubt, I think, that it fully accords with our intuitive and common-sense notions of the meaning of power to say that the actor with the highest probability of securing the response is the more powerful. Take the set of Democratic Senators in the United States Senate. Suppose that the chance that at least two-thirds of them will support the President's proposals on federal aid to education is 0.6. It is fair to say that no matter what I may do in behalf of federal aid to education, if there are no other changes in the situation except those brought about by my efforts the probability that two-thirds of them will support federal aid will remain virtually at 0.6. If, on the other hand, Senator Johnson, as majority leader, lends his full support and all his skill

of maneuver to the measure the probability may rise, let us say, to 0.8. We may then conclude (what we already virtually know is the case, of course) that Senator Johnson has more power over Democratic Senators with respect to federal aid to education than I have.

Earlier in defining the amount of power by the measure, *M*, I had already anticipated this conclusion. What I have just said is precisely equivalent to saying that the power of *A* with respect to some set of respondents and responses is greater than the power of *B* with respect to an equivalent set if and only if the measure *M* associated with *A* is greater than the measure *M* associated with *B*. To recapitulate:

$$M\!\left(\frac{A}{a}: w, x\right) = p_1 - p_2, \text{ where}$$

$$p_1 = P(a, x | A, w)$$

the probability that *a* will do *x*, given action *w* by *A*

$$p_2 = P(a, x | A, \bar{w})$$

the probability that *a* will do *x*, given no action *w* by *A*.

$$M\!\left(\frac{B}{b}: y, z\right) = p_1^* - p_2^*, \text{ where}$$

$$p_1^* = P(b, z / B, y)$$

$$p_2^* = P(b, z / B, y)$$

Now if these two situations are *power comparable* (a notion we shall examine in a moment) then *A*'s power is greater than *B*'s if and only if

$$M\!\left(\frac{A}{a}: w, x\right) > M\!\left(\frac{B}{b}: y, z\right)$$

In principle, then, whenever there are two actors, *A* and *B*, provided only that they are power comparable, they can be ranked according to the amount of power they possess, or *M*. But if it is possible to rank *A* and *B*, it is possible to rank any number of pairs. And it is obvious from the nature of M that this ranking must be transitive, i.e.,

$$\text{if } M\left(\frac{A}{a}: w, x\right) > M\left(\frac{B}{b}: y, z\right), \text{ and}$$

$$M\left(\frac{B}{b}: y, z\right) > M\left(\frac{C}{c}: u, v\right), \text{ then}$$

$$M\left(\frac{A}{a}: w, x\right) > M\left(\frac{C}{c}: u, v\right)$$

In principle, then, where any number of actors are in some relation to any number of equivalent subjects, and these relations are regarded as power comparable, then all the actors can be unambiguously ranked according to their power with respect to these subjects.

There is, as everyone knows, many a slip 'twixt principle and practice. How can one convert the theoretical measure, M, into a measure usable in practical research? Specifically, suppose one wishes to examine the power relations among some group of people—a city council, legislature, community, faculty, trade union. One wants to rank the individuals in the group according to their power. How can one do so?

The first problem to be faced is whether given the aims, substance, and possible theoretical import of his study, one does in fact have *power comparability*. One of the most important existing studies of the power structure of a community has been criticized because of what appears to have been a failure to observe this requirement. A number of leaders in a large Southern city were asked, "If a project were before the community that required *decision* by a group of leaders—leaders that nearly everyone would accept—which *ten* on the list of forty would you choose?" On the basis of the answers, individuals were ranked in such a way that a "pyramidal" power structure was inferred to exist in the city, i.e., one consisting of a small number of top leaders who made the key decisions, which were then executed by a larger middle-group of subordinate leaders. The significance of this

conclusion is considerably weakened, however, if we consider whether the question did in fact discriminate among different kinds of responses. Specifically, suppose the leaders had been asked to distinguish between decisions over local taxes, decisions on schools, and efforts to bring a new industry to the community: would there be significant differences in the rankings according to these three different kinds of issues? Because the study does not provide an answer to this question, we do not know how to interpret the significance of the "pyramidal" power structure that assertedly exists. Are we to conclude that in "Regional City" there is a small determinate group of leaders whose power significantly exceeds that of all other members of the community on all or nearly all key issues that arise? Or are we to conclude, at the other extreme, that some leaders are relatively powerful on some issues and not on others, and that no leaders are relatively powerful on all issues? We have no way of choosing between these two interpretations or indeed among many others that might be formulated.

Let us define A and B as formally power comparable (in the sense that the relative magnitudes of the measure M are held to order the power of A and B correctly) if and only if the actors, the means, the respondents and the responses or scopes are comparable. That is,

the actor, A is comparable to the actor B;
A's respondent, a is comparable to B's respondent b;
A's means, w is comparable to B's means y; and
a's response, x is comparable to b's response z.

But this is not a very helpful definition. For the important question is whether we can specify some properties that will insure comparability among actors, respondents, means, and scopes. The answer, alas, is no. So far as an explication of the term "power" is concerned, power comparability must be taken as an undefined term. That is, power comparability will have to be interpreted in the light of the specific requirements of research and theory, in the same way that the decision as to whether to regard any two objects—animals, plants, atoms, or whatnot—as comparable depends upon general considerations of classification and theoretical import. To this extent, and to this extent only, the decision is "arbitrary";

but it is not more "arbitrary" than other decisions that establish the criteria for a class of objects.

To political scientists it might seem far-fetched to compare the power of a British prime minister over tax legislation in the House of Commons with the power of the President of the United States over foreign policy decisions in the Senate. It would seem farfetched because the theoretical advantages of such a comparison are not at all clear. On the other hand, it would not seem quite so farfetched to compare the two institutional positions with respect to the "same" kind of policy—say tax legislation or foreign policy; indeed, political scientists do make comparisons of this kind. Yet the decision to regard tax legislation in the House of Commons as comparable in some sense to tax legislation in the Senate is "arbitrary." Even the decision to treat as comparable two revenue measures passed at different times in the United States Senate is "arbitrary." What saves a comparison from being genuinely arbitrary is, in the end, its scientific utility. Some kinds of comparisons will seem more artificial than others; some will be theoretically more interesting and more productive than others. But these are criteria derived from theoretical and empirical considerations independent of the fundamental meaning of the term power.

On what grounds, then, can one criticize the study mentioned a moment ago? Because the use of undiscriminating questions produced results of very limited theoretical significance. By choosing a relatively weak criterion of power comparability, the author inevitably robbed his inquiry of much of its potential richness. Considerations of comparability are, therefore, critical. But the criteria employed depend upon the problem at hand and the general state of relevant theory. The only way to avoid an arbitrary and useless definition of "power comparability" is to consider carefully the goals and substance of a particular piece of research in view of the theoretical constructs one has in mind. Thus in the case of the Senate, it may be satisfactory for one piece of research to define all Senate roll-call votes on all issues as comparable; for an-

other, only votes on foreign policy issues will be comparable; and for still another, only votes on foreign policy issues involving large appropriations; etc. In a word, the researcher himself must define what he means by comparability and he must do so in view of the purpose of the ranking he is seeking to arrive at, the information available, and the relevant theoretical constructs governing the research.

APPLICATIONS OF THE CONCEPT OF POWER COMPARABILITY

Assuming that one has power comparability, the next problem is to rank every actor whose rank is relevant to the research. Here we run into practical problems of great magnitude.

Suppose we wish to rank a number of Senators with respect to their influence over the Senate on questions of foreign affairs. Specifically, the respondent and response are defined as "all Senate roll-call votes on measures that have been referred to the Foreign Relations Committee." To begin with, let us take two Senators. What we wish to find out is the relative influence on the Senate vote of the activities of the two Senators for or against a measure prior to the roll call. "For" and "against" must be defined by reference to some standard "direction." Passage of the measure is one possible "direction" in the sense that a Senator can be for passing the measure, against it, or without a position for or against passage. This is not, however, a particularly significant or meaningful direction, and one might wish to determine the direction of a measure by reference to the President's position, or by content, or by some other standard. For this discussion, I shall assume that "for" and "against" are defined by reference to the first standard, i.e., passing the measure.

Let us not assume that a Senator does one of three things prior to a roll-call vote. He works for the measure, he works against it, or he does nothing. (The assumption, although a simplification of reality, is by no means an unreasonable simplification). Let us further assume (what is generally true) that the Senate either passes the measure or defeats it. With respect to a particular Senator, we have the following conditional probabilities:

	The Senator Works For	Works Against	Does Nothing
The Senate Passes	p_1	p_2	p_3
Defeats	$1 - p_1$	$1 - p_2$	$1 - p_3$

Since the bottom row provides no additional information we shall, in future, ignore it. Following the earlier discussion of the concept M, the measure of power, it is reasonable to define

$$M_1 = p_1 - p_3$$

$$M_2 = p_3 - p_2$$

M_1 is a measure of the Senator's power when he works for a measure and M_2 a measure of his power when he works against a measure; in both cases a comparison is made with how the Senate will act if the Senator does nothing. There are various ways in which he might combine M_1 and M_2 into a single measure, but the most useful would appear to be simply the sum of M_1 and M_2. To avoid confusion with the earlier and slightly different measure which we are now approximating, let us call the sum of M_1 and M_2, M^*. Like M, it is at a maximum of 1 when the Senate always passes the bills a given Senator works for and always defeats the bills he works against; it is at a minimum of -1 when the Senate always defeats the bills he works for and always passes the bills he works against; and it is at 0 when there is no change in the outcome, no matter what he does.

In addition, there is one clear advantage to M^*. It is easily shown that it reduces to

$$M^* = p_1 - p_2$$

In a moment we shall see how advantageous such a simple measure is.

The theoretical problem, then, is clear-cut and a solution seems reasonably well defined. It is at this point, however, that practical research procedures begin to alter the significance of a solution, for the particular operational means selected to breathe life into the relatively simple formal concepts outlined so far can produce rather different and even conflicting results.

Let me illustrate this point by drawing on a paper by Dahl, March, and Nasatir (1) on influence ranking in the United States Senate. The aim of the authors was to rank thirty-four Senators according to their influence on the Senate with respect to two different areas, foreign policy and tax and economic policy. The 34 Senators were all those who had held office continuously from early 1946 through late 1954, a long enough period, it was thought, to insure a reasonably large number of roll-call votes. The classification of measures to the two areas was taken from the *Congressional Quarterly Almanac*, as were the votes themselves. Thus the subject was well defined and the necessary data were available.

No such systematic record is maintained of course, for the positions or activities of Senators prior to a roll-call vote, and what is more it would be exceptionally difficult to reconstruct the historical record even over one session, not to say over an eight-year period. Faced with this apparently insuperable obstacle, it was necessary to adopt a rather drastic alternative, namely to take the recorded roll-call vote of a Senator as an indication of his position and activities *prior* to the roll-call. While this is not unreasonable, it does pose one major difficulty: a vote is necessarily cast either for or against a measure and hence the roll-call provides no way of determining when a Senator does nothing prior to the roll-call. But the very essence of the formal concept of power outlined earlier hinges on a comparison of the difference between what the Senate will do when a Senator takes a given position and what it does when he takes no position.

It is at this point that the advantages of the measure M^* reveal themselves. For provided only that one is prepared to take the Senator's recorded vote as a fair indication of his prior position and activities, the data permit us to estimate the following probabilities, and hence M^*

		The Senator Works For	The Senator Works Against
The Senate	Passes	p_1	p_2

One could, therefore, estimate M^* for each of the 34 Senators and rank all of them.

The validity of this method ranking would appear to be greatest, however, when all Senators are ranked on precisely the same set of bills before the Senate. To the extent that they vote on different (although mostly overlapping) sets of bills, the comparability of M^* from one Senator to another will be reduced, conceivably to the vanishing point.

For a number of reasons, including a slightly different interpretation of the characteristics of an ideal measure, the authors chose a rather different approach. They decided to pair every Senator against every other Senator in the following way. The number in each cell is an estimate of the probability that the Senate will pass a proposal, given the positions of the two Senators as indicated; the number is in fact the proportion of times that the Senate passed a foreign policy (or tax) measure in the period 1946–54, given the recorded votes of the two Senators as indicated.

	S_1 Favours the Motion	S_1 Opposes the Motion
Favors the Motion	p_{11}	p_{12}
Opposes the Motion	p_{21}	p_{22}

With 34 Senators, 561 possible pairs of this kind exist; but only 158 pairs were tabulated for foreign policy and 206 for tax and economic policy over the whole period. The measure used to enable comparisons to be made between the two Senators in each pair might be regarded as an alternative to M^*. This measure—let us call it M''—rests upon the same basic assumption, namely that we can measure a Senator's influence

by the difference between the probability that the Senate will pass a measure the Senator opposes and the probability that it will pass a measure he supports. However, there are two important differences. First, the authors decided not to distinguish between "negative" and "positive" power; consequently they used absolute values only. Second, in estimating the probability of a measure passing the Senate, the positions of two Senators were simultaneously compared in the manner shown in the table. Thus the influence of S_1 over the Senate was measured as the difference between the probability that a bill will pass the Senate when S_1 favors it and the probability that it will pass when S_1 opposes it. However, this difference in probabilities was measured twice: (1) when S_2 favors the motions before the Senate; and (2) when S_2 opposes the motions. In the same way, S_2's influence was measured twice. Thus:

$$M_1''(S_1) = |p_{11} - p_{12}|$$

that is, the change in probabilities, given S_2 in favor of the bill,

$$M_1''(S_1) = |p_{21} - p_{22}|$$

that is, the change in probabilities, given S_2 in opposition to the bill. Likewise,

$$M_1''(S_2) = |p_{11} - p_{21}|$$
$$M_2''(S_2) = |p_{12} - p_{22}|$$

The influence of S_1 was said to be greater than the influence of S_2 only if $M_1''(S_1) > M_1''(S_2)$ and $M_2''(S_1) > M_2''(S_2)$. That is, if

$$|p_{11} - p_{12}| > |p_{11} - p_{21}| \text{ and}$$
$$|p_{21} - p_{22}| > |p_{12} - p_{22}|$$

Except for the rare case of what would ordinarily be regarded as "negative" power—which, as I have already said, this particular measure was not intended to distinguish from "positive" power—the absolute values are the same as the algebraic ones. Where the algebraic differences can be taken, and this will normally be the case, both inequalities reduce to

$$p_{21} > p_{12}$$

In the ordinary case, then, using the measure M'' we can say that the power of Senator George is greater than that of Senator Knowland if the probability that the Senate will pass a measure is greater when Senator George favors a bill and Senator Knowland opposes it than when Senator Knowland favors a bill and Senator George opposes it.

The results, some of which are shown in Tables 1 to 3, are roughly consistent with expectations based on general knowledge.

Note how the formal concept of power has been subtly altered in the process of research; it has been altered, moreover,

not arbitrarily or accidentally but because of the limitations of the data available, limitations that appear to be well-nigh inescapable even in the case of the United States Senate, a body whose operations are relatively visible and well recorded over a long period of time.

The most important and at first glance the most innocent change has been to accept the roll-call position of a Senator as an indication of his position prior to the roll-call vote. This change is for most practical purposes unavoidable, and yet it generates a serious consequence which I propose to call the problem of the chameleon. Suppose a Senator takes no prior position on any bill and always decides how to vote by guessing how the Senate majority will vote; then, if he is a perfect guesser, according to the ranking method used he will be placed in the highest rank. Our common

TABLE 1.   Thirty-four U.S. Senators Ranked According to "Power" over Senate Decisions on Foreign Policy 1946–54

HIGH

Hayden	(tie) Magnuson
	Chavez
	Smith (N. J.)**
	George**
	Maybank
	Green**
	Hill*
Aiken	(tie) Wiley**
	Hoey
	Kilgore
	Ferguson*
	Murray*
	Knowland*
	Morse
Fulbright**	(tie) Saltonstall
	Johnston
	Cordon
	Hickenlooper**
	Ellender
Millikin	(tie) McClellan
	Eastland
	Russell
	Bridges*
	Johnson (Colo.)
	Byrd
	Butler (Nebr.)
	Langer*
	Young
	Capehart*
	McCarran

LOW

** member of Foreign Relations Committee five or more years.
* member of Foreign Relations Committee one to four years.

TABLE 2.   Thirty-four U.S. Senators Ranked According to "Power" over Senate Decisions on Tax and Economic Policy, 1946–54

HIGH

George††
Millikin††
Ellender
Byrd††
Saltonstall†
Cordon
McCarran
Young
Hoey††
Maybank
Johnson (Colo.) †† (tie) McClellan
Hickenlooper
Eastland
Russell
Smith (N. J.)
Knowland
Aiken
Capehart
Johnston
Bridges
Hayden   (tie) Chavez
Butler (Nebr.)†† (tie) Wiley (tie) Ferguson
Langer (tie) Hill (tie) Murray (tie) Magnuson
(tie) Fulbright (tie) Green
Morse (tie) Kilgore

LOW

†† member of Finance Committee five or more years.
† member of Finance Committee one to four years.

sense tells us, however, that in this case it is the Senate that has power over the Senator, whereas the Senator has no influence on the votes of other Senators.

If the reader will tolerate an unnatural compounding of biological and celestial metaphors, a special case of the chameleon might be called the satellite. Although I have no evidence that this was so, let us suppose that Senator Hoey took no prior positions on issues and always followed the lead of Senator George (Table 3). Let us assume that on foreign policy and tax policy, Senator George was the most powerful man in the Senate—as indeed nearly every seasoned observer of the Senate does believe. By following George, Hoey would rank as high as George; yet, according to our hypothetical assumptions, he had no influence at all on George or any other Senator.

The problem of the chameleon (and the satellite) is not simply an artifact created by the method of paired comparisons employed. It is easy to see that ranking according to

the measure M^* would be subject to the same difficulties *given the same data*. The formal concept of power, that is to say, presupposes the existence of data that in this case do not seem to be available—certainly not readily available. If one had the kinds of observations that permitted him to identify the behavior of the chameleon or satellite then no serious problem would arise. One could treat chameleon activity as equivalent to "doing nothing" to influence the passage or defeat of a measure. Since as we have seen, under the measure M^* the column "does nothing" is superfluous, the effect would be to ignore all cases of chameleon or satellite behavior and make estimates only from the instances where a Senator actually works for or works against various bills.

Thus the conceptual problem is easily solved. But the research problem remains. In order to identify chameleon behavior and

TABLE 3. *Thirty-four U.S. Senators Classified According to "Power" over Senate Decisions on Foreign Policy and Tax Policy, 1946–54*

		High influence	Medium influence	Low influence
	High influence	George**†† Hoey†† Maybank	Ellender Saltonstall† Cordon	Millikin†† Byrd†† McCarran Young Johnson (Colo.)†† McClellan
Tax and Economic Policy	Medium influence	Smith (N. J.)** Aiken* Hayden Chavez	Hickenlooper** Knowland* Johnston	Eastland Russell Capehart* Bridges*
	Low influence	Wiley** Hill* Magnuson Green**	Ferguson* Murray* Fulbright** Morse Kilgore	Butler (Nebr.)†† Langer*

** member of Foreign Relations Committee five or more years.
* member of Foreign Relations Committee one to four years.
†† member of Finance Committee five or more years.
† member of Finance Committee one to four years.

separate it from actual attempts at influence, one cannot rely on roll-calls. One needs observations of the behavior of Senators prior to the roll-calls. But if it is true, as I have been arguing, that observations of this kind are available only with great difficulty, rarely for past sessions, and probably never in large numbers, then in fact the data needed are not likely to exist. But if they do not exist for the Senate, for what institutions are they likely to exist?

CONCLUSIONS: A DIALOGUE BETWEEN A "CONCEPTUAL" THEORETICIAN AND AN "OPERATIONALIST"

The conclusions can perhaps best be stated in the form of a dialogue between a "conceptual" theoretician and a strict "operationalist." I shall call them C and O.

C. The power of an actor, A, would seem to be adequately defined by the measure M which is the difference in the probability of an event, given certain action by A, and the probability of the event given no such action by A. Because the power of any actor may be estimated in this way, at least in principle, then different actors can be ranked according to power, provided only that there exists a set of comparable subjects for the actors who are to be ranked.

O. What you say may be true in principle, but that phrase "in principle" covers up a host of practical difficulties. In fact, of course, the necessary data may not exist.

C. That is, of course, quite possible. When I say "in principle" I mean only that no data are demanded by the definition that we cannot imagine securing with combinations of known techniques of observation and measurement. The observations may be exceedingly difficult but they are not inherently impossible: they don't defy the laws of nature as we understand them.

O. True. But the probability that we can actually make these observations on, say, the U.S. Senate is so low as to be negligible, at least if we want relatively large numbers of decisions. It seems to me that from a strict operational point of view, your concept of power is not a single concept, as you have implied; operationally, power would appear to be many different concepts, depending on the kinds of data available. The way in which the researcher must adapt to the almost inevitable limitations of his data means that we shall have to make do with a great many different and not strictly comparable concepts of power.

C. I agree with all you have said. In practice, the concept of power will have to be defined by operational criteria that will undoubtedly modify its pure meaning.

O. In that case, it seems wiser to dispense with the concept entirely. Why pretend that power, in the social sense, is a concept that is conceptually clear-cut and capable of relatively unambiguous operational definitions—like mass, say, in physics? Indeed, why not abandon the concept of power altogether, and admit that all we have or can have is a great variety of operational concepts, no one of which is strictly comparable with another? Perhaps we should label them: Power 1, Power 2, etc.; or better, let's abandon single, simple, misleading words like "power" and "influence," except when these are clearly understood to be a part of a special operational definition explicitly defined in the particular piece of research.

C. I'm afraid that I must disagree with your conclusion. You have not shown that the concept of power as defined by the measure M is inherently defective or that it is never capable of being used. It is true, of course, that we cannot always make the observations we need in order to measure power; perhaps we can do so only infrequently. But the concept provides us with a standard against which to compare the operational alternatives we actually employ. In this way it helps us to specify the defects of the operational definitions as measures of power. To be sure, we may have to use defective measures; but at least we shall know that they are defective and in what ways. More than that, to explicate the concept of power and to pin-point the deficiencies of the operational concepts actually employed may often help us to invent alternative concepts and research methods that produce a much closer approximation in practice to the theoretical concept itself.

References

1. Dahl, R. A., March, J., & Nasatir, D. Influence ranking in the United States Senate. Read at the annual meeting of the American Political Science Association, Washington, D.C. September 1956 (mimeo).
2. French, J. R. P. Jr. A formal theory of social power. *Psychol. Rev.*, 1956, 63, 181–194.
3. Lasswell, H. D., & Kaplan, A. *Power and society*. New Haven: Yale Univ. Press, 1950.
4. Luce, R. D. Further comments on power distribution for a stable two-party Congress. 1956 (September) (mimeo).
5. Luce, R. D. & Rogow, A. A. A game theoretic analysis of Congressional power distributions for a stable two-party system. *Behav. Sci.*, 1956, 1, 83–95.
6. March, J. G. An introduction to the theory and measurement of influence. *Amer. pol. Sci. Rev.*, 1955, 59, 431–451.
7. March, J. G. Measurement concepts in the theory of influence. *J. Politics.* (In press).
8. March, J. G. Influence measurement in experimental and semi-experimental groups. *Sociometry.* 1956, 19, 260–271.
9. Shapley, L. S. & Shubik, M. A method for evaluating the distribution of power in a committee system. *Amer. pol. Sci. Rev.*, 1954, 48, 787–792.
10. Simon, H. Notes on the observation and measurement of political power. *J. Politics*, 1953, 15, 500–516.
11. Weber, M. *Wirtschaft und Gesellschaft.* Tubingen: J. C. B. Mohr, 1925, 2 vols. (*Grundriss der Sozialekonomik*, Vol. 3). (Manuscript received April 3, 1957).

9

Two Faces of Power[1]

Peter Bachrach
and Morton S. Baratz

In this article Peter Bachrach, Professor of Political Science at Temple University, and Morton Baratz, Professor of Economics at Bryn Mawr College, first criticized both the elitists and the pluralists (chiefly Robert Dahl and his associates) for overlooking one of the "faces of power." Originally published in 56 American Science Review (1962) 947–952, it is reprinted here with the permission of that journal and the authors.

THE CONCEPT of power remains elusive despite the recent and prolific outpourings of case studies on community power. Its elusiveness is dramatically demonstrated by the regularity of disagreement as to the locus of community power between the sociologists and the political scientists. Sociologically oriented researchers have consistently found that power is highly centralized, while scholars trained in political science have just as regularly concluded that in "their" communities power is widely diffused.[2] Presumably, this explains why the latter group styles itself "pluralist," its counterpart "elitist."

There seems no room for doubt that the sharply divergent findings of the two groups are the product, not of sheer coincidence, but of fundamental differences in both their underlying assumptions and research methodology. The political scientists have contended that these differences in findings can be explained by the faulty approach and presuppositions of the sociologists. We contend in this paper that the pluralists themselves have not grasped the whole truth of the matter; that while their criticisms of the elitists are sound, they, like the elitists, utilize an approach and assumptions which predetermine their conclusions. Our argument is cast within the frame of our central

thesis: that there are two faces of power, neither of which the sociologists see and only one of which the political scientists see.

I

Against the elitist approach to power several criticisms may be, and have been levelled.[3] One has to do with its basic premise that in every human institution there is an ordered system of power, a "power structure" which is an integral part and the mirror image of the organization's stratification. This postulate the pluralists emphatically—and, to our mind, correctly —reject, on the ground that

> nothing categorical can be assumed about power in any community. . . . If anything, there seems to be an unspoken notion among pluralist researchers that at bottom *nobody* dominates in a town, so that their first question is not likely to be, "Who runs this community?," but rather, "Does anyone at all run this community?" The first query is somewhat like, "Have you stopped beating your wife?," in that virtually any response short of total unwillingness to answer will supply the researchers with a "power elite" along the lines presupposed by the stratification theory.[4]

Equally objectionable to the pluralists— and to us—is the sociologists' hypothesis that the power structure tends to be stable over time.

> Pluralists hold that power may be tied to issues, and issues can be fleeting or persistent, provoking coalitions among interested groups and citizens, ranging in their duration from momentary to semi-permanent. . . . To presume that the set of coalitions which exists in the community at any given time is a timelessly stable aspect of social structure is to introduce systematic inaccuracies into one's description of social reality.[5]

A third criticism of the elitist model is that it wrongly equates reputed with actual power:

> If a man's major life work is banking, the pluralist presumes he will spend his time at the bank, and not in manipulating community decisions. This presumption holds until the banker's activities and participations indicate otherwise. . . . If we presume that the banker is "really" engaged in running the community, there is practically no way of disconfirming this notion, even if it is totally

94

erroneous. On the other hand, it is easy to spot the banker who really *does* run community affairs when we presume he does not, because his activities will make this fact apparent.[6]

This is not an exhaustive bill of particulars; there are flaws other than these in the sociological model and methodology[7]—including some which the pluralists themselves have not noticed. But to go into this would not materially serve our current purposes. Suffice it simply to observe that whatever the merits of their own approach to power, the pluralists have effectively exposed the main weaknesses of the elitist model.

As the foregoing quotations make clear, the pluralists concentrate their attention, not upon the sources of power, but its exercise. Power to them means "participation in decision-making"[8] and can be analyzed only after "careful examination of a series of concrete decisions."[9] As a result, the pluralist researcher is uninterested in the reputedly powerful. His concerns instead are to (a) select for study a number of "key" as opposed to "routine" political decisions, (b) identify the people who took an active part in the decision-making process, (c) obtain a full account of their actual behavior while the policy conflict was being resolved, and (d) determine and analyze the specific outcome of the conflict.

The advantages of this approach, relative to the elitist alternative, need no further exposition. The same may not be said, however, about its defects—two of which seem to us to be of fundamental importance. One is that the model takes no account of the fact that power may be, and often is, exercised by confining the scope of decision-making to relatively "safe" issues. The other is that the model provides no *objective* criteria for distinguishing between "important" and "unimportant" issues arising in the political arena.

II

There is no gainsaying that an analysis grounded entirely upon what is specific and visible to the outside observer is more "scientific" than one based upon pure speculation. To put it another way,

If we can get our social life stated in terms of activity, and of nothing else, we have not indeed succeeded in measuring it, but we have at least reached a foundation upon which a coherent system of measurements can be built up. . . . We shall cease to be blocked by the intervention of unmeasurable elements, which claim to be themselves the real causes of all that is happening, and which by their spook-like arbitrariness make impossible any progress toward dependable knowledge.[10]

The question is, however, how can one be certain in any given situation that the "unmeasurable elements" are inconsequential, are not of decisive importance? Cast in slightly different terms, can a sound concept of power be predicated on the assumption that power is totally embodied and fully reflected in "concrete decisions" or in activity bearing directly upon their making?

We think not. Of course power is exercised when A participates in the making of decisions that affect B. But power is also exercised when A devotes his energies to creating or reinforcing social and political values and institutional practices that limit the scope of the political process to public consideration of only those issues which are comparatively innocuous to A. To the extent that A succeeds in doing this, B is prevented, for all practical purposes, from bringing to the fore any issues that might in their resolution be seriously detrimental to A's set of preferences.[11]

Situations of this kind are common. Consider, for example, the case—surely not unfamiliar to this audience—of the discontented faculty member in an academic institution headed by a tradition-bound executive. Aggrieved about a long-standing policy around which a strong vested interest has developed, the professor resolves in the privacy of his office to launch an attack upon the policy at the next faculty meeting. But, when the moment of truth is at hand, he sits frozen in silence. Why? Among the many possible reasons, one or more of these could have been of crucial importance: (a) the professor was fearful that his intended action would be interpreted as an expression of his disloyalty to the institution; or (b) he decided that, given the beliefs and attitudes of his colleagues on the faculty, he would almost certainly constitute on this issue a minority of one; or (c) he concluded that, given the nature of the law-making process in the institution, his proposed remedies would be pigeonholed permanently. But whatever the case, the central point to be made is the same: to the extent that a person or group—consciously or unconsciously—creates or reinforces barriers to the public airing of policy conflicts, that person or group has power. Or, as Professor Schattschneider has so admirably put it:

All forms of political organization have a bias in favor of the exploitation of some kinds of conflict and the suppression of others because *organization is the mobilization of bias.* Some issues are organized into politics while others are organized out.[12]

Is such bias not relevant to the study of power? Should not the student be continuously alert to its possible existence in the human institution that he studies, and be ever prepared to examine the forces which brought it into being and sustain it? Can he safely ignore the possibility, for instance, that an individual or group in a community participates more vigorously in supporting the *nondecision-making* process than in participating in actual decisions within the process? Stated differently, can the researcher overlook the chance that some person or association could limit decision-making to relatively non-controversial matters, by influencing community values and political procedures and rituals, notwithstanding that there are in the community serious but latent power conflicts?[13] To do so is, in our judgment, to overlook the less apparent, but nonetheless extremely important, face of power.

III

In his critique of the "ruling-elite model," Professor Dahl argues that "the hypothesis of the existence of a ruling elite can be strictly tested only if . . . [t]here is a fair sample of cases involving key political decisions in which the preferences of the hypothetical ruling elite run counter to those of any other likely group that might be suggested,"[14] With this assertion we have two complaints. One we have already discussed, viz., in erroneously assuming that power is solely reflected in concrete decisions, Dahl thereby excludes the possibility that in the community in question there is a group capable of preventing contests from arising on issues of importance to it. Beyond that, however, by ignoring the less apparent face of power Dahl and those who accept his pluralist approach are unable adequately to differentiate between a "key" and a "routine" political decision.

Nelson Polsby, for example, proposes that "by pre-selecting as issues for study those which are generally agreed to be significant, pluralist researchers can test stratification theory."[15] He is silent, however, on how the researcher is to determine *what* issues are "generally agreed to be significant," and on how the researcher is to appraise the reliability of the agreement. In fact, Polsby is guilty here of the same fault he himself has found with elitist methodology: by presupposing that in any community there are significant issues in the political arena, he takes for granted the very question which is in doubt. He accepts as issues what are reputed to be issues. As a result, his findings are fore-ordained. For even if there is no "truly" significant issue in the community under study, there is every likelihood that Polsby (or any like-minded researcher) will find one or some and, after careful study, reach the appropriate pluralistic conclusions.[16]

Dahl's definition of "key political issues" in his essay on the ruling-elite model is open to the same criticism. He states that it is "a necessary although possibly not a sufficient condition that the [key] issue should involve actual disagreement in preferences among two or more groups."[17] In our view, this is an inadequate characterization of a "key political issue," simply because groups can have disagreements in preferences on unimportant as well as on important issues. Elite preferences which border on the indifferent are certainly not significant in determining whether a monolithic or polylithic distribution of power prevails in a given community. Using Dahl's definition of "key political issues," the researcher would have little difficulty in finding such in practically any community; and it would not be surprising then if he ultimately concluded that power in the community was widely diffused.

The distinction between important and unimportant issues, we believe, cannot be made intelligently in the absence of an analysis of the "mobilization of bias" in the community; of the dominant values and the political myths, rituals, and institutions which tend to favor the vested interests of one or more groups, relative to others. Armed with this knowledge, one could conclude that any challenge to the predominant values or to the established "rules of the game" would constitute an "important" issue; all else, unimportant. To be sure, judgments of this kind cannot be entirely objective. But to avoid making them in a study of power is both to neglect a highly significant aspect of power and thereby to undermine the only sound basis for discriminating between "key" and "routine" decisions. In effect, we contend, the pluralists have made each of these mistakes; that is to say, they have done just that for which Kaufman and Jones so severely taxed Floyd Hunter: they have begun "their structure at the mezzanine without showing us a lobby or foundation,"[18] *i.e.*, they have begun by studying the issues rather than the values and biases that are built into the political system and that, for the student of power, give real meaning to those issues which do enter the political arena.

IV

There is no better fulcrum for our critique of the pluralist model than Dahl's recent study of power in New Haven.[19]

At the outset it may be observed that Dahl does not attempt in this work to define his concept, "key political decision." In asking whether the "Notables" of New Haven are "influential overtly or covertly in the making of government decisions," he simply states that he will examine "three different 'issue-areas' in which important public decisions are made: nominations by the two political parties, urban redevelopment, and public education." These choices

are justified on the grounds that "nominations determine which persons will hold public office. The New Haven redevelopment program measured by its cost—present and potential—is the largest in the country. Public education, aside from its intrinsic importance, is the costliest item in the city's budget." Therefore, Dahl concludes, "It is reasonable to expect . . . that the relative influence over public officials wielded by the . . . Notables would be revealed by an examination of their participation in these three areas of activity."[20]

The difficulty with this latter statement is that it is evident from Dahl's own account that the Notables are in fact uninterested in two of the three "key" decisions he has chosen. In regard to the public school issue, for example, Dahl points out that many of the Notables live in the suburbs and that those who do live in New Haven choose in the main to send their children to private schools. "As a consequence," he writes, "their interest in the public schools is ordinarily rather slight."[21] Nominations by the two political parties as an important "issue-area," is somewhat analogous to the public schools, in that the apparent lack of interest among the Notables in this issue is partially accounted for by their suburban residence—because of which they are disqualified from holding public office in New Haven. Indeed, Dahl himself concedes that with respect to both these issues the Notables are largely indifferent: "Business leaders might ignore the public schools or the political parties without any sharp awareness that their indifference would hurt their pocketbooks . . . ." He goes on, however, to say that

> the prospect of profound changes [as a result of the urban-redevelopment program] in ownership, physical layout, and usage of property in the downtown area and the effects of these changes on the commercial and industrial prosperity of New Haven were all related in an obvious way to the daily concerns of businessmen.[22]

Thus, if one believes—as Professor Dahl did when he wrote his critique of the ruling-elite model—that an issue, to be considered as important, "should involve actual disagreement in preferences among two or more groups,"[23] then clearly he has now for all practical purposes written off public education and party nominations as key "issue-areas." But this point aside, it appears somewhat dubious at best that "the relative influence over public officials wielded by the Social Notables" can be revealed by an examination of their non-participation in areas in which they were not interested.

Furthermore, we would not rule out the possibility that even on those issues to which they appear indifferent, the Notables may have a significant degree of *indirect* influence. We would suggest, for example, that although they send their children to private schools, the Notables do recognize that public school expenditures have a direct bearing upon their own tax liabilities. This being so, and given their strong representation on the New Haven Board of Finance,[24] the expectation must be that it is in their direct interest to play an active role in fiscal policy-making, in the establishment of the educational budget in particular. But as to this, Dahl is silent: he inquires not at all into either the decisions made by the Board of Finance with respect to education nor into their impact upon the public schools.[25] Let it be understood clearly that in making these points we are not attempting to refute Dahl's contention that the Notables lack power in New Haven. What we *are* saying, however, is that this conclusion is not adequately supported by his analysis of the "issue-areas" of public education and party nominations.

The same may not be said of redevelopment. This issue is by any reasonable standard important for purposes of determining whether New Haven is ruled by "the hidden hand of an economic elite."[26] For the Economic Notables have taken an active interest in the program and, beyond that, the socio-economic implications of it are not necessarily in harmony with the basic interests and values of businesses and businessmen.

In an effort to assure that the redevelopment program would be acceptable to what he dubbed "the biggest muscles" in New Haven, Mayor Lee created the Citizens Action Commission (CAC) and appointed to it primarily representatives of the economic elite. It was given the function of overseeing the work of the mayor and other officials involved in redevelopment, and, as well, the responsibility for organizing and encouraging citizens' participation in the program through an extensive committee system.

In order to weigh the relative influence of the mayor, other key officials, and the members of the CAC, Dahl reconstructs "all the *important* decisions on redevelopment and renewal between 1950–58 . . . [to] determine which individuals most often initiated the proposals that were finally adopted or most often successfully vetoed the proposals of the others."[27] The results of this test indicate that the mayor and his development administrator were by far the most influential, and that the "muscles" on the Commission, excepting in a few trivial instances, "never directly initiated, opposed, vetoed, or altered any proposal brought before them. . . ."[28]

This finding is, in our view, unreliable, not so much because Dahl was compelled to make a subjective selection of what constituted *important* decisions within what he felt to be an *important* "issue-area," as because the finding was based upon an excessively narrow test of influence. To measure relative influence solely in terms of the ability to initiate and veto proposals is to ignore the possible exercise of influence or power in limiting the scope of initiation. How, that is to say, can a judgment be made as to the relative influence of Mayor Lee and the CAC without knowing (through prior study of the political and social views of all concerned) the proposals that Lee did *not* make because he anticipated that they would provoke strenuous opposition and, perhaps, sanctions on the part of the CAC?[29]

In sum, since he does not recognize *both* faces of power, Dahl is in no position to evaluate the relative influence or power of the initiator and decision-maker, on the one hand, and of those persons, on the other, who may have been indirectly instrumental in preventing potentially dangerous issues from being raised.[30] As a result, he unduly emphasizes the importance of initiating, deciding, and vetoing, and in the process casts the pluralist conclusions of his study into serious doubt.

V

We have contended in this paper that a fresh approach to the study of power is called for, an approach based upon a recognition of the two faces of power. Under this approach the researcher would begin—not, as does the sociologist who asks, "Who rules?" nor as does the pluralist who asks, "Does anyone have power?"—but by investigating the particular "mobilization of bias" in the institution under scrutiny. Then, having analyzed the dominant values, the myths and the established political procedures and rules of the game, he would make a careful inquiry into which persons or groups, if any, gain from the existing bias and which, if any, are handicapped by it. Next, he would investigate the dynamics of *nondecision-making*; that is, he would examine the extent to which and the manner in which the *status quo* oriented persons and groups influence those community values and those political institutions (as, *e.g.*, the unanimity "rule" of New York City's Board of Estimate[31]) which tend to limit the scope of actual decision-making to "safe" issues. Finally, using his knowledge of the restrictive face of power as a foundation for analysis and as a standard for distinguishing between "key" and "routine" political decisions, the researcher would, after the manner of the pluralists, analyze participation in decision-making of concrete issues.

We reject in advance as unimpressive the possible criticism that this approach to the study of power is likely to prove fruitless because it goes beyond an investigation of what is objectively measurable. In reacting against the subjective aspects of the sociological model of power, the pluralists have, we believe, made the mistake of discarding "unmeasurable elements" as unreal. It is ironical that, by so doing, they have exposed themselves to the same fundamental criticism they have so forcefully levelled against the elitists: their approach to and assumptions about power predetermine their findings and conclusions.

10

Decisions and Non-decisions: An Analytical Framework

Peter Bachrach and Morton S. Baratz

In this article Bachrach and Baratz amplify their earlier criticism of community power studies, and develop their own scheme for analyzing political decision-making. Originally published in 57 American Political Science Review *(1963) 632–642, it is reprinted here with the permission of that journal and the authors.*

IN RECENT years a rich outpouring of case studies on community decision-making has been combined with a noticeable lack of generalizations based on them. One reason for this is a commonplace: we have no general theory, no broad-gauge model in terms of which widely different case studies can be systematically compared and contrasted.

Among the obstacles to the development of such a theory is a good deal of confusion about the nature of power and of the things that differentiate it from the equally important concepts of force, influence, and authority. These terms have different meanings and are of varying relevance; yet in nearly all studies of community decision-making published to date, power and influence are used almost interchangeably, and force and authority are neglected.[1] The researchers thereby handicap themselves. For they utilize concepts which are at once too broadly and too narrowly drawn: too broadly, because important distinctions between power and influence are brushed over; and too narrowly, because other con-

cepts are disregarded—concepts which, had they been brought to bear, might have altered the findings radically.

Many investigators have also mistakenly assumed that power and its correlatives are activated and can be observed only in decision-making situations. They have overlooked the equally, if not more important area of what might be called "nondecision-making," *i.e.*, the practice of limiting the scope of actual decision-making to "safe" issues by manipulating the dominant community values, myths, and political institutions and procedures. To pass over this is to neglect one whole "face" of power.[2]

Finally, the case studies are often based upon inarticulate, perhaps unsound, premises which predetermine the findings of "fact."[3] A variety of complex factors affect decision-making—the social, cultural, economic, and political backgrounds of the individual participants; the values of the decision-making body as an entity in itself; the pressures brought to bear on the decision-makers, individually and collectively, by groups at interest; and so on. To say, as some do, that these factors are equally important is as far from the mark as it is to assume as others do, that only one is of overriding significance.[4]

What is required, then, is a model in terms of which the determinants both of decision- and nondecision-making can be appraised, taking full account of the distinct concepts of power, force, influence, and authority. In this paper we are not so ambitious. We attempt only to lay some of the groundwork for a model, seeking (1) to clarify the attributes of what we consider key concepts for any study of decision- and nondecision-making and the essential differences among them, and (2) to show how these concepts can be utilized more systematically and effectively in case studies.

I

It is customary to say that this or that person or group "has power," the implication being that power, like wealth, is a possession which enables its owner to secure some apparent future Good.[5] Another way of expressing the same point of view is to say that power is a "simple

Notes to chapter 10 are found on pages 370 to 372.

property . . . which can belong to a person or group considered in itself."[6]

For at least three reasons this usage is unacceptable. First, it fails to distinguish clearly between power over people and power over matter; and "power in the political [or economic or social] sense cannot be conceived as the ability to produce intended effects in general, but only such effects as involve other persons. . . ."[7] Second, the view that a person's power is measured by the total number of desires that he achieves is erroneous; one cannot have power in a vacuum, but only in relation to someone else. Third and most inportant, the common conception of the phenomenon mistakenly implies that possession of (what appear to be) the instruments of power is tantamount to possession of power itself. Such a notion is false because it ignores the fundamental relational attribute of power: that it cannot be possessed; that, to the contrary, the successful exercise of power is dependent upon the relative importance of conflicting values *in the mind of the recipient* in the power relationship.

A few illustrations should clarify and enlarge our position. Imagine, first, an armed military sentry who is approached by an unarmed man in uniform. The sentry levels his gun at the intruder and calls out, "Halt or I'll shoot!" The order is promptly obeyed. Did the sentry therefore have power and exercise it? So it would seem; but appearances could be deceiving. For suppose that the intruder obeyed, not because he felt compelled to do so in the face of the threatened sanction, but because he was himself a trained soldier for whom prompt obedience to a sentry's order was part of a system of values he fully accepted.[8] If that was the case, there was no conflict of goals or interests between the two principals; the sentry's threatened sanction was irrelevant, and the result would have been the same if he, and not the intruder, had been unarmed. Because the soldier put obedience to a sentry's order at the top of his schedule of values, the threat of severe deprivations had no bearing on his behavior. In such circumstances it cannot be said that the guard exerted power.

Let us now suppose that a second man approaches the sentry and, like the first, is ordered to stop or be shot. But the second stranger ignores the order, attempts to smash through the gate, and is forthwith fatally wounded. If we assume that the intruder's intention was to sabotage the military installation, we can have no doubt that his and the sentry's values were in direct conflict. Even so, the sentry's fatal shot did *not* constitute an exercise of power. For it did not bring about compliance to his order—and it did not because, apparently, the intruder valued entry to the base more highly than either obedience to the sentry's order or his own wellbeing.

Suppose, finally, that a third man approaches the sentry box, a man who wants to die but cannot bring himself to the act of self-destruction. He therefore deliberately ignores the sentry's command and is duly shot to death. Did someone in this situation have power and exercise it? As we see it, the "victim" did—for it was he, cognizant of the conflict of values between himself and the guard, who utilized the latter's supposed sanction to achieve his own objective.[9]

We reiterate that power is relational, as opposed to possessive or substantive. Its relational characteristics are threefold. First, in order for a power relation to exist there must be a conflict of interests or values between two or more persons or groups. Such a divergence is a necessary condition of power because, as we have suggested, if A and B are in agreement as to ends, B will freely assent to A's preferred course of action; in which case the situation will involve authority rather than power.[10] Second, a power relationship exists only if B actually bows to A's wishes. A conflict of interests is an insufficient condition, since A may not be able to prevail upon B to change his behavior. And if B does not comply, A's policy will either become a dead letter or will be effectuated through the exercise of force rather than through power.[11] Third, a power relation can exist only if one of the parties can threaten to invoke sanctions: power is "the process of affecting policies of others with the help of (. . . threatened) severe deprivations for nonconformity with the policies intended."[12] It must be stressed, however, that while the availability of sanctions—that is, of any promised reward or penalty by which an actor can maintain effective control over policy—is a necessary condition of power, it is not sufficient. It is necessary simply because the threat of sanctions is what differentiates power from influence[13]; it is insufficient because the availability of a sanction endows A with power over B only if the following conditions are met:

(a) The person threatened is aware of what is expected of him. In a power situation there must be clear communication between the person who initiates policy and the person who must comply.[14] If our imaginary sentry challenges a man who understands no English or is perhaps deaf, the sentry has—at least at the moment he issues his order—no power. In other words, power has a rational attribute: for it to exist, the person threatened must comprehend the alternatives which face him in choosing between compliance and non-compliance.

(b) The threatened sanction is *actually* regarded as a deprivation by the person who is so threatened. A threat by the President to "purge" a Congressman for failure to support the Administration's legislative program would be to no avail if the Congressman reckoned that his chances for reelection would be increased rather than reduced by Presidential intervention.

(c) The person threatened has greater esteem for the value which would be sacrificed should he disobey than for another value which would be foregone should he comply. Fear of physical injury did not deter those Southern Negro "sitters-in" who put greater store by the righteousness of their cause. It is worth noting at this stage that threatened deprivations are often ineffectual because the policy-initiator, in deciding what sanction to invoke, mistakenly projects his own values into the minds of his subjects.[15]

(d) The person threatened is persuaded that the threat against him is not idle, that his antagonist would not hesitate *in fine* actually to impose sanctions. To illustrate, if a famous general calculates that the President lacks the will or the popular support to employ his Constitutional prerogatives, he may ignore—even defy—the President's policy instructions.[16] Or, again, the success of a resistance movement based on the principle of nonviolence rests in large measure upon the assumption that those who can invoke sanctions will refrain from doing so, that value conflicts within A will prevent him from carrying out his threat against B. In point are the Indians who sat on the railroad tracks in defiance of the British and got away with it because (as the Indians well knew) the British put a higher value on human life than on obedience to their orders.[17]

We can now draw together the several elements of our conception of power. A power relationship exists when (a) there is a conflict over values or course of action between A and B; (b) B complies with A's wishes; and (c) he does so because he is fearful that A will deprive him of a value or values which he, B, regards more highly than those which would have been achieved by noncompliance.[18]

Several points must be made in reference to this definition. First, in speaking of power relations, one must take care not to overstate the case by saying that A has power over B merely because B, anxious to avoid sanctions, complies with a given policy proclaimed by A. This could well be an inaccurate description of their relationship, since A's power with respect to B may be extremely limited in scope, *i.e.*, in range of values affected.[19] Thus, the power of a traffic policeman over a citizen may be confined to the latter's activities as a motorist— and no more than that. Moreover, in appraising power relationships account must be taken of the weight of power, *i.e.*, the degree to which values are affected, and of its domain, *i.e.*, the number of persons affected.[20] For example, the power of the Chairman of the House Committee on Ways and Means is limited mainly to fiscal affairs; but within this scope he wields immense power in the determination of Federal tax and expenditure policies (weight), which affect a vast number of persons—up to and including at times the President himself (domain).

Finally, account must be taken of what Friedrich has dubbed the "rule of anticipated reactions."[21] The problem posed by this phenomenon is that an investigation might reveal that, though B regularly accedes to A's preferred courses of action, A in fact lacks power over B because A just as regularly tailors his demands upon B to dimensions he thinks B will accept. As an illustration, if the President submits to the Congress only those bills likely to be palatable to a majority of lawmakers, he can hardly be said to have power over the Congress simply because all his proposals are enacted into law.

II

In Robert Bierstedt's opinion, "force is manifest power . . . Force . . . means the reduction or limitation or closure or even total elimination of alternatives to the social action of one person or group by another person or group. 'Your money or your life' symbolizes a situation of naked force, the reduction of alternatives to two."[22] Force, in short, is power exercised.

We reject this view. As we see it, the essential difference between power and force is simply that in a power relationship one party obtains another's compliance, while in a situation involving force one's objectives must be achieved, if at all, in the face of *non*compliance.[23] Thus, if A's demand for B's money or his life prompts B to surrender his wallet, A has exercised power—he has won B's compliance by threat of even more severe deprivations. But if A must kill B to get the money, A has to resort to force—he must actually invoke the threatened sanction—and thereby perhaps expose himself to severer deprivations too. By the same token, if and when thermonuclear weapons are transformed from instruments of a policy of deterrence into activated missiles of death, power will have given way to force.

There is another difference between the two concepts. A person's scope of decision-making is radically curtailed under the duress of force; once the fist, the bullet, or

the missile is in flight, the intended victim is stripped of choice between compliance and noncompliance. But where power is being exercised, the individual retains this choice. Put another way, in a power relationship it is B who chooses what to do, while in a force relationship it is A.[24]

It follows from the foregoing that *manipulation* is an aspect of force, not of power. For, once the subject is in the grip of the manipulator, he has no choice as to course of action. It can be said, therefore, that force and manipulation (as a sub-concept under it) are, in contrast to power, non-rational.

An additional distinguishing attribute of force is that in some circumstances it is non-relational. For instance, if B is shot in the back by an unknown robber, he and his assailant have only a minimal interrelationship—especially when compared to a power confrontation where B must decide whether to accede to A's demands. A similarly minimal relationship obtains in cases involving manipulation, where compliance is forthcoming in the absence of recognition on the complier's part either of the source or the exact nature of the demand upon him.

In short, force and manipulation, like power, involve a conflict of values; but unlike power, they are non-rational and tend to be non-relational.

A number of implications may be drawn from this reasoning. One is that the actual application of sanctions is an admission of defeat by the would-be wielder of power. And so it is, to the extent that the prior *threat* of sanctions failed to bring about the desired behavior. A good case in point is the action of President Harry S. Truman in 1951 when he relieved General Douglas MacArthur of his command in the Pacific on grounds of insubordination. By continuing to air in public his policy differences with the Administration, MacArthur virtually compelled Truman to dismiss him. The President's decision to apply sanctions was, however, an admission of defeat, an implicit recognition that he could not, by power or authority, obtain MacArthur's compliance to the Administration's policy of a negotiated settlement of the Korean hostilities. To be sure, policy defeats of this kind may prove to be only partial. For if the resort to force against one party effectively deters noncompliance on the part of others, now or in future, the employment of sanctions becomes a fresh declaration of the existence of power. This is, of course, the rationale of all who undertake punitive actions against others: the *use* of force in one situation increases the credibility of *threats* to use it in others.

At the same time, it is important to recognize that resort to force can result in a loss of power. Two cases can be distinguished. First, the invocation of sanctions often causes a radical reordering of values within the coerced person (as well as in those persons who identify closely with him), thereby undermining the pre-existing power relationship. A good illustration is provided by the largely abortive attempts of the Nazis during World War II to pacify the populations of occupied countries by killing civilian hostages. Contrary to German expectations, this policy produced a marked stiffening of resistance; evidently, the number of "prisoners" who put a higher value on freedom than on life itself rose sharply. Second, the deprivation may prove in retrospect far less severe than it appeared in prospect, as a result of which future noncompliance is not discouraged and may even be encouraged. For example, a child whose punishment for misbehavior is the temporary loss of a prized toy may find, *ex post facto*, that the loss is entirely bearable, that the satisfactions he gained from acting up are greater at the margin than the alternative foregone. In such circumstances, obviously, future defiance of parental orders is more likely than not.

Just as power may be lessened when force is resorted to, so also may power be lessened when it is successfully exercised, *i.e.*, when compliance is obtained by mere threat of sanctions. As an illustration, Presidents of the United States have traditionally sought to exercise power over recalcitrant Congressmen by withholding patronage. But as a President exchanges a job appointment for votes—that is, as he successfully utilizes this source of power—his reserves for effecting further compliance dry up. As a corollary, repeated threats to invoke sanctions—threats never carried out—will gradually lose credibility in the minds of those threatened, until at length the threats cannot produce the desired behavior. This, in the view of many, was the basic flaw in the implementation of the stated American policy during the late 1950s of "massive retaliation at times and in places of our own choosing."[25] The same phenomenon applies to interpersonal relationships: a threat to withdraw one's love for another may be highly potent the first time, yet prove totally ineffectual if used again.

III

One person has *influence* over another within a given scope to the extent that the first, without resorting to either a tacit or an overt threat of severe deprivations, causes the second to change his course of action. Thus, power and influence are alike in that each has both rational and relational attributes. But they are different in that the exercise of power depends upon potential sanctions, while the exercise of influence does not. And there is an important difference between influence and manipulation: in situations involving the latter, but not the former, A seeks to disguise the nature and source of his demands upon B and, if A is successful, B is totally unaware that something is being demanded of him.

Although power and influence can and must be distinguished, the line between them is usually difficult to draw. This is especially true where B's reasons for acting in accordance with A's wishes are confused or multiple; in such circumstances B himself will be unable honestly to say whether his behavior was prompted by a fear of sanctions, or, rather, by his esteem for "higher" values (*e.g.*, wealth, respect, power, wisdom) than the one immediately at stake. Does the ambitious young man who submits unhappily to the every dictate of his rich uncle do so because he admires wealthy men (influence) or because he feels that unquestioning obedience is the price of a generous inheritance in the future (power)? Does the Majority Leader who unwillingly manages an Administration bill in the Senate do so because he is in awe of the Presidency and hence of the man who occupies the office (influence), or because he fears the President will actually punish him for noncompliance (power)? To say that the decisive test in situations like these turns on whether compliance is "voluntary" or "involuntary" is, in our judgment, not particularly helpful.[26]

The difficulty in distinguishing sharply and clearly between power and influence is further complicated by the fact that the two are often mutually reinforcing, that is, power frequently generates influence and *vice versa*. On this score, the case of Senator Joseph R. McCarthy of Wisconsin is especially instructive.[27] Shrewdly posing as the principal defender of the national security at the very moment when that became the dominant social value *vice* the inviolability of civil liberties, McCarthy managed for a period to stifle virtually all opposition to himself and what he stood for (influence). And from this base he was able to gain power, that is, to affect the making of actual decisions (votes in the Senate, acts of the Executive, etc.) by threats of severe deprivations (intervention in State political campaigns, destruction by accusation of the careers of appointive officials, etc.). By the same token, however, as public fears about national security subsided and concern for civil liberties grew, McCarthy's capacity to influence others sharply waned—and so, too, did his power.

Just because the distinction between power and influence is often blurred does not, however, lessen the importance of making the distinction. Nikita Khrushchev has little or no influence over Americans, yet it is obvious he exercises considerable power over us. On the other hand, the Supreme Court of the United States has widespread influence (and authority) over us both individually and collectively; its power is slight indeed.

IV

While authority is closely related to

power, it is not a form thereof; it is, in fact, antithetical to it.[28] In saying this, we reject both the traditional definition of authority as "formal power"[29] and that which conceives it as "institutionalized power."[30]

To regard authority as a form of power is, in the first place, not operationally useful. If authority is "formal power," then one is at a loss to know who has authority at times when the agent who possesses "formal power" is actually powerless; to say that Captain Queeg continued to have authority on the USS *Caine* after he was deposed of his command by the mutineers is to create needless confusion. Furthermore, to define authority as "formal power" is to fail to delineate the bounds of authority, other perhaps than to say that it ends where "real power" begins. For those who believe in limited or constitutional government such a construction is unthinkable.

To argue that "formal power" is circumscribed by law is also no answer. For it assumes without warrant the legitimacy of law. A policeman who demands obedience in the name of a law that is considered basically unjust will possess little authority in the eyes of persons steeped in the Anglo-American legal tradition. Nor is the problem completely solved by conceiving of authority in terms of constitutional legitimacy. Such a conception presupposes that all members of the community give allegiance to the constitution and the courts which interpret it. Do Federal courts have the authority to issue desegregation orders to southern school districts? According to many Southerners, including some learned in the law, the answer is in the negative.

Friedrich's analysis of authority seems to us the most appropriate. He defines the concept as "a quality of communication" that possesses "the potentiality of reasoned elaboration."[31] Like power, authority is here regarded as a relational concept: it is not that A possesses authority, but that B regards A's communication as authoritative. Also like power, an authority relationship implies rationality—although of a different order. That is, in a situation involving power, B is rational in the sense that he chooses compliance instead of defiance because it seems the less of two evils.[32] But in a situation involving authority, B complies because he recognizes that the command is reasonable in terms of his own values; in other words, B defers to A, not because he fears severe deprivations, but because his decision can be rationalized.[33] It is not essential, however, that A's directive be supported by reasoning; it is sufficient that the potentiality of such reasoning be present and recognized.[34]

If B believes that A's communication allows for reasoned elaboration when in fact it does not, it is "false" authority.[35] When the source of obedience shifts from "genuine" to "false" authority and B realizes that the communication cannot be elaborated effectively, then a relationship initially involving authority has been transformed into one involving power. For example, if a policeman demanded entrance to your house, you would probably comply on the implicit assumption that his demand was potentially supportable by reason. However, should you discover, once he was in, that his demand was *not* justifiable, your further compliance would undoubtedly derive from his exercise of power, not authority. The point is that the policeman's badge, uniform and gun—his symbols of "formal power"—do not constitute his authority. Whether he actually has that depends upon the authoritativeness of his communication, and that depends to a considerable degree upon the reasonableness of his command.

If the officer's elaboration of his demand to enter was sound in terms of the law, did he not have authority? Within the frame of our example, the answer is both no and yes. No, as far as you were concerned, since the elaboration did not make sense in terms of your own values. Yes, as far as society and its courts are concerned—provided, of course, that they themselves considered the law to be authoritative. As can readily be seen, in this kind of situation—which occurs frequently—authority is both a source of and a restraint upon the exercise of power; it both justifies and limits the use of power. But to those who believe in democracy this affords small comfort, unless authority itself is grounded upon reasoning that is meaningful to a majority of the people.

As a final note, it is worth observing that just as authority can be transformed into power, so can the reverse obtain. "Brainwashing" after the manner of George Orwell's "Big Brother" (and his real-life counterpart in Communist China) is a gruesome case in point; to obey Big Brother is not enough; you must *love* him. A different kind of illustration of the same point is the parent who uses the threat of spanking (power) to produce filial discipline which is based on acceptance of certain rules of the game (authority). Authority, in short, can cut both ways. In a humane and healthy society, it can perform the valuable function of limiting the behavior of men, especially those in official positions, to legitimate acts; for their actions must be potentially justified by "reasoned elaboration" in terms of values of a sane society. However, if the value frame of the society is pathological, authority, even as we have regarded it, can become a tool in furthering the state of pathology.

v

Perhaps the best way to summarize our effort to draw careful distinctions among power and related concepts is to apply them in a "real world" context—say, a Southern community where white citizens have decided to abide by a Federal court's desegregation order. As should be evident in the accompanying table, we assume that different persons in the community had different reasons for bowing before the law.

Local officials and local businessmen, for example, were fearful of severe deprivations —they responded to an exercise of power. Those whites we style as "moderates," on the other hand, fall into two distinct groups: (a) those (Group I) who accepted as legitimate and reasonable the *substantive logic* underlying the Court order, and (b) those (Group II) who rejected the substantive ground but accepted the *judicial procedure* as legitimate and reasonable. Both groups, that is, responded to authority, in the vital senses that both perceived the Court's decree rationally and both considered it (even though on different grounds) to be capable of "reasoned elaboration."

A third body of whites—whom, following David Riesman, we label the "other-directed"—complied not because they feared severe deprivations (power) nor because they thought the order was reasonable and legitimate (authority) but because they felt obliged to follow the lead of those in the community they most respect (influence). Stated differently, although the "other-directed" group regarded the Court's ruling as illegitimate and unreasonable both on

substantive and procedural grounds, it "went along with its betters."

Like those who were other-directed, the "masses," too, deferred to the newly dominant viewpoint in the community. But, unlike the former, the latter did so with little or no awareness of the issues at stake or of the fact that they were reversing their previous stand on the general question. The "masses," in other words, did not make a conscious choice between compliance and noncompliance with the Court order; following the pattern of manipulation, they simply conformed.

TABLE I. Hypothetical Behavior of Southern Whites to a Desegregation Court Order

Concept	Subject
Power (relational, demand rationally perceived, conflict of values, threat of severe sanctions)	Groups Which Choose Compliance State and local officials (threat of criminal contempt) Businessmen (threat of economic boycott and race strife, resulting in loss of profits)
Authority (relational, demand rationally perceived and considered reasonable, possible conflict of values, no severe sanctions)	Moderates I (substantive grounds for Court's ruling reasonable) Moderates II (substantive grounds unreasonable, but judicial process legitimate and reasonable)
Influence (relational, demand rationally perceived, conflict of values, no severe sanctions)	"Other-Directed" Persons (judicial ruling, substantively and procedurally unreasonable, but apprehensive of standing in community)
Manipulation (non-relational, non-rational, no conflict of values nor sanctions)	Groups Which Choose Neither Compliance Nor Noncompliance Mass (conform to dominant behavior in community, with little or no recognition of the problem nor awareness of complying)
Force (relational to non-relational, nonrational, application of severe sanctions)	Groups Which Choose Noncompliance Defiant official subject to contempt of Court (incarceration reflects that values underlying defiance overshadow values gained by compliance)
Power, Authority etc.	Extreme segregationists

Under the heading of groups not complying with the Court order are officials who are incarcerated and fined for criminal contempt (force) and segregationist groups that are beyond the reach of the Court. Suffice it to say that the behavior of these groups—geared as they are to a different set of values—also can be analyzed and categorized in terms of power and its related concepts.

VI

For our purposes, a decision is "a set of actions related to and including the choice of one alternative rather than another . . . ,"[36] or, more simply, "a choice among alternative modes of action. . . ."[37] Thus, we differ sharply from Lasswell and Kaplan, to whom a decision is "a policy involving severe sanctions (deprivations)."[38] The basis for the contrast between our definition and theirs is clearcut: they hold that decisions are brought about solely by the exercise of power, while we believe that power is neither the only nor even the major factor underlying the process of decision-making and reactions thereto. We believe, in fact, that in some situations power is not involved at all, that in such situations the behavior of decision-makers and their subjects alike can be explained partially or entirely in terms of force, influence, or authority.

Our position can be clarified by reference to the following diagram. Two important points may be drawn from it. First, every social decision involves interaction between the one or more persons seeking a given goal and the one or more persons whose compliance must be obtained. Thus, if A's attempt to exercise power or influence or whatever over B is ignored, there is no decision.

Second, compliance can be *sought* through the exercise of one or any combination of the four phenomena indicated on the diagram. However, if compliance is forthcoming, *it may or may not stem from the same source.* For instance, if B bows to A's wishes because A has threatened sanctions which B wishes to avoid, the resulting decision is one of "pure" power; both participants made their choices in the same

frame of reference. On the other hand, if B's compliance is grounded, not on a fear of deprivations but on acceptance of A's values, the resulting decision is a hybrid case, in the important sense that A sought to exercise power but in fact exercised authority. Similarly, cases can be identified in which A has sought to exert authority while B's compliance was given because he was influenced (see diagram). The combinations are many—particularly if the analysis also takes into account situations where two or more of the phenomena come into play simultaneously.[39] The point is, in all events, that a decision cannot be said to be a result of power or influence or authority or force unless and until it is specified from whose point of view the decision is being examined, *i.e.*, from that of the one who seeks compliance or the one who gives it.

It may be objected that this approach is unworkable for empirical analysis because it necessitates mind-reading. We think not. The courts of law do, and so can we, distinguish between "specific" intent and intent inferred from actual behavior. We believe, in other words, that it is both feasible and necessary to deduce from detailed observation of the situation why persons act as they do.[40] To put it still another way, there is no shortcut, no simple and mechanical method, for gaining a full understanding of the decision-making process.

We concede that our approach is less workable than that of Lasswell and Kaplan, Dahl, and others of that "school." On the other hand, because ours provides a broader conceptual frame within which to analyze decision-making, it makes easier the comparative study of the factors underlying

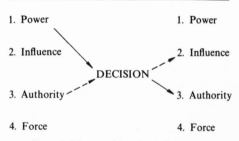

Means By Which Compliance Is Sought	Reason Why Compliance Is Forthcoming
1. Power	1. Power
2. Influence	2. Influence
3. Authority	3. Authority
4. Force	4. Force

Figure 1. Diagram of impulse and response.

different decisions on diverse circumstances. A road is thereby opened toward the development of a body of general theory with respect to the decision-making process. Moreover, because we distinguish carefully among the forces at work in any given situation, we minimize the risk of putting unwarranted emphasis upon one factor to the exclusion, wholly or partly, of others. Stated more bluntly, we put the phenomenon of power in proper perspective: we recognize that while decision-making frequently does involve power relationships, it very often does not.

VII

The other side of the coin is *non*decision-making. When the dominant values, the accepted rules of the game, the existing power relations among groups, and the instruments of force, singly or in combination, effectively prevent certain grievances from developing into full-fledged issues which call for decisions, it can be said that a nondecision-making situation exists. This phenomenon is clearly distinguishable from the negative aspects of decision-making (deciding not to act or deciding not to decide), since the mere existence of the "mobilization of bias," to use Schattschneider's phrase, is sufficient to prevent a latent issue from becoming a question for decision.

It might be objected that since a nondecision, by definition, is a nonevent, it is not observable, and, therefore, is not an operationally-useful concept. Although it is true that a nondecision is not visible to the naked eye, a latent issue is discernible and so is the mobilization of bias. Thus it can be said that the *nondecision-making process* (the impact of the mobilization of bias upon a latent issue), in distinction to a nondecision, is indeed subject to observation and analysis.

In their perceptive study, *Small Town in Mass Society*, Vidich and Bensman, without

calling it such, analyze the nondecision-making process in Springdale.[41] For example, they relate that the school administrators in the community had basic grievances but, cognizant of the dominant rural values prevailing in the community, the established tradition of deciding all town issues by unanimous vote, and the predominance of nonprofessionals in posts of leadership, the schoolmen prudently kept their grievances to themselves. In choosing this course of action, the school officials admittedly made a decision. But it was not one brought about by any decision or combination of decisions by others with respect to their grievances. Quite the contrary, it reflected the schoolmen's realization that, by sustaining the mobilization of bias, the leaders of the community—even if indirectly and unconsciously—could, would, and often did exercise authority, power and influence against them.

In those instances when a latent issue of the type which is usually kept submerged is successfully pushed forward and emerges as a public issue (for example, the recent emergence of Negro demands in the South), it is likely that the mobilization of bias will be directly and consciously employed against those who demand a redress of grievances by the decision-making organ. In such instances, the decision-making process preempts the field previously occupied by the nondecision-making process. And in so doing, it necessarily jeopardizes the previously-established mobilization of bias.

If the concept of nondecision-making proves a useful tool of analysis, it appears to us at this juncture that it can be effectively studied in terms of the categories suggested in this paper for the examination of decision-making.

11

Some Ambiguities in the Notion of Power*

William H. Riker

This article by William Riker, Professor of Political Science at the University of Rochester, provides a useful abstract summary of a number of different attempts to explicate the concept of power, and calls attention to the dependence of such efforts on different conceptions of causality. Originally published in 58 American Political Science Review (1964) 341–349, it is reprinted here with the permission of that journal and the author.

THE NOTION of power is often said to be central to the analysis of politics. But while that analysis is a very ancient activity, the conceptual clarification of the notion of power has been undertaken only in the past generation. The reason for this discrepancy I leave to the historians of political ideas. In this introduction I merely observe that the clarification has not proceeded as far as is needed, so that we are still not at all sure of what we are talking about when we use the term. Nevertheless there is light ahead, owing especially to some formal definitions that have been offered in recent years by Shapley and Shubik, March, Dahl, Cartwright, and Karlsson. By reason of the formality of these definitions the issues of meaning have been more sharply delineated than was previously possible. Hence we have reached the point, I believe, where we may confront definitions with each other and specify precisely how they differ. In so doing we may be able to resolve some of the ambiguities remaining in the concept of power. In that hope this essay is written.

* I thank Professors Robert Dahl, William Flanagan, Carl Hempel, and Dennis Sullivan for criticisms helpful in improving the argument of this paper. An earlier version was delivered at the Annual Meeting of the American Political Science Association, New York City, September 1963.

But first a personal remark: most contemporary criticism of political theory is directed, unfortunately, at the so-called giants of the past. In such an enterprise, it is not personally embarrassing—indeed it is academically fashionable and intellectually trivial—to explain where Plato went wrong or what Rousseau meant. What political theory needs, however, is criticism of contemporary theory, for this is the theory that is important in guiding political research. But such criticism may be personally embarrassing, especially when, as in this instance, it is directed at the work of men whom I regard as at the very forefront of the social sciences. I want to make it clear, therefore, that (a) I regard the theories I discuss as a great advance, one which I have in the past struggled to make and failed and (b) I utter criticism not captiously but in the spirit of contributing to the dialectic of understanding.

I. FIVE FORMAL DEFINITIONS OF "POWER"

I start with a simple statement of the basic elements of each of the five definitions, ignoring most of the subtleties of each writer's interpretations, and usually using the symbols preferred by the authors. I have also offered verbal translations of the formal definitions, translations which exhibit, I suppose, all the characteristic pitfalls of translations generally.

Shapley, a mathematician who developed his notions originally to discuss the value of n-person games, was aided in applying it to social world by an economist, Shubik.[1] Their definition relates only to the power resulting from the right to vote in a system where voting, and only voting, determines outcomes:

$$P_i = \frac{m(i)}{n!}$$

where P is the power to determine outcomes in a voting body for a participant, i, in a set of participants: $\{1, 2, \ldots, n\}$ where $m(i)$ is the number of times i is in the pivotal position and where *pivotal position* is defined thus: when the rules define q votes as winning,

$$\frac{n+1}{2} \leq q \leq n \quad \text{or} \quad \frac{n}{2} + 1 \leq q \leq n$$

Notes to chapter 11 are found on pages 372 to 373.

the pivot position is the qth position in an ordered sequence of the votes. (Note that there are $n!$ ordered sequences or permutations of n things.)

Manifestly,

$$\sum_{i=1}^{n} P_i = 1$$

In words, the Shapley-Shubik definition may be stated thus: the power of a voter to determine an outcome in a voting body is the ratio of (a) the number of possible times the voter may be in a pivotal position in an ordered sequence, to (b) the number of ordered sequences possible, *i.e.*, $n!$. What this measure is thus the participant's chance to be the last added member of a minimal winning coalition, a position that is highly attractive presumably because the last added winner can control the form or distribution of the winnings.

March's definition grows out of his desire, as a political scientist, to measure comparative amounts of influence, which I take to be substantially equivalent to power in his usage. In his most important paper on the subject he defines the phrase "has at least as much influence as" as a relation, I, between two roles, R_1 and R_2, each acting upon a set of behaviors, $\{B_1, B_2, \dots\}$.[2] The effect of R_1 and R_2 each choosing a behavior is an outcome, O_{ij}, which can be pictured as a matrix, thus:

		R_2	
		B_1	B_2
R_1	B_1	O_{11}	O_{12}
	B_2	O_{21}	O_{22}

Defining Ω_{hk} as the set of outcomes for a choice by R_h of B_k (*e.g.*, a row or column in the foregoing matrix), and using "m" to refer to some measure on the set of possible outcomes (*i.e.*, the set $\{O_{ij}\}$):

$$R_1 I R_2 \equiv m(\Omega_{1k}) \leq m(\Omega_{2k})$$

Verbally: To say "R_1 has at least as much influence as R_2" is equivalent to saying "the measure on the row of a choice of a row by Role 1 is equal to or less than the measure

on the column of a choice of a column by Role 2, where the row and column chosen are identical behaviors." The essential notion is that the greater the power the greater is the ability to restrict outcomes. If one cannot by one's own action lessen the range (or value of) outcomes in a situation, then obviously one has no control over the future. If one can lessen, then one can control to that degree. Hence follows the notion that the ability to restrict outcomes is the essence of influence or power.

Dahl, also a political scientist, defines power in a way closer to the commonsense tradition than either of the previous two. He says at the beginning: "My intuitive idea of power . . . is something like this: A has power over B to the extent he can get B to do something B would not otherwise do."[3] This sentence is formalized by the use of two conditional probabilities:

$$p_1 = P(B, x \mid A, w)$$
$$p_2 = P(B, x \mid A, \overline{w})$$

where (A, w) means that person A does act w; where $(A, \overline{w})$ means that person A does not do act w; where (B, x) means that person B does act x; and where $P(u \mid v)$ is the symbol for conditional probability and means the probability that, given the occurrence of event v, the event u also occurs. Thus p_1 and p_2 are statements of conditional probability. The amount of power, M, is defined thus:

$$M\left(\frac{A}{B}; w, x\right) = p_1 - p_2$$

Verbally: The amount of power A has over B with respect to order w (by A) and response x (by B) is (a) the probability that, when A does w, B does x, minus (b) the probability that, when A does not do w, B does x. Clearly, this is a straightforward formalization of Dahl's intuitive idea.

Cartwright, a social psychologist, has defined power in a way quite similar to Dahl's, without, however, the use of probabilities. He relies on the notion of a "psychological force" which is a sextuple of the following.[4]

> Agents: $\{A, B, C, \ldots\}$; acts of agents: $\{\alpha_A, \beta_A, \gamma_A \ldots\}$; loci: $\{a, b, c, \ldots\}$, which may be *directly joined* if they lie on a common boundary of regions; motive bases, $\{M_1, M_2, M_3, \ldots\}$ which are drives or pre-dispositions; magnitudes, m, which are real numbers measuring acts; and a time indicator t_r.

Quoting Cartwright, p. 191, "If we wish to indicate that force, f, has act α of agent A as its activator, need for g as its motive base, locus a as its location and ab as its direction, m as its strength, and t_k as its temporal position we write: $f_1 = (\alpha_A, M_q, ab, m, t_k)$." Defining the strength of an act, $|\alpha_0(ab)|$, Cartwright writes:

$$|\alpha_0(ab)| = |f_{ab}| - |f\,\overline{ab}|$$

where

$$f_{ab} = (\alpha_0, M_x, ab, m_1, t_k)$$

and where

$$f_{\overline{ab}} = (\alpha_0, M_x, ab, m_2, t_k)$$

Verbally, (f_{ab}) is a force to comply and $(f_{\overline{ab}})$ is a force to resist. Power is defined in terms of the strength of an act:

$$\text{Pow } O/P(ab) = |\chi_0(ab)|_{\max}$$

where χ_0 is an element of the set $\{O, t_k\}$ of acts which O can perform at t_k.

In Cartwright's words: "The power of O over P with respect to a change from a to b at a specified time equals the maximum strength of any act which O can perform at that time, where strength is specified for the direction ab in P's life space."

Finally, *Karlsson*, a sociologist, has defined power formally in terms of utilities.[5] Given a group of n members acting in time periods $(t_0, t_1, t_2, \ldots)$. In each time period the participants perform acts which are identified thus: $a_1(t_j), a_2(t_j), \ldots a_n(t_j)$. The outcome, x, at the end of the time period is a function, g, of these acts:

$$x(t_j) = g(a_1(t_j), \ldots, a_n(t_j))$$

For each participant there is a utility function, u_i, on the outcome,

$$u_i(t_j) = u_i(x(t_j))$$

which determines his evaluation of each outcome, x. To define the power, p, of participant i over j, assume that other participants do not act so as to influence u_i and u_j and let j choose an act to maximize u_j. Also let i choose from among his possible acts to vary u_j from a maximum to minimum, u_{ijmax} and u_{ijmin}. Power is then defined as:

$$p_{ij} = u_{ijmax} - u_{ijmin}$$

This may be expressed verbally: given the situation in which i can vary behaviors and hence outcomes in such a way as to vary j's reward (which is j's utility for an outcome), the power of i over j is the absolute difference between (1) the maximum reward for j from i's determination of an outcome and (2) the minimum such reward. Thus, the greater the range over which i can determine j's reward, the greater is i's power over j.

II. DIFFERENCES AMONG THE FORMAL DEFINITIONS

Even when stated verbally, these definitions have very little in common. One could not, for example, directly infer any one of them from any other one. There is a vague family resemblance between Dahl's and Cartwright's and it is possible that, with some modifications in vocabulary, they could be equated.[6] As between this pair and the others, and as among the other three individually, there is no possible equation, although the spirit of Karlsson's definition is closer to Dahl and Cartwright than to March and Shapley-Shubik. With five definitions there are at least four distinct meanings, each of which appears quite reasonable by itself.

An easy response to the discovery of these four aspects of power is to hope that there will soon be discovered a yet more general formulation which combines these four aspects neatly into one. And yet this hardly seems possible for in some very important ways these definitions are in part mutually exclusive. For example, in Karlsson's definition, power involves an ability to control the rewards to someone else, while in March's it involves the ability to control the outcomes of events. These are quite different potentials and indeed it is quite easy to imagine circumstances in which they vary inversely with each other (e.g., in *n*-person situations where the very ability to punish occasions coalitions against the potential punisher).

With different and contradictory meanings, even when the form of the definition has already been raised to a high level of generality, it is probably vain to hope that on an even higher level the differences and contradictions might disappear. It seems rather that we are faced with a clear instance of ambiguity which, however desirable in poetry, has no place in science or philosophy. So our immediate problem is the clarification of ambiguity, which we approach by means of a comparison of some obvious differences among the definitions.

One major difference is the size of the group to which the relation refers. Here the two extremes are Cartwright's and Shapley and Shubik's definitions; Cartwright's is specifically dyadic although at the end of his essay he expresses the hope that an *n*-adic definition might be constructed out of his dyadic one. On the other hand, Shapley and Shubik begin with an *n*-person group of voters. Their definition of power leads to a method of calculating the relative chance of each person in the system to control the outcome. Since each person's chance depends on the distribution of chances to other people, the definition is clearly *n*-adic. Of course, the *n*-adic definition subsumes the dyadic case; but its application to the dyad is trivial. In between these extremes lie the other three definitions. All three assume an *n*-person group, either specifically as in Karlsson's definition or inferentially (e.g., from the examples used). But in Dahl's and Karlsson's definition, the measure applied to events is dyadic, that is, it is a numerical comparison between attributes of a pair of persons or actors. Both writers attempt to extend the application to the whole group by means of exhaustive comparisons of each possible pair of participants. But this procedure simply emphasizes the dyadic character of the definition. March's defini-

tion seems somewhat closer to Shapley and Shubik than to the other three. Although he specifically defines the relation, *I*, as a dyadic relation between roles, still the measure on outcomes is applied to all of them, including presumably those outcomes in the *n*-person system that are not subject to comparison when *I* is evaluated for two specific roles. Thus, though the comparison is dyadic, the tools of comparison are constructed with reference to the whole set of outcomes. Because of the nature of the tools, therefore, March's definition is essentially *n*-adic, even though it is cast in the form of a dyadic relation.

It is not surprising that there should be confusion about the size of the group wherein power is measured, or that there should be contradictions between dyadic and *n*-adic definitions of power. Running throughout theory in the social sciences is a recognition of qualitative differences among one-, two- and three-unit groups. In economics, the study of price determination has sharply distinguished among monopolistic, duopolistic, and oligopolistic situations of supply. Entirely different theories have been constructed to deal with each situation. In game theory, a qualitative difference in strategic problems has been found to occur between every game of size *n* and every game of size $n + 1$, where $n = 1, 2, 3, 4$. The sharpest qualitative breaks are between one-person and two-person games and between two-person and three-person games. Two-person theory requires a different kind of mathematics from one-person theory and three-person theory requires a different set of basic definitions from two-person theory. On the other hand, three-, four-, and five-person theory can use essentially the same definitions and mathematics, although each addition of a person introduces a new kind of strategic consideration. There seems little doubt that, quite generally, there is a significant qualitative difference between dyads and *n*-ads. Not surprisingly, then, definitions generated with the dyadic situation in mind differ sharply from definitions generated with the *n*-adic situation in mind.

A second major difference among the definitions is in the postulated object of power. (This difference may well turn out to be no more than a reflection of the difference between the dyad and the *n*-ad, but superficially at least it appears to be independent.) At one extreme again is Shapley and Shubik's definition wherein the object of power is influence over the outcome. For them, power is measured as the chance to occupy a uniquely valuable position in the decision-making process, a position which one can make the final determination of the outcome. This kind of power is ego-oriented in that its object is to increase utility for ego. It is essentially indifferent to others, so long as ego wins. At the other extreme is Karlsson's definition in which the object of power is, intuitively, to inflict punishment, or, stated more closely to the formal definition, to restrict the utility of someone else. For Karlsson power is other-oriented in the sense that it is concerned only with influence over another and not with an outcome. The contrast can be stated thus: ego-oriented power (Shapley and Shubik) is the ability to increase ego's utility; other-oriented power (Karlsson) is the ability to decrease alter's utility. The other definitions under consideration range themselves in between these extremes: March's is quite close to the ego-oriented extreme, since he defines power in terms of constraints on outcomes, not people. Dahl and Cartwright's definitions are, however, close to the other-oriented extreme in the sense that they measure power as an ability to force others to do one's bidding. They are not quite so extreme in tone as Karlsson's with his emphasis on punishment, but they do have an element of personal dominance, which is the essence of the other-oriented position.

The theoretical significance of the distinction between ego-oriented and other-oriented theories is not, however, that one involves manipulating people and the other involves manipulating outcomes, but rather that they differ on whether or not power always exists. In ego-oriented theories, power always exists. It cannot be eradicated for it refers to outcomes and, so long as outcomes occur, it exists. If ego runs out of power, still someone else in the *n*-person system has the ability to influence an outcome. So power never disappears from the system. This is especially clear in the Shapley and Shubik definition, where the sum of all participants' power is always one. Suppose, in this system, the power of *i* is reduced to zero. Still there exist *j*, *k*, ... who acquire *i*'s erstwhile power over outcomes. So no power ever disappears under the Shapley-Shubik definition, although, as circumstances change, different egos may hold it. The same is to some degree true under March's definition. Roles may change in their ability to control outcomes, but some outcome is bound to occur, by definition. Some role or roles, then, can be expected to bring it about, although any particular role may be essentially powerless. Again power cannot disappear.

Under the three other-oriented definitions, however, it is quite possible that power disappears. In both the Dahl and Cartwright measures, it is possible that power be a positive number, zero, or a negative number. (Dahl specifically recognizes this range of possibilities and I infer the same range for Cartwright from the nature of the mathematical operation in his definition.) When power is a positive number, there is no problem: it clearly exists. Similarly, there is not much of a problem when power is a negative number, for a kind of ability to influence still exists. Negative power of *A* over *B* in Dahl's (and Cartwright's) terms is not, as might be initially expected, the power of *B* over *A* but rather the degree to which *A*'s orders occasion a kind of spite reaction in *B*. If *B* decides not to do something that he otherwise intended to do just and only because *A* told him to do it, then *A* has negative power over *B*. Note, however, that negative power is still a positive ability to influence. So long as *A* is aware of *B*'s probable reaction of spite, he can still manipulate *B* into doing what he wants him to do: *A* merely has to order *B* to do exactly the opposite of what *A* really wants *B* to do and *B* will comply with what *A* really wants. Hence negative power is a version of positive power and power has not disappeared. But if power is zero, then there is nothing in the relationship. In Cartwright's definition, where power is specifically dyadic, zero power means clearly that power does not exist. In Dahl's definition, however, zero power as between *A* and *B* does not preclude power between *C* and *D*. The same is true of Karlsson's definition, so we will consider these two together.

Karlsson's definition does not initially admit of power as a negative number. But he further defines relative power, r_{ij}, which is: $p_{ij} - p_{ji}$. This could, of course, be negative and would have the natural meaning, which Dahl's, does not, of a reversal in the power relationship. But Karlsson's definition, like Dahl's does admit zero power, although, if $p_{ij} = 0$, it still may be that $p_{kj} > 0$. Nevertheless, there is nothing in the Karlsson and Dahl definitions that precludes the possibility that, for all *i* and *j*, $p_{ij} = 0$, or that, for all *A* and *B*, $M(A/B) = 0$. And this is to say that power can be non-existent.

Perhaps the contrast between the other-oriented and the ego-oriented definitions can be made clearer with an example. Let there be three participants, *a*, *b*, *c*, in a system and let them have equal chances to influence the outcome and no chance to influence each other. In Shapley and Shubik's definition:

$$P_a = 1/3, \qquad P_b = 1/3, \qquad P_c = 1/3.$$

In March's definition:

$$R_a I R_b, \qquad R_a I R_c, \qquad R_b I R_c.$$

In Dahl's definition:

$$M\frac{(a)}{b} = 0, \qquad M\frac{(a)}{c} = 0, \qquad M\frac{(b)}{c} = 0,$$

$$M\frac{(b)}{a} = 0, \qquad M\frac{(c)}{a} = 0, \qquad M\frac{(c)}{b} = 0.$$

In Cartwright's definition:

Pow $a/b = 0$, Pow $a/c = 0$, Pow $b/c = 0$,

Pow $b/a = 0$, Pow $c/a = 0$, Pow $c/b = 0$,

In Karlsson's definition:

$$p_{ab} = 0, \qquad p_{ac} = 0, \qquad p_{bc} = 0,$$

$$p_{ba} = 0, \qquad p_{ca} = 0, \qquad p_{cb} = 0.$$

The one clearly ego-oriented definition (Shapley and Shubik's) defines power in this circumstance. In a less obvious way, so does March's for, while no numerical quantity is given, it is asserted that the influence of the three participants is equal. That it is equal does not preclude that it exists. In the last three definitions, however, power is clearly non-existent. The array of zeros proves the point. So I observe that ego-oriented power preserves power in the system, while other-oriented power does not.

III. THE DIFFERENCE BETWEEN DYADIC AND *n*-ADIC POWER AND BETWEEN EGO-ORIENTED AND OTHER-ORIENTED POWER

The differences just pointed out in the kinds of definitions are differences in the kinds of explanations attempted by the several theories. When I speak of kinds of explanations, I have ushered in that *bête noire* of all philosophy of science, the notion of cause. And yet unpleasant as it is, we must deal with this beast for it is beauty's lover.

The thesis of this essay is that differences in the notion of cause stand back of these differences in the notion of power. Once we have straightened out some basic problems in causality, it will be simple enough to straighten out, to explain if not to reconcile, differences in the notion of power. At least two main types of notions of causality are used in social science discourse. One is a notion of marginality, the other is a notion of necessary and sufficient condition. These usually have quite distinct meanings and applications, but sometimes they run together enough to occasion some misunderstanding. It is just such a misunderstanding that is involved in the confusion about the meaning of power.

The popular notion of cause, what the word fundamentally denotes for most speakers of English, has been brilliantly explicated by Douglas Gasking, who points out the similarity between causation and recipes.[7] He observes that a basic human experience is the production of effects by manipulating nature. Any specific rule for manipulation is, he argues, a statement of cause. For example, one says "You can make iron glow by heating it," or, alternatively, "The cause of iron glowing is heat." Hence, causation generally is the notion of rules for manipulation, or recipes. Precisely, A is said to cause B, where A and B are repeatable kinds of events, if B can be made to occur by making A occur.

While the scientist wishes to use particular causes as the basis for inference, the popular notion of cause is much too confused a relation to admit inference. There are at least two serious difficulties with it. For one thing, even the man in the street and certainly the scientist thinks of causal relations as obtaining between events that are inaccessible to human manipulation. Recipe-causality of course reflects one kind of test for the sentence "A causes B;" but one clearly does not wish to limit cause only to relations subject to this test. The more profound difficulty with recipe-causality, however, is that it takes as fixed all relevant variables except the manipulative one. Thus, to say "the monopolist's restriction of supply causes the price to rise" takes the state of demand as given, whereas in fact the level of the demand curve may itself vary independently (up or down), thus having a concomitant effect on price. If a non-manipulative variable in the antecedent condition does have a relation to the effect, then it must be involved in the cause even though recipe-causality does not admit it.

Logical confusion of this sort has rendered the popular notion of cause scientifically unusable. While most scientists have probably never successfully eliminated the popular notion from their lives or their work, still one main response to the realization of logical weakness has been a long-sustained attempt to banish the use of causality from science. The other response has been to redefine causality so that it has

the same logical form as the equivalence relation and sometimes furthermore so that the two clauses have a similar temporal and spatial reference. Thus, to say "A causes B" is to say "B occurs if and only if A has occurred." From this statement the aforementioned problems of confusion in inference could never arise because the "if and only if" requirement directs attention to variables other than the manipulative one.

The usual form of the redefined notion of causality is the assertion that the cause of an event is a necessary and sufficient condition. The proof of necessity is a proof that B would not have occurred unless A occurred, and the proof of sufficiency is a proof that, if A occurs, then B occurs too.

Necessary and sufficient conditions are not recipes, rather they are full statements of all and only the antecedents required to bring about a consequent. The full complexity of the notion of necessary and sufficient condition, which often doesn't seem so difficult to prove in the laboratory, can be illustrated by a translation I have previously devised as a guide to proving sufficiency and necessity in social situations: "One event causes another if and only if the terminal situation of the causing event is identical in space-time location and in movers and actors with the initial situation of the caused event."[8]

The redefinition of causality has not, I hasten to add, eliminated the recipe kind of causality from science, especially not from social science. Most recent discussion of causality by social scientists has been fairly close to traditional usage. It has often been on a highly sophisticated level of discourse; but it has shared the recipe character with popular discourse. Thus Herbert Simon, whose work on this subject is cited with approval by March, argues in one essay that cause is the highest order variable in a set of equations, without enquiring into whether or not the set of equations contains all the relevant variables.[9] To take his simplest example: "poor growing weather → small wheat crops → increase in price of wheat," wherein the first phase is said to cause the second and the second the third. All this, of course, assumes that the demand for wheat, not included in the system of equations, is stable and that it does not "cause" the price. Instead, the cause is said to be a marginal effect on the state of supply, something on which a low price of wheat can be blamed.

The difference between the two kinds of causality is, like the difference among definitions of power, a difference in orientation toward outcomes. In recipe-like causality, the full explanation of the effect is not the problem. Rather the problem is to explain how the effect can be made to occur. If no manipulative technique is available, cause may be non-existent.[10] By contrast, in the necessary and sufficient condition kind of causality, the center of attention is on the effect rather than on manipulative techniques. Here the full explanation of the outcome is at stake. Hence, cause cannot be non-existent, although it can be unidentified.

Thus there is a direct parallelism (a) between ego-oriented power and necessary-and-sufficient-condition causality and (b) between other-oriented power and recipe causality. It is not surprising that this parallelism exists, for power and cause are closely related concepts. Power is potential cause. Or, power is the ability to exercise influence while cause is the actual exercise of it.

This parallelism is clearest in Karlsson's and Shapley and Shubik's definitions. Karlsson's power is clearly based on a recipe notion of causality. Not only is it concerned exclusively with ego's ability to restrict alter's utility, a wholly manipulative concern; not only is his power non-existent in the absence of manipulation or the will to manipulate; but also his definition of the measure of the motivation to use power is proportional to the amount of power possessed. It is postulated thus that the desire to manipulate increases with the ability to do so, an assumption about which we have no convincing empirical information one way or another. In short, Karlsson's power is a direct reflection of recipe causality. Conversely, Shapley and Shubik's is close to a direct reflection of necessary and sufficient condition causality.[11] Since the Shapley-Shubik definition of power, though stated in terms of individual opportunities

to manipulate, involves the calculation of all possible opportunities to influence, the total picture presented is the distribution of the chance to manipulate among all participants. When the potential becomes actual we have a necessary and sufficient condition for outcomes. At no point in the analysis does power or cause cease to exist.

The parallelism in the other three definitions between kinds of power and kinds of cause is not so clear as in the two just mentioned, largely, I think, because of confusion engendered by the contrast between dyadic and *n*-adic situations. Probably the popular idea of power is similar to what Dahl calls his intuitive idea; perhaps it is even simpler, like Karlsson's intuitive idea, being merely the ability to inflict punishment on somebody. There is certainly a highly dyadic feature to punishing somebody or making somebody do something. Hence, in attempting to capture the popular and intuitive idea, there is a strong tendency to think of power as dyadic and to define it that way.

Once the notion of dyadic power is accepted there is also a strong tendency, I believe, to accept a recipe notion of cause. In the dyadic relation, especially when one actor is aggressive and the other passive, which is the usual situation in which men want to talk about power, it is very easy to see the recipe for action: "*A* uses his power over *B*." The recipe is at hand and may thus be used. Furthermore, even to those trained to look for necessary and sufficient conditions, the recipe itself looks like such a condition. Of course, it is not and cannot be, for another necessary condition is that *B* exist. Nevertheless, such background, non-marginal conditions are easy to overlook in the dyad. Hence follows the acceptance of recipe causality and other-oriented power.

The interesting, perhaps even astonishing thing about the March, and Dahl, and Cartwright definitions is the degree to which they have struggled away from the kind of power and causality suggestively imposed by the dyadic situation they purport to describe. March is the one who struggled most successfully. He retains the dyadic form of power, but he manages to import a large amount of ego-oriented power into it, so much so that previously I classified his theory as *n*-adic and almost ego-oriented. As noted, it is his emphasis on a measure over outcomes that turns his theory away from the dyad and the alter-oriented. And the emphasis on outcomes represents an approach to necessary-and-sufficient-condition causality, inasmuch as an explanation of outcomes tends toward total explanation rather than manipulative explanation. It seems to be that March started out with an other-oriented power and a recipe causality; but, as a scientist seeking complete explanations rather than manipulative techniques, he was driven toward the ego-oriented power and necessary-and-sufficient-condition causality. As a result there is a fundamental ambiguity in his definition, deeper perhaps than in any of the other writers under consideration—and for that reason more deserving of praise for scholarly integrity.

The same struggle March went through is also reflected in Dahl's and Cartwright's definitions, but in a different way. Both restrict the application of their measure: Dahl by requiring that it always be used in connection with a survey of the source, means, amount, and range of power; Cartwright by incorporating substantially these restrictions into his definition. I interpret these restrictions on an essentially manipulative theory of power that assumes an essentially manipulative theory of cause as an attempt at a total explanation and hence as an attempt at a necessary-and-sufficient-condition theory of cause. Of course, ambiguity results.

XI. CONCLUSION

Thus some fundamental ambiguities among definitions of power and inside particular definitions have been shown to reflect—and to root in—similar ambiguities about the nature of causation. Other writers, I hasten to add, have discussed the same ambiguities. Bachrach and Baratz, brilliantly criticizing Dahl's empirical work which uses a somewhat more directly manipulative definition than the theoretical definition discussed here, pointed out that a manipulative theory is far less than a complete explanation.[12] Similarly, Singer has recently observed the absence of reciprocity in power, as it has here been defined. This absence seems to me to be a function of the search for manipulative skill rather than a total explanation.[13] But I have in this essay shown that these ambiguities are not accidental features of a particular definition, but are rooted in the very conceptions of power and causality themselves.

The final question, once the full complication of the ambiguities is revealed, concerns the appropriate scientific attitude toward the conception of power itself. Ought we redefine it in a clear way or ought we banish it altogether? My initial emotion, I confess, is that we ought to banish it. But this suggestion will, I am sure, find little sympathy among my colleagues. Alternatively, I suggest minimally that each definition specify clearly the kind of theory of cause it reflects. Undoubtedly there are many kinds of situations in which one wants to investigate other-oriented power relations and recipe causality (*e.g.*, "how can the President control Congress?"); but these investigations should be clearly labelled as not likely to lead to total explanations. Beyond that I suggest that the customary definition of power be revised in the ego-oriented direction to reflect the necessary-and-sufficient-condition theory of causality. Only then will the notion of power reflect the totality of the situation it purports to describe. The Shapley-Shubik definition, which has this character, is, unfortunately, limited to committee-like situations and is not therefore general enough. What we need is a definition of power in the spirit of their definition, and applicable to a wider range of situations. But that is the subject of another paper.

ADDENDUM

There is a manipulative element in the Shapley-Shubik definition even though it is not immediately apparent. To show its existence I will construct a quite general definition of power with a necessary and sufficient condition notion of cause underlying it and then consider what is necessary to translate this more general definition into Shapley's and Shubik's.

Let there be a set of $\{1, 2, \cdots, n,\}$ participants and let $\{O_i\}$ be the set of outcomes, $i = 1, 2, \cdots, m$ and let $\{A_{1i}, A_{2i}, \cdots, A_{ni}\}$ be the set of actions to bring about O_i by a set of participants. Assume no A_{ji} alone is sufficient and some, but not necessarily all, A_{ji} are necessary for O_i.

Let

$v(A_{ji}) = 0$, if A_{ji} is not necessary

$v(A_{ji}) = 1$, if A_{ji} is necessary.

Then, for $j \neq k$,

$$P_j > P_k \equiv \sum_{i=1}^{m} v(A_{ji}) > \sum_{i=1}^{m} v(A_{ki})$$

where P_j and P_k are indices of the power of participants. Applying this definition to a simple majority voting body of $\{a, b, c\}$, where weights are $w(a) = 50$, $w(b) = 49$, and $w(c) = 1$, then A_a is necessary (i.e., is included in a minimal winning coalition) in six instances out of a possible six, A_b in four, and A_c in four. Thus, out of 14 necessary memberships, $P_a = 3/7$, $P_b = 2/7$,

$P_c = 2/7$, which is different from the Shapley-Shubik result.

To render the results identical let $u_j(O_i)$ be the utility of an outcome, O_i, for participant, j. Then let

$$P_j = \sum_{i=1}^{m} u_j(O_i)v(A_{ji}); \text{ and let } \sum_{j=1}^{n} P_j = 1$$

In the particular case of the Shapley-Shubik power index, let $u_j(O_i) = 1$, if j is pivot, and let $u_j(O_i) = 0$, if j is not pivot. In the example cited, it is now the case that $P_a = 2/3$, $P_b = 1/6$, $P_c = 1/6$, which is the Shapley-Shubik result. I conjecture that it is generally true that the Shapley-Shubik definition can be derived from the definition here set forth by a utility function for pivoting. If so, then the Shapley-Shubik definition with its apparent emphasis on outcomes contains a manipulative element, although the thing manipulated is outcomes, not people. Nevertheless, to the extent manipulation is involved, a recipe-like notion of cause has contaminated the fundamental notion of explanation, which is that of a necessary and sufficient condition, underlying their definition.

Theory Formation and Measurement

IN SECTION III we included essays which attempt to provide unambiguous definitions for the concept of power. But as Riker argues in that section, certain ambiguities associated with the concept of power seem to be a function of ambiguities in the formulation of the notion of cause. This begins to suggest, not surprisingly, that concept formation itself depends upon theory formation. This section includes essays that show the interconnections between concept formation and theoretical orientation. Along with Cartwright's wide-ranging essay we have included essays which focus upon causal analysis and game-theoretical analysis.

Apparently, a major problem in many theories of influence is identifying asymmetrical relationships. The assumption of an asymmetrical relationship informs March's efforts toward measurement; Simon addresses himself explicitly to the question, What assumptions are required in order to infer asymmetrical relationships among variables?

We include four essays having to do with game theory, which is clearly one of the most rigorous and influential orientations to the study of influence yet devised. Riker's test of the Shapley-Shubik index indicates, if there was ever any doubt about it, that the application of game theory to actual political phenomena cannot be accomplished routinely. Harsanyi's essays do not simplify the task, for in his view additional theorems are relevant to an adequate conceptualization of power.

A DEFINING characteristic of the social entity known as an organization is, as the name suggests, its state of being organized. According to common usage, an "organization" is an arrangement of interdependent parts, each having a special function with respect to the whole. Even casual observation of the behavior of members of an organization, such as an industrial firm, a hospital, or a university, reveals its organized character. The members assemble on schedule, each person engages in a limited number of activities, the range of interpersonal transactions is restricted and stable over time, and the style of social interaction is patterned. Behavior has a reasonably high degree of predictability, and people know rather well what to expect of one another. Moreover, the activities of different individuals tend to combine in such a way as to result in organizational accomplishments. The industrial firm turns out products and makes profits, the hospital provides medical care, and the university creates alumni.

The regularity of behavior and coordination of activities are remarkable in view of the heterogeneity of the organization's human elements. Participants vary greatly in ability, training, knowledge, cultural background, and needs. "Outside" the organization their activities are governed by a diversity of uncoordinated determinants, but "inside" they display regularity, dependability, and coordination. In this chapter we shall be concerned with the efforts made by social scientists to account for these phenomena.

For many years the analysis of organizations was largely guided by a set of basic assumptions, most effectively stated by Weber (1947) in his discussion of "bureaucracy." Theorists writing in this tradition assume that an organization has a primary objective (also referred to as purpose, goal, task, function, or mission). To reach this objective, subgoals must be established and specific means chosen for their attainment. This, in turn, requires a differentiation into specialized tasks which must be carried out dependably in a coordinated manner. Tasks are combined into positions (or offices or jobs), and individuals are assigned

12

Influence, Leadership, Control[1]

Dorwin Cartwright

While the essays in this section all have to do with the theory and measurement of influence, they are by no means a fair representation of the many attempts to construct theories of influence. Therefore we think it appropriate to include this bibliographical essay by Professor Cartwright, an organization theorist at the University of Michigan. This essay originally appeared in James March (ed.), Handbook of Organizations *(1965), and is reprinted here by permission from Rand McNally and Company.*

to these. Each position has a formal or informal job description which specifies what the occupant of the position is supposed to do and how he is supposed to do it. To give further assurance that the system will work properly, rules, regulations, and policies are promulgated as guides to the behavior of the participants. Finally, a control mechanism is established whereby the various positions are linked together by a chain of command so that the authority and responsibility of each position is unambiguous.

With the passage of time, and especially with the accumulation of empirical data, attacks of various sorts have been launched against this "classical" conception. In response to these attacks it is sometimes conceded that the description characterizes an ideally "rational" organization and that actual ones deviate from it in varying degrees. Nevertheless, the view prevails that every organization has a basic objective, and to be viable it must have some control system to guarantee accomplishment of this objective. As Gilman (1962, pp. 106–107) puts it, "positive control of performance down the line is possible only because one can influence, when and if necessary, the behavior of the subordinate in such a way

Notes to chapter 12 are found on page 373.

that he acts on the basis of his superior's judgment rather than his own."

Contemporary accounts of organizational control, however, are becoming more complex, for empirical research has demonstrated that behavior "down the line" is influenced by a multitude of events, only some of which are directives from superiors. The members of an organization are simultaneously members of other groups and organizations, such as a union, a peer group, a family, and the like, which also exert influence on their behavior in the organization. Many of these influences tend to conflict with those coming down the line and may interfere with the accomplishment of organization objectives. But others may serve to facilitate such accomplishment, as, for example, when a worker models his behavior after that of an "oldtimer" who happens to have a better grasp of the requirements of the job than the supervisor.

Haire (1954) traces the historical development of this more complex and more realistic account of behavior in organizations back to the research begun in 1927 by the Mayo group in the Hawthorne plant of the Western Electric Company and especially to the interpretation of this research by Roethlisberger and Dickson (1939). Its emphasis on individual needs, informal groups, and social relationships was quickly endorsed by other social scientists and led to a "philosophy of management" concerned primarily with human relationships in formal organizations. Systematic critiques of the classical theories of organization, based on research findings of the past two decades, have been presented by Argyris (1957), Likert (1961), McGregor (1960), and March and Simon (1958).

One of the most important criticisms of the classical view of organizations is directed to its assumption that the accomplishment of organizational goals requires the exercise of asymmetric, one-way control from a single source at the top of the organization. Research into the nature of democratic leadership and the benefits of participation in group decisions bolstered the attack on this "autocratic" conception of management. It would be a mistake, however, to interpret this attack as advocating the elimination of influence by an organization over its members. The early study (White & Lippitt, 1960) on styles of leadership, so frequently cited in this connection, carefully documented the negative consequences for morale and productivity of laissez-faire leadership. The main thrust of the criticism was to advocate an organization whose parts are actively interdependent as opposed to one whose parts are all dependent upon a centralized source of control.

Several recent studies (Smith & Tannenbaum, 1963; Tannenbaum, 1957; Tannenbaum, 1961; Tannenbaum & Georgopolous, 1957; Tannenbaum & Kahn, 1957; Williams, Hoffman, & Mann, 1959) have underlined the importance for organizational functioning of a sufficiently high level of social influence within the organization. These investigations have employed a research device known as the "control graph." Its horizontal axis represents the various hierarchical levels in an organization, and its vertical axis represents the amount of control exercised by those at each level over organizational policies and practices. Two aspects of an organization's control structure are indicated by such a graph: the hierarchical distribution of control, represented by the shape of the curve, and the total amount of control exercised by all levels, represented by the general height of the curve. A control curve that rises with hierarchical ascent might be said to reflect an autocratic structure, while one that declines reflects a democratic one. A low flat curve represents a laissez-faire situation, while a high flat curve represents a polyarchic one. Data for constructing graphs have been collected in a variety of organizations, revealing considerable variation between organizations in both the shape and height of the curves. In relating these curves to various symptoms of organizational effectiveness, it has been found that the distribution of control, as reflected by the shape of the curve, has diverse effects that depend on a host of other factors. However, in a majority of organizations studied there is a positive correlation between the amount of total control (i.e., the average height of the curve) and effective organizational performance. It appears, then, that organizations require for their functioning the exertion of an adequate amount of influence by one part on another, but this influence may take a variety of forms.

In this chapter, we shall take it for granted that people in an organization do exert significant influence over one another, for whatever reason or purpose, and we shall examine the processes of influence. Our purpose will be to survey the relevant literature, provide a guide to the more significant publications, and describe the present state of the field.

Anyone wishing to gain a fundamental understanding of the nature of social influence must be prepared to cope with a literature that is scattered, heterogeneous, and even chaotic. Relevant contributions have come from the disciplines of psychology, sociology, political science, economics, anthropology, and philosophy. Theorists who have attempted to impose some order upon this literature have found it to be exceedingly intractable. In fact, one could well argue that there is no single body of literature on influence but instead a collection of discrete and more or less independent literatures concerned with various aspects of influence, such as leadership, attitude change, conformity, persuasion, communication, social learning, and socialization.

A basic issue confronting the theorist, then, is whether the time is ripe to attempt a comprehensive treatment of influence per se. In discussing the concept of influence, March (1955) and Simon (1957) have argued convincingly that influence is simply a special instance of causality, namely, the modification of one person's responses by the actions of another. If this claim is correct, the study of influence must be seen as a part of the larger study of the determinants of human behavior. And progress here cannot exceed general progress in the development of the social and behavioral

sciences. The basic issue is nicely dramatized by Dahl (1957), who admits to two "suspicions" arising from his ruminations about the concept of power. First, "if so many people at so many different times have felt the need to attach the label power, or something like it, to some Thing they believe they have observed, one is tempted to suppose that the Thing must exist; and not only exist, but exist in a form capable of being studied more or less systematically." Second, "a Thing to which people attach many labels with subtly or grossly different meanings in many different cultures and times is probably not a Thing at all but many Things" (p. 201). Dahl adds that some students of the subject think that the whole study of "power" is a "bottomless swamp."

The view taken in this chapter is that the study of influence is not a bottomless swamp, although the terrain does have its soggy spots. The basic problem is how to keep from getting lost among masses of discrete data and interminable theoretical distinctions, especially since the natives appear to have no common language. A map is needed to help the student find his way. For this reason, our major objective here will be to contribute to the construction of such a map.

It will be useful to begin by taking a look at the broad outlines of the topic. One sees immediately that investigators have approached the study of influence from many different directions and have concentrated on many different features. As an aid to placing each approach within the total field and to relating one with another, we shall identify three major aspects of the influence process upon which attention may be focused. These are: (a) the *agent exerting influence*, who for convenience is denoted *O*, (b) the *method of exerting influence*, and (c) the *agent subjected to influence*, denoted *P*. When an agent, *O*, performs an act resulting in some change in another agent, *P*, we say that *O influences P*. If *O* has the capability of influencing *P*, we say that *O has power over P*.

Agent Exerting Influence

A natural starting point in the analysis of influence is to identify the agent exerting influence. Theorists differ considerably in their permissiveness as to the variety of social entities that may be conceived as exerting influence. The formalization of power proposed by Dahl (1957) represents one extreme. He speaks of influence as being exerted by "actors," which may be "individuals, groups, roles, offices, governments, nation-states, or other human aggregates." The term "actor" is also employed by Lasswell and Kaplan (1950, pp. 3–4), but they insist that this must refer ultimately to specific individuals. "An act is always that of a single person, and when we speak of 'group acts' a pattern formed by individual acts is to be understood. With this qualification, the terms 'act' and 'actor' are to be taken in the broadest possible sense as comprising all deeds and doers." In the analysis of influence proposed by March (1957), the basic elements are "roles" and the behavior of persons in them. Finally, there are theorists, like Adams and Romney (1959) or Miller and Dollard (1941), for whom the basic unit is the individual organism, in the tradition of behavioristic psychology.

Discussions of influence in the "classical" theories of organization tended to conceive of the agent exerting influence as an office or position in the organization. In these theories it was generally assumed that organizational control is, or should be, exercised by authority vested in designated positions. Orders emanating from a supervisor, or superior officer, are followed simply because they come from an authoritative position; the personal characteristics of the occupant are irrelevant. Gradually, however, the facts of organizational life began to impinge upon the theorists, and the account was subjected to revision. One of the earliest and most influential of the revisionists was Barnard (1938), who advanced a distinction between the "authority of position" and the "authority of leadership." This distinction concerns the degree to which the success of an influence attempt is dependent upon the personal ability of the agent exerting influence; authority of position is independent of personal ability, whereas authority of leadership rests on the superior ability of the agent regardless of the position he occupies. This general line of thought has been extended in various ways and now pervades the literature. A typical manifestation is the distinction proposed by Bass (1960) between "personal power" and the "power of position." It is also reflected in the frequent designation of formal versus informal aspects of organizations.

RESOURCES OF THE AGENT

Most theories of social influence assert that the ability of an agent to exert influence arises from the possession, or control, of valued resources. Dahl (1957, p. 203) refers to these as the *base* of an actor's power, which consists of "all the resources—opportunities, acts, objects, etc.—that he can exploit in order to effect the behavior of another." As an illustration he notes that "some of the possible bases of a President's power over a Senator are his patronage, his constitutional veto, the possibility of calling White House conferences, his influence with the national electorate, his charisma, his charm, and the like." It should be evident that the specific resources which constitute a base depend upon the nature of the agent and the social setting under consideration. Thus lists of "resources" contain such diverse items as wealth, military capability, prestige, skill, information, physical strength, and even personal rewards like recognition or affection.

Ownership of economic resources has been emphasized, of course, in many analyses of the basis of power in society. Individuals, or collections of people, gain the ability to exert influence in society, according to these theorists, primarily because they possess wealth and, especially, the means of production. As the corporation has become a more dominant feature of Western society, this account has been revised somewhat by such theorists as Berle and Means (1933) and Russell (1938), who observe that control of the means of production is now often more concentrated than ownership and that power tends to go with control. Thus, it is the managers of a corporation, rather than the stockholders, who wield power. This line of thought is further advanced by Harbrecht (1959) in his thesis that the United States has become a "paraproprietal society" in which "a man's relationship to things— material wealth—no longer determines his place in society (as it did in a strong proprietary system) but his place in society now determines his relationship to things." In other words, an individual gains the ability to exercise influence by occupying a position which controls economic resources.

This analysis of power in society is mirrored by treatments of power within organizations which attribute the power of an office or position to its control over resources valued by the members. Thus, it is said that a supervisor can obtain compliance with his directives because his position gives him the ability to reward or punish his subordinates by controlling promotions, salary increases, terminations of employment, or suspensions. And it is sometimes argued that union contracts which remove these matters from the control of the supervisor thereby undermine his ability to direct behavior toward the accomplishment of organizational objectives.

An empirical study of how the effectiveness of a reward system affects the amount of influence exerted by a supervisor is provided by Bennis and his associates (1958). These investigators collected data from 90 nurses in six out-patient departments in a large Eastern city. They obtained measures from each nurse concerning the rewards she hoped to get from her job and ones that were likely to be received. These included such things as salary increase, praise, promotion, better job without promotion, and educational opportunities. To measure the amount of influence exerted by the supervisor, the congruence was determined between the amount of time each nurse spent on certain activities and the amount of time her supervisor wanted her to spend. The results of this study indicate two major limitations on the effectiveness of a supervisor's influence: (a) and incorrect perception on the part of supervisors of what rewards the

nurses desire, and (b) an inability to increase or withhold these rewards. In hospitals where these limitations were less extreme, the supervisors were found to exert greater influence over the activities of the nurses.

It appears, then, that a supervisor's control over rewards is an important determinant of his influence. In many organizations managers assume that economic rewards are the primary ones at their disposal. Contemporary organization theorists tend, however, to view the supervisor's ability to influence as resting on a much broader base. They point out that participants in an organization ordinarily have many needs, in addition to economic ones, which may be satisfied or frustrated by a supervisor. As Likert (1961; p. 102) puts it, "Each of us wants appreciation, recognition, influence, a feeling of accomplishment, and a feeling that people who are important to us believe in us and respect us." The satisfaction of such "ego needs" requires resources less tangible than the economic ones, and these may be controlled by a supervisor. It would seem, however, that such resources cannot be owned by an impersonal agent, such as a position or office, but are peculiarly possessed by persons. Even so, they may affect the ability of an occupant of a position to exert influence by determining his "personal power" or his "authority of leadership." Being personal properties, they may be used by anyone who possesses them, thus permitting the rise of an informal or illicit influence structure within an organization. Finally, it should be noted that in many organizations the participants are not employees, in which case the influence needed to accomplish organizational control must rest on some base other than wages.

Unfortunately, there has been little research directly focused upon those personal properties of an agent that may serve as resources in exerting influence. A good example of how such research might proceed is the analysis of power in the classroom conducted by Gold (1958). By means of interviews, he identified 17 characteristics of children which other children viewed as valuable and important. These resources appeared to fall into five categories: (a) *expertness*—"smart at school," "has good ideas about how to have fun," "good at making things," "good at games with running and throwing"; (b) *coerciveness*—"knows how to fight," "strong"; (c) *social-emotional*—"acts friendly," "a good person to do things with," "asks you to do things in a nice way," "doesn't start fights and doesn't tease," "knows how to act so people will like him"; (d) *associational*—"plays with you a lot," "likes to do the same things you like to do"; and (e) *other*—"nice looking," "has things you'd like to have," "gives you things," "does things for you." Gold found that the importance of these resources varied with the age and sex of the child. He then showed that specific individuals who possessed many important resources were considered by their classmates as better able to influence them than individuals who possessed only a few.

The link between having a resource and having power has been examined in some detail by Levinger (1959). In an experimental study of the formation of power relationships, he brought together two previously unacquainted people to engage in a task requiring a series of joint decisions. At the outset of the experiment the critical subject was led to believe that his knowledge about the task was either superior or inferior to that of his partner. Careful observation of the decision-making process revealed that those subjects who believed they possessed superior knowledge made more influence attempts, more frequently resisted their partner's suggestions, and displayed a higher degree of assertiveness. The subjects who thought they had superior knowledge also rated themselves as having more influence over the decisions. Thus, knowledge about the distribution of a relevant resource had a clear effect upon the decision-making process.

One important feature of many kinds of resources is that they may be "pooled" so as to serve as a more effective base of in-

fluence. A single merchant may have insufficient money to launch an effective campaign for the enactment of a city ordinance, but a group of merchants, acting together, may be successful. The formation of coalitions is often a critical aspect of the exercise of influence. Indeed, some theorists (see Cyert & March, 1959) maintain that every organization is a coalition. Although we cannot review here the extensive literature on coalitions, three requirements for an effective coalition may be noted: (a) The resources contributed by the members of a coalition must be "additive" in the sense that their combination results in a more effective base of influence than that of any member alone. (b) The prospective benefits to be derived by each member must be favorable relative to his contribution to the coalition. (c) The coalition must act sufficiently as a single entity so as to convert its pooled resources into a coherent pattern of influence. As pointed out by Dahl (1958), this last requirement has sometimes been overlooked by investigators wishing to show that a particular segment of society constitutes a "ruling elite." The existence of coalitions strengthens the argument that the agent O should be conceived permissively (not necessarily as a single individual) and that the base of influence consists in the control (rather than the ownership) of resources.

MOTIVATION OF THE AGENT

Although the control of valued resources gives an agent the capacity to influence others, it does not follow that he will attempt to exert influence under all circumstances. And though it is true that the possession of certain resources may be converted by a person into power, not all people seek to acquire these resources. Thus, for example, Schulze (1958, p. 9) reports, on the basis of a historical analysis of "economic dominants" in the political power structure of a community, that over the years there has been a withdrawal of the economic dominants from participation in the public life of the community. He concludes that one should not assume the necessity of "any neat, constant, and direct relationship between *power as a potential for determinative action, and power as determinative action, itself."*

Observations of this sort focus attention upon the motivations underlying the exercise of influence. Why do people want to influence others, and what guides their influence attempts? For a great many years it was fashionable to postulate a unitary and universal motive, or desire, for power. The writings of Hobbes (1651) and Nietzsche (1912) provide outstanding examples. While Russell (1938, p. 274) agrees that "this desire is an essential part of human nature, and in energetic men it is a very large and important part," he introduces a distinction between "power desired as a means and power desired as an end in itself." Thus, people are said to attempt to influence others and to strive for positions of influence either because they seek certain objectives whose attainment requires the exercise of influence or because they gain satisfaction directly from the ability to influence others. Whatever the ultimate reason for wanting power, a person may exercise influence in order to augment his resources and thereby strengthen his base of power; he uses power to acquire power.

The distinction between instrumental and intrinsic motivation for exerting influence can be seen in much of the recent theoretical literature. It is involved, for example, in most treatments of the problem of legitimacy of authority. The right of management to supervise and to demand compliance with its directives is justified by the contribution these directives make to the attainment of organizational objectives. If an influence attempt is not guided by these objectives, as might happen when the supervisor is governed by an intrinsic power motivation, then it is illegitimate. Thus, according to this view, the exercise of legitimate authority makes use of instrumental power motivation, and a strong desire for power per se is regarded as a symptom of social pathology.

Although the desire for power, whether instrumental or intrinsic, is generally recognized by organization theorists, it is now rarely accorded a "simple and sovereign" status. A more complex set of determinants is usually assumed to be operative. These

are often stated in terms of role theory. Viewed in this perspective, the agent exercising influence is conceived as the occupant of a formal position with which a particular role is associated. Thus, for example, Stogdill (1959) identifies the function of a position as defining "the general nature of the contribution that its occupant is expected to make toward the accomplishment of the group purpose" (p. 123) and the responsibility of a role as "the specific set or range of performance that a member is expected to exhibit by virtue of the operational demands made upon his position in a formally acknowledged structure" (p. 129). An occupant of a particular position, it is said, engages in specific influence attempts because they conform to his view of the expectations that others attach to his position and role. His basic motivation, then, is not simply to exercise influence but, instead, to gain rewards given for fulfilling these expectations. Stogdill points out, however, that if a position has high status and a role has great authority, the occupant is relatively free to initiate influence attempts in keeping with his personal motives and beliefs concerning the requirements of the situation.

Costs of exerting influence. When an agent is deciding whether to exert influence it may be assumed that he "calculates," in some sense, the net advantage to him of making an influence attempt. Although little research has been aimed directly at this process, several theoretical analyses have been undertaken. Thus, for example, Harsanyi (1962, pp. 68–70), writing in the tradition of economic theory, asserts that "a realistic quantitative description of A's power over B must include, as an essential dimension of this power relation, the costs to A of attempting to influence B's behavior." He defines the costs of A's power over B as "the *expected value* (actuarial value) of the costs of his attempt to influence B. It will be a weighted average of the net total costs that A would incur if his attempt were successful (e.g., the costs of rewarding B), and of the net total costs that A would incur if his attempt were unsuccessful (e.g., the costs of punishing B)." Harsanyi indicates that costs may be calculated in physical units (e.g., bottles of beer or working hours), monetary units, or utility units. It is, of course, an empirical question whether, and in what way, a particular agent engages in a rational calculation of the costs of attempting influence.

A rather similar approach is taken by Thibaut and Kelley (1959), although their discussion is stated in a psychological, rather than an economic, vocabulary. Any interpersonal interaction, they say, results in "outcomes" for each of the participants. These outcomes are either rewards (i.e., the provision of a means whereby a drive is reduced) or costs (i.e., an inhibition or deterrence of behavior), which may be combined to yield a net "goodness" of outcome. Thibaut and Kelley construct a matrix of "possible interactions and outcomes" for a pair of people, A and B. The columns of the matrix, labeled $a_1, a_2, \ldots$, represent the items of A's "behavior repertoire," and the rows, $b_1, b_2, \ldots$, represent items of B's repertoire. Each cell corresponds to a pairing of items from the two repertoires. Within each cell is entered a pair of values (o_B, o_A), indicating the goodness of outcome to B and A, respectively. It is assumed that A and B will each seek to maximize his own gain from interaction by enacting behavior which, when matched with a behavior of the other, will yield him the best possible outcome. The similarity of this approach to that of game theory should be apparent, though these authors do not employ its mathematical apparatus.

Thibaut and Kelley state that "the power of A over B increases with A's ability to affect the quality of outcomes attained by B" (p. 101). They then identify two types of power: fate control and behavior control. A has fate control over B "if, by varying his behavior, A can affect B's outcome *regardless of what B does*" (p. 102). And, A has behavior control over B "if, by varying his behavior, A can make it desirable for B to vary his behavior too" (p. 103). The matrix

shown in Fig. 1 illustrates a situation in which A has fate control over B; whatever B does, A's behavior determines B's outcome.

	a_1	a_2
b_1	(1, 4)	(4, 4)
b_2	(1, 4)	(4, 4)

Figure 1.

In the matrix of Fig. 2, A has behavior control over B; if A enacts a_1, B will enact b_2, and if A enacts a_2, B will enact b_1.

	a_1	a_2
b_1	(1, 4)	(4, 4)
b_2	(4, 4)	(1, 4)

Figure 2.

In these two examples, it is assumed that A gains equally from enacting a_1 or a_2. He is therefore free to exercise fate control or behavior control. This assumption, however need not be made. Figs. 3 and 4 represent situations of fate control and behavior control in which A's behavior is itself constrained by differential outcomes. This possibility leads Thibaut and Kelley to observe that "power is not usable to the degree that its use penalizes the possessor, either directly or because of counterpower held by the other person" (p. 107). And they define *usable power* as "the power that it is convenient and practical for him to use" (p. 107).

	a_1	a_2
b_1	(1, 1)	(4, 4)
b_2	(1, 1)	(4, 4)

Figure 3.

	a_1	a_2
b_1	(1, 1)	(4, 4)
b_2	(4, 1)	(1, 4)

Figure 4.

Both Harsanyi and Thibaut and Kelley, then, assume that the influence attempts of an agent are guided by his evaluation of his net costs. Moreover, both admit that the agent may make errors in his evaluation of the objective outcomes. Harsanyi, however, emphasizes rational calculation on the part of the agent, whereas Thibaut and Kelley appeal more to processes of learning.

Motivation to lead. Several investigators have conducted studies to discover the conditions under which a person will engage in acts of leadership. From this research, two factors appear to be most important: The person must want to gain something for himself or the group, and he must believe that his act of leadership will heighten the probability of attaining it. Thus, Hemphill and his associates (1957) report data showing that individuals will attempt to lead more frequently if the rewards for task accomplishment are high rather than low and if they believe that their leadership will result in group success. Hemphill (1961, p. 213) concludes from a series of experiments that motivation to lead is heightened by "(1) large rewards promised by accomplishing the group's task, (2) reasonable expectancy that by working on the task it can be accomplished, (3) acceptance by other members of the group for attempting to lead, (4) a task which requires a high rate of group decisions, (5) possession of superior knowledge or competence relevant to the accomplishment of the task, and (6) previously acquired status as the group's leader." French and Snyder (1959) present additional evidence in support of the motivating effects of one's own competence and acceptance by others.

If O has power over P and wishes to accomplish something by means of P's behavior, he may have a reasonable expectation that an influence attempt will be rewarding. We should expect, therefore, to find a positive correlation between the possession of power and the use of power. In a study of professional roles conducted by Zander, Cohen, and Stotland (1957), each respondent was asked questions about the possession of authority and the exercise of this authority with respect to several different activities. The correlations between extent of possession and of use were all in the .80's or above. Hurwitz, Zander, and Hymovitch (1953) found that professional mental health workers with high attributed power talked more frequently in group discussions than did those with less power. And Lippitt

and his associates (1952) found correlations ranging from .35 to .66 between the power attributed to a member and the frequency of his attempts to influence others.

THE PROBLEM OF INTENT

Analysis of an agent's motivations for exerting influence draws attention to one other important feature of the influence process. When an agent makes an attempt to influence, he presumably has a more or less clearly formulated notion of what he wants to accomplish. And, of course, a given act may have intended or unanticipated consequences. It should be noted, however, that this possibility has not been explicitly recognized by many theorists. Thus, Merton (1957, p. 60) notes an "inadvertent confusion, often found in the sociological literature, between *conscious motivations* for social behavior and its *objective* consequences." March (1955) lists the problem of "unanticipated consequences" as a major difficulty in the analysis of influence. And March and Simon (1958) describe in some detail the embarrassment for classical theories of organization occasioned by the existence of unanticipated consequences of influence attempts.

The problem of how to deal with the intentions of the agent exerting influence is reflected in the definitions of basic concepts given by different theorists. Intention is explicitly mentioned in some definitions of power. For example, Tawney (1931, p. 230) refers to the capacity of an individual to modify conduct "in the manner which he desires"; Russell (1938, p. 35) says that power is "the production of intended effects"; and Lasswell and Kaplan (1950, p. 76) define power as the process of affecting policies of others with the help of severe deprivations for "nonconformity with the policies intended." In the definition given by Dahl (1957, p. 202) the notion of intention is only implicit: "A has power over B to the extent that he can get B to do something that B would not otherwise do." And it is not mentioned in the statement of Bierstedt (1950, p. 773) that "power is the ability to employ force," nor in the claim of Simon (1957, p. 5) that "for the assertion, 'A has power over B,' we can substitute the assertion, 'A's behavior causes B's behavior.'" Finally, we note that Cartwright (1959, pp. 193–195) employs the concept of intention in defining "control" but not "power."

A good example of the use of the concept of intention in empirical research is provided by Lippitt and his associates (1952, p. 37) in their studies of influence among participants in a summer camp. These authors distinguish between *behavioral contagion*, which is "the spontaneous pickup or imitation by other children of a behavior initiated by one member of the group where the initiator did not display any intention of getting the others to do what he did," and *direct influence*, "in which the actor initiates behavior which has the manifest objective of affecting the behavior of another member of the group." This distinction serves as a warning not to assume that all influence is brought about by deliberately calculated behavior on the part of the agent exerting influence. His resources and motivations must be taken into account, but they do not tell the whole story.

SUMMARY

In much of the literature dealing with social influence, especially that concerned with problems of administration and government, attention has been focused upon the agent exerting influence. One difficulty in integrating this literature arises from the fact that the agent has been conceived variously as an individual, role, position, group, or other collection of people. Accounts of the determinants of the agent's ability to exert influence, and readiness to do so, differ somewhat depending upon the conception employed. Most theorists agree, however, that a major base of influence is the possession, or control, of valued resources, provided these can be used to facilitate or hinder the goal attainment of another agent. Economic resources have this property, and these have been especially stressed in analyses of power in society and economic institutions. In recent years, psychologically oriented theorists have maintained that many human needs require resources, other than economic ones, which an agent may control. As a result, the concept of resource is now given a very wide range of referents.

Explanations of why an agent attempts to exert influence depend upon the way in which the agent is conceived. When the agent is taken to be a person, the account is in terms of human motivation. A person seeks to influence others, it is said, because he hopes thereby to achieve some sort of gratification, either directly from the act of influence or from the attainment of an end via the behavior of others. Recent analyses of the decision to exert influence have postulated that the person engages in some sort of calculation of the gains and costs to be expected in making an influence attempt. These have led to the suggestion that, even though an individual possesses the resources to exert influence, he is not actually free to do so when the costs to him outweigh the gains.

When the agent is viewed as the occupant of a role, the account of his motivation is more complex. In this case, his influence attempts are guided, in part at least, by the expectations others have for the role occupant. His basic motivation is to obtain rewards given for complying with these expectations. It should be apparent that according to this conception the agent exerting influence is himself subjected to influence.

Finally, we have noted that the concept of intention has an ambiguous status in theories of influence. Although some theorists object to its use because of its "subjective" nature, there is real doubt that it can be avoided, for without it one can hardly distinguish between successful and unsuccessful influence attempts or between contagion and direct influence.

Methods of Influencing

The analysis of influence is merely begun when we have identified the agent exerting

influence, specified the resources that constitute his base of influence, and described
his motives for exercising influence. Even

with these matters fixed, there are many
methods by which influence may be accomplished. As noted by Dahl (1957, p. 203), a
base is inert or passive; it must be exploited
somehow if the behavior of others is to be
altered. Thus, he defines the *means* of
power, or influence, as "a mediating activity
by A between A's base and B's response."
Dahl illustrates this concept by suggesting
that "in the case of the President, the means
would include the *promise* of patronage, the
threat of veto, the *holding* of a conference,
the *threat* of appeal to the electorate, the
exercise of charm and charism, etc."

TYPES OF INFLUENCE

This perspective is useful in attempting
to make systematic sense of the many
schemes for classifying types of influence,
or power, found in the literature. These
schemes employ a great variety of distinctions, but most involve some designation of
the means of influence. Three such systems
of classification will serve as an illustration.

Russell (1938), in his analysis of power
in society, asserts that there are three principal ways in which an agent may exert influence over a person: (a) by *direct physical
power* over his body, e.g., by imprisoning
or killing him; (b) by *rewards and punishments* employed as inducements, e.g., by
giving or withholding employment; and
(c) by *influence on opinion*, e.g., through
education or propaganda.

Gilman (1962, p. 107), who is concerned
with the problem of accomplishing control
in hierarchical organizations, identifies four
methods: (a) *coercion*, (b) *manipulation*,
(c) *authority*, and (d) *persuasion*. Coercion,
which is defined as "the substitution of
judgment with the knowledge but not the
willing consent of the subordinate," is "accomplished through the use or show of
some kind of force. Those who are influenced accept displacement of their own
judgment, and act on that supplied by a
superior, as the lesser of two evils." Manipulation "is accomplished by a controlled distortion of the appearance of reality as seen
by those affected. Their actions are based on

their own judgments of what they see, but
they are permitted to see only those things
that are calculated to call out the kind of
judgment desired by the control agent."
Gilman's analysis of authority is complex,
and we shall not do it justice here. In essence, however, authority is established by a
consensual decision by a social unit which
approves and accepts the substitution of
judgment on the basis of its usefulness to
the unit. An agent exercises authority by
appealing, explicitly or implicitly, to the
consensual decision giving him the right
to influence. Finally, persuasion, as common
usage of the term implies, is the "display of
judgment in such a way that those exposed
to it have an opportunity to become aware
of the potential value of accepting it in
place of their own."

Harsanyi (1962, p. 71), in keeping with
his interest in the "economics" of influence,
identifies four main ways by which a given
actor A can manipulate the incentives or
opportunity costs of another actor B: (a)
"A may provide certain *new* advantages or
disadvantages for B, subject to *no condition*. For instance, he may provide certain
facilities for B which make it easier or less
expensive for B to follow certain particular
policy objectives desirable to A." (b) "A
may set up *rewards* and *punishments*, i.e.,
new advantages and disadvantages subject
to certain *conditions* as to B's future behavior." (c) "A may supply *information* (or
misinformation) on (allegedly) already
existing advantages and/or disadvantages
connected with various alternative policies
open to B." (d) "A may rely on his legitimate *authority* over B, or on B's personal
affection for A, which make B attach *direct
disutility* to the very act of disobeying A."

It is apparent that these three classificatory schemes overlap to some extent but
that they also differ. Together, however,
they suggest that most of the means which
an agent, O, uses to influence another, P,
may be placed into one of the following
very broad categories.

1) O exercises physical control over *P's*
body. The soldier, policeman, or company

guard may use his gun to obtain compliance with his demands. Many forms of behavior are effectively discouraged by the judge's ability to imprison. The bully, or parent, may get his way by using his superior strength.

2) *O* exercises control over the gains and costs that *P* will actually experience. An employer may keep employees in line by firing, and blacklisting, employees who deviate from prescribed behavior. A work group may award prestige to a worker who defies a foreman. A teacher may instill good work habits among her students by judicious use of praise and blame. A father may induce his son to go to college by paying his tuition. Or, a wife may break her husband's bad habits by withholding affection.

3) *O* exercises control over the information available to *P*. In this case, the possession or control of information is used to modify *P*'s knowledge, beliefs, or skills. A salesman induces a customer to buy his product by convincing him that the product will meet his needs. A supervisor shows a subordinate how to do a better job. A shop steward persuades a new employee that hard work will reduce the need for workers. A newspaper, by selecting and slanting the news it reports, leads its readers to believe that a candidate will ruin the nation.

4) *O* makes use of *P*'s attitude toward being influenced by *O*. This category includes what Gilman and Harsanyi call authority. A good soldier complies with the orders of an officer. And, in general, whenever *P* believes that *O* has the legitimate right to influence him, *O* may appeal to this right in order to wield influence. The category also includes other cases in which the relationship between *P* and *O* is such that *P* gains satisfaction directly from complying with *O*'s wishes (e.g., *P* loves, or admires, *O*). Charismatic leaders may make use of this method of influence.

In any particular social situation it is possible, of course, that more than one type of influence will be found, and institutions are sometimes classified according to the combination of types that prevail. It has been proposed by some theorists that in the natural history of control there is an inevitable sequence starting with the "harder" types involving control over people's bodies or material resources and moving toward the "softer" types that make use of control over information or rely upon favorable attitudes toward being controlled. If at an advanced stage a softer form proves to be unsuccessful, then, according to the theory, control "regresses" to an earlier and harder type of influence. Such sequences can be observed in the history of certain political regimes, such as Nazi Germany or Communist Russia, and in the general trend of labor-management relations. It is clear, however, that many organizations begin at an advanced stage and never make use of the more primitive types of influence.

CHOICE OF MEANS

Consider hypothetically an agent who possesses all the bases required for the exercise of any type of influence. What determines which means he will actually employ? The literature does not contain a comprehensive answer to this question, but certain approaches to an answer are suggested.

McGregor (1960) proposes that the choice of means is determined by the agent's theory of the nature of man. As he puts it, "Behind every managerial decision or action are assumptions about human nature and human behavior." He identifies two broad orientations, which he calls Theory X and Theory Y. The basic assumptions of Theory X, he asserts, are implicit in most of the literature of organization and in much current managerial policy and practice. These assumptions are:

1) The average human being has an inherent dislike of work and will avoid it if he can.
2) Because of this human characteristic of dislike of work, most people must be coerced, controlled, directed, threatened with punishment to get them to put forth adequate effort toward the achievement of organizational objectives.
3) The average human being prefers to be directed, wishes to avoid responsibility, has

relatively little ambition, wants security above all (pp. 33–34).[2]

In contrast, the assumptions of Theory Y (which McGregor believes are more consistent with the findings of social science) are as follows:

1) The expenditure of physical and mental effort in work is as natural as play or rest. The average human being does not inherently dislike work. Depending upon controllable conditions, work will be a source of satisfaction (and will be voluntarily performed) or a source of punishment (and will be avoided if possible).
2) External control and the threat of punishment are not the only means for bringing about effort toward organizational objectives. Man will exercise self-direction and self-control in the service of objectives to which he is committed.
3) Commitment to objectives is a function of the rewards associated with their achievement. The most significant of such rewards, e.g., the satisfaction of ego and self-actualization needs, can be direct products of effort directed toward organizational objectives.
4) The average human being learns, under proper conditions, not only to accept but to seek responsibility. Avoidance of responsibility, lack of ambition, and emphasis on security are generally consequences of experience, not inherent human characteristics.
5) The capacity to exercise a relatively high degree of imagination, ingenuity, and creativity in the solutions of organizational problems is widely, not narrowly, distributed in the population.
6) Under the conditions of modern industrial life, the intellectual potentialities of the average human being are only partially utilized (pp. 47–48).

Although McGregor cites no evidence that individuals holding one or the other of these theories actually employ different types of influence, his general point seems well taken. One's philosophy of human nature may indeed affect expectations concerning the success of various means and thereby influence the choice among means.

Gilman (1962), accepting the point of view advanced by McGregor, asserts that the general social and cultural environment of an organization also determines the type of influence that will be employed within it. In analyzing the methods of control used by American businesses over the past 50 years, he points out that the ethics of con-

trol have changed and that the larger social system now imposes limitations upon the available alternatives. Specifically, he notes the following developments:

1) Acting through the agencies of state and federal government, American society has progressively reduced the extent and variety of economic coercion that can legitimately be employed. The yellow-dog contract, the black-list, and the interstate transportation of strike-breakers are now illegal, for example; and collective bargaining is protected by law.
2) The organization of workers has enabled them to oppose their combined economic strength to that of management. The result has been substantial additional limitation of the use of economic coercion—through contractual agreement.
3) As the result of social legislation, the prospect of prolonged unemployment resulting from discharge is no longer terrifying. It is merely unpleasant.
4) The mobility of labor and the availability of other jobs also helps make the threat of discharge less forbidding.
5) And coercion of any kind as a means of control has demonstrated its ineffectiveness in the modern enterprise. It is likely to be useful only when manpower is plentiful, when muscle power rather than skill is the employer's principal requirement, and when worker performance can be constantly and easily checked while work is in progress (pp. 108–109).

These two analyses suggest, then, that in choosing a means of influence an agent is guided by a theory of human nature and constrained by ethical and legal prescriptions deriving from the larger social environment. A rather different set of determinants are indicated by Rosenberg and Pearlin (1962) in their study of types of influence used by members of the nursing staff of a mental hospital. Using interviews and questionnaires, they attempted to discover what criteria nurses bring to bear in choosing a means to influence the behavior of a patient. Each respondent was given a hypothetical situation calling for a change in a patient's behavior and five possible actions that might be taken. Each of these actions was designed to represent one of five types of influence. The percentage of nursing personnel who reported that they would first use each type are as follows: persuasion, 54 per cent; manipulation, 38 per cent; legitimate authority, 5 per cent; coercion, 2 per cent; contractual power, 1 per cent. Analysis of the reasons given for preferring a particular means reveals a number of factors: (a) the value system of the nursing profession, (b) the predicted effectiveness of the means, (c) the immediate costs or work for the nurse, (d) delayed consequences that might be expected, (e) consequences for relationships with other patients, (f) the nurse's orientation to work, and (g) the nurse's status or position in the hospital structure.

This study by Rosenberg and Pearlin is a first exploration into a promising area of investigation. It, together with theoretical discussions like those of McGregor and Gilman, provide useful leads for more intensive research. Only after the completion of such research will we adequately understand the determinants of the choice of means of influence.

ATTRIBUTES OF MEANS

The designation of various types of influence has served a useful purpose, but, as noted above, no consensus has emerged as to which classificatory scheme is best. A more detailed and sophisticated analysis of the properties of means seems to be required. Such an analysis may start by identifying significant features that different means of influence possess. Since a means is conceived as a mediating activity on the part of O between his base and P's behavior, its attributes are properties of O's actions. Five such properties appear to be of primary significance.

1) Reasons for exerting influence. Each act of influence is interpreted by the recipient in terms of its apparent purpose, and this interpretation is a critical determinant of its effectiveness. The meaning of any act of O is colored by three critical features: (a) the degree of transparency of O's reasons for exerting influence, (b) the degree to which

O displays a concern for P's needs, and (c) the indicated source of responsibility for the influence attempt.

Careful observation of acts of influence reveals that these vary with respect to the clarity with which the purpose is conveyed; some acts are clearly structured, whereas others are ambiguous, like the pictures in a projective test. An agent may candidly reveal his purpose in exerting influence, or he may attempt to hide it. Subordinates frequently complain that the directives they receive are arbitrary or meaningless. One basis for this reaction may be that the supervisor's reasons for making the influence attempt are not evident, or if they are, that they seem to be personal rather than objective, serving only the supervisor's interests.

The literature on leadership makes it abundantly clear that agents differ greatly in their orientation to the needs of those they try to influence. Some actions convey an impression of indifference, some actual hostility, and some sympathetic support. These impressions have a profound effect upon the outcomes of any particular transaction.

In formal organizations, the ultimate responsibility for an act of influence may rest somewhere other than in the agent performing the act. A supervisor may openly assume responsibility for his directives (even when he does not actually feel free to act otherwise), or he may convey the impression that they are beyond his control, being forced by his supervisor or his role. Administrators have even been known to convey an order by saying that the required practice "has no reason; it's just policy."

2) Exchange relationships. Some theorists assert that every means of influence involves an exchange of some sort between O and P. An agent can exert influence, it is said, because he can use a resource as an inducement; the mediating activity between O's base and P's behavior is essentially bargaining. According to Homans (1958, p. 606), exchange underlies all human interaction: "Social behavior is an exchange of goods, material goods but also nonmaterial ones, such as symbols of approval or prestige. Persons that give much to others try to get much from them, and persons that get much from others are under pressure to give much to them. This process of influence tends to work out at an equilibrium to a balance in the exchanges." Gouldner (1960) has postulated a "norm of reciprocity" which serves to bring about an exchange of gratifications in social interaction. Although the concept of exchange provides considerable insight into many aspects of the influence process, there are difficulties, as we shall see, in making it universally applicable.

Transactions involving an exchange of material goods are, of course, a classical topic of economics, and we shall not consider these here. Instead, we shall concentrate upon exchanges in which O uses a resource to bring about some desired change in P; resources are traded for changes in behavior, broadly conceived.

In organizations whose members are employees, the employment contract, from which so much of the organization's control derives, is an example of such an exchange. The nature of this contract, as distinguished from a sales contract, has been analyzed by Simon (1957). In this treatment, an employee, P, enters into an employment contract with an employer, O, when P agrees to accept the authority of O and O agrees to pay P a stated wage. The critical exchange is wages for submission to authority. Although there are always limits, explicitly stated or implicitly understood, on the range of P's behavior over which O has authority, P in effect signs a blank check. Once the contract is made, O (or his delegates) can use it to justify specific directives to P, and P is bound by the contract to comply.

It seems that something analogous to an employment contract is operative even in organizations that do not pay wages to members. In this case, the member agrees to submit to organizational authority in return for whatever benefits he derives from membership. Sometimes such a contract is formalized as rules for members, but often it finds expression only in shared norms concerning the behavior of a "good" organization member.

3) *Contingency in use of a base.* An essential feature of contractual relationships is that payment is contingent upon compliance with the terms of the contract. But even in noncontractual relationships, the use of a base of influence by O may be made contingent upon P's behavior—a mother promises her child a piece of candy if he is good, or a robber threatens to shoot if a wallet is not forthcoming. Discussions of influence usually emphasize the conditional use of a base, but as Harsanyi (1962) has noted, it is possible for O to modify P's behavior by giving him, "with no strings attached," something he needs in order to accomplish some objective. In this case, O gives P unconditional help, and such actions may be expected only when O believes that P's objectives are congenial with his own. It is possible, of course, for O to give unconditional hindrance by taking an action, regardless of what P does, that serves to make expensive a particular behavior of P. When a base is used conditionally, it is necessary for O to monitor P's behavior in order to know whether his conditions have been met, and it is possible that P will comply only when he thinks that O can check on his behavior. For this reason, systems of control employing conditional means usually require some mechanism for checking up on the behavior of those controlled. The various implications of this need for monitoring have been described in some detail by Thibaut and Kelley (1959).

4) *Temporal features.* In considering the ways in which a base is converted into a means of influence, the time dimension must be kept in mind. Even though an agent's ability to influence may rest ultimately upon the resources he can exploit, influence can occur prior to any transmission of resources. The mere promise to give something of value may be sufficient to exert influence, as many a maid has sadly learned. And a successful threat eliminates the need to use its base. Much of a negotiator's skill resides in his ability to distinguish between a bluff and a genuine threat.

Since an empty promise or threat, if believed, does not require the agent actually to use his resources, there is a constant temptation not to follow through. For this reason, credibility and trust are essential ingredients of influence when threats or promises are employed as a means. In certain settings promises are "put in writing" or made part of a legal contract, but even in commercial dealings between business firms reliance is often placed on personal commitments. As the research of Macaulay (1963) indicates, legal contracts are often thought to be unnecessary because of certain widely accepted norms, such as, "Commitments are to be honored in almost all situations; one does not welsh on a deal." Similar norms are probably found in any enduring social system where influence rests upon the prospective use of a base. An interesting description of these in "street-corner society" has been provided by Whyte (1943).

5) *Change in the distribution of resources.* When it is said that an agent "uses" a base in order to exert influence, the assumption is commonly made that he "uses up" some resource. What actually happens, however, deserves careful consideration. In some situations, the exercise of influence does involve relinquishing ownership or control of a resource, as when money is paid for services. But it is possible to exert influence without giving up a resource, as illustrated by the sharing of information or by many instances of behavioral contagion. And whether O gives up or retains ownership of a particular resource, P may or may not gain its ownership. These observations suggest four possible outcomes for the distribution between O and P of ownership, or control, of the resource in question. (a) *Transfer:* O loses and P acquires the resource, e.g., the employment contract whereby the employer pays wages to the employee. (b) *Consumption:* O loses but P does not acquire possession, e.g., a foreman loses his reputation for fairness by making an unfair demand. A closely related situation is one in which a resource is not destroyed by the exercise

of influence but is transferred to a third party, as when a firm influences public opinion by buying an advertisement. (c) *Spread:* O keeps but P acquires possession, e.g., an expert shares his expertise, or a distinguished citizen "lends his name" to a fund-raising organization. (d) *No change:* O keeps and P does not acquire possession, e.g., a supervisor promises an employee a favor but does not fulfill the promise. The last three of these outcomes suggest that the exercise of influence need not be a zero-sum game.

As noted above, the attempt to conceptualize all influence as an exchange encounters severe difficulties. We now see that some of the more important of these are created by the existence of noncontingent means, influence involving the consumption or spread of resources, and influence in which no change of ownership takes place. And even when exchange may plausibly be said to occur, it is often most difficult to describe the exchange in commensurate units of value. Although these problems are serious, it would be premature to conclude that the effort is necessarily doomed to failure.

Regardless of whether influence is best conceived as an exchange of resources, it is advantageous to identify the resources involved. An illustration of the benefits to be derived from such an analysis is provided by the controversy concerning the relation between status and conformity. According to one view, a group member acquires status in a group by conforming to the expectations others have for his behavior. Thus, as Homans (1950, p. 141) puts it, "The higher the rank of a person within a group, the more nearly his activities conform to the norms of the group." But this generalization has been subjected to criticism on the ground that an accepted group member (e.g., a leader) is actually freer to deviate from group norms and to engage in more "innovative" behavior (Dittes & Kelley, 1956; Harvey & Consalvi, 1960; Kelley & Shapiro, 1954; Menzel, 1957). A theory reconciling these conflicting claims has been proposed by Hollander (1958; 1961a; 1961b), who proposes that a member acquires "idiosyncrasy credits" by behaving in ways valued by the group and that when he has acquired enough of these he may use them to justify innovative behavior. Such use, however, incurs "debits" which serve to reduce the balance in his account. Thus, both claims are correct: a member acquires status by conformity, and status permits nonconformity. Greer (1961) has criticized some features of Hollander's theory, proposing a slightly different formulation which he calls "the reciprocality of indulgences." It remains an open question whether the underlying process necessarily involves an exchange of idiosyncrasy credits. Although it is possible that others gain credits when a leader incurs debits, one may doubt that a law of "conservation of credits" is applicable to this situation.

The five attributes of means discussed above do not exhaust the properties that an act of influence may possess. Additional properties have been identified by Kounin, Gump, and Ryan (1961) on the basis of investigations of the techniques used by teachers in responding to the misbehavior of their students. These authors specify three qualities that a "desist-technique" may display: (a) clarity (defining the deviancy and stating what to do to stop it), (b) firmness, and (c) roughness (angry remarks or looks, or punishment). They find that these properties have different effects upon the behavior and attitudes of both the misbehaving child and other children who observe the interaction.

INFLUENCE BY PERSUASION

Of the many possible means of influence, persuasion is commonly advocated as most suited to a democratic, or rational, social system. And, since social science has flourished best in democratic societies, it is not surprising to find that more research has been devoted to persuasion than to any other means of influence. A detailed reporting of this research would require an entire chapter. For this reason, we merely indicate here how persuasion can be treated in a manner comparable to the other means of influence. For a more comprehensive summary, the reader is referred to the excellent publications of Hovland (1954) and Klapper (1960).

It is important to note that influence by means of persuasion requires a base. One of the most obvious of these is the ability to use an effective medium of communication; if O is to persuade P, he must be able to get his message to P. It is customary, in this connection, to think of the "mass media," such as television, radio, the press, magazines, or books. Since a given individual may be exposed to conflicting influences from the same or different media, there is an advantage in monopolizing these media. Many efforts have been made throughout the course of history to control all media available to a population, but these efforts have never succeeded completely, with the possible exception of the "brainwashing" carried out during the Korean war. The use of certain media requires the expenditure of resources, such as money or the police. Thus, these other resources become an indirect base of persuasion, giving those with wealth, or other forms of power, an advantage in the "battle for men's minds."

Assuming that an agent has access to some medium of communication, he still must possess other bases in order to exert influence. Research on persuasion has made it clear that the apparent "source" of a message greatly affects its effectiveness. If an agent has prestige, for example, his messages tend to carry weight. Thus, we may conceive of the possession of prestige as a base of influence. Other bases are credibility, expertness, and a reputation for objectivity. It is clear that an agent may acquire or lose these intangible bases and thereby gain or lose the capacity to use them in exerting influence. And sometimes their use destroys them, but other times it does not. Unfortunately, the exact nature of these processes is not well understood.

Even if an agent has access to a medium of communication and has the necessary properties to be an effective source, his effectiveness is further dependent upon certain properties of the message transmitted. The possession of skill in constructing effective messages, or the ability to control its use (e.g., by acquiring the services of an advertising agency), is thus another base of influence. Much of the research on persuasion has been concerned with the problem of how to design effective messages, raising issues both of logic and of rhetoric, in the Aristotelian sense. Eight properties, or dimensions, have received most attention: (a) rational versus emotional content, (b) positive versus negative appeals, (c) one-sided versus two-sided arguments, (d) extreme versus moderate positions, (e) degree of explicitness of conclusions to be drawn from factual propositions, (f) sequence of arguments, (g) attention-arousing devices, and (h) use of repetition. Knowledge of the results of research on these techniques of persuasion is a base of influence, and the findings obtained by commercial agencies are often carefully guarded secrets.

One should not assume, of course, that persuasion is employed exclusively via mass media. It is also used extensively in other media such as the formal channels of communication within organizations, meetings, and personal interactions. Katz and Lazarsfeld (1955) have analyzed in great detail how various informal channels of communication interact with the mass media to shape opinions, attitudes, and behavior. Of particular interest is their discussion of "opinion leaders," those individuals whose social position, experience, and personality characteristics make them especially influential in the informal communication networks of a community. The role of personal influence, persuasive or otherwise, has also been emphasized in research on the diffusion of innovation (see Katz, Levin, & Hamilton, 1963). Although most of these studies of informal, persuasive influence have been conducted in communities or rural areas, the generalizations drawn from this research appear to be applicable to formal organizations.

INFLUENCE BY ECOLOGICAL CONTROL

Contemporary theories of influence tend to emphasize methods that employ some action directed specifically to the agent being influenced. But some authors, Gilman (1962) and Rosenberg and Pearlin (1962), for example, have included *manipulation* in their lists of types of influence. Although manipulation is customarily characterized by the fact that the person influenced is not aware of the influence attempt, it usually also possesses another important feature, which we shall call *ecological control.*

When O influences P by ecological control, he takes some action which modifies P's social or physical environment, on the assumption that the new environment will subsequently bring about the desired change in P. The theory of "social gatekeepers" advanced by Lewin (1951, Ch. 8) attempts to deal with phenomena of this sort. Lewin developed this theory in an effort to answer the question, "Why do people eat what they eat?" He began by noting that once food is on the table, most of it is eaten. Thus, an answer to the question involves asking another one, "How does food come to the table?" He proposed that food moves through certain "channels" that are controlled by individuals serving as "gatekeepers." Thus, the housewife's decisions in the grocery store influence the eating behavior of her family. And since there is a tendency for people to come to like what they regularly eat, these decisions eventually shape preferences for food. Lewin indicated that the general conception of gatekeeper is also applicable to any organizational setting in which material objects, information, or personnel "flow through channels." The gatekeepers in these instances are individuals who make decisions concerning such matters as procurement, work flow, hiring, job assignment, promotion, and the spread of particular kinds of information.

In principle, O may influence P by ecological control whenever P's behavior is predictably related to some manipulable feature of P's physical or social environment. An example of this type of influence is provided by the literature on the effects of desegregation. Research into the nature of intergroup prejudice has shown that under certain conditions more favorable attitudes are generated by interaction between members of hostile groups. This finding suggests the possibility of influencing these attitudes, not by persuasion or education, but by social practices which encourage or require such interaction. Thus, an employer who wishes to modify attitudes toward members of minority groups might adopt policies of employment and job assignment designed to foster favorable conditions of interaction between members of majority and minority groups. This general procedure is applicable, of course, to other social settings such as schools, summer camps, the military establishment, and housing projects. Relevant findings from research have been reported by K. B. Clark (1953), Deutsch and Collins (1951), Sherif and associates (1961), Star, Williams, and Stouffer (1958), Wilner, Walkley, and Cook (1955), and Yarrow (1958).

Influence by ecological control can be observed in virtually every kind of social setting. The teacher exerts such influence in forming work groups, designing "projects," and making seating assignments. It has been shown by Gump and Sutton-Smith (1955) that children's games have structural properties that activate characteristic psychodynamic processes in the participants and that in therapeutic group work the choice of games is an essential part of a program of therapy. The more general possibilities of "milieu therapy" are being explored increasingly by psychiatrists. In formal organizations it is a common practice to employ a deliberate system of rotating assignments for younger managerial personnel with the purpose of instilling in them a broad perspective and identification with the organization as a whole. Role theorists have long maintained that an individual's attitudes are shaped by his role, and this proposition has been documented by Lieberman (1956) in a study of workers who become foremen or shop stewards.

One reason for exerting influence by ecological control is that many of the attitudes, values, and behaviors of individuals are determined by the groups to which they belong. Thus, Cartwright (1951), in summarizing certain findings from research in group dynamics, draws the following conclusion:

Efforts to change behavior can be supported or blocked by pressures on members stemming from the group. To make constructive use of these pressures the group must be used *as a medium of change*. . . . To change the behavior of individuals it may be necessary to change the standards of the group, its style of leadership, its emotional atmosphere, or its stratification into cliques and hierarchies. Even though the goal may be to change the behavior of *individuals*, the target of change becomes the group (p. 387).

A general theory of ecological control has not yet emerged, but a promising conceptual framework has been provided by Barker (1960) and Barker and Wright (1955). These authors employ the concept of *behavior setting* to refer to "ongoing patterns of extraindividual behavior whose identity and functioning are independent of the participation of particular persons." Each behavior setting has an associated set of physical objects arranged in a characteristic pattern at a particular temporal and physical locus. Behavior settings are such things as executive committee meetings, a work setting, a coffee break, a program of union activities, a baseball game, or the activities of a settlement house. Although many behavior settings come about "spontaneously" and without deliberate planning on the part of anyone, others are created to accomplish definite objectives. If a given individual "enters" a behavior setting, he is influenced by it in ways dependent upon the nature of the setting and his position in it. Thus, control over behavior settings and over the participation of individuals in them may be used to exert an "indirect" influence on individuals. Since much of an executive's responsibility is to design behavior settings, he is bound to exert influence by ecological control, whether he is fully aware of it or not.

SUMMARY

Once the agent of influence has been identified and his motivation for exerting influence characterized, it remains to analyze the method of influencing employed. This analysis focuses attention upon the means of influence. Following Dahl, we conceive of a means as a mediating activity by O between O's base and P's response. With this concept it is possible to impose some order on the literature concerning types of influence. Four broad classes of methods of influencing may be identified: (a) O exerts physical control over P's body, (b) O exerts control over the gains and costs experienced by P, (c) O exerts control over the information available to P, and (d) O uses P's attitudes toward being influenced by O.

Little research has been directed to ascertaining the nature of the determinants of choice of means. From the available literature it appears that at least seven determinants may be operative: (a) anticipation of the effectiveness of a given means, (b) evaluation of immediate costs, (c) assessment of delayed consequences, (d) general theory of human nature, (e) ethical evaluation of means, (f) position in social structure, and (g) legal constraints.

Although the identification of types of influence is a useful beginning in the analysis of influence, a further clarification of the nature of means is required. As a step toward such a clarification, five attributes of means need specification: (a) What are the apparent reasons for exerting influence? (b) Is there an exchange of resources? (c) Is the use of a base contingent upon compliance? (d) What is the temporal relation between O's means and P's behavior? (e) How are resources redistributed by the use of a base? Answers to these questions will provide a firmer foundation upon which to construct a comprehensive account of the processes of influence.

The topic of persuasion has been subjected to a great deal of research, especially by social psychologists. Although most attention has been directed to the problem of constructing effective messages, it is clear that the apparent nature of the source of communications is also an important feature of persuasion. If an agent is to exert influence by this means, he must possess a suitable base. Certain bases, such as prestige or

credibility, seem to be specific to persuasive influence, but others, such as wealth, may be used as a means for several types of influence.

Finally, it was noted that influence is often accomplished by actions directed to the environment of P rather than P himself. The means of such influence has been labeled *ecological control*. In this case, O attempts to modify P's behavior by manipulating those features of P's physical or social environment which determine P's behavior. The control of P's environment may itself require the exertion of influence on agents other than P. For this reason, it is useful to distinguish in any given situation between the primary target of influence and those mediating targets that are influenced in order to produce a change in the primary target.

Agent Subjected to Influence

When we say that O influences P, we mean that an action of O results in a change in some "state" of P. Thus far we have considered problems of identifying and characterizing O, with special emphasis upon O's base of influence and those activities of O that constitute means for exerting influence. A complete analysis, however, requires that we also identify and characterize P and specify the state of P that is affected.

DOMAIN AND RANGE OF INFLUENCE

In discussing the agent O, who exerts influence, we noted that theorists differ widely as to what "level" of analysis should be employed in characterizing agents. Essentially the same problem is encountered in treatments of P, the target of influence. The issue is whether one can legitimately speak of the exertion of influence on an aggregate of people, treated as a unit, or whether one must consider influence as applicable only to individuals. Regardless of the ultimate resolution of this issue, research is currently proceeding at all levels. Thus, for example, there are studies of the influence of one nation on another, of an "elite" on a nation, of mass media on culture, of a corporation on a community, of an officer on an organization, of a leader on a group, and of one person on another.

Whatever level of analysis is employed, it is clear that the number and type of agents, P_i, over whom a particular agent, O, exerts influence may vary greatly. Thus, for example, a leader may have many, or only a few, followers; a union may exert influence on blue-collar workers but not on the members of the clerical staff. We shall refer to the set of agents, $\{P_i\}$, over whom O exerts influence as *the domain of O's influence*. When we wish to refer to potential, rather than actual, influence we shall speak of the corresponding set as *the domain of O's power*. It should be apparent that the empirical meaning of a particular domain of influence (or power) will depend upon the way in which the agents are characterized.

Once the agent who is subjected to influence has been identified, it is necessary to specify further the state, or property, of the agent that is affected. Clearly, the nature of the affected state will depend upon the nature of the agent. If the agent is conceived as an individual, then the affected state might be some item of behavior, a decision, an attitude, a belief, an expectation, a value, or a motive. If the agent is conceived as an aggregate (e.g., an organization), then the affected state might be a decision, a policy, a set of norms, or its structure. Research on influence over individuals has considered most of the possible states of an individual. Research on aggregates has tended to concentrate upon decisions and policies, with less attention directed to the influencing of norms and structures.

Whether P is conceived as an individual or an aggregate, it is clear that the influence of a given agent, O, may extend differentially to various states of P. Thus, for example, the financial vice-president of a company may virtually control its investment decisions but have no effect on its policies concerning unions; a foreman may control certain items of a worker's behavior without influencing the corresponding attitudes; and a union may determine a worker's attitudes toward a company without influencing his on-the-job behavior. The set of states of P subjected to influence by O is usually called the *range* (or scope) *of O's influence* with

respect to P, and the set of P's states which O can influence is called the *range of O's power* with respect to P.

The concept of range of power is of central significance in the study of role relations among the mental health professions conducted by Zander, Cohen, and Stotland (1957). Respondents were asked to indicate power relationships in such classes of activities as diagnosis, therapy, writing social histories, and making community contacts. It was found, for example, that certain power scores for psychiatrists over social workers yielded high intercorrelations among all four classes of activities—in other words, the range of power was broad. Similar power scores for clinical psychologists, on the other hand, did not show such correlations—power in one class of activity did not assure power in another. Thus, in comparing the power of psychiatrists and clinical psychologists vis-à-vis social workers, it was necessary to specify their ranges of power.

Research on the power structure of families also emphasizes the importance of identifying the range of power. Wolfe (1959) reports a study of the relative power of husbands and wives over certain decisions of common concern. Eight such decisions were investigated: purchase of a car, purchase of life insurance, choice of house or apartment, choice of husband's job, decision as to whether the wife will work, food budget, choice of a doctor, and vacation plans. Considering these eight decisions, it was possible to identify various types of family authority structure and to assess the ways in which various factors determine which type a particular family will display. It was found, for example, that if a wife is employed, her range of power over items having economic content is enlarged. Other research, for instance that of Hoffman (1960), has found that a wife's employment reduces her range of power over certain activities carried out at home. It appears, then, that no general statement of the effects of employment upon the wife's power can be made without careful specification of the range of power in question.

A study by March (1953, p. 469) of husband-wife interactions over political issues points to a similar lesson. He found evidence that "the sharing of political power between a husband and wife tends to result in a form of specialization in which each spouse has more or less clearly defined areas of competence." And he concludes that "if the present thesis of intrafamily specialization is correct, the extent to which competing reference groups will be able to influence the behavior of either spouse in a family such as those studied here will depend in part on the subject-matter under consideration."

An important characteristic of any group is the range of its influence over its members. Although little research has been directed toward ascertaining the determinants of a group's range of influence, it is clear that some matters are "relevant" to a group while others are not. Schachter (1951) experimentally varied the relevance of certain member activities and found corresponding differences in the influence exerted on these activities. Organizations often encounter resistance to the extension of influence over certain aspects of member behavior which the members feel are not appropriately within the range of the organization's power. Rules governing the manner of dress on the job or activities off the job, for instance, frequently generate resentment and conflict. Much of the controversy over the prerogatives of management rests on a disagreement between management and unions as to the legitimate range of management's power.

Efforts to specify a particular range of influence reveal several important properties that any range may possess.[3] The time dimension provides one of these. An influence attempt may refer to a single, nonrecurring, action or to a sequence of actions. A foreman may tell a worker to do a specific task in a certain way or he may tell him always to do it that way. And even though an act may affect only a single decision, the consequences of the decision may have varying duration. Thus, in selling government bonds, the Treasury Department may attempt to persuade each citizen "to buy a bond" or it may urge him "to enroll in a payroll deduction plan." Both attempts are directed toward influencing a specific decision, but the long-range effects on the sale of bonds will be quite different in the two cases. A range may also vary with respect to the degree of abstractness of its elements. Frequently supervisory instructions are phrased in terms of functions rather than specific activities, as when a secretary is told "to keep a file up to date" rather than "to file these particular letters." Whenever a range has considerable time depth or a high degree of abstractness, it is usually necessary to specify to some degree the conditions under which certain behavior is to take place, and the definiteness of these specifications may vary greatly. As March and Simon (1958) have noted, much of the control exercised in organizations takes the form of establishing programs of behavior rather than exerting influence repetitively on specific items of behavior. Such programs usually govern behavior over long periods of time, refer to fairly abstract classes of behavior, and provide criteria for determining when the program is to be operative. When functioning properly such programs provide the organization a stable coordination of activities without the necessity of detailed and repetitive supervision.

Kahn and Katz (1960) and Likert (1961) have summarized a number of investigations concerning the effects of "closeness of supervision." These studies show that supervisors vary considerably in how frequently they check up on their subordinates, how frequently they give instructions, how detailed these instructions are, and how much freedom they allow in the pacing of work and choice of methods. Work groups with supervisors who employ more general supervision tend to produce more and to display more favorable attitudes toward the job, supervisor, and company. It is interesting to note that supervisors who employ more general methods of supervision are themselves supervised less closely. These results are obtained from a variety of settings involving both white-collar and blue-collar workers and organizations concerned with manufacturing, service, and research.

The concepts of range and domain are critical in any analysis of influence. Most theorists now agree that an adequate quantification of an agent's influence must specify both; O has more power the larger the number of states of P he can influence and the larger the number of agents he can influence. Range and domain are, moreover, at least implicit components of the widely used terms, social norm and role. The "content" of a norm, or role, is the range of characteristics subjected to its influence. The critical difference between a norm and a role consists in the fact that the domain of a norm is the entire membership of a particular social unit, whereas the domain of a role is restricted to the occupants of a particular position within the unit.

OVERT BEHAVIOR VERSUS READINESS TO ACT

Throughout the theoretical literature on influence one encounters a disagreement based on the distinction between influence on P's overt behavior and influence on P's readiness to act. Those theorists who are behavioristically inclined would restrict the study of influence to effects upon overt behavior, while more permissive theorists would include effects upon such covert states as attitudes, beliefs, or motives.

The theoretical analysis proposed by Dahl (1957) conceives of power in terms of changes in the probability of overt action. More specifically, he defines two probabilities: p_1, the probability that P will perform action x given that O employs means w; p_2, the probability that P will perform x given that O does not employ w. The *amount of power*, M, of O over P with respect to x and w is given by the equation: $M = p_1 - p_2$. Thus, for example, one indication of the amount of the President's power over Congress might be "the probability that Congress enacts a bill if it is endorsed by the President" minus "the probability that Congress enacts the bill if it is not endorsed by the President." Although this conceptualization has many attractive features, its application to concrete situations requires some procedure for measur-

ing probabilities, and this requirement is not easily met.

Apart from the difficulties in ascertaining the constituent probabilities, Dahl's reliance upon overt behavior leaves some theorists dissatisfied. March (1955, p. 433), for instance, makes the following observations: "Influence is frequently defined in terms of behavioral change over a given time interval and measured by overt motor or verbal activities. Such procedures have the major theoretical objection that they ignore changes in the individual's latent readiness to act. An adequate theory of influence must be more general than that implicit in a simple stimulus-response treatment." He points out further that an influence attempt may have delayed consequences, as Hovland and Weiss (1952) and Kelman and Hovland (1953) have shown in the "sleeper effect," or it may produce overt compliance while bringing about other latent changes so that the individual will respond in the future to influence attempts in a different manner.

Lewin (1951) conceives of influence as a change in the psychological forces operative on P that is brought about by an act of O. In this conception, a distinction is made between "component" forces and "combined" force, and behavior is coordinated to the latter. As Cartwright (1959, p. 195) puts it, "O may be able to activate a component force (i.e., have power over P) and yet not be able to change the direction of the combined force acting on P; forces activated by other agents (including P himself) may be of overwhelming magnitude. In every day terms, O may ask P to do something and P may experience a tendency to comply but not actually do so, In this case, we should say that O, by activating a component force, has influenced P in some way (producing conflict, wavering, guilt, or what not) but we could not say that O has 'controlled' P's behavior." Thus, Lewinian theory, like that of March, relates social influence directly to a readiness to act rather than to overt behavior. Both theories focus attention upon decision-making processes.

Any theory of influence stated in terms

of an individual's readiness to act must employ some conception of the psychological determinants of action. There are, of course, many such conceptions, and different theorists employ different ones. March (1955) proposes a formal model whose basic terms are evoking states, values, and connections among states. Cartwright (1959) makes use of the general theory of Lewin, whose primary concepts are valence, force, and cognitive structure. These two approaches have much in common with other theories of decision-making which employ such concepts as alternatives, expectations (subjective probability), and utility. Essentially the same phenomena are treated by Tannenbaum (1962) in terms of the event-structure conceptualization of F. H. Allport. It should be apparent that none of these theories is inconsistent with Dahl's formulation of influence as a modification in the probabilities of action; each attempts to specify the determinants of these probabilities.

Theorists who focus attention upon the readiness to act tend to conceive of the agent subjected to influence as an individual person, but there would seem to be no inherent reason for not treating aggregates in a similar manner. An executive committee, for example, makes decisions, and these decisions have identifiable determinants. An agent may exert influence on the committee's decisions by affecting these determinants. The analysis must be more complicated than in the case of an individual, since it involves both intrapersonal and interpersonal processes. For a discussion of the nature of group decision-making, see Cartwright and Zander (1960, Ch. 19).

A study reported by Dahl (1957) serves to illustrate the desirability, in assessing the influence over an aggregate, of examining its decision-making process. This study employed Dahl's conception of power in an effort to measure the relative influence of various senators over the United States Senate. The basic assumption was made that a senator's influence can be measured by the difference between the probability that the Senate will pass a bill he opposes and the

probability that it will pass a bill he supports. Voting records for bills dealing with foreign policy and taxation provided the data for the analysis. Since no evidence was available concerning actual influence processes, the roll-call position of each senator was taken to indicate his "support" or "opposition" with respect to each bill, and the probability of the bill's passage was estimated by the proportion of bills of each type actually passed. But this procedure results in an unfortunate consequence: a senator who successfully guesses the outcome of voting and sees to it that he is always on the winning side receives a score indicative of high influence. Dahl calls this "the problem of the chameleon." MacRae and Price (1959, p. 218), upon subjecting this procedure to further analysis, found additional difficulties and drew the general conclusion that "although the conceptualization of 'power' has been advanced [by Dahl], the operational definition of it has not yet been accomplished." It would seem that the measurement of influence requires more documentation than can be inferred from voting records.

A somewhat different measure of the power of an individual over the decisions of an aggregate has been proposed by Shapley and Shubik (1954). Their reasoning may be summarized as follows: Consider a committee composed of n numbers operating under some rule specifying the number of votes required for passage of a motion (e.g., a simple majority). Assume that the members vote for or against the motion in any possible sequence. Clearly, there are $n!$ such sequences. Each sequence may be regarded as a way of forming a winning coalition. A *minimal winning coalition* is defined as a coalition such that if one member is removed, it ceases to be a winning coalition. A *pivot* is the member who makes a minimal winning coalition in a sequence (i.e., the last member added to a coalition). Let s_i be the number of sequences in which individual i is a pivot. Then the *power index*, P_i, with respect to individual i, is defined by the following equation:

$$P_i = (s_i/n!)$$

Although this index is clearly defined and

has attractive formal properties, there are difficulties in relating it to substantive theories of influence. Thus, for example, Riker (1959), using this index, was unable to confirm a plausible hypothesis concerning the power of members of the French Assembly. A more direct attack on the processes of coalition formation appears to be required.

PROCESSES WITHIN P

Psychologists who have been interested in social influence have tended to focus attention on processes within the person subjected to influence. And when they refer to "types" of influence (or power), they base their distinctions upon properties displayed by these processes. One important consequence of this approach is the emphasis it places upon the part played by P in the O-P relationship; O influences P not merely because of properties possessed by O but also because, in some sense, P wants to be influenced. The classical psychological theories of social influence, which have been summarized by Allport (1954), employ such concepts as imitation, identification, and suggestion. In more recent years, these terms have been subjected to conceptual refinement and placed in the context of contemporary theories of individual behavior by such writers as Asch (1948), Bandura (1962), Bronfenbrenner (1960), Miller and Dollard (1941), Mowrer (1950), and Sears (1957). It will not be possible here to review all this literature, since its ramifications extend far into the fields of learning and personality development. Instead, we shall concentrate on those parts that deal explicitly with the social aspects of influence.

Much of this literature has been stimulated by research into the nature of the pressures people experience to make their perceptions, attitudes, and values agree with those of others. Festinger (1950) has proposed that there are two major sources of pressure toward uniformity among people. The first of these arises when opinions, attitudes, or beliefs have no firm anchorage in physical reality. Under these circumstances, a person seeks a basis for the subjective validity of his opinions, attitudes, and beliefs in their social reality, i.e., in the fact that they are shared by members of some reference group. As Festinger puts it, "An opinion, a belief, an attitude is 'correct,' 'valid,' and 'proper' to the extent that it is anchored in a group of people with similar beliefs, opinions, and attitudes." The second source of pressure toward uniformity arises when uniformity is desirable or necessary in order for a group to move toward some goal. Festinger postulates that pressures of this sort will be greater to the extent that members perceive that group movement will be facilitated by uniformity and to the extent that members are dependent upon the group in order to reach their own goals. This line of reasoning leads to the proposition that the power of a group over its members will increase with the attractiveness (cohesiveness) of the group. There is a great deal of experimental evidence (Back, 1951; Berkowitz, 1955; Converse & Campbell, 1960; Festinger, Schachter, & Back, 1950; Schachter, 1951; Schachter et al., 1951; Seashore, 1954) to support this conclusion.

Asch (1956) has shown (and many others have replicated the experiment) that when a subject finds himself disagreeing with the unanimous judgments of others concerning a simple and unambiguous stimulus, he may yield to the weight of majority opinion and distort his report of what he sees. In accounting for such pressures, Asch (1952) notes that the subject assumes that he shares the physical world with the others and that the others are normally reliable observers of this world. Thus, the subject is confronted with conflicting evidence and must choose whether to trust his own experience or the reports of others. It appears that people differ considerably in how they resolve this conflict. McClelland and his associates (1953) found, in analyzing data provided by Asch, that subjects who scored high on a test of need for achievement were much less likely to yield to the majority than those who scored low. McDavid (1959) reports that individuals who are characteristically more "content-oriented" than "source-oriented" are less likely to yield to influence. And Thibaut and Strickland (1956) find that subjects who are more oriented to cognitive clarity than toward maintaining group membership are less conforming to group pressures. On the basis of evidence of this sort Deutsch and Gerard (1955) advance a distinction between informational and normative social influence, and Bass (1960) distinguished between orientations directed toward task accomplishment and toward social interaction.

In a more detailed analysis of social influences on attitudes, Kelman (1958) has identified three forms of conformity. (a) *Compliance* occurs when P accepts influence because he hopes to achieve a favorable reaction from O. The satisfaction derived from compliance is due to the social effect of accepting influence. An example would be when P expresses agreement with an attitude of O because he expects thereby to obtain a reward from O. (b) *Identification* occurs when P accepts influence because he wants to establish or maintain "a satisfying self-defining relationship" to O. When P adopts a response through identification, he actually believes in it, but the specific content is more or less irrelevant. He adopts it because it is associated with the desired relationship, and the satisfaction is due to the act of conforming as such. Identification may be illustrated by the adolescent whose attitudes are modeled after those of a popular movie star. (c) *Internalization* occurs when P accepts influence because the content of the induced behavior is intrinsically rewarding. He may consider it useful for the solution of a problem or find it congenial to his needs. A pediatrician's influence on a mother's attitudes toward child-rearing practices exemplifies internalization.

Kelman postulates that each form of conformity on the part of P is evoked by a particular type of power possessed by O. When O's power is based on means control, conformity will take the form of compliance; when based on attractiveness, it will take the form of identification; and when based on credibility, it will take the form of internalization. He also postulates that each kind of conformity occurs under particular conditions. Thus, compliance tends to take place under conditions of surveillance by O; identification when P's relationship to O is salient; and internalization when the content of the attitude is relevant to P, regardless of surveillance or salience. In an experimental study of attitude change, Kelman employed these distinctions and hypotheses to predict relationships between the type of power employed by O and the conditions under which P will display conformity.

BASES OF POWER

A similar, but more comprehensive, conceptualization of social influence has been proposed by French and Raven (1959), who identify five "bases of power": reward, coercive, referent, legitimate, and expert. It should be noted that these are similar to some of the bases of power that O may possess (discussed above), but in this case the process of influence is viewed from P's perspective.

Reward power is based on P's belief that O has the ability to mediate rewards for him. Thus, if O is to use reward power to influence P, he must possess resources that P values, and P must believe that by conforming he will actually benefit from the resources in question. French and Raven postulate that the strength of reward power increases with the magnitude of the rewards involved and with P's subjective probability that O will mediate these rewards. They suggest that the range of reward power is limited to those matters with respect to which O can reward P for conforming. Since P's conformity is based on the prospect of being rewarded by O, reward power requires that O monitor P's behavior. Thus, any new state of P induced by a promise of reward will tend to persist only so long as P believes that O will observe it. The actual use of rewards tends to increase reward power by increasing the subjective probability attached to future promises. It also tends over time to increase the attraction of P toward O and, as we shall see, O's referent power over P.

Coercive power is based on P's belief that O has the ability to mediate punishments for him. The situation here is rather analogous to that of reward power; P must want to prevent some act of *O* and believe that through conforming he will do so. French and Raven propose that the strength of coercive power depends upon *P*'s estimate of the magnitude of the threatened punishment multiplied by the probability that he can avoid punishment if he conforms. The range of coercive power will be limited to those items of behavior which *P* believes *O* can monitor and for which *O* can administer punishments. If a new state of *P* is induced by the threat of punishment, it will not persist after the threat is withdrawn. Both the threat of punishment and its actual use reduce the attractiveness of *O* for *P* and thus *O*'s referent power over *P*. Experimental studies by French, Morrison, and Levinger (1960) and by Raven and French (1958b) lend support to this general conception of the nature of coercive power.

Referent power is based on *P*'s identification with *O*. By identification French and Raven mean "a feeling of oneness of *P* with *O*, or a desire for such an identity." If *O* is a person toward whom *P* is attracted, *P* will have a desire to become closely associated with *O*; if *O* is an attractive group, *P* will have a feeling of membership or a desire to join. The identification of *P* with *O* can be established or maintained if *P* behaves, believes, and perceives as *O* does. Accordingly, *O* has the ability to influence *P* even without an attempt to do so. A slightly different approach to the same phenomena is taken by Heider (1946; 1958), who proposes that if *P* has a positive affective attachment to *O*, "tendencies toward balance" will arise within *P* to make his relationships with a cognitive object *X* resemble those of *O*. And similar theories have been developed by Cartwright and Harary (1956), Newcomb (1953), and Osgood and Tannenbaum (1955).

The finding that the power of a group over its members increases with the attractiveness of the group might be interpreted as an instance of referent power. French and Raven argue, however, that such results may be due to the operation of any combination of referent, reward, or coercive power. If, for example, a member conforms to group pressures through fear of rejection for nonconformity, he is influenced by coercive power; if he conforms in order to obtain praise, the influence is accomplished through reward power; and if he conforms simply to be like those he admires, the influence is based on referent power. The detailed nature of conformity to the norms of attractive groups may be expected to depend upon the particular bases of power that it has for each member.

Little is known about the determinants of the range of referent power. It appears, however, that the range may be limited by *P*'s judgment as to what matters are relevant to the group. French and Raven suggest the additional hypothesis that the range of referent power is broader the more *P* is attracted to *O*. And they agree with Festinger (1953) in asserting that conformity, when based on referent power, does not depend upon the observability of the influenced behavior.

Zander and Curtis (1962), employing the distinction between coercive and referent power, make certain derivations concerning social influence on an individual's level of aspiration. They reason that a person must "internalize" the aspirations others set for him if he is to work toward their attainment and to evaluate his efforts in terms of them. They designed an experiment in which *P* was given standards for his performance either by agents who had coercive power or by ones who had referent power over him. On the assumption that coercive power does not produce internalization as much as does referent power, they successfully predicted a greater motivation to achieve these standards and a stronger feeling of failure when not achieving them under referent than under coercive power.

Ring and Kelley (1963) report a study of two methods of influence identified by McGregor (1948) as "augmentation" and "reduction." Under augmentation, *O* provides rewards in order to induce *P* to perform some desired behavior; under reduction, *O* provides punishments whenever *P* performs a behavior other than the desired one. Thus, in French and Raven's terms, augmentation employs reward power and reduction employs coercive power. Ring and Kelley reason, following Thibaut and Kelley (1959), that under augmentation P will tend to present evidence to O of his compliance (in order to receive his reward) whereas under reduction P may find it advantageous to conceal his behavior from O (since his best outcomes will be derived through either compliance or concealment). They argue further, just as French and Raven do, that when augmentation is used P will come to value O and hence come to adopt O's standards as his own, but when reduction is used P will not privately accept O's standards even though he may conform publicly. Thus, if O uses the reduction method in training P, it is likely that P will not accept O's standards even when he learns what these standards are. An experiment designed to test these derivations produced positive results: under conditions where P would be expected to disagree with O's standards there was a strong tendency for the reduction method to reduce the level of revealing one's opinions, learning the trainer's criterion, and accepting the trainer's criterion. Combining these findings with those of another experiment by Kelley and Ring (1961), the authors conclude that the best over-all strategy might be one that provides punishment for detected instances of concealment, only very mild punishment for revealed errors, and strong reward for revealed correct behavior.

It would appear that reward power corresponds most closely to Kelman's concept of compliance and that referent power is similar to identification. But since reward power (and augmentation) tends over time to generate referent power, it is sometimes difficult to distinguish between these two.

Legitimate power stems from internalized values in P which dictate that O has a right to influence P and that P has an obligation to accept this influence. In formal organizations legitimate power is usually attached to an office, and the occupant of the office then has the right to exert influence over a specified domain of people and range of activi-

ties. Clearly, the range of legitimate power may be broad or narrow, depending on a variety of circumstances. French and Raven hold that when O employs legitimate power he activates the values upon which it is based, with the result that the new state induced in P will be relatively stable and consistent across varying environment conditions. They also postulate that the attempted exercise of influence outside of the range of legitimate power decreases its strength. The concept of legitimate power, as employed by French and Raven, is closely related to Gilman's concept of authority (discussed above) and to other treatments of legitimate authority based on the writings of Weber (1947).

There are various ways in which a particular agent O may gain legitimate power over P. The election procedure is one means for designating the legitimate occupant of an office and for investing him with the legitimate power of that office. Raven and French (1958a) conducted an experiment in which two work situations were created, identical except that in one the supervisor was elected whereas in the other he assumed his position without benefit of election. They found that a standard influence attempt made by the supervisor was more effective when he had been elected than when he had not. It seems, in general, that whenever a person "accepts" the authority structure of an organization (e.g., by entering into an employment contract), he tends to award legitimate power to those designated as his supervisors.

Expert power is based on P's belief that O has some special knowledge or expertness. The term refers to essentially the same phenomenon labeled "informational power" by Deutsch and Gerard (1955). According to French and Raven, the strength of expert power varies with the extent of knowledge which P attributes to O within a given area, and its range is restricted to those cognitive systems with respect to which O is believed to have superior knowledge. Any attempt to exert influence outside of this range reduces this power by undermining P's confidence in O.

There are undoubtedly many reasons why P attributes expertness to a particular other person—O's experience, training, reputation, demonstrated ability, etc. Mausner (1954a) obtained more convergence in judgments toward partners who had previously demonstrated success in a related task than toward partners who had previously failed. Similar results were obtained by Kidd and Campbell (1955) when an entire group experienced success or failure. French and Snyder (1959) found that noncommissioned officers in the Air Force were able to exert more influence over the judgments of subordinates the more highly the subordinates rated them on general intelligence. That intelligence is not always an effective resource has been shown, however, by Lippitt and his coworkers (1952), who found intelligence to be significantly related to over-all attributed power in a middle-class summer camp but not in a lower-class camp.

In considering the effects of expert power it is necessary to distinguish between primary and secondary effects of influence. Thus, when O communicates an item of information to P, its primary effect is P's acceptance or rejection of the information. If he does accept it, then certain secondary effects may follow. One class of these secondary effects, especially interesting to psychologists, is brought about by a tendency toward consistency within cognitive systems. McGuire (1960), inspired by the Socratic method of teaching, has shown that a communication designed to modify P's belief in certain propositions may have a secondary effect upon his belief in conclusions that logically follow from the newly accepted premises. And there is considerable evidence for the general hypothesis (Rosenberg, 1960, p. 323) that "the production of inconsistency between the affective and cognitive portions of an attitude will culminate in a general attitude reorganization (through which the affective-cognitive inconsistency is reduced or eliminated) when (1) the inconsistency exceeds the individual's present tolerance limit and (2) the force producing it cannot be ignored or avoided." It is also clear that cognitive change may have secondary effects upon P's motivation by altering such things as subjective probability, perceived means-end relationships, and frames of reference.

MOTIVE BASE OF INFLUENCE

In the conception of power advanced by French and Raven, O can influence P because he can take some action that has significance for P's needs or values. P submits to O's wishes because he hopes thereby to gain a reward, avoid a punishment, become more like O, do what is right, or have a more effective relationship with his environment. This conception of power provides a link between processes of social influence and individual motivation. Cartwright (1959), who views influence as a change in the psychological forces on P brought about by an act of O, has developed this analysis a step further. If O wishes to induce a new state in P, he performs an act intended to convey a direction ("do this," "change in this way") and a motivational consequence ("you will be paid," "you will be wise," "you will be respected," "you will be loved," or "if not, you will be deprived of things valuable to you"). Thus, the force on P induced by O has a direction and a *motive base*. According to this view, every force operative on P has as its source of energy a motive base within P (i.e., his needs and values). Thus, an act of O can activate a force on P only if it "taps" a motive base of P. As an illustration, suppose that O wants to change P's attitudes toward some organizational policy and indicates that his approval of P will depend upon P's adopting the new attitude. If P desires O's approval, this act may tap P's motive base (need for approval) and thereby activate a force on P in the direction of adopting the new attitude.

This general conception, by relating social influence to the motivation of P, points to many important empirical questions about motivational determinants of influence. For example, one may ask, What determines the magnitude of a force set up by a given act of O? There is considerable evidence that the stronger the need aroused by an act of O, the greater will be the force set up by that act. In the illustration just cited, this would mean that O can activate a stronger force on P to change his attitude the

stronger P's need for social approval. Becker
and Carroll (1962) report results from a
study of conformity to majority opinion
which they interpret as indicating greater
conformity among subjects with a high need
for affiliation than among those with a
lower need. The various studies relating attraction to a group and conformity (cited
above) can be interpreted in a similar way.
Crowne and Strickland (1961), in an experiment on verbal conditioning, report
greater change in responses among subjects
with a high need for social approval than
among those with a low need. It is clear,
however, that the strength of P's need is
not the only determinant of the magnitude
of force set up by an act of O. Another determinant is P's belief concerning his chances
of actually satisfying the need through
compliance. In general, the strength of force
induced by an act of O will be greater the
greater P's subjective probability that compliance will result in a favorable outcome
with respect to a motive base. Thus, a critical condition is P's belief that O actually
controls an appropriate resource and that he
will use it in a manner favorable to P.

In discussing O's base of power, we employed two concepts: "properties" and "resources" controlled by O. We saw that a
given property of O, such as wealth or intelligence, may or may not serve as a resource, depending upon the needs of P. The
concept of motive base serves to sharpen the
distinction between these two concepts. Consider a supervisor, O, who attempts to maintain control over the behavior of his subordinates by manipulating economic rewards
for "good" performance. Suppose that two
of his subordinates, P_1 and P_2, differ in their
need for money (e.g., P_1 is the sole wage
earner in a large family, while P_2 works
mainly to keep busy). It is clear that O will
be able to induce stronger forces on P_1 than
on P_2. In general, any property controlled
by O will be a resource relative to P if and
only if it meshes with some motive base of
P. Thus, O's ability to influence P depends
not only on properties controlled by O but
also upon the motive bases of P.

The question naturally arises as to how
motive bases may be classified. What are
the needs and values that serve as motive
bases of influence? Unfortunately, there is
no universally accepted system of classification. In discussing the "base values" of influence, Lasswell and Kaplan (1950) distinguish two major types: welfare values or
"those whose possession to a certain degree
is a necessary condition for the maintenance
of the physical activity of the person" (p.
55), and deference values or "those that
consist in being taken into consideration (in
the acts of others and of the self" (p. 56)).
Specific welfare values are well-being,
wealth, skill, and enlightenment. The major
deference values are power, respect, recti-
tude, and affection. Lasswell and Kaplan
identify various "forms of influence" in
terms of these values.

Various psychologists have suggested lists
of human needs or motives. One of the
more important of these is that of Murray
(1938) who identifies twenty "manifest
needs." His "need for achievement" and
"need for affiliation" have been employed
in a few studies of social influence with
promising results. Although Murray's list
would seem to provide a rich source of
ideas for investigating various forms of influence, this possibility has not been systematically exploited.

In recent years several organization theorists, notably McGregor (1960) and Gilman
(1962), have made use of a theory of motivation advanced by Maslow (1954). As
interpreted by McGregor, this theory holds
that human needs are arranged in a hierarchy having two major properties: those at
a lower level claim priority over those at a
higher level, and when lower-level needs
are satisfied, behavior is guided by those at
the next higher level. The major types of
needs, ranging from the lowest level upward, are (a) physiological needs, (b)
safety needs, (c) social needs, (d) egoistic
needs, and (e) the need for self-fulfillment.
McGregor argues that in modern societies
the lower-level needs of most organizational
members are reasonably well satisfied and
that effective organizational control must
therefore be based on such higher-level
needs as those for acceptance, recognition,

status, and self-fulfillment. J. V. Clark (1961) and Porter (1961) have presented data which can be interpreted as consistent with this general conception. More research will be required, however, before these interesting theoretical ideas can be considered as having a firm empirical basis.

OPPOSITION AND RESISTANCE

In analyzing the processes in P that are activated by an influence attempt of O, it is important to recognize that O's action is designed to bring about a *change* in P. One should ask, therefore, what it is that maintains the pre-existing state of P. There are many possible anchorages of P's beliefs, attitudes, and behavior. The more important of these are P's own direct experience of reality, his needs and internalized values, his defense mechanisms, states previously induced by other agents, and his reference groups. It is because of such anchorages that influence attempts so often encounter opposition. Whenever O tries to change a firmly established state of P, his influence conflicts with the influence from these other sources, raising for P issues of personal integrity, self-interest, and group loyalty.

The strength of opposition to an influence attempt would seem to depend upon (a) the degree of incompatibility between the state to be induced and the pre-existing state and (b) the strength of anchorage of the pre-existing state. Thus, for example, when a person's judgment is at odds with those of others, he must choose whether to depend upon his own ability or upon that of others. And it has been repeatedly shown that the more self-confidence a person has, the less likely he is to yield to the judgments of others (Coleman, Blake, & Mouton, 1958; Goldberg & Lubin, 1958; Harvey & Rutherford, 1958; Hochbaum, 1954; Kelley & Lamb, 1957; Kelman, 1950; Mausner, 1954b; Mausner & Block, 1957; Samelson, 1957). Vaughan and Mangan (1963) report less conformity to group pressures when the subject matter is relevant to strong values of the person than when it is not. Katz (1960) has summarized a large body of literature documenting the various ways in which a person's attitudes serve important functions for him and has shown that

the conditions necessary for the modification of an attitude depend upon its motivational base. There is also evidence indicating that an attempt to change a person's attitudes so as to make them deviate from the norms of a reference group places him in conflict. Such an attempt is less effective the more salient, or important, this group is for him (Coch & French, 1948; Gerard, 1954; Kelley, 1955; Kelley & Volkhart, 1952).

In general, it appears that P's compliance with an influence attempt by O involves some cost to P, even though P may expect a net gain. For this reason, Harsanyi (1962) has proposed that in quantifying O's power over P these costs should be taken into consideration.

Cartwright (1959) and French and Raven (1959) have argued that a distinction should be made between "opposition to an influence attempt" and "resistance generated by an influence attempt." The difference in meaning may be illustrated by an example. Suppose a worker refuses to do a task assigned to him by a foreman. The reason for his refusal may be that he dislikes the task or that he believes the foreman has no right to make the assignment. In the former case, the influence attempt encounters *opposition* stemming from the worker's evaluation of the behavior to be induced, whereas in the latter the foreman's action, itself, activates *resistance*. Although any specific instance of influence is likely to contain both opposition and resistance, the conceptual distinction is useful. Opposition is the dominant process involved in the phenomena described in the preceding paragraphs, for in these cases the content of the advocated change is of primary significance. In resistance the content is quite secondary and may even be irrelevant. Resistance, in contrast to opposition, has a certain flavor of "irrationality," since it may lead a person to behave contrary to what seems to be his own best interests.

Much remains to be learned about the sources of resistance. An important begin-

ning toward understanding this problem
was made by Frank (1944), who attempted
to create resistance in the laboratory. He
found that "resistance to an activity is
readily aroused if doing it involves sub-
mitting to an arbitrary personal demand of
someone else, and is thereby equivalent to
a personal defeat," and that "resistance to
an activity is strongly inhibited by making
the activity appear to be implied by a previous agreement, so that refusal to do it
means breaking this agreement." Frank
concluded that resistance is likely to arise
whenever the recipient of an influence attempt believes that he is engaged in a
"clash of wills."

It appears, then, that resistance is stimulated when the influence process is "personalized." One of the first organizational
theorists to emphasize this point was Mary
Parker Follett (see Metcalf & Urwick,
1942), who argued that supervision should
be depersonalized—that organizational control should be exercised by "the authority
of the situation" rather than by personal
orders. She stated her case in the following
way: "One *person* should not give orders
to another *person*, but both should agree
to take their orders from the situation. If
orders are simply part of the situation, the
question of someone giving and someone
receiving does not come up. Both accept
the orders given by situation." Essentially
the same point was made in a more abstract
way by Lewin (1951) in his discussion of
"types" of forces. He proposed that *induced
forces* "correspond to the will of another"
and that *impersonal forces* have "the character of a matter-of-fact demand." He noted
that "it is of great importance . . . for the
atmosphere of the situation whether an
impersonal request or the personal will of
another individual is dominant" (p. 260).

More recently, the nature of resistance has
been investigated within the theoretical system advanced by French and Raven (1959).
These studies (French, Morrison, & Levinger, 1960; Raven & French, 1958a,
1958b; Zipf, 1960) lend support to the view
that resistance tends to arise when the basis

of power acquires negative value for *P*.
Thus, *P* is likely to resist an influence attempt from *O* whenever the attempt is
viewed by *P* as illegitimate, when it is coercive, or when *P* dislikes or mistrusts *O*.
Processes of this sort may underlie the
finding of Seashore (1954) that in a large
manufacturing firm the productivity standards of cohesive work groups were either
high or low, depending upon the degree to
which the group members felt "secure in
their relation to the company." Presumably
the company attempted to induce high
standards, but the efforts encountered
resistance when the company-employee relationship had a negative character. The generally "positive" effects produced by allow-
ing people to participate in organizational
decisions (Coch & French, 1948; Lewin,
1958; Morse & Reimer, 1956; Preston &
Heintz, 1949) may be accounted for in part
by the assumption that participation modifies the relationship between the individual
and the organization so as to reduce the
likelihood of resistance.

The view of resistance emerging from
these studies suggests that an individual's
ideology concerning power relationships,
by defining for him what is legitimate influence, will determine to some extent
whether he displays resistance in any particular situation. French, Israel, and Ås
(1960), upon repeating the Coch and
French experiment in a Norwegian factory,
found that workers' views of the legitimacy
and relevance of participation served to condition the effects of participation. Tannenbaum and Allport (1956) developed a test
of personality "trends" designed to indicate whether an individual's personality was
more "suited" to an autonomous or hierarchical form of organizational structure.
They found that those persons who were
placed in structures for which they were
"suited" were more satisfied, liked the structure better, and wanted it to continue longer
than did "unsuited" people. Thus, individuals predisposed to autonomy responded
more favorably to the structure granting
them more autonomy, whereas those predisposed to hierarchial relationships were
more comfortable in the hierarchical structure. It should be added, however, that on

the average the autonomous structure produced more satisfaction than the hierarchical one.

There is other evidence showing more
directly that certain personality traits pre-
dispose an individual to accept or resist
influence. In an experimental study of coercive influence, Zipf (1960) found that students with a stronger need for independence displayed more resistance. Vroom
(1960) reports that individuals with a
stronger need for independence or with
more "authoritarian" personalities responded less favorably to the opportunity to
participate in decisions. And several investigators (Berkowitz & Lundy, 1957; Blake &
Mouton, 1961; Mann, 1959; Wells, Weinert,
& Rubel, 1956) report a positive correlation between authoritarianism and yielding
to pressure, and between ascendance and
resisting social pressure. It should be noted,
however, that other studies (Bass, 1955;
Harvey, 1962; Steiner & Johnson, 1963) cast
some doubt on the generality of the relation
between conformity and authoritarianism.
Clearly, more research is needed to elucidate
the ways in which personality affects the
arousal of resistance to influence.

The analysis of social influence in terms
of psychological forces operating on P when
O attempts to bring about a change in P
makes it evident that influence can be accomplished by adding new forces on P,
changing the direction of pre-existing forces,
or reducing the magnitude of opposing
forces. Lewin (1951, Ch. 9) has proposed
that the first method is generally less desirable than the other two because it places
P on a higher level of conflict and thereby
engenders more emotional tension with its
symptoms of hostility, rigidity, regression,
and rebellion. If the act of O also generates
resisting forces, the conflict may be heightened further. Efforts to bring about a
change in P by the addition of new forces
(through the offer of rewards, the threat of
punishment, or the appeal to legitimacy)
leave the pre-existing opposing forces in
operation, and P must continue to cope with
these in some way even if he complies.
Festinger (1957) has argued that "forced
compliance" of this sort generates cognitive
dissonance, and he has documented some of
the behavioral manifestations of such dissonance (see also, Festinger & Aronson,
1960).

BY-PRODUCTS OF POWER AND
INFLUENCE

In the preceding sections, primary consideration was given to the conditions that
determine whether or not an influence
attempt will succeed. It was noted in the
course of this discussion that the exercise
of power may create important side effects.
Thus, for example, the use of punishment,
even though successful in producing overt
compliance, may generate hostility, and the
giving of rewards may heighten interpersonal attraction. In fact, any use of power
may be expected to have some lasting effects
on the relationship between O and P. If an
act of influence by O generates resistance
in P, this resistance may persist and color
future interactions between them. And if
an influence attempt results in public compliance but covert noncompliance, it requires surveillance by O, undermines P's
sense of personal integrity, and places strain
on the interpersonal relationship.

People with power in organizations are
often reluctant to recognize that the very
possession of power poses a threat to those
in its domain. The subordinate knows, however, that even a benevolent boss has the
potential to cause him harm, discomfort, or
inconvenience. For this reason, subordinates
tend to be especially sensitive to the behavior of their superiors. One manifestation of this sensitivity can be seen in the
communication that takes place between
levels in a formal organization. Mellinger
(1956) has analyzed some of the ways in
which status differences may distort a superior's knowledge of the attitudes of subordinates. The effects of power and status
differences have also been studied in experiments by A. R. Cohen (1958) and Kelley
(1951).

There are many ways in which people
attempt to reduce the threat inherent in
power. One of these is to restrict the range
of legitimate power or to limit the means

by which power can be exercised. Thus, subordinates in an organization may seek to reduce the rights, prerogatives, or sphere of latitude of superiors through legislation, collective bargaining, or other means for redefining the acts which a superior may legitimately perform. Another frequently employed technique is for the subordinate to avoid social situations in which the superior might perform a strong, disagreeable act. Yet another consists of attempting to influence O's motivation so that he is friendly, supportive, or cooperative with P. Forms of subordinate behavior characterized as "apple-polishing," obsequiousness, or ingratiating servility may be understood as attempts to influence O's use of power. These various devices for neutralizing the threat inherent in power have been documented by Zander, Cohen, and Stotland (1957) in their study of role relations among psychiatrists, clinical psychologists, and psychiatric social workers.

Another very important response to the threatening aspects of power is to seek "support" from others. This tendency may take the form of organizing coalitions or groups designed to counter the unwanted influence, or it may have a more purely "psychological" character. Needless to say, much of the impetus to the formation of unions arises from the needs experienced by employees to gain strength vis-à-vis management through united action. Less obvious, perhaps, is the tendency to create informal groups within a formal structure in order to protect members from what they consider to be undesirable influence. Coch and French (1948) found a sharp increase in the strength of informal group standards designed to restrict production when management imposed new production methods upon a group of workers. Burns (1955) has described in considerable detail some of the functions served by the "cliques" and "cabals" that spring up within formal organizations. On the basis of research conducted in a variety of settings (A. K. Cohen, 1955; Schrag, 1954; Yinger, 1960) it appears that when individuals find themselves power-

less, they tend to form groups whose norms and leaders represent values contrary to those of the dominant social system.

There is evidence that when a person is a member of a group he experiences more security the more cohesive the group. Seashore (1954) found that industrial workers in more cohesive work groups less often report that they feel "jumpy" or nervous than do those in less cohesive groups. Pepitone and Reichling (1955) and Wright (1943) found that members of more highly cohesive groups are more likely to express open hostility after being subjected to frustration or insults. An experiment by Stotland (1959) indicates that individuals gain support from even brief social interaction. In one of his experimental conditions pairs of subordinates were allowed to assemble for very brief meetings away from their supervisors. After these meetings they became more resistant and more aggressive toward the supervisor. In contrast, subordinates who were not given the opportunity to participate in such meetings had more favorable evaluations of the supervisor.

Because of the support people gain from group membership to resist influence, it is not uncommon for managers to try to minimize these group supports. As Schein (1960) observes, "A frequent practice in prisons, mental hospitals, educational workshops, reformatories, religious retreats, basic training centers, monasteries, nunneries, academies, and so on, is to isolate the inmates from their former social relationships. . . . There also tend to be systematic efforts on the part of the staff to destroy the internal organization of the inmate group. . . . At the same time, social alienation is fostered by the bestowing of special favors, rewards, or privileges for cooperation with the authorities" (p. 159). Schein notes, however, that in many voluntary change-producing institutions social organization is encouraged and considered to be supportive of change. Much remains to be learned about the ways in which groups affect the exercise of social control, but it is evident that their effects are important. Likert (1961) has argued that effective management consists in making constructive use of groups and that efforts to destroy or to fight them are bound to produce undesirable consequences.

There has been considerable speculation about the effects of an organization's enduring patterns of social power upon the personalities of the participants. Merton (1957), for example, has presented an extensive theoretical analysis of the Weberian concept of "bureaucratic personality." And the phrase "organization man" has been incorporated into the popular vocabulary. Satisfactory evidence concerning such effects, however, is extremely rare. It is difficult to obtain such evidence since major changes in personality ordinarily occur only over long periods of time or under extreme modifications of the environment. And correlational studies, in which personality traits are related to organizational variables, are difficult to interpret because the underlying causal network cannot be ascertained.

Some suggestive data have been provided by Tannenbaum (1957) from a field experiment in which two different programs of supervision were introduced into a clerical organization. In the autonomous program the amount of control exercised by lower-level employees was increased and that of the upper hierarchical levels decreased. In the hierarchical program the amount of control at lower levels was decreased and that at the upper levels increased. These two programs operated for over a year. Tests designated to measure 26 personality "trends" were administered near the beginning and at the end of the programs. The results provide some evidence to support the conclusion that over time there was a "movement of personality toward equilibrium with its environment."

The classical experiment by White and Lippitt (1960) on styles of leadership provides a more microscopic view of how social power may affect personality. Systematic comparisons were made of the behavior of boys in recreational clubs led by autocratic or democratic leaders. Although these clubs met only once a week for a few weeks, marked differences were observed in the occurrence of independent behavior, aggressiveness, and individuality. White and

Lippitt suggest that if these boys had been consistently subjected to one of these types of leadership over a long period of time, they would have internalized the values and personality predispositions associated with that form of social control.

Argyris (1957, p. 66) has developed the thesis that organizations that place emphasis on tight controls and directive leadership place employees in an environment where "(1) they are provided minimal control over their workaday world, (2) they are expected to be passive, dependent, and subordinate, (3) they are expected to have a short time perspective, (4) they are induced to perfect and value the frequent use of a few skin-surface shallow abilities and, (5) they are expected to produce under conditions leading to psychological failure." He concludes that these characteristics are incongruent with mature, healthy personalities and are "much more congruent with the needs of infants in our culture."

Gilman (1962, pp. 134–135) has replied to this argument by asserting that the existence of a clear, formal authority structure has certain positive values for the subordinate. "The very nature of the formal relationship through which (authority) is administered is basically ego-protecting. We should note that institutional authority is delegated to status positions rather than to individuals. The employee is not forced to admit that his boss is a better man than he is—merely that he occupies a superior status position." He adds, "There are many ways, within the bureaucratic structure of the modern enterprise, by which an individual may assert his individuality and retain his judgment of himself as competent." Gilman, however, makes the following concession: "There is, of course, a real danger in excessive use of institutional authority—which is quite different from what we might suppose. The authority of policy and procedure offers such comfortable support to the individual that he may be reluctant to venture away from it when he should. An unhealthy dependency relationship, from the point of view of the enterprise, may quite well develop when the employee is offered too much assistance through stipulations of procedure."

It should be evident from this brief summary of the literature that these important issues cannot be settled by theoretical speculation. The processes by which personality is formed are not well understood, and in view of our ignorance about these matters plausible arguments can be made for contradictory generalizations. Only carefully designed, longitudinal research can provide satisfactory knowledge about the effects of social power on personality.

SUMMARY

An adequate account of the influence of an agent specifies both the domain and range of influence; it identifies the agents affected as well as the "content" of influence. The domain has been conceived as consisting either of aggregates, such as committees, groups, and organizations, or of individuals. And the range has been described in terms of overt actions or covert properties. Some of the more interesting work has been concerned with the degree of congruence between overt and covert changes brought about by an act of influence.

Theorists who conceive of the agent subjected to influence as a person have tended to focus attention upon internal processes set up by an influence attempt. Thus, for example, Kelman has identified three forms of conformity, which he calls compliance, identification, and internalization. These three processes differ with respect to the antecedent conditions which activate them, the motivations served by them, and the resulting congruence between overt and covert manifestations of induced change.

French and Raven have illuminated certain aspects of the influence process through their designation of five bases of power. Their analysis is primarily concerned with interactions between P's motives and values,

on the one hand, and P's perceptions of his relationship with O, on the other. Thus, reward power is based on P's belief that O has the ability to mediate punishments. Both types of power activate compliance processes within P. Referent power is based on P's desire to be closely associated with O and set up processes of identification within P. Legitimate power is based on values held by P which dictate that O has a right to influence P. Since the use of legitimate power activates basic values accepted by P and related induced changes to these values, the effects of legitimate influence tend to be stable and enduring. Expert power is based on P's belief that O has knowledge or expertness of relevance to P's interests. The use of this type of power sets up in P processes of internalization and has a variety of secondary effects upon P's motivation, cognition, and action. For each type of power, French and Raven present hypotheses concerning the determinants of its range.

The significance of P's motives and values for the exercise of influence is further elucidated by means of the concept of motive base. This concept provides a thoretical linkage between properties controlled by O and influence exerted on P. Thus, a property of O becomes a resource that can serve as a base of influence only when it meshes properly with a motive base of P. Consequently, O's ability to influence P depends not only on properties controlled by O but also upon the motive bases of P. A satisfactory classification of motive bases remains to be established, but existing schemes have led to suggestive hypotheses about the nature of feasible bases of control in organizations.

In analyzing the processes in P that are activated by an influence attempt of O, it is important to recognize that P's pre-existing state has a good reason for being. If P is a person, his beliefs, attitudes, and behavior are grounded in a cognitive, motivational, and social structure. If an influence attempt runs counter to this anchorage, it encounters opposition. The strength of opposition depends upon the degree of incompatibility between the state to be induced and the pre-existing state and upon the strength of anchorage of the pre-existing state. The effective strength of an influence attempt will be reduced by such opposition. And it will be further reduced if the attempt, itself, is of such a nature as to generate resistance. Research indicates that resistance is more likely to occur when O's attempt is "personalized," arousing a "clash of wills," or when it makes use of a base that has acquired negative value for P. There is also evidence that a person's tendency to resist an act of influence is conditioned by his ideology and personality.

The central problem considered in most analyses of social influence has been to identify the conditions determining the success of influence attempts. What are the bases and means of influence? What are the sources of opposition or resistance? How can organizational procedures be designed so as to achieve an adequate degree of control? Efforts to answer questions of this sort have contributed significantly to our understanding of the nature of social influence. But there is danger in focusing too sharply on the criterion of effectiveness, for the exercise of influence has by-products. The few investigations that have examined these "unintended effects" suggest that they may be quite important. It is evident, for example, that the mere existence of power may, under certain conditions at least, pose a threat to those in its domain, producing side effects on the flow of information, the character of social interaction, and the formation of groups. And there is reason to believe that enduring systems of social control may have profound effects upon the personalities of these participating in the system. A fully satisfactory theory of influence must account for all of its effects.

CONCLUDING OBSERVATIONS

At the beginning of this chapter we expressed misgivings about the possibility of providing a comprehensive treatment of so vast a topic as "influence, leadership, and control." The reasons for uneasiness are now painfully apparent. In an effort to find a secure theoretical foundation on which to build, we have concentrated our attention primarily on the closely related topics of influence and power, believing that an under-

standing of these processes is propaedeutic to a systematic treatment of leadership and organizational control. But even within these limitations we have been forced to cope with an array of publications which in no real sense constitute a coherent literature. Our study of influence has led us to consider findings from research on such apparently diverse topics as persuasion, conformity, supervision, organizational decision-making, coalition formation, and the exercise of economic, political, or military power. One may still ask, with good reason, whether the single concept of social influence can possibly serve to bring about a theoretical integration of so heterogeneous an array of phenomena. An answer on the basis of the present review will depend largely upon one's aspirations, for we have found both promising developments and difficult problems.

One thing is clear. The accomplishment of a genuinely comprehensive theory of social influence will require an acquaintance with research conducted in all the social science disciplines. For this reason, we have tried in this chapter to take a broad perspective and to locate potentially integrative findings in a variety of fields. We have brought together in one place materials not normally considered by any one theorist. But only a first step has been taken, for it has been necessary to ignore many important contributions. From this limited effort it is clear that the task of integration will not be easy, since each body of literature has developed its own vocabulary and mode of conceptual analysis. Nevertheless, the task does not appear to be impossible. We have detected the outlines of what may become a general conceptualization of influence.

Three major topical headings have served to organize the material of this chapter: the agent O, who exerts influence, the methods of exerting influence, and the agent P, subjected to influence. This is a convenient system of classification, since so much of the existing literature concentrates upon one or another of these topics. It is not, however, a fully satisfactory one. Breaking down the process of influence in this way does violence to its essential nature, for above all influence is a social relationship. Influence cannot be properly understood by treating the properties of O or of P in isolation, and the methods of influencing make little sense without a specification of the ways they relate to the properties of both O and P. Theorists who have attempted to formalize the nature of social power now agree that power should not be conceived as a "simple property" of O but as a relationship between O and P.

In the course of this chapter we have encountered many manifestations of the relational nature of influence. The concept of "base of power," for example, was first introduced as an attribute of O, something O could use to exert influence. It quickly became apparent, however, that a property controlled by O serves as a base of power relative to P only if it meshes, in some sense, with a motive base of P. Thus, one cannot predict O's influence merely from a knowledge of the properties controlled by O. For the same reason, one cannot predict that P will be influenced by a particular agent O simply by knowing P's needs or personality traits.

The concept of "domain of influence" to cite another example, is also essentially relational. In comparing the influence of two agents, it is necessary to specify the set of agents over whom each exerts influence. Other things being equal, we would say that O_1 has more influence than O_2 if his influence extends over a wider domain. It should be noted, in passing, that the identification of a domain is always relative to some "content of influence." Thus, the concepts of domain and range of influence must be considered together.

As investigators come to recognize more fully the relational nature of influence, their formulation of research problems should change somewhat. There has been a tendency to focus attention either on O or on P at the expense of the other. Thus, for example, we tend to have one literature on leaders and one on followers rather than a single literature on the leader-follower relationship. Although it is true that much can be learned simply by considering the two literatures together, much is lost by not conceiving the central problem of research as that of understanding the relationship itself. Fortunately, there are trends in this direction, as witnessed by several studies reported in this chapter which do not fit naturally under any one of its major headings.

Research on the relational aspects of influence will be facilitated by a better understanding of the formal properties of the influence relation. March (1955) and Simon (1957) have provided useful discussions of the similarities and differences between the influence relation and the causal relation. Cartwright (1959) has proposed that certain aspects of social power may be treated as a dyadic relation on a set of agents and that the mathematical theory of directed graphs can therefore be employed to represent the power structure of an organization. And Lasswell and Kaplan (1950) have argued that influence should be viewed as a triadic relation—O over P with respect to item x. However, the formal implications of treating influence in this way have not yet been systematically explored. The time seems ripe for the construction of mathematical models of the influence relation. Those constructed by French (1956) and Harary (1959) suggest one avenue of approach.

In conclusion, it should be noted that we have found points of contact among the many different treatments of social influence. The various literatures reviewed here do seem to have much to do with one another, more than the authors appear to recognize. It is to be hoped that in the coming years integrative theories of influence will be formulated to encompass the entire field. Since influence is such a fundamental aspect of all human interaction, a general theory of influence should contribute to all the social sciences. Its construction will certainly draw upon them all. Organization theory, by its very nature, must be interdisciplinary. Perhaps it is here that a really general theory of human behavior will first arise.

Adams, J. S., & Romney, A. K. A functional analysis of authority. *Psychol. Rev.*, 1959, 66, 234–251.

Allport, G. W. The historical background of modern social psychology. In G. Lindzey (Ed.), *Handbook of social psychology.* Cambridge: Addison-Wesley, 1954. Pp. 3–56.

Argyris, C. *Personality and organization.* New York: Harper, 1957.

Asch, S. E. The doctrine of suggestion, prestige, and imitation in social psychology. *Psychol. Rev.*, 1948, 55, 250–277.

Asch, S. E. *Social psychology.* New York: Prentice-Hall, 1952.

Asch, S. E. Studies of independence and submission to group pressure. I. A minority of one against a unanimous majority. *Psychol. Monogr.*, 1956, 70, No. 9 (Whole No. 416).

Back, K. Influence through social communication. *J. abnorm. soc. Psychol.*, 1951, 46, 9–23.

Bandura, A. Social learning through imitation. In M. R. Jones (Ed.), *Nebraska symposium on motivation, 1962.* Lincoln: Univer. of Nebraska Press, 1962. Pp. 211–268.

Barker, R. G. Ecology and motivation. In M. R. Jones (Ed.), *Nebraska symposium on motivation, 1960.* Lincoln: Univer. of Nebraska Press, 1960.

Barker, R. G., & Wright, H. F. *Midwest and its children.* Evanston, Ill.: Row, Peterson, 1955.

Barnard, C. I. *The functions of the executive.* Cambridge: Harvard Univer. Press, 1938.

Bass, B. M. Authoritarianism or acquiescence. *J. abnorm. soc. Psychol.*, 1955, 51, 616–623.

Bass, B. M. *Leadership, psychology, and organizational behavior.* New York: Harper, 1960.

Becker, S., & Carroll, Jean. Ordinal position and conformity. *J. abnorm. soc. Psychol.*, 1962, 65, 129–131.

Bennis, W. G., Berkowitz, N., Affinito, M., & Malone, M. Authority, power, and the ability to influence. *Hum. Relat.*, 1958, 11, 143–155.

Berkowitz, L. Group standards, cohesiveness, and productivity. *Hum. Relat.*, 1955, 7, 509–519.

Berkowitz, L., & Lundy, R. M. Personality characteristics related to susceptibility to influence by peers or authority figures. *J. Pers.*, 1957, 25, 306–316.

Berle, A. A., & Means, G. C. *The modern corporation and private property.* New York: Macmillan, 1933.

Bierstedt, R. An analysis of social power. *Amer. sociol. Rev.*, 1950, 15, 730–736.

Blake, R. R., & Mouton, Jane S. The experimental investigation of interpersonal influence. In A. D. Biderman & H. Zimmer (Eds.), *The manipulation of human behavior.* New York: Wiley, 1961. Pp. 216–276.

Bronfenbrenner, U. Freudian theories of identification and their derivatives. *Child Develpm.*, 1960, 31, 15–40.

Burns, T. The reference of conduct in small groups: cliques and cabals in occupational milieux. *Hum. Relat.*, 1955, 8, 467–486.

Cartwright, D. Achieving change in people: some applications of group dynamics theory. *Hum. Relat.*, 1951, 4, 381–392.

Cartwright, D. A field theoretical conception of power. In D. Cartwright (Ed.), *Studies in social power.* Ann Arbor: Univer. of Michigan, Institute for Social Research, 1959.

Cartwright, D., & Harary, F. Structural balance: a generalization of Heider's theory. *Psychol. Rev.*, 1956, 63, 277–293.

Cartwright, D., & Zander, A. (Eds.) *Group dynamics: research and theory.* (2nd ed.) Evanston, Ill.: Row, Peterson, 1960.

Clark, J. V. Motivation in work groups: a tentative view. *Hum. Organ.*, 1961, 19, 199–211.

Clark, K. B. Desegregation: an appraisal of the evidence. *J. soc. Issues*, 1953, 9 (4), 2–76.

Coch, L., & French, J. R. P., Jr. Overcoming resistance to change. *Hum. Relat.*, 1948, 1, 512–532.

Cohen, A. K. *Delinquent boys.* Glencoe, Ill.: Free Press, 1955.

Cohen, A. R. Upward communication in experimentally created hierarchies. *Hum. Relat.*, 1958, 11, 41–53.

Coleman, Janet F., Blake, R. R., & Mouton, Jane S. Task difficulty and conformity pressures. *J. abnorm. soc. Psychol.*, 1958, 57, 120–122.

Converse, P., & Campbell, A. Political standards in secondary groups. In D. Cartwright & A. Zander (Eds.), *Group dynamics: research and theory.* (2nd ed.) Evanston, Ill.: Row, Peterson, 1960. Pp. 300–318.

Crowne, D. P., & Strickland, Bonnie R. The conditioning of verbal behavior as a function of the need for social approval. *J. abnorm. soc. Psychol.*, 1961, 63, 395–401.

Cyert, R. M., & March, J. G. A behavioral theory of organizational objectives. In M. Haire (Ed.), *Modern organization theory.* New York: Wiley, 1959. Pp. 76–90.

Dahl, R. A. The concept of power. *Behav. Sci.*, 1957, 2, 201–218.

Dahl, R. A. A critique of the ruling elite model. *Amer. pol. sci. Rev.*, 1958, 52, 463–469.

Deutsch, M., & Collins, M. E. *Interracial housing: a psychological evaluation of a social experiment.* Minneapolis: Univer. of Minnesota Press, 1951.

Deutsch, M., & Gerard, H. B. A study of normative and informational influence upon individual judgment. *J. abnorm. soc. Psychol.*, 1955, 51, 629–636.

Dittes, J. E., & Kelley, H. H. Effects of different conditions of acceptance upon conformity to group norms. *J. abnorm. soc. Psychol.*, 1956, 53, 100–107.

Festinger, L. Informal social communication. *Psychol. Rev.*, 1950, 57, 271–282.

Festinger, L. An analysis of complaint behavior. In M. Sherif & M. O. Wilson (Eds.), *Group relations at the crossroads*. New York: Harper, 1953. Pp. 232–256.

Festinger, L. *A theory of cognitive dissonance*. Evanston, Ill.: Row, Peterson, 1957.

Festinger, L., & Aronson, E. The arousal and reduction of dissonance in social contexts. In D. Cartwright & A. Zander (Eds.), *Group dynamics: research and theory*. (2nd ed.) Evanston, Ill.: Row, Peterson, 1960. Pp. 214–231.

Festinger, L., Schachter, S., & Back, K. *Social pressures in informal groups*. New York: Harper, 1950.

Frank, J. D. Experimental studies of personal pressure and resistance: I. experimental production of resistance. *J. gen. Psychol.*, 1944, 30, 23–41.

French, J. R. P., Jr. A formal theory of social power. *Psychol. Rev.*, 1956, 63, 181–194.

French, J. R. P., Jr. Israel, J., & Ås, D. An experiment on participation in a Norwegian factory: interpersonal dimensions of decision-making. *Hum. Relat.*, 1960, 13, 3–19.

French, J. R. P., Jr., Morrison, H. W., & Levinger, G. Coercive power and forces affecting conformity. *J. abnorm. soc. Psychol.*, 1960, 61, 93–101.

French, J. R. P., Jr., & Raven, B. The bases of social power. In D. Cartwright (Ed.), *Studies in social power*. Ann Arbor: Univer. of Michigan, Institute for Social Research, 1959. Pp. 150–167.

French, J. R. P., Jr., & Snyder, R. Leadership and interpersonal power. In D. Cartwright (Ed.), *Studies in social power*. Ann Arbor: Univer. of Michigan, Institute for Social Research, 1959. Pp. 118–149.

Gerard, H. B. The anchorage of opinions in face-to-face groups. *Hum. Relat.*, 1954, 6, 249–271.

Gilman, G. An inquiry into the nature and use of authority. In M. Haire (Ed.), *Organization theory in industrial practice*. New York: Wiley, 1962. Pp. 105–142.

Gold, M. Power in the classroom. *Sociometry*, 1958, 21, 50–60.

Goldberg, S. C., & Lubin, A. Influence as a function of perceived judgment error. *Hum. Relat.*, 1958, 11, 275–281.

Gouldner, A. W. The norm of reciprocity: a preliminary statement. *Amer. social. Rev.*, 1960, 25, 161–178.

Greer, F. L. Leader indulgence and group performance. *Psychol. Monogr.*, 1961, 75, No. 12 (Whole No. 516).

Gump, P. V., & Sutton-Smith, B. Activity-setting and social interaction: a field study. *Amer. J. Orthopsychiat.*, 1955, 25, 755–760.

Haire, M. Industrial social psychology. In G. Lindzey (Ed.), *Handbook of social psychology*. Cambridge: Addison-Wesley, 1954. Pp. 1104–1123.

Harary, F. A criterion for unanimity in French's theory of social power. In D. Cartwright (Ed.), *Studies in social power*. Ann Arbor: Univer. of Michigan, Institute for Social Research, 1959. Pp. 168–182.

Harbrecht, P. P. *Pension funds and economic power*. New York: Twentieth Century Fund, 1959.

Harsanyi, J. C. Measurement of social power, opportunity costs, and the theory of two-person bargaining games. *Behav. Sci.*, 1962, 7, 67–80.

Harvey, O. J. Personality factors in resolution of conceptual incongruities. *Sociometry*, 1962, 25, 336–352.

Harvey, O. J., & Consalvi, C. Status and conformity to pressures in informal groups. *J. abnorm. soc. Psychol.*, 1960, 60, 182–187.

Harvey, O. J., & Rutherford, Jeanne. Gradual and absolute approaches to attitude change. *Sociometry*, 1958, 21, 61–68.

Heider, F. Attitudes and cognitive organization. *J. Psychol.*, 1946, 21, 107–112.

Heider, F. *The psychology of interpersonal relations*. New York: Wiley, 1958.

Hemphill, J. K. Why people attempt to lead. In L. Petrullo & B. Bass (Eds.), *Leadership and interpersonal behavior*. New York: Holt, Rinehart, & Winston, 1961. Pp. 201–215.

Hemphill, J. K., Pepinsky, Pauline N., Kaufman, A. E., & Lipsetz, M. E. Effects of task motivation and expectancy of accomplishment upon attempts to lead. *Psychol. Monogr.*, 1957, 71, No. 22 (Whole No. 451).

Hobbes, T. *Leviathan*. (Reprint of 1st [1651] ed.) Cambridge: Cambridge Univer. Press, 1904.

Hochbaum, G. M. The relation between group members' self-confidence and their reactions to group pressures to uniformity. *Amer. sociol. Rev.*, 1954, 19, 678–687.

Hoffman, Lois W. Effects of the employment of mothers on parental power relations and the division of household tasks. *Marr. & fam. Living*, 1960, 22, 27–35.

Hollander, E. P. Conformity, status, and idiosyncrasy credit. *Psychol. Rev.*, 1958, 65, 117–127.

Hollander, E. P. Emergent leadership and social influence. In L. Petrullo & B. M. Bass (Eds.), *Leadership and interpersonal behavior. New York: Holt, Rinehart, & Winston, 1961. Pp. 30–47. (a)

Hollander, E. P. Some effects of perceived status on responses to innovative behavior. *J. abnorm. soc. Psychol.*, 1961, 63, 247–250. (b)

Homans, G. C. *The human group.* New York: Harcourt, Brace, 1950.

Homans, G. C. Social behavior as exchange. *Amer. J. Sociol.*, 1958, 63, 597–606.

Hovland, C. I. Effects of the mass media of communication. In G. Lindzey (Ed.), *Handbook of social psychology.* Cambridge: Addison-Wesley, 1954. Pp. 1062–1103.

Hovland, C. I., & Weiss, W. The influence of source credibility on communication effectiveness. *Publ. opin. Quart.*, 1952, 15, 635–650.

Hurwitz, J. I., Zander, A. F., & Hymovitch, B. Some effects of power on the relations among group members. In D. Cartwright & A. Zander (Eds.), *Group dynamics: research and theory.* Evanston, Ill.: Row, Peterson, 1953. Pp. 483–492.

Kahn, R. L., & Katz, D. Leadership practices in relation to productivity and morale. In D. Cartwright & A. Zander (Eds.), *Group dynamics: research and theory* (2nd ed.). Evanston, Ill.: Row, Peterson, 1960. Pp. 254–270.

Katz, D. The functional approach to the study of attitudes. *Publ. opin. Quart.*, 1960, 24, 163–204.

Katz, E., & Lazarsfeld, P. F. *Personal influence.* Glencoe, Ill.: Free Press, 1955.

Katz, E., Levin, M. L., & Hamilton, H. Traditions of research on the diffusion of innovation. *Amer. sociol. Rev.*, 1963, 28, 237–252.

Kelley, H. H. Communication in experimentally created hierarchies. *Hum. Relat.*, 1951, 4, 39–56.

Kelley, H. H. Salience of membership and resistance to change of group-anchored attitudes. *Hum. Relat.*, 1955, 8, 275–290.

Kelley, H. H., & Lamb, T. W. Certainty of judgment and resistance to social influence. *J. abnorm. soc. Psychol.*, 1957, 55, 137–139.

Kelley, H. H., & Ring, K. Some effects of "suspicious" versus "trusting" training schedules. *J. abnorm. soc. Psychol.*, 1961, 63, 294–301.

Kelley, H. H., & Shapiro, M. M. An experiment on conformity to group norms where conformity is detrimental to group achievement. *Amer. sociol. Rev.*, 1954, 19, 667–677.

Kelley, H. H., & Volkhart, E. H. The resistance to change of group-anchored attitudes. *Amer. sociol. Rev.*, 1952, 17, 453–465.

Kelman, H. C. Effects of success and failure on "suggestibility" in the autokinetic situation. *J. abnorm. soc. Psychol.*, 1950, 45, 267–295.

Kelman, H. C. Compliance, identification, and internalization: three processes of attitude change. *J. confl. Resol.*, 1958, 2, 51–60.

Kelman, H. C., & Hovland, C. I. "Reinstatement" of the communicator in delayed measurement of opinion change. *J. abnorm. soc. Psychol.*, 1953, 48, 327–335.

Kidd, J. S., & Campbell, D. T. Conformity to groups as a function of group success. *J. abnorm. soc. Psychol.*, 1955, 51, 390–393.

Klapper, J. T. *The effect of mass communication.* Glencoe, Ill.: Free Press, 1960.

Kounin, J. S., Gump, P. V., & Ryan, J. J., III. Explorations in classroom management. *J. teacher Ed.*, 1961, 12, 235–246.

Lasswell, H. D., & Kaplan, A. *Power and society.* New Haven: Yale Univer. Press, 1950.

Levinger, G. The development of perceptions and behavior in newly formed social power relationships. In D. Cartwright (Ed.), *Studies in social power.* Ann Arbor: Univer. of Michigan, Institute for Social Research, 1959. Pp. 83–98.

Lewin, K. *Field theory in social science.* New York: Harper, 1951.

Lewin, K. Group decision and social change. In Eleanor E. Maccoby, T. M. Newcomb, & E. L. Hartley (Eds.), *Readings in social psychology.* New York: Holt, 1958. Pp. 197–211.

Lieberman, S. The effects of changes in roles on the attitudes of role occupants. *Hum. Relat.*, 1956, 9, 385–402.

Likert, R. *New patterns of management.* New York: McGraw-Hill, 1961.

Lippitt, R., Polansky, N., Redl, F., & Rosen, S. The dynamics of power. *Hum. Relat.*, 1952, 5, 37–64.

Macaulay, S. Noncontractual relations in business. *Amer. sociol. Rev.*, 1963, 28, 55–67.

McClelland, D. C., Atkinson, J. W., Clark, R. A., & Lowell, E. L. *The achievement motive.* New York: Appleton-Century-Crofts, 1953.

McDavid, J. W. Personality and situational determinants of conformity. *J. abnorm. soc. Psychol.*, 1959, 58, 241–246.

McGregor, D. M. The staff function in human relations. *J. soc. Issues*, 1948, 4 (3), 5–22.

McGregor, D. M. *The human side of enterprise.* New York: McGraw-Hill, 1960.

McGuire, W. J. Cognitive consistency and attitude change. *J. abnorm. soc. Psychol.*, 1960, 60, 345–354.

MacRae, D., Jr., & Price, H. D. Scale positions and "power" in the Senate. *Behav. Sci.*, 1959, 4, 212–218.

Mann, R. D. A review of the relationships between personality and performance in small groups. *Psychol. Bull.*, 1959, 56, 241–270.

March, J. G. Husband-wife interaction over political issues. *Publ. opin. Quart.*, 1953, 17, 461–470.

March, J. G. An introduction to the theory and measurement of influence. *Amer. pol. sci. Rev.*, 1955, 49, 431–451.

March, J. G. Measurement concepts in the theory of influence. *J. Pol.*, 1957, 19, 202–226.

March, J. G., & Simon, H. A. *Organizations.* New York: Wiley, 1958.

Maslow, A. *Motivation and personality.* New York: Harper, 1954.

Mausner, B. The effect of partner's success in a relevant task on the interaction of observer pairs. *J. abnorm. soc. Psychol.*, 1954, 49, 557–560. (a)

Mausner, B. The effect of prior reinforcement on the interaction of observer pairs. *J. abnorm. soc. Psychol.*, 1954, 49, 65–68. (b)

Mausner, B., & Bloch, Barbara L. A study of the additivity of variables affecting social interaction. *J. abnorm. soc. Psychol.*, 1957, 54, 250–256.

Mellinger, G. D. Interpersonal trust as a factor in communication. *J. abnorm. soc. Psychol.*, 1956, 52, 304–309.

Menzel, H. Public and private conformity under different conditions of acceptance in the group. *J. abnorm. soc. Psychol.*, 1957, 55, 398–402.

Merton, R. K. *Social theory and social structure.* (Rev. ed.) Glencoe, Ill.: Free Press, 1957.

Metcalf, H. C., & Urwick, L. (Eds.) *Dynamic administration: the collected works of Mary Parker Follett.* New York: Harper, 1942.

Miller, N. E., & Dollard, J. *Social learning and imitation.* New Haven: Yale Univer. Press, 1941.

Morse, Nancy, & Reimer, E. The experimental change of a major organizational variable. *J. abnorm. soc. Psychol.*, 1956, 52, 120–129.

Mowrer, O. H. *Learning theory and personality dynamics.* New York: Ronald, 1950.

Murray, H. A. *Explorations in personality.* New York: Oxford Univer. Press, 1938.

Newcomb, T. M. An approach to the study of communicative acts. *Psychol. Rev.*, 1953, 60, 393–404.

Nietzsche, F. *Werke.* Vol. 17. *Der Wille zur Macht.* Leipzig: Kröner, 1912.

Osgood, C. E., & Tannenbaum, P. H. The principle of congruity in the prediction of attitude change. *Psychol. Rev.*, 1955, 62, 42–55.

Pepitone, A., & Reichling, G. Group cohesiveness and the expression of hostility. *Hum. Relat.*, 1955, 8, 327–337.

Porter, L. W. A study of perceived need satisfactions in bottom and middle management jobs. *J. appl. Psychol.*, 1961, 45, 1–10.

Preston, M. G., & Heintz, R. K. Effects of participatory vs. supervisory leadership on group judgment. *J. abnorm. soc. Psychol.*, 1949, 44, 345–355.

Raven, B. H., & French, J. R. P., Jr. Group support, legitimate power, and social influence. *J. Pers.*, 1958, 26, 400–409. (a)

Raven, B. H., & French, J. R. P., Jr. Legitimate power, coercive power, and observability in social influence. *Sociometry*, 1958, 21, 83–97. (b)

Riker, W. H. A test of the adequacy of the power index. *Behav. Sci.*, 1959, 4, 120–131.

Ring, K., & Kelley, H. H. A comparison of augmentation and reduction as modes of influence. *J. abnorm. soc. Psychol.*, 1963, 66, 95–102.

Roethlisberger, F. J., & Dickson, W. J. *Management and the worker.* Cambridge: Harvard Univer. Press, 1939.

Rosenberg, M. J. A structural theory of attitude dynamics. *Publ. opin. Quart.*, 1960, 24, 319–340.

Rosenberg, M., & Pearlin, L. I. Power-orientations in the mental hospital. *Hum. Relat.*, 1962, 335–350.

Russell, B. *Power: a new social analysis.* London: Allen & Unwin, 1938.

Samelson, F. Conforming behavior under two conditions of conflict in the cognitive field. *J. abnorm. soc. Psychol.*, 1957, 55, 181–187.

Schachter, S. Deviation, rejection, and communication. *J. abnorm. soc. Psychol.*, 1951, 46, 190–207.

Schachter, S., Ellertson, N., McBride, Dorothy, & Gregory, Doris. An experimental study of cohesiveness and productivity. *Hum. Relat.*, 1951, 4, 229–238.

Schein, E. H. Interpersonal communication, group solidarity, and social influence, *Sociometry*, 1960, 23, 148–161.

Schrag, C. Leadership among prison inmates. *Amer. sociol. Rev.*, 1954, 19, 37–42.

Schulze, R. O. The role of economic dominants in community power structure. *Amer. sociol. Rev.*, 1958, 23, 3–9.

Sears, R. R. Identification as a form of behavioral development. In D. B. Harris (Ed.), *The concept of development.* Minneapolis: Univer. of Minnesota Press, 1957. Pp. 149–161.

Seashore, S. E. *Group cohesiveness in the industrial work group.* Ann Arbor: Univer. of Michigan, Institute for Social Research, 1954.

Shapley, L. S., & Shubik, M. A method for evaluating the distribution of power in a committee system. *Amer. pol. sci. Rev.*, 1954, 48, 787–792.

Sherif, M., Harvey, O. J., White, B. J., Hood, W. R., & Sherif, Carolyn W. *Intergroup conflict and cooperation.* Norman, Okla.: Institute of Group Relations, 1961.

Simon, H. A. *Models of man.* New York: Wiley, 1957.

Smith, C. G., & Tannenbaum, A. S. Organizational control structure: A comparative analysis. *Hum. Relat.*, 1963, 16, 299–316.

Star, Shirley A., Williams, R. M., Jr., & Stouffer, S. A. Negro infantry platoons in white companies. In Eleanor E. Maccoby, T. M. Newcomb, & E. L. Hartley (Eds.), *Readings in social psychology.* New York: Holt, 1958.

Steiner, I. D., & Johnson, H. H. Authoritarianism and conformity. *Sociometry*, 1963, 26, 21–34.

Stogdill, R. M. *Individual behavior and group achievement.* New York: Oxford Univer. Press, 1959.

Stotland, E. Peer groups and reactions to power figures. In D. Cartwright (Ed.), *Studies in social power.* Ann Arbor: Univer. of Michigan, Institute for Social Research, 1959. Pp. 53–68.

Tannenbaum, A. S. Personality change as a result of an experimental change of environmental conditions. *J. abnorm. soc. Psychol.*, 1957, 55, 404–406.

Tannenbaum, A. S. Control and effectiveness in a voluntary organization. *Amer. J. Sociol.*, 1961, 67, 33–46.

Tannenbaum, A. S. An event-structure approach to social power and to the problem of power comparability. *Behav. Sci.*, 1962, 7, 315–331.

Tannenbaum, A. S., & Allport, F. H. Personality structure and group structure: an interpretative study of their relationship through an event-structure hypothesis. *J. abnorm. soc. Psychol.*, 1956, 53, 272–280.

Tannenbaum, A. S., & Georgopolous, B. S. The distribution of control in formal organizations. *Soc. Forces*, 1957, 36, 44–50.

Tannenbaum, A. S., & Kahn, R. L. Organizational control structure. *Hum. Relat.*, 1957, 10, 127–140.

Tawney, R. H. *Equality.* New York: Harcourt, Brace, 1931.

Thibaut, J. W., & Kelley, H. H. *The social psychology of groups.* New York: Wiley, 1959.

Thibaut, J. W., & Strickland, L. H. Psychological set and social conformity. *J. Pers.*, 1956, 25, 115–129.

Vaughan, G. M., & Mangan, G. L. Conformity to group pressure in relation to the value of the task material. *J. abnorm. soc. Psychol.*, 1963, 66, 179–183.

Vroom, V. H. *Some personality determinants of the effects of participation.* Englewood Cliffs, N. J.: Prentice-Hall, 1960.

Weber, M. *The theory of social and economic organization.* Trans. A. M. Henderson & T. Parsons. Oxford: Oxford Univer. Press, 1947.

Wells, W. D., Weinert, G., & Rubel, Marilyn. Conformity pressure and authoritarian personality. *J. Psychol.*, 1956, 42, 133–136.

White, R. K., & Lippitt, R. *Autocracy and democracy.* New York: Harper, 1960.

Whyte, W. F., Jr. *Street corner society.* Chicago: Univer. of Chicago Press, 1943.

Williams, L. K., Hoffman, R., & Mann, F. C. An investigation of the control graph: influence in a staff organization. *Soc. Forces*, 1959, 37, 189–195.

Wilner, D. M., Walkley, Rosabelle P., & Cook, S. W. *Human relations in interracial housing.* Minneapolis: Univer. of Minnesota Press, 1955.

Wolfe, D. M. Power and authority in the family. In D. Cartwright (Ed.), *Studies in social power.* Ann Arbor: Univer. of Michigan, Institute for Social Research, 1959.

Wright, M. E. The influence of frustration on the social relations of young children. *Charact. Pers.*, 1943, 12, 111–122.

Yarrow, Marian R. (Ed.) Interpersonal dynamics in a desegregation process. *J. soc. Issues*, 1958, 14, No. 1.

Yinger, J. M. Contraculture and subculture. *Amer. sociol. Rev.*, 1960, 25, 625–635.

Zander, A., Cohen, A. R., & Stotland, E. *Role relations in the mental health professions.* Ann Arbor: Univer. of Michigan, Institute for Social Research, 1957.

Zander, A., & Curtis, T. Effects of social power on aspiration and striving. *J. abnorm. soc. Psychol.*, 1962, 64, 63–74.

Zipf, Sheila G. Resistance and conformity under reward and punishment. *J. abnorm. soc. Psychol.*, 1960, 61, 102–109.

13

An Introduction to the Theory and Measurement of Influence*

James G. March

Professor March, now at the University of California, Irvine, is responsible for some of the most influential and closely reasoned essays on influence. Along with Herbert Simon, March concentrated upon constructing operational definitions of influence, and this essay shows clearly the impact of theoretical orientation upon that enterprise. We should note, moreover, that a subsequent essay by Professor March ("The Power of Power" in D. Easton, ed., Varieties of Political Theory, Englewood Cliffs, N.J., Prentice-Hall, 1966), which is not reprinted here, suggests that problems associated with the concept of power render it less useful for theory-construction than he had once supposed. This essay originally appeared in The American Political Science Review, v. 49 (1955), and is reprinted by permission from the author and The American Political Science Association.

THE SCIENCE of politics is a science of human behavior. It concerns itself with a specific segment of the activities of humans —those which either take place in, or have a clearly discernible effect upon, the formal governmental machinery of the community. The characteristic feature of a political scientist, therefore, is not his unique theoretical framework but his special empirical interest. Two main consequences follow. First, it is trivially true, and widely recognized, that the major concepts of other behavior sciences are necessarily an integral part of the study of political behavior. Second, it is equally true that, within the social sciences, it is the responsibility of

* This paper is based on work done under a grant made to the Carnegie Institute of Technology by the Ford Foundation for the study of organization theory. The author is greatly indebted to his colleagues and students in the Graduate School of Industrial Administration for their comments on earlier drafts of parts of the present article.

political science to develop those elements of behavior theory that are particularly relevant for the analysis of action in the sphere of politics.

Much of current empirical and theoretical work in political analysis is organized around the observation that many political data can be conceived to represent results of mechanisms for decision-making used (consciously or unconsciously) by individuals or collectivities.[1] In a similar fashion, students of a significant number of other types of behavior have tended to formulate their problems within a decision-making framework.[2] When one examines these apparently disparate branches of behavior theory, it is difficult to avoid the conclusion that there exist potentially fruitful parallelisms among such theories as those of consumer behavior, administrative behavior, price setting, legislative enactments, propaganda, learning, foreign affairs, and social control.

Once decision-making is accepted as one of the key focal points for empirical social science, the necessity for exploring the operational meaning and theoretical dimensions of influence is manifest. Interest in decision-making stems from the conviction that a large number of events involving the behavior of human organisms can be treated as exemplifications of pervasive mechanisms for reaching decisions. The interest in influence stems, in turn, from its conception as the fundamental intervening variable for the analysis of decision-making. Influence is to the study of decision-making what force is to the study of motion—a generic explanation for the basic observable phenomena.[3] It is the general goal of the present paper to suggest a definition of the influence concept and to explore with reference to the suggested definition some key problems in the study of influence processes. An assessment of some of the major problems in influence analysis is made in section I. In section II, a definition of influence as a causal relation is formulated. On the basis of this definition, a formal model of a decision-making organism is presented and its implications discussed; this is done in sections III, IV, and V. Finally, in section VI, measurement techniques are considered

Notes to chapter 13 are found on pages 373 to 375.

I

Some Problems in the Analysis of Influence

Problems of Generality. The empirical
study of influence has been hampered by a
tendency toward *ad hoc* formulations. As
will be indicated in greater detail below,
operational definitions of influence for
research purposes tend to be markedly
divergent and their relationship to the
general concept at best vague. Although it
may be desirable or necessary to consider
different types of influence under different
conditions, one should be in a position to
define the way in which any given type (or
its concomitant index) is related to a
theoretically formulated variable. Failure
to achieve generality in the study of influence has had two major consequences.
On the one hand, it has limited the comparability of studies of interpersonal influence (i.e., those studies that label a major
variable as "influence"). On the other hand,
it has concealed the potential relevance of
studies in quite different areas of theory and
research.[4]

Problems of Determining Influence Order.
The difficulties of identification in a system
of interacting variables have been explored
most fully by economists.[5] In the analysis
of influence the problem is frequently severe.
Consider, for example, a rather common
type of problem in the area of public
opinion. Assume that we are interested in
exploring the relationship between domestic
public opinion on foreign affairs and overseas propaganda by the State Department.
In such an investigation, there is a tendency
to take domestic public opinion as given
and ask the question: how do changes in
public opinion influence changes in overseas
propaganda? But if the propaganda has an
effect on foreign countries, and if changes
in the attitudes and/or actions of other
countries have an effect on domestic public

opinion (neither of which are entirely unreasonable conditions), one can no longer
legitimately treat public opinion as a given.
The identification of an influence order in
such systems (particularly when they are
observed in an equilibrium state) is exceptionally difficult, and many influence relations represent closed-loop[6] systems of this
type—either directly or through the operation of the so-called "rule of anticipated
reactions."

*Problems of Unanticipated or Delayed Con-
sequences.* Influence is frequently defined
in terms of behavior change over a given
time interval and measured by overt motor
or verbal activities. Such procedures have
the major theoretical objection that they
ignore changes in the individual's latent
readiness to act. An adequate theory of
influence must be more general than that
implicit in a simple stimulus-response
treatment. A slightly different manifestation
of the same difficulty results from the failure
to account for the side effects of particular
influence procedures. It is clear that in any
interpersonal relationship involving repetitive interaction, both the long and the
short run consequences of influence attempts
must be calculated. For example, it is a
commonplace observation in child psychology that although a child can be induced
to conform to parental demands by a
number of methods, these methods are
rarely neutral as to the latent alteration in
the child's propensity to meet future demands with hostility. Finally, insofar as
the "sleeper effect" discussed by Hovland
and his associates[7] is anticipated, there is a
further complication. Manifest action in
response to an influence attempt may vary
without regard to any variables other than
time.

Problems of the Dimensionality of Influence.
We wish to be able to characterize an
influence relationship between two individuals. In order to make such a characterization, it is necessary to know the dimensions
for which measurements are required. Since

the empirical study of influence is still in its infancy, it is not at all clear what the actual dimensions of an influence relationship between two individuals are. However, it is clear that such a relation frequently cannot be defined by simply citing a single influence index.[8] On the contrary, the evidence that exists indicates that the influence relationship between two individuals varies according to the subject matter under consideration.[9] One of the most obvious examples of this fact can be found in the operation of the United States Senate, where for most senators influence is highly specific to the subject matter involved.[10] It is necessary to specify one index at least for each important subject-matter area.[11] Moreover, it seems reasonable to believe that there are other dimensions and that an important function of any theoretical formulation of influence will be to provide clues to them.

Problems of Measurement. The problem of influence measurement is considered more specifically in section VI, after some theoretical considerations have been presented. However, it should be obvious from what has already been indicated with respect to other problems of analysis that measurement is one of the crucial difficulties. At the present time, available measures of influence, like influence theory, lack generality. The more obvious modes of introducing such generality into measures tend to make the measures operationally unfeasible. In addition, the major problem of comparison values remains unsolved. Insofar as possible, a measure should be in terms of an interchangeable unit that will facilitate comparisons of such things as the influence relationships between two pairs of individuals without any direct comparison between the members of the pairs involved. At present, there is lacking not only an immediately obvious unit of measurement, but even a generally feasible means of providing simple rankings.

The theoretical framework outlined in the remaining sections of the present paper was motivated by a consideration of such problems of influence analysis as these. Some of the ways in which the conceptualization of influence that is presented here contributes to at least the partial solution of these major problems, and the continuing theoretical and empirical gaps in the concept of influence, are indicated below.

II

Influence as the Inducement of Change

Consider the individual in a specified environment (i.e., reacting to a set of specified cues, both internal and external). Assuming that the behavior laws relating individual activity (neural, glandular, muscular, etc.) with the specified environment are known, it is possible to define a path of behavior that will be observed in the individual organism. For the moment, the extent to which the laws provide a complete and precise prediction is relatively unimportant, so long as they possess the minimum characteristic of delineating a boundary between behavior consistent with the prediction and behavior inconsistent with it. It is in harmony with the more frequent uses of the term "influence" and with the present sense of that term to say that if the individual deviates from the predicted path of behavior, influence has occurred, and, specifically, that it is influence which has induced the change.

Suppose that a prediction of the following form is made: "Congressman X will vote for bill Y." Suppose that a sequence of events is observed culminating in Congressman X, in fact, voting for the bill. Such an observation obviously is consistent with the proposition that no influence has occurred. But it is also consistent with the negation of that proposition. The prediction is a narrow one, dealing with only a quite limited sequence of muscular activities, and refers to only a small part of a complete definition of a behavioral path. Inasmuch as a similar observation can be made concerning virtually any prediction of human activity, it is clear that although it is frequently possible to establish the fact that interpersonal influence has occurred, it is peculiarly difficult to establish the fact that no such influence has taken place. Partly for this reason, a distinction needs to be made between the influence relationship between two events (e.g., "A votes yes," "B votes yes") and the relationship between two individuals (e.g., A, B). As has previously been mentioned, one of the fundamental problems in the assessment of interpersonal influence becomes apparent precisely at the point at which it is recognized that there is no necessary isomorphism among the causal relationships holding between the several activities of two individuals.[12]

On the other hand, suppose that a sequence of events is observed culminating in the Congressman's not voting for the bill. It can then be said that influence has occurred. Depending upon how refined are the observational instruments utilized and upon the complexity of interactions among variables within the organism, it may be possible to make more or less explicit the influencing event and the mechanisms of influence; but, in any case, one is usually prepared to say that whatever the mechanisms involved (and assuming the original prediction to be correct), what has occurred between the original prediction and the observed nonfulfillment of the prediction will fall within the general definition of influence.

For example, suppose that one of the events observed between the prediction that Congressman X will support the bill and his failure to do so is the announcement by the President of his opposition to the passage of bill Y. It might well be assumed that this latter event influenced the activities of the Congressman and specifically his inclination to support the bill.[13]

Such an assumption would presumably be based either on one or on both of two types of calculations. On the one hand, observation of the events occurring and comparison with the predicted pattern of events may reveal only two "unanticipated" observations: the President's announcement and the Congressman's failure to support

the bill. Under the prior assumption that the endogenous laws of the system are known, it is necessarily assumed that at least one (but not necessarily only one) of the unexpected events is determined by exogenous forces. So long as the two events continue to co-vary through a number of trials, parsimony and some reasonable respect for the laws of probability suggest that there exists a necessary relationship between them. On the other hand, since such an analysis fails to provide any causal ordering between the events, it fails to satisfy the intuitive feeling that an explanation of events that gives causal precedence to the Congressman's failure to vote for the bill should be rejected. Consequently, the observation of co-variation is supplemented by the attempt to find explanatory propositions for the two events.[14]

To any student of general scientific methodology, these comments on influence ring a familiar bell. As Simon has pointed out,[15] there exist some key similarities between what is ordinarily considered to be influence and that which is considered under the more general rubric of causality. Since the definition of influence to be proposed here draws heavily upon these similarities, it may be well to indicate two important characteristics of an influence relation on the one hand and a causal relation on the other by means of which their interrelation is made clear.

1) Both relations are asymmetrical. That is, the statement that A *causes* B excludes the possibility that B *causes* A. Similarly, the statement that A *influences* B excludes the possibility that B *influences* A. Here again, much of the confusion in the theoretical discussion of influence stems from the failure to distinguish the influence relationship between events (i.e., subsets of activities by individuals) and the influence relationship between individuals (i.e., the complete sets of activities by individuals). The fact that it appears to be possible to speak of asymmetries holding between events but not so frequently possible to speak of influence asymmetries between individuals (e.g., the sharing of influence may often be exhibited in the form of influence specialization according to "area") suggests that the appropriate model for the description of an influence relationship between two individuals is one in which the influence-related activities of the individuals are partitioned into mutually-exclusive sets in such a way that within each set asymmetry holds between the individual agents of the activities.[16]

2) In both cases, ordering of the relationship (i.e., causal or influence precedence) requires the specification of a set of propositions "explaining" any two observed events so that there exists a set of propositions explaining one without reference to the other, but no such set explaining the second without reference to the first. The specification of a unique ordering for the relationship requires, at the minimum, more than one observation, and under some circumstances is impossible. In particular, if all variables are explicable in terms of other variables within the system, at best only a partial ordering is possible.

In general, it appears to be true of any statement of influence that it can just as easily be formulated in terms of causality. Since in common parlance (and the present framework) it is not true that all statements of causality can be treated as statements of influence (i.e., influence and causality are not equivalent), the set of all influence relations can be understood to be a proper subset of the set of all causal relations. Specifically, the set of all influence relations is here defined to be that subset of all causal relations such that the behavior of an individual appears as the terminal point in the causal linkage. Alternatively, we can say that two individuals are in an influence relation if their behaviors are linked causally.[17]

From this, it is obvious that whether a particular causal link is considered to be a part of an influence relation will in some cases depend upon the inclusiveness in the definition of the causal system and upon the more or less arbitrary specification of the boundaries of an event. Consider, for example, the following causal chain:

a) If A places a lighted match next to the firecracker fuse, the fuse will light.

b) If the fuse lights, the fuse will burn.

c) If the fuse burns, the firecracker will explode.

d) If the firecracker explodes, a series of sound waves will travel in the direction of B.

e) If sound waves travel in the direction of B, B will contract the muscles in his hand.

Clearly, each of the specified five events could be further subdivided (i.e., the boundaries are arbitrary), and as influence has been defined above, not every segment of this particular causal chain defines an influence relation. Only those segments (four in number) terminating in B's muscle contraction fall within the definition.

Under some circumstances (i.e., if the system is an open-loop system) a lack of inclusiveness in the system is not felt to be critical. The first event in the chain can be treated as an independent variable. Some of the measurement considerations associated with the non-inclusiveness of an open-loop system are discussed below, but they should not be confused with the much more serious problems associated with the potential interaction among partially defined systems. Where the system under investigation is, in fact, closed-loop but is segmented into an apparent open-loop system, serious consequences for the measurement (or even ordering) of influence relations are introduced.

III

A Formal Model of the State of the Organism[18]

Up to this point, influence has been defined as that which induces behavior on the part of the individual at time t_1 different from that which might be predicted on the basis of a knowledge of the individual organism at time t_0. By behavior is meant any change in the state of the organism.[19] Thus, any changes in the organism are considered except those that are implicit in the original condition of the organism and, therefore, predictable on the basis of knowledge held at time t_0.[20]

The definition of influence as that which induces a change in the state of the organism makes the problem of specifying that state in meaningful terms of paramount concern for the theory of influence. At one level of abstraction, it is possible to say that this is simply a question of strategy. We consider the set of changes, of all possible types, in the organism, a set containing a perhaps finite but certainly extremely large number (n) of elements. Then, in principle, we might define the state of the organism at a given time as a vector in n-dimensional space, the components of which are the measurements made on those elements of the set at the specified time. The strategic problem becomes that of determining what subset of this extremely large set will be used as the operational definition of the state. The difficulty in approaching the organism from this point of view stems from the difficulty in measuring many of the changes in the organism.

Consider, for example, a physiological specification of changes—certainly, in one sense, the most "natural" type of characterization of the organism. At the moment, at least, the capabilities of physiological recording devices do not extend much beyond the most peripheral organismic responses.[21] Consequently, a neuro-physiological specification of the state of the organism must, in order to be useful in the study of influence, involve the creation of a series of hypothetical constructs relating the several peripheral responses to each other. In particular, some conception of the decision-making processes of the brain seems manifestly necessary. Thus far, experimental work in neural psychology has shed some important light on such questions as the areal specialization of the brain, but somewhat less light on the dynamics of its operation.[22] That this is substantially true

is borne out by an examination of the recent attempts by physiologically-oriented scientists to define a theoretical model for the brain.[23] Although the terminology is frequently different, the content of such "physiological" models is quite similar to the content of models drawn by analogy from electrical systems[24] or based directly upon inductive logic.[25] For these reasons, there appears to be no advantage to be gained by formulating the present model in the terminology of neuroanatomy. It is explicitly a logical construct, based upon a conception of the functional needs of the brain as a decision-making instrument. Nevertheless, studies of influence in the future may fruitfully utilize neuro-physiological measures of emotional alteration as a close adjunct to the more traditional attitudinal measures.

The model of the organism to be presented here represents an attempt to develop a conception of the decision-making process upon which to build a theory of influence. It is hoped that this theory will suggest at least partial solutions to the major problems of influence analysis outlined above. For example, an attempt has been made to provide sufficient generality so that any of the types of influence ordinarily considered (e.g., authority, sense of legitimacy, control over communication) fit naturally into the structure. Such a conception will provide clues both to the underlying similarities between apparently different types of behavioral premises (e.g, habit and legitimacy) and to underlying differences between apparently similar types of behavior (e.g., the private who salutes because he feels he ought to, and the private who salutes in order to avoid the guardhouse).

In the model to be developed, the formal terminology of set theory is used, as well as a series of symbols. For the following symbols, read the indicated English equivalents:

$\{\cdots\}$ "the set of $\cdots$"

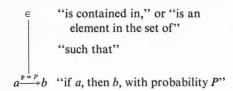

| $\in$ | "is contained in," or "is an element in the set of" |
| | "such that" |

$a \xrightarrow{p=P} b$ "if a, then b, with probability P"

Upper case letters are used to designate sets, and lower case counterparts are used to designate elements of a set (e.g., $a \in A$).

Two undefined terms are introduced. First, "*state of affairs*" (s). From previous attempts to do so, it appears to be impossible to define *state of affairs* in terms any less ambiguous than itself. Consequently, it is hoped that the intuitive meaning of the expression will be moderately clear. Some examples of states of affairs are "sleep," "the solar system destroyed," "a light blinking."

The second undefined term is the verb "to evoke." A state of affairs is said *to be evoked* when it is activated within the organism so as to impinge upon action. A state of affairs is *evocable* if it can be evoked. The term denotes a causal relationship between an evoking state of affairs and an evoked state of affairs.

The characterization of evoking as a causal relationship introduces certain difficulties into the model. As indicated above, a causal relationship is ordinarily treated as asymmetric (i.e., $aRb \rightarrow b(\sim R)a$). However, if the present model is to conform to psychological reality, one must be able to speak both of the "state of hunger" evoking the "state of eating" and of the "state of eating" evoking the "state of hunger." Consequently, the evoking set of states of affairs (E) is considered to be external to the system at the time-space point examined. In this sense it is treated as an experimental variable.

With these primitive terms, it is possible to develop a formal model of the state of the organism for purposes of influence analysis.

1) Let $S = \{$all states of affairs$\}$

2) Let $R = \{s \in S | s$ is evocable in the individual$\}$

3) Let v be a three-valued function defined over a domain consisting of all of the elements contained in the set R, such that to each element (r_i) there is associated a value, $v(r_i)$, equal to $+$, 0, or $-$.

The psychological meaning of the partitioning of R thus defined will be left unclarified in the formal structure defined here. At the same time, however, there appears to be no great advantage to be gained by suppressing the motivation for the introduction of such a function. The role of v-values in the present system is approximately the same as that performed by valences in Lewinian psychology.[26]

Alternatives to using only three equivalence relations as indicated here might be the introduction of a greater number of such relations or the use of a complete ordering of elements on the basis of a utility function. The latter possibility has long appealed more to the economist than to the behavioral scientist.[27] It offers the advantages (and they are not to be ignored) of mathematical elegance and productivity, but there is some evidence to suggest that the demands implied by a utility function are probably beyond the capabilities of the human organism and almost certainly foreign to its normal operations. On the other hand, a number of classes somewhat greater than those defined here has something to be said for it (e.g., $+ +$, $+, 0$, $-$, $- -$), and the rejection of such procedures is based primarily upon a general inclination to be most parsimonious in the definition of the model in those areas where information is the least reliable.

4) Let $G = \{r \in R | v(r_i) \neq 0\}$

5) Let $Q = R - G$

That is, the set R is partitioned into two subsets, Q and G. G is the set of all elements (in R) to which are associated a v-value of $+$ or $-$. Q is the set of all elements to which are associated a v-value of 0.

6) Let the elements of R be related by a web of probability connections.

For example:

$$q_1 \xrightarrow{p=.9} q_2 \xrightarrow{p=1} g_1$$

Given the limited discriminatory ability that is ordinarily associated with human behavior, it might be predicted that the model would most accurately approximate the decision-making activities of the individual if the values of p were restricted to extremes (e.g., p greater than .9 or less than .1). However, again by the iron law of parsimony, situations where the values of p are moderate are not excluded arbitrarily from the present model. (As will be made clear below, decision-making problems arise not only where the probability connections involve moderate p-values but also where the starting point in a chain is simultaneously associated by means of chains of high probability with two states of affairs having opposite v-values.)

7) Let $A = \{r \in R | r$ is evoked in the individual$\}$

The set A will contain at least one "alternative of action" (defined as a starting point in a chain of connections between Q and G—thus, an immediately achievable state of affairs) and at least one element of the set G. Further, each chain of probability connections among the elements of A terminates in an element of G. Thus, it is possible to say that each alternative of action in A has a probability, u, of resulting in a $g \in G$ having a v-value of $+$, and a second probability, w, of resulting in a $g \in G$ having a v-value of $-$. (Note that u and w do not necessarily sum to 1.) The set of behavior alternatives with a u-value greater than a given figure (e.g., $u > .9$) and a w-value smaller than a second figure (e.g., $w < .2$) can be considered a viable set of alternatives. Unless that set contains only a single element, the model does not uniquely determine the action of the individual.

8) Let $T = \{s \in S | s$ evokes an s in the individual$\}$

This set is implied by the interpretation of "evoking" as a causal relationship between two elements of S and by the existence of the set R.

9) To each $t \in T$ let there be associated one or more $r \in R$ by means of probability connections.

For example:

$$t_1 \xrightarrow{p=.9} r_1$$

$$t_1 \xrightarrow{p=.3} r_2$$

10) Thus, to each set A there is associated a set

$$E = \{t \in T | t \text{ is connected to an } a \in A\}$$

The set E can be called the evoking set. It conforms to what is normally called the "cue" or the "stimulus."

IV

Influence Processes

The model outlined above defines the state of the organism in terms of a number of elementary sets, v-values attached to the elements of those sets, and probability connections among the elements. One of the advantages of thus formalizing the state of the organism lies in the possibilities thereby afforded for identifying general influence processes. Since influence has previously been defined as that which induces change in the state of the organism, the present model focuses attention on four basic processes by means of which influence is exercised.

1) *By changing the v-values associated with the elements of R.* A change in $v(r_i)$ from $+$ to 0, for example, makes a potential change in the value of u (i.e., the probability of a given alternative leading to a $+v$-value) and thereby potentially alters the viable set of behavior alternatives. Such a phenomenon is that which is ordinarily called the "internalization of values." When an individual is persuaded to internalize a desire for a particular state of affairs (e.g., the election of a Republican President) which was desired previously simply for its instrumental character, the equivalent representation in the model is one in which the v-value of the state of affairs changes from 0 to $+$. Similarly, socialization falls in this category, as well as most of those forces that are commonly regarded as cultural determinates of individual activities.

2) *By changing the probability connections among the elements of R.* Such an alteration can take the form of changing the probabilities attached to an existing link or the form of introducing a new linkage into the system.[28] This is probably the form of most of the activities ordinarily called "influence." The threat of sanction, the promise of reward, or the provision of information, are examples of activities primarily directed toward restructuring the connections between different elements of *R*. For example, the President who wishes to exercise influence over the vote of a Congressman on a particular bill can (among other things) attempt to alter the Congressman's perception of the probability that a pro-administration vote will lead to desirable consequences with respect to (a) the substantive matter at hand, (b) the Congressman's re-election, and (c) the Congressman's future influence in Washington.

3) *By changing the connections between T and R.* This involves restricting or expanding the set *A* with respect to a given set *E*. Stimulus-response conditioning of any sort falls in this general category. Consider, for example, the creation and extinction of habitual reactions. Habit is based (in part) upon the inclusion of only a single alternative in *A*, and a typical form of habit-breaking is one in which the set *A* is expanded to include other alternatives. Similarly, the inculcation of a "sense of legitimacy" represents, at least in part, a case of the alteration in *T*-to-*R* connectives, as does also the phenomenon of behavioral rigidity frequently associated with old age or with organizational behavior.

4) *By changing the elements of E.* This represents an alternative way of changing the set *A*, and thereby—at least potentially—changing the content of the viable set of alternatives. The result is to induce a "change in set" in both the traditional psychological and present meaning of the expression. In problem-solving activities, the influence of a hint occurs through the mechanism of changing the elements of *E*. Similarly, the provision of information designed to define the situation for the individual actor frequently alters not only the probability connections between the elements of *R* but also the elements contained in *E*.

V

The Problem of Symbolic Learning

If one operates within the general framework outlined above, some of the more complicated problems in the study of influence tend to become, if not always simplified, at least clarified.[29] For example, some of the confusion that has found its way into influence analysis appears, from the present point of view, to stem from the identification difficulties in handling influence through symbolic communications. So long as our "rats" stay in their Skinner box and learn primarily through direct experience, we are not greatly perplexed. But when they exhibit some ability to communicate the wisdom of their experience to each other, some of our more simple-minded approaches to influence begin to break down. Consider the rule of anticipated reactions.[30] It has been suggested that whenever the reaction of alter to ego's behavior is correctly anticipated by ego (and vice-versa), it is not possible to untangle the influence relationship involved. Superficially, this appears to be the most direct application of the statements made in section I of the present paper with regard to the problems associated with identification in the absence of an exogenous variable. But in fact, if influence is defined as that which induces a change in the state of the organism different from that predictable, the common statement of the rule of anticipated reactions obscures a fundamental empirical assumption that is not always true, and, in any event, should be made explicit.

The usual statement of the difficulty follows approximately this outline: consider two conditional predictions, the first held to be true by Congressman Brown, the second held to be true by Mr. Jones, a constituent of Congressman Brown:

Brown: "If I vote against higher taxes, Jones will vote for me."

Jones: "If I vote for Brown, he will vote against higher taxes." So long as Brown votes against higher taxes and Jones votes for Brown, it is argued, it is impossible to discern who is influencing whom and to what extent. However, it is compatible with the present definition of influence, and these propositions, for Jones to have *no* influence over Brown and Brown *no* influence over Jones, since it is the source and not the form of the anticipation that is decisive.

The anticipated reaction of alter to ego's behavior is part of the states of affairs chains by means of which the state of the organism (ego) is defined at a given point in time. It is a conditional statement of the general form:

$$a \xrightarrow{p = P} b$$

The form of influence that is relevant here consists in altering this statement. Such an alteration need not be induced by the agent of the conditionally predicted event, and influence is wielded by the person inducing the alteration.

Consider the following commonly believed conditional prediction:

"If I am a good boy, Santa Claus will come to my house and leave some gifts for me. $(p = 1)$"

Santa Claus is not perceived to be exercising influence over a boy who believes this prediction; instead, influence is understood to be held by the individuals who persuade the boy to anticipate this reaction on the part of Santa Claus.

As another example, consider this proposition (representing a belief that is inculcated by the parental family in some cultures):

"If one is dishonest, he will be rejected by his associates. $(p = 1)$" Given the definition of influence used here, the individual who accepts this premise is being influenced not by his associates but by his parental family. If the attitude is subject to decay in the absence of reinforcement and to reinforcement by associates, the associates may exercise influence. But such influence is exercised through reinforcing the attitude,

not simply by virtue of their being the manifest agents of the predicted event, and is measured by the difference between what the attitude is and what it would have been in the absence of reinforcement.

If this general reasoning is applied to the example of Congressman Brown and Mr. Jones, the Brown-Jones influence relationship becomes obscure only when the action of Brown in response to his anticipation of Jones' reaction serves to reinforce Jones' anticipation of Brown's action and viceversa. This is the major empirical assumption underlying the complications foreseen. Since it is frequently a reasonable assumption, the complications remain; but it is important to distinguish the simple occurrence of an anticipated event from the contribution of the event to the reinforcement of the anticipation.

More generally, it is necessary consistently to separate the content of the learned relationship from the mechanisms by which it is learned. To be sure, there frequently is an important amount of interaction between content and learning; and, to be sure, there often is a second-level influence process between an agent of the predicted event and an agent of the symbolic communication so that the superficially perceived relationship actually does exist (though in a two-step rather than in a one-step chain). But when the distinction is maintained, the power of influence analysis is considerably augmented. This becomes particularly obvious, for example, when one considers the function and importance of the technical expert in an area of limited general knowledge.

VI

The Measurement of Influence: Some Approaches

Having explicated the concept of influence and the related concept of the "state of the organism," and having indicated at least some of the ways in which such concepts facilitate analysis, it remains to consider—within the same framework—the major problems of measurement. Previously, some of the difficulties of influence measurement were discussed in more or less general terms. In this section, the specific advantages, disadvantages, and difficulties of the chief methods of measurement currently in use are briefly considered. Three general types of measures are distinguishable in the literature: measures of attributed influence, measures of opinion change, and measures of direct interaction.

1) Measures of attributed influence.   It is possible to ask the members of the group under examination to rank each other according to influence, either over the individual respondent or over the group as a whole (*re* a particular situation).[31] Such a procedure has certain obvious advantages that should not be overlooked. In the first place, it is simple. The simplicity from the point of view of the observer is clear. The simplicity from the point of view of the respondent is less obvious, and strong reasons for anticipating considerable response difficulty can be found. However, so long as the response categories are relatively broad, no serious difficulty has been reported on this score by observers who have used this technique. In the second place, it taps unexpressed feelings and the implications of unobserved events. When overt behavior is observed over a time interval, there appear to be aspects of the influence pattern that are elusive. It is difficult to determine, for example, whether it is simply fortuitous that individual *X* changes his opinion in the direction of individual *Y*, or whether the fact that individual *Z* talks so much is indicative of his influence position or rather of a personal attraction to the tonal qualities of his own voice. By focusing on attributed power, it may be possible to distinguish real influence from pseudo-influence.

While the introspective nature of this approach provides, at least potentially, a major source of its attractiveness, it also results in a major disadvantage. One has a certain hesitancy in accepting an individual's self-evaluation of personal motivation in view of the distortions, conscious and unconscious, that may be ordinarily anticipated. In addition, this technique provides no ready means for comparing a relationship within a given ranking system on the one hand and a second relationship in a completely different ranking system on the other. Finally, in terms of the present model of the organism and the attendant specification of influence processes, this type of approach provides no clue to the form of influence involved—that is, to what sort of change in the organism has taken place (or habitually does take place).

2) Measures of opinion change.   Gauging opinion change is the approach to measuring influence that is probably most frequently used. Ordinarily, this involves defining an attitude, permitting interaction, and subsequently locating a post-interaction position on the attitude.[32] Alternatively, samples matched according to some *a priori* important characteristics can be used.[33] In such a case pre-experiment attitudes are not obtained, but the groups are exposed to different experimental treatments and then checked as to attitude. The assumption is made that the matched samples are originally substantially identical as to attitude. Such a procedure has the obvious disadvantages associated with the assumption necessarily made. On the other hand, where the situation is such that it is reasonable to presume that a pre-experimental determination of attitudes will have serious effects on the reliability of the experiment, the matched sample method has considerable merit.

As contrasted with the attributed-influence technique, these methods have the advantage of being at least somewhat external to the individual under observation. That is, although the individual is asked to indicate his own attitude, the experimenter does the measurement himself.

The method frequently requires, however, that the attitude in question be subject only to responses amenable to being located on a continuum.[34] The problem of multidimensionality is, in principle, controlled by introducing an additional continuum for each dimension. Of course, insofar as there is a desire to combine results on several trials, such a method introduces a unit problem. Ordinarily, equal distance between two points arbitrarily defined as adjacent on the continuum is assumed as well as (occasionally) equal distance between any two such points on any continuum considered. There may be circumstances under which one should be prepared to make assumptions of these types in order to facilitate the execution of a measurement program, but the transformation of "equal-appearing intervals" into "equal intervals" should be made consciously and with an awareness of the somewhat dubious foundation for the transformation.

Quite aside from the difficulties in using substantial numbers of dimensions in the absence of a common metric, one of the major tasks in attitude measurement is that of identifying the dimensions of an opinion area. In this regard, recent developments in scaling procedures (e.g., the development of latent structure analysis)[35] offer hope that this is not an impossible task, albeit it is manifestly not a simple one.

As a consequence, when one deals with opinions, whether measured by means of a Likert-type scale or by more complex scales, rankings, or perceptual judgments, the difficulties in analysis are substantial. One indication is the variety of forms that such analysis has assumed: the utilization of mean values,[36] degrees of change,[37] simple combined indices,[38] standard deviation of estimates,[39] per cent of group,[40] relative rank correlation,[41] net direction of changes,[42] and "change-no change"[43] measures for defining the existence or extent of attitude change.

Finally, two somewhat different complications introduced by the application of procedures for measuring opinion change should be mentioned. First, where such measurement is used in a group larger than two, the "satellite" individual is awkwardly handled, since any two individuals whose opinions always coincided would have equal influence. This gives a "yes-man" an influence rating equal to that of his boss, a result with which most students of decision-making would probably feel uncomfortable.[44] Second, the usual opinion-change technique and its several variations all leave unanswered a key question that is also unanswered by the attributed-power technique: what form of influence is involved? To return to an earlier example, no distinction is made between the private who salutes out of conviction and the private who salutes out of fear of conviction.

3) Measures of influence attempts. Where the opinion change technique concentrates on observing behavior (or attitude) at two different points in time and recording manifest change (resulting presumably from interaction pressures during the interval between observations), the attempted-influence technique focuses directly upon the interaction pressures themselves.[45] Influence is measured either by influence attempts alone or by some index of influence attempts accepted by the other individuals.[46]

The unit utilized varies somewhat from one observer to another. In the Bales system, the basic unit is a simple declarative sentence, with some allowance for scoring nonverbal actions (e.g., laugh, extended pause). It is possible to use other units such as a single "utterance,"[47] "message,"[48] or "influence attempt."[49] Serious objections can be raised to any of these units, the major objection being directed at the assumption that each unit is equal to every other unit. It seems reasonable to believe that there are three types of unit inequality that are ignored in such an assumption. In the first place, the impact of a given unit from a given source will vary according to the target individual. In the second place, the impact of a given unit upon a given target will vary according to the source. In the third place, the impact per unit upon a given target from a given source will vary according to the communication content.

Since this unit inequality seems fairly clear, the real assumption behind the

observation of attempts to influence appears
to be that given an interaction period of
sufficient length, the unequal units will tend
to show a mean value of 1 for each interacting individual. Of the reasonableness of
this modified assumption one may have
somewhat greater confidence, but in view of
its importance, it deserves further investigation.

In addition, concentration upon the
interaction process obscures the importance
of unobserved events. For example, it is
argued, one will over-estimate the significance of a spokesman or a person in an
authority role, where influence is based
upon previous decisive changes in the
organism. In this respect, it should be noted
that if influence is defined as "un-predicted"
change in a specific organism over a given
time interval, one is on safe theoretical
ground; but this should not be taken as an
invitation to ignore the interesting questions
raised in a hierarchical influence structure
or to spare caution in interpretation of
observations in ongoing organizations.

Like the previous two techniques, the
measures of influence attempts do not make
clear what types of changes in the organism
are involved. In some respects and under
some conditions it is possible to make
limited inferences in this direction from
interaction data, but the possibilities for
exploitation along these lines are not as
great as along others.

Finally, the techniques outlined here have
fewer non-experimental uses than either
the attributed-influence or opinion-change
techniques. This is not to say that these
methods are applicable only in a laboratory
situation, but simply to record the obvious
fact that the restraints placed upon the
utilization of such methods are, in this
respect, more severe than the similar restraints imposed on the other major techniques.

Although the methods indicated here have
considerable actual and potential utility,
their somewhat questionable integration
with the model outlined earlier in the
present paper (or with any other model)

indicates a need for some change both in
the recording procedures utilized and in the
forms of analysis undertaken. Supplementa-
tion by introspective recall methods and by
attempts to make explicit the decisional
premises held at the time of a decision seems
indicated, as does the development of techniques (possibly physiological) for localizing
more precisely the points in time at
which significant changes in the organism
occur.

There still remains the major problem of
determining comparison values. It has been
indicated that one could define the difference
between predicted and observed behavior
as a measure of influence. No attempt has
been made to indicate in what terms a
value could be assigned to that difference.
Changing the formulation from "behavior
change" to "premise reconstruction" does
not greatly improve the position *vis-à-vis*
this complication. Consider an organism
that undergoes change at two different
points in time. Is there any way of determining at which point greater influence
occurs?

Two possible ways of approaching the
problem suggest themselves (although others
might be developed). First, one can evaluate
the relative influence over a terminal act.
Make the following estimates:

a) Given the influence at t_1, in how many
different ways could the organism have
arrived at the act?

b) Given the influence at t_2, in how
many different ways could the organism
have arrived at the act?

If these "different ways" are weighted
according to some probability estimation
and those that have sufficiently small
probabilities are excluded, the change that
had the greatest positive effect upon the
probability of the event's occurring may be
called the "more influential."

As an alternative, one can evaluate the
relative influence upon the organism in
general by estimating the proportion of acts
the organism might perform which were
changed by the influence at t_1 as compared
with the influence at t_2. (Again, probability
weightings would be necessary.) Obviously,
the interaction between premises of action
makes any estimation of the sorts outlined

CONCLUSION

An attempt has been made to sketch an explication of the influence concept that is both logically consistent and operationally feasible. A formal model of a decision-making organism has been outlined and used to deduce the major forms of interpersonal influence. On the basis of this formalization of the concept, some major complications—operational and theoretical —have been explored with reference both to the conception of influence here proposed and to the procedures currently in use in empirical research. The object has been to suggest answers to some important questions and to raise questions about some answers implicit in previous research into influential processes. Althouth no attempt has been made to review the entire history of the study of influence, at least one proposition can be made with some assurance: the measurement of influence and the formalization of the concept have proceeded in an unfortunately *ad hoc* fashion, with little communication either between the "theorists" and the "empiricists" or between the several practitioners within each class of that dichotomy. For example, it is extraordinary—but true—that despite the fact that there are currently in use a significant number of distinctly different methods of measuring "influence," it is not at all clear under what conditions they provide comparable answers. It is, of course, possible, though rarely useful, to define a concept by a measurement technique; but in the absence of some knowledge of the inter-correlations involved, one cannot define the same concept by several different measurement procedures. Yet this is the current state of influence measurement. Similarly, one can find few serious attempts in the literature to relate formal definitions of influence either to measurement methods or to the main body of social science theory.

These considerations and the others introduced above imply some of the directions in which influence theory and research might fruitfully proceed. Without attempting to be exhaustive, the present writer feels constrained to indicate some of the specific questions of considerable importance as he projects the development of the theory of influence.

a) *Questions with respect to the formal theory:* What is the relationship between action theory, as formulated by Parsons and his associates, and the theory of influence? Is it possible to define a conception of the structure of the individual personality that will fit systematically into a general theory of influence? Can deductions about influence be made from the theory of information? If not, what modifications or additions would make such deductions possible? What is the extent of congruence between the present formulation of the influence concept and the formulation implicit in Lewinian field theory? What connections can be established between learning theory and the theory of influence? What is the relationship between influence theory and the formal theory of probability?

b) *Questions with respect to measurement methods:* What is the extent of intercorrelation among the standard measures of interpersonal influence? Can the differential conditions of high and low correlation be specified? What measures from the explicit process of interpersonal interaction can be used effectively as indicators of change in the state of the organism? What is the meaningful metric for comparing opinion changes? To what extent is it possible to identify the physiological manifestations of the receipt of influence?

c) *Questions with respect to the relation between formal theory and measurement techniques:* To what extent can the measurement implications of the present model of decision-making be translated into operational measurement procedures? In particular, is it possible to devise a method for discerning the decisional premises of the individual actor? What are the mechanisms involved in relating measured interactions with hypothesized organism changes? Under what conditions will measurement necessarily result in a non-unique specification of the state of the organism? What are the predictive consequences of such non-uniqueness?

Once answers are provided to questions such as these, it will be possible to proceed to the major task of influence theory and research: the formulation of a structure of propositions, defining the mechanisms of influence in an empirically-testable form.

Introduction

MANY OF the empirical and theoretical propositions in contemporary treatments of interpersonal relations reflect attempts to relate variations in interpersonal influence to other observable variables. Studies of the factors associated with leadership, of the phenomenon of authority, of the persuasion effects of different types of communication content, of the formally defined power structure in an organization, and of informal relations in a community, all assert propositions in which "influence" (sometimes provided with a different label) is a major variable. Such propositions are necessarily based on operational methods for establishing at least a partial ranking of individuals, roles, and/or specified types of behavior with respect to influence.

In general, the influence rankings found in such studies have been deduced from measurement procedures having strong intuitive appeal but relatively little formal justification. Some aspects of the general problem of influence measurement and its relationship to inter-study comparisons of research findings have been considered previously.[1] The major objective involved in the present paper is an explication of the basic measurement concepts in the theory of influence and some indication of how indices designed to deal with specific empirical situations can be constructed on the basis of the formal concepts. The concepts involved are those of influence identity, influence equality, and influence inequality. It is the fundamental contention of this paper that when one states a proposition involving rankings according to influence, one has made what is currently, but need not necessarily be, an ambiguous proposition. Some of the ambiguities in such a statement are now comparatively well recognized and will be mentioned briefly below. Other ambiguities, however—including those that appear to the writer to go to the heart of the problem—have been only partly recognized, at least in the general literature on influence.[2]

Measurement Concepts in the Theory of Influence†

James G. March

In Section III, an essay by Herbert Simon suggests that certain forms of influence could be measured in set-theoretic terms. In this essay, Professor March attempts to provide a conceptual refinement for the task by defining the influence relation in terms of pairs of roles and pairs of behaviors. This essay originally appeared in The Journal of Politics, v. 19 (1957), *and is reprinted by permission from the author and* The Journal of Politics.

The object is to define a relation (influence) between pairs of roles and pairs of behaviors. We wish the relation to be such that it will (at a minimum) identify a partial ordering of the paired objects. In formal terms, let I be a relation defined between pairs of roles (i.e., on RxR) and I′ a relation between pairs of behaviors (i.e., on BxB). We will ask that I and I′ both be reflective, transitive, and anti-symmetric.[3] The verbal translations of I and I′ would be "has at least as much influence as." Then, we can define a second pair of relations, I* and I′*, that are reflexive, transitive, and symmetric.[4] $xI*y$ if and only if xIy and yIx; and $xI′*y$ if and only if $xI′y$ and $yI′x$. The verbal meaning of I* and I′* would be "has influence equal to that of." In order to define the influence relation (I or I′), we must specify the necessary and sufficient conditions for xIy and $xI′y$. The remainder of the present paper is devoted to that.

As a background to this inquiry, it may be desirable to explain why the influence relations are not defined between pairs of "individuals" in view of the fact that in

† *This paper is based on work done while the writer was a Fellow at the Center for Advanced Study in the Behavioral Sciences. He owes a particular debt to Robert A. Dahl, James C. Davis, Howard Raiffa, and I. Richard Savage for their comments on the problem examined here.*

Notes to chapter 14 are found on pages 375 to 376.

ordinary parlance influence is conceived as a relation between persons. A formulation in terms of individuals has some serious disabilities despite its wide use in ordinary conversation. Most important among these disabilities is the fact that it combines into a single empirical observation two types of phenomena that are better kept theoretically distinct. When we say that President Eisenhower is more influential than Senator Kennedy, it is not always clear whether this is because he is President and the Senator is a senator; or because he is personally adroit and the Senator is awkward; or because he is both President and politically skillful and the Senator is neither; or because, although he is clumsy and the Senator is agile, that is not enough to overcome the difference between their two positions; or because the President's deftness overcomes his disadvantage of not being a senator, etc. It is desirable to separate the contributions made to President Eisenhower's influence by his position as President on the one hand and his personal behavior on the other (postponing for the present the problem of the interaction between position and behavior).

Similarly, the literature of influence theory currently includes two general types of propositions. First, there are propositions (e.g., Dale Carnegie) that distinguish more influential behavior from less influential behavior. Such statements deal almost exclusively with influence of behavior *qua* behavior. Second, there are propositions (e.g. those relative to the phenomenon of authority) that distinguish more influential roles from less influential roles. Typically, such statements reflect influence of a role *qua* role. For a number of reasons, such distinctions seem reasonable to maintain.

II

Identical Influence Among Roles

For simplicity, we will start with a two-role case and what can be called "identical

influence." The generalization to any number of roles and to the concepts of equality and inequality as distinct from identity will follow.

Suppose we have just two roles, R_1 and R_2, and a finite number of behaviors that are open to persons in them. The concept of behavior can be as general as we please, but for the moment it may be helpful to imagine R_1 and R_2 as having two behavior alternatives, B_1 and B_2. Then we can construct a matrix of outcomes as indicated in Table 1. The entries in the matrix (O_{11}, O_{12}, O_{21}, O_{22}) refer to the outcomes. O_{ij} is the outcome when R_2 selects B_i and R_1 selects B_j. We will say that R_1 and R_2 have identical influence if and only if O_{12} is identical to O_{21}. In general for the two-role comparison, when we allow the behaviors to run to n, we can specify the n-by-n matrix $O = ||O_{ij}||$. R_1 and R_2 have identical influence if and only if O_{ij} is identical to O_{ji} for all i and j (where i = 1, 2, . . . , n; j = 1, 2, . . . , n). Generally, we also wish to make comparisons between two roles included in a system involving additional roles. For example, this will be the case where a ranking among more than two roles is desired. We will say R_1 and R_2 are identical under such conditions if the specifications above hold under all combinations of behavior on the part of roles R_3, R_4, . . . , R_m.

From this it is clear that statements about identical influence can only be made with reference to a specified class of behaviors and a specified class of roles. The necessity of the first of these restrictions with respect to influence comparisons is now fairly widely acknowledged. The necessity however, provides a convenience that is potentially susceptible to exploitation. To

Table 1.

		R_1	
		B_1	B_2
R_2	B_1	O_{11}	O_{12}
	B_2	O_{21}	O_{22}

the extent to which large matrices are decomposable into sub-matrices in which the conditions specified above hold (or the modifications below), such decomposition should shed considerable light on interpersonal influence relationships. The restriction to a class of roles can be conceived as a special case of the general scientific problems of defining the system under investigation and controlling for factors affecting results.

Thus far we have used the notion of identity of outcome as a useful conceptual tool in order to avoid dealing with all the complications at once. What do we mean by identity? Two outcomes are identical if any statement that can be made about one can also be made (with the same truth-value) about the other. The concept of metric is a necessary complement of identity if the preceding discussion (and what follows) is to be useful in empirical work. We will specify that two outcomes are identical with respect to a given metric if any statement included in a specified class of statements that can be made about one can also be made (with the same truth-value) about the other.

The metric concept may warrant some additional comment, since its relationship to the usual connotations of "metric" may not be obvious.[5] Conceptually, we imagine a complete state-description of the world at a given moment as an "outcome." Such a description consists in an extremely large number (n) of simple observation statements. From this, imagine the class of all possible n-tuple state descriptions, that is, all possible "states of the world." This class of all possible states is susceptible to partitioning into mutually exclusive and exhaustive subsets. Any such partitioning will be called a metric. Then, an outcome (within a metric) is specified by identifying the subset in which the elementary outcome lies. The number of subsets defined by the metric is the number of possible outcomes.[6]

Consider, for example, a case where interest lies in the outcome of voting on three distinct motions in a committee. Each of the three motions can be either adopted or rejected. One possible metric on the outcomes would define the partitioning so that there were eight outcomes representing all possible combinations of adoptions and rejections on the three individual motions. A second possible metric would be defined in terms of the number of adoptions (thus defining four possible outcomes). A third possible metric would simply define two possible outcomes—more adoptions than rejections or more rejections than adoptions. Other metrics could be defined. The important point to note is that statements about the relative influence of two roles may depend on the metric employed. Suppose we are interested in studying the influence of A and B (with respect to two possible behaviors—being in favor of all three bills or being opposed to all three) over the committee's disposition of these three bills, and imagine that it is true that an individual in role A can dictate the outcome on the first motion and an individual in role B can dictate the outcome on the second motion. Query: Do A and B have identical influence over the outcomes on the three motions? The answer obviously depends on the metric of the outcome. A moment's reflection will suffice to show that if the outcome is defined either in terms of the second or the third alternatives above, A and B have identical influence, whereas with respect to the first metric they do not.

Such a result indicates an additional ambiguity in a bald statement of identity of influence.[7] Any such statement is dependent on the metric applied to the outcomes, where metric is taken to signify a specification of a class of observation statements with respect to which comparisons are made.

III

Identical Influence Among Behaviors

We have considered the case of m roles and n behaviors to provide a criterion for identity of influence among roles. Is it possible to utilize the same basic framework to indicate a criterion for identity of influence among behaviors? In general, we want to say that two behaviors are identical in influence *qua* behaviors if the outcomes resulting from one of them being performed by an individual in a given role is identical to the outcome resulting from an individual in the same role doing the other under all conditions, and that this holds for all roles. In the present case, "under all conditions" means given any pattern of behaviors on the part of the other role-players involved.

In the basic matrix notation introduced above, therefore, behaviors $B_1, B_2, \ldots, B_k$ are identical with influence with respect to two roles if $O_{1j} = O_{2j} = \ldots = O_{kj}$ and $O_{11} = O_{12} = \ldots = O_{1k}$ for all i and all j. This, however, reduces immediately to the requirement that all of the O_{1j} be equal. The extension to more than two roles is obvious.

It should be pointed out that as in the case of identity among roles, a statement of identity among behaviors is restricted to the matrix considered, in this case to a specific set of roles and a specific metric. It should also be noted that identity of influence among all behaviors considered is a sufficient (but not necessary) condition for identity of influence among roles, as is reasonable.

IV

An Influence Order Among Roles

Is it possible to say anything about matrices of outcomes where the identity criterion is not met? In particular, can we provide a sensible meaning to the proposition that R_1 is more influential than R_2? That is, can we define the relation specified above in section I? The remarks on identity of influence were expositionally convenient to introduce the general matrix formulation and the concept of metric, both of which

are assumed in what follows. (Thus, propositions of influence equality—I*—or inequality—I—, like those of influence identity, will depend on the class of behaviors specified, the roles considered, and the outcome metric employed.) However, the concept of identical influence has relatively few empirical uses. Many of the important problems in influence analysis are important precisely because such an identity does not exist.

Imagine a very simple case, consisting in two roles (R_1 and R_2), three behaviors (B_1, B_2, and B_3), and three possible outcomes, (0, 1, and 2). A possible matrix would be that indicated in Table 2. Under the criteria previously established, it is clear that the influence relationship between the two roles is not one of identity. Moreover, from any intuitive sense we would want to say that R_2 is more influential (with respect to B_1, B_2, and B_3 and the 0–1–2 metric) than R_1. Knowing the behavior of R_2, we can predict the outcome without error independently of what R_1 may do. Knowing R_1's behavior, we can make no more accurate a prediction than we could unconditionally.

Table 2.

		R_1		
		B_1	B_2	B_3
R_2	B_1	1	1	1
	B_2	0	0	0
	B_3	2	2	2

Table 3.

		R_1		
		B_1	B_2	B_3
R_2	B_1	1	1	0
	B_2	0	0	2
	B_3	2	2	1

Suppose, however, that the matrix is changed slightly, as in Table 3. Who is more influential? A possible way of thinking suggested by the previous example (Table 2) and by the definition of the outcome metric is this. We consider the class of possible outcomes under the metric. The behaviors of the individuals considered are deemed to define the outcome. That is, one of the basic statements is true, the others are false. The behavior of a specific individual restricts the possible true statements to a subset of the whole class (usually but not necessarily a proper subset). In the first example (Table 2), there are only three possible statements allowed in the metric. The behavior of R_1 does not reduce the number at all. The behavior of R_2 reduces it maximally—to one.

The second example (Table 3) is more complicated and, consequently, requires a more careful explication of the criterion to be used. In general, drawing on our intuition in the first case, we want the relevant factors to be concerned with the comparative restrictiveness (with respect to possible outcomes) exerted by the behavior of individuals in the roles compared. By "more influential" we want to mean the role that, in some sense, is more successful than the other at narrowing the range of possible outcomes.

More specifically, we will identify one role (R_1) as more influential than another (R_2) *with respect to a given behavior* if when R_1 does that behavior the possible outcomes are more constrained than they are when R_2 does the same behavior. We will consider R_1 more influential than R_2 *with respect to a set of behaviors* if the relationship above holds for each of the individual behaviors in the set. Thus, in the last example, it seems reasonable (subject to some provisos to be added below) to conceive R_2 to be more influential than R_1.

As has been indicated previously, decomposition of an arbitrarily constructed matrix may be necessary before meaningful propositions can be made. For example, consider the matrix indicated in Table 4. It is not obvious what relationship holds between R_1 and R_2. Suppose, however, that we restrict attention first to B_1 and B_3

alone and subsequently to B_2 and B_4 alone, as in Tables 5 and 6. The result is intuitively unambiguous (being identical with the first example discussed in this section): R_1 is more influential with respect to B_2 and B_4; R_2 is more influential with respect to B_1 and B_3.[8]

V

The Formal Definition of I on $R\chi R$

Let us define Ω_{ij} to be the set of possible outcomes given behavior B_i by role R_j. Thus, Ω_{21} is the set of possible outcomes given behavior B_2 by R_1. Let B_k be a specific pattern of behaviors by the roles not compared (i.e., in a comparison of R_1 and R_2, a pattern of behaviors by R_3, R_4, ..., R_m). A precise meaning for the phrase "set of possible outcomes" will be indicated below. For the present, we will assume that the expression conveys an intuitive meaning and will utilize such sets to construct a definition of an influence relation, I, between pairs of roles (i.e., as a subset of the Cartesian product of $R\chi R$). That is, we will identify those ordered pairs of roles (R_1, R_2) so that the first has at least as much influence as the second (R_1 I R_2). Since the definition depends on the range of behaviors

Table 4.

		R_1			
		B_1	B_2	B_3	B_4
R_2	B_1	0	2	0	0
	B_2	1	2	1	0
	B_3	2	0	2	2
	B_4	1	2	1	0

considered and the metric employed, the I-relation might well be written with an appropriate subscript to reflect its dependence on such factors (when the context does not make it clear).

Formally, we will say, $R_1 \; I \; R_2 \; < \; = \; >$ $m(\Omega_{11}) \leq m(\Omega_{12})$, for all i and all B_k, where m is a measure function.

VI

An Influence Order Among Behaviors

Given the conceptions already established, it is not difficult to specify a related

criterion for influence between behaviors. In order to make the motivation clear, however, a short discussion may be warranted. Suppose that we consider two roles (R_1 and R_2), two behaviors (B_1 and B_2), two outcomes (0 and 1), and a matrix of the form indicated in Table 7. On the basis of the definitions in sections 3 and 4, R_1 and R_2 clearly have identical influence, but B_1 and B_2 do not. Indeed, intuitively it seems clear that whatever definition is provided ought to define B_2 as more influential than B_1 since the former limits the outcome to just one possibility regardless of who does it.[9] In general, we will want to say that one behavior is more influential than another if the set of possible outcomes given the first behavior by a particular role-player is, in some sense, smaller than the set of possible outcomes given the second behavior by the same role-player, and that this holds for all roles considered.

VII

The Formal Definition of I on $B \chi B$

In the same way in which I depends on the outcome metric and behaviors considered, I' depends on the outcome metric and roles considered and is meaningful only when such dimensions are specified. Let Ω_{1j} be defined as before.

Formally, $B_1 \; I' \; B_2 \; < \; = \; > m(\Omega_{1j}) \leq m$ (Ω_{2j}), for all j, where m is a measure function.

VIII

Measures on the Set of Possible Outcomes

Up to this point, the discussion has assumed that the basic components of the definitions specified above were, or could be made, operationally meaningful. Explicit answers have been provided only for the simplest extreme cases. In order to make the analytical system complete, two notions need to be discussed. First, we will attempt

Table 5.

		R_1	
		B_1	B_3
R_2	B_1	0	0
	B_3	2	2

Table 6.

		R_1	
		B_2	B_4
R_2	B_2	2	0
	B_4	2	0

Table 7.

		R_1	
		B_1	B_2
R_2	B_1	1	0
	B_2	0	0

to provide a precise definition of the "set of possible outcomes." Second, we will suggest some types of measures that might be attached to such sets.

The meaning to be associated with "the set of possible outcomes given a specific behavior" depends on the outcome matrix and the structure of the set of all outcomes. Consider first the case where the outcomes are known with certainty (once the behaviors are specified) and the outcome set is without internal structure. Given a specification of row and column behaviors, the matrix unambiguously indicates the outcome, and there is no order among the outcomes. We can designate this as the *certain, unordered-outcomes* case. It is the case implicit in the previous discussion and the examples cited. Theoretically, it is the simplest case. Where there is no internal structure to the set of outcomes, it is possible to conceive any possible subset as feasible. In the unordered set [0, 1, 2], seven non-null subsets can be identified: [0], [1], [2], [0, 1], [0, 2], [1, 2], [0, 1, 2].

Consider the example cited in Table 4 and let Ω_{ij} be defined as before. In the Table 4 case:

$\Omega_{12} = [0, 2]$	$\Omega_{11} = [0, 1, 2]$
$\Omega_{22} = [0, 1, 2]$	$\Omega_{21} = [0, 2]$
$\Omega_{32} = [0, 2]$	$\Omega_{31} = [0, 1, 2]$
$\Omega_{42} = [0, 1, 2]$	$\Omega_{41} = [0, 2]$

Suppose, however, that while the outcomes are known with certainty, the set of outcomes has some internal structure. We can call this the *certain, ordered-outcomes* case. The interpretation for an order in the present schema lies in the constraints it places on feasible subsets. Where the elements of a set are ordered, only those subsets involving "touching" elements are feasible.[10] Thus, if the set [0, 1, 2] has an order $0 < 1 < 2$, the subset [0, 2] is not feasible.[11] Therefore, where we are dealing with a certain, ordered set, Ω_{12} will be the minimal feasible set containing O_{11}, O_{12}, . . . , O_{1n}. The meaning of "minimal" will depend on the (as yet undefined) measure; but typically in a complete order the minimal feasible set containing a and b will be the closed interval [a,b]. In the example above

(if $0 < 1 < 2$), all of the sets Ω_{11} and Ω_{12} are precisely [0, 1, 2].

Finally we need to consider the *uncertain-outcome* case. In general, it is not necessary here to distinguish ordered–from unordered-outcome sets since the form of the matrix entries will be probability vectors having, in each case, as many components as there are outcomes and, therefore, being in ordered form. Because of the nature of such probability vectors, the set of all possible vectors lies in a metric space (i.e., has a distance relation, ∂, specified for any two points).[12]

In the uncertain-outcome case, the feasible subsets can be defined as follows: Let O_{11} (i = 1, 2, . . . , n) be an entry in the first row of the matrix. Then Ω_{12} contains all of the O_{11} and in addition all a and b satisfying the following:

$$\partial(O_{11}, O_{i'1}), = \partial(O_{11}, a) + \partial(O_{i'1}, a)$$
$$\partial(O_{11}, a) = \partial(O_{11}, b) + \partial(a, b).[13]$$

For example, suppose that there are three outcomes (x,y,z) and four behaviors (B_1, B_2, B_3, B_4) and that the first column of the matrix is as follows (where a vector expresses, in turn, the probability of x, y, and z):

(.7, .1, .2)
(0, .5, .5)
(.2, .6, .2)
(.5, .4, .1)

Then the appropriate set, Ω_{11}, can be portrayed in two-dimensional space as a tetragon, as in Figure 1.[14]

The special case where there are only two components in the vectors is of sufficient empirical importance to warrant specific mention. It can be treated precisely as the case of certain, ordered outcomes. The relevant set becomes a closed interval. For example, if we take the previous example, but combine x and y, we have the following entries in the first column:

(.8, .2)
(.5, .5)
(.8, .2)
(.9, .1)

The set Ω_{11} then becomes the closed interval [.5:.5, .9:.1] or (without loss) the closed interval [.5, .9].

Once the meaning of "set of possible outcomes" is clear, there still remain phrases such as "in some sense smaller" and "minimal set." The ambiguities associated with such expressions have been summarized in the formal definitions by the specification of a very general measure function, m. In any specific study some interpretation must be provided for m. It is the intention here to indicate two possible forms that such a measure might assume. One of the other (or some third alternative) may seem proper in a particular instance, and there is no strong *a priori* case for either, independent of a specification of the purposes for which the research is intended.

A set-theoretic measure.   Probably the weakest form of measure that one can suggest (in the sense that the inequalities it defines would also be defined by virtually any other conceivable measure) is a set-theoretic one. If we let A and B designate sets, m(A) ≥ m(B) if and only if B is a subset of A.

The set-theoretic measure obviously avoids any necessity for assigning weights to different elements in the set of alternatives (provided an assumption of non-zero weights is accepted). One set has all of the

elements in the other plus at least one additional element. Consequently, such a measure has patent advantages where weighting of alternatives appears to be excessively arbitrary. It has the major disadvantage[15] of leaving many possible situations uncomparable—two sets are comparable only if one is the subset of the other.

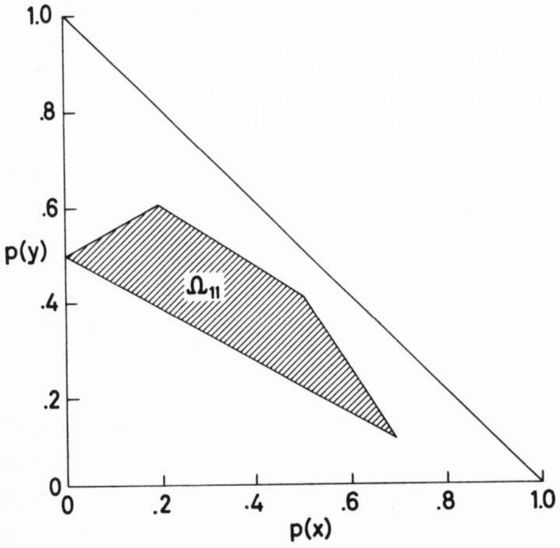

Suppose we consider the influence relationship between the President of the United States and the Speaker of the House of Representatives, with respect to outcomes defined in terms of the probability of a bill passing the House and two behaviors (announcing *for* a bill and announcing *against* a bill). A hypothetical matrix might be shown in Table 8.[16] When the President announces for a bill, the outcomes are restricted to the closed interval [.9, .6]: when the Speaker announces for a bill, the outcomes lie in the closed interval [.9, .4]. Similarly, with respect to announcing against a bill, the intervals are [.4, .1] and [.6, .1]. In both cases, the set of points defined by the President's behavior is properly included in the set defined by the Speaker's behavior and comparison is feasible under the set-theoretic measure.

Suppose, however, that the matrix in Table 9 correctly represents the situation. Under those conditions and the set-theoretic

Figure 1.

Table 8.

		President	
		For	Against
Speaker	For	.9	.4
	Against	.6	.1

Table 9.

		President	
		For	Against
Speaker	For	.4	.1
	Against	.9	.6

measure, the Speaker and the President are not comparable.[17] In general, under such a measure the ordering of individuals will be incomplete. Where the outcome set is unordered, the set-theoretic measure is also obviously easily applied and will, in general, also result in an incomplete ordering.

A weighted number of elements measure. A second possible measure function, using a weighting rule for comparing alternative outcomes, involves computing the weighted value of possible outcomes included in the relevant set. Under such a measure m(A) ≥ m(B) if and only if A has at least as large a weighted value as B.[18]

Where the set of outcomes is unordered and finite, the application of such a measure is straightforward (once weights are assigned). Where the outcomes assume the apparent form of an interval in the real numbers, however, a possible source of confusion arises. The number of real numbers in the interval [.3, .9] is infinite, but so also is the number in the interval [.1, .2]. Given the present conception of metric, however, the problem is illusory. A metric defined on the infinite set ordinarily partitions it into a finite number of subsets.[19] Consequently, under any such metric the outcome set is countable. In the case of apparent real number intervals (as in the previous examples), the usual procedure of rounding the decimals is the equivalent of partitioning an infinite set into a finite number of infinite subsets.

A counting measure such as this obviously increases the number of situations in which the relations I and I′ will be defined to hold (relative to the number under a set-theoretic measure). Whether this is desirable in a particular instance will depend on one's willingness to assign credibility (and/or meaning) to the weighting assumptions adopted. For example, in the second President-Speaker example give above if an equal-weighting assumption is made, such a measure permits the characterization of the Speaker as more influential than the President. (Readers who find this result perverse will find a discussion of at least some of the relevant problems in the appendix on the role of intention.) Whether such

a comparison statement is justified depends on factors specific to the context in which it is used.

IX

Incomplete Influence Orders

In the previous section, allusions have been made to the features of incompleteness in an influence ordering defined in the manner indicated here. Two major sources of such incompleteness appear to be implicit in the definitions proposed above. First, if the measure function is of a set-theoretic character, some sets of possible outcomes will be essentially uncomparable. Second, uncomparabilities may arise under any measure function if one role (or behavior) restricts the outcomes more than the other, given a certain behavior (or role), but the reverse inequality holds under other conditions.

This problem stems from the nature of the real world at least as much as from any arbitrary character of the criteria chosen. So long as we cannot or will not specify the comparison properties of many outcomes, any index of influence will necessarily be restricted in roughly this fashion.

In addition, a conception such as this is quite flexible in two directions. First, as has been indicated above, both the range of behaviors and the metric can be varied in order to change complex systems about which little can be said into smaller systems. Provided it is possible to specify which are which, we should not be discontent if we can say that with respect to some behaviors the President and the Speaker are equal; with respect to some the President is more influential than the Speaker; with respect to others the Speaker is more influential than the President; and with respect to some others they are not comparable. Second, once the matrix has been exploited with respect to single roles (or behaviors), there is nothing to prevent essentially multi-variate analysis in which pairs (triples, etc.) of roles or behaviors are considered jointly.

X

Outline of A Specific Empirical Application

What has been stated above consists in a set of basic criteria and some observations on them. A preliminary inquiry into the relevance of the theoretical concepts suggests that they are quite generally applicable to situations in which statements of influence order are presently attempted. However, specific empirical use of the criteria depends on establishing correspondences between the formally defined terms (behavior, roles, outcomes) and observable phenomena and ensuring that nature (or a reasonable substitute) provides all of the data relevant for a decision in the present terms. For example, it is by no means a simple problem to design an interview technique or experimental situation that will adequately simulate the attributes of reality that are theoretically desired. Yet, in many cases, the results in hypothetical situations such as can only be posed in such "artificial" contexts may be crucial to the construction of the influence matrix.

The specific example considered here is far from the most difficult one possible. In fact, it is a comparatively simple one. Nevertheless, it poses some problems that warrant attention and is illustrative of the general problem of translating theoretical formulations into empirically useful form. The specific problem chosen is one that has previously been given as an example. We wish to characterize the influence relation between the President and the Speaker of the House of Representatives, with respect to the probability of a bill passing the House. These are well-defined roles—at least the role-players are easily identified. As was done in the examples, we can limit attention to the two behaviors of being either for or against a bill, and specify outcomes (O_{ij}) as probabilities of the passage of a bill.

Two considerations of sufficient importance occur (judging by available evidence) to warrant specific preliminary notice. First, do we want to combine all cases into a single matrix independent of the party affiliations of the President and the Speaker? Although the final answer will depend on empirical results not yet in, it would seem reasonable to expect differences to be partially dependent on the party affiliations. One of the aspects of both the role of President and the role of Speaker is that of party leadership and neither can be feasibly abstracted from the party aspect. Consequently, it may be desirable at the outset to prepare four matrices:

1) Democratic President—Democratic Speaker
2) Democratic President—Republican Speaker
3) Republican President—Democratic Speaker
4) Republican President—Republican Speaker

Some of these may yield similar results (e.g., 1 and 4) but it is not obvious what the pairings will be.

The second obvious complication is similar, and susceptible to a similar preliminary solution. It is generally argued that the relative influence of the President and the Speaker depends on the subject matter involved. Consequently, it will be convenient to keep separate the results based on different substantive areas (e.g., foreign affairs, tariffs).

Any student of congressional behavior can suggest a number of other possibilities that need to be examined either by setting up *ex ante* distinctions such as these or by *ex post* sampling as will be indicated below. For the moment, however, these can be considered as representative of the possible decompositions that can be made.

Given this description of the problem, if one had complete control over nature, one could proceed in standard experimental form, providing the various possible combinations of party, governmental position, attitudes, and substance, and observing the outcome. Unfortunately,[20] such control is not available. In addition, it ordinarily is not feasible to pose hypothetical questions to the political process.[21] As a result, we are primarily dependent in this case on inadvertent "experimentation," and estimates of the outcome will be based on sample sizes defined not by the experimenter but by events. Under the circumstances, it may tax the ingenuity of the observer to ensure that all of the relevant samples will be of adequate size. For example, disagreement between a Republican Speaker and a Republican President on foreign affairs bills may well be comparatively infrequent and the resulting estimates relatively unreliable.[22]

Such problems will be substantial but perhaps not insurmountable. They assume, however, the solution to the prior observational problems which are in themselves not trivial. Observationally, we require state-descriptions of the political world assigning values to the following:

1) The political party of the President
2) The political party of the Speaker
3) The substantive area of the bill considered
4) The President's position on the bill
5) The Speaker's position on the bill
6) The outcome of the bill in the House.

In general, information on all six components is required before use can be made of the particular instance. There is no need to go into the details of securing information on these values. The techniques are the standard ones of historical and field research.

On the basis of values assigned to instances of this particular six-tuple, the matrices can be constructed involving estimates of the O_{ij}. The analysis for influence order involves (a) specifying confidence limits for the difference between adjacent cells (e.g., O_{11} and O_{12}),[23] and (b) determining a measure function. Once such steps are taken, a determination can be made.

Given the nature of the outcomes utilized in this case, however, a further analysis designed to examine the internal homogeneity of the results is in order. For the same reason that party allegiance and

substantive area were initially distinguished, it is necessary to ensure that the result in any particular matrix is not the consequence of an inadvertent amalgamation of two or more quite distinct situations.

Obviously, this is not a complete specification of how a study of the specific relationship between the President and the Speaker of the House might be executed. It is intended simply to illustrate how the necessarily abstract notions of the theoretical formulations can be utilized to pose questions for empirical research and how, in any specific empirical case, a set of operational isomorphisms between the concepts of the theory on the one hand, and the nature of available data on the other, must be established before the theoretical criteria have meaning.

XI

Summary

An attempt has been made here to provide a meaningful criterion for the definition of the influence relationships of identity, equality, and inequality holding either between individual roles or between individual behaviors. The criterion proposed distinguishes the influence of a role *qua* role and the influence of specific behavior *qua* behavior. Both have been shown to be dependent on the set of roles and the behaviors considered and on the outcome metric defined. Some of the alternative modes of treatment have been considered, and the empirical relevance of the concepts proposed has been explored.

Underlying the treatment here is the strong belief that the explication of the fundamental measurement concepts of the theory of influence is a necessary precondition for empirical research. At the same time, it should be clear from what has been said that such an explication does not obviate the need for research. The fact that an example, such as the President-Speaker one, has to be treated hypothetically is instructive in this regard.

APPENDIX ON THE ROLE OF INTENTION

Occasionally, influence is defined at least in part according to "intent" (at times only implicitly). To the present writer there are theoretical advantages in not doing so, but it may be worthwhile to indicate explicitly how the definitions proposed here will (under some conditions) lead to different results than would the introduction of intent.

Suppose that we consider the example cited in the main body of the paper with respect to the relationship between the President and the Speaker of the House, and an outcome defined as an estimate of the probability of the bill's passing the House. In that example, it is tempting to say that the President is more influential than the Speaker if $O_{21} > O_{12}$. The criterion proposed in the paper (using a counting of equally weighted elements measure) is apparently quite different, to wit: $|O_{11} - O_{12}| > |O_{11} - O_{21}|$ and $|O_{21} - O_{22}| > |O_{12} - O_{22}|$.

Given a very simple additive model it is possible to specify the differences between the two criteria. Let us say that

$$O_{ij} = aB_j + \beta B_i + C$$

Since the behavior "for" and "against" can be interpreted simply as signs ($+$ and $-$) and for the present purposes the constant, C, can be ignored, the influence matrix becomes:

President

		a	$-a$
Speaker	β	$a + \beta$	$-a + \beta$
	$-\beta$	$a - \beta$	$-a - \beta$

It is clear that a and β are coefficients of influence. It is also clear that we can now specify the alternative criteria for greater

influence in terms of a and β. The criterion proposed in the body of the paper reduces to $|a| > |\beta|$. The alternative cited above reduces to $a > \beta$. Thus, if a and β both have positive values, the two criteria yield identical results. Where a and β both have negative values, the two criteria yield opposite results. Where a and β have opposite signs, agreement between the two criteria is dependent on the specific values of the coefficients.

What meaning can be given to the signs of the coefficients? Where a coefficient is positive, the probability of passing a motion increases when an individual in the relevant role announces in favor, and decreases when he announces in opposition. This can be called positive influence. Conversely, a negative coefficient indicates that when the role-player announces in favor, the probability of passing a motion decreases. This can be called negative influence.

The differences between the two alternative criteria turn on their treatment of "negative influence." In the criteria proposed here, only magnitude is taken into account. "Direction" is ignored. Two comments may be in order: (1) Sometimes intent is imputed (as in the above case) without always an explicit warning to that effect. (2) Intent is not always the easiest thing in the world to establish.

APPENDIX ON TRANSITIVITY

It was indicated at the outset that one of the features frequently desired in the relation of influence inequality was transitivity. In the text we have not attempted to discuss the extent to which we can demonstrate that the criteria proposed are, in fact, necessarily transitive. To a limited extent, this brief note will outline our present status. I am indebted to Professor I. Richard Savage and several of his colleagues at Stanford University for their help in the exploration of this question.

1) With respect to the criterion established for inequality of influence among behaviors (e.g., the I′ relation), the proof of transitivity is trivial.

2) With respect to the criterion established for inequality of influence among roles (i.e., the I relation), the transitivity problem is more complex. On the one hand, it is possible to show that in the most general case transitivity does not necessarily follow from the criteria we have used, and a counter-example can be established. Consequently we cannot say that we are assured of transitivity in every case. On the other hand, transitivity is a necessary consequence in a number of specific cases. In particular, it should be noted that transitivity can be proved for a special case of considerable importance. Suppose we consider the empirical example suggested in section X, expanding it to include a third role, say, the majority leader of the Senate. If the sets involved are closed intervals (as in

that case) and the measure function is a set-theoretic one, the I relation is transitive. In addition, there are other situations in which transitivity can be shown to follow. Thus, the question of the transitivity of the I relation cannot be answered definitely except in the context of specific interpretations for the basic criteria. Under some conditions, as yet not realized empirically, an insistence on transitivity may place constraints on the selection of either the outcome metric or the measure function.

15

Spurious Correlation: A Causal Interpretation*

Herbert Simon

As William Riker argues in Section III, some ambiguities in the notion of power seem to inhere in ambiguities about the nature of "cause." If influence relations are conceived to be asymmetrical, then how are we to cope with the notoriously difficult problems associated with making causal inferences? This essay by Herbert Simon is one of the important early attempts in political science to come to grips with the problem of making causal inferences. Professor Simon, now at the Carnegie Institute of Technology, has written several papers on this topic. Indeed, this paper also appears in Herbert Simon, Models of Man (New York: Wiley, 1956), together with other papers on causal relations and power. This essay originally appeared in the Journal of the American Statistical Association, V. 49 (1954), and is reprinted by permission from the author and the American Statistical Association.

To test whether a correlation between two variables is genuine or spurious, additional variables and equations must be introduced, and sufficient assumptions must be made to identify the parameters of this wider system. If the two original variables are causally related in the wider system, the correlation is "genuine."

$\mathbf{E}$VEN IN the first course in statistics, the slogan "Correlation is no proof of causation!" is imprinted firmly in the mind of the aspiring statistician or social scientist. It is possible that he leaves the course (and many subsequent courses) with no very clear ideas as to what *is* proved by correlation, but he never ceases to be on guard against "spurious" correlation, that master of imposture who is always representing himself as "true" correlation.

The very distinction between "true" and "spurious" correlation appears to imply

* I am indebted to Richard M. Cyert, Paul F. Lazarsfeld, Roy Radner, and T. C. Koopmans for valuable comments on earlier drafts of this paper.

that while correlation in general may be no proof of causation, "true" correlation does constitute such proof. If this is what is intended by the adjective "true," are there any operational means for distinguishing between true correlations, which do imply causation, and spurious correlations, which do not?

A generation or more ago, the concept of spurious correlation was examined by a number of statisticians, and in particular by G. U. Yule [8]. More recently important contributions to our understanding of the phenomenon have been made by Hans Zeisel [9] and by Patricia L. Kendall and Paul F. Lazarsfeld [1]. Essentially, all these treatments deal with the three variable case —the clarification of the relation between two variables by the introduction of a third. Generalizations to *n* variables are indicated but not examined in detail.

Meanwhile, the main stream of statistical research has been diverted into somewhat different (but closely related) directions by Frisch's work on confluence analysis and the subsequent exploration of the "identification problem" and of "structural relations" at the hands of Haavelmo, Hurwicz, Koopmans, Marschak, and many others.[1] This work has been carried on at a level of great generality. It has now reached a point where it can be used to illuminate the concept of spurious correlation in the three-variable case. The bridge from the identification problem to the problem of spurious correlation is built by constructing a precise and operationally meaningful definition of causality—or, more specifically, of causal ordering among variables in a model.[2]

1

Statement of the Problem

How do we ordinarily make causal inferences from data on correlations? We begin with a set of observations of a pair of variables, *x* and *y*. We compute the coefficient of correlation, r_{xy}, between the variables and whenever this coefficient is

Notes to chapter 15 is found on pages 376 to 377.

significantly different from zero we wish to know what we can conclude as to causal relation between the two variables. If we are suspicious that the observed correlation may derive from "spurious" causes, we introduce a third variable, z, that, we conjecture, may account for this observed correlation. We next compute the partial correlation, $r_{xy \cdot z}$, between x and y with z "held constant," and compare this with the zero order correlation, r_{xy}. If $r_{xy \cdot z}$ is close to zero, while r_{xy} is not, we conclude that either: (a) z is an intervening variable—the causal effect of x on y (or vice versa) operates through z; or (b) the correlation between x and y results from the joint causal effect of z on both those variables, and hence this correlation is spurious. It will be noted that in case (a) we do not know whether the causal arrow should run from x to y or from y to x (via z in both cases); and in any event, the correlations do not tell us whether we have case (a) or case (b).

The problem may be clarified by a pair of specific examples adapted from Zeisel.[3]

I. The data consist of measurements of three variables in a number of groups of people: x is the percentage of members of the group that is married, y is the average number of pounds of candy consumed per month per member, z is the average age of members of the group. A high (negative) correlation, r_{xy}, was observed between marital status and amount of candy consumed. But there was also a high (negative) correlation, r_{yz}, between candy consumption and age; and a high (positive) correlation, r_{xz}, between marital status and age. However, when age was held constant, the correlation $r_{xy \cdot z}$, between marital status and candy consumption was nearly zero. By our previous analysis, either age is an intervening variable between marital status and candy consumption; or the correlation between marital status and candy consumption is spurious, being a joint effect caused by the variation in age. "Common sense"—the nature of which we will want to examine below in detail—tells us that the latter explanation is the correct one.

II. The data consist again of measurements of three variables in a number of groups of people: x is the percentage of

female employees who are married, y is the average number of absences per week per employee, z is the average number of hours of housework performed per week per employee.[4] A high (positive) correlation, r_{xy}, was observed between marriage and absenteeism. However, when the amount of housework, z was held constant, the correlation $r_{xy \cdot z}$ was virtually zero. In this case, by applying again some common sense notions about the direction of causation, we reach the conclusion that z is an intervening variable between x and y: that is, that marriage results in a higher average amount of housework performed, and this, in turn, in more absenteeism.

Now what is bothersome about these two examples is that the same statistical evidence, so far as the coefficients of correlation are concerned, has been used to reach entirely different conclusions in the two cases. In the first case we concluded that the correlation between x and y was spurious; in the second case that there was a true causal relationship, mediated by the intervening variable z. Clearly, it was not the statistical evidence, but the "common sense" assumptions added afterwards, that permitted us to draw these distinct conclusions.

2

Causal Relations

In investigating spurious correlation we are interested in learning whether the relation between two variables persists or disappears when we introduce a third variable. Throughout this paper (as in all ordinary correlation analyses) we will assume that the relations in question are linear, and without loss of generality, that the variables are measured from their respective means.

Now suppose we have a system of three variables whose behavior is determined by some set of linear mechanisms. In general we will need three mechanisms, each represented by an equation—three equations to determine the three variables. One such set of mechanisms would be that in which each of the variables *directly influenced* the other two. That is, in one equation x would appear as the dependent variable, y and z as independent variables; in the second equation y would appear as the dependent variable, x and z as the independent variables; in the third equation, z as dependent variable, x and y as independent variables.[5]

The equations would look like this:

$$x + a_{12}y + a_{13}z = u_1 \qquad (2.1)$$

$$a_{21}x + y + a_{23}z = u_2 \qquad \text{(I) (2.2)}$$

$$a_{31}x + a_{32}y + z = u_3 \qquad (2.3)$$

where the u's are "error" terms that measure the net effects of all other variables (those not introduced explicitly) upon the system. We refer to $A = ||a_{ij}||$ as the *coefficient matrix* of the system.

Next, let us suppose that not all the variables directly influence all the others—that some independent variables are absent from some of the equations. This is equivalent to saying that some of the elements of the coefficient matrix are zero. By way of specific example, let us assume that $a_{31} = a_{32} = a_{21} = 0$. Then the equation system (I) reduces to:

$$x + a_{12}y + a_{13}z = u_1 \qquad (2.4)$$

$$y + a_{23}z = u_2 \qquad \text{(II) (2.5)}$$

$$z = u_3 \qquad (2.6)$$

By examining the equations (II), we see that a change in u_3 will change the value of z directly, and the values of x and y indirectly; a change in u_2 will change y directly and x indirectly, but will leave z unchanged; a change in u_1 will change only x. Then we may say that y *is causally dependent on* z in (II), and that x is causally dependent on y and z.

If x and y were correlated, we would say that the correlation was genuine in the case

of the system (II), for $a_{12} \neq 0$. Suppose, instead, that the system were (III):

$$x + a_{13}z = u_1 \qquad (2.7)$$

$$y + a_{23}z = u_2 \qquad \text{(III) (2.8)}$$

$$z = u_3 \qquad (2.9)$$

In this case we would regard the correlation between x and y as spurious, because it is due solely to the influence of z on the variables x and y. Systems (II) and (III) are, of course, not the only possible cases, and we shall need to consider others later.

3

The a priori *Assumptions*

We shall show that the decision that a partial correlation is or is not spurious (does not or does indicate a causal ordering) can in general only be reached if *a priori* assumptions are made that certain *other* causal relations do *not* hold among the variables. This is the meaning of the "common sense" assumptions mentioned earlier. Let us make this more precise.

Apart from any statistical evidence, we are prepared to assert in the first example of Section 1 that the age of a person does *not* depend upon either his candy consumption or his marital status. Hence z cannot be causally dependent upon either x or y. This is a genuine empirical assumption, since the variable "chronological age" really stands, in these equations, as a surrogate for physiological and sociological age. Nevertheless, it is an assumption that we are quite prepared to make on evidence apart from the statistics presented. Similarly, in the second example of Section 1, we are prepared to assert (on grounds of other empirical knowledge) that marital status is not causally dependent upon either amount of housework or absenteeism.[6]

The need for such *a priori* assumption follows from considerations of elementary algebra. We have seen that whether a correlation is genuine or spurious depends on which of the coefficients, a_{ij}, of A are zero, and which are non-zero. But these coefficients are not observable nor are the "error" terms, u_1, u_2 and u_3. What we observe is a sample of values of x, y and z.

Hence, from the standpoint of the problem of statistical estimation, we must regard the $3n$ sample values of x, y, and z as numbers given by observation, and the $3n$ error terms, u_i, together with the six coefficients, a_{ij}, as variables to be estimated. But then we have $(3n + 6)$ variables ($3n$ u's and six a's) and only $3n$ equations (three for each sample point). Speaking roughly in "equation-counting" terms, we need six more equations, and we depend on the *a priori* assumptions to provide these additional relations.

The *a priori* assumptions we commonly employ are of two kinds:

1) A priori assumptions that certain variables are not directly dependent on certain others. Sometimes such assumptions come from knowledge of the time sequence of events. That is, we make the general assumption about the world that if y precedes x in time, then $a_{21} = 0 - x$ does not directly influence y.

2) A priori assumptions that the errors are uncorrelated—i.e., that "all other" variables influencing x are uncorrelated with "all other" variables influencing y, and so on. Writing $E(u_i u_j)$ for the expected value of $u_i u_j$, this gives us the three additional equations:

$$E(u_1 u_2) = 0; \qquad E(u_1 u_3) = 0;$$
$$E(u_2 u_3) = 0$$

Again it must be emphasized that these assumptions are "*a priori*" only in the sense that they are not derived from the statistical data from which the correlations among x, y, and z are computed. The assumptions are clearly empirical.

As a matter of fact, it is precisely because we are unwilling to make the analogous empirical assumptions in the two-variable case (the correlation between x and y alone) that the problem of spurious correlation arises at all. For consider the two-variable system:

$$x + b_{12}y = v_1 \qquad (3.1)$$
$$\text{(IV)}$$
$$y = v_2 \qquad (3.2)$$

We suppose that y precedes x in time, so that we are willing to set $b_{21} = 0$ by an assumption of type (1). Then, if we make the type (2) assumption that $E(v_1 v_2) = 0$, we can immediately obtain a unique estimate of b_{12}. For multiplying the two equations, and taking expected values, we get:

$$E(xy) + b_{12}E(y^2) = E(v_1 v_2) = 0 \qquad (3.3)$$

Whence

$$b_{12} = -\frac{E(xy)}{E(y^2)} = -\frac{\sigma_y}{\sigma_z} r_{xy} \qquad (3.4)$$

It follows immediately that (sampling questions aside) b_{12} will be zero or non-zero as r_{12} is zero or non-zero. *Hence correlation is proof of causation in the two-variable case if we are willing to make the assumptions of time precedence and non-correlation of the error terms.*

If we suspect the correlation to be spurious, we look for a common component, z, of v_1 and v_2 which might account for their correlation:

$$v_1 \equiv u_1 - a_{13}z \qquad (3.5a)$$
$$v_2 \equiv u_2 - a_{23}z \qquad (3.5b)$$

Substitution of these relations in (IV) brings us back immediately to systems like (II). This substitution replaces the unobservable v's by unobservable u's. Hence, we are not relieved of the necessity of postulating independence of the errors. We are more willing to make these assumptions in the three-variable case because we have explicitly removed from the error term the component z which we suspect is the source, if any, of the correlation of the v's.

Stated otherwise, introduction of the third variable, z, to test the genuineness or spuriousness of the correlation between x and y, is a method for determining whether in fact the v's of the original two-variable system were uncorrelated. But the test can be carried out only on the assumption that the unobservable error terms of the three variable system are uncorrelated. If we sus-

pect this to be false, we must further enlarge the system by introduction of a fourth
variable, and so on, until we obtain a system
we are willing to regard as "complete" in
this sense.

Summarizing our analysis we conclude
that:

1) Our task is to determine which of the
six off-diagonal matrix coefficients in a
system like (I) are zero.

2) But we are confronted with a system
containing a total of nine variables (six
coefficients and three unobservable errors),
and only three equations.

3) Hence we must obtain six more relations by making certain *a priori* assumptions.

a) Three of these relations may be obtained, from considerations of time precedence of variables or analogous evidence, in
the form of direct assumptions that three
of the a_{ij} are zero.

b) Three more relations may be obtained
by assuming the errors to be uncorrelated.

4

Spurious Correlation

Before proceeding with the algebra, it
may be helpful to look a little more closely
at the matrix of coefficients in systems like
(I), (II), and (III), disregarding the numerical values of the coefficients, but considering only whether they are non-vanishing (X), or vanishing (0). An example of
such a matrix would be

$$\begin{Vmatrix} X & 0 & 0 \\ X & X & X \\ 0 & 0 & X \end{Vmatrix}$$

In this case x and z both influence y, but
not each other, and y influences neither x
nor z. Moreover, a change in u_2—u_1 and
u_3 being constant—will change y, but not
x or z; a change in u_1 will change x and y,
but not z; a change in u_3 will change z and

y, but not x. Hence, the causal ordering
may be depicted thus:

In this case the correlation between x and
y is "true," and not spurious.

Since there are six off-diagonal elements
in the matrix, there are $2^6 = 64$ possible
configurations of X's and 0's. The *a priori*
assumptions (1), however, require 0's in
three specified cells, and hence for each
such set of assumptions there are only
$2^3 = 8$ possible distinct configurations. If
(to make a definite assumption) x does not
depend on y, then there are three possible
orderings of the variables (z, x, y; x, z, y;
x, y, z), and consequently 3.8 = 24 possible
configurations, but these 24 configurations
are not all distinct. For example, the one
depicted above is consistent with either the
ordering (z, x, y) or the ordering (x, z, y).

Still assuming that x does not depend on
y, we will be interested, in particular, in the
following configurations:

$$\begin{Vmatrix} X & 0 & 0 \\ X & X & X \\ 0 & 0 & X \end{Vmatrix} \quad \begin{Vmatrix} X & 0 & X \\ X & X & 0 \\ 0 & 0 & X \end{Vmatrix} \quad \begin{Vmatrix} X & 0 & 0 \\ X & X & 0 \\ X & 0 & X \end{Vmatrix}$$
$$\quad(\alpha)\qquad\qquad(\beta)\qquad\qquad(\gamma)$$

$$\begin{Vmatrix} X & 0 & X \\ 0 & X & X \\ 0 & 0 & X \end{Vmatrix} \quad \begin{Vmatrix} X & 0 & 0 \\ 0 & X & X \\ X & 0 & X \end{Vmatrix}$$
$$\quad(\delta)\qquad\qquad(\epsilon)$$

In Case α, either x may precede z, or z, x.
In Cases β and δ, z precedes x; in Cases γ
and ϵ, x precedes z. The causal orderings
that may be inferred are:

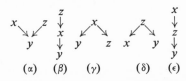

The two cases we were confronted with
in our earlier examples of Section 1 were
δ and ϵ, respectively. Hence, δ is the case of
spurious correlation due to z; ϵ the case of
true correlation with z as an intervening
variable.

We come now to the question of which of the matrices that are consistent with the assumed time precedence is the correct one. Suppose, for definiteness, that z precedes x, and x precedes y. Then $a_{12} = a_{31} = a_{32} = 0$; and the system (I) reduces to:

$$x + a_{13}z = u_1 \tag{4.1}$$

$$a_{21}x + y + a_{23}z = u_2 \tag{4.2}$$

$$z = u_3 \tag{4.3}$$

Next, we assume the errors to be uncorrelated:

$$E(u_1u_2) = E(u_1u_3) = E(u_2u_3) = 0 \tag{4.4}$$

Multiplying equations (4.1)–(4.3) by pairs, and taking expected values we get:

$$a_{21}E(x^2) + E(xy) + a_{23}E(xz)$$
$$+ a_{13}[a_{21}E(xz) + E(yz) \tag{4.5}$$
$$+ a_{23}E(z^2)] = E(u_1u_2) = 0$$

$$E(xz) + a_{13}E(z^2) \tag{4.6}$$
$$= E(u_1u_3) = 0$$

$$a_{21}E(xz) + E(yz) + a_{23}E(z^2) \tag{4.7}$$
$$= E(u_2u_3) = 0$$

Because of (4.7), the terms in the bracket of (4.5) vanish, giving:

$$a_{21}E(x^2) + E(xy) + a_{23}E(xz) \equiv 0 \tag{4.8}$$

Solving for $E(xz)$, $E(yz)$ and $E(xy)$ we find:

$$E(xz) = - a_{13}E(z^2) \tag{4.9}$$

$$E(yz) = (a_{13}a_{21} - a_{23})E(z^2) \tag{4.10}$$

$$E(xy) = a_{13}a_{23}E(z^2) - a_{21}E(x^2) \tag{4.11}$$

Case α: Now in the matrix of case α, above, we have $a_{13} = 0$. Hence:

$$E(xz) = 0 \tag{4.12a}$$

$$E(yz) = - a_{23}E(z^2) \tag{4.12b}$$

$$E(xy) = - a_{21}E(x^2) \tag{4.12c}$$

Case β: In this case, $a_{23} = 0$, hence,

$$E(xz) = - a_{13}E(z^2) \tag{4.13a}$$

$$E(yz) = a_{13}a_{21}E(z^2) \tag{4.13b}$$

$$E(xy) = - a_{21}E(x^2) \tag{4.13c}$$

from which it also follows that:

$$E(xy) = E(x^2)\frac{E(yz)}{E(xz)} \tag{4.14}$$

Case δ: In this case, $a_{21} = 0$. Hence,

$$E(xz) = - a_{13}E(z^2) \tag{4.15a}$$

$$E(yz) = - a_{23}E(z^2) \tag{4.15b}$$

$$E(xy) = a_{13}a_{23}E(z^2) \tag{4.15c}$$

and we deduce also that:

$$E(xy) = \frac{E(xz)E(yz)}{E(z^2)}. \tag{4.16}$$

We have now proved that $a_{13} = 0$ implies (4.12a); that $a_{23} = 0$ implies (4.14); and that $a_{21} = 0$ implies (4.16). We shall show that the converse also holds.

To prove that (4.12a) implies $a_{13} = 0$ we need only set the left-hand side of (4.9) equal to zero.

To prove that (4.14) implies that $a_{23} = 0$ we substitute in (4.14) the values of the cross-products from (4.9)–(4.11). After some simplification, we obtain:

$$a_{23}[E(x^2) - a_{13}{}^2E(z^2)] = 0 \tag{4.17}$$

Now since, from (4.1)

$$E(x^2) - E(u_1{}^2) + 2a_{13}E(zu_1) \tag{4.18}$$
$$= a_{13}{}^2E(z^2)$$

and since, by multiplying (4.3) by u_1, we can show that $E(zu_1) = 0$, the second factor of (4.17) can vanish only in case $E(u_1{}^2) = 0$. Excluding this degenerate case, we conclude that $a_{23} = 0$.

To prove that (4.16) implies $a_{21} = 0$, we proceed in a similar manner, obtaining:

$$a_{21}[E(x^2) - a_{13}{}^2E(z^2)] = 0 \tag{4.19}$$

from which we can conclude that $a_{21} = 0$.

We can summarize the results as follows:

1) If $E(xz) = 0$, $E(yz) \neq 0$, $E(xy) \neq 0$, we have Case α.

2) If none of the cross-products is zero, and

$$E(xy) = E(x^2)\frac{E(yz)}{E(xz)}$$

we have Case β.

3) If none of the cross-products is zero, and

$$E(xy) = \frac{E(xz)E(yz)}{E(z^2)}$$

we have Case δ.

We can combine these conditions to find the conditions that two or more of the coefficients a_{13}, a_{23}, a_{21} vanish:

4) If $a_{13} = a_{23} = 0$, we find that:
$E(xz) = 0$, $E(yz) = 0$, Call this Case (αβ).

5) If $a_{13} = a_{21} = 0$, we find that:
$E(xz) = 0$, $E(xy) = 0$. Call this Case (αδ).

6) If $a_{23} = a_{21} = 0$, we find that:
$E(yz) = 0$, $E(xy) = 0$. Call this Case (βδ).

7) If $a_{13} = a_{23} = a_{21} = 0$, then
$E(xz) = E(yz) = E(xy) = 0$. Call this Case (αβδ).

8) If none of the conditions (1)–(7) are satisfied, then all three coefficients a_{13}, a_{23}, a_{21} are non-zero. Thus, by observing which of the conditions (1) through (8) are satisfied by the expected values of the cross products, we can determine what the causal ordering is of the variables.[7]

We can see also, from this analysis, why the vanishing of the partial correlation of x and y is evidence for the spuriousness of the zero-order correlation between x and y. For the numerator of the partial correlation coefficient $r_{xy.z}$, we have:

$$N(r_{xy.z}) = \frac{E(xy)}{\sqrt{E(x^2)E(y^2)}}$$

$$- \frac{E(xz)E(yz)}{E(z^2)\sqrt{E(x^2)E(y^2)}}$$

(4.20)

We see that the condition for Case δ is precisely that $r_{xy.z}$ vanish while none of the coefficients, r_{xy}, r_{xz}, r_{yz} vanish. From this we conclude that the first illustrative example of Section 1 falls in Case δ, as previously asserted. A similar analysis shows that the second illustrative example of Section 1 falls in Case ε.

In summary, our procedure for interpreting, by introduction of an additional variable z, the correlation between x and y consists in making the six *a priori* assumptions described earlier; estimating the expected values, $E(xy)$, $E(xz)$, and $E(yz)$; and determining from their values which of the eight enumerated cases holds. Each case corresponds to a specified arrangement of zero and non-zero elements in the coefficient matrix and hence to a definite causal ordering of the variables.

5

The Case of Experimentation

In sections (3)–(4) we have treated u_1, u_2, and u_3 as random variables. The causal ordering among x, y, and z can also be determined without *a priori* assumptions in the case where u_1, u_2, and u_3 are controlled by an experimenter. For simplicity of illustration we assume there is time precedence among the variables. Then the matrix is triangular, so that $a_{ij} \neq 0$ implies $a_{ji} = 0$; and $a_{ij} \neq 0$, $a_{jk} \neq 0$ implies $a_{ki} = 0$.

Under the given assumptions at least three of the off-diagonal a's in (I) must vanish, and the equations and variables can be reordered so that all the non-vanishing coefficients lie on or below the diagonal. If (with this ordering) u_2 or u_3 are varied, at least the variable determined by the first equation will remain constant (since it depends only on u_1). Similarly, if u_3 is varied, the variables determined by the first and second equations will remain constant.

In this way we discover which variables are determined by which equations. Further, if varying u_i causes a particular variable other than the ith to change in value, this variable must be causally dependent on the ith.

Suppose, for example, that variation in u_1 brings about a change in x and y, variation in u_2 a change in y, and variation in u_3 a change in x, y, and z. Then we know that y is causally dependent on x and z, and x upon z. But this is precisely the Case β treated previously under the assumption that the u's were stochastic variables.

CONCLUSION

In this paper I have tried to clarify the logical processes and assumptions that are involved in the usual procedures for testing whether a correlation between two variables is true or spurious. These procedures begin by imbedding the relation between the two variables in a larger three-variable system that is assumed to be self-contained, except for stochastic disturbances or parameters controlled by an experimenter.

Since the coefficients in the three-variable system will not in general be identifiable, and since the determination of the causal ordering implies identifiability, the test for spuriousness of the correlation requires additional assumptions to be made. These assumptions are usually of two kinds. The first, ordinarily made explicit, are assumptions that certain variables do *not* have a causal influence on certain others. These assumptions reduce the number of degrees of freedom of the system of coefficients by implying that three specified coefficients are zero.

The second type of assumption, more often implicit than explicit, is that the random disturbances associated with the three-variable system are uncorrelated. This assumption gives us a sufficient number of additional restrictions to secure the identifiability of the remaining coefficients, and hence to determine the causal ordering of the variables.

References

1. Kendall, Patricia L., and Lazarsfeld, Paul F., "Problems of Survey Analysis," in Merton and Lazarsfeld (eds.), *Continuities in Social Research*, The Free Press, 1950, 133–96.
2. Koopmans, Tjalling C., "Identification Problems in Economic Model Construction," *Econometrica* 17: 125–44 (April 1949), reprinted as Chapter II in *Studies in Econometric Methods*, Cowles Commission Monograph 14.
3. ———, "When Is an Equation System Complete for Statistical Purposes?" Chapter 17 in *Statistical Inference in Dynamic Economic Models*, Cowles Commission Monograph 10.
4. Orcutt, Guy H., "Toward Partial Redirection of Econometrics," *The Review of Economics and Statistics*, 34 (1952), 195–213.
5. ———, "Actions, Consequences, and Causal Relations," *The Review of Economics and Statistics*, 34 (1952), 305–14.
6. Simon, Herbert A., "On the Definition of the Causal Relation," *The Journal of Philosophy*, 49 (1952), 517–28.
7. ———, "Causal Ordering and Identifiability." Chapter III in *Studies in Econometric Methods*, Cowles Commission Monograph 14.
8. Yule, G. Udny, *An Introduction to the Theory of Statistics*, Charles Griffin and Co., 10th ed., 1932, Chapters 4, 12. (Equivalent chapters will be found in all subsequent editions of Yule and Yule and Kendall, through the 14th.)
9. Zeisel, Hans, *Say It With Figures*, New York, Harper and Brothers, 1947.

16

The Linkage between Constituency Attitudes and Congressional Voting Behavior: A Causal Model*

Charles F. Cnudde
and Donald J. McCrone

This essay by Professors Cnudde and McCrone (both of
the University of Wisconsin) applies some extensions of
Simon's method to a substantive problem. As an
example of causal analysis, we believe that this essay
shows clearly the relevance of such analysis to theories of
influence. In this context (and, presumably, others as
well), to accept a given causal model as accurate is to
accept an empirical theory of influence, at least tentatively.
This essay originally appeared in 60 American Political
Science Review (1966), 66–72 and is reprinted by
permission from the authors and the American Political
Science Association.

WARREN E. MILLER and Donald E.
Stokes' publication in 1963 of a preliminary
report on the Survey Research Center's representation study is an important land-
mark in the development of empirical
political theory.[1] That report addressed
itself to the crucial theoretical question of
the linkage between mass political opinions
and governmental policy-making.[2] More
specifically, the report found considerable
policy agreement between Congressional roll
call votes and the attitudes of the individual
Congressman's constituency.[3] This policy
agreement was then interpreted through
several causal paths and the Congressman's

* The authors wish to express their gratitude to
Warren E. Miller and Donald E. Stokes for providing the data upon which this analysis is based. We
gratefully acknowledge the invaluable assistance of
Hubert M. Blalock, Jr. and James W. Prothro. The
authors, of course, are solely responsible for the
analysis.

perception of his constituency's attitudes
was found to be the main path by which
the local district ultimately influenced Congressional outputs.

The main body of the report dealt with
the broad civil rights issue dimension, and,
by specifying the perceptual path by which
constituency influence is brought to bear,
documented the effect of political issues
despite the generally low level of political
information held at the mass level. Thus,
the Congressmen, through their broad cognitive evaluations, were aware of how far
they could proceed in determining their
civil rights roll call votes on the basis of
their own attitudes before risking the
displeasure of their constituents.

Beyond such major substantive contributions the representation study introduced to
political science a variance-apportioning
technique similar to that developed by
Sewall Wright, in 1921.[4] Through this
variance-apportioning technique, the importance of the perceptual link was isolated
and evaluated. This study, then, symbolizes
the growing recognition in political science
of the importance of more sophisticated
methodological tools in the process of
theory building.

I

This essay seeks to continue this trend
toward empirical theory building in political
science. A technique for making causal inferences is utilized to resolve two theoretically important problems left unresolved in
the original constituency influence study.

In the representation study the authors report the following paradigm showing intercorrelations between constituency's attitude,
representative's perception of constituency's attitude, representative's attitude,
and representative's roll call behavior on
the civil rights dimension. Each of these
variables, which we shall call D, P, A,
and R, respectively, was linked to every
other variable through causal arrows. The
inclusion of all possible causal arrows
follows the authors' statement of the
hypothetical conditions of constituency influence.

202

Broadly speaking, the constituency can control the policy actions of the Representative in two alternative ways. The first of these is for the district to choose a Representative who so shares its views that in following his own convictions he does his constituents' will. . . . The second means of constituency control is for the Congressman to follow his (at least tolerably accurate) perceptions of district attitude in order to win re-election. . . . Out of respect for the processes by which the human actor achieves cognitive congruence we have also drawn arrows between the two intervening factors, since the Congressman probably tends to see his district as having the same opinion as his own and also tends, over time, to bring his own opinion into line with the district's.[5]

Figure 1, then, represents the model of constituency influence which the authors derive conceptually. This conceptual causal model is then evaluated empirically to determine how well it interprets constituency influence. Each conceptually possible path from D to R is assumed to be operative and the authors move directly to a test of how effective each is. Thus, each conceptually possible direct path is evaluated as an interpretation of the indirect relationship between constituency attitude and representative's roll call behavior through the computation of influence coefficients. The perceptual path, running from D to P to R, is found to be the major link accounting for the relationship between D and R. Never-

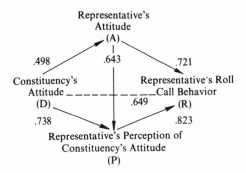

Representative's
Attitude
(A)

.498   .643   .721

Constituency's   Representative's Roll
Attitude _ _ _ _ _ _ _ _ _ _ Call Behavior
(D)   .649   (R)
.738   .823
Representative's Perception of
Constituency's Attitude
(P)

Figure 1. Intercorrelations of variables pertaining to civil rights—whole district*

* The correlations used in this essay are not taken from Warren E. Miller and Donald E. Stokes, "Constituency Influence in Congress," this Review, 57 (1963), p. 52. The original coefficients have been corrected to remove the attenuation of correlation due to the sampling variance of constituency measures based on limited samples of constituents. The basis of this correction is explained in Warren E. Miller and Donald E. Stokes, Representation in the American Congress (Englewood Cliffs, New Jersey: Prentice-Hall, in press).

theless, the path from D to A to R is found to be of some consequence in interpreting the relationship, indicating that recruitment as such has a direct effect.[6]

The use of the variance-apportioning technique also means that the authors must leave the question of the direction of causation between the two intervening variables A and P unanswered, i.e., whether the Congressman's attitudes distort his perceptions, or his perception of district attitudes influences his own attitudes. The reported influence coefficients are computed with causation going from A to P. This is consistent with general psychological theory which holds that attitudes are firmer and more long-lasting than perceptions. This model is also the "least favorable" as far as the total contribution of the Congressman's perceptions to the original relationship is concerned.[7] However, the original study declared that either causal direction is possible.

The present analysis will apply two similar theory building techniques to the civil rights model. First, the Simon-Blalock causal model analysis is used to resolve the two questions: are all the possible causal paths operative? what is the direction of causation between the representative's perception and his attitude? The Simon-Blalock technique enables us

to make causal *inferences* concerning the adequacy of casual models, at least in the sense that we can proceed by eliminating inadequate models that make predictions that are not consistent with the data.[8]

The logic of the Simon-Blalock technique, then, requires the consideration of various alternative causal models. The causal models are tested for adequacy by utilizing the empirically established intercorrelations. If the prediction equations for any given causal model do not conform to the actual relationships among the variables in the model, then it is rejected.[9] After testing each causal model, if only one fits the data, then we can infer from its adequacy that it is the causal model to adopt. If more than one model fits the data, it is necessary to resort to the use of regression coefficients to infer the most likely candidate.[10] Briefly, Blalock's additions to the Simon technique provide a basis for inferring causal relationships, not only through spurious correlations,[11] but also by establishing indirect and direct effects.

Second, Miller and Stokes' variance-apportioning technique is used to evaluate the effectiveness of various intervening variables in interpreting a relationship between independent and dependent variables.[12] This evaluation will proceed only after we have inferred the correct causal model by use of the Simon-Blalock method. The Simon-Blalock technique can also be used to evaluate intervening variables, but the value of the variance-apportioning technique is that it gives the proportion of the original relationship that the intervening paths explain.[13]

This analysis makes most of the causal assumptions made in the original study. On the theoretical level, the most important of these is that constituency attitude is the independent variable and the representative's roll call behavior is the dependent variable.

This paper also accepts the other assumptions necessary for the use of product-moment correlations in the original study: that departures from multivariate normality and normally distributed errors are not great, that relationships are additive and linear. It also assumes that the other causes of each variable are not correlated with the other variables in the system of relationships and causation is uni-directional.

II

Alternative Causal Models

The first test to be made of the constituency influence model involves whether, in fact, the direct link between *A* and *P* exists at all. If *A* and *P* are correlated only because

they are both related to *D*, then there would not be a direct relationship between *A* and *P* and the question of causal direction would be superfluous. Model I shows graphically this possibility.

Restricting our attention to the first half of the model (the relationship between *D*, *A*, and *P*), we note that Model I predicts that *D* is an independent variable producing variation directly in the variables *A* and *P*. Neither *A* nor *P* in that case would be producing variation in each other. If Model I is correct there would be no development sequence in either the direction of *D* to *A* to *P* or in the direction of *D* to *P* to *A*. The first equation in Table 1 shows the Simon-Blalock test of this model.

The very poor degree of fit between the actual correlation between *A* and *P* and the predicted correlation if there were no direct relationship between *A* and *P* indicates that Model I is incorrect empirically. The large difference between .643 and .368 indicates that at least to some degree there is a developmental sequence between *D*, *A*, and *P*. Once a direct relationship between *A* and *P* is found, the next step is to determine whether this relationship is entirely due to a developmental sequence. Model II predicts that the relationship between *A* and *P* is entirely a part of a developmental relationship from *D* to *A* to *P*.

If Model II is correct, then the causal direction of the relationship between *A* and

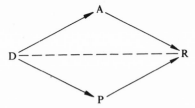

Model I. No direct link between P and A.

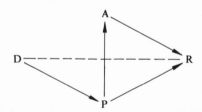

Model II. Developmental Sequence from D to A to P.

P would go from A to P. This hypothesis is a necessary part of the developmental sequence which is predicted. This, incidentally, is also the causal direction included in the "least favorable" model of the Miller and Stokes study. Were this developmental sequence to fit the data, the inference would be that no direct relationship between D and P existed. Instead, the correlation between D and P would be accounted for by the relationship from $D \rightarrow A \rightarrow P$. The second equation of Table 1 shows the test of Model II.

The poor degree of fit between .738 and .320 indicates that P is not without some independent and direct effect from D and that therefore Model II is incorrect. If there is a developmental sequence from D to A to P it does not entirely account for the correlation between D and P. To some degree, then, D also has a direct effect upon P.

Thus far, this analysis indicates two findings:

1) To some extent there is a developmental sequence involving D, A, and P.

2) To some extent D has a direct effect upon P.

The direction of causation between A and P is still unknown, but these two findings lead logically to the next test. Thus, assuming D to be a truly independent variable in this system, the fact that D has a direct effect upon P and that there is some kind of developmental sequence in the system leads to the hypothesis that the sequence goes from D to P to A. Model III shows graphically this prediction.

In model III the causal direction of the relationship between A and P is hypothesized to go from P to A. This sub-hypothesis is necessary to the total hypothesis of the predicted sequence. Also, if the correlation between D and A were found to be entirely due to the D to P to A sequence, then D

The Linkage between Constituency Attitudes and Congressional Voting Behavior: A Causal Model 205

Charles F. Cnudde and Donald J. McCrone

would have no direct effect upon A. The third equation of Table 1 tests this model.

Unlike the two previous models, this model has an almost perfect fit to the data. The close correspondence between the actual .498 and the predicted .475 correlations provides a basis for inferring that the developmental sequence does indeed go from D to P to A. This test also enables us to infer that the direction of causation which was unresolved in the original study, goes from P to A. Moreover, the accuracy of the fit indicates that the developmental sequence accounts for the entire relationship between D and A. The lack of a direct relationship between D and A is, therefore, a modification of the model presented in the original study. Two points which have implications for empirical political theory can be derived from this new model.

Model III, by showing that constituency attitude and representative's attitude are not directly related on the civil rights dimension, has important consequences for the problem of linkage between mass attitudes and governmental policy-making in democratic societies. This analysis indicates that constituencies do not influence civil rights roll calls in the House of Representatives by selecting Congressmen

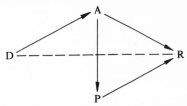

Model III. Developmental Sequence from D to P to A.

TABLE 1. *Prediction equations and degrees of fit for models of constituency influence—first half*

Predictions		Degrees of Fit	
Models	Predicted	Actual	Difference
I. *rDA rDP* = *rAP*	(.498) (.738) = .368	.643	.275
II. *rDA rAP* = *rDP*	(.498) (.643) = .320	.738	.418
III. *rDP rPA* = *rDA*	(.738) (.643) = .475	.498	.023

whose attitudes mirror their own. Instead, Congressmen vote their constituencies' attitudes (as they perceive them) with a mind to the next election. Constituency influence is not provided by candidate recruitment but by elite cognitions.

Such cognitions, in this specialized population of political elites, do not operate as psychological theory would normally indicate. Rather than finding perceptions to be influenced by attitudes, this study shows that the reverse is true. In the area of civil rights especially, Congressmen are in a political situation in which significant rewards accrue to those who perceive their constituency's attitude correctly and vote on that basis. The deprivations are so severe that little room can be allowed for the Congressman's own attitudes to distort this perception. In fact, representatives are motivated to bring their own attitudes (or, at least, their public attitudes) into line with their perceptions of constituency attitude. In the case of Congressmen voting on civil rights the dynamics of the political situation strongly influence psychological processes.

The import of these theoretical statements is dramatized by the fact that both the Congressman's perceptions and his attitudes have direct effects on his roll call votes. Table 2, testing the second half of the constituency influence model (involving the interrelationships between A, P, and R), indicates that the causal arrows between A and R and P and R cannot be removed. In order for the constituency attitude to be translated into Congressional behavior, the Congressman must perceive his constituency's attitude and vote accordingly, or he must change his attitudes to meet his perception of his constituency's attitude and then vote according to his new attitude. Model III, then, is the new constituency influence model developed through an empirical test of the conceptually possible models presented in the Miller and Stokes study.

In the original analysis, the authors of the representation study concentrated upon both the Congressman's attitude and his perception of his constituency's attitude as interpretations of the link between his constituency's attitude and his roll call votes. The new paradigm presented in this analysis points out that only his perceptions can be thought of as providing this link, while his own attitudes are related to his constituency's attitudes through his perceptions. One question remains to be dealt with by this analysis: how well do the Congressman's perceptions interpret the link between constituency attitude and roll calls on civil rights?

The Congressman's perceptions were found to provide the major link between constituency and roll call in the original analysis. The present analysis clearly confirms this point. Miller and Stokes found that the three possible paths interpreting the root relationship explained nearly all of that relationship. Of these paths, that going from constituency attitude to perception to roll call by itself explained about two-thirds of the relationship between constituency attitude and roll call.[14] Since the present analysis removes the weakest path, the two perceptual paths have to be reexamined as the sole possible interpreters of the constituency's influence on Congressional behavior. Table 3 shows the influence coefficients for these paths.

The influence coefficients for b, c, and d can be derived directly from the correlation coefficients involved, as illustrated in equa-

TABLE 2. *Prediction equations and degrees of fit for constituency influence model—second half*

	Predictions	Degrees of Fit		
Models	Predicted	Actual	Difference	
1. $rPA\ rAR = rPR$	$(.643)\ (.721) = .464$	.823	.359	
2. $rPA\ rPR = rAR$	$(.643)\ (.823) = .529$	.721	.192	

tions 1, 2, and 3. The influence coefficient for e can be derived from its correlation and from equations 2 and 3. Finally, the proportion of the root path (r^2DR) that each path explains can be calculated and added to give the proportion that they explain together.

Table 3 indicates that the paths from constituency attitude to representative's perception to roll call and from constituency to perception to representative's attitude to roll call account for an impressive 88% of the link between constituency attitude and roll call. The two paths go to this extent in solving the problem of linkage between mass attitudes and civil rights roll calls in Congress. The largest proportion of this linkage is provided by the path from constituency to perceptions to roll call. Nearly 60% of the relationship between constituency and roll call is explained by this path alone, while about 28% is explained by the path which contains the representative's attitudes. These proportions differ from the Miller-Stokes model because the direct link between constituency attitude and representative's attitude has been eliminated. Thus, these are the new weights assigned to the paths linking constituency and roll call after the model of constituency influence has been inferred by utilizing the Simon-Blalock technique.

Charles F. Cnudde and Donald J. McCrone

III

Thus far, we have evaluated the alternative causal models derived from the constituency influence paradigm based on the attitudes of the whole district. In order to strengthen our confidence in the selected causal model, let us briefly evaluate the alternative causal models based on the attitudes, not of the whole district, but only of the majority within the district.

The three alternative causal models for the direction of causation between D, P, and A are evaluated in Table 4 in the same manner as before.[15] The very poor fit between the actual and predicted correlations for Models I and II indicate that they can still be rejected as the correct causal models. Once again, the fit between the data and the predictions from Model III provides a basis for inferring that this is indeed the correct causal model.

In Table 5 variance-apportioning analysis of the two intervening paths from D to R also demonstrates that the relative weight

TABLE 3. Equations for influence coefficients for two perceptual paths as interpreters of the linkage between mass attitudes and policy

1. $b = r^2DP = .5446$
2. $c = r^2PA = .4134$ $be/r^2DR = .5978$
3. $d = r^2AR = .5198$ $bcd/r^2DR = .2778$
4. $e = r^2PR - cd = .4624$
5. $r^2DR = .4212$ Total $= .8756$

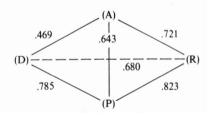

Figure 2. Intercorrelations of variables pertaining to civil rights—district majority.*

* Data provided by Warren E. Miller and Donald E. Stokes to the authors.

TABLE 4. Prediction equations and degrees of fit for models of constituency influence—District majority

	Predictions	Degrees of Fit		
Models	Predicted	Actual	Difference
I. $rDA\ rDP = rAP$	(.469) (.785) $= .368$	.643	.275
II. $rDA\ rAP = rDP$	(.469) (.643) $= .301$	.785	.484
III. $rDP\ rPA = rDA$	(.785) (.642) $= .505$	.469	.036

between the two paths remains the same. The path from D to P to R still accounts for about twice as much of the variation as does D to P to A to R. One other encouraging aspect of the influence coefficients is the slight rise in the explanatory power of the two intervening paths.

IV

Substantively, on the civil rights dimension, several important findings emerge:

1) The lack of a direct link between Congressmen's attitudes and district attitudes indicates that elite recruitment is not the basis for constituency control.

2) Unlike the private citizen, the Congressman does not distort his perceptions to coincide with his own attitudes. Because the costs of misperceiving are so high for an elected official, his perceptions are likely to cause him to modify his attitudes to fit his reasonably accurate perceptions.

3) The overwhelmingly important impact of Congressmen's perceptions in linking

mass attitudes to policy-making, as indicated by Miller and Stokes, is reconfirmed.

4) The relative importance of the indirect impact of perception through congressional attitudes was underestimated in the original study.

5) Finally, the change in the independent variable from whole district to district majority attitudes reconfirms the inferred causal model and results in only a very slight increment in the explanatory power of the model.[16]

Methodologically, this study reconfirms the implication of the Miller and Stokes article that the use of sophisticated methodological tools is essential in the process of empirical theory building. In particular, it demonstrates the utility of the Simon-Blalock method of causal inference with nonexperimental data. It also highlights the rewards to be attained by the combination of techniques for causal inference and variance-apportioning in one study.

Finally, in regard to the subject of theory building in political science, the cumulative nature of empirical model building needs to be stressed. By explicit articulation of the model of constituency influence and emphasis on establishing empirical relationships, the Miller-Stokes study provides a basis for further development. The application of new techniques and the possible inclusion of new variables is thereby facilitated. This study has focused on the cumulative nature of this model by the adoption of the Simon-Blalock method to provide answers to undeveloped or unresolved questions stemming from the original model. The resolution of these questions also results in a more parsimonious causal model of constituency influence in Congress.

TABLE 5. *Equations for influence coefficients for two perceptual paths as interpreters of the linkage between mass attitudes and policy —district majority*

1. $b = r^2DP = .6162$	$be/r^2DR = .6161$
2. $c = r^2PA = .4134$	$bcd/r^2DR = .2863$
3. $d = r^2AR = .5198$	—
4. $e = r^2PR - cd = .4624$	Total $= .9024$
5. $r^2DR = .4624$	

In the following paper we offer a method for the *a priori* evaluation of the division of power among the various bodies and members of a legislature or committee system. The method is based on a technique of the mathematical theory of games, applied to what are known there as "simple games" and "weighted majority games."[1] We apply it here to a number of illustrative cases, including the United States Congress, and discuss some of its formal properties.

The designing of the size and type of a legislative body is a process that may continue for many years, with frequent revisions and modifications aimed at reflecting changes in the social structure of the country; we may cite the role of the House of Lords in England as an example. The effect of a revision usually cannot be gauged in advance except in the roughest terms; it can easily happen that the mathematical structure of a voting system conceals a bias in power distribution unsuspected and unintended by the authors of the revision. How, for example, is one to predict the degree of protection which a proposed system affords to minority interests? Can a consistent criterion for "fair representation" be found?[2] It is difficult even to *describe* the net effect of a double representation system such as is found in the U.S. Congress (i.e., by states and by population), without attempting to deduce it *a priori*. The method of measuring "power" which we present in this paper is intended as a first step in the attack on these problems.

Our definition of the power of an individual member depends on the chance he has of being critical to the success of a winning coalition. It is easy to see, for example, that the chairman of a board consisting of an even number of members (including himself) has no power if he is allowed to vote only to break ties. Of course he may have prestige and moral influence and will even probably get to vote when someone is not present. However, in the narrow and abstract model of the board he is without power. If the board consists of an odd number of members, then he has exactly as much power as any ordinary member because his vote is

17

A Method for Evaluating the Distribution of Power in a Committee System

*L. S. Shapley
and Martin Shubik*

As Simon's essay on causal analysis shows, it is necessary to assume that variables not included in one's causal equations affect the system randomly—don't "count," in a sense—in order to make causal interpretations. This point reminds us of the importance of deductive frameworks which admit only a limited number of empirical concepts; the mathematical theory of games appears to be one such framework. This early essay by Professors Shapley and Shubik (who are both now with the Rand Corporation) presents a method for the a priori evaluation of the division of power in a committee system, based upon the chance any given member has of being critical to the success of a winning coalition. It originally appeared in 48 American Political Science Review (1954), 787–92, and is reprinted by permission from the authors and the American Political Science Association.

"pivotal"—i.e., turns a possible defeat into a success—as often as the vote of any other member. Admittedly he may not cast his vote as often as the others, but much of the voting done by them is not necessary to ensure victory (though perhaps useful for publicity or other purposes). If a coalition has a majority, then extra votes do not change the outcome. For any vote, only a minimal winning coalition is necessary.

Put in crude economic terms, the above implies that if votes of senators were for sale, it might be worthwhile buying forty-nine of them, but the market value of the fiftieth (to the same customer) would be zero. It is possible to buy votes in most corporations by purchasing common stock. If their policies are entirely controlled by simple majority votes, then there is no more

209

power to be gained after one share more than 50% has been acquired.[3]

Let us consider the following scheme: There is a group of individuals all willing to vote for some bill. They vote in order. As soon as a majority[4] has voted for it, it is declared passed, and the member who voted last is given credit for having passed it. Let us choose the voting order of the members randomly. Then we may compute the frequency with which an individual belongs to the group whose votes are used and, of more importance, we may compute how often he is *pivotal*. This latter number serves to give us our index. It measures the number of times that the action of the individual actually changes the state of affairs. A simple consequence of this formal scheme is that where all voters have the same number of votes, they will each be credited with $1/n$th of the power, there being n participants. If they have different numbers of votes (as in the case of stockholders of a corporation), the result is more complicated; more votes mean more power, as measured by our index, but not in direct proportion (see below).

Of course, the actual balloting procedure used will in all probability be quite different from the above. The "voting" of the formal scheme might better be thought of as declarations of support for the bill, and the randomly chosen order of voting as an indication of the relative degrees of support by the different members, with the most enthusiastic members "voting" first, etc. The *pivot* is then the last member whose support is needed in order for passage of the bill to be assured.

Analyzing a committee chairman's tie-breaking function in this light, we see that in an *odd* committee he is pivotal as often as an ordinary member, but in an *even* committee he is never pivotal. However, when the number of members is large, it may sometimes be better to modify the strict interpretation of the formal system, and say that the number of members in attendance is about as likely to be even as odd. The chairman's index would then be

just half that of an ordinary member. Thus, in the U.S. Senate the power index of the presiding officer is—strictly—equal to 1/97. Under the modified scheme it is 1/193. (But it is zero under either interpretation when we are considering decisions requiring a two-thirds majority, since ties cannot occur on such votes.) Recent history shows that the "strict" model may sometimes be the more realistic: in the present Senate (1953–54) the tie-breaking power of the Vice President, stemming from the fact that 96 is an even number, has been a very significant factor. However, in the passage of ordinary legislation, where perfect attendance is unlikely even for important issues, the modified scheme is probably more appropriate.

For Congress as a whole we have to consider three separate bodies which influence the fate of legislation. It takes majorities of Senate and House, with the President, or two-thirds majorities of Senate and House without the President, to enact a bill. We take all the members of the three bodies and consider them voting[5] for the bill in every possible order. In each order we observe the relative positions of the straight-majority pivotal men in the House and Senate, the President, and also the 2/3-majority pivotal men in House and Senate. One of these five individuals will be the pivot for the whole vote, depending on the order in which they appear. For example, if the President comes after the two straight-majority pivots, but before one or both of the 2/3-majority pivots, then he gets the credit for the passage of the bill. The frequency of this case, if we consider all possible orders (of the 533 individuals involved), turns out to be very nearly 1/6. This is the President's power index. (The calculation of this value and the following is quite complicated, and we shall not give it here.) The values for the House as a whole and for the Senate as a whole are both equal to 5/12, approximately. The individual members of each chamber share these amounts equally, with the exception of the presiding officers. Under our "modified" scheme they each get about 30% of the power of an ordinary member; under the "strict" scheme, about 60%. In brief, then, the power indices for the three bodies are in the proportion 5:5:2. The indices for a *single* congressman, a *single* senator, and the President are in the proportion 2:9:350.

In a multicameral system such as we have just investigated, it is obviously easier to defeat a measure than to pass it.[6] A coalition of senators, sufficiently numerous, can block passage of any bill. But they cannot push through a bill of their own without help from the other chamber. This suggests that our analysis so far has been incomplete—that we need an index of "blocking power" to supplement the index already defined. To this end, we could set up a formal scheme similar to the previous one, namely: arrange the individuals in all possible orders and imagine them casting *negative* votes. In each arrangement, determine the person whose vote finally defeats the measure and give him credit for the block. Then the "blocking power" index for each person would be the relative number of times that he was the "blocker".

Now it is a remarkable fact that the new index is exactly equal to the index of our original definition. We can even make a stronger assertion: *any scheme for imputing power among the members of a committee system either yields the power index defined above or leads to a logical inconsistency.* A proof, or even a precise formulation, of this assertion would involve us too deeply in mathematical symbolism for the purposes of the present paper.[7] But we can conclude that the scheme we have been using (arranging the individuals in all possible orders, etc.) is just a convenient conceptual device; the indices which emerge are not peculiar to that device but represent a basic element of the committee system itself.

We now summarize some of the general properties of the power index. In pure *bi*cameral systems using simple majority votes, each chamber gets 50% of the power (as it turns out), regardless of the relative sizes. With more than two chambers, power varies inversely with size: the smallest body is most powerful, etc. But no chamber is completely powerless, and no chamber holds more than 50% of the power. To

illustrate, take Congress without the provision for overriding the President's veto by means of two-thirds majorities. This is now a pure tricameral system with chamber sizes of 1, 97, and 435. The values come out to be slightly under 50% for the President, and approximately 25% each for the Senate and House, with the House slightly less than the Senate. The exact calculation of this case is quite difficult because of the large numbers involved. An easier example is obtained by taking the chamber sizes as 1, 3, and 5. Then the division of power is in the proportions 32:27:25. The calculation is reproduced at the end of this paper.

The power division in a multicameral system also depends on the type of majority required to pass a bill. Raising the majority in *one* chamber (say from one-half to two-thirds) increases the relative power of that chamber.[8] Raising the required majority in all chambers simultaneously weakens the smaller house or houses at the expense of the larger. In the extreme case, where unanimity is required in every house, each individual in the whole legislature has what amounts to a veto, and is just as powerful as any other individual. The power index of each chamber is therefore directly proportional to its size.

We may examine this effect further by considering a system consisting of a governor and a council. Both the governor and some specified fraction of the council have to approve a bill before it can pass. Suppose first that council approval has to be unanimous. Then (as we saw above) the governor has no more power than the typical councilman. The bicameral power division is in the ratio 1:N, if we take N to be the number of councilmen. If a simple majority rule is adopted, then the ratio becomes 1:1 between governor and council. That is, the governor has N times the power of a councilman. Now suppose that the approval of only one member of the council is required. This means that an individual councilman has very little chance of being pivotal. In fact the power division turns out to be N:1 in favor of the governor.[9] If votes were for sale, we might now expect the governor's price to be N^2 times as high as the average councilman's.

Several other examples of power distribution may be given. The indices reveal the decisive nature of the veto power in the United Nations Security Council. The Council consists of eleven members, five of whom have vetoes. For a substantive resolution to pass, there must be seven affirmative votes and no vetoes. Our power evaluation gives 76/77 or 98.7% to the "Big Five" and 1/77 or 1.3% to the remaining six members. Individually, the members of the "Big Five" enjoy a better than 90 to 1 advantage over the others.

It is well known that usually only a small fraction of the stock is required to keep control of a corporation. The group in power is usually able to muster enough proxies to maintain its position. Even if this were not so, the power of stockholders is not directly proportional to their holding, but is usually biased in favor of a large interest. Consider one man holding 40% of a stock while the remaining 60% is scattered among 600 small shareholders, with 0.1% each. The power index of the large holder is 66.6%, whereas for the small holders it is less than 0.06% apiece. The 400:1 ratio in holdings produces a power advantage of better than 1000:1.[10]

The preceding was an example of a "weighted majority game". Another example is provided by a board with five members, one of whom casts two extra votes. If a simple majority (four out of seven votes) carries the day, then power is distributed 60% to the multivote member, 10% to each of the others. To see this, observe that there are five possible positions for the strong man, if we arrange the members in order at random. In three of these positions he is pivotal. Hence his index is equal to 3/5. (Similarly, in the preceding example, we may compute that the strong man is pivotal 400 times out of 601.)

* * *

The values in the examples given above do not take into account any of the sociological or political superstructure that almost invariably exists in a legislature or policy board. They were not intended to be a representation of present day "reality." It would be foolish to expect to be able to catch all the subtle shades and nuances of custom and procedure that are to be found in most real decision-making bodies. Nevertheless, the power index computations may be useful in the setting up of norms or standards, the departure from which will serve as a measure of, for example, political solidarity, or regional or sociological factionalism, in an assembly. To do this we need an empirical power index, to compare with the theoretical. One possibility is as follows: The voting record of an individual is taken. He is given no credit for being on the losing side of a vote. If he is on the winning side, when n others voted with him, then he is awarded the probability of his having been the pivot (or blocker, in the case of a defeated motion), which is $1/n + 1$. His probabilities are then averaged over all votes. It can be shown that this measure gives more weight than the norm does to uncommitted members who hold the "balance of power" between extreme factions. For example, in a nine-man committee which contains two four-man factions which always oppose each other, the lone uncommitted member will always be on the winning side, and will have an observed index of 1/5, compared to the theoretical value of 1/9.

A difficulty in the application of the above measure is the problem of finding the correct weights to attach to the different issues. Obviously it would not be proper to take a uniform average over all votes, since there is bound to be a wide disparity in the importance of issues brought to a vote. Again, in a multicameral legislature (or in any more complicated system), many important issues may be decided without every member having had an opportunity to go on record with his stand. There are many other practical difficulties in the way of direct applications of the type mentioned. Yet the power index appears to offer useful information concerning the basic design of legislative assemblies and policy-making boards.

* * *

APPENDIX

The evaluation of the power distribution for a tricameral legislature with houses of 1, 3, and 5 members is given below:

There are 504 arrangements of five X's, three O's, and one ϕ, all equally likely if the nine items are ordered at random. In the following tabulation, the numbers indicate the number of permutations of predecessors ( ) and successors [ ] of the final pivot, marked with an asterisk. The dots indicate the pivots of the three separate houses. Power indices for the houses are 192/504, 162/504, and 150/504, and hence are in the proportion 32:27:25, with the smallest house the strongest. Powers of the individual members are as $32:9:9:9:5:5:5:5:5$.

O Ȯ O X X φ̇ Ẋ X X
   (60)   * [1] } 150 pivots for X

O Ȯ O X X φ̇ Ẋ O X X
   (30)   *   [3]

O X X Ẋ X X φ̇ Ȯ O
   (42)   * [1] } 162 pivots for O

O X X Ẋ X φ̇ Ȯ O X
  (30)   * [2]

O X X Ẋ φ̇ Ȯ O X X
  (20)   *   [3]

O Ȯ O X X Ẋ X X φ̇
   (56)   *

O Ȯ O X X Ẋ X φ̇ X
   (35)   * [1]

O Ȯ O X X Ẋ φ̇ X X
   (20)   *   [1]

O Ȯ X X Ẋ X X φ̇ O
   (21)   * [1] } 192 pivots for ϕ

O Ȯ X X Ẋ X φ̇ O X
   (15)   *   [2]

O Ȯ X X Ẋ φ̇ O X X
   (12) *   [3]

18

A Test of the Adequacy of the Power Index

William Riker

In this essay Professor Riker, whose work appears in Section III as well, attempts to evaluate the power index devised by Shapley and Shubik. As Riker reports, the results are ambiguous, and this could be for several reasons. All things considered, it would appear that mathematical game theory's claim to serve as a model for a descriptive theory of decision-making is tentative at best. On the other hand, game theory has provided a framework within which some of the most puzzling aspects of the notion of power begin to make sense. Accordingly we are including this sometimes ambiguous test, with many of Riker's own reservations about its interpretation. This essay originally appeared in 4 Behavioral Science *(1959) 276–90 and is reprinted by permission from the author and* Behavioral Science.

THE *a priori* power index, devised by Shapley and Shubik (1954) as an application of Shapley's theorem on the value of n-person games (1953), has seemed attractive to many political scientists as a possible base for a precise political theory and a systematic political science (Simon, 1957). By reason of this potential use of the index, it is desirable to subject it to careful scrutiny, examining both the assumptions that lie behind it and the relevance it has to concrete political events. Simon, in his comments on the index, has observed that his intuition leads him to believe that the index "agrees pretty well" with reality. But for him the adequacy of the index as a model remains untested. More recently, in using the index for a specific statistical purpose, Schaps and I have offered some indirect and slight evidence of its adequacy (1958); but this evidence is so slight that for all practical purposes our judgment of the adequacy of the model still rests on intuition. Hoping to substitute knowledge for wisdom, I have devised and conducted a test of one of the

assumptions behind the index. Although the results are essentially ambiguous, I take the trouble to report them in this essay because, ambiguous though they are, still they may lead to a slightly better understanding of this extremely important notion.

The Definition of Power

In order to spare those readers who may be unfamiliar with the notion of the power index the trouble of referring to the original essays by Shapley and Shubik, I repeat a definition of the index: Given a voting body of *n* members and a rule to define victory in a vote. (Let use assume here the usual majoritarian rule, i.e., if *n* is odd, the winning side consists of $(n + 1)/2$ or more of the members, and, if *n* is even, the winning side consists of $(n/2) + 1$ or more of the members.) Allow members to vote yea (or nay) in any possible sequence. There are *n*! (read "n factorial," that is $1 \cdot 2 \cdot \ldots \cdot n$) such sequences. Each sequence may be regarded as a way to build up a winning coalition. Define a minimal winning coalition as a coalition of members such that, if one member is subtracted, it ceases to be a winning coalition. Define a pivot as the member who makes a minimal winning coalition in a sequence, in this instance as the $[(n + 1)/2]$th or the $[(n/2) + 1]$th member. In each sequence the pivot is thus the last added or marginal member of a minimal winning coalition. The power index, *P*, with respect to any member, *i*, is this simple ratio:

$$P_i = \frac{\text{the number of sequences in which } i \text{ pivots}}{n! \text{ or the number of sequences possible}}$$

Manifestly, the sum of P_i in any voting body is one. Hence the power index of any one member is a number in the range from zero to one.

So defined, the power index may be interpreted as the *a priori* chance a member of a voting body has to be the last added member of a minimal winning coalition. As such it is analogous to the chance than any one number will turn up on a roulette wheel. (In sharp contrast to honest and uncon-

214

Notes to chapter 18 are found on page 378.

scious wheels which actually do show numbers in just about the computed expectation, consciously scheming humans manage to manipulate the process of coalition forming so that empirically observed pivoting may differ significantly from *a priori* computations of pivoting. Hence, while the odds for roulette wheels are a pretty good prediction of reality, the *a priori* power index may have no connection at all with pivoting in natural legislatures.)

Interpreting this definition of power further, it assumes that a person in a marginal position with respect to a legislative coalition is able to acquire a significantly larger portion than other members of the rewards that accrue to the coalition. In strictly mathematical terms, there is, of course, no reason for this assumption about the payoff to the marginal member. But in terms of the application of the index, there is no reason to measure the chance of marginality unless it is in fact assumed that the last added member hogs the payoff.

In popular usage, the word "power" usually means much more than this rather restricted definition allows. Popularly, "power" refers, *inter alia*, not only to (*a*) that marginal location in the bargaining system which allows a member to exact a high price, but also to (*b*) resources (such as money, arms, etc.) that can be used to dominate others and (*c*) the actual act of domination.[2] It may also have other references that I need not bother to list here. Since the word "power" has so much wider a reference in popular usage than in the precise technical sense of the power index, it is reasonable to wonder whether or not people in the real world—people who, of course, think about power in the popular sense—are actually interested in obtaining power in the technical sense. One may even ask whether or not people in the real world are conscious of the existence of power in the technical sense. The question may be put thus: Is that marginal location which the power index measures something people want to be in? In short, do people want the kind of power that the index measures?

The economist knows of course that there is no such thing in the real world as an economic man who singlemindedly maximizes profit; still the economist is quite certain that this abstraction is worth discussing because he is also quite certain that most people in the real world do want money. But the political scientist is not so certain that his abstractions have any relevance at all to life. A political man who singlemindedly maximizes power is worth discussing only if it can be shown that people in the real world want power, or at least the kind of power that is measured by the power index. Hence, one of the pressing necessities for a political *science* is some evidence on whether or not men seek power.

The Model

An approach to an answer to this question is to be found in certain features of weighted majority games. In such games, the members of the voting body have unequal weights, e.g., an unequal number of votes. (Some well-known institutional embodiments of weighted majority games are the voting procedures in business corporations in which each stockholder has as many votes as shares.) A signal feature of weighted majority games is that in them the players' power indices differ from their weights. Thus, in an extreme instance in a three person game in which the players are weighted 50, 49, and 1, the power of these players is $2/3$, $1/6$, $1/6$ respectively. The power of a player with the weight of 50 exceeds his weight by $1/6$ and the power of the player with a weight of 1 exceeds his weight by $47/300$ or only slightly less than $1/6$. The power of the player with a weight of 49 is almost $1/3$ less than his weight.[3]

One way to answer the question about whether or not people want the kind of power that the index measures is to discover whether or not participants in a weighted majority game try to increase their power index. It is not to be supposed that members of natural legislatures actually try to calculate their bargaining posi-

tion by use of Shapley's theorem. But, if
the theorem relates to anything real, members must sense gains and losses in bargaining opportunities, must note with envy
or satisfaction that their colleagues have
more or fewer opportunities, and must
behave in such ways as might increase or
maintain their opportunities. Hence, if
one can find a natural legislature that conforms somewhat to the model of a weighted
majority game, then one can examine the
behavior of the members of this legislature
in order to discover whether or not they
want this kind of power. Natural legislatures that resemble the model are those
multiparty legislatures in which the parties
have fairly strict discipline. One can then
imagine the parties as players, each player
weighted according to the number of members it has. In such a legislature the behavior that concerns us is the migration of
individual members from party to party.
In this migration do they resign from parties
with a relatively low index to join parties
with a relatively high index?

In order to answer this question one
needs to find a natural legislature characterized by at least the following features:
(a) more than two parties (b) relatively
strict party discipline so that parties may
be regarded as behaving like persons (by
strict discipline, I mean the situation in
which, if one member of a party votes on
one side of an issue, then all members of
that party vote on the same side of the
issue) and (c) relatively frequent migrations
among parties by a substantial number of
members.

One natural legislature that almost satisfies these requirements is the French National Assembly. It contains usually about
eight or ten parties with more than one
member as well as a number of single-
member parties (sometimes as many as
fifteen or twenty). Some of the multi-
member parties have quite strict discipline
so that they do in fact behave as if they were
individual persons. French parliamentary
rules rather encourage strict discipline on
most *scrutins* in that they permit one

authorized member of a party to drop bal-
lots in the urn for all other members of the
party whether these latter are physically
present or not. According to Campbell's
recent study of discipline in the National
Assembly (1953), the Communist party and
its allied group, the *Républicains Progressistes*, had perfect discipline during the nine
and a half months of the Pinay government
(from 6 March 1952 to 22 December 1952).
In only one per cent of the 673 *scrutins* did
as many as from one to five per cent of the
Socialists break party discipline. The *Indépendants d'Outre-mer* displayed discipline
almost as strict as the Socialists, and not
far behind were two rightist peasant groups,
Action Paysanne and *Paysans d'Union
Sociale*. The weakest discipline occurred
in the center parties: in only 57 per cent of
the *scrutins* were the members of the M.R.P.
strictly disciplined, while in 32 per cent of
the *scrutins* from one to five per cent of
them broke party discipline and in eleven
per cent of the *scrutins* from six to 25 per
cent broke away. The record of the Radicals
was only slightly more disciplined. In
general and as one might expect, the parties
on the left and the right were better disciplined than those in the center, with the
exception of the Gaullistes, who were in
the process of splitting in two during this
period. On the basis of this evidence, one
can say that, for the most part, French
parties are well disciplined and that, even
when their discipline is not perfect, most
French politicians think of parties as the
basic unit of coalition-construction.[4] Finally, the third requirement is satisfied by
the fact that, in recent years, about 15 per
cent of the members of the Assembly have
changed their party affiliation during the
course of a legislature. Thus, while the
French Assembly does not conform perfectly to the requirements here set forth,
it is perhaps close enough to them to be used
as a test case.

In this experiment, the inter-party migrations occurring during the two years 1953
and 1954 were used for analysis. (Since legislative and calendar years coincide in all
years except election years, the calendar
year is a convenient time unit and one that
does not admit of subjective alteration of

boundaries.) For reasons of convenience, it was determined to select years from the Second Legislature (July, 1951, to July, 1955). And in order to limit the use of computer time to a small number of hours, only two years out of the five were selected. The six months of 1951 were eliminated on the ground that a large amount of the migration among parties consisted of late arrivals enrolling in their parliamentary groups. This enrollment was felt to be accidental rather than calculated migration and thus a disturbing feature properly excluded from the experiment. The six months of 1955 were eliminated on the ground that, presumably in anticipation of the forthcoming election, very few inter-party migrations occurred. The year of 1952 was eliminated on the ground that this was the year in which occurred the disintegration of the Gaulliste party which was by far the largest party at the beginning of the year and only the fourth largest at the end of the year. Since this was an extraordinary occurrence, it was felt that a study of the session of 1952 would result in a somewhat distorted version of French parliamentary behavior. After these eliminations, the sessions of 1953 and 1954 were left. These contained a substantial amount of presumably self-seeking migration among parties. And it is this migration that is studied here.

The Migration Decision

A member's decision to migrate from one party to another presumably derives from many motives. Convictions about ideology and estimates of opportunities to be re-elected certainly appear to have deeply influenced many of the migration desisions here studied. In the cases of African members, the primary motive may well have been some attempt (doubtless doomed to failure) to discover some French party sympathetic to African points of view. But along with these readily discernible and usually verbalized motives, there may have been some effort to increase power. If so, then the migrating members' power indices should have increased in the course of the

migration, provided, of course, that the migrators could discover what actions would increase the index. And if, in fact, the migrators' indices did increase, it may be evidence that considerations of power maximization influenced the migrator's behavior and that men want the kind of power that the index measures.

It is possible, therefore, to test one of the assumptions of the power index with this simple, though tedious, calculation: Assuming that each member of a party has $1/m$ of the power of a party with m members, the power of a particular member, i, of a party, A, is defined thus:

$$P_i = \frac{P_A}{m}$$

The power that a migrator has before the migration will be designated as "$(P_i; G_\alpha)$," where G_α is the weighted majority game model of the situation before the migration. (Thus, G_α designates a particular set of weights and players, e.g., $G_1 : \{313; 105, 100, 88, 85, 75, 55, 46, 32, 23, 13, 1, 1, 1\}$, which is a 13-player game with weights totalling 625 and in which 313 are required to win.) The action of migration of course changes the game model so that the model at the end of the migration, G_β, differs from G_α. For each migration, calculate a gain or loss, R_j, where j is a member of the class, M, of events of migrations:

$$R_j = (P_i; G_\beta) - (P_i; G_\alpha)$$

The results of these calculations may be interpreted in at least the following ways:

Case 1. If $\Sigma_{j\in M}(R_j)$ is a positive number, this fact may be taken to imply either (*a*) that legislators consciously tried to increase their power indices or (*b*) that in the course of their migrations legislators accidentally increased their power indices.

Case 2. If $\Sigma_{j\in M}(R_j)$ is a negative number or zero, this fact may be taken to imply either (*a*) that legislators consciously rejected advantageous bargaining positions in order to satisfy their ideological and other

compulsions or (*b*) that legislators accidentally decreased their power indices in
the course of their migrations.

A very large positive number would, it
seems to me, indicate strongly that case 1*a*
existed. A small positive number might
indicate that either 1*a* or 1*b* existed. A large
negative number would similarly indicate
that case 2*a* existed, while a small negative
or zero might indicate that either 2*a* or 2*b*
existed. This test is, therefore, likely to
lead to unambiguous results only if a large
positive or a large negative number is
obtained. (What is to be regarded as a large
or small number will be discussed in a later
paragraph.)

An additional calculation yielding interesting information is the gain of the
party migrated to by reason of the migration. Presumably this party can reward the
migrator for his action up to the full amount
of its gain. Hence, even though the migrator's own power index may decline in the
migration, he may yet gain because the
party he joins pays him more than his loss.
This possible payment, Q_j, is calculated
thus:

$$Q_j = \frac{m'(P_A; G_\beta)}{m} - (P_A; G_\alpha)$$

where m is the number of members of A
in G_β and where m' is the number of members of A in G_α.

The Migrations

In the two years 1953 and 1954 there were
34 migrations involving 61 individual
changes of party affiliation by 46 members.
These migrations are listed in Table 1.

For the sake of the examination of some of
the individual migrations, the following material
is included in the table:

Column I: Names and departments of
migrators with the date of the migration. Note:
When an individual member moved from one
multi-member party to a single-member party
to a multi-member party in a week or less, this
double migration is interpreted as a single
migration from one multi-member party to
another.

Column II: Party left and party joined.

Column III: The structure of the game model
at the beginning and end of the migration, that
is G_α and G_β. A list of the 43 games is set forth
in Note *b* of Table 1.

Column IV: The power index at the end of
the migration, i.e., $(P_i; G_\beta)$.

Column V: The power index at the beginning
of the migration, i.e., $(P_i; G_\alpha)$.

Column VI: R_j (i.e., Column IV less Column
V).

Column VII: Q_j, if and only if Q_j is a positive
number. Manifestly, Q is nonexistent when a
member moves from a multi-member party to a
single-member party. A value for Q exists in 19
of the 34 migrations, but in only 11 of the 19 is
Q_j a positive number.

Column VIII: The percentage of advantage or
disadvantage that the migrating members possessed before the migration, that is:

$$\frac{(P_i, G_\alpha) - (1/n)}{1/n}$$

The value $1/n$, is the power index that a member
would have were this a simple majority rather
than a weighted majority game. Thus, $1/n$ is the
power index a member would have if parties did
not exist. This percentage of advantage (+) or
disadvantage (−) is of interest inasmuch as it
indicates something of the incentive a member
may or may not have for migrating. A member
at a large disadvantage (e.g., − 25 % or − 50 %)
by reason of his location in the party system
might reasonably be expected to be somewhat
restive about his party affiliation, while a
member with a large advantage (e.g. + .10)
might reasonably be expected to be stable. In
these calculations $1/n$ is one of the following
values:

$1/_{627}$, which is about .0015948963
$1/_{626}$, which is about .0015974441
$1/_{625}$, which is .0016
$1/_{624}$, which is about .0016025641

It should be noted that in the game models here
considered, disadvantages of over 25 % are
quite common, while advantages are rarely
greater than 6 to 8 per cent.

The entries in columns IV, V, VI, and VII
were calculated to ten decimal places and then
multiplied by 10^6 and rounded off so that
.0015602010 became 1560.

a. The parties, in the order of their arrangement in G_0 and with their size in G_0 are:

S: *Groupe Socialiste;* 104 members and
     one *apparenté.*

C: *Groupe Communiste;* 96 members and
     four members of the *Groupe Progres-
     siste,* which was during the entire two
     years *apparenté* to the Communist
     group. Inasmuch as the *Groupe Progres-
     siste* voted with perfect discipline in
     exactly the same way as the *Groupe
     Communiste,* it seems appropriate to
     list them as one.

William Riker

TABLE 1. The Migrations

Column I	Column II	Column III	Column IV	Column V	Column VI	Column VII	Column VIII
1. Levacher (Finistère) 6 Jan. '53	RI to CR	G_0 to G_1	1560	1548	13		−3.1%
2. Vallon (Seine-1re) Ribère (Alger-1re) 13 Jan. '53	RPF to IOM NI to IOM	G_1 to G_2	2 (1174)	1607 1215	−433 −42		+0.6% −23.9%
3. Vallon (Seine-1re) 23 Jan. '53	IOM to RPF	G_2 to G_3	1604	1174	+430	+92	−26.5%
4. Douala (Cameroun-2e) 28 Jan. '53	NI to IOM	G_3 to G_4	1169	1299	−130		−18.7%
5. Gueye (Sénégal) 12 May '53	IOM to NI	G_5 to G_6	1227	1222	+5		−23.1%
6. Caillet (Seine-5e) Nocher (Loire) 18 May '53	RPF to NI	G_6 to G_7	2 (1338)	2 (1594)	−513		−0.1%
7. Grosseaud (Seine-3e) LeFranc (Pas-de-Calais-2e) 27 May '53	URAS to IRAS	G_7 to G_8	2 (1479)	2 (1594)	−230	+1115	−0.03%
8. Gueye (Sénégal) 10 June '53	NI to IOM	G_8 to G_9	1321	1110	+211		−30.4%
9. Caillet (Seine-5e) 10 June '53	NI to UDSR	G_9 to G_{10}	1437	916	+521		−42.6%
10. Chupin (Finistère) 16 June '53	URAS to UDSR	G_{10} to G_{11}	1380	1592	−212		−0.2%
11. Bernard (Seine-et-Oise-1re) 23 Oct. '53	URAS to UDSR	G_{12} to G_{13}	1326	1609	−283		+0.7%
12. Denis (Dordogne) 23 Oct. '53	MRP to NI	G_{13} to G_{14}	863	1644	−781		+2.9%
13. Ben Aly Cherif (Constantine-2e) 17 Nov. '53	MRP to NI	G_{14} to G_{15}	1310	1648	−338		+3.2%
14. Vallon (Seine-1re) 27 Nov. '53	URAS to NI	G_{16} to G_{17}	1265	1612	−346		+1.0%
15. Trémouilhe (Lot-et-Garonne) 7 Dec. '53	UDSR to RRRS	G_{17} to G_{18}	1601	1359	+242	+347	−14.8%
16. Dommergue (Cantal) 28 Dec. '53	CR to NI	G_{18} to G_{19}	1232	1578	−346		−1.0%
17. Fifteen members of CR	CR to P	G_{19} to G_{20}	15 (1441)				
Three members of CR 30 Dec. '53	CR to CD		3 (1696)	18 (1577)	−1684		−1.1%
18. Bardoux (Puy-de-Dôme), Estèbe (Gironde-1re) 30 Dec. '53	RI to CD	G_{20} to G_{21}	2 (1719)	2 (1465)	+507	+70	−8.1%
19. Montillot (Hte. Saône) 13 Jan. '54	CR to CD	G_{22} to G_{23}	1750	1520	+230	+1	−4.8%

MRP: *Groupe du Mouvement républicain populaire;* 85 members and three *apparentés.*
RPF: *Groupe du Rassemblement du peuple*
URAS: *français;* 85 members. In May, 1953,
RS :   this group changed its name to *Groupe d'Union républicain d'action sociale* and hence, in mentioning events from May, 1953, to June, 1954, it is referred to as URAS. In June, 1954, it changed its name again to *Groupe des Républicains sociaux,* and is therefore referred to as RS for events occurring from that date to the end of the year.

RRRS: *Groupe républicain radical et radical-socialiste;* 67 members and eight *apparentés.*
RI: *Groupe des Républicains indépendants;* 47 members and nine *apparentés.*
CR: *Groupe du centre républicain d'action paysanne et sociale et des démocrates independants;* 40 members and six *apparentés.*
IARS: *Groupe des Indépendants d'action républicaine et sociale;* 30 members and two *apparentés.*
UDSR: *Groupe de l'Union démocratique et socialiste de la résistance;* 16 members and two *apparentés.*
IOM: *Groupe des Indépendants d'outre-mer;* 13 members.

TABLE 1   (cont.).

Column I	Column II	Column III	Column IV	Column V	Column VI	Column VII	Column VIII
20. Renaud (Saône-et-Loire) 18 Feb. '54	IARS to P	G_{23} to G_{24}	1442	1604	−162	+18	+0.4%
21. Lipkowski (Seine-4e) 23 Feb. '54	URAS to NI	G_{24} to G_{25}	1409	1585	−176		−0.8%
22. Béchir Sow (Tchad) 9 Apr. '54	URAS to NI	G_{26} to G_{27}	1503	1578	−75		−1.2%
23. Buron (Mayenne) Monteil (Finistère) 30 June '54	MRP to NI	G_{28} to G_{29}	2 (1432)	2 (1642)	−419		+2.5%
24. All members of CD 22 July '54	CD to P	G_{29} to G_{30}	6 (1524)	6 (1603)	−471	+1401	+0.01%
25. Moatti (Seine-2e) 23 July '54	RS to NI	G_{30} to G_{31}	1393	1584	−190		+1.2%
26. Pinvidic (Finistère) 27 July '54	RS to RI	G_{31} to G_{32}	1489	1581	−92	+225	−1.4%
27. Gailliemin (Vosges) 4 Aug. '54	RS to IARS	G_{32} to G_{33}	1619	1575	+44		−1.7%
28. Frugier (Seine-et-Oise-1re) 31 Aug. '54	RS to NI	G_{34} to G_{35}	1416	1578	−163		−1.4%
29. Sou (Tchad) 31 Oct. '54	RS to NI	G_{35} to G_{36}	1450	1574	−124		−1.6%
30. Bouret (Côtes-du-Nord) 17 Nov. '54	MRP to NI	G_{37} to G_{38}	1492	1655			+3.6%
31. Lecoeur (Pas-de-Calais-2e) 29 Nov. '54	C to NI	G_{38} to G_{39}	1501	1670	−170		+4.6%
32. Sou (Tchad) 8 Dec. '54	NI to RS	G_{39} to G_{40}	1566	1501	+66	+311	−6.1%
33. Béchir Sow (Tchad) 14 Dec. '54	NI to IOM	G_{40} to G_{41}	1296	1506	−210	+108	−5.6%
34. Frugier (Seine-et-Oise-1re) 16 Dec. '54	NI to IR	G_{41} to G_{42}	1500	1563	−63	+262	−2.2%

NI: *"non-inscrit,"* that is, parties consisting of a single member.

The foregoing order persists in G_0 to G_{19}; but in December, 1953, two new groups were formed by dissident members of CR:

P: *Groupe Paysan.*

CD: *Groupe du Centre démocratique et sociale des indépendants et paysans.*

Hence in G_{20} to G_{26} the following order of listing exists: S; C, MRP; URAS; RRRS; RI; URAS; CR; UDSR; P; IOM; CD; NI. In G_{27} to G_{29} URAS and RRRS reverse positions thus: S; C; MRP; RRRS; URAS; RI; IRAS; CR; UDSR; P; IOM; CD; NI. In G_{30} to G_{42} the following order is established as a result of the disappearance of CD: S; C; MRP; RRRS; URAS; RI; IRAS; CR; UDSR; P; IOM; NI.

b. The forty-three game models are as follows:

G_0 (314; 105, 100, 88, 85, 75, 56, 46, 32, 23, 13, 1, 1, 1)

G_1 (314; 105, 100, 88, 85, 75, 55, 47, 32, 23, 13, 1, 1, 1)

G_2 (314; 105, 100, 88, 84, 75, 55, 47, 32, 23, 15, 1, 1)

G_3 (314; 105, 100, 88, 85, 75, 55, 47, 32, 23, 14, 1, 1)

G_4 (314; 105, 100, 88, 85, 75, 55, 47, 32, 23, 15, 1)

G_5 (314; 105, 100, 89, 85, 75, 55, 47, 32, 23, 15, 1)

G_6 (314; 105, 100, 89, 85, 75, 55, 47, 32, 23, 14, 1, 1)

G_7 (314; 105, 100, 89, 83, 75, 55, 47, 32, 23, 14, 1, 1, 1, 1)

G_8 (314; 105, 100, 89, 81, 75, 55, 47, 34, 23, 14, 1, 1, 1, 1)

G_9 (314; 105, 100, 89, 81, 75, 55, 47, 34, 23, 15, 1, 1, 1)

G_{10} (314; 105, 100, 89, 81, 75, 55, 47, 34, 24, 15, 1, 1)

G_{11} (314; 105, 100, 89, 80, 75, 55, 47, 34, 25, 15, 1, 1)

G_{12} (314; 105, 100, 89, 80, 75, 55, 46, 34, 25, 15, 1, 1)

G_{13} (314; 105, 100, 89, 79, 75, 55, 46, 34, 26, 15, 1, 1)

G_{14} (314; 105, 100, 88, 79, 75, 55, 46, 34, 26, 15, 1, 1, 1)

G_{15} (314; 105, 100, 87, 79, 75, 55, 46, 34, 26, 15, 1, 1, 1, 1)

G_{16} (314; 105, 100, 87, 79, 75, 55, 47, 34, 26, 15, 1, 1, 1, 1)

G_{17} (314; 105, 100, 87, 78, 75, 55, 47, 34, 26, 15, 1, 1, 1, 1, 1)

G_{18} (314; 105, 100, 87, 78, 76, 55, 47, 34, 25, 15, 1, 1, 1, 1, 1)

G_{19} (314; 105, 100, 87, 78, 76, 55, 46, 34, 25, 15, 1, 1, 1, 1, 1, 1)

G_{20} (314; 105, 100, 87, 78, 76, 55, 34, 28, 25, 15, 15, 3, 1, 1, 1, 1, 1)

G_{21} (314; 105, 100, 87, 78, 76, 53, 34, 28, 25, 15, 15, 5, 1, 1, 1, 1, 1)

G_{22} (314; 105, 100, 87, 77, 76, 53, 34, 28, 25, 15, 15, 5, 1, 1, 1, 1, 1, 1)

G_{23} (314; 105, 100, 87, 77, 76, 53, 34, 27, 25, 15, 15, 6, 1, 1, 1, 1, 1)

G_{24} (314; 105, 100, 87, 77, 76, 53, 33, 27, 25, 16, 15, 6, 1, 1, 1, 1, 1)

G_{25} (314, 105, 100, 87, 76, 76, 53, 33, 27, 25, 16, 15, 6, 1, 1, 1, 1, 1, 1)

G_{26} (314; 105, 99, 88, 76, 76, 53, 33, 27, 25, 16, 15, 6, 1, 1, 1, 1, 1, 1)

G_{27} (314; 105, 99, 88, 76, 75, 53, 33, 27, 25, 16, 15, 6, 1, 1, 1, 1, 1, 1, 1)

G_{28} (313; 105, 99, 88, 76, 75, 53, 33, 27, 24, 16, 15, 6, 1, 1, 1, 1, 1, 1)

G_{29} (313; 105, 99, 86, 76, 75, 53, 33, 27, 24, 16, 15, 6, 1, 1, 1, 1, 1, 1, 1)

G_{30} (313; 105, 99, 86, 76, 75, 53, 33, 27, 24, 22, 15, 1, 1, 1, 1, 1, 1, 1, 1)

G_{31} (313; 105, 99, 86, 76, 74, 53, 33, 27, 24, 22, 15, 1, 1, 1, 1, 1, 1, 1)

G_{32} (313; 105, 99, 86, 76, 73, 54, 33, 27, 24, 22, 15, 1, 1, 1, 1, 1, 1, 1, 1)

G_{33} (313; 105, 99, 86, 76, 72, 54, 34, 27, 24, 22, 15, 1, 1, 1, 1, 1, 1, 1, 1)

G_{34} (313; 105, 99, 86, 76, 73, 54, 34, 27, 24, 22, 15, 1, 1, 1, 1, 1, 1, 1)

G_{35} (313; 105, 99, 86, 76, 72, 54, 34, 27, 24, 22, 15, 1, 1, 1, 1, 1, 1, 1, 1, 1)

G_{36} (313; 105, 99, 86, 76, 71, 54, 34, 27, 24, 22, 15, 1, 1, 1, 1, 1, 1, 1, 1, 1)

G_{37} (314; 105, 99, 86, 76, 71, 54, 34, 28, 24, 22, 15, 1, 1, 1, 1, 1, 1, 1, 1, 1)

G_{38} (314; 105, 99, 85, 76, 71, 54, 34, 28, 24, 22, 15, 1, 1, 1, 1, 1, 1, 1, 1, 1, 1)

G_{39} (314; 105, 98, 85, 76, 71, 54, 34, 28, 24, 22, 15, 1, 1, 1, 1, 1, 1, 1, 1, 1, 1, 1)

G_{40} (314; 105, 98, 85, 76, 72, 54, 34, 28, 24, 22, 15, 1, 1, 1, 1, 1, 1, 1, 1, 1, 1)

G_{41} (314; 105, 98, 85, 76, 72, 54, 34, 28, 24, 22, 16, 1, 1, 1, 1, 1, 1, 1, 1, 1, 1)

G_{42} (314; 105, 98, 85, 76, 72, 55, 34, 28, 24, 22, 16, 1, 1, 1, 1, 1, 1, 1, 1, 1, 1)

c. The names of the members who joined *Groupe Paysan* in migration 17 are: Antier (Hte. Loire), Ben Tounes (Alger-2e), Champierre de Villeneuve (La Réunion), Deshors (Hte. Loire), La Borbe (Rhône-2e), LeRoy Ladurie (Calvados), Oopa (Océanie), Paquet (Isère), Pébellier (Hte. Loire), Pluchet (Eure), Raffarin (Vienne), de Sesmaisons (Loire-Inf.), Toublanc (Loire-Inf.), Valle (Const.-1re), Vassor (Indre-et-Loire). Those who joined CD are: Liautey (Hte. Saône), Loustaunau-Lacau (B. Pyr), Mazel (Lozère)

d. The members involved in migration 24 are: Bardoux (Puy-de-Dôme), Estèbe (Gironde-1re), Liautey (Hte. Saône), Loustaunau-Lacau (B. Pyr.), Mazel (Lozère), Montillot (Hte. Saône) *e.* In migration 17, of the 46 members of CR, 15 resigned to form *Grpe. Paysan* and three resigned to form CD. In a major regrouping of this sort, it is somewhat difficult to specify the initiator of the action. When one or two persons resign from a party, they clearly are the ones who initiate a change in the *status quo*. But when nearly half a party resigns, the initiating force may be either the resigning minority or the majority that retains the party name. Or indeed, both majority and minority may be regarded as initiators. Here it was decided to assume that the minority, which had to take the first action, was the initiating group. If, however, it is assumed that the majority initiated the action, then the total loss (in Column VI) for the 28 members is $-.0014649320$ and the sum of Column VI should read $-.0053274262$. If it is assumed that all 46 of the members of CR initiated the split then the entry in Column VI should read $-.0031488413$ and the total for the column should be $-.0070113355$. While these two alternatives should be pointed out, the interpretation in the table seems preferred inasmuch as it was indeed the minority who initiated the action.

Interpretation of Table 1

The test figures are, of course, the sums of Columns VI and VII. The sum of Column VI ($\Sigma_{j \in M} (R_j)$) is $-.0055464035$ and ($\Sigma_{j \in M} (Q_j)$) is $+.0039307710$.

The negative sum in Column VI is somewhat surprising and deserves interpretation. In the first place, one wants to know whether or not this negative number is significant. Is it large enough to warrant the conclusion that members deliberately ignored the pursuit of power? None of the usual statistical tests of significance are here available but some indication of the significance is perhaps to be obtained from the following observation: The sum of Column V, that is the sum of the power indices of the migrators just prior to the migrations, is $.0937982241$ and the average for the 61 persons thus is $.0015376758$. The average loss for each of the 61 persons is $-.0000909246$, which is 5.9% of the average power index at the beginning of the migration. Thus it can be said that migrating members lost on the average about six per

cent of their chances to pivot. Considering the inordinate complexity of those games, a six per cent loss does not seem significant. Hence I conclude that, since $\Sigma_{j \in M} (R_j)$ is a small number, the results of the test are truly ambiguous.

This ambiguity is increased if the sum of Column VII is also considered. This sum reduces the total loss to $-.0016156325$ and the loss per member to $-.0000264858$. And then the average loss per member from the average power index at the beginning of the migration becomes 1.7%, which is surely unnoticeable and hence negligible.

In setting standards for the interpretation of this experiment it was said that only large positive or large negative numbers would yield unambiguous results. Having obtained relatively small numbers, we find ourselves in the unfortunate position of searching for meaning in ambiguity. With respect to its main object, the search is certain to result in frustration, for no method is available for resolving the ambiguity. But, as a by-product, the search may result in some further understanding both of the index and of legislators. And with the hope of picking up by-products, I here set forth some possible interpretations of the results of this test.

1. One explanation for the fact that both $\Sigma_{j \in M} (R_j)$ and $\Sigma_{j \in M} ((R_j) + (Q_j))$ were small negative numbers may be that the *a priori* power index is totally irrelevant to the actual chances of pivoting in the French Assembly in 1953 and 1954. As was remarked at the outset, the *a priori* index is a measure of the theoretical chance of pivoting on a roll call and is somewhat analogous to probabilities in games of chance. But conniving humans may alter these probabilities significantly by forming quasi-permanent coalitions. Thus, a party with a fairly large computed chance of pivoting, say $^1/_{10}$, might have in fact no chance whatsoever because it did not belong to a quasi-permanent winning coalition.[5] If this is the situation in the French Assembly, then the *a priori* index measures nothing of relevance to persons making a decision on migration. And if it measures nothing of relevance, one would expect that the outcome of these calculations would, by reason of chance

variation, be a number fairly close to zero, which was in fact what was obtained.

Whether or not this explanation is appropriate for the results obtained depends upon empirical investigation to determine the existence or non-existence of quasi-permanent coalitions. Doubtless the best way to carry out such an investigation would be to construct some sort of empirical power index. If it appeared that the empirical and *a priori* indices varied notably for particular parties, it would follow that some sort of fairly permanent coalition pattern existed and that the *a priori* indices were irrelevant to the decision on migration. But for the present at least insuperable difficulties stand in the way of the construction of an empirical index (Shapley & Shubik, 1954).

A somewhat less exact way to discover the existence of quasi-permanent coalitions has been adopted by Campbell (1953). In his previously cited study of roll calls during the Pinay government (1952), he found that on 562 divisions in which the government took part there appeared to be a government-supporting coalition consisting of the MRP, RRRS, RI, IARS, CR, and UDSR, and a government-opposing coalition consisting of Communists and their small shadow, the Progressistes. The Socialists and Gaullistes seemed genuinely in the middle. My impression (based only on cursory observation and not on measurement) is that in the two succeeding years this situation did not change basically. Inasmuch as there existed a large middle group, neither of the quasi-permanent coalitions could win all the time. Hence, while the center coalition probably won more frequently than the left coalition, an empirical power index probably would not show the center to be distinctly more powerful than other parties. Indeed, the Socialists and Gaullistes, who were often the marginal party in the making and unmaking of governments, may have had more power than the center in these crucial decisions. I conclude, therefore, that— by reason of the large number of parties and the relative fluidity of coalitions— an empirical power index would not differ notably from the *a priori* index. It follows,

then, that this first explanation of the nature of $\Sigma_{j \in M} (R_j)$ probably does not explain it satisfactorily.

2. Another possible explanation of the fact that $\Sigma_{j \in M} (R_j)$ and $\Sigma_{j \in M} ((R_j) + (Q_j))$ were small negative numbers may be that the kind of power that the index measures is difficult to estimate in practice in a legislature the size of the National Assembly. Perhaps the members, though wishing and trying to increase their power indices, could not figure out how to do so.

While, as was previously remarked, it is obvious that no legislator in this or any other large assembly has ever analyzed his bargaining position by use of Shapley's theorem on the value of *n*-person games, one of the assumptions of this experiment was that in less formal ways members might sense changes in bargaining opportunities. It was assumed that, in an assembly in which new coalitions are repeatedly formed and in which almost the chief business is coalition-forming, members with low power indices would seldom be needed in winning coalitions and would therefore sense the impotence of their positions. Feeling dissatisfied with their opportunities, they would, it was assumed, seek to better themselves. Hence it was expected that members with low indices would display a high propensity to migrate while members with high indices would display a propensity to maintain the *status quo*.

This experiment reveals some evidence— not, it must be confessed, very impressive— that this assumption is valid. Define an advantageous position in a weighted majority game as one in which the member has a power index higher than that which he would have if the game were a simple majority one. Thus, if there are 627 members and if a member's index is larger than $1/_{627}$, he is in an advantageous position. Conversely, if it is less than $1/_{627}$, he is in a disadvantageous position. In this experiment, of the 61 individual changes of party affiliation, 45 occurred when the member was in a disadvantageous position. (See Column VIII of Table 1). Thus, half again as many of the migrators were disadvantageously situated as were advantageously situated. Some of these were in an exceptionally bad position: Seven suffered a disadvantage of 15% or more and one was 43%. Furthermore, in no instance in which an advantageously situated member migrated was the advantage more than 5%; and in 9 of the 16 migrations from an advantageous position the advantage was less than one per cent. Advantages of this order are surely not perceptible in day-to-day bargaining.

Admittedly, this evidence might not have existed had the migrations of the 1952 session been used, for in that year about half the migrations were from the RPF to the IRAS or to NI. Since during a portion of the session the Gaulliste party was the largest in the Assembly, the migrators necessarily left advantageous positions. But the migrations of the 1952 session were not typical. At no other time in the Fourth Republic (and, I believe, at no time in the Third) did the largest party in the Assembly break up. Indeed, usually the rule is: the larger the party the more stable its membership. One may attribute this stability in the Fourth Republic to the fact that the largest parties (i.e. the Socialists and Communists besides the Gaullistes) have been the most rigorously disciplined ones. But beneath the effects of discipline may well be a realization of advantage in power. *Realpolitik* as well as ideology may keep the large parties together. Conversely, the great majority of migrations, except for the session of 1952, have been among the medium sized and small parties. One interesting by-product of this experiment is the realization that the instability of membership of the small and medium sized parties in multiparty assemblies may derive as much from rational attempts to increase bargaining opportunities as from irrational considerations of ideological satisfaction.

But even though, as this slight evidence suggests, the migrators may have been motivated in part by rational considerations of power maximization, still they may not have been able to calculate their potential advantages rationally. In the absence of electronic computers, a member knows that he has gained or lost by his migration only if he senses (and that grossly) a gain or loss in offers for his membership in coalitions. In day-to-day bargaining it is probable that gains and losses of less than 25% are not perceptible. Very few gains or losses of this order occurred in the two sessions under consideration. Three members (Vallon in migration 2 and Buron and Monteil in migration 23) lost more than 25% in their power index by the migration and two members (Vallon on migration 3 and Caillet in migration 9) gained more than 25%. It is perhaps notable that Vallon, having lost dramatically by his action in migration 2, perhaps attempted to recoup in migration 3. (Something of the same thing happened to Caillet: Having lost by migration 6, he recouped by migration 9. Still, his associate in migration 6 made no attempt to recoup.) But such behavior is too infrequent to be used as statistical evidence of anything. Hence, if it is assumed that only gains and losses of more than 25% are clearly perceptible in daily bargaining, then it follows that, in the 34 migrations here considered, only a statistically unreliable few involved behavior in which rational considerations might have been involved. Hence it may well be that the small negative sum of R_j may be wholly accidental.

3. A third possible explanation of the fact that $\Sigma_{j \in M} (R_j)$ and $\Sigma_{j \in M} ((R_j) + (Q_j))$ were small negative numbers may be that the migrating members in this experiment were truly indifferent to power considerations. They may have truly preferred to give expression to their ideological convictions than to increase their power. In the present context the maximization of power is equated with rational behavior (an abstraction of political man analogous to the abstraction of economic man). Assuming that ideological convictions are irrelevant to considerations of power, behavior motivated by ideology must be regarded as irrational. It is difficult to imagine that over 40 members of the national legislature in a nation whose cultural leaders pride them-

selves on their logic would allow political ideals to divert them from *realpolitik*. One hardly expects a concern for principle to appear in *la République des camarades*. But, as most observers of French politics in the Fourth Republic have remarked, party leadership is much more compelling than it was in the Third. And parties may indeed have elevated ideology above power.

I am personally inclined to favor the second explanation; but I do not exclude the possibility that the first and third may also be involved.

Unfortunately, by reason of the ambiguity of the result, this experiment proves nothing about the assumptions beneath the power index. It does, however, suggest one possibly significant conclusion: In a large assembly with many parties, the bargaining situation is so confused that members cannot determine where they stand. Indeed, in such assemblies, by reason of the complexities of relationships, members

probably cannot be expected to behave rationally.

References

Campbell, P. Discipline and loyalty in the French parliament during the Pinay government. *Pol. Stud.*, 1953, 1, 247–257.

Riker, W. H., & Schaps, R. Disharmony in federal government. *Behav. Sci.*, 1957, 2, 276–290.

Shapley, L. S. A value for n-person games. *Ann. Math. Study No. 28*, 1953, 307–317.

Shapley, L. S., & Shubik, M. A method of evaluating the distribution of power in a committee system. *Amer. Pol. Sci. Rev.*, 1954, 48, 787–792.

Simon, H. A. *Models of man.* New York: Wiley, 1957.

(Manuscript received March 5, 1958).

19

Measurement of Social Power, Opportunity Costs, and the Theory of Two-person Bargaining Games

John C. Harsanyi

These essays by Professor Harsanyi (who is now at the University of California, Berkeley) extend the interpretation of power in game-theoretic analysis beyond that of Shapley and Shubik. Formal game theory is, of course, quite devoid of empirical import; how, then, might we lend empirical interpretation on those formal statements? Harsanyi treats with this question, first in the context of two-person bargaining games, then in n-person game situations. Both of these essays appeared originally in 7 Behavioral Science *(1962) 67–80 and 81–92, and are reprinted by permission from the author and* Behavioral Science.

Introduction

RECENT PAPERS by Simon (1957), by March (1955, 1957), and by Dahl (1957) have suggested measuring person A's power over person B in terms of its actual or potential *effects*, that is, in terms of the changes that A causes or can cause in B's behavior.[1] As Dahl puts it, A has power over B to the extent to which "he can get B to do something that B would not otherwise do" (1957, p. 203).

As Simon and March have obtained very similar results, I shall restrict myself largely to summarizing Dahl's main conclusions. Dahl distinguishes the following constituents of the power relation:

(*a*) the *base* of power, i.e., the resources (economic assets, constitutional prerogatives, military forces, popular prestige, etc.) that A can use to influence B's behavior;

(*b*) the *means* of power, i.e., the specific actions (promises, threats, public appeals, etc.) by which A can make actual use of these resources to influence B's behavior;

(*c*) the *scope* of power, i.e., the set of specific actions that A, by using his means of power, can get B to perform; and finally

(*d*) the *amount* of power, i.e., the net increase in the probability of B's actually performing some specific action X, due to A's using his means of power against B (1957, pp. 203–205).

If A has power over several individuals, Dahl adds a fifth constituent:

(*e*) the set of individuals over whom A has power—this we shall call the *extension* of A's power.

Dahl points out that the power of two individuals can be compared in any of these five dimensions. Other things being equal, an individual's power is greater: (*a*) the greater his power base, (*b*) the more means of power available to him, and the greater (*c*) the scope, (*d*) the amount, and (*e*) the extension of his power. But Dahl proposes to use only the last three variables for the formal definition and measurement of social power. He argues that what we primarily mean by great social power is an ability to influence many people (extension) in many respects (scope) and with a high probability (amount of power). In contrast, a large power base or numerous means of power are not direct measures of the extent of the influence or power that one person can exert over other persons; they are only instruments by which great power can be achieved and maintained, and are indicators from which we can normally *infer* the likely possession of great power by an individual.

Among the three variables of scope, amount, and extension, amount of power is the crucial one, in terms of which the other two can be defined. For the scope of A's power over B is simply the set of specific actions X with respect to which A has a nonzero amount of power over B, i.e., the set of those actions X for which A can achieve a nonzero increase in the probability of these actions actually being performed by B. Similarly, the extension of A's power is the set of specific individuals over whom A has power of nonzero scope and amount.

While the amount of power is a difference of two probabilities, and therefore is directly

226

given as a *real number*,[2] all other dimensions of power are directly given as lists of specific objects (e.g., a list of specific resources, a list of specific actions by A or by B, or a list of specific individuals over whom A has power). But Dahl and March suggest that at least in certain situations it will be worthwhile to develop straight numerical measures for them by appropriate aggregating procedures—essentially by counting the number of comparable items in a given list, and possibly by assigning different weights to items of unequal importance (e.g., we may give more "marks" for power over an important individual than for power over a less important one) (March, 1957, pp. 213–220). In other cases we may divide up a given list into several sublists and may assign a separate numerical measure to each of them, without necessarily aggregating all these numbers into a single figure. That is, we may characterize a given dimension of power not by a single number, but rather by a set of several numbers, i.e., a vector. (For instance, we may describe the extension of President de Gaulle's power by listing the numbers [or percentages] of deputies, of army officers of various ranks, of electors, etc., who support him, without trying to combine all these figures into one index number.)

Two Additional Dimensions of Social Power

A quantitative characterization of a power relation, however, in my view must include two more variables not mentioned in Dahl's list:

(*f*) the opportunity costs to A of attempting to influence B's behavior, i.e., the opportunity costs of using his power over B (and of acquiring this power over B in the first place if A does not yet possess the required power), which we shall call the *costs* of A's power over B; and

(*g*) the opportunity costs to B of refusing to do what A wants him to do, i.e., of refusing to yield to A's attempt to influence his behavior. As these opportunity costs measure the strength of B's incentives for

Measurement of Social Power,   **227**
Opportunity Costs, and the Theory
of Two-Person Bargaining Games
John C. Harsanyi

yielding to A's influence, we shall call them the *strength* of A's power over B.[3]

More precisely, the *costs* of A's power over B will be defined as the *expected value* (actuarial value) of the costs of his attempt to influence B. It will be a weighted average of the net total costs that A would incur if his attempt were successful (e.g., the costs of rewarding B), and of the net total costs that A would incur if his attempt were unsuccessful (e.g., the costs of punishing B).

Other things being equal, A's power over B is greater the smaller the costs of A's power and the greater the strength of A's power.

Both of these two cost variables may be expressed either in physical units (e.g., it may cost A so many bottles of beer or so many working hours to get B to adopt a given policy X; and again it may cost B so many bottles of beer or so many years' imprisonment if he does not adopt policy X), in monetary units (e.g., A's or B's relevant costs may amount to so many actual dollars, or at least may be equivalent to a loss of so many dollars for him), or in utility units. (In view of the theoretical problems connected with interpersonal comparisons of utility, and of the difficulties associated with utility measurement even for one individual, in practice the costs and the strength of power will usually be expressed in physical or in monetary units.[4] But for the purposes of theoretical analysis the use of utility costs sometimes has important advantages, as we shall see.)

Unlike the power base and the means of power, which need not be included in the definition of the power relation, both the costs of power and the strength of power are essential ingredients of the definition of power. A's power over B should be defined not merely as an ability by A to get B to do X with a certain probability p, but rather as an ability by A to achieve this at a certain total cost u to himself, by convincing B that B would have to bear the total cost v if he did not do X.

The Costs of Power

One of the main purposes for which social scientists use the concept of A's power over B is for the description of the policy possibilities open to A. If we want to know the situation (or environment) which A faces as a decision-maker, we must know whether he can or cannot get B to perform a certain action X, and more specifically how sure he can be (in a probability sense) that B will actually perform this action. But a realistic description of A's policy possibilities must include not only A's ability or inability to get B to perform a certain action X, but also the *costs* that A has to bear in order to achieve this result. If two individuals are in a position to exert the same influence over other individuals, but if one can achieve this influence only at the cost of great efforts and/or financial or other sacrifices, while the other can achieve it free of any such costs, we cannot say in any useful sense that their power is equally great. Any meaningful comparison must be in terms of the influence that two individuals can achieve at comparable costs, or in terms of the costs they have to bear in order to achieve comparable degrees of influence.

For instance, it is misleading to say that two political candidates have the same power over two comparable constituencies if one needs much more electioneering effort and expenditure to achieve a given majority, even if in the end both achieve the same majorities; or that two businessmen have the same power over the city government if one can achieve favorable treatment by city officials only at the price of large donations to party funds, while the other can get the same favorable treatment just for the asking.

Of course, a power concept which disregards the costs of power is most inaccurate when the costs of using a given power become very high or even prohibitive. For instance, suppose that an army commander becomes a prisoner of enemy troops, who try to force him at gun point to give a radio order to his army units to withdraw from a

certain area. He may very well have the power to give a contrary order, both in the sense of having the physical ability to do so and in the sense of there being a very good chance of his order being actually obeyed by his army units—but he can use this power only at the cost of his life. Though the scope, the amount, and the extension of his power over his soldiers would still be very great, it would clearly be very misleading in this situation to call him a powerful individual in the same sense as before his capture.

More generally, measurement of power merely in terms of its scope, amount, and extension tends to give counterintuitive results when the possessor of power has little or no real opportunity to actually use his power. For example, take the case of a secretary who has to compile various reports for her employer, according to very specific instructions which leave her little actual choice as to how to prepare them. Suppose that her employer then uses these reports as a basis for very important decisions.[5] Physically she could exert considerable influence on her employer's policies by omitting certain pieces of information from her reports, or including misleading information. In this sense, the scope and the amount of her power over her employer is considerable. But normally she will have little opportunity for using this power, and social scientists would hardly wish to describe her as a powerful individual, as they would have to do if they used Dahl's power concept without modification.

In terms of our own power concept, however, the secretary in question has little real power if all dimensions of her power are taken into account. Though she does have power of great scope and great amount over her employer, this fact is normally more than offset by the very high costs of using her power. If she intentionally submits misleading reports she probably will be found out very soon and will be dismissed and/or punished in other ways. Moreover, if she is a loyal employee such flagrant violation of her instructions would in itself involve very high disutility costs to her.

To conclude, a realistic quantitative description of A's power over B must include, as an essential dimension of this

Measurement of Social Power,   229
Opportunity Costs, and the Theory
of Two-Person Bargaining Games
John C. Harsanyi

power relation, the costs to A of attempting to influence B's behavior.

The Strength of Power

While the costs of power must be included in the definition of our power concept in order to ensure its descriptive validity, the variable of *strength* of power must be included to ensure the usefulness of our power concept for explanatory purposes.

As March (1955, pp. 431–432) has pointed out about the concept of influence, one of the main analytical tasks of such concepts as influence or power (which essentially is an ability to exert influence) is to serve as *intervening variables* in the analysis of individual or social decision-making. Therefore we need a power or influence concept which enables us in the relevant cases to explain a decision by a given private individual or by an official of a social organization, in terms of the power or influence that another individual or some social group has over him. But fundamentally, the analysis of any human decision must be in terms of the variables on the basis of which the decision-maker concerned actually makes his decision—that is, in terms of the advantages and disadvantages he associates with alternative policies available to him. In order to explain why B adopts a certain policy X in accordance with A's wishes, we must know what *difference it makes* for B whether A is his friend or his enemy—or more generally, we must know the *opportunity costs* to B of not adopting policy X. Hence, if our power concept is to serve us as an explanatory intervening variable in the analysis of B's decision to comply with A's wishes, our power concept must include as one of its essential dimensions the opportunity costs to B of noncompliance, which measure the strength of B's incentives to compliance and which we have called the strength of A's power over B.

For instance, if we want to explain the decision of Senator Knowland to support a certain bill of the Eisenhower administration we must find out, among other things, which particular individuals or social groups influenced his decision, and to what extent.

Now suppose that we have strong reasons to assume that it was President Eisenhower's personal intervention which made Senator Knowland change his mind and decide to support the bill in question. Then we still have to explain *how* the variables governing the Senator's decision were actually affected by the President's intervention. Did the President make a promise to him, i.e., did he attach new *advantages*, from the Senator's point of view, to the policy of supporting the bill? Or did the President make a threat, i.e., did he attach new *disadvantages* to the policy of opposing the bill? Or did the President supply new information, pointing out certain already *existing* advantages and/ or disadvantages associated with these two policies, which the Senator had been insufficiently aware of before? In any case we must explain how the President's intervention increased the opportunity costs that Senator Knowland came to associate with opposing the bill.

If we cannot supply this information, then the mere existence of an influence or power relationship between President Eisenhower and Senator Knowland will not *explain* the latter's decision to support the bill. It will only pose a *problem* concerning this decision. (Why on earth did he comply with the President's request to support the bill, when it is known that he had many reasons to oppose it, and did actually oppose it for a while?)

There seem to be four main ways by which a given actor A can manipulate the incentives or opportunity costs of another actor B:

1) A may provide certain *new* advantages or disadvantages for B, subject to *no condition*. For instance, he may provide certain facilities for B which make it easier or less expensive for B to follow certain particular policy objectives desirable to A. (For example, country A may be able to induce country B to attack some third country C, simply by supplying arms to B, even if A supplies these arms "without any strings attached"—and in particular without making it a condition of her arms deliveries that B will actually attack C.) Or A may withdraw from B certain facilities that could help B in attaining policy objectives undesirable to A. More generally, A may provide for B goods or services complementary to some particular policy goal X, or competitive to policy goals alternative to X, so as to increase for B the net utility of X, or to decrease the net utility of its alternatives; or A may achieve similar results by depriving B of goods or services either competitive to X or complementary to its alternatives.[6]

2) A may set up *rewards* and *punishments*, i.e. *new* advantages and disadvantages subject to certain *conditions* as to B's future behavior.

3) A may supply *information* (or misinformation) on (allegedly) already *existing* advantages and/or disadvantages connected with various alternative policies open to B.

4) A may rely on his legitimate *authority* over B, or on B's personal *affection* for A, which make B attach *direct disutility* to the very act of disobeying A.

Of course, in a situation where A has certain power over B, either party can be mistaken about the true opportunity costs to him of various alternatives. Therefore both in discussing the costs of A's power over B, and in discussing the strength of his power, we must distinguish between *objective* costs and *perceived* costs—between what these costs actually are and what the individual bearing these costs thinks them to be. For the purpose of a formal definition of the power relation, the *costs* of A's power over B have to be stated as the *objective* costs that an attempt to influence B would actually entail upon A, while the *strength* of A's power over B has to be stated in terms of the costs of noncompliance as *perceived* by B himself. The reason is that the costs of A's power serve to describe the objective policy possibilities open to A, whereas the strength of A's power serves to explain B's subjective motivation for compliant behavior. (Of course, a full description of a given power situation would require listing both objective and perceived costs for both participants.)

The Strength of Power, and the Amount of Power in Dahl's Sense

Clearly, in general the greater the *strength* of A's power over B, the greater will be A's *amount* of power over B with respect to action X. The relationship between these two variables will take a particularly simple mathematical form if the strength of A's power is measured in *utility* terms, i.e., in terms of the disutility costs to B of noncompliance.[7]

We shall use the following model. A wants B to perform action X. But B associates disutility x with doing X. Nevertheless B would perform X with probability p_1 (i.e., would adopt the mixed strategy $s[p_1]$ assigning probability p_1 to doing X and probability $[1 - p_1]$ to not doing X), even in the absence of A's intervention.[8] B would adopt this strategy because if he completely refused to do X (i.e., if he adopted the mixed strategy $s[0]$) he would obtain only the utility payoff $u_0 -$; while if he did X with probability p_1 (i.e., if he adopted strategy $s[p_1]$), then he would obtain the higher utility payoff u_1, making his total expected utility $u_1 - p_1 x > u_0$.

Now A intervenes and persuades B that B will obtain the still higher utility payoff u_2 if he agrees to do action X with a certain probability $p_2 > p_1$ (i.e., if he adopts strategy $s[p_2]$), making his total expected utility $u_2 - p_2 x$. In view of this, B does adopt strategy $s[p_2]$.

Under these assumptions, obviously the *amount* of A's power over B will be the difference $\Delta p = p_2 - p_1$, while the *strength* of A's power over B will be the difference $u_2 - u_1$. As $p_2 \leqslant 1$, we must have $\Delta p \leqslant 1 - p_1$. Moreover, by assumption (cf. Footnote 7); $\Delta p \geqslant 0$.

If B tries to maximize his expected utility,[9] then he will adopt strategy $s[p_2]$ only if

$$u_2 - p_2 x \geqslant u_1 - p_1 x, \qquad (1)$$

that is if,

$$\Delta p = p_2 - p_1 \leqslant \frac{u_2 - u_1}{x} = \frac{\Delta u}{x} \qquad (2)$$

This gives us:

Theorem I. The maximum *amount* of power that *A* can achieve over *B* with respect to action *X* tends to be equal to the *strength* of *A*'s power over *B* (as expressed in utility units) divided by the disutility to *B* of doing action *X*—except that this maximum amount of power cannot be more than the amount of power corresponding to *B*'s doing action *X* with probability *one*.

The strength of *A*'s power over *B* divided by the disutility to *B* of doing *X* may be called the *relative strength* of *A*'s power over *B*. Accordingly, we obtain:

Theorem I'. The maximum *amount* of power that *A* can achieve over *B* with respect to action *X* tends to be equal to the *relative strength* of *A*'s power over *B* with respect to action *X* (except that, again, this maximum amount of power cannot be more than the amount of power corresponding to *B*'s doing action *X* with probability one).

Of course, in the real world we seldom observe *B* to use a randomized mixed strategy of form *s[p]*, in a literal sense. What we do find is that, if we watch *B*'s behavior over a series of comparable occasions, he will comply with *A*'s wishes in some proportion *p* of all occasions and will fail to comply in the remaining proportion $(1 - p)$ of the occasions. Moreover, the disutility to *B* of compliant behavior will vary from one occasion to another. Hence if *B* wants to comply with *A*'s wishes in *pn* cases out of *n* then, other things being equal, he will tend to select those *pn* cases where compliance is associated with the smallest disutility to him. For example, suppose that a U.S. senator, with political attitudes rather different from the administration's, decides to vote for the president's legislative program often enough to avoid at least an open break with the administration. Then he is likely to select for his support those administration bills which are least distasteful to him and to his constituents. This means that the total disutility to *B* of a given strategy *s[p]* (which now has to be defined as a strategy involving compliance in *proportion p* of all cases) will tend to increase somewhat more than proportionally as *p* increases, because should *B* decide to increase the frequency of his compliant behavior he would have to

include a higher fraction of "difficult" cases.

Accordingly, if we restate our model in terms of empirical *frequencies*, rather than theoretical *probabilities*, we must expect that the maximum *amount* of power that *A* can achieve over *B* will increase somewhat less than in proportion to increments in the *strength* of *A*'s power over *B* (measuring this strength now in terms of the *average* utility value of *B*'s incentives for compliance over all occasions). But our Theorem I is likely to retain at least its approximate validity in most empirical situations.[10]

Power in a Schedule Sense

We have just seen that the greater the strength of a person's power over other persons the greater the amount of his power over them tends to be. But likewise, the greater the strength of a person's power over other people, the greater both the scope and the extension of his power over these people. That is, the stronger incentives he can provide for compliance, the larger the number of specific actions he can get other people to perform for him will be, and the larger the number of individuals he can get to perform these actions.

But while the scope, the amount, and the extension of his power are all functions of the *strength* of his power over all individuals, the strength of his power is itself a function of the *costs* of power he is prepared to bear. The greater efforts and sacrifices he is prepared to make, the stronger incentives for compliance he will be able to provide and the greater will be the strength of his power over them.

Therefore, a given individual's power can be described not only by stating the specific values of the five dimensions of his power (whether as single numbers, or as vectors, or as lists of specific items), but also by specifying the mathematical *functions* or *schedules* that connect the costs of his power

with the other four dimensions. When
power is defined in terms of the specific
values of the five power variables we shall
speak of power in a *point* sense, and when
power is defined in terms of the functions or
schedules connecting the other four power
variables with the costs of power we shall
speak of power in a *schedule* sense.[11]

Power in a schedule sense can be regarded
as a "production function" describing how
a given individual can "transform" different
amounts of his resources (of his working
time, his money, his political rights, his
popularity, etc.) into social power of various
dimensions (of various strengths, scopes,
amounts, and extensions). The commonsense
notion of social power makes it an *ability* to
achieve certain things—an ability that the
person concerned is free to use or to leave
unused. It seems to me that this notion of
power as an ability is better captured by our
concept of power in a schedule sense than it
is by the concept of power in a point sense.
(The latter seems to better correspond to
the commonsense notion of actually exerted
influence, rather than to that of power as
such.)

If a person's power is given in a mere
schedule sense, then we can state the specific
values of his five power dimensions only if
we are also told how much of his different
resources he is actually prepared to use in
order to obtain social power of various dimensions—that is, if besides his power
schedules we know also his *utility function*.
Whereas his power defined in a schedule
sense indicates the conditions under which
his environment is ready to "supply"
power to him, it is his utility function which
determines his "demand" for power under
various alternative conditions.

Bilateral Power and the "Blackmailer's Fallacy"

So far we have tacitly assumed that, in
situations where A has power over B, A is
always in a position to determine, by his
unilateral decision, the incentives he will

provide for B's compliance, as well as the
degree of compliance he will try to enforce.
Situations in which this is actually the case
may be called unilateral power situations.
But it very often happens that not only can
A exert pressure on B in order to get him to
adopt certain specific policies, but B can do
the same to A. In particular, B may be able
to press A for increased rewards and/or decreased penalties, and for relaxing the standards of compliance required from him and
used in administering rewards and penalties
to him. Situations of this type we shall call
bilateral or reciprocal power situations. In
such situations, both the extent of B's
compliant behavior (i.e., the scope and the
amount of A's power over B) and the net
incentives that A can provide for B (i.e.,
the net strength of A's power over B) will
become matters of explicit or implicit
bargaining between the two parties.

Of the four ways in which A can increase
his strength of power discussed previously,
we tend to obtain unilateral power situations in cases 1, 3, and 4, where A's power
over B is based on providing *unconditional*
advantages or disadvantages for B, on
conveying information or misinformation
to him, or on having legitimate authority
over B and/or enjoying B's personal affection (though there are also exceptions where
these cases give rise to bilateral power). For
example, it is usually largely a matter for
A's personal discretion whether he provides
certain facilities for B, whether he discloses
certain pieces of information to him, or
whether he gives him an order as his
legitimate superior. In case 2, on the other
hand, when A's power over B is based on
A's ability to set up rewards and/or punishments for B *conditional* upon B's behavior,
normally we find bilateral power situations
(though again there are important exceptions).[12] Here B can exert pressure on A by
withholding his compliance, even though
compliance would be much more profitable
than noncompliance. He may also be able
to exert pressure on A by making the costs
of a conflict (including the costs of punishing B for noncompliance) very high to A.

For bilateral power situations Theorem I
and Theorem I′ do not hold true. For these
conclusions have been completely depend-

ent on the assumption that if a certain strategy s_1, involving some given degree of compliance by B, is more profitable to B than any alternative strategy s_2 involving a lesser degree of compliance (or none at all), then B will always choose strategy s_1 and will never choose strategy s_2—not even as a result of dissatisfaction with the terms A offers in return for B's co-operation. While in unilateral power situations this assumption is perfectly legitimate (as it amounts to no more than assuming that B tries to maximize his utility or expected utility), in bilateral power situations this assumption would involve what I propose to call the "blackmailer's fallacy" (Harsanyi, 1956, p. 156).

A would-be blackmailer A once argued that as he was in a position to cause damage worth \$1,000 to a certain rich man B, he should be able to extract from B *any* ransom r short of \$1,000, because after payment of $r < \$1,000$, B would still be better off than if he had to suffer the full \$1,000 damage.

But this argument is clearly fallacious. By similar reasoning, B could also have argued that A would accept *any* ransom r larger than nil, because after accepting a ransom $r > \$0$, A would still be better off than if no agreement were reached and he did not receive anything at all. What both of these arguments really show is that in any bargaining between two rational bargainers, the outcome must fall between what may be called the two parties' *concession limits*, which are defined by each party's refusal to accept any agreement that would make him actually worse off than he would be in the conflict situation. But the two arguments in themselves say nothing about where the two parties' agreement point will actually lie *between* these two limits. They certainly do not allow the inference that this agreement point will actually coincide or nearly coincide with one party's concession limit.[13] (Only if we know the two parties' attitudes towards risk-taking, and in particular towards risking a conflict rather than accepting unfavorable terms, can we make any predictions about where their agreement point will lie between the two concession limits.)

Either party's actual behavior will be a resultant of two opposing psychological forces. On the one hand, for example, B will admittedly have some incentive for agreeing to any ransom payment less than \$1,000. But B will also know that A will likewise have some incentive for accepting any ransom payment greater than zero, and this fact will make B expect to get away with a ransom payment of much less than \$1,000. This expectation in turn will provide B with some incentive to resist any ransom payment too close to \$1,000. Any realistic theory of B's behavior must take full account of *both* of these psychological forces—both of B's motives for compliance, and of the reasons which make him expect some concessions on A's part which will render full compliance on his own part unnecessary.

The Zeuthen-Nash Theory and the Strength of Power in Bilateral Power Situations

For analysis of the two parties' behavior in bilateral power situations, and in particular for quantitative assessment of the two opposite psychological forces governing each party's degree of compliance, we shall use the Zeuthen-Nash theory of the two-person bargaining game.[14] Our analysis will be based on the following model.[15]

Just as in the model discussed earlier. A wants B to perform action X. But B associates disutility x with doing X. Nevertheless B would perform X with probability p_1, i.e., would use the mixed strategy $s(p_1)$, even in the absence of A's intervention. This would happen because if B completely refused to do X (i.e., if he adopted strategy $s[0]$) he would obtain only the utility payoff u_0—while if he did X with probability p_1 (i.e., if he adopted strategy $s[p_1]$) then he would obtain the higher utility payoff u_1, making his total expected utility $u_1 - p_1 x > u_0$.

If B completely refused to do X, then A's utility level would be u_0^*. If B did perform X (with probability 1), then A's utility would increase by the amount x^*. Accordingly, if B did X only with probability p_1 then A's expected utility would be $u_0^* + p_1 x^*$.

Now A intervenes and offers B a reward R if B will increase the probability of his doing action X from p_1 to some mutually agreed figure p_2 (i.e., if B adopts strategy $s[p_2]$). In utility units, this reward R would represent a gain r for B, while providing this reward would cost A the amount r^*. Hence, if the two parties can agree on some probability p_2, then A's total expected utility will be

$$u_2^* = u_2^*(p_2) = u_0^* - r^* + p_2 x^* \quad (3)$$

whereas B's total expected utility will be

$$u_2 = u_2(p_2) = u_1 + r - p_2 x \quad (4)$$

A also sets up the penalty T for B if B refuses to sufficiently increase the probability of his performing action X. In utility units, this penalty T would cause a loss t to B, while enforcing this penalty would cost A the amount t^*. Hence, if the two parties could not agree on the value of p_2, A's total expected utility would be

$$u_3^* = u_0^* - t^* + p_1 x^* \quad (5)$$

(assuming that B would still perform X with probability p_1), whereas B's total expected utility would be

$$u_3 = u_1 - t_1 - p_1 x \quad (6)$$

More generally, we may assume that in a conflict situation *both* parties would use retaliatory strategies against each other, A using strategy T_A and B using strategy T_B. In such a case t should be redefined as the *total loss* that B would suffer in the conflict situation, including both the damages caused to him by his opponent's retaliatory strategy T_A, and the costs to him of his own retaliatory strategy T_B. Similarly, t^* should be redefined as the *total loss* that A would suffer in the conflict situation. But otherwise our conclusions retain their validity.

Now, what will be the equilibrium value of the probability p_2 which tends to be agreed upon in bargaining between two rational bargainers?

We already know that it must lie between the p_2 values corresponding to the two parties' concession limits. A's concession limit is reached when $u_2^* = u_3^*$. By (3) and (5), the corresponding p_2 value is

$$p_2{}^A = p_1 + \frac{r^* - t^*}{x^*} \quad (7)$$

With $p_2 = p_2{}^A$, A's total expected utility would be

$$u^*{}_2(p_2{}^A) = u_3^* = u_0^* - t^* + p_1 x^* \quad (8)$$

while B's total expected utility would be

$$u_2(p_2{}^A) = u_1 + r - \frac{x}{x^*}(r^* - t^*) - p_1 x \quad (9)$$

On the other hand, B's concession limit is reached when $u_2 = u_3$. By (4) and (6) the corresponding p_2 value is

$$p_2{}^B = p_1 + \frac{r + t}{x} \quad (10)$$

With $p_2 = p_2{}^B$, A's total expected utility would be

$$u_2^*(p_2{}^B) = u_0^* - r^* + \frac{x^*}{x}(r + t) + p_1 x^* \quad (11)$$

while B's total expected utility would be

$$u_2(p_2{}^B) = u_3 = u_1 - t - p_1 x \quad (12)$$

It is easy to see (Fig. 1) that in the utility plane $[u^*, u]$ for the two parties, all possible agreement points $U(p) = [u_2^*(p_2), u_2(p_2)]$

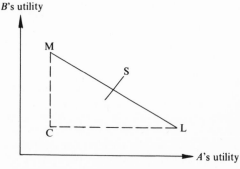

B's utility

M

S

C

L

A's utility

Figure 1. Zeuthen-Nash utility plane.

must lie on the straight-line interval connecting the two parties' concession limit points, $L = U(p_2{}^A) = [u_2{}^*(p_2{}^A), \quad u_2(p_2{}^A)]$ and $M = U(p_2{}^B) = [u_2{}^*(p_2{}^B), \quad u_2(p_2{}^B)]$. (The two parties' payoffs in the conflict situation are indicated by the conflict point $C = [u_3{}^*, u_3^-]$.)

When the locus of all possible agreement points U is a straight line, the Zeuthen-Nash solution takes a particularly simple mathematical form; it is located simply at the midpoint of the distance between the two concession-limit points L and M (i.e., at S).[16] Hence, at the solution point S, A must obtain the expected utility

$$u_4{}^* = \frac{1}{2}[u_2{}^*(p_2{}^A) + u_2{}^*(p_2{}^B)] \tag{13}$$

$$= u_0{}^* - \frac{r^* + t^*}{2} + \frac{x^*}{2x}(r + t) + p_1 x^*$$

where the last equality follows from (8) and (11); while B must obtain the expected utility

$$u_4 = \frac{1}{2}[u_2(p_2{}^A) + u_2(p_2{}^B)] \tag{14}$$

$$= u_1 + \frac{r - t}{2} - \frac{x}{2x^*}(r^* - t^*) - p_1 x$$

If we set $u_4{}^* = u_2{}^*(p_2)$ and $u_4 = u_2(p_2)$, by (13) and (3) [or by (14) and (4)] we obtain, as the equilibrium value of p_2 corresponding to the solution point S, the expression

$$p_2 = p_1 + \frac{r + t}{2x} + \frac{r^* - t^*}{2x^*} \tag{15}$$

subject, of course, to the requirement that always

$$p_2 \leqslant 1 \tag{15a}$$

The Zeuthen-Nash theory also tells us that A will choose the reward R he offers B in such a way as to maximize the expression

$$\Delta r = \frac{r}{x} - \frac{r^*}{x^*}$$

which measures, from A's point of view, the value of R as an incentive, less the cost of

providing R for B. Moreover A will select the penalty T in such a way as to maximize the expression.

$$\Delta t = \frac{t}{x} - \frac{t^*}{x^*}$$

which again measures, from A's point of view, the value of T as a deterrent, less the cost of administering T to B. This is so because, according to (13), A will maximize his own final utility payoff $u_4{}^*$, by means of maximizing Δr and Δt.

In the more general case where both parties would use retaliatory strategies in the event of a conflict, A (in order to maximize his own final payoff $u_4{}^*$) would again try to select his own retaliatory strategy T_A so as to *maximize* Δt when B's strategy T_B is given. On the other hand, B (in order to maximize his own final payoff u_4) would try to select his own retaliatory strategy T_B so as to *minimize* Δt when A's strategy T_A is given. Hence the equilibrium choice of T_A and T_B will be such as to make Δt take its maximin value.

Now clearly, if B adopts strategy $s[p_2]$ corresponding to the p_2 value defined by (15), then the *amount* of A's power over B with respect to action X will become

$$\Delta p = p_2 - p_1 = \frac{1}{2}\left(\frac{r + t}{x} - \frac{t^* - r^*}{x^*}\right) \tag{16}$$

But of course the value of Δp must be consistent with (15a). Hence (16) is subject to the restriction that

$$\Delta p \leqslant 1 - p_1 \tag{16a}$$

Let X^* denote A's action of *tolerating* B's failure to perform action X on one occasion. (We shall call action X^* the complementary action to action X.) Now suppose that A and B agree that B will perform action X with probability p_2, i.e., that B will *not* perform action X, with probability $(1 - p_2)$. This will mean that A will have to tolerate B's not performing action X, i.e., that A will have to perform action X^*, with probability $(1 - p_2)$. That is, technically, A and B will agree on a *jointly randomized* mixed strategy under which, with probability p_2, B will perform action X while A will *not* perform the complementary action X^* —whereas, with probability $(1 - p_2)$, A will perform action X^* while B will *not* perform action X.

Thus, while A's power over B will primarily consist in A's ability to get B to perform action X with a certain probability p_2; B's power over A will primarily consist in B's ability to get A to perform the complementary action X^* with probability $(1 - p_2)$.

On any given occasion where A performs action X^* (i.e., tolerates B's *not* performing action X), A will lose the utility gain x^* that he would derive from B's performing action X. Therefore A will associate disutility x^* with performing action X^*.

In equation (16), the sum $(r + t)$ is the sum of the *reward B* would obtain for compliance, and of the *penalty* he would suffer for noncompliance, both expressed in utility terms. This sum measures the *difference it would make* for B to have A as his enemy instead of having him as his friend. It represents the total opportunity costs to B of choosing noncompliance leading to the conflict situation instead of choosing compliance, i.e., some strategy $s[p_2]$ acceptable to A. In brief, it represents the *opportunity costs of a conflict*, from B's point of view. In our terminology, it measures the (gross) *absolute strength* of A's power over B. Accordingly, the quotient $(r + t)/x$ measures the *gross relative strength* of A's power over B with respect to action X.

The difference $(t^* - r^*)$ is the difference between the costs to A of *punishing B* and the costs to A of *rewarding B*, both again expressed in utility terms. This difference measures the difference it would make for A to have B as an enemy instead of having him as a friend. It represents the net opportunity costs to A of choosing the conflict situation rather than performing action X^* with a probability $(1 - p_2)$ acceptable to B, i.e., rather than tolerating B to follow some

strategy $s[p_2]$ acceptable to B. (In computing these opportunity costs, r^* has to be deducted from t^*, because in case of a conflict, A of course would save the costs of rewarding B.) In brief, this difference measures the *opportunity costs of a conflict*, this time from A's point of view. In our terminology, it measures the *gross absolute strength* of B's power over A. Moreover, as x^* is the disutility to A of performing action X^*, the quotient $(t^* - r^*)/x^*$ measures the *gross relative strength* of B's power over A with respect to action X^*.

Finally, the difference $[(r + t)/x - (t^* - r^*)/x^*]$ is the difference between the gross relative strength of A's power over B with respect to action X, and the gross relative strength of B's power over A with respect to the complementary action X^*. It may be called the *net strength* of A's power over B with respect to action X. This gives us:

Theorem II. If both parties follow the rationality postulates of the Zeuthen-Nash theory of the two-person bargaining game, then in bilateral power situtions the *amount* of A's power over B with respect to some action X tends to be equal to *half* the *net strength* of A's power over B with respect to the same action X—this net strength being defined as the difference between the gross relative strength of A's power over B with respect to action X and the gross relative strength of B's power over A with respect to the complementary action X^*. (But this theorem is subject to the qualification that the amount of A's power over B cannot be so great as to make the probability of B's performing action X become greater than *unity*.)[17]

Of course, in empirical applications the amount-of-power concept in Theorem II (and in Theorem I) must be reinterpreted in terms of empirical *frequencies*, instead of theoretical *probabilities* (see the preceding discussion of this point).

Simon (1957, pp. 66–68) has pointed out that in bilateral power situations—at least, when none of the participants seriously misjudge the situation—it is impossible to disentangle entirely by empirical methods what is due to A's power over B, and what is due to B's power over A, so that we cannot measure separately A's power over B and B's power over A. But of course this does not mean that, given a sufficiently rich theoretical framework, we cannot disentangle, and separately measure, these two power relations by theoretical analysis. In effect, our Theorem II does provide us—at least in principle—with separate measures for the gross strength of each of these two power relations, and with a theory about how these two separate measures have to be combined in order to explain the end result.

Relationships of Our Strength-of-Power Measures to Alternative Measures for Social Power

Theorems I (or I′) and II describe how the strength-of-power measures described in this paper are related to Dahl's probabilistic measure for the amount of power, in unilateral and in bilateral power situations. As March's probabilistic measure (1957, p. 224) differs from Dahl's only in taking the absolute value of the difference ($p_2 - p_1$) rather than the difference itself, these conclusions equally apply to March's measure.

The measure for the net strength of A's power over B in bilateral power situations is also related to the field-psychological measure for social power in small groups, proposed by French (1956), French and Raven (1959), and Cartwright (1959).

It was previously argued that B's (as well as A's) behavior must be explained in terms of two opposing psychological forces, one pressing B for more compliance with A's wishes in view of the rewards and penalties set up by A, and one pressing B for less compliance in view of the concessions B expects A to make in enforcing his demand for compliance. Theorem II now suggests that the strength of these two psychological forces can be measured by the *gross relative strength* of A's power over B, and of B's power over A, respectively. According to Theorem II, the strength of the resultant force, the *net strength* of A's power over B,

equals the *difference* between the separate strength of the two forces.

Similarly, French (1956, p. 183) defines his measure for social power as "the maximum force which A can induce on B minus the maximum resisting force which B can mobilize in the opposite direction." However, while the *compliance-inducing* force of French's model is closely related to the one of our own model (as both depend on B's incentives to compliance), the *compliance-resisting* force of French's model does not seem to be connected with B's expectation of obtaining concessions as to the degree of compliance that A requires from him, as is the case in our own model. Moreover, it is not clear whether the two opposing psychological forces of French's model are supposed to follow the same quantitative laws as those of our own model. But in any case the relationship between the two models would be worth further investigation.[18]

Finally, our measure for the net strength of A's power over B in bilateral power situations is also related to the *game-theoretical* measure for power in a committee system proposed by Shapley and Shubik (1954), in that both our and their measures are special cases of the *same* general game-theoretical measure for power in n-person situations.

Our measure for the net strength of power is based on the Zeuthen-Nash theory of the two-person bargaining game. In the following paper I shall discuss how this measure can be generalized for n-person reciprocal power situations, where all n participants mutually possess some power over one another and over the joint policies of their group as a whole. This generalization will be based on my bargaining model for the n-person co-operative game (Harsanyi, 1960; for an earlier version see Harsanyi, 1959), which is itself an n-person generalization of the Zeuthen-Nash theory. This generalized measure for power in n-person situations will be found to contain the Shapley-Shubik measure as a special case.

References

Cartwright, D. A field theoretical conception of power. In D. Cartwright (Ed.), *Studies in social power.* Ann Arbor: Univ. of Michigan Press, 1959. Pp. 183–220.

Dahl, R. A. The concept of power, *Behav. Sci.*, 1957, 2, 201–215.

French, J. R. P., Jr. A formal theory of social power. *Psychol. Rev.*, 1956, 63, 181–194.

French, J. R. P., Jr., & Raven, B. The bases of social power. In D. Cartwright (Ed.), *Studies in social power.* Ann Arbor: Univ. of Michigan Press, 1959. Pp. 150–167.

Harsanyi, J. C. Cardinal welfare, individualistic ethics, and interpersonal comparisons of utility. *J. polit. Econ.*, 1955, 63, 309–321.

Harsanyi, J. C. Approaches to the bargaining problem before and after the theory of games: a critical discussion of Zeuthen's, Hicks', and Nash's theories. *Econometrica*, 1956, 24, 144–157.

Harsanyi, J. C. A bargaining model for the cooperative *n*-person game, In A. W. Tucker and R. D. Luce (Eds.), *Contributions to the theory of games*, IV. Princeton: Princeton Univ. Press, 1959. Pp. 325–355.

Harsanyi, J. C. A simplified bargaining model for the *n*-person cooperative game. 1960 (hectographed). Available from author on request.

Harsanyi, J. C. On the rationality postulates underlying the theory of cooperative games. *J. Conflict Resol.*, 1961. 5, 179–196.

Luce, R. D., & Raiffa, H. *Games and decisions.* New York: Wiley, 1957.

March, J. G. An introduction to the theory and measurement of influence. *Amer. Polit. Sci. Rev.*, 1955, 49, 431–451.

March, J. G. Measurement concepts in the theory of influence. *J. Politics*, 1957, 19, 202–226.

Marschak, J. Rational behavior, uncertain prospects, and measurable utility. *Econometrica*, 1950, 18, 111–141.

Marschak, J. Three lectures on probability in the social sciences. In P. F. Lazarsfeld (Ed.), *Mathematical thinking in the social sciences.* Glencoe: The Free Press, 1954. Pp. 166–215. Reprinted as Cowles Commission Paper, N.S., No. 82.

Nash, J. F., Jr. The bargaining problem. *Econometrica*, 1950, 18, 155–162.

Nash, J. F., Jr. Two-person cooperative games. *Econometrica*, 1953, 21, 128–140.

Schelling, T. C. An essay on bargaining. *Amer. econ. Rev.*, 1956, 46, 281–306.

Shapley, L. S., & Shubik, M. A method for evaluating the distribution of power in a committee system. *Amer. Polit. Sci. Rev.*, 1954, 48, 787–792.

Simon, H. A. *Models of man: social and rational.* New York: Wiley, 1957. Pp. 62–78.

Zeuthen, F. *Problems of monopoly and economic warfare.* London: G. Routledge and Sons, 1930.

Introduction

THE PRECEDING paper argued that social power must be defined in terms of five dimensions: the *costs*, the *strength*, the *scope*, the *amount*, and the *extension* of this power. A distinction was made between unilateral and reciprocal (or bilateral) power situations. The former are situations in which a given person A is in a position to determine, by his own unilateral decision, the incentives he will provide for another person B to comply with his wishes, and also the degree of compliance he will try to enforce. The latter are situations in which both parties have the ability to exert pressure on each other, and in which the incentives provided by A and, even more important, the degree of compliance he will try to enforce, therefore become matters of explicit or implicit bargaining between the two parties. Certain simple mathematical relationships between the *strength* and the *amount* of A's power over B were established, both for unilateral and for bilateral power situations.

In *unilateral* power situations, the generalization of these results to the n-person case is quite straightforward. As a matter of fact, the situation where one given individual A has unilateral power over several individuals $B_1, \ldots, B_k$ is already covered in the preceding paper. Thus it is sufficient to consider the case where several individuals $A_1, \ldots, A_k$ simultaneously have some power over the same individual B. Here it is natural to define the *amount* of joint power that $A_1, \ldots, A_k$ have over B with respect to some action X as the *net increase* in the probability of B's actually performing action X because of the intervention of $A_1, \ldots, A_k$. On the other hand, the *strength* of their joint power may be defined as the algebraic sum of the strength of every A_i's separate power over B (giving a negative sign to the strength of the power of any individual A_i who may try to prevent B from performing action X). It is easy to see that under these definitions Theorem I (and I') retains its validity.

However, the model of bilateral power cannot be directly extended to n-person *reciprocal* power situations, where more than two individuals are able to exert pressures

20

Measurement of Social Power in n-Person Reciprocal Power Situations

John C. Harsanyi

and counterpressures upon one another. To analyze situations of this latter type, the Zeuthen-Nash theory of two-person bargaining must be replaced by a theory of n-person bargaining. The bargaining model for the n-person co-operative game (Harsanyi, 1960; for an earlier version, see Harsanyi, 1959) which will be used is an n-person generalization of the Zeuthen-Nash theory. (It is also a generalization of the Shapley [1953] value for the n-person game, in that it extends a certain modified form of the Shapley value from the special case of games with transferable utility, originally considered by Shapley, to the general case.)

To make the model of bilateral power more readily amenable to generalization for the n-person case, the measure for the *amount* of power possessed by each participant must be slightly modified. The amount of A's power over B (that is, A's power over B's *individual policy*) with respect to some action $\bar{X}$ to be performed by B was defined as the net increase Δp in the probability of B's actually performing action $\bar{X}$ because of A's intervention. Now a new measure, the amount of A's power over A and B's *joint policy* with respect to some controversial issue $X = (X_A, X_B)$, is defined as the probability p of A's being able to get the joint policy X_A adopted when A favors this policy X_A and B favors a different policy X_B.

Clearly the old model is a special case of the new one, as the controversial issue between A and B may be that B would prefer *not* to perform some action $\bar{X}$ which A wants B to perform. If we denote by $\bar{X}^*$ A's possible action of *tolerating* B's failure to perform action $\bar{X}$, then the joint policy X_A

239

preferred by A will involve B's performing action $\bar{X}$ and A's *not* performing action $\bar{X}^*$, whereas the joint policy X_B preferred by B will involve B's *not* performing action $\bar{X}$ and A's performing action $\bar{X}^*$.

Quantitatively these two measures for the amount of A's power are related as follows. Suppose that, without A's intervention, B would perform action $\bar{X}$ with probability p_1; but because of A's intervention, and as a result of mutual agreement between the two parties, B increases the probability of his performing action $\bar{X}$ to p_2. Then the amount of A's power *over B* (i.e., A's power over B's *policy* concerning action $\bar{X}$) would be the difference $\Delta p = p_2 - p_1$. On the other hand, the amount of A's power over A and B's *joint policy* would be defined as the *conditional probability* p of B's performing action $\bar{X}$, given that on the present occasion he would not perform action $\bar{X}$ without A's intervention (because a controversial issue between A and B exists only on occasions where B would not perform action $\bar{X}$ without A's intervention). This conditional probability is $p = (p_2 - p_1)/(1 - p_1)$.

It is easy to see that our new measure for the amount of A's power is simply a normalized version of the old measure. For in any particular situation where p_1 is given, the new measure p is proportional to the old measure Δp, as $p = \Delta p/(1 - p_1)$. But while Δp varies[1] between 0 and $1 - p_1$, the new measure p varies between 0 and 1. (However, our main concern will be with the n-person analogue of the case where A's and B's preferences are completely opposed with respect to some particular action $\bar{X}$, i.e., where $p_1 = 0$. Then of course $p = \Delta p$ and the two measures coincide.)

Definitions of the Amount of Power in Three Types of n-Person Situations

CASE A. SINGLE PREFERENCES AND NO COMPROMISE POLICIES

Power relations become relevant in a social group when two or more individuals have conflicting preferences and a decision has to be made as to whose preferences shall prevail. Thus special theoretical interest attaches to the extreme case where n individuals have preferences so dissimilar that no two of them agree in preferring some particular policy X_i to some other policy X_j, and where no "pure" compromise policies (i.e., policies having the nature of *pure strategies*) exist among the policies preferred by different individuals.

This can be represented by the following model. There are n individuals, called 1, ..., n. Each individual i prefers a different joint policy X_i, but is completely indifferent among all alternative policies X_j, X_k, ... preferred by various other individuals j, k, ... (This we shall call the *single preferences* assumption. Its purpose is to rule out the possibility that two or more individuals *jointly* prefer some policy X_i over some alternative policy X_j. For instance, suppose to the contrary that while individual 1's first preference is policy X_1, he is not indifferent between policy X_2 (favored by individual 2) and policy X_3 (favored by individual 3), in that his second preference goes to X_2 and his third preference to X_3. Here 1 and 2 will *jointly* prefer X_2 to X_3, contrary to our assumption.)

Let v_{ij} be the utility that individual i assigns to joint policy X_j. By the single preferences assumption we can write

$$v_{ij} = \begin{cases} w_i & \text{if } i \neq j \\ w_i + x_i & \text{if } i = j \end{cases} \quad (1)$$

It will also be assumed that between any policy X_i, favored by i, and any policy X_j, favored by j, there is no pure compromise policy X_k that would be preferred by *both* individuals to the policy favored by the *other* individual. (This will be called the *no compromise* assumption.) This implies that all possible joint policies other than the policies $X_1, \ldots, X_n$ representing the first preference of one of the n individuals, are inefficient policies and can be disregarded. Therefore we shall identify the controversial issue at stake among the n individuals with the n-tuple $X = (X_1, \ldots, X_n)$.

In this situation it is natural to define the *amount* of individual i's power over the *joint policy* of all n individuals as the probability p_i of his being able to get his favorite joint policy X_i adopted by all individuals. Of course, $\Sigma p_i = 1$. We shall write $\bar{p}$ for the probability vector $\bar{p} = (p_1, \ldots, p_n)$.

CASE B. MULTIPLE PREFERENCES AND NO COMPROMISE POLICIES

There are again n individuals, with each individual i giving his *first* preference to a different[2] joint policy X_i. But now each individual i may also have definite preferences between policies X_j and X_k, even if $j, k \neq i$ (*multiple preferences* assumption).

We shall still assume, however, that X_1, $\ldots$, X_n are the only efficient policies (*no compromise* assumption).

We may again try to define individual i's power as the probability p_i of his being able to get policy X_i accepted. But for most purposes this probability will not be an adequate measure of his power. If, e.g., out of three possible policies, individual 1 assigns 10 units of utility to policy X_1, 9 units of utility to policy X_2, and 1 unit of utility to policy X_3, we shall not be able to assess the magnitude of his power if we know only that he has a 10 per cent chance of getting X_1 adopted and do not know how the remaining 90 per cent probability is distributed between policies X_2 and X_3.

Thus we may call p_i, the probability of individual i's favorite policy X_i being adopted by the whole group, the *amount* of i's *specific power*, because it measures his power to determine exactly the nature of the specific policy to be adopted by the group. (Again, $\Sigma p_i = 1$.) For most purposes, however, we need a different measure.

A more satisfactory measure will be the whole probability vector $\bar{p} = (p_1, \ldots, p_n)$ giving the probabilities for the adoption of each of the alternative policies $X_1, \ldots, X_n$. This may be called the *vector measure* for i's power.

But we can also define a more satisfactory scalar measure as follows. Let v_{ij} again denote the utility that individual i assigns to joint policy X_j. Suppose that X_k is the policy alternative least preferred by i so that

$$v_{ik} = \min_j v_{ij} = w_i \qquad (2)$$

We define $x_{ij} = v_{ij} - w_i$. Then for each policy x_j we can write

$$v_{ij} = w_i + x_{ij} \qquad (3)$$

with $x_{ik} = 0$ for the least-preferred policy X_k.

Let $Y(\bar{p})$ be the prospect corresponding to the probability vector $\bar{p}$, i.e., the prospect that adoption by the group of joint policies $X_1, \ldots, X_n$ has the probabilities $p_1, \ldots, p_n$ respectively. The expected utility value to individual i of prospect $Y(\bar{p})$ will be

$$y_i = w_i + \sum_j p_j x_{ij} \qquad (4)$$

In order to compare Case B with Case A, we may also consider certain simpler hypothetical prospects $\tilde{Y}_i(\tilde{p}_i)$ which would involve only two possibilities; adoption of policy X_i, most preferred by i, and adoption of policy X_k, least preferred by i, the former having probability $\tilde{p}_i$ and the latter having probability $1 - \tilde{p}_i$. The expected utility value to i of any such hypothetical prospect $\tilde{Y}_i(\tilde{p}_i)$ would be

$$\tilde{y}_i = w_i + \tilde{p}_i x_{ii} \qquad (5)$$

There will be a unique prospect $\tilde{Y}_i(\tilde{p}_i)$ which would have the same utility value to individual i as prospect $Y(\bar{p})$, making $\tilde{y}_i = y_i$. This $\tilde{Y}_i(\tilde{p}_i)$ will correspond to the probability

$$\tilde{p}_i = \sum_j p_j x_{ij} / x_{ii} \qquad (6)$$

This hypothetical two-way prospect $\tilde{Y}_i(\tilde{p}_i)$ may be said to measure the value to i of the n-way prospect $Y(\bar{p})$, and the corresponding probability $\tilde{p}_i$, may be used as a scalar measure of individual i's power. What $\tilde{p}_i$ measures is not i's power to get the group to adopt some specific joint policy X_i; this is measured by p_i, the amount of i's *specific* power. Rather, $\tilde{p}_i$ measures i's power to get the group to adopt *some* policy reasonably satisfactory to him, even if this policy is not necessarily the policy *most preferred* by him. This quantity $\tilde{p}_i$ we shall call the amount of *i*'s *generic* power over the group's joint policy. For most purposes it represents the best scalar measure for the amount of *i*'s power.[3]

Of course in Case A previously considered $\tilde{p}_i = p_i$, and the amount of *i*'s power (without qualification), the amount of *i*'s *specific* power, and the amount of *i*'s *generic* power are all the same thing.

CASE C. MULTIPLE PREFERENCES AND
POSSIBLE COMPROMISE POLICIES

Finally, we shall consider the more general case where the number of efficient alternative policies available is $n + m$, i.e., is greater than n, the number of individuals.[4] Policies $X_1, \ldots, X_n$ will represent the first preferences of individuals $1, \ldots, n$. Policies $X_{n+1}, \ldots, X_{n+m}$ will not represent any individual's first preference, but they still may be adopted as joint policies by the n individuals (or they may be used with positive probability weights in the jointly randomized mixed strategy adopted by them) because they may represent a suitable compromise among the conflicting interests of different individuals.

In Case C, individual *i*'s power can again be measured by the amounts of his specific or generic power, or by the vector measure for the amount of his power. But there are the following differences. The amounts of specific power, p_i, for the n individuals now need not add up to unity (because some probability now may be allocated to policies other than $X_1, \ldots, X_n$). The vector measure $\tilde{p}$ for the amount of power now is an $(n + m)$-vector, not an n-vector as in Case B.[5] Finally, in Case C the amount of *i*'s *specific* power is an even less satisfactory measure for his power than it was in Case B, and the use of the amount of his *generic* power will become even more necessary. (For instance, if the n individuals agree to adopt some particular compromise policy, say, with probability 1; then every individual will have zero amount of *specific* power, as he had to give up all his chances to achieve his own favorite policy. At the same time, the compromise actually adopted may very well be highly

satisfactory to all of them, giving all of them a near-unity amount of *generic* power.)

Definition of the Strength of Power

As Cases A and B are special cases under Case C, we shall define the strength of each participant's power for the *general* Case C, and shall later mention some of the simplifications applying in special cases.

The n participants will have more or less conflicting interests concerning a certain controversial issue $X = (X_1, \ldots, X_{n+m})$, i.e., concerning how much probability p_j to allocate to each of the $(n + m)$ policy alternatives X_j. Therefore we shall assume that these probabilities p_j will be determined by explicit or implicit bargaining among the n participants.[6] By definition, the amount of individual *i*'s specific power will be simply p_i. By equation (6), the amount of his generic power, $\tilde{p}_i$, will also be defined in terms of the probabilities p_j. Thus both of these measures for each individual's power can be regarded as results of bargaining among these individuals.

The outcome of this bargaining will depend on two main factors. One is the physical and legal ability of each individual or coalition of individuals to carry through certain policies independently of the consent of other individuals, which we shall call the *independent power* of this individual or coalition. (For instance, in many policy-making bodies a simple or qualified majority coalition of the members will have full independent power to decide on policies.) The other factor is the ability of each individual, or coalition of individuals, to provide incentives (i.e., rewards and penalties) for other individuals to give their consent to policies favored by this individual or coalition, which we shall call the *incentive power* of this individual or coalition. (For instance, a minority which could not decide policies by its own rights may be able to bribe or intimidate the majority into consenting to its policy proposals.)

My bargaining model for the *n*-person game—on the assumption that each participant's behavior will satisfy certain rationality postulates—predicts the outcome of bargaining among the n participants in terms of all individuals' and all possible coalitions' independent power and incentive power. Thus the *theoretically predicted value* of the amount of a given individual i's *generic power*, $\tilde{p}_i$, can be regarded as a measure of the *strength* of i's *bargaining position*, or of his power to get some policy alternative reasonably acceptable to him adopted by the group. This quantity I propose to call the *strength* of individual i's power.[7] (I propose to use the theoretically predicted value of $\tilde{p}_i$, the amount of i's *generic* power, rather than the predicted value of p_i, the amount of i's *specific* power, because for reasons already indicated I consider $\tilde{p}_i$ as being a much better measure for i's power than p_i.)

We shall consider a bargaining situation of the following kind. The n individuals agree to adopt the jointly randomized mixed strategy $\bar{p}$ assigning the probabilities $p_1, \ldots, p_{n+m}$ to the *policy alternatives* $X_1, \ldots, X_{n+m}$. By equation (4), strategy $\bar{p}$ will yield for individual i the expected utility

$$y_i = w_i + \sum_{j \in M} p_j x_{ij} \tag{7}$$

where $M = (1, \ldots, n + m)$.

At the same time, the n participants also agree on a reward strategy ρ, under which each individual i will give each other individual j a *reward* R_{ij} in order to get j to agree to a strategy $\bar{p}$ favorable to i. (Of course, some or all of these rewards R_{ij} may be nil.) These rewards may take the form of money, commodities, power in *other* fields (i.e., concessions concerning controversial issues other than X—this restriction is necessary to avoid double counting), etc.

Let r_i be the total *net* utility gain that individual i obtains as a result of reward strategy ρ.[8] The total utility payoff of individual i as a result of strategies $\bar{p}$ and ρ will be

$$u_i = w_i + r_i + \sum_{j \in M} p_j x_{ij} \tag{8}$$

We also need a set of notations to describe the situation that would arise if the n individuals could not agree on the joint strategies $\bar{p}$ and ρ, in particular to describe the situation that would arise if the n

individuals split into two opposing coalitions S and $\bar{S}$, the former having s members and the latter having $\bar{S} = n - s$ members.

We shall assume that, in case of a conflict between coalitions S and $\bar{S}$, coalition S would have the choice among the policy alternatives $X_1, \ldots, X_{n+m}$ with probability π^S, while coalition $\bar{S}$ would have the choice among these alternatives with probability $\pi^{\bar{S}} = 1 - \pi^S$. If the choice were made by coalition S, alternative X_j would be selected with probability $q_j{}^S$; if the choice were made by coalition $\bar{S}$, alternative X_j would be selected with probability $q_j{}^{\bar{S}}$. Hence, in case of a conflict between coalitions S and $\bar{S}$, the total probability of X_j being selected would be

$$p_j{}^S = p_j{}^{\bar{S}} = \pi^S q_j{}^S + (1 - \pi^S) q_j{}^{\bar{S}} \tag{9}$$

If policy alternatives $X_1, \ldots, X_{n+m}$ have probabilities $p_1{}^S, \ldots, p_n{}^S{}_{+m}$ associated with them, equation (4) would give individual i the expected utility

$$y_i{}^S = w_i + \sum_{j \in M} p_j{}^S x_{ij} \tag{10}$$

We shall also assume that in the event of a conflict between coalitions S and $\bar{S}$, coalition S would use the retaliatory as well as defensive conflict strategy ϑ^S, while coalition $\bar{S}$ would use the conflict strategy $\vartheta^{\bar{S}}$. To a given member i of coalition S, the conflict strategies ϑ^S (of which he would be a participant) and $\vartheta^{\bar{S}}$ (of which he would be a target of attack) would cause the total *net* utility loss $t_i{}^S$. Thus $t_i{}^S$ would be the total net *cost* to i of a conflict between S and $\bar{S}$ (if, to avoid double counting, we disregard the losses that i would suffer because the conflict might change the probabilities associated with the various policy alternatives X_j).[9]

Thus the total payoff to individual i in case of a conflict between S and $\bar{S}$ would be

$$u_i{}^S = w_i - t_i{}^S + \sum_{j \in M} p_j{}^S x_{ij} \tag{11}$$

Under these assumptions, according to my bargaining model (Harsanyi, 1960, equation |8.7|) the n individuals will agree on such strategies $\bar{p}$ and ρ which will give each individual i the final utility payoff u_i, defined by the generalized Shapley-value expression:

$$u_i = w_i + z_i \cdot \frac{1}{n}(1 + R)$$

$$+ z_i \cdot \sum_{\substack{S \ni i \\ S \subset N}} \frac{(s - 1)!(n - s)!}{n!} \quad (12)$$

$$\times [(P^S - P^{\bar{S}}) - (T^S - T^{\bar{S}})]$$

where N denotes the set $N = (1, \ldots, n)$, and where $z_1, \ldots, z_n$ are certain variables,[10] whereas

$$R = \sum_{k \in N} \frac{r_k}{z_k} \quad (13)$$

$$P^S = \sum_{k \in S} \sum_{j \in M} \frac{p_j^S x_{kj}}{z_k} \quad (14)$$

and

$$T^S = \sum_{k \in S'} \frac{t_k^S}{z_k} \quad (15)$$

The quantities x_{kj} are the constants defined by equations (2) and (3). On the other hand, the variables of form z_i, r_i, p_i^S, t_i^S are defined implicitly in terms of a set of simultaneous optimizational equations[11] (equations $(\alpha\alpha)$, $(\beta\beta)$, and (γ) .to (η) in Harsanyi, 1960), whose numerical solution in general requires an iterative procedure.

In special cases, however, a more direct approach is possible, In particular, in Case A it is often possible to treat the assumed bargaining game as a game with (locally) *transferable utility*,[12] owing to the participants' ability to redistribute probability, by mutual agreement, between different policy alternatives X_i and X_j. In Case A, equation (8), in view of equation (1), takes the simple form

$$u_i = w_i + r_i = p_i x_i \quad (16)$$

In order to obtain transferable utility, we have to subject all individuals' utility functions to linear transformations, by choosing the quantities x_i as the new units of measurement for each individual i's utility. The transformed value of u_i will be

$$u_i' = \frac{w_i + r_i}{x_i} + p_i \quad (17)$$

Summing these quantities, we obtain

$$\sum_{i \in N} u_i' = \sum_{i \in N} \frac{w_i + r_i}{x_i} + 1 \quad (18)$$

which is a constant independent of the probabilities p_i and so satisfies the transferable-utility requirement.

Similarly, equation (11), in view of (1), now takes the simple form

$$u_i^S = w_i - t_i^S + p_i^S x_i \quad (19)$$

The transformed value of u_i^S will be

$$(u_i^S)' = \frac{w_i - t_i^S}{x_i} + p_i^S \quad (20)$$

Summing these quantities, in view of (9), we obtain

$$\sum_{i \in S} (u_i^S)' = \sum_{i \in S} \frac{w_i - t_i^S}{x_i} + \pi^S \sum_{i \in S} q_i^S$$

$$= \sum_{i \in S} \frac{w_i - t_i^S}{x_i} + \pi^S \quad (21)$$

The last equality applies because in Case A coalition S will obviously distribute all probability among the policies X_i favored by its own members i so that

$$\sum_{i \in S} q_i^S = 1 \quad (22)$$

We see that the summation in equation (21) also yields a constant independent of the probabilities q_i^S, and so satisfies the transferable-utility requirement.

However, the possibility of utility transfers satisfying equations (20) or (21) is restricted by the fact that the probabilities p_i and q_i^S can never become negative. For our purposes it is sufficient if the transferable-utility requirement is *locally* satisfied in the neighborhood of the solution payoff vector $\bar{u} = (u_1, \ldots, u_n)$ of the game, which will be so if the equilibrium values for all n probabilities $p_1, \ldots, p_n$ are positive (i.e., nonzero).[13] In actual fact, it can be shown that the method to be discussed always furnishes the correct solution in any situation under Case A where it yields positive or zero values for all probabilities $p_i = \tilde{p}_i$. But when our method gives negative values for some of the p_i's, then the whole solution (including those p_i's for which we have obtained positive or zero values) must be recomputed by means of the general iterative method not assuming transferable utility.

In cases where the transferable-utility assumption is admissible, equation (12) can be supplemented by the following simple equilibrium conditions:

$$z_i = x_i \qquad i = 1, \ldots, n \qquad (23)$$

$$R = \max_{\rho} R(\rho) \qquad (24)$$

$$T^s - T^{\bar{s}}$$
$$= \min_{\vartheta^s} \max_{\vartheta^{\bar{s}}} [T^s(\vartheta^s, \vartheta^{\bar{s}}) - T^{\bar{s}}(\vartheta^s, \vartheta^{\bar{s}})] \qquad (25)$$

Moreover, by (22), (1), and (23), we have

$$P^s = \pi^s \qquad (26)$$

(In the general case without transferable utility, we obtain equilibrium conditions fairly similar to (24) and (25). But the *max* and *min* operators are subject to constraints involving some of the other variables, in such a way that the constraints together form a nonrecursive circular system. This nonrecursiveness generally necessitates the use of an iterative procedure for finding the solution.)[14]

From equations (12), (8), and (6), we obtain the predicted value of $\tilde{p}_i$, the amount of individual i's generic power, as

$$\tilde{p}_i = \frac{z_i}{x_{ii}} \left[\frac{1}{n} + \sum_{\substack{S \ni i \\ S \subset N}} \frac{(s-1)!\,(n-s)!}{n!} \right.$$

$$\times (P^s - P^{\bar{s}}) \Big]$$

$$+ \frac{z_i}{x_{ii}} \left[\frac{1}{n} \left(R - \frac{r_i}{z_i} \right) \right.$$

$$- \sum_{\substack{S \ni i \\ S \subset N}} \frac{(s-1)!\,(n-s)!}{n!} (T^s - T^{\bar{s}}) \Big] \qquad (27)$$

The expression on the right of this equation is what we propose to call the *strength of* individual i's *power*.

Let us consider the meaning of this mathematical expression more closely. If we interpret equation (14) in the light of equation (6), we can see that each variable P^s is essentially a weighted sum of the amounts of *generic power* that the various members of coalition S would possess in case of a conflict between coalitions S and $\bar{S}$. Similarly, by equation (13), the variable R is a weighted sum of the net *rewards* r_i that the different individuals would receive from one another in case of full agreement. Finally, by equation (15), each variable T^s is a weighted sum of the *penalties* (or conflict costs) that the members of coalition S would suffer in case of a conflict between coalitions S and $\bar{S}$.

Accordingly, the first term on the right of equation (27) is a weighted sum (of a constant $1/n$ and) of the amounts of generic power that individual i and his coalition partners would possess in various possible conflict situations, less a weighted sum of the amounts of generic power that members of the opposing coalitions would possess. This term can be regarded as a measure of the *net strength* of individual i's (and of his potential allies') *independent power*, i.e., of his ability to implement his policy preferences without the consent, or even against the resistance, of various individuals who may oppose him (and of his ability to prevent the latter from implementing their policy preferences without his consent).

On the other hand, the second term is a weighted sum of the net rewards that all other individuals would obtain in case of full agreement, and of the net penalties that they would suffer in various possible conflict situations if they opposed individual i, less a weighted sum of the net reward that individual i would obtain if full agreement were reached, and of the net penalties that he and his coalition partners would suffer in conflict situations. This term can be regarded as a measure of the *net strength* of individual *i*'s *incentive power*, i.e., of his ability to provide incentives (or to use incentives provided by nature or by outside agencies) to induce other participants to consent to implementing his own policy preferences.

Finally, the *sum* of these two terms, i.e., the whole expression on the right of equation (27), which we have called the *strength of i's power*, can be taken as a measure for the full strength of *i*'s *bargaining position*, or of his power to get his policy preferences satisfied within the group, based both on his independent power and on his incentive power. (Under the models in the preceding paper for 2-person situations involving either unilateral power or reciprocal power, *A* had no independent power with respect to action *X* to be performed by *B*, as *A* was unable to perform an action of *B*'s in place of *B*. The only way *A* could get an action of *B*'s performed was to provide incentives for *B* to perform it. Hence the total strength of *A*'s power over *B* was simply equal to the strength of his incentive power. But in *n*-person reciprocal power situations we need a more general definition for the strength of a person's power, admitting the strength of his independent power as a separate term.)

We have derived the mathematical expression defining the strength of an individual's power from a bargaining model for the *n*-person game, based on certain specific rationality postulates. But the above analysis shows that this expression is a suitable measure for the strength of each participant's *bargaining position* or *power* even in situations where the participants do not follow the rationality postulates of this bargaining model. (Of course, in such situations the observed *amount* of each participant's generic power will usually *not* be equal to its theoretically predicted value, i.e., to the *strength* of this participant's power.) To put it differently, the rationality postulates of our bargaining model are based on the assumption that all participants will use the strategical possibilities open to them in the best possible and most rational ways. In empirical situations this assumption will not always be fulfilled. But what the outcome would be if all participants did make full rational use of their strategical possibilities will still be a question of great theoretical interest; because the answer to this question will help us to assess quantitatively *what their strategical possibilities actually are*, i.e., what each participant's objective *bargaining position* is, even if the actual outcome does not correspond very closely to the different participants' objective bargaining positions.

To sum up our results, we now state our:

Theorem III.[15] In *n*-person reciprocal power situations, if the participants follow the rationality postulates of the writer's bargaining model for the *n*-person game, then the *amount* of each participant's *generic power* will tend to be equal to the *strength* of his power, defined as the sum of the strength of his *independent power* and the strength of his *incentive power*.[16]

Relationship Between Our Strength-of-Power Concept and the Shapley-Shubik Measure for Power

Shapley and Shubik (1954) have proposed a quantitative measure for the power of each participant in a committee system, e.g., in a constitutional structure. (For instance, they have found that under the U.S. Constitution the power indices for the President, for an individual senator, and for an individual congressman are in the proportion of 350:9:2.) In our notations, their power index can be defined as

$$p_i{}^* = \frac{1}{n} + \sum_{\substack{S \ni i \\ S \subset N}} \frac{(s-1)! \, (n-s)!}{n!}$$

$$\times \, (\pi^S - \pi^{\bar{S}}) \tag{28}$$

which is identical with our measure for the *strength* of individual *i*'s *independent power* alone in Case A (cf. equations [23], [26], and [27]).

Shapley and Shubik's power measure is based on the Shapley value for the *n*-person game (Shapley, 1953), while our strength-of-power concept is based on our own bargaining model for the n-person game. But in view of the very close mathematical relationship between our bargaining model and the Shapley value, it is not surprising that our strength-of-power concept and their power index are also closely related.

Of course, the intuitive interpretation Shapley and Shubik give to their power index is not the same that we have given to our measure for the strength of independent power, in that their power index is supposed to express (roughly speaking) the *a priori* probability that a given participant i will have the *decisive vote* in getting policy proposals finally accepted. But Shapley and Shubik are fully aware of the fact that their power index admits of a number of alternative intuitive interpretations—in effect, they point out that any intuitive interpretation consistent with the axioms defining the Shapley value would necessarily lead to numerically the same power index.

But even at an intuitive level it is possible to translate their definition in terms of our own model. Let us consider the case of n individuals each of whom wants to have the decisive vote on some particular policy problem. Let us also make the following two restrictive assumptions:

1) Each of the n participants would be perfectly indifferent as to who should have the decisive vote in case he could not have it himself.

2) None of the n participants can provide any incentives for the other participants.

Assumption 1 brings the situation under our Case A, while assumption 2 makes the strength of each participant's incentive power equal to zero.

We may consider that the Shapley-Shubik model deals with the special case corresponding to these assumptions. Given these assumptions, both our strength-of-power measure and the Shapley-Shubik power index for a given individual i are defined as being equal to the probability p_i that the decisive vote will be cast by this individual i. Moreover, both our own model and the Shapley-Shubik model yield for this probability the value $p_i = p_i^*$ defined by equation (28). Thus, under these assumptions their power measure and ours coincide.

In short, the Shapley-Shubik power measure can be regarded as that special case of our own strength-of-power concept where the *single-preferences* and the *no-compromise* assumptions of Case A are satisfied, and where at the same time the *incentive power* of every participant is *nil* (or is disregarded).

That is, compared with the Shapley-Shubik measure, our own strength-of-power measure has the advantage of taking account of the effects that the *incentive power* of various participants has on each participant's power position. For instance, if the participant's utility functions are sufficiently known then our measure makes it possible to compute the increase in the American President's strength of power (and the corresponding decrease in the strength of the power of the Congress), due to a given amount of patronage that he can promise to senators and congressmen, or due to a given amount of influence with the electorate he can promise or threaten to mobilize at the next election for the Congress, etc.

Our strength-of-power measure can also take account of the effects of alliances and party alignments among the participants. Under Case A this can be done only by assuming that the very act of co-operation with the other members of a given possible coalition S would be a source of direct utility or disutility to certain individuals i, with corresponding effects on the values of the quantities $t_i{}^s$ and T^s.[17] But under Cases B and C, alliances and party alignments can be represented also by similarities among the policy preferences of various participants. In the analysis of most empirical situations one will presumably need both of these methods for representing alliances among the participants. (Shapley and Shubik [1954, pp. 791–792] take account of party alignments by noting the possible discrepancies between their theoretical measure and an analogous empirical measure they introduce, but the existence of a party structure does not enter into their theoretical measure as such.)

Finally, our strength-of-power measure can also take account of improvements in *all* participants' power positions when suitable *compromise policies* are discovered, which may increase the chances, for all participants at the same time, of a reasonably satisfactory outcome (Case C).

References

Harsanyi, J. C. A bargaining model for the co-operative *n*-person game. In A. W. Tucker and R. D. Luce (Eds.), *Contributions to the theory of games*, IV. Princeton: Princeton Univ. Press, 1959. Pp. 325–355.

Harsanyi, J. C. A simplified model for the *n*-person cooperative game, 1960 (hectographed). Available from author on request.

Harsanyi, J. C. Measurement of social power, opportunity costs, and the theory of two-person bargaining games, *Behav. Sci.*, 1962, 1. Pp. 67–80.

Shapley, L. S. A value for *n*-person games. In H. W. Kuhn and A. W. Tucker (Eds.), *Contributions to the theory of games*, II. Princeton, Princeton Univ. Press, 1953. Pp. 307–317.

Shapley, L. S., & Shubik, M. A method for evaluating the distribution of power in a committee system. *Amer. Polit. Sci. Rev.*, 1954, 48, 787–792.

The Concept of Power and Theories of Political Systems

THE SELECTIONS reproduced in this section are important because they attempt to explicate the concept of power in the context of an empirical theory of politics. The essays by Parsons and Boulding emphasize the definition of a group of concepts around which empirical theory might be organized, while the essays by Blau, Banfield, Brams, and Waltz are more nearly attempts to develop partial theories. Moreover, the essays by Boulding, Parsons, and Blau concentrate on theories about the construction of political systems out of interpersonal relations which theories of political power have often emphasized, while Banfield, Brams, and Waltz are more concerned with the consequences of the distribution of power (variously defined) for the working of domestic and international political systems. But all the essays are united by a concern for the construction of empirical theory around the concept of power.

A close reading of these essays will reveal considerable disagreement about the meaning of this elusive word, and in one or two cases some vagueness of definition. But definitional disputes become less significant once a term is given an unambiguous definition in the context of an empirical theory. The adequacy of the definition can then be judged by the success of the theory itself. It will be obvious that these essays vary widely in their success in giving the concept of power both empirical and theoretical significance. But they do succeed in raising some of the most important theoretical questions implied in discourse about political power, and define these questions in a slightly more precise way than much previous literature on the subject. By doing so, they provide some support for the belief that progress depends as much on making one's desire for explanations more precise, and thus one's hypotheses more specific, as upon refining one's definitions or measurement techniques.

POWER is one of the key concepts in the great Western tradition of thought about political phenomena. It is at the same time a concept on which, in spite of its long history, there is, on analytical levels, a notable lack of agreement both about its specific definition, and about many features of the conceptual context in which it should be placed. There is, however, a core complex of its meaning, having to do with the capacity of persons or collectivities "to get things done" effectively, in particular when their goals are obstructed by some kind of human resistance or opposition. The problem of coping with resistance then leads into the question of the role of coercive measures, including the use of physical force, and the relation of coercion to the voluntary and consensual aspects of power systems.

The aim of this paper is to attempt to clarify this complex of meanings and relations by placing the concept of power in the context of a general conceptual scheme for the analysis of large-scale and complex social systems, that is of societies. In doing so I speak as a sociologist rather than as a political scientist, but as one who believes that the interconnections of the principal social disciplines, including not only these two, but especially their relations to economics as well, are so close that on matters of general theory of this sort they cannot safely be treated in isolation; their interrelations must be made explicit and systematic. As a sociologist, I thus treat a central concept of political theory by selecting among the elements which have figured prominently in political theory in terms of their fit with and significance for the general theoretical analysis of society as a whole.

There are three principal contexts in which it seems to me that the difficulties of the concept of power, as treated in the literature of the last generation, come to a head. The first of these concerns its conceptual diffuseness, the tendency, in the tradition of Hobbes, to treat power as simply the generalized capacity to attain ends or goals in social relations, independently of the media employed or of the status of "authorization" to make decisions or impose obligations.[1]

The effect of this diffuseness, as I call it,

21

On the Concept of Political Power

Talcott Parsons

In this article Talcott Parsons attempts to explicate the concept of power as part of a more general scheme which also defines the polity as a subsystem of the social system. In doing so, he calls our attention to the dependence of the political system on a certain type of interpersonal relationship which he attempts to define precisely. The reader will find it helpful in understanding this article first to familiarize himself with Professor Parson's earlier and more elaborate analysis of the economy. See Talcott Parsons and Neil Smelser, Economy and Society *(New York: The Free Press, 1956). The essay reprinted below originally appeared in 107* Proceedings of the American Philosophical Society *(June, 1963), 232–62, and is reprinted in Talcott Parsons,* Sociological Theory and Modern Society *(New York: The Free Press, 1967). It is reproduced here with the permission of the American Philosophical Society and the author.*

is to treat "influence" and sometimes money; as well as coercion in various aspects, as "forms" of power, thereby making it logically impossible to treat power as a *specific* mechanism operating to bring about changes in the action of other units, individual or collective, in the processes of social interaction. The latter is the line of thought I wish to pursue.

Secondly, there is the problem of the relation between the coercive and the consensual aspects. I am not aware of any treatment in the literature which presents a satisfactory solution of this problem. A major tendency is to hold that somehow "in the last analysis" power comes down to one or the other, i.e., to "rest on" command of coercive sanctions, *or* on consensus and the will to voluntary cooperation. If going to one or the other polar solution seems to be unacceptable, a way out, taken for example by Friedrich, is to speak of each of these as different "forms" of power. I shall propose a solution which maintains that both aspects are essential, but that neither of the above two ways of relating them is satisfactory, namely subordinating either one to the other or treating them as discrete "forms."

Finally the third problem is what, since the Theory of Games, has widely come to be called the "zero-sum" problem. The dominant tendency in the literature, for example in Lasswell and C. Wright Mills, is to maintain explicitly or implicitly that power is a zero-sum phenomenon, which is to say that there is a fixed "quantity" of power in any relational system and hence any gain of power on the part of A must by definition occur by diminishing the power at the disposal of other units, B, C, D. . . . There are, of course, restricted contexts in which this condition holds, but I shall argue that it does not hold for total systems of a sufficient level of complexity.

Some General Assumptions

The initial assumption is that, within the conception of society as a system, there is an essential parallelism in theoretical structure between the conceptual schemes appropriate for the analysis of the economic and the political aspects of societies. There are four respects in which I wish to attempt to work out and build on this parallel, showing at the same time the crucial substantive differences between the two fields.

First "political theory" as here interpreted, which is not simply to be identified with the meaning given the term by many political scientists, is thought of as an abstract analytical scheme in the same sense in which economic theory is abstract and analytical. It is not the conceptual interpretation of any concretely complete category of social phenomena, quite definitely not those of government, though government is the area in which the political element comes nearest to having clear primacy over others. Political theory thus conceived is a conceptual scheme which deals with a restricted set of primary variables and their interrelations, which are to be found operating in all concrete parts of

social systems. These variables are, however, subject to parametric conditions which constitute the values of other variables operating in the larger system which constitutes the society.

Secondly, following on this, I assume that the empirical system to which political theory in this sense applies is an analytically defined, a "functional" subsystem of a society, not for example a concrete type of collectivity. The conception of the economy of a society is relatively well defined.[2] I should propose the conception of the *polity* as the parallel empirical system of direct relevance to political theory as here advanced. The polity of a given society is composed of the ways in which the relevant components of the total system are organized with reference to one of its fundamental functions, namely effective collective action in the attainment of the goals of collectivities. Goal-attainment in this sense is the establishment of a satisfactory relation between a collectivity and certain objects in its environment which include both other collectivities and categories of personalities, e.g. "citizens." A total society must in these terms be conceived, in one of its main aspects, as a collectivity, but it is also composed of an immense variety of sub-collectivities, many of which are parts not only of this society but of others.[3]

A collectivity, seen in these terms, is thus clearly not a concrete "group" but the term refers to groups, i.e. systematically related pluralities of persons, seen in the perspective of their interests in and capacities for effective collective action. The political process then is the process by which the necessary organization is built up and operated, the goals of action are determined and the resources requisite to it are mobilized.

These two parallels to economic theory can be extended to still a third. The parallel to collective action in the political case is, for the economic, production. This conception in turn must be understood in relation to three main operative contexts. The first is adjustment to the conditions of "demand" which are conceived to be external to the economy itself, to be located in the "consumers" of the economic process. Secondly, resources must be mobilized, also from the environment of the economy, the famous factors of production. Thirdly, the internal economic process is conceived as creatively combinatorial; it is, by the "combination" of factors of production in the light of the utility of outputs, a process of creating more valuable facilities to meet the needs of consuming units than would be available to them without this combinatorial process. I wish most definitely to postulate that the logic of "value added" applies to the political sphere in the present sense. [4]

In the political case, however, the value reference is not to utility in the economic sense but to effectiveness, very precisely, I think in the sense used by C. I. Barnard. [5] For the limited purposes of political analysis as such the givenness of the goal-demands of interest groups serves as the same order of factor in relation to the political system as has the corresponding givenness of consumer's wants for purposes of economic analysis—and of course the same order of qualifications on the empirical adequacy of such postulates.

Finally, fourth, political analysis as here conceived is parallel to economic in the sense that a central place in it is occupied by a generalized medium involved in the political interaction process, which is also a "measure" of the relevant values. I conceive power as such a generalized medium in a sense directly parallel in logical structure, though very different substantively, to money as the generalized medium of the economic process. It is essentially this conception of power as a generalized medium parallel to money which will, in the theoretical context sketched above, provide the thread for guiding the following analysis through the types of historic difficulty with reference to which the paper began.

The Outputs of Political Process and the Factors of Effectiveness

The logic of the combinatorial process which I hold to be common to economic theory and the type of political theory advanced here, involves a paradigm of inputs and outputs and their relations. Again we will hold that the logic is strictly parallel to the economic case, i.e. that there should be a set of political categories strictly parallel to those of the factors of production (inputs) on the one hand, the shares of income (outputs) on the other.

In the economic case, with the exception of land, the remaining three factors must be regarded as inputs from the other three cognate functional subsystems of the society, labor from what we call the "pattern-maintenance" system, capital from the polity and organization, in the sense of Alfred Marshall, from the integrative system. [6] Furthermore, it becomes clear that land is not, as a factor of production, simply the physical resource, but essentially the commitment, in value terms, of any resources to economic production in the system independent of price.

In the political case, similarly the equivalent of land is the commitment of resources to effective collective action, independent of any specifiable "pay-off" for the unit which controls them. [7] Parallel to labor is the demands or "need" for collective action as manifested in the "public" which in some sense is the constituency of the leadership of the collectivity in question—a conception which is relatively clear for the governmental or other electoral association, but needs clarification in other connections. Parallel to capital is the control of some part of the productivity of the economy for the goals of the collectivity, in a sufficiently developed economy through financial resources at the disposal of the collectivity, acquired by earnings, gift, or taxation. Finally, parallel to organization is the legitimation of the authority under which collective decisions are taken.

It is most important to note that none of these categories of input is conceived as a form of power. In so far as they involve media, it is the media rooted in contiguous functional systems, not power as that central to the polity—e.g. control of productivity may operate through money, and constituents' demands through what I call "influence." Power then is the *means* of acquiring control of the factors in effectiveness; it is not itself one of these factors, any more than in the economic case money is a factor of production; to suppose it was, was the ancient mercantilist fallacy.

Though the analytical context in which they are placed is perhaps unfamiliar in the light of traditional political analysis, I hope it is clear that the actual categories used are well established, though there remain a number of problems of exact definition. Thus control of productivity through financing of collective action is very familiar, and the concept of "demands" in the sense of what constituents want and press for, is also very familiar.[8] The concept legitimation is used in essentially the same sense in which I think Max Weber used it in a political context.[9]

The problem of what corresponds, for the political case, to the economist's "shares of income" is not very difficult, once the essential distinction, a very old one in economic tradition, between monetary and "real" income is clearly taken into account. Our concern is with the "real" outputs of the political process—the analogue of the monetary here is output of power.

There is one, to us critically important revision of the traditional economic treatment of outputs which must be made, namely the bracketing together of "goods and services," which then would be treated as outputs to the household as, in our technical terms, a part of the "pattern-maintenance" system. The present position is that goods, i.e., more precisely property rights in the physical objects of possession, belong in this category, but that "services," the commitment of human role-performances to an "employer," or contracting agent constitute an output, not to the household, but to the polity, the type case (though not the only one) being an employing organization in which the role-incumbent commits himself to performance of an occupational role, a job,[10] as a contribution to the effective functioning of the collectivity.

There is, from this consideration, a con-clusion which is somewhat surprising to economists, namely that service is, in the economic sense the "real" counterpart of interest as monetary income from the use of funds. What we suggest is that the political control of productivity makes it possible, through combinatorial gains in the political context, to produce a surplus above the monetary funds committed, by virtue of which under specified conditions a premium can be paid at the monetary level which, though a result of the combinatorial process as a whole, is most directly related to the output of available services as an economic phenomenon, i.e. as a "fluid resource." Seen a little differently, it becomes necessary to make a clear distinction between labor as a factor of production in the economic sense and service as an output of the economic process which is utilized in a political context, that is one of organizational or collective effectiveness.

Service, however, is not a "factor" in effectiveness, in the sense in which labor is a factor of production, precisely because it is a category of power. It is the point at which the economic utility of the human factor is matched with its potential contribution to effective collective action. Since the consumer of services is in principle the employing collectivity, it is its effectiveness for collective goals, not its capacity to satisfy the "wants" of individuals, which is the vantage point from which the utility of the service is derived. The output of power which matches the input of services to the polity, I interpret to be the "opportunity for effectiveness" which employment confers on those employed or contract offers to partners. Capital in the economic sense is one form of this opportunity for effectiveness which is derived from providing, for certain types of performances, a framework of effective organization.[11]

The second, particularly important context of "real" output of the political process is the category which, in accord with much tradition, I should like to call capacity to assume leadership responsibility. This, as a category of "real" output also is not a form of power, but this time of influence.[12] This is an output not to the economy but to what I shall call the integrative system, which in its relevance to the present context is in the first instance the sector of the "public" which can be looked on as the "constituencies" of the collective processes under consideration. It is the group structure of the society looked at in terms of their structured interests in particular modes of effective collective action by particular collectivities. It is only through effective organization that genuine responsibility can be taken, hence the implementation of such interest demands responsibility for collective effectiveness.[13] Again it should be made quite clear that leadership responsibility is not here conceived as an output of power, though many political theorists (e.g. Friedrich) treat both leadership and, more broadly influence, as "forms" of power. The power category which regulates the output of leadership influence takes this form on the one side of binding policy decisions of the collectivity, on the other of political support from the constituency, in the type case through franchise. Policy decisions we would treat as a factor in integration of the system, not as a "consumable" output of the political process.[14]

Finally, a few words need to be said about what I have called the combinatorial process itself. It is of course assumed in economic theory that the "structures" of the factors of production on the one hand, the "demand system" for real outputs on the other hand, are independent of each other. "Utility" of outputs can only be enhanced, to say nothing of maximized, by processes of transformation of the factors in the direction of providing what is wanted as distinguished from what merely is available. The decision-making aspect of this transformative process, what is to be produced, how much and how offered for consumption, is what is meant by economic production, whereas the physical processes are not economic but "technological"; they are controlled by economic considerations, but are not themselves in an analytical sense economic.

The consequence of successful adaptation of available resources to the want or demand system is an increment in the value of the resource-stock conceived in terms of utility as a type of value. But this means recombination of the components of the resource-stock in order to adapt them to the various uses in question.

The same logic applies to the combinatorial process in the political sphere. Here the resources are not land, labor, capital, and organization, but valuation of effectiveness, control of productivity, structured demands and the patterning of legitimation. The "wants" are not for consumption in the economic sense, but for the solution of "interest" problems in the system, including both competitive problems in the allocative sense and conflict problems, as well as problems of enhancement of the total effectiveness of the system of collective organization. In this case also the "structure" of the available resources may not be assumed spontaneously to match the structure of the system of interest-demands. The increment of effectiveness in demand-satisfaction through the political process is, as in the economic case, arrived at through combinatorial decision-processes. The organizational "technology" involved is not in the analytical sense political. The demand-reference is not to discrete units of the system conceived in abstraction from the system as a whole—the "individual" consumer of the economist—but to the problem of the share of benefits and burdens to be allocated to subsystems of various orders. The "consumption" reference is to the interest-unit's place in the allocative system rather than to the independent merits of particular "needs."

The Concept of Power

The above may seem a highly elaborate setting in which to place the formal introduction of the main subject of the paper, namely the concept of power. Condensed and cryptic as the exposition may have been, however, understanding of its main structure is an essential basis for the special way in which it will be proposed to combine the elements which have played a crucial part in the main intellectual traditions dealing with the problems of power.

Power is here conceived as a circulating medium, analogous to money, within what is called the political system, but notably over its boundaries into all three of the other neighboring functional subsystems of a society (as I conceive them), the economic, integrative, and pattern-maintenance systems. Specification of the properties of power can best be approached through an attempt to delineate very briefly the relevant properties of money as such a medium in the economy.

Money is, as the classical economists said, both a medium of exchange and a "measure of value." It is symbolic in that, though measuring and thus "standing for" economic value or utility, it does not itself possess utility in the primary consumption sense—it has no "value in use" but only "in exchange," i.e. for possession of things having utility. The use of money is thus a mode of communication of offers, on the one hand to purchase, on the other to sell, things of utility, with and for money. It becomes an essential medium only when exchange is neither ascriptive, as exchange of gifts between assigned categories of kin, nor takes place on a basis of barter, one item of commodity or service directly for another.

In exchange for its lack of direct utility money gives the recipient four important degrees of freedom in his participation in the total exchange system. (1) He is free to spend his money for any item or combination of items available on the market which he can afford, (2) he is free to shop around among alternative sources of supply for desired items, (3) he can choose his own time to purchase, and (4) he is free to consider terms which, because of freedom of time and source he can accept or reject or attempt to influence in the particular case. By contrast, in the case of barter, the negotiator is bound to what his particular partner has or wants in relation to what he has and will part with at the particular time. The other side of the gain in degrees of freedom is of course the risk involved in the probabilities of the acceptance of money by others and of the stability of its value.

Primitive· money is a medium which is still very close to a commodity, the commonest case being precious metal, and many still feel that the value of money is "really" grounded in the commodity value of the metallic base. On this base, however, there is, in developed monetary systems, erected a complex structure of credit instruments, so that only a tiny fraction of actual transactions is conducted in terms of the metal—it becomes a "reserve" available for certain contingencies, and is actually used mainly in the settlement of international balances. I shall discuss the nature of credit further in another connection later. For the moment suffice it to say that, however important in certain contingencies the availability of metallic reserves may be, no modern monetary system operates primarily with metal as the actual medium, but uses "valueless" money. Moreover, the acceptance of this "valueless" money rests on a certain institutionalized confidence in the monetary system. If the security of monetary commitments rested only on their convertibility into metal, then the overwhelming majority of them would be worthless, for the simple reason that the total quantity of metal is far too small to redeem more than a few.

One final point is that money is "good," i.e. works as a medium, only within a relatively defined network of market relationships which to be sure now has become world-wide, but the maintenance of which requires special measures to maintain mutual convertibility of national currencies. Such a system is on the one hand a range of exchange-potential within which money may be spent, but on the other hand, one within which certain conditions affecting the protection and management of the unit are maintained, both by law and by responsible agencies under the law.

The first focus of the concept of an institutionalized power system is, analogously, a relational system within which certain categories of commitments and obligations, ascriptive or voluntarily assumed —e.g. by contract—are treated as binding, i.e. under normatively defined conditions their fulfillment may be insisted upon by the appropriate role-reciprocal agencies. Furthermore, in case of actual or threatened resistance to "compliance," i.e. to fulfillment of such obligations when invoked, they will be "enforced" by the threat or actual imposition of situational negative sanctions, in the former case having the function of deterrence, in the latter of punishment. These are events in the situation of the actor of reference which intentionally alter his situation (or threaten to) to his disadvantage, whatever in specific content these alterations may be.

Power then is generalized capacity to secure the performance of binding obligations by units in a system of collective organization when the obligations are legitimized with reference to their bearing on collective goals and where in case of recalcitrance there is a presumption of enforcement by negative situational sanctions —whatever the actual agency of that enforcement.

It will be noted that I have used the conceptions of generalization and of legitimation in defining power. Securing possession of an object of utility by bartering another object for it is not a monetary transaction. Similarly, by my definition, securing compliance with a wish, whether it be defined as an obligation of the object or not, simply by threat of superior force, is not an exercise of power. I am well aware that most political theorists would draw the line differently and classify this as power (e.g. Dahl's definition), but I wish to stick to my chosen line and explore its implications. The capacity to secure compliance must, if it is to be called power in my sense, be generalized and not solely a function of one particular sanctioning act which the user is in a position to impose,[15] and the medium used must be "symbolic."

Secondly, I have spoken of power as involving legitimation. This is, in the present context, the necessary consequence of conceiving power as "symbolic," which therefore, if it is exchanged for something intrinsically valuable for collective effectiveness, namely compliance with an obligation, leaves the recipient, the performer of the obligation, with "nothing of value." This is

to say, that he has "nothing" but a set of expectations, namely that in other contexts and on other occasions, he can invoke certain obligations on the part of other units. Legitimation is therefore, in power systems, the factor which is parallel to confidence in mutual acceptability and stability of the monetary unit in monetary systems.

The two criteria are connected in that questioning the legitimacy of the possession and use of power leads to resort to progressively more "secure" means of gaining compliance. These must be progressively more effective "intrinsically," hence more tailored to the particular situations of the objects and less general. Furthermore in so far as they are intrinsically effective, legitimacy becomes a progressively less important factor of their effectiveness—at the end of this series lies resort, first to various types of coercion, eventually to the use of force as the most intrinsically effective of all means of coercion.[16]

I should like now to attempt to place both money and power in the context of a more general paradigm, which is an analytical classification of ways in which, in the processes of social interaction, the actions of one unit in a system can, intentionally, be oriented to bringing about a change in what the actions of one or more other units would otherwise have been—thus all fitting into the context of Dahl's conception of power. It is convenient to state this in terms of the convention of speaking of the acting unit of reference— individual or collective—as *ego*, and the object on which he attempts to "operate" as *alter*. We may then classify the alternatives open to ego in terms of two dichotomous variables. On the one hand ego may attempt to gain his end from alter either by using some form of control over the situation in which alter is placed, actually or contingently to change it so as to increase the probability of alter acting in the way he wishes, or, alternatively, without attempting to change alter's situation, ego may attempt to change alter's intentions, i.e. he may manipulate symbols which are meaningful to alter in such a way that he tries to make alter "see" that what ego wants is a "good thing" for him (alter) to do.

The second variable then concerns the type of sanctions ego may employ in attempting to guarantee the attainment of his end from alter. The dichotomy here is between positive and negative sanctions. Thus through the situational channel a positive sanction is a change in alter's situation presumptively considered by alter as to his advantage, which is used as a means by ego of having an effect on alter's actions. A negative sanction then is an alteration in alter's situation to the latter's disadvantage. In the case of the intentional channel, the positive sanction is the expression of symbolic "reasons" why compliance with ego's wishes is "a good thing" independently of any further action on ego's part, from alter's point of view, i.e. would be felt by him to be "personally advantageous," whereas the negative sanction is presenting reasons why noncompliance with ego's wishes should be felt by alter to be harmful to interests in which he had a significant personal investment and should therefore be avoided. I should like to call the four types of "strategy" open to ego respectively (1) for the situational channel, positive sanction case, "inducement"; (2) situational channel negative sanction, "coercion"; (3) intentional channel, positive sanction "persuasion," and (4) intentional channel negative sanction "activation of commitments" as shown in the following table:

Sanction type	Channel	
	Intentional	Situational
Positive	Persuasion 3	1 Inducement
Negative	Activation of 4 Commitments	2 Coercion

A further complication now needs to be introduced. We think of a sanction as an intentional act on ego's part, expected by him to change his relation to alter from what it would otherwise have been. As a means of bringing about a change in alter's action, it can operate most obviously where the actual imposition of the sanction is made contingent on a future decision by alter. Thus a process of inducement will operate in two stages, first contingent offer on ego's part that, if alter will "comply" with his wishes, ego will "reward" him by the contingently promised situational change. If then alter in fact does comply, ego will perform the sanctioning act. In the case of coercion the first stage is a contingent threat that, unless alter decides to comply, ego will impose the negative sanction. If, however, alter complies, then nothing further happens, but, if he decides on noncompliance, then ego must carry out his threat, or be in a position of "not meaning it." In the cases of the intentional channel ego's first-stage act is either to predict the occurrence, or to announce his own intention of doing something which affects alter's sentiments or interests. The element of contingency enters in in that ego "argues" to alter, that if this happens, on the one hand alter should be expected to "see" that it would be a good thing for him to do what ego wants—the positive case—or that if he fails to do it it would imply an important "subjective cost" to alter. In the positive case, beyond "pointing out" if alter complies, ego is obligated to deliver the positive attitudinal sanction of approval. In the negative case, the corresponding attitudinal sanction of disapproval is implemented only for noncompliance.

It is hence clear that there is a basic asymmetry between the positive and negative sides of the sanction aspect of the paradigm. This is that, in the cases of inducement and persuasion, alter's compliance obligates ego to "deliver" his promised positive sanction, in the former case the promised advantages, in the latter his approval of alter's "good sense" in recognizing that the decision wished for by ego and accepted as "good" by alter, in fact turns out to be good from alter's point of view. In the negative cases, on the other hand, compliance on alter's part obligates ego, in the situational case, not to carry out his threat, in the intentional case by withholding disapproval to confirm to alter that his compliance did in fact spare him what to him, without ego's intervention, would have been the undesirable subjective consequences of his previous intentions, namely guilt over violations of his commitments.

Finally, alter's freedom of action in his decisions of compliance versus noncompliance is also a variable. This range has a lower limit at which the element of contingency disappears. That is, from ego's point of view, he may not say, if you do so and so, I will intervene, either by situational manipulations or by "arguments" in such and such a way, but he may simply perform an overt act and face alter with a *fait accompli*. In the case of inducement a gift which is an object of value and with respect to the acceptance of which alter is given no option is the limiting case. With respect to coercion, compulsion, i.e. simply imposing a disadvantageous alteration on alter's situation and then leaving it to alter to decide whether to "do something about it" is the limiting case.

The asymmetry just referred to appears here as well. As contingent it may be said that the primary meaning of negative sanctions is as means of prevention. If they are effective, no further action is required. The case of compulsion is that in which it is rendered impossible for alter to avoid the undesired action on ego's part. In the case of positive sanctions of course ego, for example in making a gift to alter, cuts himself out from benefiting from alter's performance which is presumptively advantageous to him, in the particular exchange.

Both, however, may be oriented to their effect on alter's action in future sequences of interaction. The object of compulsion may have been "taught a lesson" and hence be less disposed to noncompliance with ego's wishes in the future, as well as prevented from performance of a particular undesired act and the recipient of a gift may feel a "sense of obligation" to reciprocate in some form in the future.

So far this discussion has dealt with sanctioning acts in terms of their "intrinsic" significance both to ego and to alter. An offered inducement may thus be possession of a particular object of utility, a coercive threat, that of a particular feared loss, or other noxious experience. But just as, in the initial phase of a sequence, ego transmits his contingent intentions to alter symbolically through communication, so the sanction involved may also be symbolic, e.g. in place of possession of certain intrinsically valuable goods he may offer a sum of money. What we have called the generalized media of interaction then may be used as types of sanctions which may be analyzed in terms of the above paradigm. The factors of generalization and of legitimation of institutionalization, however, as discussed above, introduce certain complications which we must now take up with reference to power. There is a sense in which power may be regarded as the generalized medium of coercion in the above terms, but this formula at the very least requires very careful interpretation—indeed it will turn out by itself to be inadequate.

I spoke above of the "grounding" of the value of money in the commodity value of the monetary metal, and suggested that there is a corresponding relation of the "value," i.e. the effectiveness of power, to the intrinsic effectiveness of physical force as a means of coercion and, in the limiting case, compulsion.[17]

In interpreting this formula due account must be taken of the asymmetry just discussed. The special place of gold as a monetary base rests on such properties as its durability, high value in small bulk, etc., and high probability of acceptability in exchange, i.e. as means of inducement, in a very wide variety of conditions which are not dependent on an institutionalized order. Ego's primary aim in resorting to compulsion or coercion, however, is deterrence of unwanted action on alter's part.[18] Force, therefore, is in the first instance important as the "ultimate" deterrent. It is the means which, again independent of any institutionalized system of order, can be assumed to be "intrinsically" the most effective in the context of deterrence, when means of effectiveness which *are* dependent on insti-

tutionalized order are insecure or fail.
Therefore, the unit of an action system
which commands control of physical force
adequate to cope with any potential counter
threats of force is more secure than any
other in a Hobbesian state of nature.[19]

But just as a monetary system resting
entirely on gold as the actual medium of
exchange is a very primitive one which
simply cannot mediate a complex system of
market exchange, so a power system in
which the only negative sanction is the
threat of force is a very primitive one which
cannot function to mediate a complex
system of organizational coordination—it
is far too "blunt" an instrument. Money
cannot be only an intrinsically valuable
entity if it is to serve as a generalized
medium of inducement, but it must, as we
have said, be institutionalized as a symbol;
it must be legitimized, and must inspire
"confidence" within the system—and must
also within limits be deliberately managed.
Similarly power cannot be only an intrinsically effective deterrent; if it is to be the
generalized medium of mobilizing resources for effective collective action, and
for the fulfillment of commitments made by
collectivities to what we have here called
their constituents; it too must be both
symbolically generalized, and legitimized.

There is a direct connection between the
concept of bindingness, as introduced above,
and deterrence. To treat a commitment or
any other form of expectation as binding is
to attribute a special importance to its fulfillment. Where it is not a matter simply of
maintenance of an established routine, but
of undertaking new actions in changed
circumstances, where the commitment is
thus to undertake types of action contingent
on circumstances as they develop, then the
risk to be minimized is that such contingent
commitments will not be carried out when
the circumstances in question appear. Treating the expectation or obligation as binding
is almost the same thing as saying that
appropriate steps on the other side must be
taken to prevent nonfulfillment, if possible.
Willingness to impose negative sanctions is,

seen in this light, simply the carrying out
of the implications of treating commitments
as binding, and the agent invoking them
"meaning it" or being prepared to insist.

On the other hand there are areas in
interaction systems where there is a range
of alternatives, choice among which is
optional, in the light of the promised advantageousness, situational or "intentional," of one as compared to other choices.
Positive sanctions as here conceived constitute a contingent increment of relative
advantageousness, situational or intentional,
of the alternative ego desires alter to
choose.

If, in these latter areas, a generalized,
symbolic medium, is to operate in place of
intrinsic advantages, there must be an
element of bindingness in the institutionalization of the medium itself—e.g. the fact
that the money of a society is "legal
tender" which must be accepted in the
settlement of debts which have the status
of contractual obligations under the law.
In the case of money, I suggest that, for the
typical acting unit in a market system,
what specific undertakings he enters into is
overwhelmingly optional in the above
sense, but whether the money involved in
the transactions is or is not "good" is not
for him to judge, but his acceptance of it is
binding. Essentially the same is true of the
contractual obligations, typically linking
monetary and intrinsic utilities, which he
undertakes.

I would now like to suggest that what is
in a certain sense the obverse holds true of
power. Its "intrinsic" importance lies in its
capacity to ensure that obligations are
"really" binding, thus if necessary can be
"enforced" by negative sanctions. But for
power to function as a generalized medium
in a complex system, i.e. to mobilize resources effectively for collective action, it
must be "legitimized" which in the present
context means that in certain respects compliance, which is the common factor among
our media, is not binding, to say nothing of
being coerced, but is optional. The range
within which there exists a continuous
system of interlocking binding obligations
is essentially that of the internal relations of
an organized collectivity in our sense. and

of the contractual obligations undertaken on its behalf at its boundaries.

The points at which the optional factors come to bear are, in the boundary relations of the collectivity, where factors of importance for collective functioning other than binding obligations are exchanged for such binding commitments on the part of the collectivity and *vice versa*, nonbinding outputs of the collectivity for binding commitments to it. These "optional" inputs, I have suggested above, are control of productivity of the economy at one boundary, influence through the relations between leadership and the public demands at the other.[20]

This is a point at which the dissociation of the concept of polity from exclusive relation to government becomes particularly important. In a sufficiently differentiated society, the boundary-relations of the great majority of its important units of collective organization (including some boundaries of government) are boundaries where the overwhelming majority of decisions of commitment are optional in the above sense, though once made, their fulfillment is binding. This, however, is only possible effectively within the range of a sufficiently stable, institutionalized normative order so that the requisite degrees of freedom are protected, e.g. in the fields of employment and of the promotion of interest-demands and decisions about political support.

This feature of the boundary relations of a particular political unit holds even for cases of local government, in that decisions of residence, employment, or acquisition of property within a particular jurisdiction involve the optional element, since in all these respects there is a relatively free choice among local jurisdictions, even though, once having chosen, the citizen is, for example, subject to the tax policies applying within it—and of course he cannot escape being subject to any local jurisdiction, but must choose among those available.

In the case of a "national" political organization, however, its territorial boundaries ordinarily coincide with a relative break in the normative order regulating social interaction.[21] Hence across such boundaries an ambiguity becomes involved in the exercise of power in our sense. On the one hand the invoking of binding obligations operates normally without explicit use of coercion within certain ranges where the two territorial collectivity systems have institutionalized their relations. Thus travelers in friendly foreign countries can ordinarily enjoy personal security and the amenities of the principal public accommodations, exchange of their money at "going" rates, etc. Where, on the other hand, the more general relations between national collectivities are at issue, the power system is especially vulnerable to the kind of insecurity of expectations which tends to be met by the explicit resort to threats of coercive sanctions. Such threats in turn, operating on both sides of a reciprocal relationship, readily enter into a vicious circle of resort to more and more "intrinsically" effective or drastic measures of coercion, at the end of which road lies physical force. In other words, the danger of war is endemic in uninstitutionalized relations between territorially organized collectivities.

There is thus an inherent relation between both the use and the control of force and the territorial basis of organization.[22] One central condition of the integration of a power system is that it should be effective within a territorial area, and a crucial condition of this effectiveness in turn is the monopoly of control of paramount force within the area. The critical point then, at which the institutional integration of power systems is most vulnerable to strain, and to degeneration into reciprocating threats of the use of force, is between territorially organized political systems. This, notoriously, is the weakest point in the normative order of human society today, as it has been almost from time immemorial.

In this connection it should be recognized that the possession, the mutual threat, and possible use of force is only in a most proximate sense the principal "cause" of war. The essential point is that the "bottleneck" of mutual regression to more and more primitive means of protecting or advancing collective interests is a "channel" into which all elements of tension between the collective units in question may flow. It is a question of the many levels at which such elements of tension may on the one hand build up, on the other be controlled, not of any simple and unequivocal conception of the "inherent" consequences of the possession and possible uses of organized force.

It should be clear that again there is a direct parallel with the economic case. A functioning market system requires integration of the monetary medium. It cannot be a system of N independent monetary units and agencies controlling them. This is the basis on which the main range of extension of a relatively integrated market system tends to coincide with the "politically organized society," as Roscoe Pound calls it, over a territorial area. International transactions require special provisions not required for domestic.

The basic "management" of the monetary system must then be integrated with the institutionalization of political power. Just as the latter depends on an effective monopoly of institutionally organized force, so monetary stability depends on an effective monopoly of basic reserves protecting the monetary unit and, as we shall see later, on centralization of control over the credit system.

The Hierarchical Aspect of Power Systems

A very critical question now arises, which may be stated in terms of a crucial difference between money and power. Money is a "measure of value," as the classical economists put it, in terms of a continuous linear variable. Objects of utility valued in money are more or less valuable than each other in numerically statable terms. Similarly, as medium of exchange, amounts of money differ in the same single dimension. One acting unit in a society has more money—or assets exchangeable for money—than another, less than, or the same.

Power involves a quite different dimension which may be formulated in terms of the conception that A may have power over B. Of course in competitive bidding the holder of superior financial assets has an advantage in that, as economists say, the "marginal utility of money" is less to him than to his competitor with smaller assets. But his "bid" is no more binding on the potential exchange partner than is that of the less affluent bidder, since in "purchasing power" all dollars are "created free and equal." There may be auxiliary reasons why the purveyor may think it advisable to accept the bid of the more affluent bidder; these, however, are not strictly economic, but concern the interrelations between money and other media, and other bases of status in the system.

The connection between the value of effectiveness—as distinguished from utility—and bindingness, implies a conception in turn of the focussing of responsibility for decisions, and hence of authority for their implementation.[23] This implies a special form of inequality of power which in turn implies a priority system of commitments. The implications of having assumed binding commitments, on the fulfillment of which spokesmen for the collectivity are prepared to insist to the point of imposing serious negative sanctions for noncompliance, are of an order of seriousness such that matching the priority system in the commitments themselves there must be priorities in the matter of which decisions take precedence over others and, back of that, of which decision-making agencies have the right to make decisions at what levels. Throughout this discussion the crucial question concerns bindingness. The reference is to the collectivity, and hence the strategic significance of the various "contributions" on the performance of which the effectiveness of its action depends. Effectiveness for the collectivity as a whole is dependent on hierarchical ordering of the relative strategic importance of these contributions, and hence of the conditions governing the imposition of binding obligations on the contributors.

Hence the power of *A* over *B* is, in its legitimized form, the "right" of *A*, as a decision-making unit involved in collective process, to make decisions which take precedence over those of *B*, in the interest of the effectiveness of the collective operation as a whole.

The right to use power, or negative sanctions on a barter basis or even compulsion to assert priority of a decision over others, I shall, following Barnard, call authority. Precedence in this sense can take different forms. The most serious ambiguity here seems to derive from the assumption that authority and its attendant power may be understood as implying opposition to the wishes of "lower-order" echelons which hence includes the prerogative of coercing or compelling compliance. Though this is implicit, it may be that the higher-order authority and power may imply the prerogative is primarily significant as "defining the situation" for the performance of the lower-order echelons. The higher "authority" may then make a decision which defines terms within which other units in the collectivity will be expected to act, and this expectation is treated as binding. Thus a ruling by the Commissioner of Internal Revenue may exclude certain tax exemptions which units under his jurisdiction have thought taxpayers could claim. Such a decision need not activate an overt conflict between commissioner and taxpayer, but may rather "channel" the decisions of revenue agents and taxpayers with reference to performance of obligations.

There does not seem to be an essential theoretical difficulty involved in this "ambiguity." We can say that the primary function of superior authority is clearly to define the situation for the lower echelons of the collectivity. The problem of overcoming opposition in the form of dispositions to noncompliance then arises from the incomplete institutionalization of the power of the higher authority holder. Sources of this may well include overstepping of the bounds of his legitimate authority on the part of this agent. The concept of compliance should clearly not be limited to "obedience" by subordinates, but is just

as importantly applicable to observance of the normative order by the high echelons of authority and power. The concept of constitutionalism is the critical one at this level, namely that even the highest authority is bound in the strict sense of the concept bindingness used here, by the terms of the normative order under which he operates, e.g. holds office. Hence binding obligations can clearly be "invoked" by lower-order against higher-order agencies as well as *vice versa*.

This of course implies the relatively firm institutionalization of the normative order itself. Within the framework of a highly differentiated polity it implies, in addition to constitutionalism itself, a procedural system for the granting of high political authority, even in private, to say nothing of public organizations, and a legal framework within which such authority is legitimized. This in turn includes another order of procedural institutions within which the question of the legality of actual uses of power can be tested.

Power and Authority

The institutionalization of the normative order just referred to thus comes to focus in the concept of authority. Authority is essentially the institutional code within which the use of power as medium is organized and legitimized. It stands to power essentially as property, as an institution, does to money. Property is a bundle of rights of possession, including above all that of alienation, but also at various levels of control and use. In a highly differentiated institutional system, property rights are focussed on the valuation of utility, i.e. the economic significance of the objects, e.g. for consumption or as factors of production, and this factor comes to be differentiated from authority. Thus, in European feudalism the "landlord" had both property rights in the land, and political jurisdiction over persons acting on the same land. In modern legal systems these

components are differentiated from each
other so the landowner is no longer the
landlord; this function is taken over mainly
by local political authority.

Precisely with greater differentiation the
focus of the institution becomes more generalized and, while specific objects of possession of course continue to be highly important, the most important object of property comes to be monetary assets, and
specific objects are valued as assets, i.e.,
in terms of potentials of marketability.
Today we can say that rights to money
assets, the ways in which these can be
legitimately acquired and disposed of, the
ways in which the interests of other parties
must be protected, have come to constitute
the core of the institution of property.[24]

Authority, then, is the aspect of a status
in a system of social organization, namely
its collective aspect, by virtue of which the
incumbent is put in a position legitimately
to make decisions which are binding, not
only on himself but on the collectivity as a
whole and hence its other member-units, in
the sense that so far as their implications
impinge on their respective roles and
statuses, they are bound to act in accordance with these implications. This includes the right to insist on such action
though, because of the general division of
labor, the holder of authority very often is
not himself in a position to "enforce" his
decisions, but must be dependent on specialized agencies for this.

If, then, authority be conceived as the
institutional counterpart of power, the
main difference lies in the fact that authority
is not a circulating medium. Sometimes,
speaking loosely, we suggest that someone
"gives away his property." He can give
away property rights in specific possessions
but not the institution of property. Similarly the incumbent of an office can relinquish authority by resigning, but this is
very different from abolishing the authority
of the office. Property as institution is a code
defining rights in objects of possession, in
the first instance physical objects, then
"symbolic" objects, including cultural ob-

jects such as "ideas" so far as they are
valuable in monetary terms, and of course
including money itself, whoever possesses
them. Authority, similarly, is a set of rights
in status in a collectivity, precisely in the
collectivity as actor, including most especially right to acquire and use power in
that status.

The institutional stability, which is
essential to the conception of a code, then
for property inheres in the institutional
structure of the market. At a higher level
the institution of property includes rights,
not only to use and dispose of particular
objects of value, but to participate in the
system of market transactions.

It is then essentially the institutionalized
code defining rights of participation in the
power system which I should like to think
of as authority. It is this conception which
gives us the basis for the essential distinction between the internal and the external
aspects of power relative to a particular
collectivity. The collectivity is, by our conception, the definition of the range within
which a system of institutionalized rights
to hold and use power can be closed. This is
to say, the implications of an authoritative
decision made at one point in the system can
be made genuinely binding at all the other
relevant points through the relevant processes of feed-back.

The hierarchical priority system of authority and power, with which this discussion started can, by this criterion, only
be binding within a given particular
collectivity system. In this sense then a
hierarchy of authority—as distinguished
from the sheer differences of power of other
coercive capacities—must be internal to a
collectivity organized system in this sense.
This will include authority to bind the
collectivity in its relations to its environment, to persons and to other collectivities.
But bindingness, legitimized and enforced
through the agency of this particular collectivity, cannot be extended beyond its
boundaries. If it exists at all it must be by
virtue of an institutionalized normative
order which transcends the particular collectivity, through contractual arrangements
with others, or through other types of
mutually binding obligation.

Power, Influence, Equalization, and Solidarity

It is on this basis that it may be held that at the boundaries of the collectivity the closed system of priorities is breached by "free" exercise, at the constituency or integrative boundary, of influence. Status in the collectivity gives authority to settle the terms on which power will be exchanged with influence over this boundary. The wielder of influence from outside, on the collectivity, is not bound in advance to any particular terms, and it is of the essence of use of power in the "foreign relations" of the collectivity, that authority is a right, within certain limits of discretion, to spend power in exchange for influence. This in turn can, through the offer of accepting leadership responsibility in exchange for political support, replenish the expenditure of power by a corresponding input.

By this reasoning influence should be capable of altering the priority system within the collectivity. This is what I interpret policy decision as a category of the use of power as a medium to be, the process of altering priorities in such a way that the new pattern comes to be binding on the collectivity. Similarly, the franchise must be regarded as the institutionalization of a marginal, interpenetrating status, between the main collectivity and its environment of solidary groupings in the larger system. It is the institutionalization of a marginal authority, the use of which is confined to the function of selection among candidates for leadership responsibility. In the governmental case, this is the inclusion in a common collectivity system of both the operative agencies of government and the "constituencies" on which leadership is dependent, a grant not only in a given instance of power to the latter but a status of authority with respect to the one crucial function of selection of leadership and granting them the authority of office.

In interpreting this discussion it is essential to keep in mind that a society consists, from the present point of view, not in one collectivity, but in a ramified system of collectivities. Because, however, of the basic imperatives of effective collective action

already discussed, these must in addition to the pluralistic cross-cutting which goes with functional differentiation, also have the aspect of a "Chinese box" relation. There must be somewhere a paramount focus of collective authority and with it of the control of power—though it is crucial that this need not be the top of the total system of normative control, which may for example be religious. This complex of territoriality and the monopoly of force are central to this, because the closed system of enforceable bindingness can always be breached by the intervention of force.[25]

The bindingness of normative orders other than those upheld by the paramount territorial collectivity must be defined within limits institutionalized in relation to it. So far as such collectivities are not "agencies" of the state, in this sense, their spheres of "jurisdiction" must be defined in terms of a normative system, a body of law, which is binding both on government and on the nongovernmental collectivity units, though in the "last analysis" it will, within an institutionalized order either have to be enforced by government, or contrariwise, by revolutionary action against government.

Since independent control of serious, socially organized force cannot be given to "private" collectivities, their ultimate negative sanctions tend to be expulsion from membership, though many other types of sanction may be highly important.

Considerations such as these thus do not in any way eliminate or weaken the importance of hierarchical priorities within a collective decision-system itself. The strict "line" structure of such authority is, however, greatly modified by the interpenetration of other systems with the political, notably for our purposes the importance of technical competence. The qualifications of the importance of hierarchy apply in principle at the boundaries of the particular collective system—analytically considered —rather than internally to it. These I would interpret as defining the limits of authority. There are two main contexts in which norms of equality may be expected to modify the concrete expectations of hierarchical decision-systems, namely on the one hand, the context of influence over the right to assume power, or decision-making authority and, on the other hand, the context of access to opportunity for status as a contributing unit in the specific political system in question.

It is essential here to recall that I have treated power as a circulating medium, moving back and forth over the boundaries of the polity. The "real" outputs of the political process, and the factors in its effectiveness—in the sense corresponding to the real outputs and factors of economic production—are not in my sense "forms" of power but, in the most important cases, of financial control of economic resources, and of influence, in the meaning of the category of influence, defined as a generalized mechanism of persuasion. These are very essential elements in the total political process, but it is just as important to distinguish them from power as it is to distinguish financially valuable outputs and factors of production from money itself. They may, in certain circumstances, be exchangeable for power, but this is a very different thing from being forms of power.

The circulation of power between polity and integrative system I conceive to consist in binding policy decisions on the one hand, which is a primary factor in the integrative process, and political support on the other, which is a primary output of the integrative process. Support is exchanged, by a "public" or constituency, for the assumption of leadership responsibility, through the process of persuading those in a position to give binding support that it is advisable to do so in the particular instance—through the use of influence or some less generalized means of persuasion. In the other political "market" vis-à-vis the integrative system, policy decisions are given in response to interest-demands in the sense of the above discussion. This is to say that interest groups, which, it is most important to note as a concept says nothing about the moral quality of the particular interest, attempt to

persuade those who hold authority in the relevant collectivity, i.e. are in a position to make binding decisions, that they should indeed commit the collectivity to the policies the influence-wielders want. In our terms this is to persuade the decision makers to use and hence "spend" some of their power for the purpose in hand. The spending of power is to be thought of, just as the spending of money, as essentially consisting in the sacrifice of alternative decisions which are precluded by the commitments undertaken under a policy. A member of the collectivity we conceive as noted to have authority to "spend" power through making binding decisions through which those outside acquire claims against the collectivity. Its authority, however, is inalienable; it can only be exercised, not "spent."

It has been suggested that policies must be hierarchically ordered in a priority system and that the power to decide among policies must have a corresponding hierarchical ordering since such decisions bind the collectivity and its constituent units. The imperative of hierarchy does not, however, apply to the other "market" of the power system in this direction, that involving the relations between leadership and political support. Here on the contrary it is a critically important fact that in the largest-scale and most highly differentiated systems, namely the leadership systems of the most "advanced" national societies, the power element has been systematically equalized through the device of the franchise, so that the universal adult franchise has been evolved in all the Western democracies.[26] Equality of the franchise which, since the consequences of its exercise are very strictly binding,[27] I classify as in fact a form of power, has been part of a larger complex of its institutionalization, which includes in addition the principle of universality—its extension to all responsible adult citizens in good standing and the secrecy of the ballot, which serves to differentiate this context of political action from other contexts of involvement, and protect it against pressures, not only from hierarchical superiors but, as Rokkan points out, from status-peers as well.

Of course the same basic principle of one member, one vote, is institutionalized in a vast number of voluntary associations, including many which are subassociations of wider collectivities, such as faculties in a university, or boards and committees. Thus the difference between a chairman or presiding officer, and an executive head is clearly marked with respect to formal authority, whatever it may be with respect to influence, by the principle that a chairman, like any other member, has only one vote. Many collectivities are in this sense "truncated" associations, e.g. in cases where fiduciary boards are self-recruiting. Nevertheless the importance of this principle of equality of power through the franchise is so great empirically that the question of how it is grounded in the structure of social systems is a crucial one.

It derives, I think, from what I should call the universalistic component in patterns of normative order. It is the value-principle that discriminations among units of a system, must be grounded in intrinsically valued differences among them, which are, for both persons and collectivities, capacities to contribute to valued societal processes. Differences of power in decision-making which mobilizes commitments, both outward in relation to the environment of the collectivity and internally, to the assignment of tasks to its members, are ideally grounded in the intrinsic conditions of effectiveness. Similarly, differences on the basis of technical competence to fulfill essential roles are grounded in the strategic conditions of effective contribution.

These considerations do not, however, apply to the functions of the choice of leadership, where this choice has been freed from ascriptive bases of right, e.g. through kinship status or some imputed "charismatic" superiority as in such a case as "white supremacy." There is a persistent pressure of the sufficiently highly valued functions or outcomes, and under this pressure there seems to have been a continual, though uneven, process of erosion of discriminations in this critical field of the distribution of power.

It may be suggested that the principle of universalistic normative organization which

is immediately superordinate to that of political democracy in the sense of the universal equal franchise, is the principle of equality before the law; in the case of the American Constitution, the principle of equal protection of the laws. I have emphasized that a constitutional framework is essential to advanced collective organization, given of course levels of scale and complexity which preclude purely "informal" and traditional normative regulation. The principle in effect puts the burden of proof on the side of imposing discriminations, either in access to rights or in imposition of obligations, on the side that such discriminations are to be justified only by differences in sufficiently highly valued exigencies of operation of the system.

The principle of equality both at the level of application of the law and of the political franchise, is clearly related to a conception of the status of membership. Not all living adults have equal right to influence the affairs of all collectivities everywhere in the world, nor does an American have equal rights with a citizen of a quite different society within its territory. Membership is in fact the application to the individual unit of the concept of boundary of a social system which has the property of solidarity, in Durkheim's sense. The equal franchise is a prerogative of members, and of course the criteria of membership can be very differently institutionalized under different circumstances.

There is an important sense in which the double interchange system under consideration here, which I have called the "support" system linking the polity with the integrative aspect of the society, is precisely the system in which power is most directly controlled, both in relation to more particularized interest-elements which seek relatively particularized policies—which of course includes wanting to prevent certain potential actions—and in relation to the more general "tone" given to the directionality of collective action by the character of the leadership elements which assume responsibility and which, in exchange, are invested, in the type case by the electoral process, with authority to carry out their responsibilities. One central feature of this control is coming to terms with the hierarchical elements inherent in power systems in the aspects just discussed. Certain value systems may of course reinforce hierarchy, but it would be my view that a universalistically oriented value system inherently tends to counteract the spread of hierarchical patterns with respect to power beyond the range felt to be functionally necessary for effectiveness.[28]

There is, however, a crucial link between the equality of the franchise and the hierarchical structure of authority within collectivities, namely the all-or-none character of the electoral process. Every voter has an equal vote in electing to an office, but in most cases only one candidate is in fact elected—the authority of office is not divided among candidates in proportion to the numbers of votes they received, but is concentrated in the successful candidate, even though the margin be very narrow, as in the U.S. presidential election of 1960. There are, of course, considerable possible variations in electoral rules, but this basic principle is as central as is that of the equality of the franchise. This principle seems to be the obverse of the hierarchy of authority.

The hierarchical character of power systems has above been sharply contrasted with the linear quantitative character of wealth and monetary assets. This has in turn been related to the fundamental difference between the exigencies of effectiveness in collective action, and the exigencies of utility in providing for the requirements of satisfying the "wants" of units. In order to place the foregoing discussion of the relations between power and influence in a comparable theoretical context, it is necessary to formulate the value-standard which is paramount in regulating the integrative function which corresponds to utility and effectiveness in the economic and political functions respectively.

This is, with little doubt, the famous con-

cept of solidarity as formulated by Durkheim.[29] The two essential points of reference for present purposes concern the two main aspects of membership, as outlined above, the first of which concerns claims on executive authority for policy decisions which integrate the total collective interest on the one hand, the "partial" interest of a subgroup on the other. The second concerns integration of rights to a "voice" in collective affairs with the exigencies of effective leadership and the corresponding responsibility.

The principle is the "grounding" of a collective system in a consensus in the sense of the above discussion, namely an "acceptance" on the part of its members of their belonging together, in the sense of sharing, over a certain range, common interests, interests which are defined both by type, and by considerations of time. Time becomes relevant because of the uncertainty factor in all human action, and hence the fact that neither benefits nor burdens can be precisely predicted and planned for in advance; hence an effective collectivity must be prepared to absorb unexpected burdens, and to balance this, to carry out some sort of just distribution of benefits which are unexpected and/or are not attributable to the earned agency of any particular subunit.

Solidarity may then be thought of as the implementation of common values by definition of the requisite collective systems in which they are to be actualized. Collective action as such we have defined as political function. The famous problem of order, however, cannot be solved without a common normative system. Solidarity is the principle by virtue of which the commitment to norms, which is "based" in turn on values, is articulated with the formation of collectivities which are capable of effective collective action. Whereas, in the economic direction, the "problem" of effective action is coping with the scarcity of available resources, including trying to facilitate their mobility, in the integrative direction it is orderly solution of competing claims, on the one hand to receive benefits—or minimize losses—deriving from memberships, on the other to influence the processes by which collective action operates. This clearly involves some institutionalization of the subordination of unit-interest to the collective in cases where the two are in conflict, actual or potential, and hence the justification of unit interests as compatible with the more extensive collective interest. A social system then possesses solidarity in proportion as its members are committed to common interests through which discrete unit interests can be integrated and the justification of conflict resolution and subordination can be defined and implemented. It defines, not the modes of implementation of these common interests through effective agency, but the standards by which such agency should be guided and the rights of various constituent elements to have a voice in the interpretation of these standards.

Power and Equality of Opportunity

We may now turn to the second major boundary of the polity, at which another order of modifications of the internal hierarchy of authority comes to focus. This is the boundary vis-à-vis the economy where the "political" interest is to secure control of productivity and services, and the economic interest lies in the collective control of fluid resources and in what we may call opportunity for effectiveness. I shall not attempt here to discuss the whole interchange complex, but will confine myself to the crucial problem of the way that here also the hierarchical structure of power can, under certain conditions, be modified in an egalitarian direction.

Productivity of the economy is in principle allocable among collective (in our sense political) claimants to its control as facilities, in linear quantitative terms. This linear quantification is achieved through the medium of money, either allocation of funds with liberty to expend them at will, or at least monetary evaluation of more specific facilities.

In a sufficiently developed system, services must be evaluated in monetary terms also, both from the point of view of rational budgeting and of the monetary cost of their employment. In terms of their utilization, however, services are "packages" of performance-capacity, which are qualitatively distinct and of unequal value as contributions to collective effectiveness. Their evaluation as facilities must hence involve an estimate of strategic significance which matches the general priority scale which has been established to regulate the internal functioning of the collectivity.

Services, however, constitute a resource to be acquired from outside the collectivity, as Weber puts it through a "formally free" contract of employment. The contracts thus made are binding on both sides, by virtue of a normative system transcending the particular collectivity, though the obligation must articulate with the internal normative order including its hierarchical aspect. But the purveyors of service are not, in advance, bound by this internal priority system and hence an exchange, which is here interpreted to operate in the first instance as between strategic significance expressed as power-potential, and the monetary value of the service, must be arrived at.

Quite clearly, when the purveyor of service has once entered into such a contract, he is bound by the aspect of its terms which articulates the service into this internal system, including the level of authority he exercises and its implications for his power position in the collectivity. If the collectivity is making in any sense a rational arrangement, this must be tailored to an estimate of the level of the value of his strategic contribution, hence his performance-capacity.

Since, however, the boundary interchange is not integral to the internal system of bindingness, the hierarchical imperatives do not apply to the opportunity aspect of this interchange on the extra-political side. This is to say that the same order of pressures of a higher-order universalistic normative system can operate here that we suggested operated to bring about equality in the franchise. Again the principle is that no particularistic discriminations are to be legitimized which are not grounded in essential functional exigencies of the system of reference.

In the case of the franchise there seems to be no inherent stopping place short of complete equality, qualified only by the minimum consideration of competence attached to fully responsible membership—excluding only minors, "defectives," through retardation and mental illness, and those morally disqualified through crime. In the service case, on the other hand, given commitments to optimum performance which in the present context can be taken for granted, the limit to the equating of universalism and equality lies in the concept of competence. Hence the principle arrived at is the famous one of equality of opportunity, by which there is equalization of access to opportunity for contribution, but selection on criteria of differential competence, both quantitative and qualitative.

Whereas the equalization of the franchise is a control on differential power "from above" in the hierarchy of control and operates mainly through the selection of leadership, equality of opportunity is (in the corresponding sense) a control from below, and operates to check particularistic tendencies which would tend to exclude sources of service which are qualified by competence to contribute, and/or to check tendencies to retain services which are inferior to those available in competition with them.

It is the combination of these two foci of universalization, the equalitarianism of upper rights to control through the franchise, and of rights to participate through service on the basis of competence, which account for the extent to which the "cumulative advantage,"[30] which might seem to be inherent in the hierarchical internal structure of power systems, often in fact fails either to materialize at all, or to be as strong as expected.

Long and complex as it is, the above discussion may be summed up as an attempted solution of the second of the three main problems with which this paper began, namely that of the relation between the coercive and the consensual aspects of the phenomenon of power. The answer is first premised on the conception of power as a specific but generalized medium of the functioning of social relationships in complex, differentiated systems of social interaction.

Power is secondly specifically associated with the bindingness of obligations to performance within a range of circumstances which may arise in a varying and changing situation. The obligations concerned are hence in some important degree generalized so that particularities under them are contingent on circumstances. The bindingness of obligations implies that they stand on a level of seriousness such that the invoking agent, ego, may be put in the position of asserting that, since he "means it" that alter must comply, he is prepared to insist on compliance. Partly then as a symbolic expression of this seriousness of "meaning it" and partly as an instrument of deterrence of noncompliance,[31] this insistence is associated with command of negative situational sanctions the application of which is frequently contingent on noncompliance, and in certain cases deterrence is achieved by compulsion. We would not speak of power where situational negative sanctions or compulsion are in no circumstances attached to noncompliance in cases where a legitimate agent insists on compliance.

Thirdly, however, power is here conceived as a generalized medium of mobilizing commitments or obligation for effective action. As such it ordinarily does not itself possess intrinsic effectiveness, but symbolizes effectiveness and hence the bindingness of the relevant obligations to contribute to it. The operative validity of the meaningfulness of the symbolization is not a function of any one single variable but, we argue, of two primary ones. One of these is the willingness to insist upon compliance, or at least to deter noncompliance, a line of reasoning which leads to the understanding of willingness to resort to negative sanctions, the nature of which will vary, as a function of the seriousness of the question, on the dimension of their progressively more drastic nature, in the last analysis force.

The other variable concerns the collective reference and hence the justification[32] of invoking the obligations in question in the situation. This aspect concerns the dependence of power on the institutionalization of authority and hence the rights of collective agents to mobilize performances and define them as binding obligations. This justification inherently rests on some sort of consensus among the members of the collectivity of reference, if not more broadly, with respect to a system of norms under which authority and power are legitimized on a basis wider than this particular collectivity by the values of the system. More specifically, authority is the institutionalized code within which the "language of power" is meaningful and, therefore, its use will be accepted in the requisite community, which is in the first instance the community of collective organization in our sense.

Seen in this light the threat of coercive measures, or of compulsion, without legitimation or justification, should not properly be called the use of power at all, but is the limiting case where power, losing its symbolic character, merges into an intrinsic instrumentality of securing compliance with wishes, rather than obligations. The monetary parellel is the use of a monetary metal as an instrument of barter where as a commodity it ceases to be an institutionalized medium of exchange at all.

In the history of thought there has been a very close connection between emphasis on the coercive element in power systems and on the hierarchical aspect of the structure of systems of authority and power. The above discussion has, I hope, helped to dissociate them by showing that this hierarchical aspect, important as it is, is only part of the structure of power systems. The view advanced is that it is an inherent aspect of the internal structure of collectivities. No collectivity, even the nation, however, stands alone as a total society since it is integrated with norms and values; subcollectivities can even less be claimed to be societies. The collectivity aspect of total social structure may in a particular case be dominant over others, but always in principle it impinges on at least two sorts of boundary-problems, namely that involved in its "support" system and that involved in

the mobilization of services as sources of contribution to its functioning.

In both these cases, we have argued, quite different principles are operative from that of the hierarchy of authority, namely the equality of franchise on the one hand, equality of opportunity on the other. In both cases I envisage an interchange of power, though not of authority, over the boundary of the polity, and in neither case can the principle governing the allocation of power through this interchange be considered to be hierarchical in the line authority sense. The empirical problems here are, as elsewhere, formidable, but I definitely argue that it is illegitimate to hold that, from serious consideration of the role of power as a generalized medium, it can be inferred that there is a general trend to hierarchization in the total empirical social systems involved.[33]

The Zero-sum Problem

We are now in a position to take up the last of the three main problems with which the discussion started, namely whether power is a zero-sum phenomenon in the sense that, in a system, a gain in power by a unit A is in the nature of the case the cause of a corresponding loss of power by other units, $B, C, D. \ldots$ The parallel with money on which we have been insisting throughout should give us clues to the answer, which clearly is, under certain circumstances yes, but by no means under all circumstances.

In the monetary case it is obvious that in budgeting the use of a fixed income, allocation to one use must be at the expense of alternative uses. The question is whether parallel limitations apply to an economy conceived as a total system. For long this seemed to many economists to be the case; this was the main burden of the old "quantity theory of money." The most obvious political parallel is that of the hierarchy of authority within a particular collectivity. It would seem to be obvious that, if A, who has occupied a position of substantial power, is demoted, and *B* takes his place, *A* loses power and *B* gains it, the total in the system remaining the same. Many political theorists like Lasswell and C. Wright Mills, generalized this to political systems as a whole.[34]

The most important and obvious point at which the zero-sum doctrine breaks down for money is that of credit-creation through commercial banking. This case is so important as a model that a brief discussion here is in order. Depositors, that is, entrust their money funds to a bank, not only for safe keeping, but as available to the bank for lending. In so doing, however, they do not relinquish any property rights in these funds. The funds are repayable by the bank in full on demand, the only normal restrictions being with respect to banking hours. The bank, however, uses part of the balances on deposit with it to make loans at interest, pursuant to which it not only makes the money available to the borrower, but in most cases assumes binding obligations not to demand repayment except on agreed terms, which in general leave the borrower undisturbed control for a stipulated period—or obligates him to specified installments of amortization. In other words, the same dollars come to do "double duty," to be treated as possessions by the depositors, who retain their property rights, and also by the banker who preempts the rights to loan them, as if they were "his." In any case there is a corresponding net addition to the circulating medium, measured by the quantity of new bank deposits created by the loans outstanding.[35]

Perhaps the best way to describe what happens is to say that there has occurred a differentiation in the functions of money and hence there are two ways of using it in the place of one. The ordinary deposit is a reserve for meeting current expenses, whether "private" or "business," which is mainly important with respect to the time element of the degrees of freedom mentioned above. From the point of view of the depositor the bank is a convenience, giving him safekeeping, the privilege of writing checks rather than using cash, etc., at a cost which is low because the bank earns interest through its loaning operations. From the point of view of the borrower, on the other hand, the bank is a source of otherwise unavailable funds, ideally in the economist's sense, for investment, for financing operations promising future increments of economic productivity, which would not otherwise have been feasible.

The possibility of this "miracle of loaves and fishes" of course rests on an empirical uniformity, namely that depositors do in fact, under normal circumstances, keep sufficient balances on hand—though they are not required to—so that it is safe for the bank to have substantial amounts out on loan at any given time. Underlying this basic uniformity is the fact that an individual bank will ordinarily also have access to "reserves," e.g. assets which, though earning interest, are sufficiently liquid to be realized on short notice, and in the last analysis such resources as those of a federal reserve system. The individual bank, and with it its depositors, is thus ordinarily relatively secure.

We all know, however, that this is true only so long as the system operates smoothly. A particular bank can meet unusual demands for withdrawal of deposits, but if this unusual demand spreads to a whole banking system, the result may be a crisis, which only collective action can solve. Quite clearly the expectation that all depositors should be paid, all at once, in "real" money, e.g. even "cash" to say nothing of monetary metal, cannot be fulfilled. Any monetary system in which bank credit plays an important part is in the nature of the case normally "insolvent" by that standard.

Back of these considerations, it may be said, lies an important relation between bindingness and "confidence" which is in certain respects parallel to that between coercion and consensus in relation to power, indeed one which, through the element of bindingness, involves a direct articulation between money and power. How is this parallel to be defined and how does the articulation operate?

First the banking operation depends on mutual confidence or trust in that depositors entrust their funds to the bank, knowing, if they stop to think about it, that the bank will have a volume of loans outstanding which makes it impossible to repay all deposits at once. It is well known with what hesitation, historically, many classes have been brought to trust banks at all in this simple sense—the classical case of the French peasant's insistence on putting his savings in cash under the mattress is sufficient illustration. The other side of the coin, however, is the bank's trust that its depositors will not panic to the point of in fact demanding the complete fulfillment of their legal rights.

The banker here assumes binding obligations in two directions, the honoring of both of which depends on this trust. On the one hand he has loaned money on contract which he cannot recover on demand, on the other he is legally bound to repay deposits on demand. But by making loans on binding contractual terms he is enabled to create money, which is purchasing power in the literal sense that, as noted above, the status of the monetary unit is politically guaranteed—e.g. through its position as "legal tender"—and hence the newly created dollars are "as good as" any other dollars. Hence I suggest that what makes them good in this sense is the input of power in the form of the bindingness of the contractual obligation assumed by the banker—I should classify this as opportunity for effectiveness. The bank, as collectivity, thus enjoys a "power position" by virtue of which it can give its borrowers effective control of certain types of opportunity.

It is, however, critically important that in general this grant of power is not unconditional. First it is power in its form of direct convertibility with money, and second, within that framework, the condition is that, per unit of time, there should be a surplus of money generated, the borrower can and must return more money than he received, the difference being "interest." Money, however, is a measure of productivity, and hence we may say that increasing the quantity of money in circulation is economically "functional" only if it leads after a sequence of operations over a period of time to a corresponding increase in

productivity—if it does not the consequence is inflationary. The process is known as investment, and the standard of a good investment is the expected increment of productivity which, measured in money terms, is profitability. The organizational question of allocation of responsibility for decisions and payments should of course not be too directly identified with the present level of analytical argument.

It may help round out this picture if the concept of investment is related to that of "circular flow" in Schumpeter's sense.[36] The conception is that the routine functioning of economic processes is organized about the relation between producing and consuming units, we may say firms and households. So long as a series of parametric constants such as the state of demand and the coefficients of cost of production hold, this is a process in equilibrium through which money mediates the requisite decisions oriented to fixed reference points. This is precisely the case to which the zero-sum concept applies. On the one hand a fixed quantity and "velocity of circulation" of the monetary medium is an essential condition of the stability of this equilibrium, whereas on the other hand, there is no place for banking operations which, through credit expansion, would change the parametric conditions.

These decisions are governed by the standard of solvency, in the sense that both producing and consuming units are normally expected to recoup their monetary expenditures, on the one hand for factors of production, on the other for consumers' goods, from monetary proceeds, on the producing side, sale of output, on the consuming, sale of factors of production, notably labor. Solvency then is a balance between monetary cost and receipts. Investment is also governed by the standard of solvency, but over a longer time period, long enough to carry out the operations necessary to bring about an increase of productivity matching the monetary obligations assumed.

There is here a crucial relation between

the time-extension of the investment process and use of power to make loan contracts binding. Only if the extension of control of resources through loans creates obligations can the recipients of the loans in turn assume further obligations and expect others to assume them.

The essential principle here is that, in the sense of the hierarchy of control, a higher-order medium is used as a source of leverage to break into the "circle" of the Schumpeterian flow, giving the recipients of this power effective control of a share of fluid resources in order to divert them from the established routine channels to new uses. It is difficult to see how this could work systematically if the element of bindingness were absent either from loan contracts or from the acceptance-status of the monetary medium.

One further element of the monetary complex needs to be mentioned here. In the case of investment there is the element of time, and hence the uncertainty that projected operations aiming at increase in productivity will in fact produce either this increase or financial proceeds sufficient to repay loans plus interest in accordance with contract. In the case of the particular borrower-lender relationship this can be handled on an individual contract-solvency basis with a legally determined basis of sharing profits and/or losses. For the system, however, it creates the possibility of inflation, namely that the net effect of credit-extension may not be increase in productivity but decline in the value of the monetary unit. Furthermore, once a system involves an important component of credit, the opposite disturbance, namely deflation with a rearrangement of the meaning of the whole network of financial and credit expectations and relationships, is also a possibility. This suggests that there is, in a ramified credit economy, a set of mechanisms which, independently of particular circular flow, and credit-extension and repayment transactions regulates the total volume of credit, rates of interest, and price-level relations in the economy.

Let us now attempt to work out the parallel, and articulating, analysis for power systems. There is, I suggest, a circular flow operating between polity and economy in the interchange between factors in political effectiveness—in this case a share of control of the productivity of the economy—and an output to the economy in the form of the kind of control of resources which a loan for investment provides—though of course there are various other forms. This circular flow is controlled by the medium of power in the sense that the input of binding obligations, in particular through commitment to perform services, broadly balances the output of offer of opportunity for effective performance.

The suggestion is that it is a condition of the stability of this circulation system that the inputs and outputs of power on each side should balance. This is another way of saying that it is ideally formulated as a zero-sum system, so far as power is concerned, though because it includes the investment process, the same is not true for the involvement of monetary funds in the interchanges. The political circular flow system then is conceived as the locus of the "routine" mobilization of performance expectations either through invoking obligations under old contractual—and in some cases, e.g. citizenship, ascriptive—relations, or through a stable rate of assumption of new contractual obligations, which is balanced by the liquidation, typically through fulfillment, of old ones. The balance applies to the system, of course, not to particular units.

Corresponding to utility as the value-pattern governing economic function I have put forward effectiveness as that governing political function. If it is important to distinguish utility, as the category of value to which increments are made by the combinatorial process of economic production, from solvency as the standard of satisfactory performance in handling money as the medium of economic process, then we need to distinguish effectiveness as the political value category, from a corresponding standard for the satisfactory handling of power.

The best available term for this standard seems to be the success of collective goal-attainment. Where the polity is sufficiently differentiated so that power has become genuinely a generalized medium we can say that collective units are expected to be successful in the sense that the binding obligations they undertake in order to maintain and create opportunities for effectiveness, is balanced by the input of equally binding commitments to perform service, either within the collectivity in some status of employment, or for the collectivity on a contractual basis.

The unit of productive decision-making, however, is, in a sense corresponding to that applying to the household for the economic case, also expected to be successful in the sense that its expenditure of power through not only the output of services but their commitment to utilization by particular collectivities, is balanced by an input of opportunity which is dependent on collective organization, that is a unit in a position to undertake to provide opportunities which are binding on the unit.

In the light of this discussion it becomes clear that the business firm is in its aspect as collectivity in our technical sense, the case where the two standards of success and solvency coincide. The firm uses its power income primarily to maintain or increase its productivity and, as a measure of this, its money income. A surplus of power will therefore in general be exchanged for enhancement of its control of economic productivity. For a collectivity specialized in political function the primary criterion of success would be given in its power position, relative that is to other collectivities. Here there is the special problem of the meaning of the term power position. I interpret it here as relative to other collectivities in a competitive system, not as a position in an internal hierarchy of power. This distinction is of course particularly important for a pluralistic power system where government is a functionally specialized subsystem of the collectivity structure, not an approximation to the totality of that structure.[37] In somewhat corresponding fashion a collectivity specialized in integrative function would measure its success in terms of its

"level of influence"—for example, as a political interest-group in the usual sense, its capacity to influence public policy decisions. A consequence of this reasoning is that such an influence group would be disposed to "give away" power, in the sense of trading it for an increment of influence. This could take the form of assuring political support, without barterlike conditions, to leadership elements which seemed to be likely to be able to exercise the kind of influence in question.

Is there then a political equivalent of the banking phenomenon, a way in which the circular flow of power comes to be broken through so as to bring about net additions to the amount of power in the system? The trend of the analytical argument indicates that there must be, and that its focus lies in the support system, that is the area of interchange between power and influence, between polity and integrative system.

First I suggest that, particularly conspicuous in the case of democratic electoral systems, political support should be conceived as a generalized grant of power which, if it leads to electoral success, puts elected leadership in a position analogous to that of the banker. The "deposits" of power made by constituents are revocable, if not at will, at the next election—a condition analogous to regularity of banking hours. In some cases election is tied to barterlike conditions of expectation of carrying out certain specific measures favored by the strategically crucial voters and only these. But particularly in a system which is pluralistic not only with reference to the composition of political support, but also to issues, such a leadership element acquires freedom to make certain types of binding decision, binding in the nature of the case on elements of the collectivity other than those whose "interest" is directly served. This freedom may be conceived to be confined to the circular flow level, which would be to say that the input of power through the channel of political support should be exactly balanced by the output through policy decisions, to interest groups which have specifically demanded these decisions.

There is, however, another component of the freedom of elected leadership which is crucial here. This is the freedom to use influence—for example through the "prestige" of office as distinguished from its specified powers—to embark on new ventures in the "equation" of power and influence. This is to use influence to create additions to the total supply of power. How can this be conceived to work?

One important point is that the relation between the media involved with respect to positive and negative sanctions is the obverse of the case of creating money through banking. There it was the use of power embodied in the binding character of loan contracts which "made the difference." Here it is the optional capacity to exert influence through persuasion. This process seems to operate through the function of leadership which, by way of the involvements it possesses with various aspects of the constituency structure of the collectivity, generates and structures new "demands" in the specific sense of demands for policy decision.

Such demands then may be conceived, in the case of the deciders, to justify an increased output of power. This in turn is made possible by the generality of the mandate of political support, the fact that it is not given on a barter basis in exchange for specific policy decisions, but once the "equation" of power and influence has been established through election, it is a mandate to do, within constitutional limits, what seems best, in the governmental case "in the public interest." Collective leadership may then be conceived as the bankers or "brokers" who can mobilize the binding commitments of their constituents in such a way that the totality of commitments made by the collectivity as a whole can be enhanced. This enhancement must, however, be justified through the mobilization of influence; it must, that is, both be felt to be in accordance with valid norms and apply to situations which "call for" handling at the level of binding collective commitments.

The critical problem of justification is, in one direction, that of consensus, of its bearing on the value-principle of solidarity as we have outlined this above. The standard therefore which corresponds to the value principle of solidarity is consensus in the sense in which that concept has been used above.

The problem then is that of a basis for breaking through the circular stability of a zero-sum power system. The crucial point is that this can only happen if the collectivity and its members are ready to assume new binding obligations over and above those previously in force. The crucial need is to justify this extension and to transform the "sentiment" that something ought to be done into a commitment to implement the sentiment by positive action, including coercive sanctions if necessary. The crucial agency of this process seems to be leadership, precisely conceived as possessing a component analytically independent of the routine power position of office, which defines the leader as the mobilizer of justifications for policies which would not be undertaken under the circular flow assumptions.

It may be suggested that the parallel to credit creation holds with respect to time-extension as well as in other respects. The increments of effectiveness which are necessary to implement new binding policies which constitute an addition to the total burden on the collectivity cannot simply be willed into being; they require organizational changes through recombinations of the factors of effectiveness, development of new agencies, procurement of personnel, new norms, and even changes in bases of legitimation. Hence leadership cannot justifiably be held responsible for effective implementation immediately, and conversely, the sources of political support must be willing to trust their leadership in the sense of not demanding immediate—by the time of the next election—"pay-off" of the power-value of their votes in their decisions dictated by their own interests.[38]

It is perhaps legitimate to call the responsibility assumed in this connection specifically leadership responsibility and distinguish it in these terms from administrative responsibility which focuses on the routine functions. In any case I should like to conceive this process of power-enhancement as strictly parallel to economic investment, in the further sense that the pay-off should be an increment to the level of collective success in the sense outlined above, i.e. enhanced effectiveness of collective action in valued areas which could not have been expected without risk-taking on the part of leadership in a sense parallel to entrepreneurial investment.

The operation of both governmental and nongovernmental collectivities is full of illustrations of the kind of phenomenon I have in mind, though because this type of formal analysis is somewhat unfamiliar, it is difficult to pin them down exactly. It has, for example, often been pointed out that the relation of executive responsibility to constituency-interests is very different in domestic and in foreign affairs. I suggest that the element of "political banking" in the field of foreign affairs is particularly large and that the sanction of approval of policy decisions, where it occurs, cannot infallibly be translated into votes, certainly not in the short run. Similar considerations are very frequently involved in what may be called "developmental" ventures, which cannot be expected to be "backed" by currently well-structured interests in the same sense as maintenance of current functions. The case of support of research and training is a good one since the "community of scholars" is not a very strong "pressure group" in the sense of capacity directly to influence large blocks of votes.

It would follow from these considerations that there is, in developed polities, a relatively "free-floating" element in the power system which is analogous to a credit-system. Such an element should then be subject to fluctuations on a dimension of inflation-deflation, and be in need of controls for the system as a whole, at a level above that of the activities of particular units.

The analogue of inflation seems to me to touch the credibility of the assertion of the bindingness of obligations assumed. Power, as a symbolic medium, is like money in that it is itself "worthless," but is accepted in the expectation that it can later be "cashed in," this time in the activation of binding obligations. If, however, "power-credit" has been extended too far, without the necessary organizational basis for fulfillment of expectations having been laid, then attempting to invoke the obligations will result in less than a full level of performance, inhibited by various sorts of resistance. In a collectivity undergoing disintegration the same formal office may be "worth less" than it otherwise would have been because of attrition of its basis of effectiveness. The same considerations hold when it is a case of overextension of new power-expectations without adequate provision for making them effective.

It goes without saying that a power-system in which this creditlike element is prominent is in a state analogous to the "insolvency" of a monetary system which includes an important element of actual credit, namely its commitments cannot be fulfilled all at once, even if those to whom they have been made have formally valid rights to such fulfillment. Only a strict zero-sum power system could fulfill this condition of "liquidity." Perhaps the conservation of political ideologies makes it even more difficult to accept the legitimacy of such a situation—it is all too easy to define it as "dishonest"—than in the corresponding economic case.

There is, however, a fine line between solid, responsible and constructive political leadership which in fact commits the collectivity beyond its capacities for instantaneous fulfillment of all obligations, and reckless overextendedness, just as there is a fine line between responsible banking and "wild-catting."

Furthermore, under unusual pressures, even highly responsible leadership can be put in situations where a "deflationary" spiral sets in, in a pattern analogous to that of a financial panic. I interpret, for instance McCarthyism as such a deflationary spiral in the political field. The focus of the commitments in which the widest extension had

taken place was in the international field—
the United States had very rapidly come into
the position of bearing the largest share of
responsibility for maintenance of world
political order against an expansionist Communist movement. The "loss of China"
was in certain quarters a particularly trau-
matic experience, and the Korean war a
highly charged symbol of the costs of the
new stewardship.

A pluralistic political system like the
American always has a large body of latent
claims on the loyalty of its citizens to their
government, not only for the "right
sentiments" but for "sacrifices," but equally
these are expected to be invoked only in
genuine emergencies. The McCarthy definition of the situation was, however, that
virtually anyone in a position of significant
responsibility should not only recognize
the "in case" priority—not necessarily by
our basic values the highest—of national
loyalty, but should explicitly renounce all
other loyalties which might conceivably
compete with that to the nation, including
those to kith and kin. This was in effect a
demand to liquidate all other commitments
in favor of the national, a demand which in
the nature of the case could not be met
without disastrous consequences in many
different directions. It tended to "deflate"
the power system by undermining the
essential basis of trust on which the influence
of many elements bearing formal and informal leadership responsibilities, and which
in turn sustained "power-credit," necessarily rested. Perhaps the most striking
case was the allegation of communist in-
filtration and hence widespread "disloyalty"
in the army, which was exploited to try to
force the army leadership to put the commitments of all associated personnel,
including e.g. research scientists, in completely "liquid" form. Two features of the
McCarthy movement particularly mark it
as a deflationary spiral, first the vicious
circle of spreading involvement with the
casting of suspicion on wider and wider
circles of otherwise presumptively loyal
elements in the society and secondly the
surprisingly abrupt end of the spiral once
the "bubble was pricked" and "confidence
restored," events associated particularly
with the public reaction to McCarthy's
performance in the televised army hearings,
and to Senator Flanders' protest on the
floor of the Senate.[39]

The focus of the McCarthy disturbance
may be said to have been in the influence
system, in the relation between integrative
and pattern-maintenance functions in the
society. The primary deflationary effect was
on the "credit" elements of pluralistic
loyalties. This in turn would make leadership elements, not only in government but
private groups, much less willing to take
risks in claiming loyalties which might
compete with those to government. Since,
however, in the hierarchy of control the
influence system is superordinate to the
power system, deflation in the former is
necessarily propagated to the latter. This
takes in the first instance the form of a rush
to withdraw political support—which it
will be remembered is here treated as a
form of power—from leadership elements
which could in any sense be suspected of
"disloyalty." The extreme perhaps was the
slogan propagated by McCarthy and played
with by more responsible Republican
leaders like Thomas E. Dewey, of "twenty
years of treason" which impugned the
loyalty of the Democratic Party as a whole.
The effect was, by depriving opposition
leadership of influence, to make it unsafe
even to consider granting them power.

The breaking through of the zero-sum
limitations of more elementary power
systems opens the way to altogether new
levels of collective effectiveness, but also,
in the nature of the case, involves new levels
of risk and uncertainty. I have already
dealt briefly with this problem at the level
of the particular collectivity and its extension of commitments. The problem of
course is compounded for a system of
collectivities because of the risk not only of
particular failures, but of generalized inflationary and deflationary disturbances. There
are, as we have noted, mechanisms of
control which operate to regulate investment, and similarly extension of the commitments of particular collectivities, both

of which have to do with the attempt to ensure responsibility, on the one hand for solvency over the long run, on the other for success of the larger "strategy" of extension. It is reasonable to suppose that beyond these, there must be mechanisms operating at the level of the system as a whole in both contexts.

In the monetary case it was the complex of central banking, credit management and their relations to governmental finance which has been seen to be the focus of these highest-level controls. In the case of power it is of course the first crucial point that there was to be some relatively paramount apex of control of the power and authority system, which we think of as in some sense the "sovereign" state.[40] This has mainly to do with the relations between what we have called justification and legitimacy, in relation to government as the highest-order tightly integrated collectivity structure—so far. This is the central focus of Weber's famous analysis of authority, but his analysis is in need of considerable extension in our sense. It seems, among other things, that he posed an unduly sharp alternative between charismatic and "routine" cases, particularly the rational-legal version of the latter. In particular it would be my view that very substantial possibilities of regulated extension of power-commitments exist within the framework of certain types of "legal" authority, especially where they are aspects of a political system which is pluralistic in general terms. These problems, however, cannot further be explored at the end of what is already a very long paper.

Conclusion

This paper has been designed as a general theoretical attack on the ancient problem of the nature of political power and its place, not only in political systems, narrowly conceived, but in the structure and processes of societies generally. The main point of reference for the attack has been the conception that the discussion of the problem in the main traditions of political thought have not been couched at a sufficiently rigorously analytical level, but have tended to treat the nation, the state, or the lower-level collectively organized "group," as the empirical object of reference, and to attempt to analyze its functioning without further basic analytical breakdown. The most conspicuous manifestation of this tendency has been the treatment of power.

The present paper takes a radically different position, cutting across the traditional lines. It takes its departure from the position of economic theory and, by inference, the asymmetry between it and the traditional political theory,[41] which has treated one as the theory of an analytically defined functional system of society—the economy—and the other as a concrete substructure, usually identified with government. Gradually the possibility has opened out both the extension of the analytical model of economic theory to the political field and the direct articulation of political with economic theory within the logical framework of the theory of the social system as a whole, so that the *polity* could be conceived as a functional subsystem of the society in all its theoretical fundamentals parallel to the economy.

This perspective necessarily concentrated attention on the place of money in the conception of the economy. More than that, it became increasingly clear that money was essentially a "symbolic" phenomenon and hence that its analysis required a frame of reference closer to that of linguistics than of technology, i.e. it is not the intrinsic properties of gold which account for the value of money under a gold standard any more than it is the intrinsic properties of the sounds symbolized as "book" which account for the valuation of physically fixed dissertations in linguistic form. This is the perspective from which the conception of power as a *generalized symbolic medium* operating in the processes of social interaction has been set forth.

This paper has not included a survey of the empirical evidence bearing on its ramified field of problems, but my strong conviction is not only that the line of analysis adopted is consistent with the broad lines of the available empirical evidence, but that it has already shown that it can illuminate a range of empirical problems which were not well understood in terms of the more conventional theoretical positions—e.g. the reasons for the general egalitarian pressure in the evolution of the political franchise, or the nature of McCarthyism as a process of political deflationary spiral.

It does not seem necessary here to recapitulate the main outline of the argument. I may conclude with the three main points with which I began. I submit, first, that the analytical path entered upon here makes it possible to treat power in conceptually specific and precise terms and thus gets away from the theoretical diffuseness called to attention, in terms of which it has been necessary to include such a very wide variety of problematical phenomena as "forms" of power. Secondly, I think it can advance a valid claim to present a resolution of the old dilemma as to whether (in the older terms) power is "essentially" a phenomenon of coercion or of consensus. It is both, precisely because it is a phenomenon which integrates a plurality of factors and outputs of political effectiveness and is not to be identified with any one of them. Finally, light has been thrown on the famous zero-sum problem, and a definite position taken that, though under certain specific assumptions the zero-sum condition holds, these are not constitutive of power systems in general, but under different conditions systematic "extension" of power spheres without sacrifice of the power of other units is just as important a case.

These claims are put forward in full awareness that on one level there is an inherent arbitrariness in them, namely that I have defined power and a number of related concepts in my own way, which is different from many if not most of the definitions current in political theory. If theory were a matter only of the arbitrary choice of defini-

tions and assumptions and reasoning from there, it might be permissible to leave the question at that and say simply, this is only one more personal "point of view." Any claim that it is more than that rests on the conception that the scientific understanding of societies is arrived at through a gradually developing organon of theoretical analysis and empirical interpretation and verification. My most important contention is that the line of analysis presented here is a further development of a main line of theoretical analysis of the social system as a whole, and of verified interpretation of the empirical evidence presented to that body of theory. This body of theory must ultimately be judged by its outcomes both in theoretical generality and consistency, over the whole range of social system theory, and by its empirical validity, again on levels which include not only conventionally "political" references, but their empirical interrelations with all other aspects of the modern complex society looked at as a whole.

Technical Note

The above analysis has been presented in wholly discursive terms. Many decisions about categorization and detailed steps of analysis were, however, referred to a formalized paradigm of the principal structural components and process categories and relations of a society considered as a social system. For the benefit of readers with more technical interests in social system theory it has seemed advisable to present a very brief outline of the most directly relevant parts of the general paradigm here, with a brief elucidation of its relevance to the above discussion.[42]

The structural reference points are essentially two, namely first that at a sufficiently high level of differentiation of a society, economy, polity and integrative system become empirically distinct in terms of the primacy of function of structural units e.g. there is an important structural difference between a private business firm, an administrative agency of government and a court of law. Secondly every such unit is involved in plural interchange relations with other units with respect to most of its functional requirements from its situation—i.e., for factor inputs—and the conditions of making its contributions to other units in the "division of labor"—i.e., disposal of "product" outputs. This order of differentiation requires *double* interchanges between all the structural components belonging to each category-pair, e.g. firms and households, firms and political agencies (not necessarily governmental, it should be remembered) etc. The double interchange situation precludes mediation of processes in terms either of ascriptive expectations or barter arrangements, or a combination of the two. It necessitates the development of generalized symbolic media, of which we have treated money, power, and influence as cases.

At a sufficiently high level of generalized development the "governing" interchanges (in the sense of cybernetic hierarchy) take place between the media which are anchored in the various functional subsystems —as power is anchored in the polity. These media in turn serve as instrumentalities of gaining control of "lower-order" resources which are necessary for fulfillment of expectations. Thus the expenditure of money for "goods" is not, at the system or "aggregate" level (as analyzed by Keynes), acquisition of the possession of particular commodities, but consists in the generalized expectation of availability of goods on "satisfactory" market terms. This is the primary output of the economy to consumers. Similarly, when we speak of control of productivity as a factor of effectiveness, it is not managerial control of particular plants which is meant, but control of a share of general productivity of the economy through market mechanisms, without specification of particulars.

Figure 1. Format of the Societal Interchange System.

The paradigm of interchange between general media of communication is presented in figures 1 and 2. Figure 1 simply designates the format in which this part of the paradigm is conceived. The assumptions of this format are three, none of which can be grounded or justified within the limits of the present exposition. These are (1) that the patterns of differentiation of a social system can be analyzed in terms of four primary functional categories, each of which is the focus of a primary functional subsystem of the society. As noted in the body of the essay, economy and polity are conceived to be such subsystems; (2) The primary interchange processes through which these subsystems are integrated with each other operate through generalized symbolic media of the type which I have assumed money and power to be,[43] and (3) at the level of differentiation of interest here, each interchange system is a double interchange, implying both the "alienation" of resources and products from their system of origin and the transcending of the barter level of exchange. Under these assumptions all figure 1 does is to portray a system of six double interchanges operating between each logically given pair among the four primary functional subsystems of a society. For convenience tentative names are given to each of these six double interchange systems.

Figure 2, then, places each of the six interchange systems on a horizontal axis, simply because they are easier to read that way. It adds to figure 1 only by introducing names of categories, directions of flow and designations as to medium (money, power, etc.) for each of the four places in each of the six interchange systems, thus presenting twenty-four categories, each of the four basic media appearing in four "forms."

Among the six interchange sets, power as a medium is involved, by our analysis, in only three, namely the interchanges of the polity (*G*) with each of the other three. These are the system of "resource mobilization," *vis-à-vis* the economy, the support system which involves the input of political support and the output of decisions (*vis-à-*

vis the integrative system) and the system of legitimation, as I have called it, *vis-à-vis* the value aspect of the pattern-maintenance system. The last of these three is a special case which does not involve power as a medium, but rather the structure of the code governing authority as defining the institutionalized uses of power, hence the legitimation of authority. Primary attention can thus be given to the other two.

The categories included in the *A-G* (economy-polity, or resources mobilization) interchange can be described as "forms" of power and of money (or wealth) respectively. They will be seen to be the categories which have been used in the appropriate parts of the discursive exposition of the body of the paper. The double interchange here, as in the classic economy—or labor-consump-

tion case, involves first one factor-interchange, namely control of productivity as factor of effectiveness exchanged for opportunity for effectiveness (in the particular case of capital, as a factor of production). Productivity is a monetary factor because it is a pool of resources controlled through monetary funds—which of course in turn can be exchanged for the particular facilities needed, notably goods and services. Opportunity, however, is a form of power in the sense discussed.

The second part of the double interchange is one of "product" outputs. This takes place between commitment of services to organization—typically through employment—which I have interpreted to be a form of power, and the allocation of fluid resources to the purveyors of service as facilities essential to the performance of their obligations—typically the control of budgeted funds, though often generaliza-

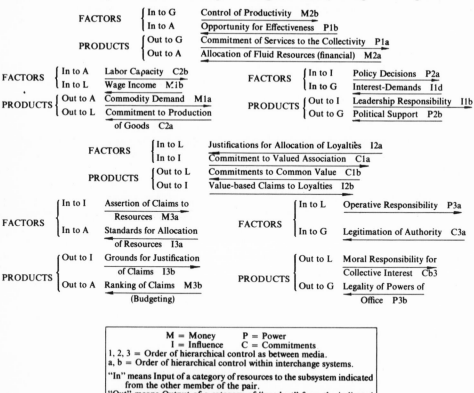

Figure 2. The Categories of Societal Interchange.

tion does not extend as high as this. Thus fluid resources in the ideal type case take the form of money funds. [44]

The second primary interchange system, which for convenience I shall call the support system, is that between polity and integrative system (*G-I*), which latter involves the associational aspect of group structure and solidarity in relation to the system of norms (legal and informal)—as distinguished from values. The basic difference lies in the fact that power here is interchanged not with money but with influence, and that whereas *vis-à-vis* money it was the "controlling" medium, *vis-à-vis* influence it is controlled. This difference is symbolized by the placing of the power categories here in the outside positions whereas in the *A-G* case they were placed inside (as the monetary categories were in *L-A*).

The relevant factor interchange here is between policy decisions as a "factor of solidarity" and interest-demands as a factor of effectiveness, in the senses in which these concepts were used above. Essentially we may say that interest-demands "define the situation" for political decision-making—which of course is by no means to say that demands in their initial form are or should be simply "granted" without modification. Like other factors they are typically transformed in the course of the political process.

Correspondingly policy decisions are a factor in solidarity in that they constitute commitments for collective action on which "interested parties" within limits can count.

The interchange of "product" outputs then consists of leadership responsibility as output of the polity (a form of influence, note, *not* of power), and political support as an output of the "associational" system—in the governmental case e.g. the electorate, which is a source of the political "income" of power. It will of course be noted that the units involved in any particular case of these two interchanges typically are not the same—thus party leaders may bid for support whereas administrative officials make certain policy decisions. This type of "split" (carried out to varying degrees) is characteristic of any highly differentiated system.

Figure 3 attempts to look at the generalized media from the point of view not only of their hierarchical ordering, but of the relation between the code and message components, and the position of the latter as sanctions controlling on the one hand factors essential to the various functional subsystems, on the other hand product outputs from these subsystems. The rows are arranged from top to bottom in terms of the familiar hierarchy of control—each row

FIGURE 3
THE MEDIA AS SANCTIONS

COMPONENTS OF MEDIA AND INTERCHANGE RECIPROCALS / MEDIA IN HIERARCHY OF CONTROL	CODES		MESSAGES (SANCTIONS)		TYPES OF SANCTION AND OF EFFECT
	VALUE-PRINCIPLE	COORDINATION STANDARD	FACTORS CONTROLLED	PRODUCTS CONTROLLED	
L COMMITMENTS	INTEGRITY	PATTERN-CONSISTENCY	SOURCE WAGES A JUSTIFICATION OF LOYALTIES I	DESTINATION CONSUMERS' DEMAND A CLAIMS TO LOYALTIES I	NEGATIVE-INTENTIONAL (ACTIVATION OF COMMITMENTS)
I INFLUENCE	SOLIDARITY	CONSENSUS	COMMITMENTS TO VALUED ASSOCIATION L POLICY DECISIONS G	COMMITMENT TO COMMON VALUES L POLITICAL SUPPORT G	POSITIVE-INTENTIONAL (PERSUASION)
G POWER	EFFECTIVENESS	SUCCESS	INTEREST-DEMANDS I CONTROL OF PRODUCTIVITY A	LEADERSHIP RESPONSIBILITY I CONTROL OF FLUID RESOURCES A	NEGATIVE-SITUATIONAL (SECURING COMPLIANCE)
A MONEY	UTILITY	SOLVENCY	CAPITAL G LABOR L	COMMITMENT OF SERVICES G EXPECTATION OF GOODS L	POSITIVE-SITUATIONAL (INDUCEMENT)

Figure 3. The Media as Sanctions.

designating one of the four media. The columns, on the other hand, designate components into which each medium needs to be broken down if some of the basic conditions of its operation in mediating interaction are to be understood.

In the body of the paper I have discussed the reasons for which it seems necessary to distinguish two components in the code aspect of each medium, namely what have been called the relevant value principle on the one hand, the "coordinative standard" on the other. The most familiar example concerns the paradigmatic economic case. Here the famous concept of utility seems to be the relevant principle whereas that of solvency is the coordinative standard. Utility is the basic "measure" of value in the economic sense, whereas the imperative to maintain solvency is a category of norm for the guidance of units in economic action. For the political case I have adopted the concept of effectiveness in Barnard's sense as the parallel to the economist's utility. Success, for the unit in question, notably the collective ease, seems to be the best available term for the corresponding coordinative standard. (Possibly, used with proper qualifications, the term sovereignty might be still more appropriate for this standard.)

At the other most important direct boundary of the polity, solidarity in Durkheim's sense seems to be the value-principle of integration which is parallel to utility and effectiveness, whereas the very important (to political theory) concept of *consensus* seems adequately to formulate the relevant integrative coordinative standard. Since they are not directly involved in the interchange systems of immediate concern here, I merely call attention to the designation of the value-principle of the pattern-maintenance system as *integrity* and the corresponding coordinative standard as *pattern-consistency*.

The *A* and *G* columns of figure 3 then designate contexts of operation of each of the four media as sanctions, but arranged not by interchange system as in figure 2, but by control of factor inputs and product

outputs respectively. Thus money though not itself a factor of production, "controls," i.e. buys, labor and capital as the primary factors, in the *A-L* and the *A-G* interchange systems respectively, whereas for "consuming" systems money buys outputs of the economy, namely goods (in *A-L*) and services (in *A-G*) respectively.

The involvement of power is conceived to be parallel. On the one hand it "commands" the two primary mobile factors of effectiveness, namely control of productivity (in *G-A*) and interest-demands (in *G-I*) (as justified in terms of appeal to norms). On the other hand the "consumers" or beneficiaries of the outputs from the process can use power to command these outputs in the form of fluid resources (e.g. through budget allocation in *G-A*) and of leadership responsibility for valued goals (in *G-I*).

It will be noted that in figure 3 negative and positive sanction types alternate in the hierarchy of control. Power, as the medium depending on negative situational sanctions is "sandwiched" between money (below it) with its positive situational sanctions and influence (above it) with its positive intentional sanctions.

Returning to figure 2, power is also involved in the legitimation system (*L-G*), but this time as code, as aspect of authority. This may be conceived as a mechanism for linking the principles and standards in the *L* and *G* rows. What is called the assumption of operative responsibility (*P3a*), which is treated as a "factor of integrity" is responsibility for *success* in the implementation of the value-principles, not only of collective effectiveness, but of integrity of the paramount societal value-pattern. It may be said that the legitimation of authority (*C3a*) "imposes" the responsibility to attempt such success. Legality of the powers of office on the other hand (*P3c*), as a category of output to the polity, is an application of the standard of pattern-consistency. At the various relevant levels action may and should be taken consistent with the value-commitments. In exchange for legal authorization to take such action, the responsible office-holder must accept moral responsibility for his use of power and his decisions of interpretation (*C3b*).

THE WORLD of the economist is organized fundamentally by exchange. This relationship, by which each of two parties gives up something to the other and receives something in return, is indeed a powerful social organizer. It is capable of organizing the division of labor and the allocation of resources, and it guides specialized production, as every elementary student of economics knows. In its general form it starts off as a conditional promise: "You do something nice to me and I will do something nice to you." If the other party to whom the communication is addressed accepts the invitation, the promises are fulfilled and the exchange is consummated. In this consummation we have a positive-sum game, provided that the exchange has been a free one in which both parties benefit, at least in their own opinion at the time. There may be later regrets which could turn the operation as it actually takes place into a negative-sum game, but the economist has generally assumed that these are small, and that such disappointments as may occur in exchange constitute a learning process by which everybody eventually learns to make wise choices among the opportunities which are open to him in the market. Exchange, furthermore, is the key relationship in what we might call unconscious or ecological economic development. It encourages the division of labor and this in turn encourages the increase in "skill and dexterity," and the growth, ultimately, of a specialized class of "philosophers," as Adam Smith called them, who practice research and development—all of which leads to increase in the "productive power of labor."

Exchange, however, is not the only system by means of which social organization is built up. Economists have always recognized that exchange can develop a process of social organization and growth only if certain prerequisites are fulfilled in the way of institutions of property, law and order, and so on. The economist however, has tended to identify these other organizers as essentially static or given in nature and providing merely the preconditions or the framework within which exchange does the real work. Milton Friedman and the "Chicago School" (if there is one) represent the

22

Toward a Pure Theory of Threat Systems

Kenneth E. Boulding

Like Parsons, Kenneth Boulding, Professor of Economics at the University of Colorado, an authority on the applications of game theory in societal analysis, and the author of Conflict and Defense, *here attempts to define a sub-system analogous to the economic system which rests on interpersonal relationships which students of political power have long emphasized. Originally published in 53* American Economic Review *(1963) 424–34, this article is reprinted here with the permission of that journal and the author.*

extreme of this point of view. This, however, would seem to be an unrealistic appraisal of the way in which the dynamics of most societies operate. Exchange is by no means the only human relationship which is capable of producing differentiation, division of labor, role structure, communication patterns, and all the other marks of organizational development. I distinguish at least two other types of human relationship which have the property of organizing social systems. The first of these is the threat, which is the main subject of this paper, the second may be called the integrative relationship, which involves a "meeting of minds" (that is, a convergence in the images and the utility functions of the parties toward each other). There is, of course, a negative of this relationship: the disintegrative relationship, in which the images move further apart. The integrative relationship is itself a complex of many different types of relationship, such as, for example, the teaching-learning relationship between the teacher and the student, the persuasive relationship between an orator and his audience or between an advertiser and his addressees, and a great variety of relationships, such as respect, affection, love, and

so on, which lead toward similarity in value
or utility functions over the domain of
various states of the world in the minds of
the parties concerned. Economists pay very
little attention to these integrative systems,
and indeed have generally tended to assume,
what in a dynamic sense is sheer nonsense,
that utility functions are given—whereas,
as Veblen pointed out, they are the product
of human interaction. I would add that they
are especially the product of the integrative
relationships in society.

It must be emphasized that threat
systems, exchange systems, and integrative
systems are practically never found in a
pure form. All actual social systems are
likely to contain all three elements. Even
under slavery, for instance, which has a high
proportion of threat, there are elements of
exchange and even of integration. At the
other extreme, in the family, the monastery,
or the utopian community, where the integrative system is dominant, there are also
elements of exchange and threat. Even in
the most loving family or community there
is a point below which the terms of trade of
an individual member cannot deteriorate
without causing serious trouble, and the
threat of expulsion always remains an ultimate sanction. Just as economics, however,
has prospered by abstracting from the complexity of the social system as a whole a
single relationship and element, that of exchange, and has built an elaborate theoretical and empirical structure on this foundation, which can then throw light on the
more complex processes of the real world,
so the phenomena of threat systems on the
one side or integrative systems on the other
can be abstracted out of the social complex
and developed in a pure form. It is tempting,
indeed, to try to assign the threat systems to
the political scientist and integrative systems
to the sociologist, as we assign exchange to
the economist, though this division is too
neat to correspond to the untidy facts of
academic specialization.

Let us then look at the threat as an abstract human relationship, as an economist
might look at exchange, and consider how
this might be used as an organizer of society.
Like exchange, threat in its simplest form is
a relationship between two parties. Exchange, however, originates in a conditional promise to do something good if
something good is done in return, whereas
a threat originates in a promise to do something bad. The threat relationship begins
when the threatener says to the threatened,
"You do something nice to me or I will do
something nasty to you." The exchange-
like form of the threat can be seen in the
threat of the holdup man. "Your money or
your life," which looks like "Give me my
money and I will give you your life." There
is a real difference, however, between the
commodity which is offered in exchange and
the discommodity which is offered in the
threat. "I will give you your life" means "I
will not take away your life." In order for
the threat to be perceived as a threat by
the threatened, the threatener must be able
to create a perception of credibility; that is
of both capability and will of carrying out
the threat if the threatened does not do
what the threatener wants him to do. We
may note that we have exactly the same
problem of credibility in exchange, but it is
less prominent because the information is
usually more obvious. We visualize the
exchanger as handing out the object which
he offers to exchange. In financial exchanges,
however, when what is offered is a promise
to pay in the future, the problem of credibility becomes very real and takes much the
same form that it does in threat systems.

The subsequent course of the system
depends very much on the nature of the
response to the initial threat. Four responses may be distinguished which may be
labeled submission, defiance, counterthreat,
and the integrative response.

Submission is a not infrequent, though
seldom popular, response to threat. When
the holdup man threatens us we give him
our wallet. When the parent says, "Don't
steal the cookies or you'll be spanked," the
child refrains from stealing the cookies.
When the master says to the slave, "Work
for me or I will kill you," the slave frequently obeys. When the state says, "Become a soldier or I will put you in prison,"
the young man allows himself to be con-

scripted. The threat-submission system is likely to be a conflict system; that is, it is likely to move the parties to a state in which the threatener is better off and the threatened is worse off than in the initial condition. The welfare situations can be illustrated in a field such as Figure 1, in which we plot A's welfare horizontally and B's welfare vertically. Suppose P_1 represents the welfare of both parties before the threat is made. The very act of making the threat is likely to change the positions of the parties in this field. They may, for instance, move to P_2, where both parties are worse off; the threat creates a state of anxiety in the minds of both parties. On the other hand it is possible that A, the threatener, may enjoy making threats, in which case the actual making of the threat might move the parties to P_2'. When submission takes place, we may move to a position like P_3, where A is better off and B is worse off. This is a typical conflict move. On the other hand, it is not impossible that B's submission to the threat may make him better off as well as A, though this is unlikely; that is, submission might move us from P_2 to a position such as P_3'. This is the situation where A is threatening to make B do something for B's own good which B would not be motivated to do in the absence of threat. The moral justification for threat frequently revolves around this hypothesis. We threaten to spank the child or to fail the student or to hang the murderer strictly for his own good, even if a little skepticism as to these protestations may not be out of order.

The threat-submission relationship has been a powerful social organizer. It is indeed, one of the major organizers of classical civilization insofar as this rests on slavery. It is also the foundation of a good deal of obedience to the law and of the authority of the state. As Baumol has pointed out in his *Welfare Economics and the Theory of the State*, we may quite rationally vote to threaten ourselves where there is something, like paying taxes, which everybody wants to do if everybody does it, but which nobody wants to do if other people do not. The possibility of nonconflictual threat-submission relationships, therefore, is not to be taken lightly. A key concept here is that

of the legitimacy of threat. We submit to the traffic cop and the stoplight because we all recognize their legitimacy. The concept of legitimacy is perhaps more in the domain of integrative systems than of threat systems, but this only illustrates how intertwined these two systems may be.

Threats can be perceived as legitimate only if they are also perceived as appropriate; the threatened punishment must fit the deterred crime. Even if what we are trying to accomplish is not perceived as preventing a crime by the threatened party, that is, even if the threat is not perceived as legitimate, its credibility still depends on its appropriateness. To say to a child, "If you steal the cookies I will kill you," is only credible, and only deters, if not taken literally. This is why "massive retaliation" is impotent against "salami-slicing," to slip once more into the repulsive jargon of strategic science.

The second possible response to threat is defiance. This is somewhat analogous to the nonconsummation of exchange because of a refusal to trade. A says to B, "You give me X and I will give you Y"; B simply says, "No, it's not worth it to me," and the situation returns to the *status quo ante*. In threat systems the situation is more complicated

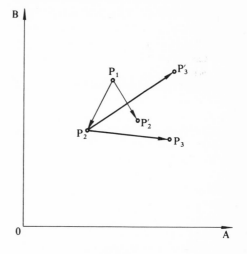

Figure 1.

because defiance puts a burden of response on the threatener and hence is in some sense a challenge to him. The threatener then has to decide whether or not to carry out the threat. If he does carry out the threat, this is likely to have a cost to him as well as to the threatened. We have here a very clear negative-sum game. If he does not carry out the threat his credibility is impaired; there is still a cost to him. Defiance therefore always imposes a cost to the threatener which is not found in the corresponding situation in exchange. The probability of this should presumably be taken into account by a rational threatener in deciding whether or not to make the initial threat.

The third alternative is the counter-threat; that is, "If you do something nasty to me, I will do something nasty to you." This is deterrence. This also imposes upon the original threatener a choice of whether or not to carry out the threat. If he is in fact deterred, his credibility is thereby apt to be weakened the next time he makes a threat; that is, there is a decline, as it were, in the capital value of his threat potentiality. If he carries out his original threat, there is likely to be a mutual exchange of "bads," or carried-out threats, which is very clearly a negative-sum game. This is perhaps the greatest difference between threat systems and exchange systems, for when exchange is consummated it is almost always positive-sum, whereas when threats are consummated they are usually negative-sum. This is why exchange systems have a much higher horizon of development than threat systems. This explains, I think, why in the long pull the free labor market, for instance, has always been able to outdo slavery, and why all classical civilizations have ultimately perished whereas the world of trade has grown slowly but persistently from its very origins.

Perhaps the most important single feature of systems of deterrence is their long-run instability. The whole history of threat systems is summed up succinctly in two verses from St. Luke (11:21–22): "When a strong man armed keepeth his palace, his goods are in peace; but when a stronger than he shall come upon him and overcome him, he taketh from him all his armor wherein he trusted and divideth his spoils." It is indeed a source of the basic long-run instability of all threat systems that the unilateral threat system, or the threat-submission system, which may be fairly successful for a time, almost inevitably degenerates into the bilateral threat system, or deterrence. Deterrence is successful as long as it deters, but deterrence itself seems to be unstable. The reason for this, I suspect, is that the credibility of threats depreciates with time if threats are not carried out. Hence threats occasionally need to be carried out in order to re-establish the credibility. Another reason is that threat capability declines if threats are not occasionally carried out, particularly where this capability is enshrined in complex social organizations and in apparatus such as armed forces.

For both these reasons, a state of stable deterrence is rarely stable for long. Eventually either the capability or the credibility, or both, of one of the parties will depreciate to the point where the other party will make new demands. At this point deterrence breaks down and the system slips either into submission or into defiance. Submission is particularly hard if the parties have lived under stable deterrence for a while, so the outcome of a new demand is likely to be defiance. This, then, forces on the imposer of the new demand the choice between carrying out the threat or acceptance of the defiance, which would further destroy his credibility. He is likely, therefore, to carry out the threat, which will lead to the carrying out of the counterthreat, which will result in a negative-sum game known as war. In this, it is true, one party may emerge relatively better off than the other, and indeed if the loser is very much worse off the victor may even be absolutely better off. In this case we may pass again to a unilateral threat system. This is the "successful" period of the new civilization, and this again leads to counterthreats and ultimate downfall. Thus the rise and fall of civilizations seems to be implicit in the very nature of the threat system itself—as, indeed, a

pure exchange system is also likely to experience ultimate cycles of boom and col-
lapse. It may be that, ultimately, only
integrative systems can provide stability,
and I am not sure even of that.

This brings us to the fourth possible response to threat, which is the integrative
response. This is harder to analyze and to
describe. It may take a great many different
forms because of the very richness of the
integrative system itself. The integrative
response is that which establishes community between the threatener and the
threatened and produces common values and
a common interest. The integrative response may be mixed with any one of the
first three responses. Submission, for instance, may be made in such a way that the
threatener is eventually absorbed into a
larger culture and the threat system disappears. The experience of the Negro in the
United States may be such a case. By
accepting and illuminating the ostensible
value system of his conquerors, the Negro
both made and produced an integrative response which eventually made slavery impossible. In the Gandhian experience in
India we have an example of defiance mixed
with an integrative response; this is the
essence of nonviolent resistance. The
threatened party, by defying the threatener
and by accepting the consequences without
bitterness or complaint, eventually undermines the morale of the threatener and the
threat system disintegrates. Examples of
counterthreat used as an integrative response seem to be rarer, for whereas both
submission and defiance, in a sense, unite
the threatener and the threatened in some
sort of a social system in which integrative
factors may operate, the counterthreat
divides the threatener from the threatened,
breaks any bond which might develop between them, and hence is apt to be disintegrative rather than integrative. This perhaps
is another reason for the fundamental
instability of deterrence, and its ultimate
certainty of failure. It is still not inconceivable, however, that a carefully controlled counterthreat might be combined
with an integrative response. We may have
seen something like this happen in the industrial relationship, where the threat to

fire on the part of the employer may produce either the counterthreat to quit or the
more organized counterthreat of the strike.
In this case, however, the very nature of the
relationship and the fact that if there is to
be an industrial organization at all the
parties have to live together, opens up the
possibility of integrative solutions to counterthreat systems. Where, for instance, the
threat or even the actuality of the counterthreat is used to obtain union recognition
and a contract, we see counterthreat being
used as a device to establish an essentially
integrative system of industrial jurispru-
dence. Parallel to this in international
systems might be a counterthreat system
used to achieve a disarmament organization of a world government.

Like exchange systems, threat systems
have a geographical structure which is imposed on them by the fact that threats, like
commodities, have a cost of transport.
Because of this there are many striking
parallels as I have pointed out in *Conflict
and Defense* (Harper and Row, New York,
1962), between the competition of states by
means of threats and the competition of firms
by means of exchange. Thus the theory of
duopoly is very much like that of a bipolar
system in international relations. Each of
the competing organizations has a certain
"home strength" as represented by the
threat capacity in the case of the nation or
the cost of production at the mill in the case
of the firm. As it goes away from home it has
to incur a cost of transport, so that the
further from home the organization operates the smaller the threat that it can bring
to bear or the higher the price it must
charge. In each case this represents an
application of the general principle of "the
further the weaker." Between two states as
between two firms there is likely to be a
boundary of equal strength, with each
organization dominating the area between
itself and the boundary. Such a situation
can easily lead to an arms race or a price
war, as each organization tries to push the
boundary of equal strength further from its

home base, either by increasing its armaments or by cutting its mill price. This is pretty clearly a negative-sum game, from which the parties can usually only be rescued by an integrative system of some kind, for instance a merger in the case of the firms, or in less extreme forms a gentlemen's agreement, and in the case of states a federation or a "security community."

These considerations lead to an interesting theory of viability which I have also expounded in some detail in *Conflict and Defense*. An organization may be said to have unconditional viability if no other organization has the capability of destroying it; that is, an organization is unconditionally viable if it is dominant over all other organizations at its home base. A system of unconditional viability is only possible if each organization is stronger than any other or any reasonable combination of others. This paradoxical result is attainable if the organizations are far enough apart and if their strength, that is, their threat capability, diminishes rapidly enough for each one as he goes away from home, that is, if there is what I call a high loss-of-strength gradient. A system of stable unconditional viability is threatened either by an increase in the number of organizations in a given field or by diminution of the loss-of-strength gradient. The less the loss-of-strength gradient, the fewer organizations can coexist in unconditional viability.

I have argued that the peculiar crisis of national defense today is a result of the loss of unconditional viability even by the largest nations in the light of nuclear threat. If we are to exist at all, it must be on conditions of conditional viability, in which each organization can destroy the other but refrains from doing so. This is not an altogether unfamiliar system—indeed, in interpersonal relations we have had to live with it. In the age of the sword, unconditional viability for the individual was at least not inconceivable, even though one had to be a pretty good swordsman to achieve it. The crossbow and, following that, firearms, ruined this system and in our personal

relations we now live in a world in which we are literally all at each other's mercy. One would think that, in these circumstances, mercy would be taken seriously and studied, but this is the last thing that anyone seems to want to do. In international relations, especially, we are still living under the illusion of unconditional viability, and we may have a very rude awakening.

Concepts of liquidity and inflation which have been developed in economics have also some applicability to threat systems. The concept of generalized military capability is closely related to the economic concept of liquidity. A liquid asset is something with which anything can be bought; a military capability is something with which anything can be destroyed. It is, as it were, money for the doing of harm. Another reason for the instability of threat systems, incidentally, is that harm can be done much faster than good (I am indebted to T. C. Schelling for this observation). One might add, however, as a corollary that the ultimate victory of exchange and integrative systems over threat systems is assured by the fact that more good can be done than harm. The doing of harm has a limit of total destruction; that is, of zero good. The doing of good has no definite upper limit. The liquidity or the lack of specificity of a military capability is another factor which is likely to lead to the instability of the threat system. The military capability of A is a generalized threat directed, say, at B, C, D, and E. Each of these parties, however, perceives the threat as if it were directed wholly at him. The perception of the threat, therefore, on the part of the threatened is four times the amount of the threat on the part of the threatener at a maximum. It is not surprising that under these systems threat systems produce armament races which almost inevitably lead to the carrying out of the threat.

When threat systems become embodied in military organizations, we have problems arising which are strikingly parallel to those which develop for economics when production and exchange get to be concentrated in firms. The military organization, which I have elsewhere called the "milorg," is the equivalent in the threat system of the firm in the exchange system. It possesses many of the qualities and characteristics of the firm. It has a hierarchical organization, it is organized by a budget, it has flows of expenditures most of which are laid out in the purchase of inputs, and it has a flow of receipts. The major difference between the milorg and the firm arises from the source of the receipts: in the case of the firm, receipts are derived from the sale of a product on the market; in the case of the milorg, the receipts are derived from a government budget and ultimately from taxation or from the creation of money. The milorg, that is to say, does not produce a clearly defined product in the way that a firm does; its receipts have more the character of transfer payments than of returns from sales; that is, exchange. In this respect it is more like a philanthropy than it is like a firm. If we ask what it produces, we would have to answer in terms of a generalized threat; that is, a capability of doing harm to unspecified persons or things.

We may go further, indeed, and distinguish a number of different "commodities" which the milorg produces. One in the currently fashionable terminology is the "counterforce." This is the diminution of a potential enemy's capacity to harm the home organization. This might take the form of a defensive work such as a wall, a buffer state, a Maginot Line, or anything which would sharply increase the potential opponent's loss-of-strength gradient as he moved toward the defended center. It might also take the form of an ability to destroy the opponent's milorg or those aspects of it which have capability of destroying the home organization. Another product of the milorg might be, again in the fashionable terminology, "countervalue." This is the ability to threaten, not the threat-makers of the opponent, but the things which he values—his cities, people, social organizations, and so on. Countervalue weapons and organization are generally associated with deterrents, that is, with counter-threats, but they may also be used unilaterally to threaten the opponent into doing something which the threatener wants. The great difficulty of operating a threat system

is that all these different threat-commodities are very hard to distinguish in practice, and hence an action which is intended to be one kind of threat may be interpreted at the other end as a totally different kind. Insofar as threats are used as instruments of persuasion to change people's opinions or behavior, they tend to suffer from a defect of all persuasion systems; that what is persuasive to the persuader is not always persuasive to the persuadee. The threatener or the persuader has an image of the order which is derived largely from his own experience, and hence is likely to be false in many important regards. Our threats, like our persuasions, tend to be directed at some imaginary person whom we have made in our own image, not at the real person at whom the activity is directed.

The analogue of inflation in threat systems is found in the arms race, in which both parties continually increase the amount of economic resources which they are putting into organized threats (milorgs) without changing their relative power position. Today, indeed, we may be approaching a hyperinflation of the threat system under the impact of military research and development, which effectively destroys any validity which the system once may have had. We can then look at arms control as an attempt at stabilizing the "price level" after a hyperinflation.

The subject could be pursued much further, and there seems to me to be no reason why a science of threat systems should not be developed at least as elaborately as economics builds from exchange. This science, perhaps, still has to find its Adam Smith, but one feels that so much development has gone on in it in recent years that its "Wealth of Nations" must be just around the corner. The need for this science, furthermore, is very urgent. Because of the development of the nuclear weapon and the consequent disappearance of unconditional viability, the whole threat system, that is, the system of national defense, is suffering a grave crisis—indeed, I would argue, a breakdown. The control of the threat system, therefore, is a matter of the topmost priority for the human race. Unless we do this we may not have a chance to develop any other systems. In order to control a threat system, however, we must understand it. It is one of the most astonishing features of human society that governments are willing to invest so much money in threat systems with only crude folk knowledge as to how these systems actually work, and without being at all interested, apparently, in finding out more about them. This is perhaps because the threat system is an important element in the integrative system of most societies. Nations are built on the solid foundations of violence and cruelty, threats and counterthreats. Our national heroes are soldiers and our national mythology is a mythology of successful threat. A threat to the threat system, therefore, is seen as a threat to the integrity of the society itself. We love making threats and it satisfies our masculine demand for "strength" to make them, and hence a threat to the threat system is seen as a threat to that which we love. To make a science of threats, however, is to threaten the threat system itself, for a system so inefficient in producing welfare as the threat system is can only survive as long as it is supported on folk ignorance. It is little wonder, therefore, that the science of threat systems has been so slow to develop.

My thesis may perhaps be summarized in the following lines of verse:

> Four things that give mankind a shove
> Are threats, exchange, persuasion, love;
> But taken in the wrong proportions
> These give us cultural abortions.
> For threats bring manifold abuses
> In games where everybody loses;
> Exchange enriches every nation
> But leads to dangerous alienation;
> Persuaders organize their brothers
> But fool themselves as well as others;
> And love, with longer pull than hate,
> Is slow indeed to propagate.

[Power] is both awful and fragile, and can dominate a continent, only in the end to be blown down by a whisper. To destroy it, nothing more is required than to be indifferent to its threats, and to prefer other goods to those which it promises. Nothing less, however, is required also.

R. H. Tawney, *Equality*

" 'Power' (*Macht*) is the probability that one actor within a social relationship will be in a position to carry out his own will despite resistance," according to Weber.[1] Tawney's definition similarly centers on imposing one's will on others, except that he explicitly directs attention to the asymmetry of power relations: "Power may be defined as the capacity of an individual, or group of individuals, to modify the conduct of other individuals or groups in the manner which he desires, and to prevent his own conduct being modified in the manner in which he does not."[2]

Broadly defined, power refers to all kinds of influence between persons or groups, including those exercised in exchange transactions, where one induces others to accede to his wishes by rewarding them for doing so. Neither Weber nor Tawney, however, used the term that broadly. Although the customer technically imposes his will upon the jeweler when he makes him surrender a diamond ring by paying for it, this situation clearly should not be confused with that of the gangster who forces the jeweler to hand over the ring at the point of a gun. Physical coercion, or its threat, is the polar case of power, but other negative sanctions, or the threat of exercising them, are usually also effective means of imposing one's will on others. People can be made to do things for fear of losing their jobs, of being ostracized, of having to pay fines, or of losing social standing. This suggests a distinction between coercive power, which rests on the deterrent effect of negative sanctions, and influence based on rewards, as that characteristic of exchange transactions.[3]

Defining power as control through negative sanctions implies that an individual exercises power when he gets another to perform a service by threatening to take 100 dollars from him if he refuses, whereas he does not when he gets the other to per-

23

Differentiation of Power

Peter Blau

The following selection is chapter five from Peter Blau's important book, Exchange and Power in Social Life (New York: John Wiley, 1964). This chapter analyzes the differentiation of a subsystem based on power, analogous to the earlier schemes of Parsons and Boulding. Reprinted here with the permission of John Wiley and Sons, Inc., and the author.

form the same service by promising him 100 dollars for it. The objection may be raised that the net difference is the same in both cases—the other is 100 dollars better off if he performs the service than if he does not—but this objection does not seem valid. The crucial factor is the baseline from which an individual starts when another seeks to influence him, and the only difference between punishments and rewards is in relation to this initial baseline, whether he is worse or better off than he was before the transaction started. The necessity to avert a loss is probably also experienced as more of an external compulsion than the temptation to make a gain. A more serious objection, however, is that the baseline itself is obscured once rewards become recurrent.

Regular rewards make recipients dependent on the supplier and subject to his power, since they engender expectations that make their discontinuation a punishment. A person who has a job is rewarded for performing his duties by his earnings, and as his wages are positive sanctions it seems at first that no power is involved in terms of the definition presented. However, being fired from a job cannot plausibly be considered to constitute merely the absence of rewards; it clearly is a punishing experience. The threat of being fired is a negative sanction that gives an employer power over his employees, enabling him to enforce their

*Unilateral Dependence and
Obligations*

compliance with his directives. Regular rewards create expectations that redefine the baseline in terms of which positive sanctions are distinguished from negative ones. The air we breathe is not conceived by us to be a special reward, nor is the freedom to move about the streets as we please, but being suffocated or imprisoned is experienced as a punishment. Correspondingly, a man who has reason to expect to remain in his job does not think of his regular earnings as distinctive rewards, and the loss of his income is a punishment for him. Only a raise in income is a specific reward, although even raises that occur regularly come to be expected, and in these cases failure to receive a raise tends to be experienced as a punishment and may be so intended by the employer.

The definition of power should be amplified, therefore, to read that it is the ability of persons or groups to impose their will on others despite resistance through deterrence either in the forms of withholding regularly supplied rewards or in the form of punishment, inasmuch as the former as well as the latter constitute, in effect, a negative sanction.[4] Three further implications should be noted. First, following Parsons, the concept of power is used to refer to an individual's or group's ability *recurrently* to impose his or its will on others, not to a single instance of influencing a decision of theirs, however important.[5] Second, the punishment threatened for resistance, provided it is severe, makes power a compelling force, yet there is an element of voluntarism in power—the punishment could be chosen in preference to compliance, and it sometimes is—which distinguishes it from the limiting case of direct physical coercion.[6] Finally, power is conceptualized as inherently asymmetrical and as resting on the *net* ability of a person to withhold rewards from and apply punishments to others—the ability that remains after the restraints they can impose on him have been taken into account. Its source is one-sided dependence. Interdependence and mutual influence of equal strength indicate lack of power.

By supplying services in demand to others, a person establishes power over them. If he regularly renders needed services they cannot readily obtain elsewhere, others become dependent on and obligated to him for these services, and unless they can furnish other benefits to him that produce interdependence by making him equally dependent on them, their unilateral dependence obligates them to comply with his requests lest he cease to continue to meet their needs. Providing needed benefits others cannot easily do without is undoubtedly the most prevalent way of attaining power, though not the only one, since it can also be attained by threatening to deprive others of benefits they currently enjoy unless they submit. The threat of punishment, although it exerts the most severe restraints, creates the dependence that is the root of power indirectly, as it were, while recurrent essential rewards that can be withheld do so directly. The government that furnishes needed protection to its citizens, the employer who provides needed jobs to his employees, and the profession that supplies needed services to the community, all make the others dependent on them and potentially subject to their power.

Emerson has presented a schema for examining "power-dependence" relations and their consequences, which can be reformulated to specify the conditions that produce the imbalance of power itself.[7] Individuals who need a service another has to offer have the following alternatives: *First, they can supply him with a service* that he wants badly enough to induce him to offer his service in return, though only if they have the resources required for doing so; this will lead to reciprocal exchanges. *Second, they may obtain the needed service elsewhere*, assuming that there are alternative suppliers; this also will lead to reciprocal exchanges but in different partnerships. *Third, they can coerce him to furnish the service*, provided they are capable of doing so, in which case they would establish domination over him. *Fourth, they may learn to resign themselves to do without this service*, possibly finding some substitute for it, which would require that they change the values that determine their needs. Finally, if they are not able or willing to choose any of these alternatives, they have no other choice but to comply with his wishes, since he can make continued supply of the needed service contingent on their compliance. In the situation specified, the supply of services inevitably generates power. The absence of the first four alternatives defines the conditions of power in general.

This schema can be employed to indicate the conditions of social independence, the requirements of power, the issues in power conflicts, and their structural implications. The conditions of social independence are characterized by the availability of the first four alternatives, which enables people to evade the fifth one of dependence on services from a given source. First, strategic resources promote independence. Specifically, a person who has all the resources required as effective inducements for others to furnish him with the services and benefits he needs is protected against becoming dependent on anyone. The possession of generalized rewards, such as money, is evidently of major significance in this connection, although wealth is not a perfect safeguard against dependence, since many benefits a person may want, such as fame or love, cannot be obtained for money but only with other resources.

The fact that there are alternative sources from which a needed service can be obtained is a second condition that fosters independence. If there is only one employer in a community, or only one expert consultant in a work group, others are likely to become dependent on him. The situation, however, does not have to be that extreme. As a matter of fact, any commitment to a social relationship entails a degree of dependence by excluding alternatives. An employee presumably remains in a job either because alternative employment opportunities are less attractive to him or because his investment in this job is so great that moving to another would be too costly for him. Whatever the reason, his lack of equally preferable alternatives

makes him dependent on his employer.[8] The degree of dependence of individuals on a person who supplies valued services is a function of the difference between their value and that of the second-best alternative open to them. The more employees prefer their own job to any possible alternative, the more dependent are they on their employer and the more power does he have over them. The employer can cut the salary of employees who are very dependent on their job, assign them unpleasant duties, or force them to work harder, and they have no choice but to accept the decisions and to comply. Yet by doing so the employer makes the job less attractive to the employees and other employment opportunities relatively more attractive, decreasing the difference between the present job and alternatives, and thus reducing his employees' dependence on him and his power over them. Generally, the greater the difference between the benefits an individual supplies to others and those they can obtain elsewhere, the greater is his power over them likely to be. Hence, others can increase their independence of a person who has power over them simply by accepting fewer benefits from him—no more than they can get for their services elsewhere—except that this is often not so simple for them.[9]

A third condition of independence is the ability to use coercive force to compel others to dispense needed benefits or services. The inability to use force may be due to weakness or to normative restraints that effectively prohibit resort to coercion, or it may be due to the fact that the desired benefit loses its significance if given under duress, as is the case for love and for social approval. Superior coercive power makes people relatively independent of others inasmuch as power includes the ability to prevent others from interfering with one's conduct. Since there is strength in numbers, independence can be won through forming coalitions capable of enforcing demands.[10]

A lack of need for various services constitutes the fourth condition of independence. The fewer the wants and needs of an individual, the less dependent he is on others to meet them. Needs, however, do not remain constant. By providing individuals with goods and services that increase their satisfaction, their level of expectations tends to be raised, and while they were previously satisfied without these benefits, they are now desirous of continuing to obtain them. The development of new needs in this fashion underlies the increasing consumer demand that is an essential element in an expanding economy. But emergent needs serve this function by strengthening the dependence of people on those who can supply the resources required to meet these needs, notably employers. Religious and political ideals derive their driving force in large part from imbuing adherents with values that make the satisfaction of material wants comparatively unimportant and that, consequently, lessen men's dependence on those who can supply material benefits. By reducing material needs, revolutionary ideologies become a source of independent strength and resistance to power.

The fourfold schema can also help to delineate the strategies required to attain and sustain power, which are complementary to the conditions of independence just discussed. To achieve power over others with his resources, a person must prevent others from choosing any of the first four alternatives, thereby compelling them to comply with his directives as a condition for obtaining the needed benefits at his command. This requires, first, that he remain indifferent to the benefits they can offer him in exchange for his. The strategies of power designed to preserve this indifference include denying others access to resources that are vital for the welfare of a group or individual, for example, by fighting attempts of working-class parties to take over the government; securing needed benefits from outside sources rather than subordinates, as illustrated by the gang leader's disinclination to borrow money from his more affluent followers;[11] and

encouraging competition among the suppliers of essential service, for instance, by opposing the formation of unions that would restrict competition for jobs among workers.

A second requirement of power is to assure the continued dependence of others on the services one has to supply by barring access to alternative suppliers of these services. Monopolization of needed rewards is the typical means of achieving this purpose. The only firm in town where jobs can be found, the only child on the block who has a bicycle, the political society that is the sole source of national security and glory, the church that is the only avenue to salvation, and the police that alone can offer protection against violence—all these have power due to their monopoly over important benefits.

The ability to prevent others from resorting to coercive force to effect their demands is a third prerequisite of maintaining power. Discouraging coalitions among subordinates that would enable them to extract demands is a strategy that serves this end, as is blocking their access to political power. Such organizations as unions and working-class parties have two analytically distinct, though actually inseparable, functions in the fight against existing powers. Their success threatens those in positions of power, on the one hand, by making them dependent for essential services on these organizations (for example, for labor supply) and, on the other, by subjecting them to their coercive power (for instance, the union's sit-down strike or the executive power of the labor-party government). Obstructing such coalitions, therefore, protects power against being undermined either by withholding vital services or by employing coercive force. Probably the most important strategies for safeguarding the power that rests on the possession of important resources, however, are support for law and order and resistance against political control of exchange processes. These defenses protect the power potential that resides in superior vital resources not only from the threat of violence but also from being curbed by the legitimate power of the state.

Fourth, power depends on people's needs for the benefits those in power have to offer. Materialistic values, which make money and what it can buy of great significance, strengthen the power of employers. Patriotic ideals, which identify people with the success of their country in war and peace, fortify the power of the government. Religious convictions, which make the blessings of a church and the spiritual counsel of its representatives rewards of great saliency, reinforce the power of church dignitaries. Revolutionary ideologies, which define the progress of a radical movement as inherently valuable for its members, bestow power on the movement's leadership. Groups and individuals in power have a stake in helping to perpetuate and spread the relevant social values and in opposing counter-ideologies that depreciate these values. Dominant groups whose power rests on different social values have some conflicting interests, therefore, although their common interest in preserving the existing power structure may well override these differences.

The conflict between the powerful (who have an interest in fortifying their power) and the people over whom they have power (who have an interest in strengthening their independence) centers around four types of issues, which again correspond to the four alternatives outlined. First, there is the issue of the resources of subordinates. If their resources were sufficient to obtain the benefits they need in exchange for them, they would cease to be subject to the power of the others. Granted that every single subordinate's resources are inadequate for this purpose, the issue becomes that of pooling the resources of all subordinates who confront a superior or group of superiors to extract demands from him or them. The second issue is that of the alternative opportunities available to subordinates for obtaining needed benefits. Competition among superiors for the services of subordinates increases the subordinates' independence, whereas monopolistic practices increase the superiors' power. These two conflicts are complementary, since the question in both cases is the degree of collective organization per-

missible to restrain free competition, although it is the organization of the powerless that would husband their resources in one case, and the organization of the powerful that would monopolize needed benefits in the other.

The third conflict is political. At issue here is the use of coercive force in the fight against powers based on superior resources. The prototype is the conflict over the use of the legitimate coercive power of the state to regulate exchange transactions and restrict power that rests on economic strength. Fourth, there is the ideological conflict between social values that intensify the need for the services the powerful have to offer and counterideologies that mitigate this need. In the process of decreasing the need for some services, however, radical ideologies increase the need for others—namely, those that contribute to the reform movement—with the result that ideologies make adherents less dependent on the power of some but more dependent on power of others.

Finally, tracing the implications of each of the four alternatives leads to the analysis of basic problems of social structure. First, the fact that benefits can be obtained by reciprocating for them with others directs attention to the study of exchange processes and the distribution of resources. Second, the exploration of alternative opportunities points to the investigation of the emerging exchange structures, the competitive processes in them, the going rates of exchange, and the normative standards that tend to develop. Third, the study of coercive power raises questions concerning the establishment of coalitions and organizations to mobilize power, the differentiation of power in social structures, and the processes that govern the struggle over political power in a society.[12] Fourth, the ability to get along without something originally needed calls attention to the modifications of social values that occur under various conditions, the formation of new ideologies, and conflicts between ideologies.[13]

The main points of the entire discussion

presented are summarized in the schema at the foot of this page.

Dependence on the benefits a person can supply does not make others subject to his power but gives him only potential power over them. Realization of this power requires that he actually supply the benefits or commit himself to do so. In a technical sense, we are dependent on all employers who are in a position to offer us better jobs than those we have, but these employers have no power over us, while our employer has the power to command our compliance with his directives, because the salary and other benefits he furnishes obligate us to comply lest we cease to continue to receive them. He alone can withdraw from us benefits to which we have become accustomed, whereas other employers can only tempt us with greater rewards.

The ability to provide superior benefits than are available elsewhere, in a situation where these benefits are needed and cannot be extracted by force, constituted a very strong claim to power, although not a completely inescapable one. If the power demands are too severe, relinquishing these benefits may be preferable to yielding to the demands. Moreover, a person's or group's resources may not be adequate to

obligate others to comply. For these reasons coercive force, which can hardly be resisted, is important as a last resort for exercising power over individuals who cannot otherwise be made to yield. Whereas physical force is a perfect protection against power—killing a man or incarcerating him disposes of his threat—it is an imperfect tool for exercising power, since people can choose even death over compliance. Hence, coercive force differs only in degree from the power that rests on the supply of needed benefits, albeit an important degree.

Competition for Status

Competition arises in the process of social integration and gives rise to differentiation of status in groups, as noted in chapter two. At this point processes of social differentiation in groups will be traced in greater detail, focusing on the ultimate differentiation of power and drawing attention to some parallels between the differentiating processes in face-to-face groups and those in complex structures.

The initial competition in newly forming groups is for participation time. Whatever attracts individuals to the group, whether they seek to gain simply acceptance, social support, respect, or positions of leadership and power, obtaining these social rewards

Alternatives to Compliance	Conditions of Independence	Requirements of Power	Structural Implications
1. Supply inducements	Strategic resources	Indifference to what others offer	Exchange and distribution of resources
2. Obtain elsewhere	Available alternatives	Monopoly over what others need	Competition and exchange rates
3. Take by force	Coercive force	Law and order	Organization and differentiation
4. Do without	Ideals lessening needs	Materialistic and other relevant values	Ideology formation

requires opportunities for proving oneself worthy of them. Others must devote time to interact with and listen to an individual to enable him to impress them with his outstanding qualities, but time is scarce since not everyone can be attended to at once. Time, then, is a generalized means in the competition for a variety of social rewards, equivalent in this respect to profitable sales in economic competition, which also are needed whether the aim is to distribute profits, increase assets, buy new equipment, or achieve a dominant position in the market. The unequal distribution of speaking time produces an initial differentiation that gives some an advantage in subsequent competitive processes, just as the unequal distribution of sales among firms does.

The group allocates time among various members in accordance with their estimated abilities to make contributions to its welfare based on the initial impressions. In a discussion group confronted with the task of resolving some issue or solving some problem, for example, most speaking time is allocated to those who appear most likely to advance the solution. Having speaking time available, however, is not sufficient for an individual's purpose, whatever it is; he must properly use the opportunity it provides to obtain social rewards from the rest of the group. The member who makes important contributions to the discussion is first rewarded by the approval of others, by having them increasingly turn to him for his suggestions and for his approval of theirs, and if his suggestions continue to prove viable, he is further rewarded by their respect for his abilities. The group member who makes lesser contributions—for instance, relieving the tensions generated by conflicts of opinions through his good humor and congeniality—is likely to earn the approval and acceptance of others, though not their high respect.

The object of competition shifts in this process from having time made available for originating interaction with others first to receiving interaction from them that express their positive evaluation of oneself, and then from there to commanding their respect and compliance or, at least, earning

their acceptance and social support. Lack of success in the earlier competition for speaking time puts an individual at a disadvantage in the later competition for respect and leadership. Once competition has become refocused on social status, however, speaking time is no longer of central concern and there are even occasions when it is most advantageous to refrain from talking. These processes reveal again some close parallels to economic competition. Firms must compete for sales to maximize profits, and great profits are necessary to compete for a dominant position in the industry. But once a dominant position is the central focus of competitive endeavors considerations other than profitable sales must be taken into account, such as possible anti-trust action of the government. Indeed a situation may arise in which the maintenance of a firm's dominant position is best served by refraining from further increasing sales. Gary's management of United States Steel is reported to have followed such a policy of restraint, in sharp contrast to Carnegie's earlier management under which the firm achieved its dominant position.[14]

Earning superior status in a group requires not merely impressing others with outstanding abilities but actually using these abilities to make contributions to the achievement of the collective goals of the group or the individual goals of its members. It requires, for example, suggestions that advance the solution of the common problem of a discussion group or advice that helps individual colleagues in a work group to improve their performance. Having his suggestions usually followed by others is a mark of respect that raises an individual's social standing in a group, while others' social standing simultaneously suffers for two reasons, because they often follow his suggestions and because their own are rarely accepted. Initially, the high respect of the rest of the group may be sufficient reward for the contributions a group member makes, and short-term discussion groups in laboratories may never advance beyond this stage, but in the long run it is likely to prove insufficient. Since the value of a person's approval and respect is a function of his own social standing, the process of recurrently paying respect to others depreciates its value. Hence, respect often does not remain an adequate compensation for contributions that entail costs in time and effort to the one who makes them, such as assistance with complex problems. Those who benefit from such instrumental help, therefore, become obligated to reciprocate in some other way, and deferring to the wishes of the group member who supplies the help is typically the only thing the others can do to repay him. As a result of these processes in which the contributions of some come to command the compliance of others, a differentiated power structure develops.

Exchange relations become differentiated from competitive ones concurrently with the differentiation of social status that emerges in the course of competition. In rudimentary social structures, all members compete with each other for the output of each other. Thus, each group member competes with all the other members for the respect of these same other members. As status begins to become differentiated, those whose abilities win the respect of others go on to compete among themselves for positions of power and leadership, whereas those who must acknowledge inferiority by paying respect have no chance in this continuing competition. In consequence, exchange relations are' no longer identical with competitive ones. The high-status members furnish instrumental assistance to the low-status ones in exchange for their respect and compliance, which help the high-status members in their competition for a dominant position in the group. Without the contribution of the highs to the performance of collective or individual tasks, the lows would be deprived of the benefits that accrue to them from improved performance and joint achievements. Without the compliance and support of the lows, the highs cannot attain positions of power and leadership. Sometimes the members of work groups compete in their performance. If this is the case, the exchange relations between the highs and the lows that develop out of competitive relations as the result of status differentiation help both the highs in their competition for superior status and the lows in their competition for better performance.

These processes, in which competitive and exchange relations become differentiated in the course of the development of increasing status differences, are also manifest in entire communities, as the class structure of the Ifugao in the Philippines illustrates.[15] There are three broad classes, and class position depends primarily on wealth. Everybody competes for wealth as a means of improving his social status. The middle class is composed of property holders who work on the land, ranging from those with such poor land that they are continually threatened by bankruptcy, which would put them into the propertyless lower class, to those with such large holdings and surplus incomes that they have some chance to move into the upper class. In effect, families in the lower-middle class compete for staying in the middle class, while families in the upper-middle class compete for entry into the upper class, and since they are too far apart to compete, exchange relations develop between these two strata that serve the members of each in their distinct competitive struggles. Members of the upper-middle class often furnish loans, at interest, to those of the lower-middle class, which help them to retain their land and thus stay in the middle class, and which increase the wealth of the upper-middle class and thus their chances of moving into the upper class. It is evident that the situation in Western societies, though more complex, is strikingly similar.

In sum, the development of structural differentiation occurs along several different lines, partly in succession, and in part concurrently. The initial competition for participation time in newly forming groups turns into endeavors to prove oneself attractive to others and ultimately into competition for respect, power, and leadership. The group first allocates participation time differentially, then centers interaction disproportionately on some members, and successively differentiates respect, power, and dominance. Success at each step of differential allocation constitutes a competitive advantage for the next. Simultaneous with the increasing differentiation of social status, exchange relations become differentiated from competitive ones, because only those successful in the earlier competition for respect continue to compete for dominance, while the unsuccessful ones cease to compete with the successful members and instead offer compliance and support for their competition in exchange for instrumental services from them. Furthermore, role specialization develops, particularly in complex social structures, where a great variety of contributions are needed. Individuals who have been unsuccessful in their attempts to earn respect and power have incentives to find new ways of making contributions that would gain them superior status, and individuals in dominant positions have the power to assign specialized tasks to various others, both of which processes promote specialization.

A stratified system of differential status, however, involves more than differences in the respect and compliance various individuals command among others. The fact that one individual's ability and judgment are more widely respected in a group than another's means that the one is more highly esteemed than the other, but for these evaluations to crystallize into status differences requires that they be publicly acknowledged and that consensus is reached regarding them. As Homans put it: "In the early stages of the development of a group, several members may give one of their companions much social approval so that he is in fact enjoying high esteem, and yet no single member may have come to recognize what the others are doing."[16] Only the consensus that emerges among the rest of a group that the qualities of one member are worthy of high respect transforms their personal esteem of him into social status rooted in shared valuations,

which implies that newcomers would be expected to accord him high respect even before they personally have acquired a high estimation of his qualities. Public recognition of the relative respect deserved by various members of the group makes the prestige structure a social reality independent of the attitudes of specific individuals. Our behavior to the President of the United States would undoubtedly reflect the high prestige he generally commands, whatever we personally may think of him. Consensus concerning the obligation to comply with the requests of a person similarly transforms his personal power into authoritative leadership, but analysis of this problem is deferred to chapter eight.

The stratification systems of entire communities, which consist of ranked classes rather than ranked individuals, exhibit still another way in which social status is grounded in public consensus that reflects the social structure, and so do organized hierarchies of authority. Once an individual is not only accepted by the members of a social class but is also recognized by outsiders as belonging to it, and perhaps even as having more or less social standing within it, the existing social agreement on the class ranking further secures his social status by rooting it in the class structure. For sheer membership in a social class, if generally acknowledged, bestows a certain prestige upon an individual.[17] Correspondingly, the institutionalized authority in a hierarchical order gives officials some authority simply on the basis of occupying a given office, as illustrated by military rank, although this authority is usually fortified and expanded in actual processes of interaction, as we shall see. In contrast to prestige and authority structures, power structures rest not primarily on social consensus concerning the privileges or rights that must be granted to the members of various strata but on the distribution of resources with which compliance with demands can be enforced.

A person of superior status in a group, who usually commands respect as well as compliance, exerts two types of influence, only one of which should be designated properly as power to impose his will on others. The respect others have for his judgment prompts them to follow his advice. The obligations they incur by accepting his contributions to their welfare induce them to reciprocate by complying with his directives. While these constitute two types of influence a person with superior status exerts, exception may be taken to Homans' conclusion concerning them: "In both cases, whether he gives them advice they take or orders they obey, the important point is that he controls their behavior; and the fact that a new occasion may call for his advising them jointly is a nonessential detail."[18] There is a crucial distinction between following advice and following orders, and orders are not simply joint advice, although there is a mixed case that involves both joint advice and directives.

If others follow a person's advice he influences them by enabling them to do something that is to their advantage, but if they follow his orders he influences them to do something that is to his advantage. Although their interests are served in both cases, they profit directly from taking his competent advice, whereas they incur a cost by complying with his directives in order to profit from services he renders them in exchange, such as advice on their problems. The individual whose advice is accepted does not impose his will on others —if he were to advise them to do what he wants rather than what corresponds to his best judgment, his poor advice would soon be ignored—but the one whose orders are obeyed does; only the latter exercises power. Indeed, giving advice and issuing orders have opposite consequences; advising another creates obligations, while ordering him to do something uses them up, as it were, by enabling him to discharge his obligations through his compliance.[19]

The status implications of asking a person to perform a task depend largely on its effect on the imbalance of obligations. Homans conceptualized this differently: "If I ask you to do something I cannot do, I recognize you as my superior. . . . But if I ask you to do something that I can also do, and there are other valuable things I can do but you cannot, you are my inferior. . . ."[20] However, although I cannot clean house or iron or cook as well as our maid, I do not acknowledge her superiority by asking her to do it, since I pay her for it. If a person repeatedly asks another to do something that benefits himself, he becomes obligated to comply with the other's wishes, which means that he implicitly subordinates himself to the other's power by asking, *unless* he repays him for it, financially or otherwise. The assumption is that the maid's wages, given her needs, obligate her to perform services for and comply with the directives of her employer, and asking a person who is under obligation to one to do something does *not* imply subordination, or equality, for that matter.

If a group of individuals who work on a collective task regularly follow the good suggestions of one of them, thus marking him as their leader, a mixed situation exists. Carrying out his suggestions that advance their work benefits the entire group, those who accept them as well as the one who gives them. They are apt to continue to follow his lead, not only because his suggestions are respected, but also because the others become obligated to him for his contribution to their welfare, enabling him to make them accede to his wishes even when this is not to their immediate advantage. Since the leader benefits as much as the rest do from their following his good suggestions, rather than somebody else's poorer ones, the compliance his contributions earn him constitutes a surplus profit of leadership.

Status as Expendable Capital

Status can be considered as capital, which an individual can draw on to obtain benefits, which is expended in use, and which can be expanded by profitably investing it at interest. Thus, sociable intercourse tends to occur predominantly among people whose social standing is roughly equal.[21]

This is due in part to differences in style of life between social classes, which impede relaxed sociability between widely different classes, and in part to the deference owed superiors, which too hampers easy socializing. Sometimes, however, individuals are willing to put up with these discomforts, because they find it gratifying to be accepted by superiors as sociable companions. The striver is an extreme example of this tendency, although it should be noted that the individual who appears a striver is a poor one indeed, but few of us are entirely free of it. The person is rare who would not enjoy an invitation to a dinner at the White House. The fact that many people find it rewarding to associate with superiors means that those of superior status can furnish rewards, and expect a return for them, merely by associating with others of lower status.[22]

The same principle holds for power. The subordination of a person who has power over many others is more valuable than the subordination of one with little or no power, just as acceptance by a prestigeful person is usually more highly valued than acceptance by one with little prestige. The subordination of a powerful person has a multiplier effect on the power of the one to whom he submits, since it usually carries with it the subordination of those over whom he has power. This is how power hierarchies that are not formally instituted emerge. In political conventions, for example, the delegate who has the power to deliver a large block of votes is a more valuable supporter of a candidate—that is, contributes more to a candidate's power —than the one who can only offer his own vote. The process may be more subtle and thus have still wider repercussions. The powerful delegate's reputation and the weight of his support may influence other delegates who are not pledged to him and who are not directly under his power to vote for the candidate to whom he throws his support.[23] Inasmuch as a powerful person's willingness to accept a subordinate position is more valuable than that of a powerless one, the powerful can expect more rewards for doing so than the powerless.

Status, like capital, is expended in use.

An individual's prestige depends largely on his class position, that is, on the prestige of those who accept him and socialize with him as an equal. If he associates with persons of superior prestige on an egalitarian basis, this helps to raise his own, which is the reason it is rewarding to associate with prestigeful people. By the same token, an individual who regularly socializes with others of inferior prestige is in danger of being considered by the community to be on their level and, hence, of losing prestige. The rewards he can obtain from socializing with social inferiors who prize associating with him—for instance, from the deference they accord him in social interaction— entails the possible cost of losing social standing. Correspondingly, the person who submits to another's power is not only no longer his own master but also indicates to others that his strength is not as great as they might have thought, which may well encourage them to comply less strictly with his requests in the future. These losses, in addition to his submission itself, are the price he pays for using his power over subordinates to obtain benefits from a superior.

There is, however, a more direct expenditure of power. By directing others to do what he wants, a person enables them to discharge their obligations to himself for whatever services he has rendered them, thereby depleting his power over them, although continuing services to them would replenish his power. Moreover, people submit to a superior's power because all other alternatives they have are still less attractive to them. By exercising power and making demands on subordinates, a superior makes remaining under his power less attractive and alternatives to it relatively more attractive than they were before, thus decreasing his subordinates' dependence on which his power rests.

A person with a large capital can live on its interest without using up any of it, and the case of the person whose superior social status is pronounced and secure is analogous. The upper-class Brahmin can freely

associate with middle-class friends should
he find it rewarding, since his secure social
position is not in the least endangered by
doing so. But the parvenue who still seeks
to prove that he belongs to the upper class
must do so by socializing with others who
evidently do belong and thus tends to be
reluctant to risk his insecure social standing
by being seen with middle-class associates.
An interviewing study of psychiatrists (who
were generally acknowledged to be the
superior group), psychologists, and social
workers found that psychiatrists of high
status (measured by self-perceived power)
thought more highly of psychologists and
social workers and showed more interest in
associating with them than low-status
psychiatrists did.[24] Although the medical
degree makes the position of psychiatrists
immune to any threat by psychologists or
social workers, it tends to require a secure
status in the superior stratum to feel free
to express approval of, and associate with,
the members of the subordinate strata.

Superiors obtain much satisfaction from
associating with inferiors, who usually look
up to them and follow their suggestions.
The rewards that high status yields are
undoubtedly an incentive for engaging in
social intercourse, which may be a main
reason why socioeconomic status has been
consistently found to be directly correlated
with social participation, specifically, with
membership in voluntary associations,
active participation within them, and participation in discussions of various sorts.[25]
But insecure superior status, which can be
jeopardized by social contacts with others
of lower status, puts pressure on individuals
to forego these satisfactions. Only firmly
grounded social standing enables a person
to benefit from such social contacts without the risk of losing his superior status or
some of it.

The case of power is again closely parallel.
If an individual has much power over
others, which means that they are obligated
to and dependent on him for greatly needed
benefits, they will be eager to do his bidding and anticipate his wishes in order to
maintain his good will, particularly if there
are still others who compete for the benefits he supplies them. If an individual has
little power over others, however, they will
be less concerned with pleasing him, and he
may even have to remind them that they
owe it to him to follow his requests.[26] Such
reminders demonstrate to them that he
really needs the services they render him,
just as they need his services, which implies
that the relation between him and them is
not one of unequal power but one of
egalitarian exchange. The power of accu-
mulated obligations is depleted by asking
others to repay their debts, because doing
so transforms, at least in part, the power
relations into exchange relations, which
presume relative equality of status. Great
inequality of power typically obviates the
need for such reminders, and the profound
obligations on which it rests cannot be
fully repaid by the services furnished at any
one time, thus keeping the others continually indebted. The great power produced
by a large asset of obligations permits a
person to live on its interest without depleting it. Indeed, if he is willing to risk
some of it, he can increase it further.

An individual who has power over an
entire group can coordinate their activities
in the pursuit of various ends by telling
each what to do. This principle underlies
political government, formal organizations
generally, and also the organizing activities
of informal leaders. By giving orders to
others and imposing his will upon them,
the ruler or leader cashes in on some of the
obligations they owe him for whatever
services he has rendered and thus depletes
his power. Actually, coordination often
entails credit, that is, compliance with
demands in excess of obligations.[27] But if
the coordination is effective, it furthers the
achievement of some goals, that is, it brings
rewards that would not have been obtained
otherwise. These rewards may be indivisible
—a country's national strength, the trophy
of the winning team—or allocated by outside authority—the earnings of the workers
in a unit under the group incentive system.
In these cases the benefits group members
derive due to the leader's effectiveness more
than replenish his credit and their obligations

to him, which were partly used up by their compliance with his directives. If the rewards are divisible, as illustrated by the income of the firm or the political offices of the winning party, the leader can distribute some of the extra benefits resulting from his contribution to his subordinates and still maintain a surplus for himself, increasing his power over subordinates while making special profits besides, whether they are financial or the highest political office. Should his guidance prove unrewarding, however, he will lose power over followers. If the leader has used up their obligations to him and they have nothing to gain by remaining under his direction, he will even cease to be their leader. Without having money to pay employees a person cannot remain their employer; without having patronage to dispense to "ward heelers" he cannot remain their political boss; without winning some contests for the gang he cannot remain its leader. It is by taking this risk of losing some or all his power that the superior earns surplus profits, in the form of increased power and other rewards, if the chances he takes pay off.[28] A person with great power can more easily risk some of it to gain more; hence the rich in power tend to get richer in power.

Very high status, firmly rooted in large resources and in the social structure, is a signal asset, the implications of which differ from those of slight superiority qualitatively as well as quantitatively. Superior status that empowers a person to command a variety of services from others enables him to gain many advantages. But if securing these advantages requires making too stringent demands, he depletes his power and endangers his status for several reasons. The costly services he forces others to supply to him may make it profitable for them to relinquish the benefits on which his power rests in favor of the lesser benefits that can be had from another person at lesser cost. If he must often prod others into furnishing services to him, moreover, it shows them that he is dependent on them and thus reduces his power over them. Finally, his exploitation of subordinates, though they may not be able to escape from it, may draw upon him community disapproval and weaken his position in the community at large. The distinctive asset of vast power is that it obviates the need for making excessive demands that undermine power. This means not merely that individuals or groups with much power still have a great deal left after using some of it, by commanding services, but that their exercise of power usually does not deplete it at all and often actually helps them further to enhance it. For highly superior status and resources facilitate making profits by risking investments under conditions of uncertainty.

Great achievements are usually the result of having taken risks in striving for them. It is precisely when success is uncertain that it tends to be most highly valued and most generously rewarded. Knight has emphasized that profit, strictly speaking, is due to uncertainty and is the reward for assuming responsibility for uncertainty, that is, for risking investments whose return cannot be predicted with accuracy in advance.[29] People seem to prefer to be sure of the rewards they receive for the services they render and to be willing to pay a price for such security.[30] The entrepreneur provides this security by guaranteeing his employees certain rewards for their services and by assuming the responsibility for deciding on investments under conditions of uncertainty. The profits he reaps from the enterprise are his reward for having taken these risks. Leadership generally involves making decisions whose outcome is uncertain and furnishing services expected to (but not certain to) further the attainment of collective objectives. The increment in power the successful leader earns is his reward for having made these risky decisions and investments.

The larger the initial scope of a man's power, the easier it is for him to take the risks that are likely to augment his power. An important reason for this is the principle of insurance.[31] Although the outcome of any single decision may be quite uncertain, it is often possible to predict with a high degree of accuracy the statistical probability of the outcome of a large number of decisions of a given kind. For example, while it is difficult to estimate in advance whether a single employee is going to quit or not, the proportion of several thousands of employees who are likely to quit in any one year can often be predicted rather accurately on the basis of past experience. Whereas there is uncertainty concerning the single event or decision, there is virtually none concerning many events or decisions that can be grouped under a general category, since the proportion of unsuccessful ones can be predicted in advance and taken into account as part of the cost through some form of insurance. Given a knowledge of the proportion of unsuccessful outcomes—for example, warehouses annually destroyed by fire or quitting rate of experienced employees—the man with a large number of investments can completely assure himself against loss and does not operate under uncertainty at all, but this knowledge does not relieve the man with a single investment of uncertainty (unless he buys insurance from another with sufficiently large investments to provide it). The man with one investment risks it and may lose all, while the man with many investments discounts a proportionate loss and assumes, in fact, no risk. In other words, the sheer scope of a man's operations or power decreases the risk involved in assuming what is, in absolute terms, the same amount of risk. The consequent security of individuals with much power and resources makes them less responsive to social pressures but also more tolerant toward inferiors and outsiders than are those whose superior status rests on less secure foundations.

"In the South the master is not afraid to raise the slave to his own standing, because he knows that he can reduce him in a moment to the dust at his pleasure. In the North the white no longer distinctly perceives the barrier that separates him from the degraded race, and he shuns the Negro with the more pertinacity since he fears lest they should some day be confounded together."[32] If this observation of de Tocqueville does not exactly correspond to the situation any more, it is because Negroes are no longer slaves and the advances they have made in the last century, disappointingly small though they are in view of our democratic values, have made them a threat to the superior status of the whites in the South, except to those in the highest social strata, who are generally more tolerant toward Negroes than lower-class Southerners. A group's tolerant attitude toward, and encouragement of, the efforts of another group to raise its power and social standing requires that the first group's secure social status is not endangered by these efforts.[33] There is something smug about tolerance, despite best intentions, since it implicitly assert's one's own superiority.[34] Our attitudes toward opponents and deviants, too, can remain permissive only as long as we do not feel threatened by them; once their actions are experienced as a threat, we can hardly help becoming intolerant toward them, often fiercely so.

The social conditions of tolerance can be illustrated by the difference between what might be called the "psychiatric" and the "political" orientation toward offenders of basic values. The psychiatric orientation toward delinquents conceives of them as individuals with personality problems who should be helped and not punished. Although such an orientation is most appropriate for the sex deviant, the parents of children immediately threatened by his activities can rarely muster such a tolerant attitude toward him, not to speak of the parents of children who have actually been attacked by him. Hitler was undoubtedly a person who, though not insane, had serious personality defects that deserved psychiatric treatment. But the Jews, and later most of the world, could not and did not think of him as a pitiful neurotic who should be cared for but as a dangerous foe who should be crushed. The power he held to subjugate people had to be taken seriously, which made any psychiatric understanding of his maladjusted personality completely irrelevant and required instead a political orientation on him as an opponent. This extreme illustration serves to highlight the principle that for people to be tolerant of the actions of others, the latter must not have the power to subjugate them or to endanger their security; if they do, intolerance is required to avert the threat.

Intolerance is an admission of weakness that acknowledges the power of another, just as tolerance is a sign of strength that confirms the other's inferiority. Power over others is greatly desired by many men, since it is a generalized means with the aid of which a large variety of objectives can be accomplished, and since the ability to impose one's will on others often comes to be valued in its own right. A man can demonstrate his power to himself and to the world by forcing others to take his threats seriously. By treating the juvenile delinquet as a boy in need of rehabilitation, we deny his claim to being a strong man through our condescending tolerance. We cannot remain equally permissive in the face of the gangster or fascist hoodlum, who poses a more serious threat to our lives and fortunes and freedom, yet our intolerant opposition to him in attempts to suppress him serves to validate the power that he craves. The gangster's or fascist's power over followers has its source in the rewards they derive from following him, whether these are material or ideological, and their willingness to do his bidding gives him coercive power in the community. Endeavors to suppress his power, as long as they are unsuccessful, confirm and reinforce it, for they show others the apparent futility of resistance and tempt them to submit to him. Power is undeniable, and its serious threats must be opposed, but unsuccessful opposition further strengthens it.

Conclusions

Imbalances of obligations incurred in social transactions produce differences in power. Unreciprocated, recurrent benefits obligate the recipient to comply with the requests of the supplier and thus give the latter power over the former. The conditions of power are defined by the four basic alternatives to it. One method for obtaining needed benefits from a person who can furnish them is to provide services he needs in return. This raises the problems of the exchange processes that develop and of the distribution of resources in a community that governs them and is modified by them. A second possibility is to obtain the needed benefits from another source. Tracing the implications of this alternative leads to the study of competitive processes, of the exchange rates that become established in social structures, and of monopolization. Third, benefits can be secured by force. This fact calls attention to the differentiation of power in a group or society, to the organizations in which power is mobilized, and to political processes and institutions. Fourth, benefits can be renounced and the need for them can be overcome, notably when identification with profound ideals makes material satisfactions appear relatively insignificant. The implications here point toward the analysis of common values, changing needs, and the emergence of ideologies in various social situations.

The four conditions of power are circumscribed by the absence of these four alternatives. If men have insufficient resources, if no satisfactory alternatives are available to them, if they cannot use coercive force, and if their needs are pressing, a person or group who can supply benefits that meet these needs attains power over them. Under these conditions, their subordination to his power is inescapable, since he can make the fulfillment of essential needs contingent on their compliance.

Differentiation of power arises in the course of competition for scarce goods. In informal groups, the initial competition is for participation time, which is scarce, and which is needed to obtain any social reward from group membership. In communities the primitive competition is for scarce means of livelihood. At first, all members of the collectivity compete against all others, but as status differences emerge in consequence of differential success in the initial competition, the object of the competition changes, and exchange relations become differentiated from competitive ones. Those successful in the earlier stages of competition tend to compete later for dominant positions and, in communities, for movement into higher social classes, while the unsuccessful ones cannot compete with them for dominance but become their exchange partners, who receive instrumental benefits in exchange for subordination and status support. In class structures of communities, the exchange relations between members of different classes or substrata complement and support their respective competitive struggles for social status. Public recognition that a person belongs to a given stratum in the hierarchy of classes consolidates his social status.

Not all types of influence reflect power to impose one's will on another. Inducing a person to render a service by rewarding him for doing so does not involve exercising power over him, unless continuing rewards obligate him not only to furnish services but also to comply with directives. Moreover, a person whose advice others follow influences them without imposing his will on them. In contrast, the person whose orders others follow does exercise power over them. His orders prompt them to do what he wants, whereas his advice permits them to do better what they want. His advice benefits them and thus obligates them to him; it does not entail the exercise of power, though it may well be a source of power. On the other hand, their compliance with his orders benefits him and thus discharges their obligations to him; it does entail an exercise of power, and it depletes the power in the process.

Power is expended in use, but it can be invested at some risk to yield more power. A person who calls on others to discharge their obligations to him reveals his dependence on their services and weakens his power over them. But if a man has much power, he need not remind subordinates, who are eager to maintain his good will, to discharge their obligations, and he can use his power to organize their activities more effectively to achieve various objectives. The benefits that accrue to them due to his effective leadership further obligate others to him and strengthen his power over them. This increment in power is his reward for taking the risks of leadership, for leadership entails the danger of losing power should its guidance fail to bring additional rewards.

A firmly established, secure social status that is not endangered by efforts of others to improve theirs is a prerequisite for tolerant encouragement of these efforts. To be sure, democratic values demand that all people who have the opportunity to improve their social status and that they are free to organize political opposition in attempts to achieve political power. Institutional restraints are needed to protect these opportunities and freedoms, however, because groups whose social standing and power is endangered by the economic and political endeavors of others cannot be expected to look upon them with tolerant benevolence but are likely to meet these threats to themselves with intolerant opposition. It is the duty of those citizens of a democratic society who are not immediately involved in particular power struggles to help safeguard equality of opportunity and political tolerance, since the involvement of the participants makes them incapable of doing so.

THE CHICAGO area from a *purely formal standpoint*, can hardly be said to have a government at all. There are hundreds, perhaps thousands, of bodies each of which has a measure of legal authority and none of which has enough of it to carry out a course of action which other bodies oppose. Altogether, these many bodies are like a great governing committee each member of which has, in matters affecting it, an absolute veto. Moreover, the "committee" is (from a formal standpoint) one in which the members can have no communication with each other. Each legally separate body acts (from a formal standpoint) independently and without knowledge of the others. This being the case, it is of course extremely easy (from a formal standpoint) for any opponent to forestall any action. An opponent has only to find, among the countless independent bodies whose consent is required, one which can be induced to withhold consent in order to obstruct action. From a formal standpoint, virtually nothing can be done if anyone opposes—and, of course, everything is always opposed by someone—and therefore every opponent's terms must always be met if there is to be action. Every outcome must therefore be an elaborate compromise if not a stalemate.

For example, the government of Chicago proper consists of executive, legislative, and judicial bodies which are formally separate. The City Council may check the executive. The executive may check the Council. The courts may check them both.

The executive, however, is not a single body. It is several. The mayor is one. The city treasurer and the city clerk, both elected and therefore no more responsible to the mayor than he to them, are others. Schools are run by a board appointed by the mayor but not removable by him. Public housing is run by another such board, the transit authority by another, and parks by still another.

The City Council consists of the mayor and fifty aldermen, each of whom represents a ward. From a formal standpoint, the mayor can only preside, offer recommendations, and exercise a veto. Each of the aldermen has (from a formal standpoint) equal power. A majority of the Council can

24

The Structure of Influence

Edward C. Banfield

The following selections are Chapters 8 and 11 from Edward C. Banfield's study of Chicago, Political Influence *(New York: The Free Press, 1961). In these chapters Banfield attempts to explain much of the political behavior he has described by an analysis of the distribution of authority and other forms of power in Chicago. In the second of the chapters reprinted here he attempts to develop a formal model and to elaborate some hypotheses of general significance. These chapters are reprinted here with the permission of The Free Press and the author.*

check the mayor (and of course all of the other executives) in almost anything.

Cook County (from a formal standpoint) is not a government but a congeries of unrelated governing bodies. It has several executives, all of whom are elected and therefore independent of each other. (These include the president of the County Board, the sheriff, the coroner, the county clerk, the state's attorney, and the county treasurer). It has a legislative body whose fifteen members have equal authority, and it has courts of co-ordinate standing. There are, in addition, various other county governing bodies: the Zoning Board of Appeals, the Forest Preserve District, the Sanitary District, and so on. From a purely formal standpoint, all are independent, or nearly so, and thus able to check each other.

Even if all of these bodies were to agree upon a course of action (and if only the formal elements of the situation are regarded, it is hard to see how they ever could agree), they might be checked or overruled by the state of Illinois. Legally, the city is a creature of the state, and the county is an arm of the state. The state can reverse any decision that may be made by the city or county; it can even abolish them

309

both. But the state is not a single body either. It consists of several elected executives, one of whom is called governor; of two legislative bodies, a senate and a house of representatives, with ample authority to check each other and the governor at every turn (but subject also to being checked by him), and of independent courts.

This account of the formal fragmentation of authority in the Chicago area could be carried much further. What has been said should suffice, however, to make clear that a single actor—say, the mayor of Chicago—can pursue a course of action only insofar as the formal decentralization is somehow overcome by informal centralization.

By far the most important mechanism through which this is done is the political party or machine. (A "machine" is a party of a particular kind: one which relies characteristically upon the attraction of material rewards rather than enthusiasm for political principles). The Mayor of Chicago is chairman of the Cook County Democratic Committee.[1] (Although it is not necessary that the same person occupy both offices, a mayor has good opportunities to take control of the party machinery, and the head of the party has much to say about who will be nominated for mayor.)[2] As party "boss," the mayor plays the principal part in making up the "ticket." One who defies his control may be "dumped" at the next primary, and one who is loyal to him may be chosen for rapid advancement. In addition, he has a vast amount of patronage at his disposal; he can give or withhold the hundreds of jobs without which most ward committeemen could not maintain their positions. Without being dishonest himself, he can regulate the "take" of those who profit financially from their connection with politics. Having control of the police force, he can decide how rigorously laws are to be enforced.

Normally, the Cook County Board is controlled by a Democratic president much as the City Council is controlled by the mayor. Between the two Democratic political heads—the mayor and the county

president—there is a good understanding of relative power and mutual interest. Each runs his own bailiwick, but when the need for joint action arises, the mayor, who is the more powerful, is the senior partner.

The governor is normally a Republican. He is the boss of a machine whose greatest strength lies in the suburbs of Chicago and in the towns and villages downstate. His supply of patronage and other favors, although large, is not sufficient to assure him control as complete or dependable as that of the Democratic political heads. Nevertheless, he can usually—if he wishes to pay the price—control the action of the Republicans in the legislature on the few measures he deems crucial.

Although the machines go far toward overcoming the constitutional decentralization of authority, they do not overcome it entirely. There remain some obstacles which a political head may circumvent only with difficulty, and others which he may not get around at all. The latter are of three general kinds:

1) He may be checked by elected official whose co-operation is essential. In general, elected officials are subject to the discipline of the party machines and thus of the political heads; to this extent their "independence" is nominal rather than real. The machine and its head are not all-powerful, however, and there are usually "irregulars" within the party who can afford to defy its discipline. Thus, it happens sometimes that a political head is checked absolutely by an elected official of his own party. In the Exhibition Hall case, many people hoped that would happen: the state treasurer-elect, an "independent" Democrat, was expected to refuse to buy certain bonds, thus frustrating a plan which the Mayor and the Governor strongly supported.

Usually, of course, the checking is done by an elected official of the opposite party. In the most common and important case, the governor checks the mayor. Although Chicago has what is called "home rule," it is nevertheless the creature of the General Assembly.[3] The governor usually dominates the legislature, and he is always in a position to give or withhold co-operation essential to the success of many of the mayor's undertakings. Those who wish to check the mayor are therefore likely to turn to the governor for help, as was done in the Welfare Merger case.

The mayor is not entirely at the governor's mercy, however. Occasions arise when the governor needs some of the votes the mayor controls in the legislature and then the mayor can demand a *quid pro quo*. The mayor's main defense, however, is public opinion. He can arrange matters so that the governor, if he withholds co-operation, will bear the onus of "playing politics" or of obstructing a program which the voters approve. In the Chicago Transit Authority case, for example, the Governor, whatever his personal inclinations, could not afford openly to refuse collaboration with the Mayor in an effort to solve the city's transit problems. This circumstance gave the Mayor some bargaining power.

2) Courts are often impervious to the influence of the political head. The principle of the separation of powers, which assures the courts their independence, is generally respected by politicians, most of whom are lawyers. In civil cases especially, political heads rarely attempt to exercise influence. When the issue is public and essentially political (e.g., the Exhibition Hall), judges frequently take cues from the appropriate political heads. They may do so because the political head can give or withhold some advantage (like all who run for office, judges must be "slated"; but because they have long terms and the party is not likely to "dump" a judge who is endorsed by the Bar Association, they are relatively independent); more often, however, a judge accepts cues from the political head out of friendship or respect (the judge and the political head are likely to have gone to school and to have risen in politics together) or because he feels that it is right and proper to give the views of the chief executive special weight. As a rule, the political head and the judge are not in direct communication, although there is nothing to stop the political head from picking up the telephone and calling the judge if he wants to. The judge gets his cues by reading the newspapers and by discussing public affairs as other people do with friends and associates. In the Exhibition Hall case, for example, it may be taken for granted that the judges knew, without being told, where the Governor and the Mayor stood and why the proponents wanted the decision expedited.

The one sure way to remove an issue entirely from the influence of the political heads is to take it to the United States Supreme Court.

3) The political head may be checked by the voters at the polls. It goes without saying that he is checked when he is voted out of office. But there are other checks which the voters may apply. Bond issues, usually, and constitutional amendments, always, require the approval of the voters. So long as they turn down a proposal that has been placed upon the ballot, nothing can be done about it.

This element of decentralization has also been partially overcome in practice. A proposal may be put on the ballot in an off-year or a primary election when the total vote is sure to be light. The machine can then turn out enough disciplined voters to carry the day. But even so, the referendum is an important check. Some proposals would certainly be voted down even in a primary election, even in Chicago, where the machine is strongest. There are many more which could never pass a state-wide referendum.

These three obstacles—i.e., elements of decentralization which remain effective despite the enormous amount of informal centralization brought about by the machines—tend to generate civic controversies of the kind described here and, in general, to make political issues out of what otherwise would be administrative decisions. That a real possibility exists of checking the political head encourages people to try to do so. Interests that are adversely affected by the course of action he proposes endeavor to maneuver the situation so that one or another of these obstacles can be placed in his way. If they are fortunate, they may check him absolutely. But even if they do not succeed in this, they may compel him to make compromises.

When it is the mayor who is to be checked, the most readily available obstacle to place in his way is, normally, the opposition of the governor. Thus, in the Welfare Merger case, when IPAC found itself unable to get along with the city welfare commissioner, it asked the Governor to transfer the city department to the county. If the governor has decided to follow the same course of action as the mayor, some other obstacle must be found. In the Exhibition Hall case, proponents of the hall eluded one obstacle, to begin with, by securing the agreement of the Mayor and the Governor. This enabled them to secure legislation providing for the financing of the hall without the necessity of a referendum, thus eluding another obstacle. Not being able to use the Governor against the Mayor or the voters against them both, the opponents of the hall relied upon the only obstacles left to them: the courts (six suits were filed against the hall) and the independent powers of an elected official, the State Treasurer, who might defy the Mayor and the Governor.

The importance to the structure of influence of this formal decentralization of authority does not, however, rest solely upon the possibility of bringing one or more of these three obstacles into play so as to check the political head absolutely. Even where formal decentralization is entirely overcome by informal arrangements, decentralization of formal structure is of great importance. For the overcoming of it almost always represents a cost to the political head (i.e., he has to give up something, if only time and effort, to secure it), and this cost is often so great as to deter him altogether from the course of action he would otherwise pursue or to incline him to make compromises and concessions.

There are, indeed, a few circumstances in which formal decentralization can be overcome at trivial cost. Use and wont give the political head the right to issue instructions to some "independent" bodies almost as if they were a part of his office. (Even here, however, a certain amount of protocol must usually be observed by him, and this may be regarded as a cost.) But such cases are the exception. As a rule, the political head must give up something or incur some disadvantage of consequence—he must "pay"—in order to acquire for his own use the authority which the law places in other hands. For example, had he wanted to do so, it is likely that Mayor Daley could have acquired control over Ryan and the County Board in the Branch Hospital case. But to have acquired it would have been costly in one way or another. He would have had to give Ryan some juicy plum, or else he would have had to incur his enmity and run the risk of splitting the party. Even if the branch hospital matter had been very important to him, he might well have decided that the cost of acquiring control (giving up a plum or creating a split) was more than he wanted to pay. It is often the case that the "price" of acquiring control is so high that the political head decides that the transaction is out of the question. Thus, formal decentralization, even when it does not present an insuperable obstacle, may check the political head by imposing costs so high as to render action "unprofitable."

In a system in which the political head must continually "pay" to overcome formal decentralization and to acquire the authority he needs, the stock of influence in his possession cannot all be "spent" as he might wish. Some of it is "working capital." He gets his stock of influence by "buying" a bit here and a bit there from the many small "owners" who were endowed with it by the constitution-makers. Those who "sell" him their bits of influence demand something in return: jobs, favors, party preferment, *or other bits of influence*. Thus, some of the influence he has centralized he must again decentralize by trading it for other bits that he particularly needs. He may have a sizable "inventory" and many "accounts receivable," but if his "accounts payable" are large, his net position is not good. If, for example, he has control over a state senator in a certain matter, it may be because he has given the senator control over him in another matter. With regard to this other matter he may still *seem* to have control, but he does not really have it, for he has traded it.

It goes without saying that if he is to stay in business very long, the political head must, like any trader, maintain his capital and support himself while doing so. He must, in other words, employ the incentives at his disposal so as to: (a) secure the co-operation he needs to accomplish his immediate purposes (e.g., get certain bills passed and ordinances adopted), and (b) replenish the supply of incentives (and if possible increase it) so that he can accomplish other purposes on future occasions. In the CTA subsidy case, for example, it may possibly have been within the Mayor's ability to offer the Governor such incentives as to induce him to exert himself to the limit to get the subsidy bill through the legislature. But the Mayor had to consider whether this would be a wise investment of his limited stock of influence. He had to consider whether passage of the subsidy bill would so much increase his standing with an important bloc of voters or would bring him such patronage or other benefits as in the long run to make the transaction "profitable," i.e., as to yield a net gain in his influence. To be sure, on any particular occasion the Mayor might indulge himself in the luxury of "consuming" rather than "investing" influence, i.e., of using it for present purposes without regard to its replenishment. But if he consumed it for very long, he would be out of business.

It need hardly be remarked that if the political head had formal authority commensurate with requirements of the tasks he undertakes, he would not have to engage in this kind of trading. He would not have to offer jobs, favors, party preferment, and bits of influence in order to induce others to act as if they were his subordinates; they would have to act so because he could replace them if they did not.[4]

In some instances, it must be acknowledged, control acquired and used informally is more reliable in its operation than control provided by law. But this is not the general case, and it must be counted a disadvantage of informal control that its operation is, generally, highly uncertain. Here again the question is often one of "profitability." If the political head pays a high enough price, he may be able to buy the certainty of being obeyed. But there seems to be a principle of increasing costs at work: beyond a point, each increase in the probability of being obeyed costs more than the one before it, and the total cost becomes prohibitively high long before certainty is reached.

In part, the reason for this is that "debts" of influence owed to the political head, like gamblers' debts, cannot be collected in courts of law. If business is to be done in these circumstances, it must be under a set of extra-legal rules which will secure enforcement of contracts. Such rules exist. In some instances they are effective because politicians feel a moral obligation to abide by them, just as traders in the grain pit respect commitments the evidence of which is no more substantial than a raised eyebrow. In some instances they are effective because the one who "owes" influence fears his "creditor's" ability to make reprisals. When this motivation is paramount, the debtor is likely to test the influence of the creditor by acts of insubordination. This process of testing, which is a means that politicians use to get and to give information about their relative influence, has the incidental effect of introducing an element of uncertainty into the operation of the whole system of influence. Thus, for example, the governor may find that one of his leaders in the General Assembly unexpectedly refuses to carry out his wishes; the leader, it may be, has nothing more in mind than to establish the fact that he is strong enough to "buck" the governor and that, accordingly, his "price" must be raised.

Since he takes and uses authority which the constitution-makers intended to put beyond his reach, the political head is frequently excoriated in the press and elsewhere as an enemy of democracy. He is told that he ought to be ashamed of himself for being a boss, although the system of government could not possibly do the things

the critics want done unless the decentralization of authority were somehow overcome.
He must, therefore, boss while pretending
not to. Although he is well aware that the
system could not function satisfactorily if
he did not assume powers that do not
legally belong to him, he is likely to share
somewhat in the general misgivings, and he
must therefore either convince himself that
he is not bossing or else feel guilty for doing
so.[5]

To understand how the political heads
evaluate their opportunities, i.e., how they
decide the terms on which they will use
influence or allow it to be used upon them,
it is necessary to look at some salient facts
of political geography.

"Downstate" (all of Illinois outside of
Cook County) is white, Protestant, Anglo-
Saxon, rural, and normally Republican. It
elects the governor (a Democrat has held
the office in only 16 of the last 58 years), and
it controls the General Assembly. Under a
recent reapportiontment, the Senate is safely
downstate and Republican; a narrow
majority of the House may be from Cook
County, but some of the Cook County
representatives are sure to be Republicans,
and some downstate Democrats are almost
sure to vote with the Republicans. Downstate hates and fears Chicago, which it regards as an alien land.

Chicago is heavily Democratic. The
Democratic heartland is the slums and
semi-slums of the inner city; here, in wards
which are predominantly Negro, Italian,
Polish, Lithuanian, or Irish, and (except for
the Negroes) almost entirely Catholic, the
machine gets the hard core of its support.
The lower the average income and the less
average education, the more reliably Democratic is the ward.

The vote is less Democratic as one moves
outward from the center of the city. Some
of the outlying wards are usually Republican. So are most of the "country
towns" (that part of Cook County which
lies outside Chicago); for the most part, the
suburbanites of the "country towns" are
white, Protestant, and middle-class. Their

affinity is with downstate rather than the
inner city.

The inner city wards are so populous and
so heavily Democratic that they can usually
offset the Republican vote of the outlying
wards. In the future, the ascendancy of the
inner city wards is likely to be even more
complete. White, middle-class families are
moving to the suburbs, and their places are
being taken by Negroes and poor whites
from the South. Since the newcomers are
almost all Democrats, and since many of
those who leave are either Republicans or
upward mobile types likely to become
Republican, the proportion of Democrats
in the inner city is increasing.

One might expect, then, that a mayor of
Chicago would make the maintenance of the
Democratic machine his most important
business. So long as he controls the machine
and it controls primary elections in the
inner wards, he is invincible. And, of
course, the way to maintain the machine is
to pass out "gravy" with a generous hand
—to give jobs, favors, and opportunities for
graft and bribery to those who can deliver
votes in the primaries.

This is, in fact, the strategy followed by
the bosses of the most powerful machine
wards.

It is not, however, the strategy of the
mayor. He is normally the chairman of the
county Democratic committee and therefore the leading figure in the party in
Illinois and one of its leading figures
nationally. Consequently, it is not enough
for him merely to maintain himself in office
in Chicago. He must take a wider view. He
must carry the county and, if possible, the
state, and he must contribute all that he can
to the success and prestige of the party
nationally. When the interests of the party
on the larger scene conflict with its interests
in the inner city of Chicago, the interests of
the party in the inner city must usually be
sacrificed.

As the table shows, to win a county-wide
election a heavy vote in the inner city wards
is not enough. There must also be a fairly
strong Democratic vote in the outlying
wards and in the suburban "country
towns." The voters in these places are not
in the habit of doing what the precinct

captains tell them to do; their incomes are generally high enough, and their positions in society secure enough, to make them indifferent to the petty favors and advantages the machine has to offer. Many of them even seem to have absorbed the idea that "independence," i.e., splitting the ticket, is a mark of middle-class sophistication. To get the vote it needs from these outlying areas, the Democratic party must appear not as a "machine" but as a "force for clean and progressive government." To do this it must offer "blue-ribbon" candidates, and it must give the city and county the kind of administration that will win the approval of the press and of "good government" forces generally. ("Good government" is some kind of a mixture—the proportions vary greatly from context to context—of the following principal ingredients: (a) "reform" of the old-fashioned kind, i.e., the suppression of vice, crime, and political corruption; (b) "efficiency" in the sense of doing what public administration "experts" recommend with respect to organization structure and "house-keeping" functions like budgeting and personnel management; (c) following "progressive" policies in the fields of housing, planning, race relations, and welfare; and (d) executing big projects —airports and exhibition halls, for example—to boost the size, business, and repute of the city.)

The preference of the outlying wards and "country towns" for good government has for a good many years been a force which the inner city machine has had to take into

account. Its importance, moreover, is growing every year. In part, this is because the whole population—and especially that of the outlying wards and "country towns"— is becoming more discriminating in its voting behavior. In part, also, it is because the numerical strength of the outlying areas is growing while that of the inner city remains approximately the same.

In this situation, a rational county Democratic leader will be less attentive to the inner city wards, whose vote he can count on, than to the outlying areas, whose independence is a danger. His strategy in dealing with these outlying areas is clear: he must help his party live down its reputation as a "corrupt machine" and establish a new one as the honest and energetic servant of the people. The welfare of the suburbs must be his special concern; he must show the suburbanites that they have nothing to fear and much to hope for from the Democratic organization in the central city.

By the same token, a rational Republican leader will endeavor to keep alive the old image of the "boss-ridden" and "crooked" machine. He will do his best to frighten suburbanites and downstaters with stories of the growth and spread of the machine and of its designs on them.

These strategies are the ones the Democratic and Republican political heads do, in fact, follow. Mayor Daley, whose slogan

Relative Importance in the Cook County Electorate of Inner City Wards of Chicago, Outlying Wards of Chicago, and "Country Towns"

	Population (in thousands)		Per Cent Change	Per Cent Contributed to County Democratic Vote	
	1950	1960*		1948	1956
18 Inner City Wards	1,257	1,291	3	37	31
Outlying Wards (Rest of Chicago)	2,364	2,616	11	50	51
"Country Towns" (Suburbs)	888	1,532	73	13	18
Total Cook County	4,509	5,439	20	100	100

*Estimate

is "good government is good politics and
good politics is good government," has
made it clear that he will not tolerate corruption in office and has kept a very tight rein
on gambling, prostitution, and other organized crime. At the same time, he has in-
augurated many reforms: he established an
executive budget, introduced the perform-
ance-type budget, passed a performance
zoning ordinance and housing code, extended
the merit system, established a centralized
purchasing system under a respected administrator, took control over contracts
from the City Council, and transferred
authority to issue zoning variation permits
from the City Council to a Zoning Board of
Appeals. His policy toward the suburbs has
been sympathetic and generous: through
James Downs, the highly respected businessman who is his consultant on housing
and planning, he has offered them the
assistance of the city-planning department
and of such other technicians as might help
with their transportation, water, drainage,
and other problems. In his campaign for re-
election in 1958, the Mayor presented himself as an efficient and non-partisan administrator. His principal piece of campaign
literature did not so much as mention the
Democratic party or the Democratic slate.

The Republicans have also followed a
rational strategy. They have tried to paint
the Mayor as a "boss" and the Democratic
organization as a corrupt and rapacious
"machine." In the 1958 election, for example, Daley was dubbed Dictator Dick,
and the Republican organizations distributed buttons marked "S.O.S."—"Save Our
Suburbs from the Morrison Hotel Gang"
(the Morrison Hotel is Democratic head-
quarters in Chicago). Some buttons showed
the Democratic machine as an octopus
reaching out to grasp the unprotected suburbs.

These and other antagonisms put adoption of any plan of metropolitan area
organization out of the question. Because of
their strength in the outlying wards and in
the suburbs the Republicans would have a
good chance of controlling a metropolitan

area government. But in order to avail
themselves of the chance, they would have
to relinquish their present control of most
of the suburbs. For if the whole metropolitan area were, so to speak, put in the
same pot, the Democrats might now and
then win the whole pot, and even when they
could not win it they could offer a troublesome and expensive contest. Therefore,
although the bolder Republicans and the
Republicans whose interests are mainly
metropolitan favor proposals for putting
one or more functions on an area-wide
basis, the more timid ones and those whose
interests are in particular "safe" suburbs
are opposed to it. With the Democrats the
situation is similar. Mayor Daley would
probably be glad to take his chances with
the electorate of the metropolitan area. But
the leading ward committeemen of Chicago
much prefer certain success in the central
city to occasional success in the metropolitan area.

The central city-suburban cleavage is the
fundamental fact of party politics in the
metropolitan area. But the cleavage is not
simply a party one. As the Welfare Merger,
Transit Authority, and Chicago Campus
cases show, party differences reflect differences of interest and outlook that are deep-
seated and pervasive.[6]

It will be seen that the influence of the
mayor depends largely upon his being
"boss" of the party in the county and that
this in turn depends upon his ability to maintain the inner city machine while attracting
support from the "good government" forces
in the outlying wards and suburbs. In short,
the mayor must bring the machine and the
independents into a working alliance.

To become the county boss, one need
only have the backing of the principal ward
bosses of the inner city. There are 80 members of the county committee, 50 from the
central city and 30 from the "country
towns," and their votes are weighed according to the number of Democratic votes cast
in each district in the previous general
election. The inner city wards are therefore
in a decided majority. These are grouped
into ethnic blocs each of which has its own
boss: there is a bloc of Negro wards under
the control of Congressman William L.

Dawson, a bloc of Italian wards under an Italian leader, a bloc of Polish wards under a Polish leader, and certain mixed wards under Irish leaders. Four or five of the most powerful bloc leaders, together with the president of the County Board, can, by agreeing among themselves, choose the county chairman.

Left to themselves, the bloc bosses would doubtless prefer someone who would not trouble them with reform. They realize, however, that the voters in the outlying areas will not leave them to themselves and that, unless the machine's reputation is improved, it will be swept out of existence altogether. They accept, therefore—although, no doubt, as a necessary evil and probably without fully realizing the extent of the evil—the need of a leader who will make such reforms as will maintain the organization.

In choosing a leader, the bloc bosses look for someone whose identifications are with the inner city wards (he has to be a Catholic, of course, and one whom ward politicians will feel is "their kind"), whose "nationality" will not disturb the balance between the Italians and the Poles (this virtually means that he must be Irish), who knows the workings of the organization from long experience in it and who is felt to have "earned" his promotion, who has backers with money to put up for campaign expenses (for it will be assumed that the county chairman will have himself nominated for office), who is perfectly "clean" and has a creditable record of public service, and who has demonstrated sufficient vigor, force, and shrewdness to maintain the organization and lead it to victory at the polls.

Once he has taken charge of the machine, a new leader need pay very little attention to the ward bosses who selected him. If he can win elections, he is indispensable to them. Moreover, possession of office—of the county chairmanship and the mayoralty —gives him legal powers (patronage, slate-making, and control of city services, including police) which make the ward bosses dependent upon him. Without them to hold the ladder, he could not climb into his position. But once he is in it, they cannot

compel him to throw something down to them.

He is likely, therefore, to prove a disappointment to them and a pleasant surprise to the friends of good government. The bloc bosses need him more than he needs them. They want "gravy" to pass out to their henchmen. But he is a county, state, and national leader, and as such his task is to limit or suppress the abuses upon which they fatten. To win the respect and confidence of the independent voters in the outlying wards and the suburbs, he must do the things that will hurt the bosses most.

The requirements of his role as a leader who must win the support of the independent voters are enough to account for his zeal to show himself honest and public-spirited. But it is likely that another circumstance will be working in the same direction. Ethnic pride may swell strongly in him and make him want to show the skeptics and the snobs that a man from the wrong side of the tracks can be as much a statesman as anyone from an "old family" or an Ivy League college.[7]

The political head is not likely to take a lively interest in the content of policy or to be specially gifted in the development of ideas or in their exposition. If ideas and the content of policy interested him much, or if he were ideologically-minded, he would not have made his career in the machine, for the machine is entirely without interest in such matters. Similarly, he is not likely to be a vivid public personality, to be eloquent, or to have a flair for the direct manipulation of masses. The qualities that make a popular or charismatic leader would tend to prevent a man from rising within the organization. The kind of leader produced by it is likely to be, above all, an executive.

Any mayor of Chicago must "do big things" in order to be counted a success. It is not enough merely to administer honestly and efficiently the routine services of local government—street cleaning, garbage collection, and the like. An administration that did only these would be counted a failure,

however well it did them. As a businessman
member of the Chicago Plan Commission
explained to an interviewer:

> The Mayor—no public official—is worth
> his salt if he isn't ambitious. That's true of
> you and everyone else. Now, what's a politi-
> cal person's stock in trade? It's government,
> of course. For a public official to just sit back
> and see that the police enforce the laws is not
> dynamic enough. I don't know that he would
> reason it out this way, but you have to get
> something with a little sex in it to get votes.
> In the old days, there were ward-heelers
> with a fistful of dollar bills. But that, even in
> Chicago, is passé.
>
> What makes a guy have civic pride? A
> worker in a factory, a cab driver? He gets
> a sense of pride in taking part in an active
> community. The Mayor's smart enough to
> realize it. Today the tendency all over the
> country is for the public officials to take the
> lead more than they did a few years ago. . . .

Wanting to do "big things" and not
caring very much which ones, the political
head will be open to suggestions. (When
Mayor Daley took office, he immediately
wrote to three or four of the city's most
prominent businessmen asking them to list
the things they thought most needed doing.)
He will be receptive, particularly, to proposals from people who are in a position to
guarantee that successful action will win a
"seal of approval" from some of the "good
government" groups. He may be impressed
by the intrinsic merit of a proposal—the
performance budget, for example—but he
will be even more impressed at the prospect
of being well regarded by the highly respectable people whose proposal it is. Taking
suggestions from the right kind of people
will help him get the support he needs in
order to win the votes of independents in
the outlying wards and suburbs.

For this reason, he will not create a strong
staff of policy advisers or a strong planning
agency. The preparation of policies and
plans will be done mainly within those
private organizations having some special
stake in the matters involved and by the
civic associations. Quite possibly, the
political head might, if he wished, assemble
a technical staff of first-rate ability and,

working closely with it, produce a plan far
superior to anything that might be done by
the private organizations and the civic
associations. But a plan made in this way
would have one fatal defect: its makers
could not supply the "seal of approval"
which is, from the political head's standpoint, its chief reason for being. On the
other hand, a plan made by the big business
organizations, the civic associations and the
newspapers, is sure to be acclaimed. From
the political head's standpoint it is sure-fire,
for the people who make it and the people
who will pass judgment upon it are the same.

Under these circumstances, the city planning department will have two main functions: (a) to advise the mayor on the technical aspects of the various alternatives put
before him by private groups, and (b) to
assemble data justifying and supporting the
privately-made proposals that the mayor
decides to "merchandise," and to prepare
maps, charts, perspective drawings, and
brochures with which to "sell" the plans
to the public.

This division of labor is illustrated in the
Fort Dearborn case. There the Mayor, not
satisfied with various private proposals that
had been made to him, instructed the head
of the City Planning Department and his
adviser on housing and planning matters,
Downs, to prepare a comprehensive plan
for the central area. The plan they prepared
was essentially a listing of the probable
outcomes of several site selection controversies then underway, and it showed remarkable agreement with the views of a
committee of big businessmen who had
made a plan for the central area on their
own. Actually, political and other circumstances had so narrowed the site possibilities
that there was little the Planning Department could do but record the results of the
battles that had been waged and—a very
important function—legitimate them by
conferring upon them an aura of technical
impartiality. ("The plan," the commissioner
of city planning told the Mayor in his
letter of transmittal, "represents the basic
thinking of the technicians.")

There are often fundamental differences
of opinion among those whose approval
the political head wants. Chicago is too

big a place, and the interests in it too diverse, for agreement to occur very often. When there is a disagreement within the "good government" forces, the rational strategy for the political head usually is to do nothing. Watchful waiting will offend no one, and to be negative when one does not have to be is (as Mayor Daley recognized in the Fort Dearborn case) bad politics. The political head is therefore inclined to let a civic controversy develop in its own way without interference from him, in the expectation that "public opinion" (the opinion of "civic leaders" and the newspapers) will "crystallize." Controversies like those described in this book serve the function of forming and preparing opinion; they are the process by which an initial diversity of views and interests is reduced to the point where a political head feels that the "community" is "behind" the project.

The political head, therefore, neither fights for a program of his own making nor endeavors to find a "solution" to the conflicts that are brought before him. Instead, he waits for the community to agree upon a project. When agreement is reached, or when the process of controversy has gone as far as it can, he ratifies the agreement and carries it into effect.

In the Branch Hospital case, for example, President Ryan had no strong personal views for or against a South Side hospital. Had he tried, he might have found a course of action satisfactory to everyone (he might, for instance, have asked the General Assembly to offer capital grants to private hospitals willing to take county patients on a non-discriminatory basis). However, he made no effort to find a "solution" to the problem. Instead, he postponed matters as long as possible by assuring the Welfare Council that it would be heard in due course. When further postponement was impossible, he appointed a committee of "civic leaders" to bring in recommendations. In these ways he managed to avoid antagonizing either the radical or the conservative Negroes and to make it appear that he was honest, impartial, and tax-minded. To be sure, the question at issue remained unsettled and had to be fought over again two years later. Eventually, however, there

might be agreement, and then Ryan would doubtless carry the agreement quickly into effect.

If this account of the structure of influence is correct, it should be possible to draw some inferences as to how the political head will respond to efforts to influence him.

It would be rational for the political head to pay a rather high "price" for newspaper support. If his only aim were to maintain himself in the machine wards of the inner city, he could afford to be indifferent to the newspapers. But he must lead his party to victory in the county and state, and to do this he must establish a good opinion both of himself and of it in the outlying wards and the suburbs. It is with the voters in these outlying areas that the newspapers can help him or hurt him. They can present him to their readers as the "boss" of a "machine" or as an honest and progressive administrator laboring mightily to make Chicago the greatest city in the world.

The behavior of the politicians seems to bear out this inference. The leaders of the heavily Democratic inner city wards—for example, Dawson, the Negro Congressman—are notoriously indifferent to criticism in the press. On the other hand, those politicians who have a county-wide constituency are very sensitive to it. In the public housing case, John J. Duffy as alderman paid no attention to the newspapers; when he decided to run for president of the Cook County Board, however, he became extremely amenable to pressure from the *Sun-Times*.[8] In the Branch Hospital case, Ryan compromised only when proponents of a South Side hospital threatened to start a newspaper campaign against the bond proposals. Mayor Daley and Governor Stratton both exerted themselves greatly in support of the Exhibition Hall, which was a *Tribune* "must."

It is to the advantage of the newspapers to harp on the faults of the boss and the "machine." The newspapers are all Republican, and of course it is "good politics" to make the Democrats look bad. Then, too, in enlarging upon the threat to civic virtue represented by the boss and his henchmen, they enlarge by implication—and sometimes expressly as well—upon the importance of their own role as guardians of that virtue. The embattled newspaper editor, fighting to save the people from crooks in office, is a popular culture hero whom the owners of newspapers, as well as the editors, would probably hate to see forgotten. Even if they were not attached, sentimentally and otherwise, to this image, they would not want their readers to forget that the mayor is the "boss" of a "machine," for their bargaining power with him rests largely upon his need for their assistance in eradicating the old image and creating a new one.

Whatever may be their reasons, the newspapers often attack the machine for doing what (as they well know) absolutely must be done in order to make a government so formally decentralized work at all. They want vast and controversial projects like the Exhibition Hall and the Fort Dearborn project pushed through at top speed, but at the same time they affect to believe that it is highly reprehensible for a party leader to impose discipline upon his followers in the General Assembly and the City Council. In general, they pretend that any departure from the formally prescribed procedures is an arrogant and probably corrupt usurpation of authority.[9]

The newspapers must be careful not to carry their attacks too far, however. It is one thing to pillory a ward boss and quite another to make an irreparable break with a political head who can give or withhold assistance in matters of great importance to the newspaper. Newspapers, no less than department stores and real estate operators, want favors from local government. Sometimes they want them for business reasons; sometimes for what they regard as public purposes. A political head who knows that he will not get a kind word from a newspaper under any circumstances is not likely to be very co-operative with it. If the newspaper wants a Fort Dearborn project or an Exhibition Hall, it must be moderate in its treatment of those in power in order not to deny them all incentive to co-operate. Violent as their Republicanism sometimes is in national matters, the Chicago papers get along well with the local Democratic political heads. The late Colonel Robert R. McCormick was on friendly personal terms with Mayor Kelly, and the *Tribune* today, although not failing in its duty to warn its readers of the evils of machine politics, sometimes praises Mayor Daley.

A Democratic political head can also be expected to pay a "price," although not a high one, for the support of the most prestigious "civil leaders." If it is known that prominent and respected men think highly of him and of his administration, something is gained toward overcoming the handicap of the machine's reputation and attracting the support that is needed in the outlying wards and the suburbs. What the most important of the "civic leaders" think influences what the civic associations do and thus what the newspapers report. Doubtless, too, the views of the more prestigious influence those of the less, and thus eventually help to shape middle-class opinion.

The number of "civic leaders" (unlike the number of newspapers) is large enough so that no one of them can ask a monopoly "price" for co-operation. Moreover, the "civic leader" (like the newspaper) wants something from the political head or expects to want something soon, and has, therefore, more incentive to get on good terms with the political head than the political head has to get on good terms with him. An overwhelming proportion of the "civic leaders" are Republican in national politics. Very few of them, however, are active in local Republican affairs, and still fewer are outspoken critics of the mayor. That Mayor Daley has conducted affairs well is not enough to explain this. There is always room for differences. Moreover, in other administrations, when there was much to criticize, the Republican "civic leaders" were not much more critical.

The influence structure that has been described is not stable. Although it has existed for many years without change, it is now moving rapidly toward a new and very different state.[10]

The principal dynamic factor is the tension between the demands for "good government" from the outlying areas and the maintenance requirements of the inner city machine. The outlying areas, as explained above, are constantly becoming more important to the success of the Democratic party in the metropolitan area. But all of the measures that will conciliate and attract the voters in these areas are in some way at the expense of the machine. In order to maintain itself in the outlying areas, the party must weaken the machine in its inner city heartland. Before long, it will have liquidated it altogether.

Even such a seemingly innocuous reform as the establishment of an information bureau in City Hall has weakened the machine. Helping a constituent find his way through the maze of local governmental organizations was one of the few favors the ward committeeman had left to give. When constituents found that they could get better service by calling the mayor's information bureau, another tie to the machine was cut. If a new tie took its place, it was the mayor himself or to the City Hall bureaucracy.

The most serious blows to the machine have been the wide-scale extension of the merit system and the partial suppression of graft and corruption. There are still plenty of incentives for people at the top of the party hierarchy to give their time and effort: if the taste for "glory," "power," and being on the "inside" is not enough, there is still much "honest graft" to be had from the sale of legal service and insurance. At the lower levels of the hierarchy the case is very different. With few patronage jobs, and with those few much depreciated in value by the high level of general employment, there are not many incentives for ward and precinct workers. It is not surprising, then, that bribes and payoffs tend to supplement the value of patronage. If putting an old uncle on the street-cleaning force is not a sufficient incentive to make the precinct worker work nowadays, then letting his brother, a policeman, take bribes from burglars may be necessary. This is an effect of inflation.

If it is to survive, the machine must tolerate a certain amount of corruption at least until such time as competent precinct captains can be induced to work from other motives than personal gain. At present, in the working-class districts at least, the other motives do not exist. Therefore the boss must—if he is to keep his organization from falling to pieces—"look the other way" to avoid seeing the inevitable corruption. If he saw it he would have to put a stop to it, and if he put a stop to it he would weaken both his personal political position and the whole structure of governmental power.

No matter whether he looks the other way or not, some corruption is inevitable in a city like Chicago. The inevitability of corruption—and therefore the inevitability of occasional exposures of corruption—is another element in the dynamics of the situation. An occasional scandal will keep the machine in ill-repute no matter what its achievements may be, and a large scandal occurring at a particular inopportune time may possibly destroy it forever.[11]

The inner city machine, then, is being dismantled bit by bit in order to improve the position of the party in the outlying areas. Its liquidation will not result in a net loss in the Democratic vote in the country; on the contrary, it is being liquidated in the expectation of gaining votes or, at least, of cutting losses below what they would be if the reforms were not made. Democrats who run for county and for state office will be the special beneficiaries of its demise, for the inner wards will almost certainly continue to be heavily Democratic, and the party, by its reforms, will have gained much credit with the "independents" and the "good government" voters in the outlying areas.

The demise of the inner city machine, however, will nevertheless produce changes throughout the entire structure of influence—changes that are probably not anticipated by reformers and that in the long run may not be pleasing to them.

To the extent that the party is weakened, other means must be found for mitigating the effects of the extreme decentralization of formal authority that is so important a feature of government in the metropolitan area and the state. Chicago, like most large cities, has in recent years strengthened the formal powers of its chief executive (the mayor now prepares the budget and has control of purchases). But despite all of the reforms that have been made and all that are likely to be made, the formal decentralization is still so great that, unless it is somehow overcome by informal arrangements, the government cannot function effectively. When the mayor ceases to be a boss, he will not have power to run the city as it should be run, unless—a very unlikely possibility—fundamental changes are made in the constitution. In all probability, his loss of informal control will weaken the city government disastrously.

This weakening will both provoke civic controversies of the kind described here and prevent them from being settled. When every interest has a real chance of affecting an outcome by asserting itself vigorously, incitement to controversy is strong. When there is a very powerful political head, interests may make representations but they cannot bring *pressure* to bear (for the very powerful political head is impervious to pressure). Under the circumstances, the interests will accept, without challenge, decisions that they would contest bitterly if there were any chance of success. In the absence of a strong political head, the limitless opportunities for obstruction inherent in the system of decentralized formal authority will be used to the full. No decision will ever go unchallenged, and contests will often be fought to the draw because (as the Chicago Campus case suggests), with no strong political head to intervene, each side can check the others.

To the extent that the machine is weakened, the mayor will have to depend upon other means to get the heavy vote he needs from the inner city wards. There are two possibilities:

1) Voluntary associations—e.g., labor unions, organizations of businessmen, churches—may enter politics actively, using their resources to influence primary elections more or less as the machine does now. This, of course, would mean city administrations dominated by "labor" or "business," and probably sudden shifts back and forth between the two.

2) The mayor may make his appeal directly to the mass of voters. In this event —the more likely of the two—his power would depend ultimately upon his ability to manipulate a mass audience by television. If he appealed to the mass taste, perhaps by being "handsome," "folksy," or "colorful," he might have as much success with the voters as the machine ever had.[12] For such a candidate, one of the best formulas for success (but by no means the only one, of course) would be to appeal to ethnic pride and prejudice while at the same time distributing welfare services with a lavish hand.

Whether manipulating the inner city voter through television by appeals to ethnic pride is morally better than manipulating him through precinct captains with petty favors and phoney "friendship" may well be doubted. Certainly, there are dangers in "personality" politics, especially in a city highly charged with racial antagonisms. Relying as it has on its ability to buy the voter's support, the machine has never found it necessary to exploit these antagonisms. But a candidate who has no favors to give will have to deal with "issues," and one of these is likely to be race. The machine, moreover, must, like any organization, be preoccupied with its own maintenance and, therefore, with reconciling and harmonizing conflicting tendencies and with checking and subordinating extreme and erratic movements. The "personality" candidate will probably be a good deal freer to follow where the impulses of his mass audience lead.

Such a candidate will be constrained in one important way, however. He will require a very large campaign fund. (The boss pays for his campaign in part by promising his supporters an "in" at City Hall, but the "personality" must have cash for television time.) He will therefore be subject to the influence of large contributors. This may discourage him from some forms of demagoguery, but it will leave him little discretion in the matters that are of most interest to his backers. The boss has an extraordinary amount of discretion in important matters because his position depends upon doing petty favors for a large number of people. The "personality" candidates will have to do big favors for the big organizations—labor as well as business, perhaps—which alone can give the large sums required.

The difference between machine and "personality" politics is well illustrated by the Negro communities of Chicago and New York.[13] Negro political life in Chicago is dominated by an old-fashioned boss, Congressman William L. Dawson, who is not only extremely energetic in doing small favors for his constituents and in seeing to it that his precinct workers are "taken care of" but also quite indifferent to issues and principles, including those of special importance to the race. Dawson seldom speaks in Congress or from a platform, and when he does he never raises racial issues when he can avoid it. On some notable occasions, when others have raised racial issues, he has emphatically and publicly opposed the "race" position. In New York, an opposite style prevails. There, the leading Negro politician is Congressman Adam Clayton Powell, who has no organization to speak of (he is pastor of a large church) and who addresses the voters directly. Powell, unlike Dawson, is interested in nothing but race and never takes a position which is not an extreme "race" one. He is a vivid personality, an eloquent speaker, and an uncompromising rabble-rouser.

Chicago's influence structure has been formed to a large extent by the machine: the machine has been the dominant institution to which subsidiary ones have had to adjust. With its demise, the adaptations these subsidiary institutions have made will be obsolete, and the new ones will have to be made.

This also can be illustrated by reference to Negro politics. The Dawson machine exists because the larger Democratic machine brought it into being and sustains it with patronage. (If Tammany Hall were strong in New York, a Negro organization

leader would probably soon displace Powell.) And because the Dawson machine exists, other institutions within the Negro community must take it into account and act accordingly. The NAACP, for example, is "practical" in its approach because Dawson arranged for the defeat of a president who was too "radical." The *Defender*, the Negro newspaper, is "reasonable" because Dawson helped its owner get credit. Conservatives like Robert E. Taylor[14] and Theophilus M. Mann (the Branch Hospital case) "represent" the Negro community in white-dominated organizations partly because they are acceptable to Dawson and his organization. Potential leaders know that anyone who wants recognition or who wants to achieve concrete gains must come to terms with the organization and must work through it. A Negro physician who is temperamentally a "race man" and an aggressive leader told an interviewer: "Now in Wisconsin, where I have a farm, I might very well be a Republican. You have to support the person who can get things done for you, and if the Republicans have the power then you have to be a Republican. But I can't see being anything but a Democrat in Chicago. I've never been anything but one here . . . . "

The influence of the machine on the Negro community is a special case of a more general phenomenon. The form and content of white politics, too, is affected by the presence of the machine. It is reasonable, then, to suppose that the demise of the machine and its eventual replacement by something else will produce a set of adjustments throughout the influence structure and that these will give rise to a different style of politics. If the new style were sure to be one in which every citizen's convictions on matters of principle were taken equally into account, no believer in democracy could doubt the desirability of the change. The alternative, however, is not that. Whether, in the long run, "personality" politics will be preferable to machine politics—whether the Powell style will be preferable to the Dawson style—is a question which each person may judge according to his own ideas of what is good and of what is probable. Where the electorate is largely middle-class, as it is in the outlying wards of the city and in the suburbs, it is reasonable to expect that voters will continue to be more discriminating in their choices and more exacting in their demands. In such places, the choice does not necessarily lie between "personality" and machine politics. In the slums of the inner city, however, the case is different; there it is likely to be many years before democracy, in something approaching the classical sense, can be made to work. Perhaps, in the final analysis, the Chicago machine should be judged by how well it facilitates the transition from itself to something better. By this standard, there is certainly much to be said against it. But here, too, the machine must be judged against real, not ideal, alternatives. If this is done, the case seems by no means clear.

In earlier chapters, attention was centered upon the extreme formal decentralization of authority which is so striking a feature of the Chicago political system.[1] This formal decentralization, it was pointed out, must somehow be overcome by an informal centralization before anything can be done. The case studies may therefore be read as accounts of how informal centralization is achieved, or, more precisely, how it is attempted. The paradigm is as follows: the actions of many persons, each of whom has independent authority, must be concerted for a proposal to be adopted; the proponents of the proposal try to concert these actions by exercising influence—by persuading, deceiving, inveigling, rewarding, punishing, and otherwise inducing; meanwhile the opponents exercise influence either to prevent the actions from being concerted or to concert them in behalf of some alternative proposal which they prefer.

In this chapter, this simple conceptual scheme is elaborated into a formal model having application to all situations in which the activity of two or more actors, each of whom is free to give or withhold his activity, is to be concerted. Although intended primarily to describe politics in a metropolitan area, the model treats what Barnard and some others make the defining characteristic of all organization, namely, the conscious concerting of action to achieve a purpose.

It will be seen that the frame of reference, the principal concepts, and the basic assumptions and hypotheses about relations among concepts (approximately the first three-fourths of the chapter) are all based upon the empirical findings of the earlier chapters. These empirically-grounded assumptions and hypotheses are not "proved" by the data of these chapters (strictly speaking, they could only be disproved), but the data do not contradict them and they give some support to some of them. Some additional hypotheses (presented in the remaining fourth of this chapter) are derived by logical deduction from the empirically-grounded ones which constitute the basic framework of the model. If when tested—and some of them cannot be

---

25

Concerting Action by Influence

Edward C. Banfield

---

tested by any data in this volume—these derived hypotheses prove false, doubt will be cast upon the factual premises from which they were deduced. Thus the model is both a way of generating hypotheses (for some of the derived hypotheses could not possibly have been suggested by the data and others would probably have been overlooked if attention had not been turned in the right directions by the model) and of testing the basic assumptions and hypotheses upon which it is built. Some of these assumptions and hypotheses cannot be tested directly: disproving what is logically implied by them is the only way of disproving them; here the model is particularly useful.

To explain to the reader what support the findings of this volume give each of the premises of the model and how far each of the logically derived hypotheses accords with the evidence would involve much repetition and would get in the way of the explication of the model itself. It is left to the reader, therefore, to decide for himself how far the data of this and other studies fit the assumptions and hypotheses. References in this chapter to the case studies are intended only to illustrate the meaning of statements, not to supply evidence of the truth of them.

The frame of reference, then, is one in which a proposal is to be adopted or not adopted. In Chicago, proposals arise, proximately if not ultimately, from the maintenance and enhancement needs of large formal organizations. This fact, however, need not enter into the model: it is enough for present purposes that a proposal exists

325

and that it is to be adopted or not adopted. Performance of a specified set of actions by specified actors, or by a specified number of, or proportions of, the actors who constitute a specified group,[2] constitutes *adoption*, i.e., adoption is defined as the performance by these actors of these actions, which will be called *requisite* actions. (In the Branch Hospital dispute, for example, the casting of affirmative votes by a majority of the county board and by a majority of voters in a referendum were the requisite actions.) An actor who can perform a requisite action has *authority* over the action. He may perform it or not as he likes, or, in the language to be used here, he may *give* or *withhold* it from the system of activity being concerted toward adoption of the proposal.

An actor may, if he chooses, place himself under the control of another, either of one who has authority or of one who has not. One actor is under another's *control* when he gives or withholds action at the other's direction, i.e., becomes the other's agent. (The Democratic majority of the County Board gave and withheld its vote according to instructions from Ryan; it was therefore under his control.)

Control may be pyramided. That is, an actor who has authority may accept control by a second actor, who in turn accepts control by a third, who in turn accepts control by a fourth, and so on. (The Cook County Democrats in the legislature were controlled by Senator Lynch, who was himself controlled by Mayor Daley.) Such a situation is represented in Diagram 1.

When, as in Diagram 1, all requisite actions are under the control of a single actor, control is *centralized*. Centralization decreases as the number of requisite actions under separate control increases. Thus if L were to lose control of a, there would be a decrease in centralization, and if D were to lose control of 8, there would be a further decrease.

In any situation there may be (but not always are) actors who cannot be controlled. These will be called *autonomous*. (A judge who bases his decisions solely upon the law is autonomous; so is a voter who votes on principle rather than in return for favors.) An autonomous actor may or may not take a position with respect to a proposal.[3]

There is no way of knowing in advance whether an autonomous actor will give or withhold his action.

Unless control over all controllable actors is centralized and unless all autonomous actors give the requisite actions under their control (either by affirmative action or by their failure to withhold them), a proposal cannot be adopted. Adoption (by definition) is constituted by the contribution of the entire set of requisite actions.

It follows that whether a system of activity can be concerted for the adoption of a proposal always remains uncertain until it has been discovered whether there are autonomous actors in the situation and, if there are, whether they will give their activity. (In the Chicago Transit Authority case it turned out, contrary to the general expectation, that the Governor's chief legislative leaders were—if their story be believed—autonomous in that matter; they withheld their activity, and the subsidy

Diagram 1.

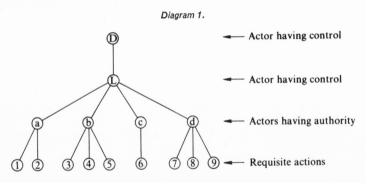

— Actor having control

— Actor having control

— Actors having authority

— Requisite actions

proposal failed of adoption. In the Exhibition Hall case, on the other hand, the courts, which presumably were autonomous upheld the Authority—"gave their activity"—and the proposal was adopted.)

Essentially, then, the adoption of a proposal may be viewed as a process in which: (a) there exists some initial distribution of authority, which (b) is overcome by (i) the creation of a centralized system of control, and, if there are any autonomous actors in the situation, by (ii) contributions of activity from all autonomous actors.

If we think not of a single proposal but of a flow of them, we may describe two stages by which the system of control comes into being. In the first stage there occurs a partial centralization, which is stable from proposal to proposal, and in the second, centralization is completed (or not completed) by the laying down of *ad hoc* lines of control.

1) When two or more actors come under the control of another on a continuing basis, i.e., from proposal to proposal, a *structure* of control exists. (Thus, for example, the Mayor's control of the city council, the Governor's control of the legislature, and a newspaper's control of "civic leadership" constitute structures, since they exist with respect to all proposals in a series.)

Centralization of control therefore necessitates a linkage of structures where structures exist. In the situation presented in Diagram 2, some requisite actions are controlled on a continuing basis by A (the mayor), others by B (the governor), others by C (the president of the county board), and still others by D (a newspaper). Control is thus partially centralized in four structures, and a proposal may be adopted if the action of the four actors (A, B, C, and D) who control the structures can be concerted.

2) In the second stage of centralization, the remaining elements of decentralization

must be overcome by the creation of *ad hoc* lines of control. In other words, structures must be linked by control relationships established to secure adoption of a particular proposal (when structures are linked on a continuing basis they constitute, by definition, a single larger structure); this in a given case may involve the laying down of many *ad hoc* lines of control or of few. If, for example, in the situation presented in Diagram 3 the newspaper (D) were to establish control with respect to a particular matter (an exhibition hall, let us say) over the three political heads (A, B, and C) and thus over the structures they control, control would thus have been centralized by the laying down of three *ad hoc* lines of control.

There must always be at least one *ad hoc* relationship in a centralized system of control. This is because sets of requisite actions, although they may be nearly the same from proposal to proposal, cannot be exactly the same. (If they were, one centralized structure of control would suffice for the adoption of all proposals, and the problem under discussion here would cease to exist.)

Control over an actor may be secured only by an exercise of power. Or, to say the same thing in another way, *power* is the ability to establish control.[4] For the purposes of the model, it is not useful to distinguish whether power rests upon ability to persuade by logical argument, to offer material reward, or something else.

No actor—except, of course, an autonomous one—ever gives a requisite action unless control over him has first been established by an exercise of power. That is to say, the actor must be persuaded, deceived, bribed, or otherwise induced to accept control, or else he will not give the requisite actions.

Diagram 2.

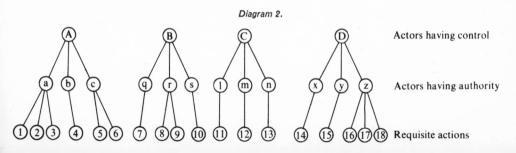

A — Actors having control

a b c q r s l m n x y z — Actors having authority

① ② ③ ④ ⑤ ⑥ ⑦ ⑧ ⑨ ⑩ ⑪ ⑫ ⑬ ⑭ ⑮ ⑯ ⑰ ⑱ — Requisite actions

An actor has a limited stock of power which he gives up piecemeal, or "spends." His power is like capital: he can either "consume" it or "invest" it.[5] If he consumes it, it is "used up," and he does not have it any more. To say, then, that a certain actor could by exercising all of his power achieve a certain effect is seldom much to the point. For there are likely to be circumstances— especially the need to maintain a stock of power for use on future occasions—which prevent him from exercising all of it. (In the Chicago Transit Authority case, for example, the Governor probably could have induced his legislative leaders to support the subsidy proposal by offering them large favors in return. But he had to think of the other things he could do with the same expenditure of his limited stock of influence —other items of his legislative program that he could get adopted, for example—, and he may have concluded that he could not afford to pass the subsidy proposal, even though it was within his ability to do so.)

Every actor seeks to maintain or increase his stock of power. That is, capital is always "invested," never "consumed." An actor exercises power only when he thinks doing so will improve his net power position (he may, of course, invest to minimize losses); when there are alternative investment possibilities, he always chooses the one he thinks will be most profitable.

To maintain control of a structure, repeated investments of power are required. (Daley, for example, could maintain control of the City Council only by continual outlays of patronage to ward committeemen.)[6] It is not useful to try to specify in the model how frequent these outlays must be; it is enough to say that the maintenance of a structure is a continuing cost to the actor who controls it.

In making his choice of investments, an actor takes into account the uncertainty of the return as well as its probable value. Uncertainty characterizes the situation in three ways particularly:

1) It is seldom clear who controls requisite actions. (In the Chicago Campus case, for example, it was not clear whether Ryan could dispose of Miller Meadows or whether he had given control of it to the Advisory Committee.) Power may be wasted by establishing control over actors who, it turns out, do not control requisite actions. Or an actor may fail to acquire control because he guesses incorrectly either that the other does not control certain requisite actions or that the actions are not worth the price asked for them. (The Chicago Housing Authority, for example, vastly underrated the value to it of control over the leading aldermen.)[7]

2) The terms upon which control may be acquired (assuming that it may be acquired at all) are established through a process of bargaining.[8] Therefore the terms cannot be known in advance. The actor may waste power in futile efforts to acquire control, or he may spend more power than he would have to spend if he had perfect information. (There was no doubt that Mayor Daley was the key to the situation in the Fort Dearborn case, but how he could be

Diagram 3.

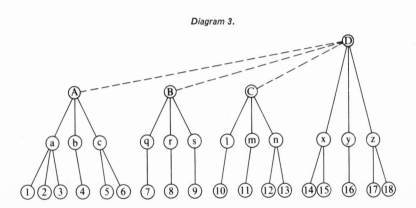

influenced and whether he could be influenced were matters of great uncertainty.)

3) These and other uncertainties (e.g., how the actor will evaluate the investment opportunities open to him) make it difficult or impossible to predict whether or not an actor will exercise power in a given situation. (The Exhibition Hall controversy, for example, was sustained for a time by the proponents' hope that the Mayor would intervene to prevent building on the lakefront.)

The matter is further complicated because there are various *kinds* of power, and an actor who will respond to one kind may not respond to another. Even if an actor does respond to a certain kind of power, a larger (i.e., costlier to the powerholder) investment of it may be required to secure control over him. In other words, the kinds of power (and this is the defining characteristic of a kind) are very imperfectly substitutable one for another; the terms of substitutability, when substitutability exists, are unique to the transaction. This, of course, introduces additional uncertainty into the situation.

For present purposes, it is useful to distinguish four kinds of power. These belong to two (cross-cutting) categories, each of which is comprised of two classes:

Category I

Class A. Power which arises from the sacrifice of a proposal. A proposal is sacrificed when it is either killed or compromised. It is *killed* when its adoption is rendered impossible, it is *compromised* when an anomaly or inconsistency is introduced into it. Compromises may occur incrementally: the proposal has, so to speak, detachable features which can be given up one at a time to "buy" control. Power of this kind will be called *proposal-costly.* (In the Branch Hospital case, Ryan was able to get the proponents of the South Side branch to withdraw their opposition to the bond issue only by dropping plans for building on the West Side and by promising to build eventually on the South Side. Thus this exercise of power depended upon a sacrifice of his

initial proposal: it was the sacrifice which generated the only power which would work in the circumstances.)

Class B. Power which arises otherwise than from the sacrifice of proposals. This kind of power, which will be called *proposal-costless*, is a residual category. It is not necessary to inquire where it comes from.

Category II

Class A. Power which makes its effect by offering gains or losses which the responding actor values for his own sake or for the sake of some small private circle belonging to him (e.g., family, friends). Power which operates in this way will be called *private-regarding.*

Class B. Power which makes its effect by offering gains or losses which the responding actor values for the sake of something (e.g., value, group, public) that transcends (although it may include) him and his small private circle. Power which operates in this way will be called *public-regarding.* (If Mayor Daley had had only public-regarding power, he could not have controlled the City Council. For the councilmen, in most instances, responded only to private-regarding power, e.g., jobs, favors, and recognition. Daley himself, on the other hand, responded to public-regarding as well as to private-regarding power: in the Fort Dearborn case, for example, considerations of the public interest had more weight with him than did private political advantage.)

In some situations a rule specifies that certain types of private-regarding power may not be exercised (offered or responded to). Violation of this rule is *corruption.* Whether in particular circumstances control can be secured corruptly is always problematic. The larger the bribe, however, the better the chance that it will succeed. Even where corruption is possible, the cost of it may be so high that the powerholder finds the investment unprofitable.

Although the several kinds of power cannot be used with perfect interchangeability, there may exist in the situation mechanisms by which one kind is linked to another. In Diagram 4, A (a civic association) has only public-regarding power and B (a mayor) will respond only to public-regarding power. But B's control of x, y, and z (councilmen) depends entirely upon private-regarding power: that is, x, y, and z will not respond to public-regarding power. Thus A is able to control x, y, and z because—and only because—B responds to one kind while exercising another. An actor (or a grouping of actors) who performs this function will be called a *connector*.

Any proposal is likely to be opposed. An opponent follows one or more of five strategies.[9]

1) He may attempt to prevent the centralization necessary for adoption of the proposal which he opposes. This he may do: (a) by discouraging a key actor from acquiring control over some requisite action (e.g., by raising the "price" of that action through competitive bidding or by offering the actor other and more profitable opportunities for the investment of his power) or (b) by himself acquiring control over a requisite action and then withholding the action. (In the Exhibition Hall case, the opponents hoped to control the newly elected State Treasurer and thus to withhold the requisite action—purchase of the Authority's bonds—over which he had authority. In the Branch Hospital case, opponents of the West Side branch threatened to withhold votes needed in a bond referendum.)

2) He may by an act of power establish *ad hoc* control over the centralized system. He may, in other words, secure control over that single actor who can give or withhold the entire set of requisite actions and may then use this control to kill the proposal. (This happens when someone persuades the governor to veto a bill.) Such a situation is represented in Diagram 5.

3) He may exercise power so as to cause autonomous actors to take positions (as, for example, by appealing to a court for an injunction). Since there is always some chance that an autonomous actor who takes a position will withhold his action, it is to the opponent's interest both to discover which actors in a situation (if any) are autonomous and to cause them to take positions.

4) He may secure adoption of an alternative proposal which will vitiate the one he opposes. To do this he must of course establish control over the set of actions requisite to the alternative. (In the Branch Hospital case, for example, one set of actors tried to centralize control on behalf of a South Side site; another set tried to centralize control on behalf of a West Side one, and still a third set—the "race men" —tried to centralize control on behalf of having no county hospital at all.)

5) He may secure adoption of a proposal changing the set of actions requisite for adoption of the proposal he opposes. This is *constitutional revision*. Ordinarily an opponent finds it more difficult to revise a constitution than to kill a particular proposal: the set of requisite actions needed for

Diagram 4.

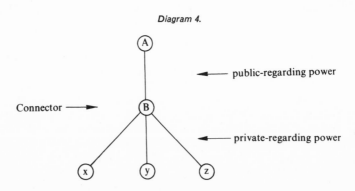

revision is usually large and difficult to centralize. But if the opponent can change the set of actions requisite for adoption, he may make adoption more difficult, or perhaps altogether impossible, either by increasing the distribution of authority or by introducing autonomous actors. (If, for example, the opponents of the Exhibition Hall could have revised the constitution to require voter approval of such expenditures, they might have rendered adoption impossible.)

From this framework of hypotheses and assumptions the following propositions may be inferred:

1) The wider the distribution of authority, the larger the stock of power that is required if proposals are to be adopted. This is not an invariant relationship: the power required to secure one requisite action from one actor may sometimes be in some sense "greater" than that required to secure all of the other requisite actions in a given set. There is, however, a presumption that the larger the number of actors over whom control must be established, the larger the stock of power must be. One can imagine a political system in which there is seldom or never enough power to overcome the decentralization of authority. Similarly, one can imagine one in which the authority is so highly centralized that little power need be exercised to secure adoptions. One would expect fewer proposals to be adopted in the first than in the second.

In Chicago, the previous chapters have shown, the distribution of authority is so wide that a large apparatus of informal power—notably the Democratic machine—is required to overcome it if anything is to be done. Mayor Daley, it was suggested,

could cease being a boss if his authority were very greatly increased. On the other hand, if the machine were dismantled without there occurring any compensating centralization of authority, the city government would be paralyzed.[10]

2) As the number of autonomous actors in a situation increases, the probability of adoptions decreases. This is so because there is some probability that an autonomous actor will choose to withhold a requisite action.

3) As the number of autonomous actors increases, control tends to become less structured. Structures of control, i.e., relationships which are stable from proposal to proposal, are expensive to maintain. The value of a structure—and thus the amount that will be invested in it—tends to decline as the outcome of the process (viz., adoption or non-adoption) becomes less and less subject to control. If, for example, it is made easier to bring a proposal before the voters or the courts (assuming these to be autonomous), the value of a political head's control of the legislature (i.e., a structure) is thereby depreciated, and his incentive to maintain control is reduced.

4) In a situation where there are good investment opportunities (e.g., wide distribution of authority, few autonomous actors or none, relatively small structures of control, scarcity of capital, little uncertainty, and many proposals), there is a tendency toward capital accumulation and investment: large numbers of actors try to enter the game and by the investment of small amounts of power to acquire more.

Diagram 5.

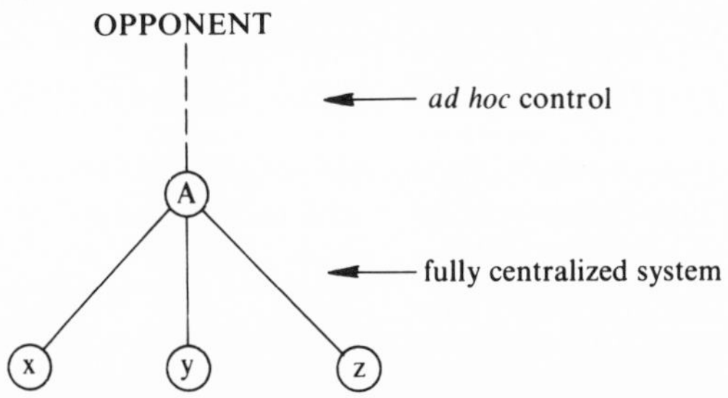

OPPONENT

◄——— *ad hoc* control

Ⓐ

◄——— fully centralized system

ⓧ   ⓨ   ⓩ

Throughout most of its history, the political system of Chicago (as contrasted with that of, say, London, where authority is highly centralized and most actors are autonomous) has favored political entrepreneurship. To be sure, Mayor Daley has in recent years created a monolithic structure of influence. But, as an earlier chapter explained, he encourages efforts to influence him because such efforts give him a sense of the intensity with which views are held and of the representativeness of the would-be influencers.[11] Thus, although he has a virtual monopoly of the final decisions, there remain strong incentives for others to get power and to bring it to bear upon him. As the case studies show, many people play hard at this game.

5) Conditions causing uncertainty (e.g., presence of autonomous actors, absence of structures, and specialization in kinds of power) tend to encourage investment by those who want to make quick gains ("speculators")[12] and to discourage investment by those who are content with relatively small and safe returns.

6) Circumstances which tend to increase the level of investment (particularly, perhaps, of speculative investment) tend also to increase the probability that any given proposal will be opposed. Opposing proposals in order to extort a payment from the proponents (e.g., perhaps a compromise on another, logically unrelated, proposal) may in some situations be a most profitable form of investment. If so, it will be one of the channels into which new investment is attracted. (In the Exhibition Hall case, Craven sued the Authority in order to improve his bargaining position with the State Department of Agriculture on another matter. Thus, presumably, the possibility of influencing the Department of Agriculture—i.e., an opportunity to make a good investment of power—had the effect of engendering opposition to the Exhibition Hall.)

7) An actor who controls a structure (i.e., whose control is maintained from proposal to proposal) can trade control over requisite actions belonging to one set (i.e., having reference to one proposal) for control over requisite actions belonging to another set (i.e., having reference to a different proposal). Control of a structure also puts an actor in a position to "borrow": he can secure control of certain actions now by pledging to give control over other (perhaps unspecified) actions at a later time. Such trading and borrowing increase the amount of power available to the actor with respect to a particular proposal, or at a particular time, over what it would be if there were no trading or borrowing. This gives him an advantage over actors who, since they do not control structures, must operate on an *ad hoc* basis.

8) The more power an actor has, the less he will be affected by uncertainty in his efforts to secure control. For the small powerholder, there may be uncertainty *whether* he can obtain the control he wants. For the large one, the uncertainty is only as to the amount of the investment that will be required.

9) The more kinds of power an actor has, the greater the probability that he can secure control in a given case. An actor who has only one kind runs the risk, no matter how much of that one kind he has, that it will prove to be the "wrong" kind: i.e., that it will not work in particular cases.

10) The probability of adoptions (and the probability that there will not be much compromise) tends to increase as the correspondence improves between the kinds of power that powerholders have at their disposal and the kinds to which actors will respond. The probability is highest where the kinds are perfectly matched.

11) Where the distribution of power is highly specialized by kind (i.e., where the actors over whom control is sought respond differentially to many kinds of power) and where the kinds of power at the disposal of powerholders do not match this distribution well, connectors perform an indispensable function. In such situations, the more connectors (up to a point) the greater the probability that proposals will be adopted (and that they will be little compromised).

12) The "economies of scale" that arise from controlling a structure and from

having a large and varied "inventory" of power to give a cumulative advantage to certain actors and thus may lead to structural centralization: i.e., oligarchy or dictatorship (oligopoly or monopoly). (Mayor Daley's power, for example, has "snowballed": having control of a few key wards, he got control of the party machinery in the county; having that, he elected himself mayor; being mayor he could give or withhold jobs, favors, and advantages of all kinds; his position thus became so preeminent that political possibilities—"investment opportunities"—are presented to him first as a matter of course.)

13) The structuring of control (i.e., creation of a stable partial centralization) may make possible adoption of proposals which could not be adopted if control were completely unstructured. A proposal which would not attract investments of power if it were necessary to construct an entirely *ad hoc* system of influence to secure its adoption may attract investment if it is possible to make use of a partial centralization which is already in existence and which will cost no more to maintain because of the added use. (Daley maintains complete control of the City Council; all but two of its members are Democrats and no Democrat has ever voted against a Daley proposal. The costs of maintaining this structure are fixed ones: to have an additional measure passed by the Council does not ordinarily cost the Mayor anything extra. If he did not maintain control on a continuing basis—if he had to establish it *de novo* for each proposal—the cost of passing an additional measure would seldom be negligible.)

14) In situations where there is a shortage of power in relation to profitable opportunities for its exercise (i.e., a shortage of investment capital), there will be a tendency to kill some proposals and to compromise others in order to increase the supply of power. It need not be assumed that powerholders will (assuming interchangeability) exhaust their stocks of proposal-costless power before using any of their proposal-costly power: whenever proposal-costless power is used up, the other—if there is any of it left—*must* be resorted to. It follows that an increase in the supply of

power may—but need not necessarily—reduce the sacrifice of proposals. (The Mayor never sacrifices proposals to get them through the City Council: in the Council he has ample proposal-costless power resting upon patronage and favors. In his dealings with the Governor, on the other hand, he does not have, or cannot use, patronage and favors. To get power to bargain with the Governor, he must therefore sacrifice proposals. If his stock of proposal-costless power were to increase—as it would, for example, if occasion arose for him to decide whether to slate a strong or a weak candidate against the Governor—it would then be possible for him to make fewer sacrifices in proposals. He might, however, choose to sacrifice them rather than to employ the other power at his disposal.)

15) When public-regarding power does not suffice to meet the needs of a system (either because there is not enough of it or because those over whom control is to be established will not respond to it), there will be a tendency to employ private-regarding power in its place. Where this is against the rule, corruption occurs (by definition). Other factors (especially the supply of and demand for public-regarding power) being held constant, corruption will tend to increase as the distribution of authority widens. (To get anything done in Chicago, numerous independent office-holders must be induced to act otherwise than as their official roles prescribe. In some cases reasonable argument based upon a conception of the public interest is a sufficient inducement. But the number who must be induced is usually large, and there are likely to be some who must be offered patronage, favors, and other bribes. Many kinds of bribes are generally considered legitimate [it is not dishonorable, for example, for a political head to endorse a legislator as the price of getting his vote][13] and most of them are technically legal. But legitimate bribes shade off by imperceptible degrees into illegitimate and illegal ones, and even though the illegality of a bribe is beyond question, it may as a practical matter be impossible to establish that it has been given. For example, a mayor may much against his inclination tacitly tolerate inefficiency and even graft by "looking the other way" because to do otherwise would destroy informal control essential to his main purposes. If he had more authority, or if the independent office-holders would respond to arguments about the public interest or to legitimate bribes, he would not find it necessary to tolerate graft.)

It will be seen that the model may be employed normatively. Any political system incorporates or exemplifies values lying along continua having the following extreme positions:

1) All proposals should be adopted (radicalism).

2) No proposal should be adopted (conservatism).

3) No proposal should be compromised (planning).

4) The distribution of authority should be very wide (checks and balances).

5) All actors would be autonomous (democracy, classical conception).

6) Only public-regarding power should be employed.

7) There should be no corruption.

Obviously these requirements cannot all be met at once. Any political system must somehow compromise the competing values; even if overwhelming importance is attached to one value, the others cannot usually be entirely neglected: some weight must be accorded to all, even though this be at the expense of the most valued. Gains in terms of some values must be weighed against losses in terms of others. (Chicago might decrease corruption, but doing so would either require centralization of authority or—since the supply of power would be less—would make adoption of proposals harder and compromise of them more frequent.) It is very difficult to judge in even an approximate way how a change in respect to one value would affect the situation with respect to all of the others. And if these functions were known, it would be even more difficult to judge what should be the terms of the compromise.

BALANCE OF power is the hoariest concept in the field of international relations. Elaborated in a variety of analyses and loaded with different meanings, it has often been praised or condemned, but has seldom been wholly rejected. In a fascinating historical account of balance-of-power concepts, Martin Wight has distinguished nine meanings of the term.[1] For purposes of theoretical analysis a tenth meaning, cast in causal terms, should be added.

Balance-of-power theory assumes that the desire for survival supplies the basic motivation of states, indicates the responses that the constraints of the system encourage, and describes the expected outcome. Beyond the survival motive, the aims of states may be wondrously varied; they may range from the ambition to conquer the world to the desire merely to be left alone. But the minimum responses of states, which are necessary to the dynamics of balance, derive from the condition of national co-existence where no external guarantee of survival exists. Perception of the peril that lies in unbalanced power encourages the behavior required for the maintenance of a balance-of-power system.

Because of the present narrow concentration of awesome power, the question arises whether the affairs of the world can any longer be conducted or understood according to the balance-of-power concept, the main theoretical prop of those traditionally called realists. Even many who share the realist concern with power question its present relevance. They do so for two reasons.

It is, in the first place, widely accepted that balance-of-power politics requires the presence of three or more states. Political thought is so historically conditioned that the balance of power as it is usually defined merely reflects the experience of the modern era. In Europe for a period of three centuries, from the Treaty of Westphalia to the Second World War, five or more great powers sometimes sought to coexist peacefully and at other times competed for mastery. The idea thus became fixed that a balance of power can exist only where the participants approximate the customary number. But something more than habit is

26

International Structure, National Force, and the Balance of World Power

Kenneth N. Waltz

In this article Kenneth Waltz, Professor of Politics at Brandeis University, discusses two important questions about political resources in international politics: What is the significance of nuclear weapons as a political resource, and what are the effects of the current pattern of distribution of those resources on other aspects of international politics? Originally published in 21 Journal of International Affairs *(1967) 215–31, it is reprinted here with the permission of that journal and the author.*

involved. Also mixed into ideas about necessary numbers is the notion that flexibility in the alignment of states is a requirement of balance-of-power politics. The existence of only two states at the summit of power precludes the possibility of international maneuver and national realignment as ways of compensating for changes in the strength of either of them. Excessive concentration of power negates the possibility of playing the politics of balance.

Second, war or the threat of war, another essential means of adjustment, is said to be of only limited utility in the nuclear age. In balances of power, of course, more is placed on the scales than mere military force. Military force has, however, served not only as the *ultima ratio* of international politics but indeed as the first and the constant one. To reduce force to being the *ultima ratio* of politics implies, as Ortega y Gasset once noted, "the previous submission of force to methods of reason."[2] Insufficient social cohesion exists among states and the instruments of international control are too weak to relegate power to the status of

335

simply the *ultima ratio*. Power cannot be separated from the purposes of those who possess it; in international politics power has appeared primarily as the power to do harm.[3] To interdict the use of force by the threat of force, to oppose force with force, to annex territory by force, to influence the policies of other states by the threat or application of force—such uses of force have always been present at least as possibilities in the relations of states. The threat to use military forces and their occasional commitment to battle have helped to regulate the relations of states, and the preponderance of power in the hands of the major states has set them apart from the others. But, it is now often said, nuclear weapons, the "best" weapons of the most powerful states, are the least usable. At the extreme, some commentators assert that military force has become obsolete. Others, more cautious in their claims, believe that the inflated cost of using military force has seriously distorted both the balance between the militarily strong states and the imbalance between the strong and the weak ones. National military power, though not rendered wholly obsolete by nuclear weapons, nevertheless must be heavily discounted. The power of the two nuclear giants, it would seem, is then seriously impaired.[4]

A weird picture of the political world is thus drawn. The constraints of balance-of-power politics still operate: each state by its own efforts fends for its rights and seeks to maintain its existence. At the same time, the operation of balance-of-power politics is strangely truncated; for one essential means of adjustment is absent, and the operation of the other is severely restricted. In the nineteenth-century liberals' vision of a world without power, force was to be banished internationally by the growing perfection of states and their consequent acceptance of each other as equals in dignity. The liberal utopia has reappeared in odd form. The limitation of power—or in extreme formulations, its abolition—is said to derive from the nuclear armament of some states; for nuclear armament makes at once for gross inequality in the power of states and for substantial equality among all states through the inability of the most powerful to use force effectively. Those who love paradox are understandably enchanted. To examine the ground upon which the supposed paradox rests is one of the main aims of this essay.

I

This first reason for believing that balance-of-power politics has ended is easy to deal with, for only its relevance, not its truth, is in question.

If the balance-of-power game is really played hard it eventuates in two participants, whether states or groupings of them. If two groupings of states have hardened or if the relation of major antagonism in the world is simply between two nations, the balance-of-power model no longer applies, according to the conventional definition. This conclusion is reached by placing heavy emphasis on the process of balancing (by realignments of states) rather than on altering power (which may depend on the efforts of each state).[5] In a two-power world, emphasis must shift from the international process of balancing to the prospect of altering power by the internal efforts of each participant.

Admittedly, the old balance-of-power model cannot be applied without modification to a world in which two states far exceed all others in the force at their disposal. Balance-of-power analysis, however, remains highly useful if the observer shifts his perspective from a concentration upon international maneuver as a mode of adjustment to an examination of national power as a means of control and national effort as a way of compensating for incipient disequilibria of power. With this shift in perspective, balance-of-power politics does not disappear; but the meaning of politics changes in a manner that can only be briefly suggested here.

In a world of three or more powers the possibility of making and breaking alliances exists. The substance of balance-of-power politics is found in the diplomacy by which alliances are made, maintained, or disrupted.

Flexibility of alignment then makes for rigidity in national strategies: a state's strategy must satisfy its partner lest that partner defect from the alliance. A comparable situation is found where political parties compete for votes by forming and reforming electoral coalitions of different economic, ethnic, religious, and regional groups. The strategies (or policies) of the parties are made so as to attract and hold voters. If it is to be an electoral success, a party's policy cannot simply be the policy that its leaders may think would be best for the country. Policy must at least partly be made for the sake of party management. Similarly in an alliance of approximately equal states, strategy is at least partly made for the sake of the alliance's cohesion. The alliance diplomacy of Europe in the years before World War I is rich in examples of this. Because the defection or defeat of a major state would have shaken the balance of power, each state was constrained to adjust its strategy and the deployment of its forces to the aims and fears of its partners. This is in sharp contrast to the current situation in NATO, where de Gaulle's disenchantment, for example, can only have mild repercussions. Though concessions to allies will sometimes be made, neither the Soviet Union nor the United States alters its strategy or changes its military dispositions simply to accommodate associated states. Both superpowers can make long-range plans and carry out their policies as best they see fit, for they need not accede to the demands of third parties. That America's strategy is not made for the sake of de Gaulle helps to explain his partial defection.

Disregarding the views of an ally makes sense only if military cooperation is relatively unimportant. This is the case in NATO, which in fact if not in form consists of unilateral guarantees by the United States to its European allies. The United States, with a preponderance of nuclear weapons and as many men in uniform as all of the Western European states combined,[6] may be able to protect her allies; they cannot possibly protect her. Because of the vast differences in the capacities of member states, the approximately equal sharing of burdens found in earlier alliance systems is

no longer conceivable. The gross inequality between the two superpowers and the members of their respective alliances makes any realignment of the latter fairly insignificant. The leader's strategy can therefore be flexible. In balance-of-power politics, old style, flexibility of alignment made for rigidity of strategy or the limitation of freedom of decision. In balance-of-power politics, new style, the obverse is true: rigidity of alignment in a two-power world makes for flexibility of strategy or the enlargement of freedom of decision.

Those who discern the demise of balance-of-power politics mistakenly identify the existence of balances of power with a particular mode of adjustment and the political means of effecting it. Balances of power tend to form so long as states desire to maintain their political identities and so long as they must rely on their own devices in striving to do so. With shrinking numbers, political practices and methods will differ; but the number of states required for the existence and perpetuation of balance-of-power politics is simply two or more, not, as is usually averred, some number larger than two.

II

The reduction in the number of major states calls for a shift in conceptual perspective. Internal effort has replaced external realignment as a means of maintaining an approximate balance of power. But the operation of a balance of power, as previously noted, has entailed the occasional use of national force as a means of international control and adjustment. Great-power status was traditionally conferred on states that could use force most handily. Is the use of force in a nuclear world so severely inhibited that balance-of-power analysis has lost most if not all of its meaning?

Four reasons are usually given in support of an affirmative answer. First, because the nuclear might of one superpower balances that of the other, their effective power is reduced to zero. Their best and most distinctive forces, the nuclear ones, are least usable. In the widely echoed words of John Herz, absolute power equals absolute impotence.[7] Second, the fear of escalation strongly inhibits even the use of conventional forces, especially by the United States or the Soviet Union. Nuclear powers must fear escalation more than other states do, for in any war that rose to the nuclear level they would be primary targets. They may, of course, still choose to commit their armies to battle, but the risks of doing so, as they themselves must realize, are higher than in the past. Third, in the nuclear age enormous military power no longer ensures effective control. The Soviet Union has not been able to control her Asian and European satellites. The United States has found it difficult to use military force for constructive purposes even against weak opponents in Southeast Asia. Political rewards have not been proportionate to the strength of the states that are militarily most powerful. Finally, the weak states of the world, having become politically aware and active, have turned world opinion into a serious restraint upon the use of force, whether in nuclear or conventional form. These four factors, it is argued, work singly and in combination to make the use of force more costly and in general to depreciate its value.

Never have great powers disposed of larger national products, and seldom in peacetime have they spent higher percentages of them on their military forces. The money so lavishly expended purchases more explosive power and more varied ways of delivering it than ever before in history. In terms of world distribution, seldom has military force been more narrowly concentrated. If military force is less useful today, the irony of history will have yet another vivid illustration. Has force indeed so depreciated as to warp and seriously weaken the effects of power in international relations? The above arguments make it seem so; they need to be re-examined. The following analysis of the use of force deals with all four arguments, though not by examining them one by one and in the order in which they are stated.

E. H. Carr long ago identified the error of believing "in the efficacy of an international public opinion," and he illustrated and explained the fallacy at length.[8] To think of world opinion as a restraint upon the military actions of states, one must believe that the strong states of the world—or for that matter the weak ones—would have used more military force and used it more often had they not anticipated their condemnation. Unless in a given instance world opinion can be defined, its source identified, and the mode of its operation discerned, such a view is not plausible. To believe in the efficacy of world opinion is to endow a non-existent agent and an indefinable force with effective restraining power. Not world opinion but national views, shaped into policies and implemented by governments, have accounted for past events in international relations. Changes that would now permit world opinion, whatever that might be, to restrict national policies would have to lie not in the operation of opinion itself but in other changes that have occurred in the world. With "world opinion," as with Adam Smith's "invisible hand," one must ask: What is the reality that the metaphor stands for? It may be that statesmen pay their respects to world opinion because they are already restrained by other considerations.

Are such considerations found, perhaps, in changes that have taken place in the nature and distribution of force itself? If the costs of using military force have lessened its value, then obeisance paid to world opinion is merely a cloak for frustration and a hypocritical show of politeness. That the use of force is unusually costly, however, is a conclusion that rests on a number of errors. One that is commonly committed is to extend to all military force the conclusion that nuclear force is unusable. After listing the changes effected by nuclear weapons, one author, for example, concludes that these changes tend to restrict "the usability and hence the political utility of national military power in various ways."[9] This may represent merely a slip of the pen; if so, it is a telling one. A clearer and more interesting form of the error is found in the argument that the two super-powers, each stalemated by the other's nuclear force, are for important political purposes effectively reduced to the power of middle-range states. The effective equality of states apparently emerges from the very condition of their gross inequality. We read, for example, that "the very change in the nature of the mobilizable potential has made its actual use in emergencies by its unhappy owners quite difficult and self-defeating. As a result, nations endowed with infinitely less can behave in a whole range of issues as if the difference in power did not matter." The conclusion is driven home— or, rather, error is compounded—by the argument that the United States thinks in "cataclysmic terms," lives in dread of all-out war, and bases its military calculations on the forces needed for the ultimate but unlikely crisis rather than on what might be needed in the less spectacular cases that are in fact more likely to occur.[10]

Absolute power equals absolute impo-tence, at least at the highest levels of force represented by the American and Soviet nuclear armories. At lesser levels of violence many states can compete as though they were substantially equal. The best weapons of the United States and the Soviet Union are useless, and the distinctive advantage of these two states is thus negated. But what about American or Soviet nuclear weapons used against minor nuclear states or against those who are entirely without nuclear weapons? Here again, it is claimed, the "best" weapon of the most powerful states turns out to be the least usable. The nation that is equipped to "retaliate massively" is not likely to find the occasion to use its capability. If amputation of an arm were the only remedy available for an infected finger, one would be tempted to hope for the best and leave the ailment untreated. The state that can move effectively only by committing the full power of its military arsenal is likely to forget the threats it has made and acquiesce in a situation formerly described as intolerable. Instruments that cannot be used to deal with small cases—

those that are moderately dangerous and damaging—remain idle until the big case arises. But then the use of major force to defend a vital interest would run the grave risk of retaliation. Under such circum-stances, the powerful are frustrated by their very strength; and although the weak do not thereby become strong, they are, it is said, nevertheless able to behave as though they were.

Such arguments are often made and have to be taken seriously. In an obvious sense, part of the contention is valid. When great powers are in a stalemate, lesser states acquire an increased freedom of movement. That this phenomenon is now noticeable tells us nothing new about the strength of the weak or the weakness of the strong. Weak states have often found opportunities for maneuver in the interstices of a balance of power. This is, however, only part of the story. To maintain both the balance and its by-product requires the continuing efforts of America and Russia. Their instincts for self-preservation call forth such efforts: the objective of both states must be to per-petuate an international stalemate as a minimum basis for the security of each of them—even if this should mean that the two big states do the work while the small ones have the fun. The margins within which the relative strengths of America and Russia may vary without destroying the stalemate are made wide by the existence of second-strike retaliatory forces, but per-missible variation is not without limit. In the years of the supposed missile gap in America's disfavor, Khrushchev became unpleasantly frisky, especially over Berlin and Cuba. The usefulness of maintaining American nuclear strength was demonstra-ted by the unfortunate consequences of its apparent diminution.

Strategic nuclear weapons deter strategic nuclear weapons (though they may also do more than that). Where each state must tend to its own security as best it can, the means adopted by one state must be geared to the efforts of others. The cost of the American nuclear establishment, maintained in peaceful readiness, is functionally comparable to the costs incurred by a government in order to maintain domestic order and provide internal security. Such expenditure is not productive in the sense that spending to build roads is, but it is not unproductive either. Its utility is obvious, and should anyone successfully argue otherwise, the consequences of accepting his argument would quickly demonstrate its falsity. Force is least visible where power is most fully and most adequately present.[11] The better ordered a society and the more competent and respected its government, the less force its policemen are required to employ. Less shooting occurs in present-day Sandusky than did on the western frontier. Similarly in international relations, states supreme in their power have to use force less often. "Non-recourse to force"—as both Eisenhower and Khrushchev seem to have realized—is the doctrine of powerful states. Powerful states need to use force less often than their weaker neighbors because the strong can more often protect their interests or work their wills in other ways—by persuasion and cajolery, by economic bargaining and bribery, by the extension of aid, or finally by posing deterrent threats. Since states with large nuclear armories do not actually "use" them, force is said to be discounted. Such reasoning is fallacious. Possession of power should not be identified with the use of force, and the usefulness of force should not be confused with its usability. To introduce such confusions into the analysis of power is comparable to saying that the police force that seldom if ever employs violence is weak or that a police force is strong only when policemen are swinging their clubs. To vary the image, it is comparable to saying that a man with large assets is not rich unless he spends little money or that a man is rich only if he spends a lot of it.

But the argument, which we should not lose sight of, is that just as the miser's money may grossly depreciate in value over the years, so the great powers' military strength has lost much of its usability. If military force is like currency that cannot be spent or money that has lost much of its worth, then is not forbearance in its use merely a way of disguising its depreciated value? Conrad von Hötzendorf, Austrian Chief of Staff prior to the First World War, looked upon military power as though it were a capital sum, useless unless invested. In his view, the investment of military force was ultimately its commitment to battle.[12] It may be permissible to reason in this way, but it makes the result of the reasoning a foregone conclusion. As Robert W. Tucker has noted, those who argue that force has lost its utility do so "in terms of its virtually uncontrolled use." But, he adds, "alter the assumption on which the argument proceeds—consider the functions served by military power so long as it is not overtly employed or employed only with restraint—and precisely the opposite conclusion may be drawn."[13]

In the reasoning of Conrad, military force is most useful at the moment of its employment in war. Depending on a country's situation, it may make much better sense to say that military force is most useful when it deters an attack, that is, when it need not be used in battle at all. When the strongest state militarily is also a status-quo power, non-use of force is a sign of its strength. Force is most useful, or best serves the interests of such a state, when it need not be used in the actual conduct of warfare. Again, the reasoning is old-fashioned. Throughout a century that ended in 1914, the British navy was powerful enough to scare off all comers, while Britain carried out occasional imperial ventures in odd parts of the world. Only as Britain's power weakened did her military forces have to be used to fight a full-scale war. By being used, her military power has surely become less useful.

Force is cheap, especially for a status-quo power, if its very existence works against its use. What does it mean then to say that the cost of using force has increased while its utility has lessened? It is highly important, indeed useful, to think in "cataclysmic terms," to live in dread of all-out war, and to base military calculations on the forces needed for the ultimate but unlikely crisis. That the United States does so, and that the Soviet Union apparently does too, makes the cataclysm less likely to occur. But not only that. Nuclear weapons deter nuclear weapons; they also serve as a means of limiting escalation. The temptation of one country to employ larger and larger amounts of force is lessened if its opponent has the ability to raise the ante. Conventional forces may be used more hesitantly than it would be in the absence of nuclear weapons because it cannot be assumed that escalation will be perfectly regulated. But force can be used with less hesitation by those states able to parry, to thrust, and to threaten at varied levels of military endeavor.

Where power is seen to be balanced, whether or not the balance is nuclear, it may seem that the resultant of opposing forces is zero. But this is misleading. The vectors of national force do not meet at a point, if only because the power of a state does not resolve into a single vector. Military force is divisible, especially for the state that can afford a lot of it. In a nuclear world, contrary to some assertions, the dialectic of inequality does not produce the effective equality of strong and weak states. Lesser states that decide to establish a nuclear arsenal by slighting their conventional forces render themselves unable to meet any threat to themselves other than the ultimate one (and that doubtfully). By way of contrast, the military doctrine of the United States, to which the organization of her forces corresponds, is one of flexible response. Great powers are strong not simply because they have nuclear weapons but also because their immense resources enable them to generate and maintain power of all types, military and other, at different technological levels.

Just as the state that refrains from applying force is said to betray its weakness, so the state that has trouble in exercising control is said to display the defectiveness of its power. In such a conclusion, the elementary error of identifying power with control is evident. Absence of control or failure to press hard to achieve it may indicate either that the would-be controller noticed that,

try as he might, he would have insufficient force of inappropriate types of force at his command; or it may indicate that he chose to make less than a maximum effort because imposition of control was not regarded as very important. One student of international relations has remarked that "though the weapons of mass destruction grow more and more ferociously efficient, the revolutionary guerrilla armed with nothing more advanced than an old rifle and a nineteenth-century political doctrine has proved the most effective means yet devised for altering the world power-balance."[14] But the revolutionary guerilla wins civil wars, not international ones, and no civil war can change the balance of power in the world unless it takes place in the United States or the Soviet Union. Enough of them have occurred since the Second World War to make the truth of this statement clear without need for further analysis. Even in China, the most populous of states, a civil war that led to a change of allegiance in the cold war did not seriously tilt the world balance.

Two states that enjoy wide margins of power over other states need worry little about changes that occur among the latter. Failure to act may then not betray the frustrations of impotence; instead it may demonstrate the serenity of power. The United States, having chosen to intervene in Vietnam, has limited the use of its military force. Because no realignment of national power in Vietnam could in itself affect the balance of power between the United States and the Soviet Union—or even noticeably alter the imbalance of power between the United States and China—the United States need not have intervened at all. Whether or not it could have safely "passed" in Southeast Asia, the American government chose not to do so; nor have its costly, long-sustained efforts brought success. If military power can be equated with control, then the United States has indeed demonstrated its weakness. The case is instructive. The People's Republic of China has not moved militarily against any country of Southeast Asia. The United States could successfully counter such a move, one would expect, by opposing military force with military force. What has worried some people and led others to sharpen their statements about the weakness of the powerful is that the United States, hard though it has tried, has been unable to put down insurrection and halt the possible spread of Communist ideology.

Here again old truths need to be brought into focus. As David Hume long ago noted, "force is always on the side of the governed."[15] The governors, being few in number, depend for the exercise of their rule upon the more or less willing assent of their subjects. If sullen disregard is the response to every command, no government can rúle. And if a country, because of internal disorder and lack of coherence, is unable to rule itself, no body of foreigners, whatever the military force at its command, can reasonably hope to do so. If Communism is the threat to Southeast Asia, then military forces are not the right means for countering it. If insurrection is the problem, then it can hardly be hoped that an alien army will be able to pacify a country that is unable to govern itself. Foreign troops, though not irrelevant to such problems, can only be of indirect help. Military force, used internationally, is a means of establishing control over a territory, not of exercising control within it. The threat of a nation to use military force, whether nuclear or conventional, is pre-eminently a means of affecting another state's external behavior, of dissuading a state from launching a career of aggression and of meeting the aggression if dissuasion should fail.

Dissuasion or deterrence is easier to accomplish than "compellence," to use an apt term invented by Thomas C. Schelling.[16] Compellence is more difficult to achieve than deterrence, and its contrivance is a more intricate affair. In Vietnam, the United States faces not merely the task of compelling a particular action but of promoting an effective political order. Those who argue from such a case that force has depreciated in value fail in their analyses to apply their own historical and political knowledge. The master builders of imperial rule, such men as Bugeaud, Galliéni, and Lyautey, played both political and military roles. In like fashion, successful counter-revolutionary efforts have been directed by such men as Templer and Magsaysay, who combined military resources with political instruments.[17] Military forces, whether domestic or foreign, are insufficient for the task of pacification, the more so if a country is rent by faction and if its people are politically engaged and active. To say that militarily strong states are feeble because they cannot easily bring order to minor states is like saying that a pneumatic hammer is weak because it is not suitable for drilling decayed teeth. It is to confuse the purpose of instruments and to confound the means of external power with the agencies of internal governance. Inability to exercise *political* control over others does not indicate *military* weakness. Strong states cannot do everything with their military forces, as Napoleon acutely realized; but they are able to do things that militarily weak states cannot do. The People's Republic of China can no more solve the problems of governance in some Latin American country than the United States can in Southeast Asia. But the United States can intervene with great military force in far quarters of the world while wielding an effective deterrent against escalation. Such action exceeds the capabilities of all but the strongest of states.

Differences in strength do matter, though not for every conceivable purpose. To deduce the weakness of the powerful from this qualifying clause is a misleading use of words. One sees in such a case as Vietnam not the *weakness* of great military power in a nuclear world but instead a clear illustration of the *limits* of military force in the world of the present as always.

III

Only a sketch, intended to be suggestive, can here be offered of the connections between the present structure of the global balance of power, the relations of states, and the use of force internationally.

Unbalanced power is a danger to weak states. It may also be a danger to strong ones. An imbalance of power, by feeding the ambition of some states to extend their control, may tempt them to dangerously adventurous activity. Safety for all states, one may then conclude, depends upon the maintenance of a balance among them. Ideally, in this view, the rough equality of states gives each of them the ability to fend for itself. Equality may then also be viewed as a morally desirable condition. Each of the states within the arena of balance will have at least a modest ability to maintain its integrity. At the same time, inequality violates one's sense of justice and leads to national resentments that are in many ways troublesome. Because inequality is inherent in the state system, however, it cannot be removed. At the pinnacle of power, only a few states coexist as approximate equals; in relation to them, other states are of lesser moment. The bothersome qualities of this inevitable inequality of states should not cause one to overlook its virtues. In an economy, in a polity, or in the world at large, extreme equality is associated with instability. To draw another domestic analogy; where individualism is extreme, where society is atomistic, and where secondary organizations are lacking, government tends either to break down into anarchy or to become highly centralized and despotic. Under conditions of extreme equality, the prospect of oscillation between those two poles was well described by de Tocqueville; it was illustrated by Hobbes; and its avoidance was earnestly sought by the authors of the *Federalist Papers*. In a collection of equals, any impulse ripples through the whole society. Lack of secondary groups with some cohesion and continuity of commitment, for example, turns elections into auctions with each party in its promises tempted to bid up the others. The presence of social and economic groups, which inevitably will not all be equal, makes for less volatility in society.

Such durable propositions of political theory are lost sight of in the argument,

frequently made, that the larger the number of consequential states the more stable the structure of world politics will be.[18] Carried to its logical conclusion, the argument must mean that perfect stability would prevail in a world in which many states exist, all of them approximate equals in power.

The analysis of the present essay leads to a different conclusion. The inequality of states, though not a guarantee of international stability, at least makes stability possible. Within the structure of world politics, the relations of states will be as variable and complex as the movements and patterns of bits of glass within a kaleidoscope. It is not very interesting to ask whether destabilizing events will occur and disruptive relations will form, because the answer must always be yes. More interesting are such questions as these: What is the likely durability of a given political structure, whether international or domestic? How does it affect the relations of states, or of groups and individuals? How do the relations of constituent units and changes within them in turn affect the political structure? Within a state, people use more violence than do governments. In the United States in 1965, 9,814 people were murdered, but only seven were executed.[19] Thus one says (with some exaggeration, since fathers still spank their children) that the state enjoys a monopoly of *legitimate* violence. Too much violence among individuals will jeopardize the political structure. In international relations it is difficult to say that any particular use of violence is illegitimate, but some states have the ability to wield more of it. Because they do, they are able both to moderate others' use of violence and to absorb possibly destabilizing changes that emanate from uses of violence that they do not or cannot control. In the spring of 1966, Secretary McNamara remarked that in the preceding eight years there had been "no less than 164 internationally significant outbreaks of violence...."[20] Of course, not only violence is at issue. To put the point in more general terms, strong structures are able to moderate and absorb destabilizing changes; weak structures succumb to them.

No political structure, whether domestic or international, can guarantee stability. The question that one must ask is not whether a given distribution of power is stable but how stable different distributions of power are likely to be. For a number of reasons, the bipolar world of the past two decades has been highly stable.[21] The two leading states have a common interest in stability: they would at least like to maintain their positions. In one respect, bipolarity is expressed as the reciprocal control of the two strongest states by each other out of their mutual antagonism. What is unpredictable in such a two-party competition is whether one party will try to eliminate the other. Nuclear forces of second-strike capacity induce an added caution. Here again force is useful, and its usefulness is reinforced in proportion as its use is forestalled. Fear of major war induces caution all round; the Soviet Union and the United States wield the means of inducing that caution.

The constraints of duopolistic competition press in one direction: duopolists eye each other warily, and each is very sensitive to the gains of the other. Working in the opposite direction, however, is the existence of the immense difference in power between the two superpowers and the states of middle or lesser rank. The condition of inequality makes it unlikely that any shifts in the alignment of states would very much help or hurt either of the two leading powers. If few changes can damage the vital interests of either of them, then both can be moderate in their responses. Not being dependent upon allies, the United States and the Soviet Union are free to design strategies in accord with their interests. Since the power actually and potentially at the disposal of each of them far exceeds that of their closest competitors, they are able to control in some measure the possibly destablizing acts of third parties or

to absorb their effects. The Americans and Russians, for example, can acquire the means of defending themselves against the nuclear assaults that the Chinese and French may be able to launch by the mid-1970's. Anti-ballistic-missile systems, useful against missiles launched in small number, are themselves anti-proliferation devices. With considerable expectation of success, states with vast economic, scientific, and technological resources can hope to counter the armaments and actions of others and to reduce their destabilizing effects.[22] The extent of the difference in national capabilities makes the bipolar structure resilient. Defection of allies and national shifts of allegiance do not decisively alter the structure. Because they do not, recalcitrant allies may be treated with indifference; they may even be effectively disciplined. Pressure can be applied to moderate the behavior of third states or to check and contain their activities. The Suez venture of Britain and France was stopped by American financial pressure. Chiang Kai-shek has been kept on a leash by denying him the means of invasion. The prospective loss of foreign aid helped to halt warfare between Pakistan and India, as did the Soviet Union's persuasion. In such ways, the wielding of great power can be useful.

The above examples illustrate hierarchical control operating in a way that often goes unnoticed because the means by which control is exercised are not institutionalized. What management there now is in international relations must be provided, singly and occasionally together, by the duopolists at the top. In certain ways, some of them suggested above, the inequality of states in a bipolar world enables the two most powerful states to develop a rich variety of controls and to follow flexible strategies in using them.

A good many statements about the obsolescence of force, the instability of international politics, and the disappearance of the bipolar order are made because no distinction has been clearly and consistently drawn between international structure, on the one hand, and the relations of states on the other. For more than two decades, power has been narrowly concentrated; and force has been used, not orgiastically as in the world wars of this century, but in a controlled way and for conscious political purposes. Power may be present when force is not used, but force is also used openly. A catalogue of examples would be both complex and lengthy. It would contain such items, on the American side of the ledger, as the garrisoning of Berlin, its supply by airlift during the blockade, the stationing of troops in Europe, the establishment of bases in Japan and elsewhere, the waging of war in Korea and Vietnam, and the "quarantine" of Cuba. Seldom if ever has force been more variously, more persist-

International Structure, National   **345**
Force, and the Balance of World
Power
Kenneth N. Waltz

ently, and more widely applied; and seldom has it been more consciously used as an instrument of national policy. Since the war we have seen, not the cancellation of force by nuclear stalemate, but instead the political organization and pervasion of power; not the end of balance of power owing to a reduction in the number of major states, but instead the formation and perpetuation of a balance *à deux*.

27

Measuring the Concentration of Power in Political Systems

Steven J. Brams

In this article Brams, Assistant Professor of Political Science at Syracuse University, seeks to analyze the distribution of power defined as interpersonal relationships, rather than resources. He attempts to use the theory of directed graphs as a means of measuring the concentration or dispersion of power defined in those terms. Originally published in 62 American Political Science Review *(1968) 461–75, it is reprinted here with the permission of that journal and the author.*

I

Introduction

THE UNEQUAL distribution of power among the members of a political system is one of the most pervasive facts of political life. Yet, while many studies have confirmed the fact that a few members exercise disproportionate control over many others in most systems, the configurations of power relations that occur *among* the few have generally not been subjected to systematic comparative analysis. In a few notable empirical studies, attempts have been made to compare the exercise of power in different issue-areas and across different decisions.[1] Comparative analyses have suffered, however, from the lack of any means to make tractable and compare, except in a qualitative way, schematic representations of power relations either in different political systems or over different issue-areas in the same system.[2] When diagrams of power structures become complex and unwieldy, it is easiest to forget about making precise comparisons about the way power is distributed among decision-makers somehow identified as being influential in the political process.

In this article I shall develop a quantitative index that measures the *degree of concentration* of power among the actors in a political system. For this purpose I shall assume that three things can be said about the political system (which might comprise anything from a committee of people to a group of conglomerate actors like nation-states) under consideration:

1) Which actors have influence (or power) over what other actors;

2) For each pairwise influence relationship, whether or not the influence is symmetrical (two-way) or asymmetrical (one-way);

3) If asymmetrical, the direction in which influence flows.

The only restriction placed on the influence relation is that no actor can influence himself.

Most systems of actors and relations about which the above things can be said can be considered *partly ordered structures*, by which I mean loosely structures that are not completely chaotic: they have elements of both order and disorder.[3] The task of this article is to suggest one way to make perspicuous the element of order embedded in a system of organized complexity like that defined above—and, in the process, to show how modern mathematics, in its focus on questions of order and relation instead of questions of magnitude and quantity, can serve as a powerful tool in revealing the anatomy of political systems, just as it has illuminated structures of elements and relations in the natural sciences.[4] The articulation of the structural order or form of a system whose actors have nondesultory relations with each other makes possible the explanation of recurring patterns of behavior within it, and I shall conclude by suggesting some possible factors associated with power concentration patterns in political systems.

II

Simplifying Relational Power Structures

To illustrate the analysis which follows, consider as examples three types of decision-

346

making systems postulated by Charles E. Lindblom.[5] As depicted in Figures 1a, 1b, and 1c, $x \rightarrow y$ means x has influence over y, or in Lindblom's terminology y's decisions are adjusted to x's decisions. Symmetrical influence relationships are indicated by double arrows between two decision-makers and asymmetrical relationships by a single arrow.

As suggested by the diagrams, and discussed by Lindblom, the hierarchical structure can be considered as one extreme form and the mutual adjustment structure, characterized by a variety of symmetrical and asymmetrical relationships, as another; in between we find a mixture of central and non-central decision-making, in which, for example, L in Figure 1c is both a central supervisor (of d, b, and k) and a mutual adjuster (to a, g, and k). From the figures it would appear that power in the mixed system is more concentrated than in the "disorganized" mutual adjustment system and less concentrated than in the "organized" hierarchical system.

At a conceptual level, the identification of different types of decision-making systems, and the power structures associated with each, has considerable heuristic value. But if we were asked to measure and rank the degree of centralization of decision-making, and concentration of power, in several mixed political systems (few systems in practice are pure types), the qualitative categories set forth above would be useless. Can we summarize a diagrammatic power structure in an intuitively reasonable quantitative index of power concentration?

Let us start by grouping into sets those decision-makers in Figures 1a, 1b, and 1c who can influence (directly or indirectly), and be influenced (directly or indirectly),

only by every other decision-maker in their sets. These *mutual influence sets* (or more properly subsets, if we regard the universe as the union of all decision-makers in a system) are given in Figures 2a, 2b, and 2c. At a collective level these sets are defined by the above property that all of the sets possess, and at an individual level by a list of the decision-maker members in each set. These are respectively intensional (or connotative) and extensional (or denotative) definitions of mutual influence sets, and both are necessary to the analysis that follows.[6]

The mutual influence sets are disjoint, for if there were a common member of two different sets this member would connect together all members of the two sets into a single mutual influence set.[7] Further, as well as having a geometric representation these sets have a clear and unambiguous substantive interpretation, which clusters of units generated by statistical (e.g., factor analysis) and iterative grouping and ordering procedures often do not possess.[8] As Stephen C. Johnson remarked in setting forth criteria for the application of hierarchical clustering methods to similarity measures between pairs of objects:

> There should be a clear, explicit, and intuitive description of the clustering, *i.e.*, the clusters should mean something. Some of the published clustering methods have nice algorithms, but when they have been carried out it is difficult to see exactly what problem has been solved.[9]

Most mutual influence sets consist of only one decision-maker, who is not in a mutual

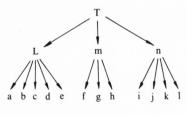

Hierarchical
System

Figure 1a.

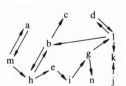

Mutual
Adjustment
System

Figure 1b.

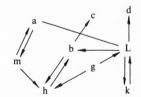

Mixed
System

Figure 1c.

influence relationship with any other decision-maker. There are some sets of two decision-makers, and one which contains seven! Since each decision-maker in this latter set in Figure 2b is connected in a closed sequence with every other decision-maker (including *d*, which forms a cycle with *I*, so that the closed sequence, *heigldlbh*, includes the cycle *ldl*), each can ultimately influence and be influenced by, every other.[10]

Grouping decision-makers into mutual influence sets constitutes the first step in the analysis.[11] These sets, each of which can be influenced (as an entity) by power being exerted on only one of its members, now become our new units of analysis. In approaching a definition of the concept of power concentration, our next step is to find a principle that would somehow allow us to describe the "concentration" of flows of influence occurring between or among these mutual influence sets.

To this end, let us define an influence relationship between these sets to be *concentrated* if one mutual influence set can directly influence one or more other mutual influence sets that together contain more constituent decision-makers than the influencing set.[12] Clearly, what we mean by use of the term "concentrated" influence relationship is one characterized by the exercise of minority control—that is, where the "few" influence the "many." Given this notion of power concentration, it now remains for us to define what we mean by the *degree* of power concentration.

To do this, we must find a way to count up the number of times minority control is exerted between mutual influence sets. (Recall that control between mutual influence sets can never be reciprocal, because our mutual influence sets subsume all instances of symmetrical influence relationships between decision-makers). We shall do this by defining a mutual influence set to be a *minority control set* if it directly influences one or more other mutual influence sets containing a total of more constitutent decision-makers. (Instances of indirect forms of minority control will be considered later.) In Figures 3a, 3b, and 3c, we have drawn dashed lines around all mutual influence sets that are also minority control sets. In Diagram 3c, for example, the minority control sets $\{a, m\}$ and $\{g\}$ influence both $\{b, h\}$ and $\{L, k\}$ with a combined total of four constituent decision-makers; $\{L, k\}$ is also a minority control set, because it influences $\{b, h\}$ and $\{d\}$ with a combined total of three constituent decision-makers.

III

An Index of Power Concentration

Let us assume that there is at least one nonempty minority control set in a political system.[13] Given this assumption, we now define an index of power concentration (PC) as follows:

$$\text{PC} = 1 - \frac{N_{MC}}{N_T} \qquad 0 < \text{PC} < 1,$$

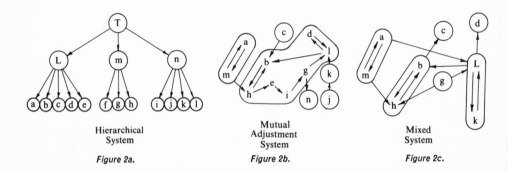

Hierarchical
System

Figure 2a.

Mutual
Adjustment
System

Figure 2b.

Mixed
System

Figure 2c.

where

N_{MC} = the number of decision-makers in all minority control sets,

N_T = the total number of decision-makers in the political system.

We see that when N_{MC} is small relative to N_T, control will be concentrated in the hands of relatively few decision-makers and PC will be large. (PC = 1 only when N_{MC} = 0, which is the many-controlling-the-few case we have restricted from the present analysis.) On the other hand, when N_{MC} is large relative to N_T (it will never equal N_T), control will be concentrated in the hands of a relatively large number of decision-makers and PC will be small.

Do values of PC for the hierarchical, mutual adjustment, and mixed systems conform to our previous commonsense notions of the concentration of power in each of these systems? The answer seems to be no: PC = .85 for the mutual adjustment system, .75 for the hierarchical system, and .44 for the mixed system. While we would have expected power to be least, not most, concentrated in the mutual adjustment system, inspection of Diagram 3b reveals what intuition does not—that just two decision-makers (*a* and *m*) have direct or indirect influence over all other decision-makers in the rest of the system (except *j*).[14] Nevertheless, though this would explain the mutual adjustment system's higher concentration of power vis-a-vis the mixed system—in which a total of five decision-makers, *a*, *m*, *g*, *k*, and *l*, exercise influence over the rest of the system (and themselves)—does the mutual adjustment system really outrank the hierarchical system in its concentration of power?

IV

Hierarchical Levels of Influence: the Index Refined

It does only if we do not take account of the fact that in the hierarchical system there are two different *levels* of minority control sets. In this system, unlike the other systems, one minority control set {*T*} influences *all* the other minority control sets, {*L*}, {*m*}, and {*n*}. As only intermediaries between {*T*} and the mutual influence sets, the sets {*L*}, {*m*}, and {*n*} hardly qualify as minority control sets in the same way that {*T*} does. Since decision-maker *T* influences directly or indirectly *all* other decision-makers in the hierarchical system, {*T*} in an important sense can be considered to be the *only* minority control set. Provisionally accepting this interpretation of a minority control set, the value of the PC index for the hierarchical system would be .94, which would make it the highest of the three systems and more consonant with our intuitive ranking of power concentration in the systems. Diagrammatically, this interpretation would mean that the hierarchical system would be equivalent to a system in which {*T*} influenced {*a*}, {*b*}, . . . , {*n*} directly.[15]

In the mixed system there is a related problem in determining which mutual influence sets should be considered minority control sets. As can be seen from Figure 3c, two of the three initially-postulated minority

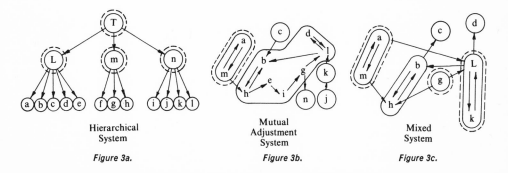

Hierarchical System

Figure 3a.

Mutual Adjustment System

Figure 3b.

Mixed System

Figure 3c.

control sets, $\{a, m\}$ and $\{g\}$, influence *both* a mutual influence set and another minority control set which together have a total of more constituent decision-makers. Thus, in this system there are not even clear-cut hierarchical levels of minority control: two minority control sets exercise influence at both lower and higher levels, and the argument given above for excluding lower-level minority control sets in the calculation of the PC index is not applicable to these mixed-level sets.

Consistent with our previous interpretation, however, we shall adopt the provisional rule that minority control sets which are influenced *exclusively* by other minority control sets, regardless of the hierarchical level (or levels) of the sets which they in turn influence, will not be counted in the calculation of the index. Thus, because $\{L, k\}$ is influenced exclusively by $\{a, m\}$ and $\{g\}$ in the mixed system, we count only the three members of the latter two (mixed-level) minority control sets in the N_{MC} term of the index. The value of the PC index then becomes .67 for the mixed system, which still leaves it lowest in power concentration behind the hierarchical system (.94) and the mutual adjustment system (.85), though not by such a wide margin as before (when its value was .44).

Even interpreting the index according to the above rules, the PC index as it stands is

not entirely satisfactory as a descriptive statistic. In a decision-making system with more than two hierarchical levels, the index may mask important information about influence relations among lower-level minority control sets which are influenced exclusively by higher-level minority control sets and thus are not counted in the numerator of the index. To arrive at a more refined index that illuminates the configuration of influence relations at *all* levels, it is first necessary to show how different hierarchical levels can be distinguished.

To do this, consider the condensations of the digraphs of the three decision-making systems in which the mutual influence sets (and minority control sets) are points and only the directed lines between the mutual influence sets (and minority control sets) are preserved.[16] As we previously noted, all influence relations between mutual influence and minority control sets are asymmetrical and acyclic (free of cycles of influence), so the reduced digraphs with these sets as points are themselves acyclic. If p is the length of a longest path of such a digraph—that is, the maximal number of directed lines along which influence may be transmitted from one point to another— each mutual influence or minority control set (point of the reduced digraph) can be assigned to one of $(p + 1)$ hierarchical levels in such a way that it receives influence only from higher levels and transmits it only to lower levels.[17] The procedures set forth below make the level assignments for each point unique.

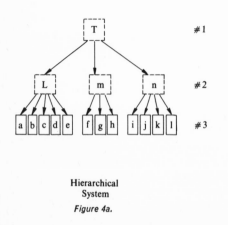

Hierarchical
System

Figure 4a.

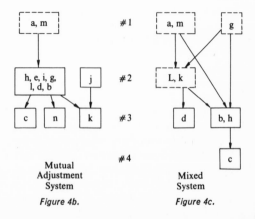

Mutual
Adjustment
System

Figure 4b.

Mixed
System

Figure 4c.

For the three decision-making systems, hierarchical levels are numbered in descending order from the highest ($\#1$) to the lowest in Figures 4a, 4b, and 4c, with the solid and dashed rectangles (points of the reduced digraph) circumscribing the members of the mutual influence sets and minority control sets, respectively, of Figures 3a, 3b, and 3c. In Diagram 4c, for example, a longest path in the digraph includes a path of length 1 from $\{a, m\}$ to $\{L, k\}$, a path of length 2 from $\{a, m\}$ to $\{b, h\}$, and a path of length 3 from $\{a, m\}$ to $\{c\}$; there is also another longest path of length 3 from $\{g\}$ to $\{L, k\}$ to $\{b, h\}$ to $\{c\}$. Since the two paths of length 3 are the longest paths in the digraph, there are four hierarchical levels in this system ($\#1$, $\#2$, $\#3$, and $\#4$), with each point in a longest path assigned to a different level as shown.

Each point not in a longest path of the reduced digraph, but influenced by a point in a longest path, is given level assignment $\#(q + 1)$, where q is the length of a maximal path of the digraph terminating at the point in question. Thus, $\{L, k\}$ of level assignment $\#2$ in Figure 4c, which is in a longest path, influences $\{d\}$, which is the terminal point of two maximal paths of length 2, so the level assignment of $\{d\}$ is $\#(2 + 1)$, or $\#3$.

On the other hand, each point not in a longest path of the reduced digraph, but which influences a point in a longest path, is given level assignment $\#(p - r + 1)$, where p, as above, is the length of a longest path in the digraph and r is the length of a maximal path in the digraph originating with the point in question. Thus, $\{k\}$ of level assignment $\#3$ in Figure 4b, which is in a longest path, is influenced by $\{j\}$, which is the originator of a maximal path of length 1; since a longest path in the digraph is of length 2, the level assignment of $\{j\}$ is $\#(2 - 1 + 1)$ or $\#2$.

For more complicated digraphs, similar procedures can be followed for ordering more "remotely" connected points at unique hierarchical levels. These ordering procedures, which have been incorporated into a computer program called DE-COMP,[18] allow us to define an index of power concentration between any two hierarchical levels, m and n ($m < n$), of a

political system:

$$PC(m, n) = 1 - \frac{N_{MC(m)}}{N_{T(m,n)} - N_{U(m,n)}}$$
$$\text{if } N_{MC(m)} > 0$$

$$PC(m, n) = 0 \qquad\qquad \text{if } N_{MC(m)} = 0$$

where $0 \leqslant PC(m, n) < 1$ and

$N_{MC(m)}$ = the number of decision-makers in minority control sets at level m,

$N_{T(m,n)}$ = the total number of decision-makers in the political system at levels m through n,

$N_{U(m,n)}$ = the number of decision-makers (not in minority control sets at level m) at levels m through n uninfluenced by any minority control sets at level m.

$N_{U(m,n)}$ will not be equal to zero whenever there is a mutual influence set at level m, or a mutual influence or minority control set at levels $(m + 1)$ through n which is only a "transmitter"—that is, which exerts influence but is not influenced from above.[19] Only in the mutual adjustment system (Figure 4b), where $N_{U(1,2)} = N_{U(1,3)} = 1$ because of $\{j\}$, is this term not equal to zero.

It is apparent that a single index like PC which summarizes a complex system from the top to the bottom levels may cover up where and to what extent power is concentrated in the system. Therefore, there is an obvious advantage in a "movable" index which allows one to describe the concentration of power between *any* two levels of a political system.

In Table 1 the values of this index for all one-step levels, and for the highest and lowest levels (i.e., the entire system), are given for the hierarchical, mutual adjustment, and mixed systems. When there are no minority control sets exerting influence from a higher to a lower level, the index assumes the arbitrary value 0, which is indicative of the "many" influencing the "few" and thus the low concentration of power between two levels.

The higher the value of PC(m, n), the more concentrated power is between levels m and n. In the hierarchical system, for example, power is more concentrated between levels #2 and #3 (PC(2, 3) = .80) than between levels #1 and #2 (PC(1, 2) = .75); for the system as a whole PC(1, 3) = .94, since {T} at level #1 is the only decision-maker counted in the $N_{MC(m)}$ term of the index.

In the mixed system PC(1, 2) = .40, suggesting that, contrary to our definition of minority control sets, the "many" may exert influence on the "few" and drop the value of the index below .50. Examination of Figure 4c explains this phenomenon: minority control indeed exists, but it exists because of influence directly exerted by {a, m} and {g} at level #3 as well as level #2. When we look at the concentration of power between levels #1 and #3 (PC(1, 3) = .63), the index assumes a value > .50.

In general, PC(m, n) ≤ .50 (but not equal to the arbitrary value 0) if and only if the minority control sets at level m, considered together, have more constituent members than the sets at lower levels, down to n, which they influence. This circumstance cannot occur in a system unless multiple influence from two or more sources, at or above level n, impinges on at least one mutual influence or minority control set, perhaps below level n, in the system.

Because the mixed system contains an influence relationship that traverses more than one level ({g} → {b, h} goes from level #1 to level #3 in Figure 4c), its reduced digraph is not "gradable." In a gradable reduced digraph all the directed lines fall between adjacent levels, so the length of every path connecting two points in such a digraph is equal in all cases to the absolute difference in the levels of the points. As a consequence, influence exerted by mutual influence or minority control sets at one level in both the hierarchical and mutual adjustment systems, each of which is representable by a gradable reduced digraph, will reach all mutual influence and minority control sets (connected by a path) at any given lower level in the same amount of time.[20] It is also worth noting that, in every system representable by a nongradable reduced digraph, there will be influence from two or more sources at different levels impinging on at least one mutual influence or minority control set, suggesting the possibility of conflicting orders from different levels that create cross-pressures on the actors in such systems.

So far we have shown how actors in a political system can be grouped into mutual influence and minority control sets and assigned unique hierarchical levels according to the structure of their pairwise influence relations. Having formulated an index to measure the concentration of power between any two levels of a political system, we shall now discuss what this index does *not* measure and some possible variations that might be made in it to suit the particular needs of a study. For convenience we shall assume in the next section that levels m and n have been chosen and shall refer only to the PC index instead of the PC(m, n) index.

TABLE 1. *Values of* PC(m, n) *for three decision-making systems*

PC(m, n)	Hier-archical System	Mutual Adjust-ment System	Mixed System
One-Step Levels			
PC(1, 2)	.75	.78	.40
PC(2, 3)	.80	0	.60
PC(3, 4)	—	—	0
Entire System			
PC(1, 3)	.94	.83	—
PC(1, 4)	—	—	.67

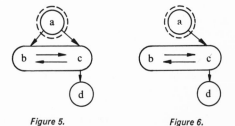

Figure 5.   Figure 6.

What the Index Does Not Measure

One kind of decision-maker occupies a special position in a power structure. This is the *linkage* decision-maker, of which we may distinguish two types. One type is the *upward* linkage decision-maker, as represented by decision-maker b in Figure 5, who links decision-makers from higher levels to the members of his mutual influence set. The other type is the *downward* linkage decision-maker, as represented by decision-maker c in Figure 5, who links decision-makers at lower levels to the members of his mutual influence set. In both cases the influence of these linkage decision-makers "overlaps" their mutual influence sets and joins decision-makers at different levels in the system.[21] As we shall see below, the type of linkage of a linkage decision-maker may be different with respect to the different decision-makers that he joins above and below him.

When a linkage decision-maker is both upward- and downward-linked, as is decision-maker c in Figure 6, the flow of influence in the system from higher to lower levels will be most direct. However, this fact will not be reflected in the value of the PC index, which is the same (.75) between the top and bottom levels for both of the systems in Figures 5 and 6, because the index treats mutual influence sets as indecomposable units of analysis and gives no special recognition to the types of linkage decision-makers within these units.

While information on linkage decision-makers, or the "tightness' of influence relations within mutual influence sets, is not taken into account in the formulation of the PC index, it is certainly recoverable at a later stage in the analysis. Having observed from Figure 4c, for instance, that the mixed system can be represented by a nongradable reduced digraph of four levels, with different PC values for each pair of levels, we can then go back to Figure 3c for more detailed information and ascertain that: (1) with respect to minority control set $\{L, k\}$ at level #2, decision-maker b in mutual influence set $\{b, h\}$ is both an upward and downward linkage decision-maker; (2) with respect to minority control sets $\{a, m\}$ and $\{g\}$ at level #1, however, decision-maker b is only a downward linkage decision-maker (decision-maker h in $\{b, h\}$ is the upward linkage decision-maker); (3) thus, we may conclude that the flow of influence to mutual influence set $\{c\}$ at the bottom level takes a more direct route from $\{L, k\}$ through $\{b, h\}$ than from $\{a, m\}$ or $\{g\}$ through $\{b, h\}$.

One form of indirect influence which we have not allowed for in our definition of a minority control set is that occurring when a mutual influence set directly *and* indirectly, but not directly alone, influences one or more other mutual influence sets containing a total of more constituent decision-makers. If we restrict minority control only to instances where the "few" directly exert influence on the "many," then we can reserve the term *minority influence* (and minority influence sets) for those other cases where the "few," both directly and indirectly, exert influence on the "many." If $\{c\}$ influenced $\{j\}$, for example, in Diagram 3b, it would be considered a minority influence set because $\{j\}$ influences $\{k\}$— and thus $\{c\}$ directly or indirectly would influence two decision-makers. Minority influence is a remote form of minority control.

Obviously, the appropriateness of either the inclusion or exclusion of indirect influence in the PC index will depend on whether or not direct and indirect forms of influence can be considered equivalent to each other. This judgment in turn will depend on the nature of the political system under investigation—in particular, the speed with which influence flows from one actor to another—and in what time perspective (short-run, long-run) one seeks to describe behavior within the system. The distribution of influence among the members of a system in the short run may look quite different than in the long run, after indirect influence has had time to "spread."[22]

Given the availability of additional information, the PC index could be modified in another way. If numerical weights could be assigned to decision-makers, minority control (and minority influence) sets could be defined on the basis of the combined weights of the decision-makers in one mutual influence set being less than the combined weights (rather than the combined numbers) of those in other sets which they influence.

It seems evident that what the best index is for any particular study will depend on the nature and purposes of the study. The point I wish to emphasize is that all variations in the power concentration index ultimately depend on variations in the definition of mutual influence sets, minority control (and minority influence) sets, and hierarchical levels of control, the building-block concepts in this analysis.[23] I have attempted to show how these concepts can help us to simplify visually and summarize quantitatively complex power configurations in a political system.

VI

*An Illustrative Application to
Empirical Data*

Unfortunately, few attempts have been made to represent power relations in a political system schematically. The paucity of work in this area undoubtedly stems in part from the lack of analytic tools that enable one to simplify, and extract meaning from, complex power structures. No less an obstacle, however, has been the obdurate problem of identifying a relational concept of power that can be defined operationally and used to measure the exercise of power between actors in a political system.

As a very rudimentary approach to this problem, we shall consider two actors to be in a power relationship when they appear to be responsive to each other's behavior. When one actor responds more frequently than the other, we shall assume that the actor responding less frequently exercises asymmetrical influence over the actor responding more frequently; when the actors respond to each other with equal frequency, we shall assume that they are involved in a symmetrical influence relationship.[24] As Thibaut and Kelley explain, the possession of superior (or asymmetrical) power tends to relieve an actor in a dyadic relationship of the necessity of paying close attention to his partner's actions.[25] In this sense, power is "the ability to afford not to learn."[26]

In order to apply these simplifying assumptions to the identification of symmetrical and asymmetrical forms of power in dyadic relationships, it is first necessary to try to infer the "responses" of actors to each other's behavior. For this purpose, we shall use data collected by Zbigniew K. Brzezinski on the number and location of all Politburo-level bilateral and multilateral meetings of delegations from eight Communist countries in the two periods November 1956–November 1957 (the "stabilization" period) and 1958–1959.[27] Two countries will be considered to be in an influence relationship if their meetings with each other exceed a specified number. If an equal number occurs in each country, their influence relationship will be considered symmetrical; otherwise, the country *receiving* the most visits (responses) will be considered the country exercising asymmetrical influence over the other.

Influence is thus conceived not as a substance or possession (e.g., GNP) but as a relational property that appears in the transactions of nations.[28] In particular, we have conceptualized it as a property associated with the recurring movements of government officials. From the symmetrical or asymmetrical pattern of such movements, we seek to infer the responses of these officials and their governments to each other's actions.[29]

In the November 1956–November 1957 period, the bilateral and multilateral meetings represented occasions for the eight countries to meet with each other 60 times in pairs.[30] Since there are 28 possible combinations in which eight countries can meet in pairs, one would expect that the average pair of countries would meet $60/28 = 2.14$ times in this period. If we assume that two countries are in an influence relationship if their Politburo-level delegations met a greater-than-expected number of times, then any pair of countries that met three or more times (i.e., at least 40 percent above the expected number of meetings in this case) would qualify as being in an influence relationship.

In the 1958–1959 period, there were 109 occasions for the 28 pairs of countries to meet with each other in bilateral or multilateral meetings, or an expected number of 3.90 meetings per pair of countries. Instead of assuming that two countries were in an influence relationship if they met four or more times during this period (i.e., at least 3 percent above the expected number of meetings), we shall assume five meetings as the minimum number necessary for an influence relationship to exist (i.e., at least 28 percent above the expected number) in order to make the cutoff point for this period more comparable with the cutoff point for the earlier period.[31]

Based on the above criteria, the symmetrical influence relations among the eight Communist countries for the two periods are shown in Figures 7a and 7b.[32] The grouping of these countries into mutual influence and minority control sets reveals that there are three hierarchical levels of influence in the earlier period (longest path: {USR, GME} → {CZE} → {CHN}), but only two in the later period, so PC(m, n) for the entire system in the earlier period is PC(1, 3) in the later period, PC(1, 2).

The value of PC(1, 3) in the earlier period is .71 (with Rumania not in an influence relationship, the system comprises seven countries), and the value of PC(1, 2) in the later period (with the system comprising all eight countries) is .63, suggesting that power became less concentrated in the Communist political system in the late 1950's. This finding seems to be in agreement with the observations of many experts that the bloc had begun to assume a more polycentric character at this time.[33]

As host to frequent delegations from abroad the Soviet Union stands as the dominant influence on other bloc members in both periods. Its association with neo-Stalinist East Germany in the early period, and more revisionist Hungary and Poland in the later period, are particularly worthy of note.[34] Rumania's disattachment from the bloc in the early period—perhaps indicative of its neglect by the rest of the bloc—might in part explain recent signs it has given of disaffection with Soviet policies and the Warsaw Treaty Organization.

VII

Some Broader Implications of the Analysis

Needless to say, the diagrams of influence relations of the eight Communist countries

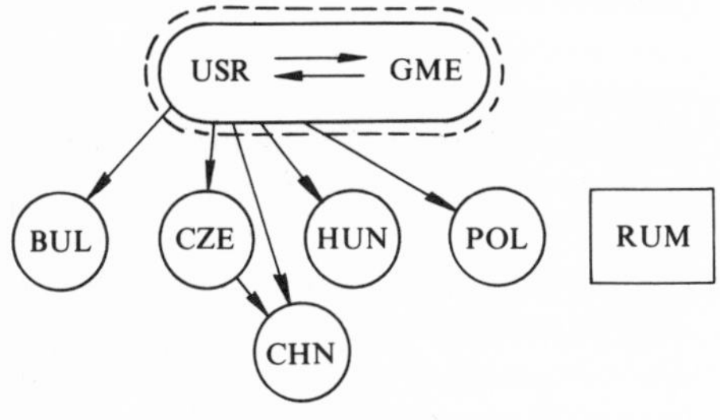

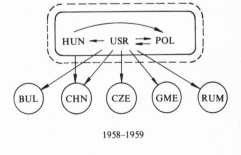

Nov. 1956–Nov. 1957

1958–1959

Figure 7a.

Figure 7b.

are vastly oversimplified representations of very complex phenomena and processes. Although my measure of influence is based upon the movement of high-level officials in policy-making positions—and thus, presumably, indicative of more than just a lack of indifference between two countries—it ignores the substance of their meetings, the power resources available to the participants, their goals, motives, and opportunity costs, the scope of issues over which influence was exercised, the forms which it took, and the effects of the exercise of influence on the subsequent behavior of the officials and the countries they represented.

Unfortunately, these are matters on which reliable information is generally lacking, even if means could be devised for distilling it and combining it in a way which would make meaningful comparisons possible. For now we must settle for more available and manageable types of data, but there is no impenetrable upper limit on the types of manipulations that we can perform on these data to elicit *patterns* of influence relations among actors in political systems—a heretofore neglected area of political inquiry.[35] Indeed, these manipulations as much as the data themselves will determine how rapidly our knowledge advances.

Why has the search for patterns been neglected? At least in part because

> ... statistical techniques are not appropriate to realms of organized complexity where some statements can be made only of the two or more things considered in their interrelationship, where the pertinent fact is not the presence or absence of something in such and such quantity but rather the nature of the arrangement of the observable entities.[36]

Toward dealing with the arrangement of such entities, I have defined a political system as something set-theoretic in nature consisting of a set of actors and certain kinds of relations between pairs of actors. Then, by relating the actors and their relations to the points and directed lines of a digraph, which were primitive (undefined) terms in the analysis, I was able to utilize the findings of digraph theory to highlight some structural properties of the systems under consideration.

In this way, modern mathematics provides a powerful means to simplify and bring order out of complex systems of actors and their relations where either the empirical structure of a system cannot adequately be interpreted numerically or where the assumptions and concepts of a non-numerical model better describe relevant aspects of the structure. There is necessarily arbitrariness in the choice of a particular model—numerical or non-numerical—and the concomitant simplifications it imposes on the reality one is trying to describe, but a fruitful model can rearrange and discipline the way in which personal bias is introduced so as to evoke new and interesting patterns that intuitive methods cannot reveal.[37]

While different systemic models may produce different patterns that "fit the data," *explanation* of the data requires that a model's mathematical assumptions (e.g., a digraph is an irreflexive relation), primitives (e.g., point), and derived concepts (e.g., strong component of a digraph) underlying the way in which the parts of a system are pieced together be explicitly related to behavioral assumptions (e.g., no actor can influence himself), primitives (e.g., actor), and derived concepts (e.g., mutual influence set) in the model. Having established such a correspondence, the mathematical theory can then be used to draw out nonobvious theoretical implications linking the mathematical primitives and derived concepts (e.g., every point is contained in exactly one strong component), which may then be replaced by their behavioral counterparts (e.g., every actor is a member of exactly one mutual influence set).

At a mathematical level, we end up with not only a set of theorems but an understanding of how they were arrived at, step by deducible step; at a behavioral level, we end up with a set of hypotheses, some of which (those whose constituent terms can be interpreted empirically) are capable of test by reference to observable phenomena. Thus, the statement "every actor is a member of exactly one mutual influence set" is a logically necessary consequence of the assumptions of the digraph model; its formal correctness has nothing to do with how we choose to interpret its behavioral terms empirically.[38] As applied to an empirical situation, however, it is a hypothesis whose corroboration by empirical data would require operationally defining its terms independently of each other and testing the truth of the empirical relationship. For example, we might define an actor to be a member of a legislative body and a mutual influence set to be a party caucusing group in the legislature; in testing the hypothesis, we would not only be confirming or disconfirming *its* empirical validity but mediately strengthening or weakening the primitive hypotheses—of which there may be more than one set—from which it was derived in the model (e.g., all influence relationships are either symmetrical or asymmetrical), which may not be directly testable because their constituent terms (i.e., symmetrical and asymmetrical influence relationships) do not refer to observable phenomena.[39]

Finally, some concepts of the model, when combined with our knowledge of the empirical world, may suggest how characteristics of a system (e.g., "gradability" of its reduced digraph) may be related to characteristics of its members (e.g., extent of cross-pressures on them) and thus lead to new insights into the possible effect of a system on the behavior of its members and vice versa. Other insights might be generated "retroductively" from the data when diverse phenomena are observed (e.g., Rumania's early neglect by Communist bloc members and its independence today) which may be made explicable by supposing a hypothesis to obtain (e.g., neglect of a member of a system will loosen his attachment to the norms of the system).[40] In the conclusion of this article I shall suggest some individual and systematic characteristics associated with the degree of power concentration in a system.

The approach outlined above, heterodox by traditional standards, seems more relevant to the construction of fruitful models and testable theories than simply positing physical analogues of political systems (e.g., an airport traffic control center), whose structural correspondence to real political systems is impossible to validate. Such an approach also seems useful in the face of the welter of uncoordinated findings that new methods of quantitative analysis, particularly with the aid of the computer, have made possible. To give theoretical coherence to our knowledge of the political world, it is essential that we begin to investigate *structural* properties associated with complex and observable patterns of relations instead of focusing attention exclusively on the quantifiable properties of the constituent units of systems.[41] In their allusions to the "exact sciences," social and behavioral scientists generally have not recognized that some of the greatest advances in modern physics, particularly in mathematical theories of symmetry and invariance, have been characterized by a concern with relational patterns and spatial order of geometrical configurations of elementary particles— what might be called the architecture of matter—rather than with properties of the featureless constituent units or the forces that produced them.[42] Indeed, Marshall McLuhan asserts that "it has been the consensus of modern science and philosophy that we have now shifted from 'cause' to 'configuration' in all fields of study and analysis."[43]

My operationalization of the direction of influence flows in terms of the symmetrical and asymmetrical movement of government officials, though supported by experimental studies, should be recognized as a high-order abstraction of the generally unobservable succession of demands and responses of governments in influence relationships to which we are not privy. Different measures of and assumptions about influence may produce different findings, but these will be a matter of concern only if one insists that power is a unidimensional concept whose essence can be revealed by some single best method of analysis.[44] Hopefully, my illustrative application of the power concentration index to empirical data will stimulate the search for reliable and valid indicators of relational power as well as the application of the index—or the kinds of methods which underlie its formulation—to more complex systems which reveal more fully its utility as a comparative measure.[45] In different behavioral contexts, particularly sociometry, the index would seem useful as a measure of the concentration of communications, friendship choices, and other interaction phenomena and processes.[46]

The digraph model on which the index is based might also be used to construct a logical hierarchy of if-then propositions. Such a hierarchical ordering of causal relations could be obtained by letting the points of a digraph symbolize a set of characteristics $\{c_1, c_2, \ldots, c_n\}$ (e.g., bicameral legislature), a single directed line from characteristic c_i to c_j symbolize the implication relation for conditional statements (if c_i then c_j) that are true (for a particular universe), and two directed lines going in opposite directions between characteristics c_i and c_j symbolize the equivalence relation for biconditional statements (c_i if and only if c_j) that are true. Since the characteristics in every "mutual influence set" form an equivalence class, the presence of only one in a set could be used to establish the presence of all in the set; and the presence of characteristics forming a point basis (see footnote 19) could be used to establish the presence of all characteristics in the hierarchy.

VIII

Conclusion

I shall conclude by suggesting some possible correlates and consequences of the concentration (or dispersion) of power in political systems. First and most obviously, the concentration of power might be correlated with itself—that is to say, its concentration in one issue-area might tend to be associated with its concentration in other issue-areas, as Robert A. Dahl found in New Haven.[47] On the other hand, the dispersion of powerful forces on one decision might be associated with their dispersion, through different alignment, on others, as apparently was the case in Chicago in the late 1950's.[48] Further, the concentration of power in one functional area may breed its concentration in others, as the rapid centralization of supranational authority in Western Europe a decade ago demonstrated.[49]

Second, the high concentration of power in a decision-making system may increase its vulnerability, especially if the structure of the system is a tree in which the disruption of one channel of influence would affect all decision-makers below the decision-maker directly serviced by this channel. In such a system there would be few opportunities for coalitions with overlapping members to form, which would increase the probability of disruptive conflict in the system and decrease its chances of long-run survival and growth. Growth, Deutsch has argued,[50] is fostered by an increase in the levels of autonomy of a system, which might in graph-theoretic terms be reflected in the development of systems whose power structures are nongradable graphs with centers (or subsystems) of influence connected by linkages spanning several different hierarchical levels.[51]

Finally, at least in small groups, the distribution of power is related to the communications network through which power is exerted. The greater a person's "relative centrality" in a communications network, for example, the higher his morale and the more likely he is to emerge as leader of his group.[52] Analogously in political systems, high concentration of power is probably correlated with the emergence of single rather than collective leaders within elite structures. Furthermore, satisfaction probably accrues to people in these positions, and those who find such positions attractive at the recruitment stage probably possess a distinctive set of psychological predispositions.

Considerably more research is needed, however, to test and confirm how and under what circumstances the concentration of power affects political behavior. Being better able to measure and compare how and to what extent power is relationally distributed among the members of political systems should better enable us to understand and predict its effects.

From a broader perspective, I believe the usefulness of the kind of configurative analysis outlined here—or synthesis, from the viewpoint of combining constituent units—is not limited to the study of power. Other manifold phenomena and processes are amenable to systemic types of analysis, and other models or indices, such as the influence concentration index suggested by Bruce M. Russett in this issue of the REVIEW, will illuminate this kind of pursuit.[53] By taking the trouble to explain the substantive meaning and behavioral

significance of the abstract assumptions and concepts of a mathematical theory, we can translate the theory into a model, and the model with operational concepts and data into a testable empirical theory, and thus raise the concept of a political system from the level of vocabulary to the level of analysis. Otherwise, the way in which we try to fit the erratic properties of the parts of a system into a less erratic and more coherent whole will remain in the hocus-pocus world of magic, leaving us with either no visible trace of how a result was obtained or no clue as to its theoretical significance.

Notes

Notes

Reflections on the Place of Force in the Social Process," and "On the Concept of Power," reprinted in Parsons, *Sociological Theory and Modern Society* (New York: The Free Press, 1967), pp. 264–354.

2. POLITICAL POWER: THE PROBLEM OF MEASUREMENT
Roderick Bell

1. THE CONCEPT OF POWER AND THE STUDY OF POLITICS
R. Harrison Wagner

1. Robert Bierstedt, "An Analysis of Social Power," 15 *American Sociological Review* (1950), p. 732.
2. Robert Dahl, "The Concept of Power," 2 *Behavioral Science* (1957), p. 202. Although "influence" is a verb which takes an object, it does not necessarily refer unambiguously to a relationship between people either. One may influence a decision, just as one may decide (and thus have the power to decide). In neither case is the nature of the interpersonal relationships assumed by such statements made clear. Moreover, the criteria for attributing an influence on B to A are as unclear as those for attributing power to A. Thus most of the discussion of "power" which follows applies to "influence" as well.
3. Cf. William Riker, "Some Ambiguities in the Notion of Power," 58 *American Political Science Review* (1964) 341–349. One might ask how one knows when to stop listing necessary conditions. The answer to this question is provided by one's theory, which limits the number of terms permitted in its vocabulary. The completeness of the list of necessary and sufficient conditions is a formal property of the theory. I owe this point to my colleague, Roderick Bell.
4. The former case is not as simple as it may appear. It includes any effort by A to convince B that some consequences which he had ignored are really relevant, arguments about the probability of the occurrence of certain consequences, etc.
5. The significance of the writings on power by John Harsanyi is that they are explicitly formulated in these terms. See especially John Harsanyi, "Measurement of Social Power, Opportunity Costs, and the Theory of Two-Person Bargaining Games," 7 *Behavioral Science* (1962) 67–80.
6. Cf. Carl Hempel, *Aspects of Scientific Explanation* (New York: The Free Press, 1965), pp. 457–63.
7. Kenneth Boulding, "Toward a Pure Theory of Threat Systems," 53 *American Economic Review* (1963) 424–34; Peter Blau, *Exchange and Power in Social Life* (New York: John Wiley, 1964); Talcott Parsons, "Some

1. For this portion of the essay I rely heavily upon Brian Ellis, *Basic Concepts of Measurement* (Cambridge: Cambridge University Press, 1966; Warren S. Torgerson, *Theory and Method of Scaling* (New York: John Wiley & Sons, 1958), esp. chaps. 1–3; and Marx W. Wartofsky, *Conceptual Foundations of Scientific Thought* (New York: Macmillan, 1968), esp. chap. 7.
2. Ellis, *loc. cit.*, p. 39.
3. For an elaboration of this view of science, see May Brodbeck, "Models, Meaning, and Theories," in Llewellyn Gross, ed., *Symposium on Sociological Theory* (New York: Harper & Row, 1959).
4. Carl Hempel, *Fundamentals of Concept Formation in Empirical Science*, v. II., No. 7 of *International Encyclopedia of Unified Science* (Chicago: University of Chicago Press, 1952).
5. Of course, this argument is only illustrative. Presumably, in most reasonably developed actual theories there will be more than one term which is directly operationalized. The point here is that, in principle, at least one term *must* be.
6. Torgerson, *op. cit.*, p. 8.
7. Brodbeck, *loc. cit.*
8. Political science is certainly not devoid of mathematics, however. See, *e.g.*, Hayward Alker, *Mathematics and Politics* (New York: Macmillan, 1965).
9. Ellis, *op. cit.*, p. 1.
10. Wartofsky, *op. cit.*, p. 154.
11. Torgerson, *op. cit.*, p. 14.
12. Ellis, *op. cit.*, p. 20.
13. Torgerson, *op. cit.*, p. 17.
14. Wartofsky, *op. cit.*, p. 160.
15. Torgerson, *op. cit.*, p. 15.
16. Torgerson, *op. cit.*, and Brodbeck, *op. cit.*, both make such suggestions.
17. Wartofsky, *op. cit.*, p. 163.
18. *Ibid.*, p. 164.
19. *Ibid.*
20. It is instructive to note as well that Euclidean geometry does *not* "work" (*i.e.*, does not yield accurate predictions) when very great magnitudes are involved. Euclidean geometry is appropriate for Newtonian mechanics; a different, "curved" geometry (in which the shortest distance between two points is not a straight line) is appropriate for the theory of relativity. Such considerations illustrate the severe dependence of measurement observations upon theory.

21. Wartofsky, *op. cit.*, p. 170.

22. *Ibid.*, p. 171.

23. Torgerson, *op. cit.*, p. 22.

24. The measurement of player utilities in game theory depends upon similar associative measurement. See Anatol Rapoport, *Two-Person Game Theory* (Ann Arbor: The University of Michigan Press, 1966), chap. 2.

25. Wartofsky, *op. cit.*, p. 172.

26. Robert E. Lane, *Political Life* (Glencoe: The Free Press, 1959), p. 5.

27. See, for example, May Brodbeck, "Methodological Individualisms; Definition and Reduction," *Philosophy of Science*, vol. 25, 1958, pp. 1–22.

28. See page 6, this volume.

29. Rapaport, *op. cit.*, esp. chap. 12.

30. See page 348, this volume.

31. Page 347, this volume.

32. Page 354, *Ibid.*

33. There is by now a long list of efforts in causal analysis in political science; good introductions, with bibliography, can be found in Alker, *op. cit.*, chap. 6, and Hubert N. Blalock, *Causal Inferences in Nonexperimental Research* (Chapel Hill: University of North Carolina Press, 1961).

34. Page 76, this volume.

35. Refer to citations in footnote 33.

36. Page 196, this volume.

37. Rapoport, *op. cit.*, p. 5.

38. Ellis, *op. cit.*, p. 63.

39. *Ibid.*, p. 60.

40. Rapoport, *op. cit.*, p. 29.

41. *Ibid.*

42. *Ibid.*

43. Torgerson, *op. cit.*, provides an excellent textbook for the bibliography of attitude measurement; Rapoport, *op. cit.*, discusses some of the problems in measurement in chap. 2.

44. Rapoport, *Ibid.*, p. 202.

45. Page 76, this volume.

3. HOW TO STUDY COMMUNITY POWER:
   THE PLURALIST ALTERNATIVE

Nelson W. Polsby

1. For indications that disenchantment is setting in among political scientists, see the following: Robert A. Dahl, "A Critique of the Ruling Elite Model," *American Political Science Review*, 52 (June, 1958), 463–469; Herbert Kaufman and Victor Jones, "The Mystery of Power," *Public Administration Review*, 14 (Summer, 1954), 205–212; Norton E. Long, "The Local Community as an Ecology of Games," *American Journal of Sociology*, 64 (November, 1958), 251–261; Nelson W. Polsby,

"The Sociology of Community Power: A Re-assessment," *Social Forces*, 37 (March, 1959), 232–236 and "Three Problems in the Analysis of Community Power," *American Sociological Review*, 24 (December, 1959), 796–803; Raymond E. Wolfinger, "Reputation and Reality in the Study of 'Community Power'," *American Sociological Review*, 25 (December, 1960), in press. Sociologists also seem to be re-examining studies of community power: Reinhard Bendix and Seymour M. Lipset, "Political Sociology," *Current Sociology*, 6 (1957), 79–99; Peter H. Rossi, "Community Decision-Making," *Administrative Science Quarterly*, 1 (March, 1957), 415–443. Writings praising community power studies are quite extensive, and include the following: Gordon Blackwell, "Community Analysis," in Roland Young (ed.), *Approaches to the Study of Politics* (Evanston, 1958), 305–317; William J. Gore and Fred S. Silander, "A Bibliographical Essay on Decision-Making," *Administrative Science Quarterly*, 4 (June, 1959), 106–121; Lawrence J. R. Herson, "The Lost World of Municipal Government," *American Political Science Review*, 51 (June, 1957), 330–345.

2. For example, Robert S. Lynd and Helen M. Lynd, *Middletown* (New York, 1929) and *Middletown in Transition* (New York, 1937); Floyd Hunter, *Community Power Structure* (Chapel Hill, 1953); August B. Hollingshead, *Elmtown's Youth* (New York, 1949); W. Lloyd Warner *et. al.*, *Democracy in Jonesville* (New York, 1949); C. Wright Mills, "The Middle Classes in the Middle-Sized Cities," *American Sociological Review*, 11 (October, 1946), 520–529; Robert O. Schulze, "Economic Dominants and Community Power Structure," *American Sociological Review*, 23 (February, 1958), 3–9; Roland Pellegrin and Charles H. Coates, "Absentee-Owned Corporations and Community Power Structure," *American Journal of Sociology*, 61 (March, 1956), 413–419; Delbert C. Miller, "Industry and Community Power Structure," *American Sociological Review*, 23 (February, 1958), 9–15 and "Decision-Making Cliques in Community Power Structure," *American Journal of Sociology*, 64 (November, 1958), 299–310.

3. Warner *et. al.*, *op. cit.*, p. xviii.

4. See, *e.g.*, Kaufman and Jones, *op. cit.*

5. See Polsby, *op. cit.*

6. See *ibid.*, Dahl, *op. cit.*, and Kaufman and Jones, *op. cit.*

7. I am well aware that for other purposes the "pluralist" approach can be divided into several schools of thought. However, all variations of pluralist theory contrast effectively with stratification theory. Pluralist presumptions can be found, for example, in the writings of de Tocqueville and Madison, and in Arthur Bentley, *The Process of Government* (Chicago, 1908); E. Pendleton Herring, *The Politics of Democracy* (New York, 1940); David B. Truman, *The Governmental Process* (New York,

1953); V. O. Key, Jr., *Politics, Parties and Pressure Groups* (New York, 4th ed., 1959).

8. Among the researchers who have found pluralist presumptions about the nature of the political system useful are Robert A. Dahl ("The New Haven Community Leadership Study," Working Paper Number 1, December, 1957, mimeo); Harry Scoble ("Yankeetown: Leadership in Three Decision-Making Processes," presented at the meeting of the American Political Science Association, 1956); and George Belknap and Norton E. Long. See Long, *op. cit.*, Long and Belknap, "A Research Program on Leadership and Decision-Making in Metropolitan Areas" (New York, Governmental Affairs Institute, 1956), mimeo; Belknap and John H. Bunzel, "The Trade Union in the Political Community," *PROD*, 2 (September, 1958), 3–6; Belknap, "A Plan for Research on the Socio-Political Dynamics of Metropolitan Areas" (presented before a seminar on urban leadership of the Social Science Research Council, New York, August, 1957). See also a paper presented to this same seminar by Peter H. Rossi, "The Study of Decision-Making in the Local Community."

9. I present some of the characteristics of a stratification theory of community power in other papers, *e.g.*, "Power in Middletown: Fact and Value in Community Research," (March, 1960), mimeo; "Power as a Variable of Social Stratification" (November, 1959), mimeo.

10. See Kaufman and Jones, *op. cit.*

11. Wolfinger, *op. cit.*, has summarized findings on this point, pp. 7 *ff.*

12. See Dahl, "The New Haven . . .," *op. cit.*, Polsby, *op. cit.*, and Wolfinger, *op. cit.*, and forthcoming publications of the New Haven Community Leadership Study.

13. Scoble, *op. cit.*

14. Long and Belknap, *op. cit.*

15. Belknap, *op. cit.*

16. See, for example, Pellegrin and Coates, *op. cit.*, and Lynd and Lynd *Middletown in Transition, op. cit.*, p. 89.

17. See Dahl, "Critique . . .," *op. cit.*

18. See, for example, Belknap, *op. cit.*, for an explicit discussion of this point. One stratification writer who has attempted to take account of the time factor is Jerome K. Myers, "Assimilation in the Political Community," *Sociology and Social Research*, 35 (January-February, 1951), 175–182. Myers plots a secular trend which indicates slow increases in the number of Italians and Italian-descended persons employed by a New Haven municipal government over a fifty year period ending in 1940. Myers claims to have discovered "discrimination" against Italians, because they did not participate in city government jobs to an extent proportional with their representation in the total population of the city. His conclusion was that "the early or quick assimilation of New Haven Italians in the political system does not seem very probable. . . . All

indications are that political assimilation is inevitable, although it is at least several generations away."

By taking account of shorter-term cyclical movements within the allegedly "basic" structure, we may be able to explain the delay in the political assimilation of Italians.

First, New Haven Italo-Americans were and are predominantly Republican in local politics, because in New Haven the Republican organization early and energetically courted the Italo-American vote. From 1920 to 1940, years in which that ethnic group would "normally" have been expected to come into their own as a politically significant minority group, the city government was in Democratic hands two-thirds of the time. It might be expected, therefore, that Italo-Americans would be less well represented among officeholders than if these circumstances were reversed. Second, in 1945, a Republican of Italian descent was elected Mayor, whereupon Italian-Americans invaded the top echelons of city government to such an extent that the Mayor pleaded in vain with one who was a candidate for President of the City Council to withdraw in favor of a Yankee Republican, on the grounds that there were "too many Italians" in City Hall, and that the Yankee members of the Republican coalition should have some recognition.

19. See, especially, Wolfinger, *op. cit.*

20. See C. Wright Mills, "The Middle Classes . . .," *op. cit.*, and my "The Sociology of Community Power," *op. cit.*, on this point.

21. See Anthony Downs, *An Economic Theory of Democracy* (New York, 1957); Robert E. Lane, *Political Life: How People Get Involved in Politics* (Glencoe, 1959); Samuel Stouffer, *Communism, Conformity and Civil Liberties* (New York, 1955), pp. 58 *ff.*

22. Lane, *op. cit.*, pp. 220–234.

23. Arthur J. Vidich and Joseph Bensman, *Small Town in Mass Society* (Princeton, 1958), pp. 69–70, 290–291. Studies of social status have been hampered by a similar problem of upper-class-centeredness. See the criticism of Warner on this point by Seymour M. Lipset and Reinhard Bendix, "Social Status and Social Structure," *British Journal of Sociology*, 2 (June, 1951), esp. pp. 163 *ff.*

24. See Bentley, *op. cit.*, pp. 175–222. Note, at p. 202: "If we can get our social life stated in terms of activity, and of nothing else, we have not indeed succeeded in measuring it, but we have at least reached a foundation upon which a coherent system of measurements can be built up. . . . We shall cease to be blocked by the intervention of unmeasurable elements, which claim to be themselves the real causes of all that is happening, and which by their spook-like arbitrariness make impossible any progress towards dependable knowledge."

25. Only one sociologist seems to have realized what this implies for the methods and conclusions of political analysis. See Rudolf Herberle, *Social Movements* (New York, 1951). The relevant theory is compactly expounded by Herbert Blumer in "Collective Behavior," in Alfred M. Lee (ed.), *Principles of Sociology* (New York, 1953), pp. 167–220.

26. Indeed, Max Weber, the most important "founding father" of modern stratification analysis, makes just this point. See Weber's "Class, Status, Party," in H. H. Gerth and C. W. Mills (eds.), *From Max Weber: Essays in Sociology* (New York, 1946), pp. 180–195, esp. p. 184.

27. See, for example, Lynd and Lynd, *Middletown in Transition, op. cit.*, pp. 454–455, 509; Alfred W. Jones, *Life, Liberty and Property* (Philadelphia, 1941), pp. 336–354; Warner *et. al., op. cit.*, p. 27; C. Wright Mills, "The Middle Classes," *op. cit.* Compare also Richard Centers, *The Psychology of Social Classes* (Princeton, 1948), and note the extent to which his conclusions outrun his data.

28. See, for example, Truman, *op. cit., passim.* Alexis de Tocqueville, *Democracy In America* (New York, 1954), esp. Vol. I, pp. 181–205, 281–342, Vol. II, pp. 114–135.

29. See Robert A. Dahl, *A Preface to Democratic Theory* (Chicago, 1956).

30. Truman, *op. cit.*, summarizes a tremendous amount of this material.

31. Long and Belknap, *op. cit.*, pp. 9–11. See Polsby, "The Sociology of Community Power," *op. cit.*, and Edward C. Banfield, "The Concept 'Leadership' in Community Research" (delivered at the meeting of the American Political Science Association, 1958), for similar lists.

32. In papers cited in note 9 above.

33. Robert A. Dahl, "The Analysis of Influence in Local Communities," (May, 1959), mimeo., p. 10.

34. Long and Belknap, *op. cit.*, pp. 13–14. This corresponds to the findings—but not the interpretations—of Schulze, *op. cit.*, and of Pellegrin and Coates, *op. cit.*

35. This presumes that the researcher wants to make some generalizations about the "normal" distributions of power in community decision-making.

4. A CRITIQUE OF THE RULING ELITE MODEL
Robert A. Dahl

1. See Robert A. Dahl, "The Concept of Power," *Behavorial Science*, Vol. 2 (July 1957), pp. 201–215.

2. C. Wright Mills, *The Power Elite* (New York, 1956), *passim.*

3. Mills, *op. cit.;* Floyd Hunter, *Community Power Structure* (Chapel Hill, 1953).

5. "POWER ELITE" OR "VETO GROUPS"?
William Kornhauser

1. Page references in the text for remarks by C. Wright Mills refer to *The Power Elite* (New York: Oxford University Press, 1956).

2. Page references in the text for remarks by David Riesman refer to *The Lonely Crowd* (New York: Doubleday Anchor, 1953).

3. C. Wright Mills, "The Power Elite," in A. Kornhauser (ed.), *Problems of Power in American Society* (Detroit: Wayne State University Press, 1957), p. 161.

4. *White Collar* (New York: Oxford University Press, 1951).

5. *The New Men of Power* (New York: Harcourt, Brace and Company, 1948).

6. *White Collar*, p. 327.

7. David Riesman and Nathan Glazer, "Criteria for Political Apathy," in Alvin W. Gouldner (ed.), *Studies in Leadership* (New York: Harper & Brothers, 1950).

8. *White Collar*, pp. 342–350.

9. "Criteria for Political Apathy," p. 520.

6. THE BALANCE OF POWER: PRESCRIPTION, CONCEPT, OR PROPAGANDA
Ernst B. Haas

1. W. Stubbs, *Seventeen Lectures on the Study of Medieval and Modern History*, Oxford, 1886, p. 225.

2. R. Cobden, *Political Writings*, London, 1878, pp. 111–14.

3. E. V. Gulick, *The Balance of Power*, Philadelphia, 1943, pp. 14–15; A. F. Pollard, "The Balance of Power," *Journal of the British Institute on International Affairs*, II (1923), pp. 60 ff.

4. A. Stern, "Das politische Gleichgewicht," *Archiv für Politik und Geschichte*, IV (1923), pp. 48–49.

5. L. Bucher, "Über politische Kunstausdrücke. II. Politisches Gleichgewicht," *Deutsche Revue*, XII (1887), pp. 333–39.

6. E. Kaeber, *Die Idee des Europäischen Gleichgewichts in der publizistichen Literatur vom 16. bis zur Mitte des 18 Jahrhunderts*, Berlin, 1906, pp. 22–25, 31–33, 33–35; see also E. Nys, "La théorie de l'équilibre européen," *Revue de droit international et de législation comparée*, XXV (1893), pp. 49–54.

7. H. J. Morgenthau, *Politics Among Nations*, New York, 1948, pp. 125, 134–45.

8. Q. Wright, *A Study of War*, Chicago, 1942, II, pp. 743–66.

9. It is of some significance that the terminological confusion is not confined to Western writing. Raymond L. Garthoff has shown that even though the Russian political vocabulary has separate expressions for most of the usages cited, in practice loose application creates exactly the same difficulty as in English so far as classification and analysis are concerned. Garthoff concludes that, from an examination of 250 citations using some form of balance of power expression, this summary can be made: 136 instances of balance meaning general "relation of forces," especially in the class struggle; 87 instances meaning a "general distribution" of power; 17 instances of balance meaning "equilibrium"; and 10 instances of balance meaning "preponderance" or hegemony. In discussions of international relations, the Soviet use of the term "balance of power" generally connotes an equilibrium of forces between the "imperialist" and "socialist" worlds, and is therefore associated with short-term policies of peaceful coexistence. "The Concept of the Balance of Power in Soviet Policy-Making," *World Politics*, IV (October 1951), pp. 88–90, 102–3, 108–9.

10. Bolingbroke, *Works*, Philadelphia, 1841, II, p. 257.

11. U.P. despatch in *Los Angeles Times*, September 1940, cited in Alfred Vagts, "The Balance of Power: Growth of an Idea," *World Politics*, I (October 1948), p. 86.

12. Réal de Curban, *La Science du gouvernement*, Paris, 1764, VI, pp. 443 ff.

13. Henri de Rohan, *De l'intérest des princes et estats de la Chréstienté*; Duplessis-Mornay, *Sur les moyens de diminuer l'Espagnol;* both cited in A. de Stieglitz, *De l'équilibre politique, du légitimisme et du principe des nationalités*, Paris, 1893–1897, I, pp. 21 ff. This work contains brief analyses of all the major pamphlets and treatises on the balance of power before 1800, and an analysis of the opinions of most writers on international law since Grotius.

14. K. Frantz, *Untersuchungen über das Europäische Gleichgewicht*, cited in K. Jacob, "Die Chimäre des Gleichgewichts," *Archiv für Urkundenforschung*, VI (1918), pp. 359–60.

15. Pollard, *op. cit.*, p. 59 (italics in original).

16. H. D. Lasswell, *World Politics and Personal Insecurity*, New York, 1935, ch. III.

17. Hauterive, *De l'état de la France à la fin de l'an VIII*, cited in Stern, *op. cit.*, p. 32.

18. L. Donnadieu, *Essai sur la théorie d'équilibre*, Paris, 1900, p. 111.

19. N. Spykman, *America's Strategy in World Politics*, New York, 1942, pp. 21–25.

20. F. G. Leckie, *An Historical Research into the Nature of the Balance of Power in Europe*, London, 1817, pp. 4, 242 ff., 292, 303, 350 ff.

21. O. Höijer, *La théorie de l'équilibre et le droit des gens*, Paris, 1917, pp. 52–59.

22. D. de Pradt, *Du Congrés de Vienne*, Paris, 1815, 1, pp. 67–69, 75 ff., 84 ff., 95, 104.

23. Stern, *op. cit.*, pp. 31–34.

24. Bucher, *op. cit.*, pp. 336, 338.

25. Bolingbroke, *op. cit.*, pp. 249, 258, 266, 291; W. T. R. Fox, *The Super Powers*, New York, 1944, pp. 161 ff.

26. J. B. Moore, *International Law and Some Current Illusions*, New York, 1924, p. 310.

27. Morgenthau, *op. cit.*, *passim.;* also F. L. Schuman, *International Politics*, New York, 1941, pp. 281 ff.

28. J. J. Rousseau, *Extrait du projet de paix perpetuelle de M. l'abbé de Saint-Pierre*, cited in Donnadieu, *op. cit.*, pp. 9–10.

29. F. Ratzel, *Politische Geographie*, Munich, 1908, cited in Kaeber, *op. cit.*, p. 4.

30. Donnadieu, *op. cit.*, p. xx. See also the description of Sir Eyre Crowe in the famous State Paper of 1907, in which the "universal law" approach predominates.

31. A. Sorel, *L'Europe et la Révolution française*, Paris, 1908, I, pp. 19–20, 30–35.

32. S. B. Fay, *Encyclopedia of the Social Sciences*, article on the balance of power, I, pp. 395–99.

33. G. P. Gooch, "European Diplomacy Before the War in the Light of the Archives," *International Affairs*, XVIII (1939), p. 78.

34. Fay, *op. cit.*, p. 396. Stieglitz is to be counted among those in agreement with the guide-and-system theory.

35. D. Hume, "On the Balance of Power," *Essays Moral, Political and Literary*, London, 1889, I, pp. 352–53.

36. For a study of the relationship between balance of trade and balance of power theories, cf. K. Pribram, "Die Idee des Gleichgewichts in der älteren nationalökonomischen Theorie," *Zeitschrift für Volkswirtschaft, Sozialpolitik und Verwaltung*, XVII (1908), pp. 1–28; see also Felix Gilbert, "The 'New Diplomacy' of the Eighteenth Century," *World Politics*, IV (October 1951), pp. 1–38.

37. C. Dupuis, *Le principe d'équilibre et le concert européen*, Paris, 1909, pp. 104–5.

38. E. de Vattel, *Le droit des gens ou principes de la loi naturelle*, III, pt. 3, pars. 28, 33, 42, 43, 44, 47, 48, 49, 50; Sir R. Phillimore, *Commentaries upon International Law*, London, 1871, I, pp. 468–511. Examples of this usage are found most commonly in the writings of statesmen. They will be cited below.

39. Réal de Curban, *op. cit.*, VI, p. 442.

40. See, e.g., H. N. Brailsford and G. Lowes Dickinson, as quoted in Georg Schwarzenberger, *Power Politics*, London, 1940, p. 123, and also the author's own comments, which also tend to equate power politics with power balance.

41. Spykman, *op. cit.*, pp. 1–21, 103–4.

42. The extreme example of this body of thought is represented by Wolff with his concept of the *civitas maxima* and the role of the balance of power in preventing its destruction

(*Ius Gentium Methoda Scientifica Pertactantum, pars.* 642–43, 646, 651, *Classics of International Law,* no. 13, 1934). Also Pufendorf, *Ius Naturae et Gentium.* Book VIII, ch. 6, *ibid.,* no. 17, 1934.

43. This difficulty may be demonstrated by the perhaps unconscious ease with which some modern writers present a balance of power picture as *description* and then readily switch to a *prescriptive* continuation of their discussion, despite the semantic and logical problems implied in this procedure.

44. I am indebted for this suggestion to Professor Oliver J. Lissitzyn.

7. NOTES ON THE OBSERVATION AND MEASUREMENT OF POWER
Herbert A. Simon

1. On the relation between nominalism and the arbitrariness of definitions see Morris Weitz's stimulating comments on "What Does Russell Mean by Analysis," pp. 110–121 in Paul Arthur Schilpp (ed.), *The Philosophy of Bertrand Russell* (Evanston: The Library of Living Philosophers, 1946). On the importance of clear and "appropriate" definitions to the early development of classical mechanics, see Ernst Mach, *The Science of Mechanics* (Chicago: The Open Court Publishing Company, 1902) especially pp. 358–367.

2. As we shall see, Harold D. Lasswell and Abraham Kaplan, in their otherwise very incisive analysis of power in *Power and Society* (New Haven: Yale University Press, 1950) came dangerously close to this latter error, being saved from it only by distinguishing between "influence" and "exercise of influence." Since their terminological convention is certainly inconvenient and confusing, I shall not follow it. Instead, I shall retain "value position" and "value potential" in place of their "influence," and use "influence" for their "exercise of influence."

3. It is not necessary, for present purposes, to distinguish between influence and power, and I shall continue to use the two words as synonyms.

4. On the other hand, if power is independently defined, this proposition becomes an empirical statement about the dynamics of power.

5. Lasswell and Kaplan, *op. cit.,* p. 71.

6. I refer here to the phenomenon of unilateral coupling, of great importance in electrical network theory, and more recently, business cycle theory. See Richard M. Goodwin, "Dynamical Coupling with Especial Reference to Markets Having Production Lags," *Econometrica,* 15 (July, 1947), 181–204.

7. For a technical discussion of the mathematical and statistical aspects of the problem, see Herbert A. Simon, "Causal Ordering and Identifiability," Tjalling Koopmans (ed.), *Econometric Methods* (New York: Wiley, 1953), Cowles Commission for Research in Economics Monograph, No. 14.

3. Carl J. Friedrich, *Constitutional Government and Democracy* (Boston: Little, Brown and Company, 1941), pp. 589–91.

9. Lasswell and Kaplan, *op. cit.,* p. 83.

10. To be sure, the connection can be even more complicated in a society where persons having a high value position are regarded as possessing the legitimate right to exercise influence. An example would be a prestigious scientist whose pronouncements on theology and politics are given respectful attention. But, properly speaking, the influence base in this case is not prestige but the rules of legitimacy in the society. I think the point will be clear after we have discussed, in the next paragraphs, the concept of legitimacy.

11. Lasswell and Kaplan, *op. cit.,* (a) p. 71, (b) p. 75, and (c) p. 133.

12. Lasswell and Kaplan take a middle ground on this question. According to them, legitimacy has real force (pp. 121–3, 134), but the holders of effective power, because they can interpret the essentially ambiguous rules of legitimacy, can rationalize almost any power structure they prefer (pp. 126–130). But the authors, while tending to discount the limits on the process of rationalization, do recognize that limits exist (p. 130).

13. I believe that most of the arguments against "quantitizing" or "measuring" the "qualitative" variables encountered in the social sciences stem from ignorance of how flexible the concept "quantity" is, and how indefinite the lines between quantity and quality. Such arguments are particularly suspect when it is asserted in one sentence that a particular variable is "essentially qualitative" and in the next that the adjectives "more" or "less" can be predicated of it.

14. As has been stated previously, in *Power and Society,* authority denotes power based on legitimacy.

15. Herbert A. Simon, "A Formal Theory of the Employment Relation," *Econometrica,* 19 (July, 1951), 293–305 and "A Comparison of Organization Theories," *The Review of Economic Studies,* 20, No. 1 (1952–3), 40–48.

8. THE CONCEPT OF POWER
Robert A. Dahl

1. By demonstrating the importance of concepts such as power and influence, particularly in political analysis, and by insisting upon rigorous conceptual clarity, Harold Lasswell has had a seminal influence. Cf. especially Reference 3. A similar approach will be found

in References 6, 7, 8, 10. For the approach of the present articles I owe a particularly heavy debt to March, with whom I had countless profitable discussions during a year we both spent as fellows at the Center for Advanced Study in the Behavioral Sciences. I have drawn freely not only on our joint work but on his own published and unpublished writings on the subject. The comments of Jacob Marschak on this paper have also been most helpful. There are, of course, approaches radically different from the one employed here and in the works mentioned above. John R. P. French, Jr. (2), has developed a model that assumes "a unidimensional continuum of opinion which can be measured with a ratio scale," and he defines "the power of A over B (with respect to a given opinion) [to be] equal to the maximum force which A can induce on B minus the maximum resisting force which B can mobilize in the opposite direction." Game theory provides still another approach. Cf. References 4, 5, 9.

9. TWO FACES OF POWER
Peter Bachrach and Morton S. Baratz

1. This paper is an outgrowth of a seminar in Problems of Power in Contemporary Society, conducted jointly by the authors for graduate students and undergraduate majors in political science and economics.

2. Compare, for example, the sociological studies of Floyd Hunter, *Community Power Structure* (Chapel Hill, 1953); Roland Pellegrini and Charles H. Coates, "Absentee-Owned Corporations and Community Power Structure," *American Journal of Sociology*, Vol. 61 (March 1956), pp. 413–19; and Robert O. Schulze, "Economic Dominants and Community Power Structure," *American Sociological Review*, Vol. 23 (February 1958), pp. 3–9; with political science studies of Wallace S. Sayre and Herbert Kaufman, *Governing New York City* (New York, 1960); Robert A. Dahl, *Who Governs?* (New Haven, 1961); and Norton E. Long and George Belknap, "A Research Program on Leadership and Decision-Making in Metropolitan Areas" (New York, Governmental Affairs Institute, 1956). See also Nelson W. Polsby, "How to Study Community Power: The Pluralist Alternative," *Journal of Politics*, Vol. 22 (August, 1960), pp. 474–84.

3. See especially N. W. Polsby, *op. cit.*, p. 475f.

4. *Ibid.*, p. 476.

5. *Ibid.*, pp. 478–79.

6. *Ibid.*, pp. 480–81.

7. See especially Robert A. Dahl, "A Critique of the Ruling-Elite Model," this REVIEW, Vol. 52 (June 1958), pp. 463–69; and Lawrence J. R. Herson, "In the Footsteps of Community Power," this REVIEW, Vol. 55 (December 1961), pp. 817–31.

8. This definition originated with Harold D. Lasswell and Abraham Kaplan, *Power and Society* (New Haven, 1950), p. 75.

9. Robert A. Dahl, "A Critique of the Ruling-Elite Model," *loc. cit.*, p. 466.

10. Arthur Bentley, *The Process of Government* (Chicago, 1908), p. 202, quoted in Polsby, *op. cit.*, p. 481n.

11. As is perhaps self-evident, there are similarities in both faces of power. In each, A participates in decisions and thereby adversely affects B. But there is an important difference between the two: in the one case, A openly participates; in the other, he participates only in the sense that he works to sustain those values and rules of procedure that help him keep certain issues out of the public domain. True enough, participation of the second kind may at times be overt; that is the case, for instance, in cloture fights in the Congress. But the point is that it need not be. In fact, when the maneuver is most successfully executed, it neither involves nor can be identified with decisions arrived at on specific issues.

12. E. E. Schattschneider, *The Semi-Sovereign People* (New York, 1960), p. 71.

13. Dahl *partially* concedes this point when he observes ("A Critique of the Ruling-Elite Model," pp. 468–69) that "one could argue that even in a society like ours a ruling elite might be so influential over ideas, attitudes, and opinions that a kind of false consensus will exist—not the phony consensus of a terroristic totalitarian dictatorship but the manipulated and superficially self-imposed adherence to the norms and goals of the elite by broad sections of a community. . . . This objection points to the need to be circumspect in interpreting the evidence." But that he largely misses our point is clear from the succeeding sentence: "Yet here, too, it seems to me that the hypothesis cannot be satisfactorily confirmed without something equivalent to the test I have proposed," and that is "by an examination of a series of concrete cases where key decisions are made. . . . "

14. *Op. cit.*, p. 466.

15. *Op. cit.*, p. 478.

16. As he points out, the expectations of the pluralist researchers "have seldom been disappointed." (*Ibid.*, p. 477).

17. *Op. cit.*, p. 467.

18. Herbert Kaufman and Victor Jones, "The Mystery of Power," *Public Administration Review*, Vol. 14 (Summer 1954), p. 207.

19. Robert A. Dahl, *Who Governs?* (New Haven, 1961).

20. *Ibid.*, p. 64.

21. *Ibid.*, p. 70.

22. *Ibid.*, p. 71.

23. *Op. cit.*, p. 467.

24. *Who Governs?*, p. 82. Dahl points out that "the main policy thrust of the Economic

Notables is to oppose tax increases; this leads them to oppose expenditures for anything more than minimal traditional city services. In this effort their two most effective weapons ordinarily are the mayor and the Board of Finance. The policies of the Notables are most easily achieved under a strong mayor if his policies coincide with theirs or under a weak mayor if they have the support of the Board of Finance .... New Haven mayors have continued to find it expedient to create confidence in their financial policies among businessmen by appointing them to the Board." (pp. 81–2).

25. Dahl does discuss in general terms (pp. 79–84) changes in the level of tax rates and assessments in past years, but not actual decisions of the Board of Finance or their effects on the public school system.

26. *Ibid.*, p. 124.

27. *Ibid.*, "A rough test of a person's overt or covert influence," Dahl states in the first section of the book, "is the frequency with which he successfully initiates an important policy over the opposition of others, or vetoes policies initiated by others, or initiates a policy where no opposition appears." (*Ibid.*, p. 66).

28. *Ibid.*, p. 131.

29. Dahl is, of course, aware of the "law of anticipated reactions." In the case of the mayor's relationship with the CAC, Dahl notes that Lee was "particularly skillful in estimating what the CAC could be expected to support or reject." (p. 137). However, Dahl was not interested in analyzing or appraising to what extent the CAC limited Lee's freedom of action. Because of his restricted concept of power, Dahl did not consider that the CAC might in this respect have exercised power. That the CAC did not initiate or veto actual proposals by the mayor was to Dahl evidence enough that the CAC was virtually powerless; it might as plausibly be evidence that the CAC was (in itself or in what it represented) so powerful that Lee ventured nothing it would find worth quarreling with.

30. The fact that the initiator of decisions also refrains—because he anticipates adverse reactions—from initiating other proposals does not obviously lessen the power of the agent who limited his initiative powers. Dahl missed this point: "It is," he writes, "all the more improbable, then, that a secret cabal of Notables dominates the public life of New Haven through means so clandestine that not one of the fifty prominent citizens interviewed in the course of this study—citizens who had participated extensively in various decisions—hinted at the existence of such a cabal. . . " (p. 185).

In conceiving of elite domination exclusively in the form of a conscious cabal exercising the power of decision-making and vetoing, he overlooks a more subtle form of domination; one

in which those who actually dominate are not conscious of it themselves, simply because their position of dominance has never seriously been challenged.

31. Sayre and Kaufman, *op. cit.*, p. 640. For perceptive study of the "mobilization of bias" in a rural American community, see Arthur Vidich and Joseph Bensman, *Small Town in Mass Society* (Princeton, 1958).

10. DECISIONS AND NONDECISIONS: AN ANALYTICAL FRAMEWORK
Peter Bachrach and Morton S. Baratz

1. See, *e.g.*, Floyd Hunter, *Community Power Structure* (Chapel Hill, 1953); and Robert A. Dahl, *Who Governs?* (New Haven, 1961).

2. Peter Bachrach and Morton S. Baratz, "Two Faces of Power," *American Political Science Review*, Vol. 56, (December 1962), pp. 947–52. A somewhat similar view, arrived at independently, may be found in Thomas J. Anton, "Power, Pluralism, and Local Politics," *Administrative Science Quarterly*, Vol. 7 (March 1963), p. 453.

3. See Bachrach and Baratz, *op. cit.*, pp. 947, 952.

4. *Cf.* Peter Rossi, "Community Decision-Making," in Roland Young (ed.), *Approaches to the Study of Politics* (Evanston, Ill., 1958), p. 359.

5. Thomas Hobbes, as paraphrased by C. J. Friedrich, *Constitutional Government and Politics* (New York, 1937), p. 12.

6. Harold D. Lasswell and Abraham Kaplan, *Power and Society* (New Haven, 1950), p. 75, draw this implication from the definition of power, *i.e.*, "the production of intended effects," in Bertrand Russell, *Power: A New Social Analysis* (New York, 1938), p. 35.

7. Lasswell and Kaplan, *loc. cit.*

8. Agreement based upon reason represents another kind of interpersonal relationship—authority—which is discussed below.

9. It might be argued that the "victim" did not actually exercise power in this instance, because he had no sanctions with which to threaten the sentry. This objection misses the obvious point: the "victim" threatened the guard with severe deprivations (dishonor, imprisonment) if the guard did not perform his soldierly duty by complying with the "victim's" command that he (the "victim") be killed.

10. See part IV below.

11. See part II below.

12. Lasswell and Kaplan, *op. cit.*, p. 76. We have deleted "actual or" from the parenthetical expression because *actual* deprivation for nonconformity is a property of force, rather than power. This point is discussed further below.

The Lasswell-Kaplan definition is open to another criticism. They observe (p. 77) that "to have power is to be taken into account in others' acts (policies)." Strictly construed, this must mean that any and every person or group involved—in whatever degree—in decision-making must have power. For is not the farmer who markets .001 percent of the total supply of wheat "taken into account" by other buyers and sellers in just the same sense—though not, of course, in the same degree—as in the General Motors Corporation in the determination of automobile prices? Or, to change the illustration, is it not the case that, in the literal interpretation of the word, nonvoters as well as voters "participate," and therefore have power, in deciding close elections? We should think so. But if this is what is meant by power, how can we avoid concluding that no matter where we look, we shall always find that power is broadly diffused? To rephrase, if (a) we analyze the distribution of power solely in terms of decision-making and (b) we ascribe power to all who participate in whatever measure or with whatever "weight" ("The weight of power is the degree of participation in the making of decisions . . . " [*Ibid.*], then (c) do we not necessarily prejudge that power in real-world situations will be widely dispersed? For further discussion of this general question, see Bachrach and Baratz, *op. cit.*

13. See part III below.

14. See Richard E. Neustadt, *Presidential Power* (New York, 1960), p. 21. Compare Thomas C. Schelling, *The Strategy of Conflict* (Cambridge, Mass., 1960), pp. 38–9.

15. This error, compounded by that of regarding power as something which is possessed, may well have underlain the policy of the United States toward Chiang Kai-Shek during the period (1944–49) of the Chinese civil war. It is entirely possible, that is to say, that in providing substantial amounts of armament to the Kuomintang regime, we mistook the instruments of power for power itself; and, in addition, by interpreting the Kuomintang-Communist struggle in terms of our own values, we utterly misread the temper of the great majority of the Chinese people.

The abortive invasion of Cuba in April 1961 is perhaps another example of the inherent dangers in projecting our values onto a populace holding a different collection of interests. Looking at the great body of Cuban nationals who were apparently bereft both of individual freedom and personal dignity, we concluded that we need only provide the opportunity, the spark, which would ignite nationwide uprisings against the Castro regime. But hindsight has indicated how badly we misread popular feeling in Cuba. See Stewart Alsop, "Lessons of the Cuban Disaster," *Saturday Evening Post*, 24 June 1961, pp. 26–27.

16. Neustadt, *op. cit.*, pp. 12–13. On the general point, see also Schelling, *op. cit.*, p. 6.

17. The point is also well illustrated by Franco-American policy differences in the early 1960s. Committed both to the defense of Western Europe and to strict limitation on the number of nations with independent nuclear forces, the United States was caught in a dilemma in its dealings with General de Gaulle. In the words of a contemporary observer, "De Gaulle . . . has played a judo trick on the United States . . . [He] means to fashion his 'European construction,' based on the *force de frappe* and the Franco-German axis and excluding the British and Americans. And he means to do this *under the umbrella of the American nuclear deterrent* . . . There is precious little the Kennedy Administration can do about de Gaulle's judo trick—short of removing its nuclear protection. And this has not even been seriously considered . . . . 'We're a bit like that little Dutch boy with his finger in the dike,' says one Kennedy adviser. Remove the American commitment to defend Europe, and the result is unmitigated disaster, not only to Europe but to the United States. Thus the United States, like the little Dutch boy, is immobilized. The strongest power in the Western alliance has amazingly little bargaining power in the alliance." Stuart Alsop, "Should We Pull Out of Europe?" *Saturday Evening Post*, 13 April 1963, p. 80. Emphasis in original.

The main point is made more pithily by "President Hudson" in Allen Drury's novel, *A Shade of Difference* (New York, 1962), p. 82: "The more real power you have, the less you can afford to exercise it, and the less real power you have, the more you can throw it around."

For further discussion of the relationship between power and commitment, see E. Abramson *et al.*, "Social Power and Commitment Theory," *American Sociological Review*, Vol. 23 (February 1958), pp. 15–22.

18. With Lasswell and Kaplan, *op. cit.*, p. 16, we define a value as "a desired event—a goal event. That X values Y means that X acts so as to bring about the consummation of Y."

19. *Ibid.*, p. 76.

20. *Ibid.*, p. 77.

21. *Op. cit.*, pp. 17–18. A corollary proposition could be called the "rule of *mis*anticipated reactions." We refer to a situation in which one person grudgingly conforms to what he *thinks* another wants, but finds after the fact either that he misread the other's preferences or that the latter never intended to invoke sanctions for behavior contrary to his preferences.

22. "An Analysis of Social Power," *American Sociological Review*, Vol. 15 (December 1950), p. 733.

23. A major defect of Lord Russell's conception of power (see above, note 6) is that it utterly ignores this distinction. One can produce an "intended effect" through the exercise of either power or force.

24. It is often true, when force is operative, that A gives B the option to comply with his demands *between* blows. But in such circumstances, should B bend to A's wishes, he does so out of fear of further sanctions, in which case force is transformed into power.

25. One of the more penetrating critiques along these lines may be found in General Maxwell D. Taylor, *The Uncertain Trumpet* (New York, 1959).

26. According to Bierstedt, *op. cit.*, p. 731, "... influence is persuasive while power is coercive. We submit voluntarily to influence while power requires submission." In our view, if B submits voluntarily, power is operative; but if he submits under duress, force is operative.

It is worth noting that under our definition it would be incorrect to say that Marx "influenced" Lenin, or that Haydn "influenced" Mozart, or that Jesus Christ "influenced" the Conquistadores. In each of these cases the second *shared* the values of the first, *i.e.*, the relationship involved neither power nor influence, but *authority*. See part IV below.

27. See Richard H. Rovere, *Senator Joe McCarthy* (New York, 1959).

28. C. J. Friedrich, "Authority, Reason and Discretion," in C. J. Friedrich (ed.), *Authority* (Cambridge, Mass., 1958), p. 37.

29. Lasswell and Kaplan, *op. cit.*, p. 133.

30. Bierstedt, *op. cit.*, p. 733.

31. *Authority*, pp. 35, 36.

32. As is perhaps obvious, if B chooses to defy A, the relationship no longer will involve power. This notion of rationality of choice is analogous to Thomas Hobbes's treatment of the relationship between fear and liberty. "Feare, and Liberty," he wrote, "are consistent; as when a man throweth his goods into the Sea for *feare* the ship should sink, he doth it nevertheless very willingly, and may refuse to doe it if he will: It is therefore the action, of one that was free." *Leviathan*, Everyman Edition, p. 110.

33. Friedrich, *Authority*, p. 36. Reasoning also underlies the difference between authority and influence. Thus, if B complies with A's demand neither because he fears deprivations nor because his compliance is based upon reasoning, B has been influenced. This distinction will be further elaborated below.

34. *Ibid.*, p. 38.

35. *Ibid.*, p. 47.

36. Robert A. Dahl, "The Analysis of Influence in Local Communities," in Charles Adrian (ed.), *Social Science and Community Action* (East Lansing, Mich., 1960), p. 26.

37. Peter Rossi, "Community Decision-Making," in Roland Young (ed.), *Approaches to the Study of Politics* (Evanston, Ill., 1958), p. 364.

38. *Op. cit.*, p. 74.

39. For example, A may employ both authority *and* power to gain B's agreement, and B's response may have a similarity dual basis. An apparent case in point is the relationship between Adolf Hitler and some of his military chiefs during World War II. On this, consult William L. Shirer, *The Rise and Fall of the Third Reich* (New York, 1960), pp. 366 ff. and *passim*.

40. The approach we have in mind is exemplified by the untutored, but nevertheless penetrating, study of "Springdale" by Joseph Vidich and Arthur Bensman, *Small Town in Mass Society* (Princeton, N.J., 1958). For further discussion of this point, see following section.

41. *Ibid.*

11. SOME AMBIGUITIES IN THE NOTION OF POWER
William H. Riker

1. L. S. Shapley and Martin Shubik, "A Method for Evaluating the Distribution of Power in a Committee System," this REVIEW, Vol. 48 (1954), pp. 787–92; L. S. Shapley, "A Value for *N*-Person Games," *Annals of Mathematics Study No. 28* (Princeton, 1953) pp. 307–17 and "Simple Games," *Behavioral Science*, Vol. 7 (1962), pp. 59–66.

2. James G. March, "Measurement Concepts in the Theory of Influence," *Journal of Politics*, Vol. 19 (1957), pp. 202–226; see also his "An Introduction to the Theory and Measurement of Influence," this REVIEW, Vol. 49 (1955), pp. 431–51.

3. Robert A. Dahl, "The Concept of Power," *Behavioral Science*, Vol. 2 (1957), pp. 201–15, at pp. 202–03. Note that Harsanyi has modified Dahl's definition (and also Shapley's) by adding opportunity costs. Since these modifications do not affect the basic theory, I have not discussed them here. John C. Harsanyi, "Measurement of Social Power, Opportunity Costs, and the Theory of Two-Person Bargaining Games," and "Measurement of Social Power in *N*-Person Reciprocal Power Situations," *Behavioral Science*, Vol. 7 (1962), pp. 67–80, 81–92.

4. Dorwin Cartwright, "A Field Theoretical Conception of Power," pp. 183–220, in Dorwin Cartwright, ed., *Studies in Social Power* (Ann Arbor, 1959).

5. Georg Karlsson, "Some Aspects of Power in Small Groups," in Joan H. Criswell, Herbert Solomon, and Patrick Suppes (eds.), *Mathematical Methods in Small Group Processes* (Stanford, 1962), pp. 193–202.

6. If Cartwright's force to comply, f_{ab}, and force to resist, $f_{\overline{ab}}$, could be translated into conditional probabilities of compliance and resistance, then Cartwright's definition would be exactly the same as Dahl's formula, $p_1 - p_2$.

7. Douglas Gasking, "Causation and Recipes," *Mind*, Vol. 64 (1955), pp. 479–87.

8. William H. Riker, "Causes of Events," *The Journal of Philosophy*, Vol. 55 (1958), pp. 281–91. This essay depends for its terminology on my "Events and Situations," *The Journal of Philosophy*, Vol. 54 (1957) pp. 57–90.

9. Herbert Simon, *Models of Man* (New York, 1957), chap. 1, 3.

10. G. J. Warnock, " 'Every Event Has a Cause' " in Anthony Flew, ed., *Logic and Language*, Second Series (Oxford, 1953) p. 101 ff.

11. But see the addendum of this paper for evidence of a manipulative element in their definition.

12. Peter Bachrach and Morton Baratz, "Two Faces of Power," this REVIEW, Vol. 56 (1962), pp. 957–52.

13. J. David Singer, "Inter-nation Influence," this REVIEW, Vol. 57 (1963), pp. 420–30.

12. INFLUENCE, LEADERSHIP, CONTROL
Dorwin Cartwright

1. The preparation of this chapter was facilitated by a grant-in-aid from the Ford Foundation.

2. From *The Human Side of Enterprise*, by D. M. McGregor. Copyright 1960. McGraw-Hill Book Company. Used by permission.

3. I am indebted to Daniel Katz and Robert L. Kahn for letting me read parts of their forthcoming book, *The Social Psychology of Organizations*. Many of the ideas presented here were stimulated by this manuscript.

13. AN INTRODUCTION TO THE THEORY AND MEASUREMENT OF INFLUENCE
James G. March

1. See, for example, Robert A. Dahl, *Congress and Foreign Policy* (New York, 1950), Part I; Harold D. Lasswell and Abraham Kaplan, *Power and Society* (New Haven, 1950), pp. 74–83; Seymour M. Lipset, Paul F. Lazarsfeld, Allen H. Barton, and Juan Linz, "The Psychology of Voting: An Analysis of Political Behavior," in the *Handbook of Social Psychology*, ed. Lindzey (Cambridge, 1954), Vol. 2, pp. 1124–75; Martin Shubik, *Readings in Game Theory and Political Behavior* (New York, 1954); Herbert A. Simon, Donald W. Smithburg, and Victor A. Thompson, *Public Administration* (New York, 1950), Ch. 3; Richard C. Snyder, H. W. Bruck, Burton Sapin, *Decision-Making as an Approach to the Study of International Politics* (Princeton, 1954).

2. Ward Edwards, "The Theory of Decision-Making," *Psychological Bulletin*, Vol. 51, pp. 380–417 (July, 1954); Paul F. Lazarsfeld, Elihu Katz, et al., *Personal Influence* (Glencoe, 1954); L. J. Savage, *The Foundations of Statistics* (New York, 1954); *Decision Processes*, ed. Thrall, Coombs, and Davis (New York, 1954).

3. Note that this does not commit one to a Newtonian psychology; nor is it anticipated that an analogical approach to the theory of influence will prove particularly useful.

4. Because it partially avoids this pitfall by relying heavily on learning theory, the recent Yale volume on persuasion has considerable merit. See Carl I. Hovland, Irving L. Janis, and Harold H. Kelley, *Communication and Persuasion* (New Haven, 1953).

5. See, for example, Tjalling C. Koopmans, "Identification Problems in Economic Model Construction," in *Studies in Econometric Method*, ed. Hood and Koopmans (New York, 1953), pp. 27–48.

6. A "closed loop" system is one in which the variables within the system are related in such a way that one can trace a chain of relationships from a given variable through other variables and back to the original starting point without retracing one's steps. Thus a fairly common set of hypotheses in voting behavior forms the following closed loop: voting intention→exposure to party position on the state of the economy→perception of the state of economy→voting intention. An "open loop" system is one in which such circles do not exist. The terms were borrowed originally from servomechanics, where they are used primarily to describe different types of automatic control devices.

7. Hovland, *Communication and Persuasion*, Ch. 8, and the articles there cited.

8. To be sure, one can define something in any way he pleases. What is meant is that a uni-dimensional influence index will rarely be of much utility.

9. James G. March, "Husband-Wife Interaction over Political Issues," *Public Opinion Quarterly*, Vol. 17, pp. 461–70 (Winter, 1953–54); Albert H. Rubenstein, "Problems in the Measurement of Interpersonal Communication in an Ongoing Situation," *Sociometry*, Vol. 16, p. 86 (Feb., 1953).

10. George Galloway, *The Legislative Process in Congress* (New York, 1953), Ch. 14.

11. If the index has only two values, it is possible to talk of a set theoretical model for describing the relationship, defining a partitioning of the joint decisions of A and B into mutually exclusive sets of decisions made by either A or B alone. Comparison of influence positions then depends either upon the development of comparison values or upon the existence of a situation in which the set of decisions made by A alone at time t_0 is properly included in the set made by A alone at time t_1,

or in the set made by B alone at some given time. If a multi-valued index is used, vector notation seems to be indicated and the development of standard measurement units to be of central importance.

12. Lasswell and Kaplan, *Power and Society*, p. 76; David B. Truman, *The Governmental Process* (New York, 1951), pp. 188–93.

13. For the moment, at least, we will not consider the complications introduced by the possibility that the President's announcement is induced by certain previous activities on the part of the Congressman.

14. H. O. A. Wold, "Causality and Econometrics," *Econometrica*, Vol. 22, pp. 162–77 (April, 1954). For a general discussion of the function of explanatory laws in the construction of theory, see Clark L. Hull, *Principles of Behavior* (New York, 1943), Ch. 1.

15. Herbert A. Simon, "On the Definition of the Causal Relation," *Journal of Philosophy*, Vol. 49, pp. 517–28 (July 31, 1952); and "Notes on the Observation and Measurement of Political Power," *Journal of Politics*, Vol. 15, pp. 500–16 (Nov., 1953).

16. Simon, "Notes" (cited in note 15), pp. 513–14; March, "Husband-Wife Interaction" (cited in note 9), pp. 469–70.

17. Note the problem of spurious correlation that exists here as elsewhere in the treatment of causality. The fact that the behaviors of the premiers of Hungary and Roumania appear to co-vary is not sufficient evidence upon which to establish an influence relationship between them.

18. Special acknowledgement is due to Professors Harold Guetzkow and Herbert Simon and to Messrs. Douglas K. Mims, Frederick Stern, and Fred M. Tonge for their criticisms and suggestions with respect to the model outlined in this section.

19. For a similar definition, see Donald B. Lindsley, "Electroencephalography," in *Personality and the Behavior Disorders*, ed. Hunt (New York, 1944), Vol. 2, p. 1033.

20. Excluded, consequently, from the present discussion is the influence analysis of a wholly self-contained system—that is, one in which all variables are determined by system variables exclusively. This applies whether the system involved is the individual personality or a number of such personalities.

21. Charles E. Osgood, *Method and Theory in Experimental Psychology* (New York, 1953).

22. Donald B. Lindsley, "Emotion," in the *Handbook of Experimental Psychology*, ed. Stevens (New York, 1951), pp. 473–516.

23. William R. Ashby, *Design for a Brain* (New York, 1952); Donald O. Hebb, *The Organization of Behavior* (New York, 1949).

24. Norbert Wiener, *Cybernetics* (Cambridge, 1948).

25. Rudolph Carnap and Y. Bar-Hillel, *An Outline of a Theory of Semantic Information*, Technical Report No. 247, Research Laboratory of Electronics, Massachusetts Institute of Technology, October 27, 1952.

26. Kurt Lewin, *The Conceptual Representation and the Measurement of Psychological Forces* (Durham, 1938).

27. Kenneth J. Arrow, "Alternative Approaches to the Theory of Choice in Risk-Taking Situation," *Econometrica*, Vol. 19, pp. 404–32 (Oct., 1951); John von Neumann and Oskar Morganstern, *Theory of Games and Economic Behavior* (Princeton, 1947), pp. 15–31.

28. The latter can be treated as a special case of the former if the probability web be taken as completely defined but having frequent instances where $p = 0$.

29. One example of such clarification is presented in the present section. The writer is persuaded it is far from an isolated case. For example, some of the respects in which the problem of generality is attacked have been indicated in the discussion of influence processes (e.g., the elements of similarity between habit—and therefore the extended literature on habit—and legitimacy). With respect to the dimensionality of an influence relationship, the model suggests that in addition to the subject matter under consideration it may be necessary to differentiate influence over alternative suggesting from influence over choice among given alternatives, influence over highly specific acts or attitudes from influence over underlying value premises, etc.

30. Carl J. Friedrich, *Constitutional Government and Democracy* (Boston, 1941), pp. 589–91; Simon, "Notes" (cited in note 15), pp. 505–6.

31. For example, Floyd Hunter, *Community Power Structure* (Chapel Hill, 1953); J. I. Hurwitz *et al.*, "Some Effects of Power on the Relations among Group Members," in *Group Dynamics*, ed. Cartwright and Zander (Evanston, 1953), pp. 483–92; Ronald Lippitt *et al.*, "The Dynamics of Power," *ibid.*, pp. 462–82.

32. For example, James Bieri, "Changes in Interpersonal Perceptions Following Social Interaction," *Journal of Abnormal and Social Psychology*, Vol. 48, pp. 61–66 (Jan., 1953); Harvey Cromwell and Richard Kunkel, "An Experimental Study of the Effect on the Attitude of Listeners of Repeating the Same Oral Propaganda," *Journal of Social Psychology*, Vol. 35, pp. 175–84 (May, 1952); James C. Davies, "Some Relations between Events and Attitudes," this REVIEW, Vol. 46, pp. 777–8, (Sept., 1952); Leon Festinger *et al.*, "The Influence Process in the Presence of Extreme Deviates," *Human Relations*, Vol. 5, pp. 327–46 (Nov., 1952).

33. For example, Harold H. Kelley, "The Warm-Cold Variable in First Impressions of Persons," *Journal of Personality*, Vol. 18, pp. 431–39 (June, 1950); Malcolm Moos and

B. Koslin, "Prestige Suggestion and Political Leadership," *Public Opinion Quarterly*, Vol. 16, pp. 77–93 (Spring, 1952); Jack A. Parrish and Donald T. Campbell, "Measuring Propaganda Effects with Direct and Indirect Attitude Tests," *Journal of Abnormal and Social Psychology*, Vol. 48, pp. 3–9 (Jan., 1953); Stanley Schachter and Robert Hall, "Group-Derived Restraints and Audience Persuasion," *Human Relations*, Vol. 5, pp. 397–406 (Nov., 1952).

34. One variation of the more standard opinion-change techniques warrants specific mention. Where the influence relationship studied involves a simple dyad, it is possible to use the revealed-differences method. Two respondents are presented with problems, each of which admits of only two possible responses. They are then asked to reconcile any differences that arise and arrive at a joint position for each question. The proportion of decisions "won" by the most-winning person forms an index of the influence differential. To the extent that it is possible to assume the equal weighting of decisions, such a method is feasible and provides a reasonably straightforward way of comparing different relationships. See Fred L. Strodtbeck, "Husband-Wife Interaction over Revealed Differences," *American Sociological Review*, Vol. 16, pp. 468–73 (Aug., 1951). Recently, Strodtbeck has been experimenting with a similar technique in three-person groups.

35. Samuel A. Stouffer *et al.*, *Measurement and Prediction* (Princeton, 1950).

36. Herbert C. Kelman, "Attitude Change as a Function of Response Restriction," *Human Relations*, Vol. 6, pp. 185–214 (Aug., 1953).

37. Raymond L. Gorden, "Interaction between Attitude and the Definition of the Situation in the Expression of Opinion," *American Sociological Review*, Vol. 17, pp. 50–58 (Feb., 1952).

38. Rheem F. Jarrett and Alex C. Sheriffs, "Propaganda, Debate, and Impartial Presentation as Determiners of Attitude Change," *Journal of Abnormal and Social Psychology*, Vol. 48, pp. 33–41 (Jan., 1953).

39. Everett W. Bovard, "Group Structure and Perception," *Journal of Abnormal and Social Psychology*, Vol. 46, pp. 398–405 (July, 1951).

40. Irving, L. Janis *et al.*, "Effects of Preparatory Communications on Reactions to a Subsequent News Event," *Public Opinion Quarterly*, Vol. 15, pp. 487–518 (Fall, 1951).

41. Malcolm G. Preston and Roy K. Heintz, "Effects of Participatory vs. Supervisory Leadership on Group Judgment," *Journal of Abnormal and Social Psychology*, Vol. 44, pp. 345–55 (July, 1949).

42. Carl I. Hovland and Walter Weiss, "The Influence of Source Credibility on Communication Effectiveness," *Public Opinion Quarterly*, Vol. 15, pp. 635–50 (Winter, 1951–52).

43. Solomon E. Asch, "Effects of Group Pressure upon the Modification and Distortion of Judgments," in *Groups, Leadership, and Men*, ed. Guetzkow (Pittsburgh, 1951) pp. 177–90.

44. One method of avoiding this difficulty is to prohibit communication between respondents and present them with problems completely alien to their experience. Such procedures pose considerable problems of interpretation, but they do provide interesting and important data on the mechanisms of personal adjustment used by the satellite individual in a situation of uncertainty.

45. The recording of interactive events has been used by several observers in one form or another, probably the best known being those developed by Bales and Carter. See Robert F. Bales, *Interaction Process Analysis* (Cambridge, 1950); Launor Carter *et al.*, "A Note on a New Technique of Interaction Recording," *Journal of Abnormal and Social Psychology*, Vol. 46, pp. 258–60 (April, 1951). In essence, the observation of influence in this case is made by attempting to observe the in-process interaction.

46. Theodore M. Mills, "Power Relations in Three-Person Groups," *American Sociology Review*, Vol. 18, pp. 351–57 (Aug., 1953); Norman Polansky *et al.*, "An Investigation of Behavioral Contagion in Groups," *Human Relations*, Vol. 3, pp. 319–48 (Nov., 1950).

47. Kurt W. Back, "Influence through Social Communication," *Journal of Abnormal and Social Psychology*, Vol. 46, pp. 9–23 (Jan., 1951).

48. Festinger *et al.*, "Influence Process" (cited in note 32).

49. Lippitt *et al.*, "Dynamics of Power" (cited in note 31).

14. MEASUREMENT CONCEPTS IN THE THEORY OF INFLUENCE
James G. March

1. James G. March, "An Introduction to the Theory and Measurement of Influence," *American Political Science Review*, Vol. 49, (June, 1955), pp. 431–451; James G. March, "Influence Measurement in Experimental and Semi-Experimental Groups," *Sociometry*, in press.

2. It should be clear below that the distinctions made here are not unknown to the literature. In particular, the studies by Hovland, Janis and Kelley (Carl I. Hovland, Irving L. Janis, and Harold H. Kelley, *Communication and Persuasion* (New Haven, 1953) appear to make the same general types of distinctions. Where studies are less closely tied to an experimental tradition, however, they tend to be less

satisfactory in this respect. I hasten to add that this appears to stem primarily from a mode of thinking about the problem rather than from any insurmountable advantage of laboratory experimentation over at least some other forms of investigation.

3. A relation (R) is reflexive if aRa. It is transitive if aRb and bRc imply aRc. It is anti-symmetric if aRb and bRa imply a = b. The transitivity problem with respect to the criteria proposed in the present paper is discussed in the appendix on transitivity.

4. A relation is symmetric if aRb implies bRa.

5. The appellation "metric" is not arbitrary, however. The present conception is closely related to formal measures theory. See Raymond L. Wilder, "Point Sets," in *Encyclopaedia Britannica* (Chicago, 1954), Vol. 18, p. 117.

6. This will be important to the discussion in section VIII below.

7. It should be noted that in the example just given the dependency of the statements on the class of behaviors specified is also manifest. Had all possible voting patterns on the part of the two role-players been considered, a different result would have been obtained.

8. It is, of course, true that not all matrices will decompose so neatly.

9. It may be worth noting that this is the situation involved in a multiple-house legislative process where unanimity among the houses is required (equate B_1 with passage in one house, B_2 with failure in one house, 1 with ultimate passage, and 0 with ultimate failure). It has frequently been observed that such a process has a built-in bias against change. This bias is here accurately portrayed as greater influence attaching to one behavior than to another.

10. Two elements (a and b) of an ordered set "touch" if there is no other element in the set (x) such that either $a > x > b$ or $b > x > a$.

11. It will be noted that the explication here is closely related to the general measure concept of distance. The justification for making set-restriction basic rather than distance lies primarily outside the formal system in the possible behavioral interpretations of the two and in the writer's intuitive sense of the proper fundamental-derived relationship. Since neither of these is necessarily persuasive, others may well find it more sensible to reverse the order and start with the distance concept. Such a course of action is both feasible and unexceptionable.

12. See Garrett Birkhoff, *Lattice Theory* (New York, 1948), p. x.

13. Thus, a convex hull for persons more familiar with the theory of convex bodies.

14. Note that although there are three components to the vectors, there are only two degrees of freedom. Consequently, a two-dimensional representation is possible. Note also that if the last vector had been (.3, .4, .3) a triangular set would have been sufficient.

15. Of course, the disadvantage ultimately lies not with the measure but with the inadequacies of knowledge or the character of the situation that make it necessary. Where the measure is appropriate, it should be used.

16. Although it is not necessary to the present argument, the matrices in the examples of this section have been constructed so that the diagonals sum to 1. This is based on the fact that the positions "for" and "against" depend critically on the parliamentary accident of phrasing of a bill. The argument would have been stronger if the referent were motions rather than bills, but in any event nothing in the present paper depends in any way on this special feature of a particular case.

17. This particular matrix represents a type of situation having considerable theoretical importance. The case and its relevance to the concepts proposed here are examined in detail in the appendix on intent.

18. The most frequent weighting scheme would probably be one of equal weights, particularly in the uncertain outcome case. Where equal weights are assumed, the measure becomes a simple counting of the number of elements.

19. If, in fact, the metric does not do so, the problem becomes real but can still be overcome by an appropriate weighting rule that provides non-zero weights to only a finite number of outcomes. It is hard to imagine a situation in which this would make sense, however.

20. Speaking loosely!

21. In some cases an approximation to asking hypothetical questions of the system can be achieved by asking detailed hypothetical questions of the individuals involved in the system. These can then be validated against those cases were nature provides an actual experiment.

22. Typically, the costs of unreliability of the estimates would have to be compared with such other costs as those of combining classes to increase sample size.

23. Such limits depend, of course, on the confidence level chosen and the statistical tests used. Provided the frequencies are moderately large, normal theory and a t-test seems appropriate.

15. SPURIOUS CORRELATION: A CAUSAL INTERPRETATION
Herbert Simon

1. See Koopmans (2) for a survey and references to the literature.

2. Simon (6) and (7). See also Orcutt (4) and (5). I should like, without elaborating it here, to

insert the *caveat* that the concept of causal ordering employed in this paper does not in any way solve the "problem of Hume" nor contradict his assertion that all we can ever observe are covariations. If we employ an ontological definition of cause—one based on the notion of the "necessary" connection of events—then correlation cannot, of course, prove causation. But neither can anything else prove causation, and hence we have no basis for distinguishing "true" from "spurious" correlation. If we wish to retain the latter distinction (and working scientists have not shown that they are able to get along without it), and if at the same time we wish to remain empiricists, then the term "cause" must be defined in a way that does not entail objectionable ontological consequences. That is the course we shall pursue here.

3. Zeisel [9], pp. 192–95. Reference to the original source will show that in this and the following example we have changed the variables from attributes to continuous variables for purposes of exposition.

4. Zeisel [9], pp. 191–92.

5. The question of how we distinguish between "dependent" and "independent" variables is discussed in Simon (7), and will receive further attention in this paper.

6. Since these are empirical assumptions it is conceivable that they are wrong, and indeed, we can imagine mechanisms that would reverse the causal ordering in the second example. What is argued here is that these assumptions, right or wrong, are implicit in the determination of whether the correlation is true or spurious.

7. Of course, the expected values are not, strictly speaking, observables except in a probability sense. However, we do not wish to go into sampling questions here, and simply assume that we have good estimates of the expected values.

16. THE LINKAGE BETWEEN CONSTITUENCY ATTITUDES AND CONGRESSIONAL VOTING BEHAVIOR: A CAUSAL MODEL

Charles F. Cnudde and Donald J. McCrone

1. Warren E. Miller and Donald E. Stokes, "Constituency Influence in Congress," this REVIEW, 57 (1963), 45–56.

2. For other material on the linkage problem, see especially V. O. Key, Jr., *Public Opinion and American Democracy* (New York: Alfred A. Knopf, 1961), pp. 441–531.

3. Briefly, the representation study interrelates three types of data collected in 1958. First, a mass survey was conducted according to probability sampling methods. From this survey central tendencies on attitudinal dimensions were computed for 116 congressional districts. Second, interviews were conducted with incumbent and non-incumbent candidates running for

the House of Representatives from these constituencies. The third set of data consisted of Guttman scales of roll call votes taken in Congress on civil rights, social welfare and foreign policy. For a fuller description of the study, see Warren E. Miller and Donald E. Stokes, *Representation in the American Congress* (Englewood Cliffs, N. J.: Prentice-Hall, in press).

4. Sewall Wright, "Correlation and Causation," *Journal of Agricultural Research*, 20 (1921), 557–585.

5. Miller and Stokes, "Constituency Influence in Congress," *op. cit.*, pp. 50–51.

6. *Ibid.*, p. 53.

7. *Loc. cit.*

8. Hubert M. Blalock, Jr., *Causal Inferences in Nonexperimental Research* (Chapel Hill: The University of North Carolina Press, 1964), p. 62. Also see Herbert A. Simon, "Spurious Correlations: A Causal Interpretation," *Journal of the American Statistical Association*, 49 (1954), 467–479.

9. In the three-variable model, for example, if we predict that the relationship between B and C is spurious because they are both dependent variables of A, the Simon-Blalock method predicts that the product of the correlations between A and C, and A and B will equal the correlation between C and B. Thus: $rCB = rAC\,rAB$.

10. At the very least, then, this method allows us to eliminate logically possible alternative models from our store of explanations. For the utility of regression coefficients, see Blalock, *op. cit.*, pp. 85–87.

11. For a recent application of the Simon technique, see Thad L. Beyle, "Contested Elections and Voter Turnout in A Local Community: A Problem in Spurious Correlation," this REVIEW, 59 (March, 1965), 111–117.

12. Miller and Stokes, "Constituency Influence in Congress," *op. cit.*, pp. 52–53.

13. If B is an intervening variable between A and C, then the product of the amount of variation A explains in B, and B explains in C, gives the proportion of the relationship between A and C that is accounted for by the path from A to B to C. Thus: the proportion of A to C explained by A to B to $C = (r^2AB \times r^2BC)/r^2AC$.

14. Miller and Stokes, "Constituency Influence in Congress," *op. cit.*, p. 53.

15. It is not necessary to make prediction equations for the relationships between A, P, and R in the latter half of the model for their intercorrelations remain the same. Only the correlations between D and other variables are affected.

16. The degree to which these substantive findings (and many others) apply to other issue dimensions is the subject of Miller and Stokes' forthcoming book on representation. *Representation in the American Congress, op. cit.*

17. A METHOD FOR EVALUATING THE DISTRIBUTION OF POWER IN A COMMITTEE SYSTEM
L. S. Shapley and Martin Shubik

1. See J. von Neumann and O. Morgenstern, *Theory of Games and Economic Behavior* (Princeton, 1944, 1947, 1953), pp. 420 ff.

2. See K. J. Arrow, *Social Choice and Individual Values* (New York, 1951), p. 7.

3. For a brief discussion of some of the factors in stock voting see H. G. Gothman and H. E. Dougall, *Corporate Financial Policy* (New York, 1948), pp. 56–61.

4. More generally, a minimal winning coalition.

5. In the formal sense described above.

6. This statement can be put into numerical form without difficulty, to give a quantitative description of the "efficiency" of a legislature.

7. The mathematical formulation and proof are given in L. S. Shapley, "A Value for N-Person Games," *Annals of Mathematics Study No. 28* (Princeton, 1953), pp. 307–17. Briefly stated, any alternative imputation scheme would conflict with either *symmetry* (equal power indices for members in equal positions under the rules) or *additivity* (power distribution in a committee system composed of two strictly independent parts the same as the power distributions obtained by evaluating the parts separately).

8. As a general rule, if one component of a committee system (in which approval of all components is required) is made less "efficient" —i.e., more susceptible to blocking maneuvers— then its share of the total power will increase.

9. In the general case the proportion is $N - M + 1:M$, where M stands for the number of councilmen required for passage.

10. If there are two or more large interests, the power distribution depends in a fairly complicated way on the sizes of the large interests. Generally speaking, however, the small holders are better off than in the previous case. If there are two big interests, equal in size, then the small holders actually have an advantage over the large holders, on a power per share basis. This suggests that such a situation is highly unstable.

med the computations for an IBM 650 electronic computer and who, by his mathematical skill, rendered relatively simple what appeared to be an incredibly tedious problem even for the computer. Finally, I express my gratitude to the Political Science Department of the University of Wisconsin and its acting chairman, Professor James McCamy, who graciously allowed a visiting lecturer to draw on the research funds of the department.

2. See, Dahl, R. A., "The Concept of Power," *Behav. Science*, 1957, 2, 201–15, in which it is noted that the intuitive idea of power includes, as well as the act of influence, the basis, means, amount, and scope of influence.

In Dahl's terms, the power index is at least a measure of a base of power, and also probably of the amount of potential domination.

3. It may be helpful to show how this example in the text is worked out. In a three-person game there are six possible sequences of voting for members a, b, and c. Thus: $a\overset{*}{b}c$, $a\overset{*}{c}b$, $b\overset{*}{a}c$, $bc\overset{*}{a}$, $c\overset{*}{a}b$, $cb\overset{*}{a}$. If all three members have equal weight (as in a simple majority game), and if it takes two votes to win, then the second member in each sequence pivots. There are thus two pivots out of six sequences for each member and $P_i = {}^2/_6 = {}^1/_3$. Now assume, for a weighted majority game, that a is weighted 50, b is 49, and c is one. If it takes 51 votes to win, b and c pivot once each and a pivots four times, as marked with asterisks in the foregoing list of sequences. The several power indices are thus: $P_a = {}^4/_6 = {}^2/_3$; $P_b = {}^1/_6$; $P_c = {}^1/_6$.

4. While I have made no formal study of discipline during the period to be studied in this essay, my impression, based on the examination of numerous roll-calls, is that discipline in 1953 and 1954 was about the same as in 1952, except that, since the Gaullistes were split, they had better discipline than during the Pinay government.

5. For a game theoretic interpretation of the role of limiting factors in the formation of coalitions, see R. D. Luce and A. Rogow, "A game theoretic analysis of congressional power distributions, for a stable 2-party system," *Behavioral Science*, 1956, 1, 83–95 and the literature there cited on the notion of ψ-stability.

18. A TEST OF THE ADEQUACY OF THE POWER INDEX
William Riker

1. The calculations for this experiment were carried out in the Numerical Analysis Laboratory of the University of Wisconsin. I express my deep gratitude to the members of its staff for their interest in this project and the energy they expended on it. Especially, I express my gratitude to Mr. George Struble, who program-

19. MEASUREMENT OF SOCIAL POWER, OPPORTUNITY COSTS, AND THE THEORY OF TWO-PERSON BARGAINING GAMES
John C. Harsanyi

1. I am indebted to Professor Jacob Marschak, of U.C.L.A., and to Professors Herbert A. Simon and James G. March, of Carnegie Institute of Technology, for helpful discussion on this and related topics.

2. But as the probability that B will actually perform a specific action X suggested by A will in general be different for different actions X and for different individuals B, the total amount of A's power (or even the amount of A's power over a given individual B) will also have to be described by a vector rather than by a single number, except if some sort of aggregation procedure is used.

3. Of course, instead of taking the opportunity costs (i.e. the net disadvantages) associated for B with noncompliance, we could just as well take the net advantages associated for him with compliance—they both amount to the same thing.

4. A good deal of recent experimental work shows that it is possible, at least under certain conditions, to measure the utilities that a given individual assigns to various alternatives. Interpersonal comparisons of utility can also be given operationally meaningful interpretation (Harsanyi, 1955, pp. 316–320). Note, however, that the main conclusions of this paper, in particular Theorems I and II, do not require interpersonal utility comparisons.

5. I owe this example to Professor Jacob Marschak.

6. Case 1 is discussed in somewhat greater detail because power based on providing services or diservices without any conditions attached is often overlooked in the literature. For our purposes, the distinction between unconditional advantages or disadvantages on the one hand, and conditional rewards or punishments on the other hand, is important because the latter lend themselves to *bargaining* much more easily than the former do.

7. To simplify our analysis, in what follows we shall be concerned only with the case where A is able to influence B in the intended direction, i.e., has a nonnegative amount of power over him. (A can have a negative amount of power over B only if he seriously misjudges the situation, because otherwise he can always make the amount of his power at worst *zero*, by simply refraining from intervention.)

8. We follow Dahl in considering the more general case where B would do action X with some probability p_1 (which of course may be zero), even in the absence of A's intervention.

9. On the assumption of expected-utility maximization, see Marschak (1950; 1954, Section 1).

10. More exactly, in most unilateral power situations. The distinction between unilateral and bilateral power situations will be discussed below.

Note that in empirical applications based on a *frequency* interpretation, a further complication may arise owing to the fact that the utilities to A, and the disutilities to B, of a set of several compliant actions $X_1, \ldots, X_k$ by B may *not* be simply *additive* (as they may have the nature of complementary or of competitive

"goods" from A's point of view, and/or the nature of complementary or of competitive "evils" from B's point of view).

11. In analogy to the distinction in economic theory between demand or supply in a point sense and in a schedule sense.

12. Viz. in cases when A is able to persuade B that he, A, has irrevocably committed himself in advance to not making any concessions to B. See Schelling (1956, pp. 282–287), Harsanyi (1961.)

13. Only in ultimatum games (cf. Footnote 12 above), including all unilateral power situations, is it generally true that one party can extract any degree of concession or compliance from the other party up to the latter's actual concession limit point.

14. I have set out my reasons for accepting the Zeuthen-Nash theory, and have discussed the theory in some detail, in Harsanyi (1956, 1961). The original references are Zeuthen (1930) and Nash (1950, 1953). For an excellent introduction to game theory in general, see Luce and Raiffa (1957).

15. See Footnotes 7 and 8 above.

16. This is obviously true in the special case where the game is perfectly symmetric with respect to the two players. Generally the result follows from the invariance of the Zeuthen-Nash solution with respect to order-preserving linear transformations.

17. In other words, Theorem II is subject to conditions (15a) and (16a).

18. Cartwright (1959, p. 193) mentions the fact that while he himself defines social power as a *difference* of two opposing forces, Lewin proposed to measure it as a *quotient* of two opposing forces. According to Theorem II, in bilateral power situations the net force that A can exert on B is proportional to the *difference* of two psychological forces. More generally, if a person has both incentives for and incentives against doing a certain action, then the net strength of his incentives will be the difference between the strength of his positive and negative incentives. (For instance, if B's doing X yields him both rewards and penalties, then his net incentive will be the total value of the rewards less the total value of the penalties.) But note that in the former case Theorem II brings in a coefficient 1/2, which does not occur in the latter case. On the other hand, both in unilateral and in bilateral power situations the gross strength of the force moving B toward compliance is the *quotient* of the strength of his incentives to compliance, and of the disutility to B of performing the required action X. Here the quotient formula arises because the disutility of doing X enters into the definition of B's expected utility as a *multiplicative* factor (it multiplies the probability of B's actually doing X).

20. MEASUREMENT OF SOCIAL POWER IN n-PERSON RECIPROCAL POWER SITUATIONS
John C. Harsanyi

1. To simplify our analysis, we disregard the case of negative power, where $\Delta p < 0$, i.e., where A's intervention actually *decreases* the probability of B's performing action X which A wants him to perform. (This can occur only as a result of A's seriously misjudging the situation. For if he knew the effects of his intervention, he always could achieve at least a *zero* amount of power by simply refraining from any intervention.)

2. As to the case where two individuals i and j prefer the *same* policy $X_i = X_j = X_{ij}$, see Footnote 3 below.

3. If two individuals i and j prefer the same policy $X_i = X_j = X_{ij}$, we of course have only one probability p_{ij} for the adoption of policy X_{ij}, instead of having two separate probabilities p_i and p_j for the adoption of X_i and X_j. This probability p_{ij} may be regarded as a measure for the amount of *joint* specific power of these two individuals. (We cannot regard p_{ij} as a measure for each individual's separate specific power, because if we counted p_{ij} two times, the specific-power measures of all n individuals would not add up to unity.) On the other hand, using equation (6), we can define separate measures for the amounts of *generic* power, $\tilde{p}_i$ and $\tilde{p}_j$, possessed by the two individuals. If, apart from their common first preference for policy X_{ij}, their utility functions for the various policy alternatives are otherwise not identical, then we actually may have $\tilde{p}_i \neq \tilde{p}_j$.

4. For a situation where the number of policy alternatives is smaller than the number of individuals, see Footnote 3.

5. But this $(n + m)$-vector will normally have no more than n nonzero components (and in most cases is likely to have much fewer than that). Let $\bar{v}_j = (v_{1j}, \ldots, v_{nj})$ be the vector of the utilities that individuals, $1, \ldots, n$ associate with each policy alternative X_j. Let us call a set of policies $X_j, X_k, \ldots$ linearly independent if the corresponding utility vectors $\bar{u}_j, \bar{u}_k, \ldots$ are linearly independent. Then no efficient probability mixture of the policy alternatives $X_1, \ldots, X_{n+m}$ can use more than n linearly independent policies with nonzero probability weights. Moreover, any efficient utility vector that can be attained by a probability mixture of more than n linearly dependent policies can also be attained by a mixture of *at most* n linearly independent policies. Therefore there is never any advantage in using a probability mixture of more than n different policies.

6. In the real world, of course, the bargaining parties will usually trade in statistical *frequencies*, not in *probabilities* as such. That is, if

no direct (i.e., pure) compromise policy is available, they will reach an indirect compromise by letting one party have his way on one occasion and another party on another occasion, with frequencies dependent on each party's bargaining position. But reinterpretation of our model in terms of frequencies rather than probabilities tends to make little difference to our conclusions (see pages 72–73).

7. A more exact definition will be given below (see equation [27]).

8. When all rewards R_{ij} happen to be *independent goods* for both the giver i and the receiver j, i.e., when they are neither complementary nor competitive goods, then we can analyze each net utility gain r_i into an algebraic sum of the separate utilities of all rewards received, and the separate utility costs of all rewards given away, by individual i. But in general such analysis is not possible because these quantities are not simply additive.

9. Again, in special cases we may be able to analyze $t_i{}^s$ into a sum of the *losses* that i would suffer by the opposing coalition's conflict strategy $\vartheta^{\bar{s}}$, and of the *costs* to him of his own coalition's conflict strategy ϑ^s. The latter in turn may possibly admit of analysis into the costs of retaliatory actions against members of the opposing coalition, the costs of defensive measures, the costs of subsidies (rewards) to be paid to members of his own coalition *less* the value of subsidies he receives from them, etc. But in general such analysis is not possible because these items are not simply additive.

10. They are the reciprocals of the quantities $a_1, \ldots, a_n$, which I have called the *weights* of the game (Harsanyi, 1960).

11. By an *optimizational* equation I mean an equation containing the *max* and/or the *min* operator(s).

12. We speak of a game with *transferable utility* if any player i can transfer money or other values (or can transfer power in our case) to any other player j in such a way that the *sum* of their utilities (as well as the utilities of all other players) remains *constant* because j's utility gain is exactly equal to i's utility loss.

13. More exactly, the transferable-utility requirement must be satisfied also for each coalition S in the neighborhood of the vector $\bar{u}^S$ formed out of the conflict payoffs $u_i{}^S$ of all members i of coalition S. This in turn requires that the equilibrium values (as defined by equations $(\alpha\alpha)$, $(\beta\beta)$, and (γ) to (η) of my 1960 paper) of the probabilities $q_j{}^S$ for each $j\epsilon M$, and for each $S \subset N$, should be nonnegative.

14. In cases B and C, also, the solution of the game takes a simpler form when the solution uses n different policy alternatives X_j with nonzero probabilities p_j. (By Footnote 5 the solution never has to use more than n different policies, but of course it may use a smaller number of them.) Then the n variables z_i become the roots of the following set of n simultaneous equations, linear in the reciprocals of

$$\sum_{i \in N} \frac{x_{ij}}{z_i} = 1 \qquad \text{for each } j \epsilon J$$

where J is the set of all j corresponding to a policy X_j actually used. The equilibrium values of R and of the T^s's are again determined by equations (24) and (25). But the equilibrium values of the P^s's are now determined by conditions more complex than equation (26).

15. For easier reference I am calling this Theorem III, to follow Theorems I and II of the preceding paper.

16. Theorem III is a direct generalization of Theorem II. But formally there is no full parallelism, because in Theorem II the strength-of-power measure has to be multiplied by a factor $1/2$ while in Theorem III no multiplication is necessary. This is so because we have found it convenient to incorporate the factor $1/n$ (corresponding to factor $1/2$ of Theorem II) into the expression we have chosen to define the strength of a person's power in n-person situations.

We do not have to add a qualification, as we did in the cases of Theorems I and II, concerning the range of variation of the amount of generic power (viz. that $0 \leqslant \tilde{p}_i \leqslant 1$), because under the definition given the strength of a person's power always remains within the required range.

17. The pairs of opposing coalitions S and $\bar{S}$ in my bargaining model are assumed in general to be based merely on *tactical considerations*. But some particular coalitions of course may also exhibit emotional ties and/or similarities in policy preferences among their members. This fact in our model would find expression in the utility functions of the relevant individuals.

21. ON THE CONCEPT OF POLITICAL POWER
Talcott Parsons

1. Thus E. C. Banfield, *Political Influence* (New York, The Free Press of Glencoe, 1962), p. 348, speaks of control as the ability to cause another to give or withold action, and power as the ability to establish control over another. Similarly Robert Dahl, "The Concept of Power," *Behavioral Scientist* 2 (July, 1957), says that "*A* has power over *B* to the extent that he can get *B* to do something that *B* would not otherwise do." C. J. Friedrich takes a similar position in his forthcoming book, the tentative title of which is "Man and his Government."

2. *Cf.* Talcott Parsons and Neil J. Smelser, *Economy and Society* (Illinois, The Free Press of Glencoe, 1956), chapter I, for a discussion of this conception.

3. E.g. the American medical profession is part of American society, but also it is part of a wider medical profession which transcends this particular society, to some extent as collectivity. Interpenetration in membership is thus a feature of the relations among collectivities.

4. For discussions of the concept of "valued-added" in spheres of application broader than the economic alone, *cf.* Neil J. Smelser, *Social Change in the Industrial Revolution* (Glencoe, Illinois, The Free Press of Glencoe, 1959), chapter II, pp. 7–20, and Neil J. Smelser, *Theory of Collective Behavior* (New York, The Free Press of Glencoe, 1963), chapter II, pp. 23–47.

5. C. I. Barnard, *The Functions of the Executive* (Cambridge, Harvard University Press, 1938), chapter V, pp. 46–64.

6. On the rationale of these attributions, see *Economy and Society*, *op. cit.*, chapter II.

7. "Pay-off" may be a deciding factor in choice between particular contexts of use, but not as to whether the resource shall be devoted to collective effectiveness at all.

8. I have in fact adopted the term "demands" from the usage of David Easton, "An Approach to the Analysis of Political Systems," *World Politics* 9 (1957): 383–400.

9. *Cf.* Max Weber, *The Theory of Social and Economic Organization* (New York, Oxford University Press, 1947), p. 124. Translation by A. M. Henderson and Talcott Parsons; edited by Talcott Parsons.

10. The cases of services concretely rendered to a household will be considered as a limiting case where the roles of consumer and employer have not become differentiated from each other.

11. In the cases treated as typical for economic analysis the collective element in capital is delegated through the *bindingness* of the contracts of loan of financial resources. To us this is a special case, employment being another, of the binding obligation assumed by an organization, whether it employs or loans, by virtue of which the recipient can be more effective than would otherwise be the case. It is not possible to go further into these complex problems here, but they will, perhaps, be somewhat illuminated by the later discussion of the place of the concept of bindingness in the theory of power.

12. See my paper "On the Concept of Influence," to be published in the *Public Opinion Quarterly* 27 (Spring, 1963).

13. Here again Barnard's usage of the concept of responsibility seems to me the appropriate one. See Barnard, *op. cit.*

14. In order not to complicate things too much, I shall not enter into problem of the interchange system involving legitimation here. See my paper "Authority, Legitimation, and Political Process," in *Nomos* 1, reprinted as chapter V of my *Structure and Process in*

Modern Societies (Glencoe, Illinois, The Free Press, 1960), chapter V, pp. 170–198.

15. There is a certain element of generality in physical force as a negative sanction, which gives it a special place in power systems. This will be taken up later in the discussion.

16. There are complications here deriving from the fact that power is associated with *negative* sanctions and hence that, in the face of severe resistance, their effectiveness is confined to deterrence.

17. I owe the insight into this parallel to Professor Karl W. Deutsch of Yale University (personal discussion).

18. "Sadistic" infliction of injury without instrumental significance to ego does not belong in this context.

19. I have attempted to develop this line of analysis of the significance of force somewhat more fully in "Some Reflections of the Role of Force in Social Relations," in Harry Eckstein, ed., *The Problems of Internal War* (New Jersey, Princeton University Press, 1963).

20. Thus, if control of productivity operates through monetary funds, their possessor cannot "force" e.g. prospective employees to accept employment.

21. This, of course, is a relative difference. Some hazards increase the moment one steps outside his own home, police protection may be better in one local community than the next, and crossing a state boundary may mean a considerable difference in legal or actual rights.

22. *Cf.* my paper "The Principal Structures of Community," *Nomos* 2 and *Structure and Process, op. cit.*, chapter 8. See also W. L. Hurst, *Law and Social Process in the United States* (Ann Arbor, University of Michigan Law School, 1960).

23. As already noted, in this area, I think the analysis of Chester I. Barnard, in *The Function of the Executive, op. cit.*, is so outstandingly clear and cogent that it deserves the status of a classic of political theory in my specific sense. See especially chapter X.

24. Two particularly important manifestations of this monetization of property are, first the general legal understanding that executors of estates are not obligated to retain the exact physical inventory intact pending full statement, but may sell various items—their fiduciary obligation is focussed on the money value of the estate. Similarly in the law of contract increasing option has been given to compensate with money damages in lieu of the specific "performance" originally contracted for.

25. Since this system is the territorially organized collectivity, the state with its government, these considerations underlie the critical importance of foreign relations in the sense of the relations to other territorially organized, force-controlling collectivities, since, once in-

ternal control of force is effectively institutionalized, the danger of this kind of breach comes from the outside in this specific sense of outside. The point is cogently made by Raymond Aron.

26. See, on this process, Stein Rokkan, "Mass Suffrage, Secret Voting, and Political Participation," *European Journal of Sociology* 2 (1961): 132–152.

27. I.e., the aggregate of votes, evaluated by the electoral rules, determines the incumbency of office.

28. Of course where conditions are sufficiently simple, or where there is sufficient anxiety about the hierarchial implications of power, the egalitarian element may penetrate far into the political decision-making system itself, with, e.g. insistence that policy-decisions, both external and internal in reference, be made by majority vote of all members, or even under a unanimity rule. The respects in which such a system—which of course realistically often involves a sharply hierarchical stratification of influence—is incompatible with effectiveness in many spheres, can be said to be relatively clear, especially for *large* collectivities.

29. It is the central concept of *The Division of Labor in Society*. For my own relatively recent understanding of its significance, see "Durkheim's Contribution to the Theory of Integration of Social Systems," in Kurt Wolff, Ed., *Émile Durkheim, 1858–1917* (Ohio, Ohio State University Press, 1960), pp. 118–153.

30. *Cf.* C. Wright Mills, *The Power Elite* (New York, Oxford University Press, 1956) and my commentary in *Structure and Process in Modern Societies, op. cit.*, chapter 6.

31. *Cf.* Durkheim's famous essay, "Deux lois de l'évolution pénale," *L'Année Sociologique* 4 (1899–1900): 65–95.

32. *Cf.* my paper "On The Concept of Influence," *op. cit.*, for a discussion of the concept of justification and its distinction from legitimation.

33. Failure to see this seems to me to be a major source of the utopian strain in Marxist theory, expressed above all by the expectation of the "withering away of the state." There is perhaps a parallel to the confusion connected for many centuries with the Aristotelian doctrine of the "sterility" of money.

34. H. D. Lasswell and A. Kaplan, *Power and Society* (New Haven, Yale University Press, 1950) and Mills, *The Power Elite, op. cit.*

35. Whether this be interpreted as net addition to the medium or as increase in the velocity of circulation of the "slow" deposit funds, is indifferent, because its economic effects are the same.

36. Joseph Schumpeter, *The Theory of Economic Development* (Cambridge, Harvard University Press, 1955), translated by Redvers Opie.

37. If very carefully interpreted, perhaps the old term "sovereignty" could be used to

38. Perhaps this is an unusually clear case of the relativity of the formal legal sense of the bindingness of commitments. Thus the populistic component in democratic government often ties both executive and legislative branches rather rigidly in what they can formally promise. However, there are many *de facto* obligations assumed by Government which are very nearly binding. Thus legally Congress could withdraw the totality of funds recently granted to universities for the support of scientific research and training, the formal appropriations being made year by year. Universities, however, plan very much in the expectation of maintenance of these funds and this maintenance is certainly something like a *de facto* obligation of Congress.

39. I have dealt with some aspects of the McCarthy episode in "Social Strains in America," *Structure and Process, op. cit.,* chapter 7, pp. 226–249. The inherent impossibility of the demand for "absolute security" in a pluralistic system is very cogently shown by Edward Shils in *The Torment of Secrecy* (New York, The Free Press of Glencoe, 1956), especially in chapter VI.

40. In saying this I am very far from maintaining that "absolute" sovereignty is an essential condition of the minimal integration of political systems. On the contrary, first it is far from absolute internally, precisely because of the pluralistic character of most modern political systems and because of the openness of their boundaries in the integrative economic and other directions. Externally the relation of the territorial unit to norms and values transcending it is crucial, and steadily becoming more so. See my paper "Polarization of the World and International Order" in Quincy Wright, William M. Evan and Morton Deutsch, eds., *Preventing World War III* (New York, Simon and Schuster, 1962), pp. 310–331.

41. I myself once accepted this. *Cf. The Social System* (Illinois, The Free Press of Glencoe, 1951), chapter V, pp. 161–163.

42. The paradigm itself is still incomplete, and even in its present state has not been published as a whole. The first beginning statement dealing with process was made by Parsons and Smelser in *Economy and Society,* esp. Chapter II, and has been further developed in certain respects in Smelser's two subsequent independent books (*Social Change in the Industrial Revolution,* and *Theory of Collective Behavior*). In my own case certain aspects, which now need further revision, were published in the article "Pattern Variables Revisited" (*American Sociological Review,* August, 1960). Early and partial versions of application to political subject-matter are found in my contributions to Roland Young, ed., *Approaches to the Study of Politics,* and Burdick and Brodbeck, eds., *American Voting Behavior.*

43. There is a very crucial problem area which concerns the nature of the interchanges between a society as a system in our sense and its environment. This set of problems unfortunately cannot be entered into here.

44. The process of investment, which I conceive to be one very important special case of the operation of this interchange system, seems to work in such a way that the power component of a loan is a grant of opportunity, through which an increment of otherwise unavailable control of productivity is gained. The recipient of this "grant" is then, through committing (individual or collective) services, in a position to utilize these resources for increasing future economic productivity in some way. This is a special case because the resources might be used in some other way, e.g. for relieving distress or for scientific research.

23. DIFFERENTIATION OF POWER
Peter Blau

1. Max Weber, *The Theory of Social and Economic Organization,* New York: Oxford University Press, 1947, p. 152.

2. R. H. Tawney, *Equality,* London: Allen and Unwin, 1931, p. 229.

3. This corresponds to John P. R. French, Jr., and Bertram Raven's distinction between coercive and reward power, in addition to which they specified three types not contingent on external sanctions (legitimate, referent, and expert power); "The Bases of Social Power," in Dorwin Cartwright, *Studies in Social Power,* Ann Arbor: Institute for Social Research, University of Michigan, 1959, pp. 150–167. Talcott Parsons makes a parallel distinction between coercive power that rests on deterrence through negative sanctions and inducements in exchange transactions that rest on positive sanctions; "On the Concept of Influence," *Public Opinion Quarterly,* 27 (1963), 43–45, and "On the Concept of Political Power," *Proceedings of the American Philosophical Society,* 107 (1963), 238–239.

4. A technical problem of definition, to which Arnold Kaufman has called my attention, arises if there is disagreement between superior and subordinates as to whether a given reward is regularly supplied or not. For example, an employer may think of a Christmas bonus as a special reward, whereas his employees have come to think of it as part of their regular income and to consider not receiving the bonus a penalty. It is necessary to decide depending on the purpose at hand, whether the defining criterion is the subordinates' expectation or the superior's intent.

5. *Ibid.,* pp. 237–238.

6. Parsons' emphasis on legitimacy in this connection (*ibid.*, pp. 236–244), however, seems to confound the distinction between power and the special case of authority, which will be discussed in chapter viii.

7. Richard M. Emerson, "Power-Dependence Relations," *American Sociological Review*, 27 (1962), 31–41. Suggestive as the underlying conception is, the focus on balancing operations is unfortunate and somewhat confusing inasmuch as it diverts attention from the analysis of power imbalance. His schema deals with the balancing operations consequent to given differences in power-dependence, whereas the reformulation derives power imbalances from the conditions of exchange.

8. The counterdependence of the small employer on the employee's services may create interdependence and neutralize the small employer's power, but the large employer is not so much dependent on single employees as on a labor force whose turnover can and must be taken into account in management, and his independence of any one employee sustains his power over all of them, unless it is reduced by their collective action.

9. Accepting a job at a higher salary than one can command in the market, buying from an acquaintance at wholesale prices, gaining acceptance in a more eminent group than one's achievements warrant, and generally obtaining any recurrent benefit that is superior to what could be obtained elsewhere entails dependence and loss of power.

10. Emerson, *op. cit.*, p. 37.

11. William F. Whyte, *Street Corner Society* (2nd ed.), University of Chicago Press, 1955, pp. 257–258.

12. These could also be considered to be implications of the fifth alternative. The third and fifth alternatives are complementary, as they are concerned with power from the perspectives of the two different parties.

13. Some aspects of the first problem have been discussed in chapter iv; some of the second will be discussed in this chapter and in chapters vi and vii; of the third, in chapters viii and ix (as well as in the present one); and of the fourth, in chapters ix and xi.

14. Charles H. Hession, S. M. Miller, and Curwen Stoddart, *The Dynamics of the American Economy*, New York: Knopf, 1956, pp. 193–208.

15. Irving Goldman, "The Ifugao of the Philippine Islands," in Margaret Mead, *Cooperation and Competition Among Primitive Peoples*, New York: McGraw-Hill, 1937, pp. 153–179.

16. George C. Homans, *Social Behavior*, New York: Harcourt, Brace and World, 1961, p. 150.

17. The existence of ranked social classes makes even low standing in any class except the lowest something for which people compete. Hence, most exchange relations between high status and low status individuals contribute to two different competitive systems—that among the highs, and that among the lows.

18. *Ibid.*, p. 372.

19. On separate occasions Homans made essentially each of these two points: that his rewarding advice entitles a man later to tell others what to do (*loc. cit.*), and that their doing what he tells them reduces their debt to him (*ibid.*, p. 298). But the two points together conflict with his statements quoted above.

20. *Ibid.*, p. 151.

21. *Ibid.*, pp. 320–331, where several empirical findings in support of this statement are cited.

22. *Ibid.*, pp. 366–370, and Blau, *The Dynamics of Bureaucracy* (2nd ed.), University of Chicago Press, 1963, pp. 146–150. Similarly, since inferiors usually take the initiative in approaching superiors, "if you can get another man, hitherto considered your equal, to come to your office rather than your going to his, to discuss some problem, you are to that extent one-up on him." Homans, *op. cit.*, p. 202.

23. For an analysis of the circulation and expansion of influence and power, see Parsons, "On the Concept of Influence," and James S. Coleman's "Comment," *Public Opinion Quarterly*, 27 (1963), 37–92, esp. pp. 72–73.

24. Alvin Zander, Arthur R. Cohen, and Ezra Stotland, "Power and the Relations Among Professions," in Cartwright, *op. cit.*, pp. 15–34.

25. On voluntary associations, see Mirra Komarowski, "The Voluntary Associations of Urban Dwellers," in Logan Wilson and William Kolb, *Sociological Analysis*, New York: Harcourt, Brace, 1949, pp. 378–392; on unions, see William Spinrad, "Correlates of Trade Union Participation," *American Sociological Review*, 25 (1960), 237–244; on participation in discussions, see Fred. L. Strodtbeck, Rita M. James, and Charles Hawkins, "Social Status in Jury Deliberations," *American Sociological Review*, 22 (1957), 713–719, William A. Caudill, *The Psychiatric Hospital as a Small Society*, Cambridge: Harvard University Press, 1958, pp. 243–252, 295–296, and Blau, *op. cit.*, p. 154.

26. Homans, *op. cit.*, pp. 298–299; on a gang leader's reluctance to call in the debts of his followers to him lest his dominant position suffer, see Whyte, *op. cit.*, pp. 106–107.

27. "Force alone can establish Power, habit alone can keep it in being, but to expand it it must have credit—a thing which, even in its earlier life, it finds useful and has generally received in practice." Bertrand de Jouvenel, *On Power*, New York: Viking, 1949, p. 25.

28. Homans, *op. cit.*, pp. 296–297.

29. Frank H. Knight, *Risk, Uncertainty and Profit* (2nd ed.), Boston: Houghton Mifflin, 1933, esp. chapters i, ii, and viii.

30. See Herbert A. Simon, *Models of Man,* New York: Wiley, 1957, pp. 183–195.

31. Knight, *op. cit.,* chapter vii.

32. Alexis de Tocqueville, *Democracy in America,* New York: Vintage, 1954, Vol. I, 374.

33. See de Jouvenel, *op. cit.,* pp. 345–346.

34. John Updike illustrates this aspect of tolerance nicely in a story about a conversation the only white woman resident on an island has with the husband of one of the few white tourist couples there. Thus, the woman talks about his wife and the attitude of the Negro inhabitants to her: " 'You see how dark she is,' she explained. 'How tan.... They say your wife's being part Negro has kept you out of the hotels on the better islands.' " Later, wondering about his defensiveness in answer to this remark, the husband reflects what the attitude of his progressive wife would have been: "His seriousness had been unworthy of her. She would have wanted him to say yes, her grandfather picked cotton in Alabama, in America these things are taken for granted, we have no problem. But he saw, like something living glimpsed in a liquid volume, that the comedy of this response depended upon, could only live within, a vast unconscious pride of race." "The Doctor's Wife," in *Pigeon Feathers,* New York: Knopf, 1962, pp. 208–209.

24. THE STRUCTURE OF INFLUENCE
Edward Banfield

1. For an account of the Chicago machine although in the transitional period just before the rise of Mayor Daley), see Martin Meyerson and E. C. Banfield, *Politics, Planning, and the Public Interest* (Glencoe, Ill.: The Free Press, 1955), especially Chapter 3.

2. In this and the following chapters, the term "political head" will be used to refer to one who is both the chief executive of an administration and the "boss" of a party machine; the three political heads on the Chicago scene are the governor, the mayor, and the president of the Cook County Board.

3. See the Chicago Home Rule Commission, *Modernizing a City Government* (Chicago: University of Chicago Press, 1954).

4. Having formal authority to discharge an employee, although it may sometimes be a necessary condition for controlling him, may not be a sufficient one: there may be many reasons why the political head cannot "afford" to discharge him. But if he has authority, he can discharge him *if he is willing to pay the price,* whereas if he lacks authority he may not be able to get rid of him in any way at all. Usually, therefore, having authority gives the political head some measure of control that he would not otherwise have, for the employee knows that there is a point beyond which he cannot go without convincing the political

head that it would pay (in the sense of minimizing his losses) to get rid of him.

It may be useful to employ the concepts "costless formal authority," the exercise of which is not attended with any disadvantages or "costs" at all, and "net formal authority," which in the circumstances the possessor can "afford" to exercise, notwithstanding certain attendant costs. The statements in the text may then be made more precise: if the political head had costless or net formal authority commensurate with the requirements of his tasks, he would not have to engage in trading. To this it may be added that if surrounding ("cost") conditions are held constant, an increase in formal authority produces an increase in net formal authority.

5. The Leader of the London County Council, although he dominates the LCC very much as the Mayor dominates the Chicago City Council (the Leader consults a policy committee, but its members are selected by him), does not have to bear the onus of being a "boss." His position, much more than that of the Mayor of Chicago, is extra-legal; he is not elected at large, and nothing in law gives him the right to call the tune. But while his influence is extra-legal, it is not informal. There are explicit understandings which give him a right to issue orders; consequently, he need not "buy" control in the Chicago manner.

Nevertheless, a Democrat in the Chicago City Council is a paragon of independence compared to his opposite number in the LCC. As the chief whip of the LCC recently explained to a visitor:

"It rarely happens that a member votes against his party. If it did happen, we would probably say, 'We are prepared to overlook it this time, but not again.' If it happened a second time, we would not admit that person to party meetings and he would be reported to the London Labour Party. In effect, it would bar him from standing again.

"We do have what we call the 'conscience rule.' If there is something that a member can't vote for because of religious or conscientious scruples—for example, selling liquor in public parks, or Sunday games in parks—he will be allowed to absent himself from the vote. The Party is always very generous about that."

6. This argument is developed and applied to other metropolitan areas in E. C. Banfield, "The Politics of Metropolitan Area Organization," *Midwest Journal of Political Science,* I No. 1 (May, 1957), 77–91.

7. According to Robert Moses, "Smith and LaGuardia had quite a lot in common. First and foremost, they shared the same fierce determination to demonstrate to skeptics and bigots that boys from the sidewalks of lower Manhattan could run great governments honestly,

intelligently, progressively and, to an astonishing degree, without degrading politics, and thus wring reluctant admiration from the sticks, the crossroads, the Southern Tier and Park Avenue. One had the curious sense in observing Governor Smith that he was living up to a model or an example he had established for himself and that the executive was something apart from and superior to the man. It was the same with LaGuardia." (*New York Times Magazine*, September 8, 1957).

8. Meyerson and Banfield, *op. cit.*, pp. 196–99.

9. Here, for example, is a *Chicago Tribune* editorial (April 13, 1955) which ridicules the City Council without acknowledging that in a body of fifty formally independent representatives shortcuts may be indispensable:

"Ald. Keane (31st) arrived 11 minutes late for a meeting Tuesday morning of the council committee on traffic and public safety, of which he is chairman. The committee had a sizeable agenda, 286 items in all to consider.

"Ald. Keane took up the first item. For the record, he dictated to the committee secretary that Ald. A moved and Ald. B seconded its approval, and then, without calling for a vote, he declared the motion passed. Neither mover nor seconder had opened his mouth. He followed the same procedure on six more proposals, again without a word from the aldermen whose names appeared in the record. Then he put 107 items into one bundle for passage, and 172 more into another for rejection, again without a voice other than his own having been heard.

"Having disposed of this mountain of details in exactly 10 minutes, Ald. Keane walked out. The aldermen he had quoted so freely without either their concurrence or their protest, sat around looking stupid.

"Most likely they are."

10. The argument that follows develops some points made in Meyerson and Banfield, *op. cit.*, Chapter 11.

11. In 1959 and 1960, scandals in the traffic court, the assessor's office, and the police department put the Chicago machine in a very bad light. Mayor Daley was not personally involved; there was no question regarding his integrity. Nevertheless, the scandals prohibited him from running for governor at that time (he might not have run anyway, of course). If he had been up for re-election just then against a strong candidate, he might possibly have been beaten.

12. New York's Mayor LaGuardia is a good example of a mayor who appealed directly to the mass. As Robert Moses has written (*op. cit.*):

"It must be admitted that in exploiting racial and religious prejudices LaGuardia could run circles around the bosses he despised and derided. When it came to raking ashes of Old World hates, warming ancient grudges, waving the bloody shirt, tuning the ear of ancestral voices, he could easily out-demagogue demagogues. . . . He knew that the aim of the rabble-rousers is simply to shoo into office for entirely extraneous, illogical and even silly reasons the municipal officials who clean city streets, teach in schools, protect, house, and keep healthy, strong and happy the millions of people crowded together there."

13. See the much more elaborate discussion of these matters in James Q. Wilson, *Negro Politics: The Search for Leadership*.

14. Meyerson and Banfield, *op. cit.*

25. CONCERTING ACTION BY INFLUENCE
Edward C. Banfield

1. Especially Chapter 8, pp. 235–41.

2. The specified group might be "registered voters" and the specified proportion "a majority." If there are 100 voters, any 51 who vote in favor contribute all of the requisite actions. If more than 51 vote in favor, it is impossible to say which favorable voters contributed the requisite actions. The actions of voters other than the 51, whether these actions are in favor or opposed, are not requisite and so do not enter into the situation at all.

3. There is a special class of autonomous actor (empirically, the courts) whose activity is counted as given unless it is withheld by affirmative action. (A court's contribution of activity is not withheld if the proposal does not come before it; it is withheld only if, when the proposal comes before it, the court decides negatively.)

4. The following glossary may be helpful: (a) *Authority* is the right to give or withhold action requisite to adoption of a proposal; only an actor who can perform such actions (who is "authorized") has authority. (b) *Control* is the ability to cause another to give or withhold action; one who is controlled acts as the agent of the one who controls. (c) *Power* is the ability to establish control over another. (d) *Influence* is a generic term including authority, control, and power.

5. See Chapter 8, especially p. 242.

6. If Daley does not mean to use this control eventually to acquire more control, this is not an "investment." The assumption here is that he *does* mean to use it so.

7. Meyerson and Banfield, *op. cit.*, p. 260.

8. See the discussion of the logic of bargaining by T. C. Schelling, in *The Strategy of Conflict* (Cambridge, Mass.: Harvard University Press, 1960).

9. See Chapter 8, especially pp. 238–40.

10. See Chapter 8, especially pp. 258–59.

11. See Chapter 9, pp. 275–76.

12. See, for example, the important part played in the public housing site controversy by George Stech, the truckdriver who wanted to get into politics (Meyerson and Banfield, *op. cit.*, especially pp. 109–11).

13. *Cf.* Lincoln Steffens, *Autobiography* (New York: Harcourt, Brace & Co., 1931), p. 577.

26. INTERNATIONAL STRUCTURE, NATIONAL FORCE, AND THE BALANCE OF WORLD POWER
Kenneth N. Waltz

1. Martin Wight, "The Balance of Power," in *Diplomatic Investigations: Essays in the Theory of International Politics*, ed. by Herbert Butterfield and Martin Wight (Cambridge: Harvard University Press, 1966), p. 151.

2. Quoted in Chalmers Johnson, *Revolutionary Change* (Boston: Little, Brown, 1966), p. 13.

3. I do not mean to imply that this exhausts the purpose of power. In this essay, however, I cannot analyze other aspects of power either in themselves or in relation to the power to do harm.

4. The point has been made most extensively by Klaus Knorr and most insistently by Stanley Hoffmann. See Knorr, *On the Uses of Military Power in the Nuclear Age* (Princeton: Princeton University Press, 1966). See also Hoffmann, "Obstinate or Obsolete? The Fate of the Nation-State and the Case of Western Europe," *Daedalus*, Vol. XCV (Summer 1965), especially pp. 897, 907; "Europe's Identity Crisis: Between the Past and America," *Daedalus*, Vol. XCIII (Fall 1964), especially pp. 1287–88; "Nuclear Proliferation and World Politics," in *A World of Nuclear Powers?*, ed. by Alastair Buchan (Englewood Cliffs, N.J.: Prentice-Hall, 1966); and two essays in *The State of War* (New York: Praeger, 1965), "Roulette in the Cellar: Notes on Risk in International Relations," especially pp. 140–47, and "Terror in Theory and Practice," especially pp. 233–51.

5. See, for example, Inis L. Claude, Jr., *Power and International Relations* (New York: Random House, 1962), p. 90; and Morton A. Kaplan, *System and Process in International Politics* (New York: John Wiley & Sons, 1957), p. 22.

6. See "The Text of Address by McNamara to American Society of Newspaper Editors," *The New York Times*, May 19, 1966, p. 11.

7. John Herz, *International Politics in the Atomic Age* (New York: Columbia University Press, 1959), pp. 22, 169.

8. Edward Hallett Carr, *The Twenty Years' Crisis, 1919–1939*, 2nd ed. (New York: Harper & Row, 1964), p. 140.

9. Knorr, *On the Uses of Military Power*, p. 87.

10. Hoffmann, "Europe's Identity Crisis," pp. 1279, 1287–88.

11. *Cf.* Carr, *The Twenty Years' Crisis*, pp. 103, 129–32.

12. "The sums spent for the war power is money wasted," he maintained, "if the war power remains unused for obtaining political advantages. In some cases the mere threat will suffice and the war power thus becomes useful, but others can be obtained only through the warlike use of the war power itself, that is, by war undertaken in time; if this moment is missed, the capital is lost. In this sense, war becomes a great financial enterprise of the State." Quoted in Alfred Vagts, *Defence and Diplomacy: The Soldier and the Conduct of Foreign Relations* (New York: King's Crown Press, 1956), p. 361.

13. Robert W. Tucker, "Peace and War," *World Politics*, Vol. XVII (Jan. 1965), p. 324 fn. For a comprehensive and profound examination of the use of force internationally, see Robert Osgood and Robert Tucker, *Force, Order, and Justice* (forthcoming).

14. Coral Bell, "Non-Alignment and the Power Balance," *Survival*, Vol. V (Nov.–Dec. 1963), p. 255.

15. "The soldan of Egypt or the emperor of Rome," he went on to say, "might drive his harmless subjects like brute beasts against their sentiments and inclination. But he must, at least, have led his *marmalukes* or *praetorian bands*, like men, by their opinion." "Of the First Principles of Government," in *Hume's Moral and Political Philosophy*, ed. by Henry D. Aiken (New York: Hafner, 1948), p. 307.

16. Thomas C. Schelling, *Arms and Influence* (New Haven: Yale University Press, 1966), pp. 70–71.

17. The point is well made by Samuel P. Huntington, "Patterns of Violence in World Politics," in *Changing Patterns of Military Politics*, ed. by Samuel P. Huntington (New York: The Free Press of Glencoe, 1962), p. 28.

18. By "structure" I mean the pattern according to which power is distributed; by "stability," the perpetuation of that structure without the occurrence of grossly destructive violence.

19. U.S. Bureau of the Census, *Statistical Abstract of the United States: 1966* (Washington, D.C.: Government Printing Office, 1966), p. 165.

20. *The New York Times*, May 19, 1966, p. 11.

21. For further examination of the proposition, see Kenneth N. Waltz, "The Stability of a Bipolar World," *Daedalus*, Vol. XCIII (Summer 1964), pp. 881–909. On the possibility of exercising control, see Waltz, "Contention and Management in International Relations," *World Politics*, Vol. XVII (July 1965), pp. 720–44.

22. On the limitations of a small nuclear force, see Waltz, *Foreign Policy and Democratic Politics* (Boston: Little, Brown, 1967), pp. 145–48.

27. MEASURING THE CONCENTRATION OF POWER IN POLITICAL SYSTEMS
Steven J. Brams

1. See, for example, Robert A. Dahl, *Who Governs? Democracy and Power in an American City* (New Haven: Yale University Press, 1961); Edward C. Banfield, *Political Influence* (New York: Free Press of Glencoe, 1961); and Robert E. Agger, Daniel Goldrich, and Bert E. Swanson, *The Rulers and the Ruled: Political Power and Impotence in American Communities* (New York: John Wiley & Sons, Inc., 1964).

2. For an imaginative effort to develop a classification of generalized issue-areas relevant to different political systems, see James N. Rosenau, "Pre-theories and Theories of Foreign Policy," in R. Barry Farrell (ed.), *Approaches to Comparative and International Politics* (Evanston, Ill.: Northwestern University Press, 1966), pp. 27–96. See also Theodore J. Lowi, "American Business, Public Policy, Case Studies, and Political Theory," *World Politics*, 16 (July 1964), pp. 677–715.

3. See Lancelot L. White, "Atomism, Structure and Form: A Report on the Natural Philosophy of Form," in Gyorgy Kepes (ed.), *Structure in Art and in Science* (New York: George Braziller, 1965), pp. 20–21; and more generally, Lancelot L. White, *Essay on Atomism: From Democritus to 1960* (New York: Harper and Row, 1963).

4. For some examples of the use of modern mathematics in the social sciences, see John G. Kemeny, "Mathematics Without Numbers," *Daedalus*, 88 (Fall 1959), pp. 577–591.

5. *The Intelligence of Democracy: Decision Making through Mutual Adjustment* (New York: Free Press of Glencoe, 1965), pp. 25–28.

6. See Irving M. Copi, *Introduction to Logic* (New York: Macmillan Company, 1953), pp. 100–105.

7. This verbal explanation of a mathematical theorem does not, of course, constitute a formal proof. Instead of encumbering the exposition of the analysis which follows with mathematical derivations, I have endeavored wherever possible to give references where a rigorous treatment of relevant points can be found.

8. For a review of some of the recent literature on "cluster seeking techniques," see Geoffrey H. Ball, "Data Analysis in the Social Sciences: What about the Details?," *Proceedings—Fall Joint Computer Conference, 1965*, pp. 533–559; also, Hayward R. Alker, Jr.,

"Statistics and Politics: The Need for Causal Data Analysis" (Paper presented at the Annual Meeting of the American Political Science Association, Sept. 5–8, 1967, Chicago).

9. Stephen C. Johnson, "Hierarchical Clustering Schemes," *Psychometrika*, 32 (Sept. 1967), p. 242. I am indebted to Rudolph J. Rummel for this reference.

10. A formal definition of a closed sequence and cycle in the theory of directed graphs (digraphs) is given in Frank Harary, Robert Z. Norman, and Dorwin Cartwright, *Structural Models: An Introduction to the Theory of Directed Graphs* (New York: John Wiley & Sons, Inc., 1965), pp. 40–41. The remainder of the analysis is devoted to showing how a digraph can be behaviorally coordinated with, or serve as a model of, a simplified political system.

11. Since the construction of mutual influence sets is equivalent to the condensation of points of a digraph with respect to its strong components (with the mutual influence sets points of the condensation), the construction is unique. See *ibid.*, p. 55, Theorem 3.2.

12. *Cf.* this concept of concentration with the concept of *evenness*, or lack of concentration, of a nation's transaction flows in my "Trade in the North Atlantic Area: An Approach to the Analysis of Transformations in a System," *Peace Research Society: Papers*, VI (1967), pp. 149–152. Another related concept is that of *cosmopolitanism* in my "A note on the Cosmopolitanism of World Regions," *Journal of Peace Research*, 1968, No. 1, pp. 87–95.

13. Presumably, this condition will hold in most political systems of interest.

14. Decision-maker j's exclusion suggests that we should not count j in N_T, the denominator of the PC index, because he is not directly or indirectly influenced by the minority control set, $\{a, m\}$. Accordingly, we define a revised power concentration index,

$$PC' = 1 - \frac{N_{MC}}{N_T - N_U} \qquad 0 < PC' < 1,$$

where

N_U = the number of decision-makers (not in minority control sets) *uninfluenced* by any minority control set.

PC' is the same as PC for the hierarchical and mixed systems (because $N_U = 0$ for these systems), but PC' ($= .83$) is slightly less than PC ($= .85$) for the mutual adjustment system.

15. A system in which all influence relationships are asymmetrical and never flow "upward" can also be described as one in which (1) a decision-maker cannot be both the superior and subordinate of another, and (2) a subordinate of a subordinate is a subordinate. A necessary and sufficient condition for these requirements to hold is that the digraph of the system be free of cycles. See John G. Kemeny and J. Laurie Snell, *Mathematical Models in the Social*

16. If there is more than one directed line between two mutual influence or minority control sets, which is not the case in any of the Lindblom systems, only one is preserved. Some of the consequences of this simplification for the PC index are discussed in Footnote 23, where a refinement in the index is suggested.

17. Harary, Norman and Cartwright, *op. cit.*, p. 270, Theorem 10.2.

18. Steven J. Brams, "DECOMP: A Computer Program for the Condensation of a Directed Graph and the Hierarchical Ordering of Its Strong Components," *Behavioral Science*, 13 (July, 1968), 344–45. A write-up and source deck of this program are available from the Syracuse University Computing Center, Syracuse, N.Y.

19. In digraph theory, the sets of points with outgoing but no incoming directed lines at all levels (but the lowest) of the reduced digraph—the originators of influence in the system—is the unique point basis of the reduced digraph. In the original digraph (containing cycles), a point basis is not unique and will consist of one member from each of the originator mutual influence and/or minority control sets. See Harary, Norman, and Cartwright, *op. cit.*, pp. 85–89.

20. *Ibid.*, p. 276.

21. Such "linking pins," when operating at different hierarchical levels, have been found to perform a valuable integrative function in an organization. See Rensis Likert, *New Patterns of Management* (New York: McGraw-Hill Book Company, Inc., 1961), ch. 8. In digraph theory, linkage decision-makers b and c in Figure 5 are cut points whose removal would reduce the strength of connectedness of the digraph. See Harary, Norman, and Cartwright, *op. cit.*, ch. 8. For a method to identify "liaison persons" in symmetric graphs, see Ian C. Ross and Frank Harary, "Identification of the Liaison Persons of an Organization Using the Structure Matrix," *Management Science*, 1 (April–July 1955), 251–258.

22. See John R. P. French, Jr., "A Formal Theory of Social Power," in Dorwin Cartwright and Alvin Zander (eds.), *Group Dynamics: Research and Theory* (2nd ed.; New York: Harper and Row, 1960), pp. 727–744; and Frank Harary, "A Criterion for Unanimity in French's Theory of Social Power," in Dorwin Cartwright (ed.), *Studies in Social Power* (Ann Arbor, Michigan: Research Center for Group Dynamics, University of Michigan, 1959), pp. 168–182.

23. Another elementary concept, influence relationship sets, might be usefully employed to build greater precision into the power concentration index. These sets would consist of all asymmetrical influence *relationships* occurring between each minority control set and the set or sets which it influences. For example, the values of the PC index for the three-actor

systems pictured below are the same (.67), but the influence relationship set for the system on the left has one member (one directed line from the minority control set to the mutual influence set) while the influence relationships set for the system on the right has two members (two directed lines from the minority control set to the mutual influence set). Because minority control set {a} can exert direct influence on actor c in the right-hand system, a reasonable argument could be made to weight the influence of {a}, and the concentration of power in the system, by the number of members of the influence relationship sets. The more influence relationships which these sets contain, the more direct will be minority control—and, in one sense, the more concentrated power will be in the system.

24. For experimental evidence on this point, see Jacob I. Hurwitz, Alvin Zander, and Bernard Hymovitch, "Some Effects of Power on the Relations Among Group Members," in Cartwright and Zander, *op. cit.*, pp. 800–809; Arthur R. Cohen, "Upward Communication in Experimentally Created Hierarchies," *Human Relations*, 11 (Feb. 1958), 41–53; and David L. Watson, "Effects of Certain Social Power Structures on Communication in Task-Oriented Groups," *Sociometry*, 28 (Sept. 1965), 322–336.

25. John W. Thibaut and Harold H. Kelly, *The Social Psychology of Groups* (New York: John Wiley & Sons, Inc., 1959), p. 125.

26. Karl W. Deutsch, *The Nerves of Government: Models of Political Communication and Control* (New York: Free Press of Glencoe, 1963), p. 111.

27. Zbigniew K. Brzezinski, "The Organization of the Communist Camp," in his *The Soviet Bloc: Unity and Conflict* (rev. ed.; New York: Frederick A. Praeger, 1961), pp. 445–479.

28. For an actor-oriented measure of influence in dominance situations (system representable by a complete asymmetric digraph where each actor either dominates or is dominated by—but not both—every other actor), see John G. Kemeny, J. Laurie Snell, and Gerald Thompson, *Introduction to Finite Mathematics* (2nd ed.; Englewood Cliffs, N.J.: Prentice-Hall, Inc., 1966), pp. 390–391.

29. For an extended treatment of this idea, see Charles A. McClelland, *Theory and the*

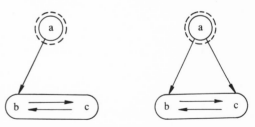

International System (New York: Macmillan Company, 1966), Ch. 3. In a recent paper, McClelland has used digraph theory to study international crises. See his "The Beginning, Duration, and Abatement of International Crises: Comparisons in Two Conflict Areas," in Charles F. Hermann (ed.), *International Crises*, forthcoming.

30. A bilateral meeting represents an occasion for the meeting of one pair of countries whereas a multilateral meeting represents an occasion for several pairs of countries to meet with each other. Brzezinski did not distinguish between the meetings of pairs of delegations in bilateral and multilateral meetings.

31. If we assumed six meetings per pair as the cutoff point in the second period (i.e., 54 percent above the expected number), then only 5 of the 28 pairs of countries would be in influence relationships and at least two of the eight countries would therefore not be in influence relationships with any others. At the five-meeting-per-pair cutoff point, on the other hand, 9 of the 28 pairs of countries are in influence relationships, and each of the eight countries is in an influence relationship with at least one other. In the first period, one country (Rumania) is not in an influence relationship with any other, but the three-meetings-per-pair cutoff point for this period cannot be lowered without violating the criterion that the cutoff point be greater than the expected number of visits per pair for the system.

32. The eight countries, and their code abbreviations, are: Bulgaria—BUL; China—CHN; Czechoslovakia—CZE; East Germany—GME; Hungary—HUN; Poland—POL; Rumania—RUM; and Soviet Union—USR.

33. See, for example, Robert H. McNeal (ed.), *International Relations Among Communists* (Englewood Cliffs, N.J.: Prentice-Hall, Inc., 1967), pp. 76–78.

34. For a discussion of these points, see Brzezinski, *op. cit.*, pp. 482–483.

35. *Cf.* Riker's argument for *n*-adic, rather than dyadic, definitions of power. William H. Riker, "Some Ambiguities in the Notion of Power," this REVIEW, 58 (June, 1964), 341–349.

36. Clyde Kluckhohn, "Cultural Anthropology," in Lynn White, Jr. (ed.), *Frontiers of Knowledge in the Study of Man* (New York: Harper and Brothers, 1956), p. 39.

37. See Christopher Alexander, *Notes on the Synthesis of Form* (Cambridge, Mass.: Harvard University Press, 1964), p. 194, Footnote 12. It should be noted that the non-numerical digraph model was used to formulate the numerical PC(*m, n*) index.

38. See Rudolph Carnap, "Elementary and Abstract Terms," in Arthur Danto and Sidney Morgenbesser (eds.), *Philosophy of Science* (Cleveland: World Publishing Company, 1960),

p. 155. The above analytic (nonfactual) statement illustrates the great advantage of translating an already developed mathematical theory into a mathematical model of a political system: the model inherits from the theory a stock of proven theorems with a logically unassailable theoretical structure.

39. Carl G. Hempel, "Operationism, Observation, and Theoretical Terms," *ibid.*, pp. 117–120.

40. Retroduction, which involves reasoning back from diverse phenomena to a pattern within which they appear intelligible, should be distinguished from induction, which involves the discovery of regularities (empirical correlations) in repetitive observations of details in phenomena. See Norwood R. Hanson, *Patterns of Discovery: An Inquiry into the Conceptual Foundations of Science* (Cambridge, Eng.: Cambridge University Press, 1958), pp. 85 ff. I am indebted to Wayne A. Kimmel for this reference.

41. This is not to say that study of the isolated parts of systems is not useful but rather that we must also direct our attention to ways of putting the parts together into a palpable whole. This point is developed more fully in my "Transaction Flows in the International System," this REVIEW, 60 (Dec. 1966), 880–881. For a discussion of these complementary approaches in biology, see C. H. Waddington, *The Nature of Life* (London: George Allen & Unwin Ltd., 1961), esp. pp. 21–24.

42. Jacob Bronowski, "The Discovery of Form," in Kepes, *op. cit.*, esp. pp. 56, 59–60.

43. Marshall McLuhan, *The Gutenberg Galaxy: The Making of Typographic Man* (Toronto: University of Toronto Press, 1962), p. 252.

44. On this point, see James D. Barber, *Power in Committees: An Experiment in the Government Process* (Chicago: Rand McNally & Company, 1966), p. 129.

45. For an analysis of changes in the structure of influence relationships over time based on visits between heads-of-state and other high-level officials for all nations in the world in 1964–65, see Steven J. Brams, "The Structure of Influence Relationships in the International System," in James N. Rosenau (ed.), *International Politics and Foreign Policy; A Reader in Research and Theory* (rev. ed.; New York; Free Press, forthcoming 1969). In *ibid.*, it is suggested that the kind of influence tapped by data on international visits tends to reflect the visited nation's control over broad policy areas, but not specific actions related to the vital national interests, of the visiting nation.

46. One concept making use of interaction data that has been of particular interest in the structural analysis of organizations is status. See Leo Katz, "A New Status Index Derived from Sociometric Analysis," in J. L. Moreno (ed.), *The Sociometry Reader* (Glencoe, Ill.; Free Press of Glencoe, 1960), pp. 266–271; and

Frank Harary, "Status and Contra-status," *Sociometry*, 22 (March 1959), 23–43.

47. Dahl, *op. cit.*

48. Banfield, *op. cit.*

49. Ernst B. Haas, *The Uniting of Europe: Political, Social, and Economical Forces*, 1950–1957 (London: Stevens & Sons, 1958).

50. Deutsch, *op. cit.*, p. 253.

51. One kind of algebraic ordering which has been proposed as a model for the structure of cities and organizations is the semilattice. See Christopher Alexander, "A City is Not a Tree," *Architectural Forum*, 122 (2 parts; April, May 1965), pp. 58–62, 58–61; and Morris R. Friedell, "Organizations as Semilattices," *American Sociological Review*, 32 (Feb. 1967), 46–54.

52. Alex Bavelas, "Communication Patterns in Task-Oriented Groups," in Cartwright and Zander, *op. cit.*, pp. 669–682. At a more theoretical level, see Terence K. Hopkins, *The Exercise of Influence in Small Groups* (Totowa, N.J.: Bedminster Press, 1964).

53. For various measures of the "concentration of authority" based on asymmetric dominance relationships between all pairs of actors in a system, see Otomar J. Bartos, *Simple Models of Group Behavior* (New York: Columbia University Press, 1967), pp. 56–61. These measures, like Russett's are algebraic in nature and do not presuppose a decomposition that depicts the geometric order in a system.

Bibliography

Bibliography

Abramson, E., H. A. Cutter, R. W. Kautz, and M. Mendelson, "Social Power and Commitment: A Theoretical Statement," 23 *American Sociological Review* (1958) 15–22.

Abu-Laban, Baha, "The Reputational Approach in the Study of Community Power: A Critical Evaluation," 8 *Pacific Sociological Review* (1965) 35–42.

Adams, J. S., and Romney, A. K., "A Functional Analysis of Authority," 86 *Psychological Review* (1959) 234–251.

Agger, Robert A., "Power Attributions in the Local Community: Theoretical and Research Considerations," 34 *Social Forces* (1956) 322–331.

———, and Daniel Goldrich, "Community Power Structures and Partisanship," 23 *American Sociological Review* (1958) 383–392.

———, and Bert E. Swanson, *The Rulers and the Ruled: Political Power and Impotence in American Communities* (New York: John Wiley, 1964).

Anton, Thomas J., "Power, Pluralism, and Local Politics," 7 *Administrative Science Quarterly* (1963) 425–457.

Aron, Raymond, "Social Structure and Ruling Class," 1 *British Journal of Sociology* (1950) 1–17, 126–144.

Ash, Maurice, "An Analysis of Power, with Special Reference to International Politics," 3 *World Politics* (1950) 218–237.

Bachrach, Peter, "Elite Consensus and Democracy," 24 *Journal of Politics* (1962) 439–452.

———, and Morton Baratz, "Decisions and Nondecisions: An Analytical Framework," 57 *American Political Science Review* (1963) 632–642.

———, "Two Faces of Power," 56 *American Political Science Review* (1962) 947–952.

Back, K., "Influence Through Social Communication," 46 *Journal of Abnormal and Social Psychology* (1951) 9–23.

Bales, Robert F., *Interaction Process Analysis* (Cambridge: Addison-Wesley, 1950).

Banfield, Edward C., *Political Influence* (New York: The Free Press, 1961).

———, and James Q. Wilson, *City Politics* (Cambridge: Harvard University Press, 1963).

Banton, M. (ed.), *Political Systems and the Distribution of Power* (London: Tavistock, 1965).

Barber, James D., *Power in Committees: An Experiment in the Government Process* (Chicago: Rand McNally, 1966).

Barkley, R., "Theory of the Elite and the Mythology of Power," 19 *Science and Society* (1955) 97–106.

Barnard, C. I., *The Functions of the Executive* (Cambridge: Harvard University Press, 1938).

Barth, Ernest A. T., "Community Influence Systems: Structure and Change," 40 *Social Forces* (1961) 58–63.

———, and Baha Abu-Laban, "Power Structure and the Negro Sub-community," 24 *American Sociological Review* (1959) 69–76.

———, and Stuart D. Johnson, "Community Power and a Typology of Social Issues," 38 *Social Forces* (1959) 29–32.

Bass, B. M., *Leadership, Psychology, and Organizational Behavior* (New York: Harper & Bros., 1960).

Belknap, George M., "Political Power Relations in a Mid-West City," 20 *Public Opinion Quarterly* (1956) 73–81.

Bell, Daniel, "The Power-Elite Reconsidered," 64 *American Journal of Sociology* (1958) 238–250.

Bell, Wendell, and Maryanne T. Force, "Social Structure and Participation in Different Types of Formal Associations," 34 *Social Forces* (1956) 345–350.

Beth, Marian W., "The Elite and the Elites," 47 *American Journal of Sociology* (1942) 746–755.

Bennis, W. G., Berkowitz, M. Altinito, M. Malone, "Authority, Power, and the Ability to Influence," 11 *Human Relations* (1958) 143–155.

Biderman, A. D., and H. Zimmer, eds., *The Manipulation of Human Behavior* (New York: John Wiley, 1961).

Bierstedt, Robert, "An Analysis of Social Power," 15 *American Sociological Review* (1958) 730–738.

Birch, A. H., *Small-Town Politics: Study of Political Life in Glossop* (New York: Oxford University Press, 1959).

Blackwell, Gordon W., "Community Analysis," in Roland Young, ed., *Approaches to the Study of Politics* (Evanston: Northwestern University Press, 1958), pp. 305–317.

Blackwell, Gordon W., "A Theoretical Framework for Sociological Research in Community Organization," 33 *Social Forces* (1954) 57–64.

Blankenship, Vaughn, "Community Power and Decision-Making: A Comparative Evaluation of Measurement Techniques," 43 *Social Forces* (1964) 207–216.

Blau, Peter M., *Bureaucracy in Modern Society* (New York: Random House, 1956).

———, *Exchange and Power in Social Life* (New York: John Wiley, 1964).

Bloomberg, Warner, and Morris Sunshine, *Suburban Power Structures and Public Education* (Syracuse: Syracuse University Press, 1963).

Bonjean, Charles M., "Class, Status, and Reputation," in 49 *Sociology and Social Research* (1964) 69–75.

——, and David M. Olson, "Community Leadership: Directions of Research," 9 *Administrative Science Quarterly* (1964) 278–300.

——, and Charles R. Adrian, "Elections and Community Power," 25 *Journal of Politics* (1963) 107–118.

——, "Power Structure and Community Change: A Replication Study of Community A," 6 *The Midwest Journal of Political Science* (1962) 277–296.

——, "Simplifying the Discovery of Elites," 5 *The American Behavioral Scientist* (1961) 14–16.

Boulding, Kenneth, "Toward a Pure Theory of Threat Systems," 53 *American Economic Review* (1963) 424–434.

Brady, Robert A., *Business as a System of Power* (New York: Columbia University Press, 1943).

Brams, Steven J., "Measuring the Concentration of Power in Political Systems," 62 *American Political Science Review* (1968) 461–475.

Brzezinski, Zbigniew, and Samuel Huntington, *Political Power: USA/USSR* (New York: Viking, 1964).

Burns, Arthur Lee, "From Balance to Deterrence: A Theoretical Analysis," 9 *World, Politics* (1957) 494–529.

Canetti, Elias, *Crowds and Power* (New York: Viking, 1962).

Cartwright, Dorwin, "Influence, Leadership, Control," in James G. March, ed., *Handbook of Organizations* (Chicago: Rand McNally, 1965) 1–47.

——, ed., *Studies in Social Power* (Ann Arbor: University of Michigan Press, 1959).

Catlin, G. E. G., *The Science and Method of Politics* (New York: Alfred Knopf, 1927).

——, *A Study of the Principles of Politics* (New York: Macmillan, 1930).

——, *Systematic Politics* (Toronto: University of Toronto Press, 1962).

Clark, Terry N., ed., *Community Structure and Decision-Making: Comparative Analyses* (San Francisco: Chandler, 1968).

——, "The Concept of Power: Some Overemphasized and Underrecognized Dimensions—An Examination with Special Reference to the Local Community," 48 *Southwestern Social Science Quarterly* (1967) 271–286.

——, "Power and Community Structure: Who Governs, Where, and When?" 8 *Sociological Quarterly* (1967) 291–316.

Claude, Inis, *Power and International Relations* (New York: Random House, 1962).

Clelland, Donald A., and William H. Form, "Economic Dominants and Community Power: A Comparative Analysis," 69 *American Journal of Sociology* (1964) 511–521.

de Crespigny, Anthony, "Power and Its Forms," 16 *Political Studies* (1968) 192–205.

Crozier, Michel. *The Bureaucratic Phenomenon* (Chicago: University of Chicago Press, 1964).

Dahl, Robert A., "The Analysis of Influence in Local Communicites," in Charles R. Adrian, ed., *Social Science and Community Action* (East Lansing: Institute for Community Development and Services, Michigan State University, 1961) 25–42.

——, "The Concept of Power," 2 *Behavioral Science* (1957) 201–215.

——, "A Critique of the Ruling Elite Model," 52 *American Political Science Review* (1958) 463–469.

——, *Modern Political Analysis* (Englewood-Cliffs, N.J.: Prentice-Hall, 1963).

——, *Political Oppositions in Western Democracies* (New Haven: Yale University Press, 1966).

——, "Power," *International Encyclopedia of the Social Sciences* (New York: The Free Press, 1968).

——, *Who Governs?* (New Haven: Yale University Press, 1961).

Dahrendorf, Ralf, *Class and Class Conflict in Industrial Society* (Stanford: Stanford University Press, 1959).

D'Antonio, William V., H. J. Ehrlich, and E. C. Erickson, "Further Notes on the Study of Community Power," 27 *American Sociological Review* (1962) 848–854.

——, Howard J. Ehrlich, and Eugene C. Erickson, eds., *Power and Democracy in America* (Notre Dame: University of Notre Dame Press, 1961).

Danzger, M. Herbert, "Community Power Structure: Problems and Continuities," 29 *American Sociological Review* (1964) 707–717.

Davison, W. P., *Power—The Idea and Its Communication*, P-1869. Santa Monica, Calif., The RAND Corporation, 1959.

Deutsch, Karl, and Singer, J. D., "Multipolar Power Systems and International Stability," *World Politics* 16 (1964) 390–406.

Deutsch, Karl W., *The Nerves of Government* (New York: The Free Press, 1962).

Domhoff, G. William. *Who Rules America?* (Englewood Cliffs, N.J.: Prentice-Hall, 1967).

Domhoff, G. William, and Hoyte B. Ballard, eds., *C. Wright Mills and the Power Elite* (Boston: Beacon Press, 1968).

Easton, David, *The Political System* (New York: Alfred Knopf, 1953).

——, *A Systems Analysis of Political Life* (New York: John Wiley, 1965).

——, ed., *Varieties of Political Theory* (Englewood Cliffs, N.J.: Prentice-Hall, 1966).

Edwards, Ward, "The Theory of Decision-Making," 51 *Psychological Bulletin* (1954) 380–417.

Ehrlich, Howard J., "The Reputational Approach to the Study of Community Power," 26 *American Sociological Review* (1961) 926–927.

Emerson, Richard M., "Power-Dependence Relations," 27 *American Sociological Review* (1962) 31–41.

Emmet, Dorothy, "The Concept of Power," 54 *Proceedings of the Aristotelian Society* (1954).

Etzioni, Amitai, *A Comparative Analysis of Complex Organizations* (New York: The Free Press, 1961).

Freeman, Linton C., Thomas J. Fararo, W. Bloomberg, and S. M. Sunshine, "Locating Leaders in Local Communities: A Comparison of Some Alternative Approaches," in 28 *American Sociological Review* (1963) 791–798.

French, J. R. P., Jr., "A Formal Theory of Social Power," 63 *Psychological Review* (1956) 181–194.

French, F. W., *The Turkish Political Elite* (Cambridge: MIT Press, 1965).

Friedrich, Carl J., *Constitutional Government and Democracy* (Boston: Ginn and Co., 1950).

———, *Man and His Government* (New York: McGraw-Hill, 1963).

———, ed., *Nomos I: Authority* (Cambridge: Harvard University Press, 1958).

Gamson, William A., *Power and Discontent* (Homewood, Ill.: Dorsey, 1968).

Gibb, G. A., "Leadership," in G. Lindsey, ed., *Handbook of Social Psychology* (Cambridge: Addison-Wesley, 1954).

Gilbert, Claire W., "Community Power and Decision-Making: A Quantitative Examination of Previous Research," in Terry Clark, ed., *Community Structure and Decision-Making: Comparative Analyses* (San Francisco: Chandler, 1968).

Gitlin, Todd, "Local Pluralism as Theory and Ideology," 5 *Studies on the Left* (1965) 21–45.

Goffman, Irwin W., "Status Consistency and Preference for Change in Power Distribution," 22 *American Sociological Review* (1957) 275–281.

Gold, M., "Power in the Classroom," in 21 *Sociometry* (1958) 50–60.

Goldhamer, Herbert, and Edward Shils, "Types of Power and Status," 45 *American Journal of Sociology* (1939) 171–182.

Haas, Ernst B., "The Balance of Power: Prescription, Concept, or Propaganda," 5 *World Politics* (1953) 442–477.

Harris, E. E., "Political Power," 68 *Ethics* (1957) 1–10.

Harsanyi, John C., "Measurement of Social Power in N-Person Reciprocal Power Situations," 7 *Behavioral Science* (1962) 81–92.

———, "Measurement of Social Power, Opportunity Costs, and the Theory of Two-Person Bargaining Games," in 7 *Behavioral Science* (1962) 67–80.

Hellenbrand, Martin J., *Power and Morals* (New York: Columbia University Press, 1949).

Herson, J. R., "In the Footsteps of Community Power," 55 *American Political Science Review* (1961) 817–830.

Holsti, J. K., "The Concept of Power in the Study of International Relations," 7 *Background* (1964) 179–200.

Homans, G. C., "Social Behavior as Exchange," 63 *American Journal of Sociology* (1958) 597–606.

Hunter, Floyd, *Community Power Structure: A Study of Decision Makers* (Chapel Hill: University of North Carolina Press, 1953).

———, "Studying Association and Organization Structures," in Roland Young, ed., *Approaches to the Study of Politics* (Evanston: Northwestern University Press, 1958) 343–362.

James, Alan, "Power Politics," 12 *Political Studies* (1964) 307–326.

Janowitz, Morris, "Community Power and 'Policy Science' Research," 26 *Public Opinion Quarterly* (1962) 398–410.

———, ed., *Community Political Systems*. (New York: The Free Press, 1960).

Jennings, M. Kent, *Community Influencials* (New York: The Free Press, 1964).

James, Stephen B., "The Power Inventory and National Strategy," 6 *World Politics* (1954) 421–452.

de Jouvenel, Bertrand, *On Power* (New York: Viking, 1949).

Kemmerer, Gladys M., *et. al.*, *The Urban Political Community* (Boston: Houghton Mifflin Co., 1963).

Kaplan, Abraham, "Power in Perspective," in Robert Kahn and Elise Boulding, eds., *Power and Conflict in Organizations* (New York: Basic Books, 1964), pp. 11–32.

Kaplan, Morton, Arthur L. Burns, and Richard E. Quandt, "Theoretical Analysis of the 'Balance of Power,'" 5 *Behavioral Science* (1960) 240–252.

Kariel, Henry, *The Decline of American Pluralism* (Stanford: Stanford University Press, 1961).

Karlsson, Georg, "Some Aspects of Power in Small Groups," in Joan H. Criswell, Herbert Salomon, and Patrick Suppes, eds., *Mathematical Methods in Small Group Processes* (Stanford: Stanford University Press, 1962), pp. 193–202.

Kaufman, Herbert, and Victor Jones, "The Mystery of Power," 14 *Public Administration Review* (1954) 205–212.

Keller, Suzanne, *Beyond the Ruling Class* (New York: Random House, 1963).

Kimball, S. T., and M. Pearsall, "Event Analysis as an Approach to Community Study," 34 *Social Forces* (1955) 58–63.

Kimbrough, Ralph, *Political Power and Educational Decision-Making* (Chicago: Rand McNally) 1964.

King-Hall, Stephen, *Power Politics in the Nuclear Age: A Policy for Britain* (London: Gollancz, 1962).

Klapp, Orrin E., and L. Vincent Padgett, "Power Structure and Decision-Making in a Mexican Border Town," 65 *American Journal of Sociology* (1960) 400–406.

Knorr, Klaus, *On the Uses of Military Power in the Nuclear Age* (Princeton: Princeton University Press, 1966).

————, *The War Potential of Nations* (Princeton: Princeton University Press, 1956).

Kornhauser, Arthur, ed., *Problems of Power in American Democracy* (Detroit: Wayne State University Press, 1957).

————, *The Politics of Mass Society* (New York: The Free Press, 1959).

Kuhn, Alfred, *The Study of Society: A Unified Approach* (Homewood, Ill.: Irwin and Dorsey, 1963).

Lammers, C. J., "Power and Participation in Decision-Making in Formal Organizations," 73 *American Journal of Sociology* (1967) 201–216.

Lasswell, Harold D., *Power and Personality* (New York: Norton, 1948).

————, *Politics: Who Gets What, When, and How?* (reprinted, New York: The Free Press, 1951).

Lasswell, Harold D., and Abraham Kaplan, *Power and Society* (New Haven: Yale University Press, 1950).

Lenski, Gerhard, *Power and Privilege* (New York: McGraw-Hill, 1966).

Leoni, Bruno, "The Meaning of 'Political' in Political Decisions'," 5 *Political Studies* (1957) 225–239.

Lewin, Kurt, *Field Theory in Social Science* (New York: Harper, 1951).

Lindblom, Charles, *The Intelligence of Democracy* (New York: The Free Press, 1965).

Lindzey, Gardner, ed., *Handbook of Social Psychology* (Cambridge: Addison-Wesley, 1954).

Lippitt, R., N. Polansky, F. Redl, and S. Rosen, "The Dynamics of Power," 5 *Human Relations* (1952) 37–64.

Long, Norton E., "The Local Community as an Ecology of Games," 64 *American Journal of Sociology* (1958) 251–261.

————, "Power and Administration," 9 *Public Administration Review* (1949) 257–264.

Luce, R. D., and A. A. Rogow, "A Game Theoretic Analysis of Congressional Power Distributions for a Stable Two-Party System," 1 *Behavioral Science* (1956) 83–95.

————, and Howard Raiffa, *Games and Decisions* (New York: John Wiley, 1957).

Lynd, Robert S., "Power in American Society as Resource and Problem," in Arthur Kornhauser, ed., *Problems of Power in American Democracy* (Detroit: Wayne State University Press, 1957) pp. 1–45.

————, and Helen Lynd, *Middletown* (New York: Harcourt, Brace, 1929).

————, *Middletown in Transition* (New York: Harcourt, Brace, 1937).

McClelland, Charles A., *Theory and the International System* (New York: Macmillan, 1966).

McKee, James B., "Community Power and Strategies in Race Relations," 6 *Social Problems* (1958–59) 195–203.

MacRae, D., Jr., and H. D. Price, "Scale Positions and 'Power' in the Senate," 4 *Behavioral Science* (1959) 212–218.

March, James G., "An Introduction to the Theory and Measurement of Influence," 59 *American Political Science Review* (1955) 431–435.

————, "Measurement Concepts in the Theory of Influence." 19 *Journal of Politics* (1957) 202–226.

————, "The Power of Power," in David Easton, ed., *Varieties of Political Theory* (Englewood Cliffs, N.J.: Prentice-Hall, 1966), pp. 39–70.

Martin, Roscoe, *et al.*, *Decisions in Syracuse* (Garden City: Doubleday Anchor, 1965).

Meisel, James, *The Myth of the Ruling Class: Gaetano Mosca and the Elite* (Ann Arbor: University of Michigan Press, 1958.)

Merriam, Charles, *Political Power* (new ed., New York: Collier, 1964).

Merton, Robert K., *Social Theory and Social Structure* (New York: Free Press, rev. ed., 1957).

Miller, Delbert C., "Town and Gown: The Power Structure of a University Town," 68 *American Journal of Sociology* (1963) 432–443.

Mills, C. Wright, *The New Men of Power* (New York: Harcourt, Brace, 1948).

————, *The Power Elite* (New York: Oxford University Press, 1956).

————, *Power, Politics, and People: Collected Essays* (New York: Ballantine, 1963).

————, "The Structure of Power in American Society," 9 *British Journal of Sociology* (1958) 29–41.

Minogue, K. R., "Power in Politics," 7 *Political Studies* (1959) 269–289.

Morgenthau, Hans, *Politics Among Nations* (New York: Alfred Knopf, 1960).

————, "Power as a Political Concept," 17 *Review of Politics* (1955) 431–460.

————, *Scientific Man vs. Power Politics* (Chicago: University of Chicago Press, 1946).

Mosca, Gaetano, *The Ruling Class*, trans. Hannah Kahn (New York: McGraw-Hill, 1939).

Nagel, Jack H., "Some Questions About the Concept of Power," 13 *Behavioral Science* (1968) 129–137.

Naville, Pierre, "Technical Elites and Social Elites," 37 *Sociology of Education* (1963) 27–29.

Neumann, Franz, "Approaches to the Study of Political Power," 65 *Political Science Quarterly* (1950) 161–180.

Neustadt, Richard E., *Presidential Power* (New York: John Wiley, 1960).

Nuttal, Ronald L., Erwin K. Scheuch, and Chad Gordon, "On the Structure of Influence," in Terry Clark, ed., *Community Structure and Decision-Making: Comparative Analyses* (San Francisco: Chandler, 1968).

Olson, Mancur, *The Logic of Collective Action* (Cambridge: Harvard University Press, 1965).

Oppenheim, Felix, *Dimensions of Freedom* (New York: St. Martin's Press, 1961).

Ossowski, Stanislaw, *Class Structure in the Social Consciousness* (New York: The Free Press, 1963.)

Parsons, Talcott, "The Distribution of Power in American Society," 10 *World Politics* (1957) 123–143.

———, "On the Concept of Influence," with a comment by James S. Coleman and a rejoinder by Parsons, 27 *Public Opinion Quarterly* (1963) 37–92.

———, "On the Concept of Political Power," 107 *Proceedings of the American Philosophical Society* (1963) 232–262.

———, "Some Reflections on the Place of Force in Social Processes," in Harry Eckstein, ed., *Internal War* (New York: The Free Press, 1964), pp. 33–70.

Partridge, P. H., "Some Notes on the Concept of Power," 11 *Political Studies* (1963) 107–125.

Pilisuk, Marc, and Thomas Hayden, "Is There a Military Industrial Complex Which Prevents Peace?" 21 *Journal of Social Issues* (1965) 67–117.

Polsby, Nelson W., *Community Power and Political Theory* (New Haven: Yale University Press, 1963).

———, "How to Study Community Power: The Pluralist Alternative," 22 *Journal of Politics* (1960) 474–484.

———, "Power in Middletown: Fact and Value in Community Research," 26 *Canadian Journal of Economics and Political Science* (1960) 592–603.

———, "The Sociology of Community Power: A Reassessment," 37 *Social Forces* (1959) 232–236.

———, "Three Problems in the Analysis of Community Power," 24 *American Sociological Review* (1959) 796–803.

Presthus, Robert V., *Men at the Top: A Study in Community Power* (New York: Oxford University Press, 1964).

Raths, Louis, "Power in Small Groups," 28 *Journal of Educational Sociology* (1954) 97–103.

Raven, B. H., and J. R. P. French, Jr., "Legitimate Power, Coercive Power, and Observability in Social Influence," 21 *Sociometry* (1958) 83–97.

Reiss, Albert J., Jr., "Some Logical and Methodological Problems in Community Research," 33 *Social Forces* (1954) 51–57.

Riker, William H., "Some Ambiguities in the Notion of Power," 58 *American Political Science Review* (1964) 341–349.

———, *The Study of Local Politics* (New York: Random House, 1959).

———, "A Test of the Adequacy of the Power Index," 4 *Behavioral Science* (1959) 276–290.

Rosecrance, R. N., "Bipolarity, Multipolarity, and the Future," 10 *Journal of Conflict Resolution* (1966) 315–327.

Rossi, Peter H., "Community Decision-Making," 1 *Administrative Science Quarterly* (1957) 415–443.

———, "Power and Community Structure," 4 *Midwest Journal of Political Science* (1960) 390–401.

Russell, Bertrand, *Power* (New York: Norton, 1938).

Russett, Bruce, "Probabilism and the Number of Units Affected: Measuring Influence Concentration," 62 *American Political Science Review* (1968) 476–480.

Sayre, Wallace S., and Herbert Kaufman, *Governing New York City* (New York: Russell Sage Foundation, 1960).

Schattschneider, E. E., *The Semi-Sovereign People* (New York: Holt, Rinehart, and Winston, 1960).

Schelling, Thomas C., *Arms and Influence* (New Haven: Yale University Press, 1966).

———, *The Strategy of Conflict* (Cambridge: Harvard University Press, 1960).

Schermerhorn, Richard A., *Society and Power* (New York: Random House, 1961).

Schulze, Robert O., "The Role of Economic Dominants in Community Power Structure," 23 *American Sociological Review* (1958) 3–9.

Schulze, Robert O., and Leonard V. Blumberg, "The Determination of Local Power Elites," 63 *American Journal of Sociology* (1957) 290–296.

Schwarzenberger, George, *Power Politics—A Study of International Society* (New York: Stevens, 2nd ed., 1951), or (N.Y.: Praeger, 3rd ed., 1964).

Shapley, L. S., and M. Shubik, "A Method for Evaluating the Distribution of Power in a Committee System," 48 *American Political Science Review* (1954) 787–792.

Shubik, Martin, ed., *Game Theory and Related Approaches to Social Behavior* (New York: John Wiley, 1964).

Simmel, Georg, *The Sociology of Georg Simmel*, ed. Kurt Wolff (New York: The Free Press, 1950).

Simon, Herbert, "Notes of the Observation and Measurement of Political Power," 15 *Journal of Politics* (1953) 500–516.

Singer, J. David, "Inter-Nation Influence," 57 *American Political Science Review* (1963) 420–430.

Smelser, Neil J., *Theory of Collective Behavior* (New York: The Free Press, 1963).

Smith, P. A., "The Game of Community Politics," 9 *Midwest Journal of Political Science* (1965) 37–60.

Snyder, Richard C., H. W. Bruck and Burton Sapin, "The Decision-Making Approach," in H. Eulau, S. J. Eldersveld, and M. Janowitz, eds., *Political Behavior* (New York: The Free Press, 1956), pp. 352–358.

Spinrad, William, "Power in Local Communities," 12 *Social Problems* (1965) 335–356.

Sussman, Marvin B., ed., *Community Structure and Analysis* (New York: Crowell, 1959).

Swanson, Bert E., ed., *Current Trends in Comparative Community Studies*, Public Affairs Monograph Series, No. 1 (Kansas City: Community Studies, Inc.; 1962).

Sweezy, Paul M., "Power Elite or Ruling Class," 8 *Monthly Review* (1956) 138–150.

Tannenbaum, A. S., "An Event Structure Approach to Social Power and to the Problem of Power Comparability," 7 *Behavioral Science*, (1962) 315–331.

———, and Georgopolous, B. S., "The Distribution of Control in Formal Organizations," 36 *Social Forces* (1957) 44–50.

Thibaut, John W., and Harold H. Kelley, *The Social Psychology of Groups* (New York: John Wiley, 1959).

Thometz, Carol Estes, *The Decision-Makers* (Dallas: Southern Methodist University Press, 1963).

Van den Berghe, Pierre, "Dialectic and Functionalism: Toward Theoretical Synthesis," 28 *American Sociological Review* (1963) 695–705.

Vidich, Arthur, Joseph Bensman, and Maurice Stein, eds., *Reflections on Community Studies* (New York: John Wiley, 1964).

———, *Small Town in Mass Society*, Princeton: Princeton University Press, 1959).

Wahlke, John C., *et al.*, *The Legislative System* (New York: John Wiley, 1962).

Walter, B., "On the Logical Analysis of Power-Attribution Procedures," 26 *Journal of Politics* (1964) 850–866.

Walter, E. V., "Power and Violence," 58 *American Political Science Review* (1964) 350–360.

Walton, John, "Disciple, Method, and Community Power: A Note on the Sociology of Knowledge," 31 *American Sociological Review* (1966) 684–689.

———, "Substance and Artifact: The Current Status of Research on Community Power Structure," 71 *American Journal of Sociology* (1966) 403–438.

———, "The Vertical Axis of Community Organization and the Structure of Power," 48 *Southwestern Science Quarterly* (1967) 353–368.

Waltz, Kenneth, "International Structure, National Force, and the Balance of World Power," 21 *Journal of International Affairs* (1967) 215–231.

Warner, W. Lloyd, *et. al.*, *Democracy in Jonesville* (New York: Harper, 1949).

Weber, Max, *The Theory of Social and Economic Organization*, ed. Talcott Parsons (New York: The Free Press, 1947).

West, James, *Plainville, USA* (New York: Columbia University Press, 1945).

White, R. K., and R. Lippitt, *Autocracy and Democracy* (New York: Harper, 1960).

Wildavsky, Aaron, *Leadership in a Small Town* (Totowa, N.J.: Bedminster Press, 1964).

Wolfinger, Raymond E.; "A Plea for a Decent Burial," 27 *American Sociological Review* (1962) 841–847.

———, "Reputation and Reality in the Study of 'Community Power'," 25 *American Sociological Review* (1960) 636–644.

Worsley, Peter, "The Distribution of Power in Industrial Society," *Sociological Review Monograph 8* (1964) 15–41.

Yinger, J. M., "Contraculture and Subculture," 25 *American Sociological Review* (1960) 625–635.